Culture, Power, and History

Studies in Critical Social Sciences

Series Editor

DAVID FASENFEST
College of Urban, Labor and Metropolitan Affairs
Wayne State University

VOLUME 4

Culture, Power, and History

Studies in Critical Sociology

Edited by

Stephen Pfohl, Aimee Van Wagenen, Patricia Arend,
Abigail Brooks and Denise Leckenby

BRILL

LEIDEN · BOSTON

2006

This book is printed on acid-free paper.

Library of Congress Cataloging-in-Publication Data

Culture, power, and history : studies in critical sociology / edited by Stephen Pfohl . . . [et al.].
    p. cm. — (Studies in critical social sciences, ISSN 1573-4234 ; v. 4)
    Includes bibliographical references and index.
    ISBN 90–04–14659–8 (alk. paper)
    1. Culture. 2. Power (Social sciences) 3. Social change. 4. Sociology—Philosophy.
I. Pfohl, Stephen J. II. Title. III. Series.

HM621.C862 2005
303.3'01—dc22
                           2005050797

ISSN 1573-4234
ISBN 90 04 14659 8

PRINTED IN THE NETHERLANDS

Contents

History

Stephen Pfohl and Aimee Van Wagenen

Culture, Power, and History: an Introduction

Culture is what gives human social life its meaning. Cultural practices delineate the real, imaginary, and symbolic boundaries between specific groups of human animals and the wider realm of energetic materiality in which we humans find ourselves. Power is what shapes, gives form to, and animates the stuff of culture. It is the terrain upon which human cultural productions are made. Power both enables and constrains, enlivening culture like an energetic field of forces. Within particular fields of power certain ways of imagining and enacting social life are privileged, while others are marginalized, cursed, silenced, or unconsciously abandoned. History is the dynamic social realm in which struggles over culture and power take place. Within history, cultural formations of power are routinely enacted and ritually challenged. It is in history that some powerful cultural practices are established as commonsensical or taken-for-granted while others are materially and psychically excluded by specific conjunctures of culture and power. These exclusions haunt the everyday practices of culture in specific times and places. This book is about social intersections between culture, power, and history; it is about what these intersections give to us and what they sacrifice or take away.

The theme of this book – *Culture, Power, and History* – is, at once, broad and specific. While the book

is broad enough to include a wide range of convergent theoretical and empirical concerns, each chapter situates the specific cultural meanings or practices under consideration within the historical landscapes of power out of
which such meanings and practices arise, are challenged, and change. In referring to culture, we have in mind social practices which are both symbolic
and deeply material – the rituals of everyday life; the economic production
and consumption of language, images, and discourse; the spatial and temporal mediation of subjective experience; the psychic and bodily impact of
communicative technologies; and the historically-situated enactment of what
we are attracted to or repulsed by.

The cultural practices with which we are concerned are situated at the complex sociological crossroads between the historical intricacies of structured
power and the biographical intimacies by which we come to know, make
sense of, and act within the social world. This is where C. Wright Mills sought
to locate what he called *the sociological imagination*. In Mills words, this represents a "quality of mind" that

> enables us to grasp history and biography and the relations between the
> two in society. . . . For that imagination is the capacity to shift from one per-
> spective to another – from the political to the psychological; from exami-
> nation of a single family to comparative assessments of the national budgets
> of the world; from the theological school to the military establishment; from
> considerations of an oil industry to studies of contemporary poetry. It is the
> capacity to range from the most impersonal and remote transformations to
> the most intimate features of the human self – and to see the relations
> between the two (1959: 6–7).

Culture, Power, and History is, in large measure, guided by Mills' vision of the
sociological imagination. In recent years this vision has been amplified and
made more complex by the convergent perspectives of feminist, queer, anti-
racist, cultural Marxist, poststructuralist, social psychoanalytic, and post-
colonial approaches to cultural economies of meaning. Such economies of
meanings are, at the same time, historical economies of power. The influence
of these convergent approaches to critical social thought are evident in each
of the essays collected here. In different ways, each deals with culture, power,
and history, not as discrete sociological variables, but as interrelated aspects
of what Patricia Hill Collins refers to as a complex matrix of both domination and resistance (1990). In this sense, grouping some of the essays under
the heading of culture and others under the terms power and history is some-

what deceptive. These groupings are for organizational purposes only, and are based simply on which thematic appears as more central to a particular chapter. In truth, all the included essays address culture, power, and history as interrelated and mutually constitutive social vectors of force.

Culture

Few terms have proved more controversial for the sociological study of power in history over the last two decades than the term culture. For mainstream sociologists, culture, particularly when linked to interdisciplinary programs of "cultural studies," has often been interpreted as a mantra for abstract and empirically ungrounded theoretical work, laced with relativism, concerned almost exclusively with micro-level phenomenon, and seemingly inattentive to macro social structural dynamics. For the would-be guardians of a time-warn left sociological orthodoxy, cultural studies has also often been viewed as a threat. In this case what was supposedly threatened were the rational values and frameworks that were said to have once unified critical thought – a commitment to the centrality of working class struggles against capitalist domination, a transcendent ethical vantage-point on what constitutes a just society, and the determinant importance of economic analysis.

Inspired in significant ways by feminist and anti-racist analyses that sought to complicate critical approaches to domination, and by a variety of unorthodox Marxisms, including those set into motion by several generations of the Frankfurt school, the Birmingham Centre for Contemporary Cultural Studies, and poststructuralist approaches to historical materiality, the work contained in this book seeks to engage with culture in ways that go beyond the simplistic orthodoxies of both mainstream sociology and an earlier generation of critical thinkers. As such, the papers included in this volume typically intersect empirical and theoretical concerns in ways that recognize the symbolic and imaginary dynamics of culture as material aspects of the natural history of the human species itself. This is to affirm that human language and the artful use of visual, acoustic, and tactile cultural imagery are concrete bodily aspects of the means by which we humans productively secure and/or endanger our historically-specific modes of economic survival in relation to other humans and the natural world. This is also to deliberately blur distinctions between micro and macro-levels of analysis by attending to the material specificity of sense-making cultural practices situated at the crossroads between lived biographical experience and the constraints of patterned historical structures.

Methodologically, such crossroads are the location from which sociological knowledge is produced as well. This is not to simply suggest that all sociological knowledge is relative to the social positioning of its producers. It is also an invitation to rigorously and reflexively situate sociological knowledge within the power-driven historical contexts in which it is produced and consumed, and to make such power-reflexivity an epistemological characteristic of critical sociological inquiry as such.

The section of this book designated as "Culture" embodies key features of the critical approach to culture depicted above. It opens with Abigail Brooks' analysis of the recent skyrocketing of cosmetic surgical practices within advanced western capitalist societies. These "extreme makeovers" of the body are interpreted as both an historical outgrowth of a deregulated consumer economy and as gendered mechanisms of social control. "Under the Knife and Proud of It" traces the increased normalization of the "choice" for cosmetic surgery to new body-altering technologies, to intensified media portraits of the "courage" of those who undergo such operations, and to a cultural discourse that valorizes a seemingly infinite will to technological flight from the flesh and from the finite contingencies of first-hand bodily knowledge and natural wisdom. Brooks also documents the increasingly positive portrayal of elective cosmetic surgeries in four popular contemporary magazines, demonstrating the normalization of these procedures as they are dressed in the language of scientific wonder, casual consumer choice, and sensible health and beauty. In addition, Brooks reflexively situates her critical cultural analysis within a historical context where personal dreams and desires are overwritten by powerful and anxiety-producing mass-marketed messages.

Whereas Abigail Brooks seeks to historically account for the cultural normalization of powerful new technological alterations in bodily images, Steven Farough's "The Social Geography of White Masculinities" seeks to denormalize something which all too many white men routinely take-for-granted – their own seemingly "nonracial" senses of self. Drawing upon intensive interviewing and several recent critical analytic approaches to the study of culture, including social cartography and a sociologically informed approach to psychoanalysis, Farough constructs a map depicting the transformation of racialized senses of whiteness as white men of varying economic class backgrounds move between urban geographies marked by racially-charged definitions of everyday social space. In this sense, Farough's work points not only to the cultural specificity of gendered discourses about race, but makes racial identity itself a dynamic and contestable phenomenon within contemporary urban geographies of experience and power. Of particular importance is the paranoiac-like fear and anxiety experienced by white men when they cross out of urban spaces that are implicitly recognized as white into zones of the city where they become subject to what Farough, following bell hooks, depicts as the "oppositional gaze" of color-coded "others." Here, being looked at both exposes the otherwise taken-for-granted cultural privileges of whiteness and provides a complex sociological mapping of institutionalized racism that extends well beyond the realm of conscious self-awareness.

In "The Commodification of Childhood," Juliet Schor takes us to the "kidspace" – another place where watching and being watched is a central feature. Schor's powerful critique of the contemporary practice of marketing and advertising to children begins with an examination of new methods marketers have borrowed from the social sciences to research children – in particular, naturalistic research methods. Using techniques like naturalistic ethnographic observation, marketers watch every aspect of children's lives; playing, eating, grooming, socializing, learning and shopping are all targets of surveillance. Schor finds this trend disturbing – and not just because of the constant and encroaching surveillance over kids' lives. Even more disturbing, this extensive surveillance is coupled with a discourse of "kid empowerment" and a practice called "viral marketing" where agencies recruit trend-setting children to host parties to do research and to spread the word about products to their friends. In Schor's analysis, these trends give shape to an advertising industry that is constructing children as marketable objects by "empowering" and recruiting them to participate in their own commodification. Marketers, Schor concludes, corrupt the bonds of friendship by teaching kids that their friends are a resource to be bought and sold rather than a place of refuge from the pressures of the marketplace.

While Juliet Schor brings a consideration of culture to bear to study of the marketing and the economy, William Gamson in "Movement Impact on Cultural Change" brings a consideration of culture to bear to study of social movement outcomes. Heeding the call to "bring culture back in" to social movement theory, Gamson here updates his 1990 work, *The Strategy of Social Protest*, with a framework for measuring social movement impact upon cultural change. Typically movement outcome is measured in terms of change to public policy, supplanting any examination of the impact of movements on culture. Gamson here makes a persuasive case for considering the cultural sphere as distinct from the policy domain by arguing that neglect for the cultural sphere underplays the success of those movements whose primary struggle is not with an antagonistic and clearly identifiable authority, but is with taken-for-granted cultural codes. To operationalize cultural change, Gamson suggests examining public discourse – talk, argumentation, information, and images in a range of public communication including the news media, advertising, entertainment, music and the arts.

The chapters by Charles Sarno and Aimee Van Wagenen meditate upon innovative methodological approaches to the critical historical sociology of culture. Sarno's essay, "On the Place of Allegory in the Methodological Conventions of a Critical Sociology" represents a case study of the deployment of allegory in Max Weber's classic work, *The Protestant Ethic and the Spirit of Capitalism*. This paper also addresses a crucial cultural dimension of critical sociological analysis – the complex way in which fictive and/or literary aspects of meaning become embedded in the analytic construction of social facts. Of central concern for Sarno is the relationship between the "moral impulses" embedded in historical uses of allegory and the allegorical character of sociological analyses of power. Rather than denying or suppressing fictive aspects of critical sociological analysis, Sarno engages with recent interdisciplinary reflections on ethnographic story-telling in arguing for a reflexive form of social science narrative that is attentive to its own constructive relation to power and which troubles the easy identifications and literalness of mainstream sociological accounts. This is not to argue that sociological inquiry is entirely allegorical in nature. But as Sarno contends, it is to suggest that critical approaches to sociology can only ignore its literary dimensions at its own peril and in willful ignorance of its own material historical specificity.

Aimee Van Wagenen's essay, "An Epistemology of Haunting" conjures up related questions about the literary status of sociological analysis. The jump-off point is Avery Gordon's book, *Ghostly Matters: Haunting and the Sociological Imagination*. Gordon demands that sociologists reckon with the historically specific practices of power and knowledge that constitute the commonsense of our discipline. As such, Van Wagenen contends that Gordon's provocative book confronts sociology with the task of critically engaging with the messy complexities of excluded histories and missing subjectivities, sentenced to ghostly exile by the repressive dynamics of normative social science inquiry.

Van Wagenen introduces readers to Gordon's innovative epistemology of haunting, a strategy aimed at grappling with the uncanny psychic and material traces of those whose lives lie buried beneath the manufacture of even the most compelling of scientific sociological stories. Van Wagenen also explores the political implications of Gordon's dialectic of presence and absence as this bears upon the cultural dynamics of gender, race, class and the haunting world historical legacies of colonialism. At issue here is not only the redemptive illumination of ghostly pasts, but also a utopian prefiguration of future transformations in the material and affective structuring of culture and power.

Like both Sarno and Van Wagenen, Eva Garroutte considers the culture of social scientific knowledge production – in this case, social scientific knowledge of and about American Indians. Garroutte takes up the call from indigenous scholars for the development of a new intellectual agenda for American Indian scholarship. She suggests a new perspective – Radical Indigenism – that might accomplish a methodological and theoretical basis for a new agenda. While Radical Indigenism has affinities with postcolonial critiques of the culture of Western knowledge production, Garroutte here takes postcolonial critique on an Indigenist turn, arguing that the production of knowledge about Indigenous people must proceed from Indigenous philosophy of knowledge. Attentive to multiple Indigenous philosophies of knowledge, Garroutte makes a powerful case for the importance of including the spiritual and sacred elements in the doing of American Indian scholarship generally. In so doing, Garroutte questions not just particular products of Western knowledge, but also its central epistemological premises. Garroutte's essay puts Radical Indigenism into practice by examining what such a perspective would add to contests around authenticity and identity in Native America.

Power

Like culture, power is a term that has undergone significant conceptual transformations in recent critical sociology. From the early twentieth century until the present, sociology's most consistent understanding of power was derived from Max Weber. Weber defined power as the ability of one set of social actors to exert influence over others, despite the resistance of others. This definition has proved useful in underscoring inequalities in the ability to influence social actions that are derived from the hierarchical organization of social resources.

But this is also a limited imagination of power and one that assumes that power is itself a resource that can be owned or controlled by some persons, while being exercised as a weapon against others.

The chapters of this book grouped around the theme of power supplement traditional sociological understandings of power by highlighting additional dimensions of power as well. Implicit here is the recognition that power is itself a feature of all social life and that for a social group to exist at all that group must exert some degree of influence over its environment, if for no other reason that to distinguish itself from what lies outside its borders. But to exert influence does not necessarily mean that someone or some group must possess power. It can also mean that people make use of their differential positioning within a dynamic field of relational forces arranged so as to bless some, while cursing others. This is to view power as a field of forces within which cultural practices are historically situated.

This vision of power as a dynamic and historically contingent field of forces that both constrains and enables the actions of those who move about within power's terrain resonates with the writings of both Michel Foucault and Pierre Bourdieu. It is also shared by many of the authors writing within this volume. So too are two other aspects of recent critical analyses of power – the distinction between coercive and hegemonic (or consent winning) power and attention to what Peruvian sociologist Aníbal Quijano (2000) refers to as the "coloniality of power." Quijano's work argues that no aspects of contemporary culture or economy are ever entirely free of the haunting shadows of colonialism and the complex ways that colonial formation of power impact upon all social processes, from the constitution of social definitions of success to historical practices that grant pleasure, produce pain, or shape subjective experience. Power: a constitutive field of transformative social relationships within which hierarchical impositions and resistances take place; both coercive and hegemonic in form; the shadow of the continuing colonialisms that inhabit the cultural and economic interstices of both world historical institutions and the exigencies of daily social life – these are all working definitions of power that are to be found within this collection of essays.

The section called "Power" begins with R. Danielle Egan's essay, "Eyeing the Scene: The Uses and (Re) uses of Surveillance Cameras in an Exotic Dance Club." Rooted in eighteen months of ethnographic fieldwork and participant observation, Egan's text maps a critical sociological story about the contested construction of social space in a context charged by the power of sex, commerce, and strategies aimed at the control of labor. In this, readers are invited inside the social cartography of an exotic dance club, not to gaze upon the nude bodies of dancers draped in the garb of marketable male fantasies, but to critically examine the shifting cultural-spatial resonances and resistances enacted by both women sex workers and the men who manage their labor. Egan's analysis of the spaces of power within the exotic dance club draws upon Michel Foucault's ideas concerning panoptic technologies of surveillance. By deploying such technologies of control club managers attempt to create an environment charged by hyper-visibility. While managers typically speak about the use of things such as surveillance cameras as necessary for the protection of dancers, Egan shows how this also induces a degree of self-surveillance within those subject to the camera's electronic eye. Nevertheless, just as Foucault argues that vectors of power inevitably produce, not only compliance, but also resistance, Egan empirically displays subtle and creative forms of resistance to omnipresent surveillance on the part of the dancers she studies. In this sense, dancers both refuse and strategically reinscribe the cultural meaning of the spaces in which they are "eyed."

The power of space is also a central concern in Delario Lindsey's "To Build a More *Perfect Discipline*." This time the focus is the space of New York City as it is made subject to what Lindsey theorizes as "ideologies of the normative." These are material aspects of the discourse of crime-control promulgated by the administration of Mayor Rudolph Giuliani in the years leading up to the terrorist attacks of September 11, 2001. Lindsey tells a sociological story of a different kind of terrorism, perpetrated, not by those who would attack America from the outside, but by racialized discourse that remains an omnipresent feature of the coloniality of power within the USA today. The result is the militaristic deployment of "over-control" strategies on the part of the New York City Police Department. Making use of *frame critical analysis* in interpreting accounts of "Giuliani time" from four different New York newspapers, Lindsey examines police efforts to "own the night" and implement "zero-tolerance" for crimes and images of crime that Giuliani associated with moral depravity and the deteriorating quality of city life. As Lindsey argues, one major result of Giuliani's powerful discourse was to cast vast shadows of suspicion upon persons and groups discredited by the Mayors' rhetoric. As such, it should come as no surprise that of those subjected to the aggressive "stop and frisk" operations by the Giuliani Administration's special Street Crimes Unit, 62% were African Americans, a group comprising but 25.6% of the city's population in its entirety. Lindsey's work focuses upon the powerful material effects of culturally orchestrated political discourse. The violence of this troubling aspect of New York's history is nowhere more evident than in Lindsey's portrayal of the shooting death of the unarmed African immigrant Amadou Diallo, the outcome of what police described as a "good stop" and one that followed proper police procedures.

The material impact of powerful forms of cultural discourse is also a central dimension of Karen McCormack's chapter, "Resisting the Welfare Mother." Based on in-depth interviews with impoverished women living in two distinct social geographies, one inner city and the other rural-suburban, McCormack tells a story of both the differential impact of stigmatizing language and of resistance to stigma. In the inner city context where the collective nature of living on public assistance had become an omnipresent feature of everyday life, although blighted by lack of access to good jobs, transportation and various forms of cultural capital, for the most part, mothers receiving welfare were not subject to the same experiences of stigma and ill-treatment that were aspects of the everyday lives and culture of their rural-suburban counterparts.

McCormack's important finding suggests that the power of demeaning popular culture and political stereotypes about welfare mothers, while real, is hardly homogeneous. Nor is the ability of women to resist such stereotypes. Again, this is culturally mediated by social location. Mothers in both locations found themselves routinely engaged in words and deeds that accommodated dominant stereotypes, while distinguishing themselves as "deserving" and, thus, separate from the imagined "welfare mother" of dominant discursive lore. Nevertheless, women belonging to the inner city community where welfare mothers, relatives, and relations were in regular contact with each other did have access to a variety of cultural tactics that enabled them to resist the power of some of the most pernicious aspects of stigmatizing discourse. The availability of such tactics allowed these mothers to emphasize such matters as the independence from bad relations with men granted to them by welfare and to voice critiques of structural, rather than individual, underpinnings of poverty.

The thematic consideration of power's material and psychic impact on the discursive production of subjectivity continues with Leslie Salzinger's "From Gender as Object to Verb: Rethinking How Global Restructuring Happens." Building upon fieldwork in several factories in the city of Juárez (Mexico's largest maquila labor market), Salzinger tells a complex story about the role of the production of gendered subjectivity in the constitution of globalization. This story is a remarkable illustration of how global power works not unilaterally or monolithically to make over the local, but instead works in complex and contradictory fields of force that are always embedded in local processes of meaning-making and subjectivity. In Ciudad Juárez, Salzinger observes that transnational managerial discourse depicts women as malleable, docile supplementary earners ideally suited to repetitive and tedious assembly work. This social imagination of the feminine maquila worker actively shapes the concrete exigencies of everyday factory production and materially influences the dynamics of global economic restructuring – making gender a verb in the process of globalization. Managers hire women as a result of these gendered tropes and resist changing their hiring practices even as the growth of industry in the maquila region makes young women workers scarce. Moreover, the material power of dominant cultural discourses portraying women as docile persist even as allegedly docile women workers collectively strike, subversively show up late for work, or willfully leave their current jobs for others available just across the street. While such actions seemingly challenge the image of the docile feminine assembly worker, managers continue to organize production in accord with the dominant discourse – maintaining the belief that assembly work is fundamentally feminine, while resisting the recruitment and hiring of men. In this, as Salzinger's account skillfully demonstrates, even a force as powerful as global economic restructuring is performatively enacted with contradictions that simultaneously constrain *and* enable social relations of production, at once serving *and* undermining the valorization of capital.

In the interview conducted with Canadian social theorists Arthur and Marilouise Kroker by William Wood, historical modalities of power are thematized at a more general level. Arthur and Marilouise Kroker are the editors of the influential electronic publication, *CTHEORY*, an international of journal of theory, technology, and culture. Several years ago *CTHEORY* was ranked by the French newspaper *Le Monde* as one of the world's three top electronic journals. Over the last two decades Arthur and Marilouise have also been the authors and/or editors of a large number of works examining the political fate of the human body and spirit in an age characterized by an unprecedented merger between technology and culture.

In their conversation with William Wood, the Krokers address a variety of important themes pertaining to the intersections of culture, power, and history. Of particular note is their discussion of the relation between viral power – the digitally coded and omnipresent circulation of disembodied electronic information moving at the speed of light – and the strategic emergence of a new form of American empire in the period following the terrorist attacks of September 11, 2001. This, suggest the Krokers, is an empire of light, speed, and violence, which plays itself out in aggressive US military-economic strikes the globe over and in a dazzling mixture of legal repression and mass-mediated fears and fascinations within the US itself. Over the course of the interview the Krokers also discuss the collective religious impulses and theology that lie beneath the American technological imagination, connections between biotechnological control mechanisms and the US security state, and the media scripting of the current war against terrorism as a facet of what Arthur and Marilouise call the hegemonic technological culture of pan-capitalism. This provocative interview closes with the Kroker's reflections on cultural and political relations between the US and Canada.

History

While the interview with Arthur and Marilouise Kroker speaks to cultural matters of great relevance to contemporary history, each of the next five chapters in *Culture, Power, and History* address matters in the past with importance to critical understandings of the present. As such, using terms formulated by Michel Foucault (1979: 31), each might be described as offering an effective *history of the present*. Each, in other words, seeks not simply to recapture past events, but to intervene within contemporary cultural understandings and politics by making connections between historical lineages of power that shape or give structure to the contemporary order of things. This confines contemporary avenues of action by facilitating the ritual transfer of past structures of power into the present. Sometimes this transference occurs in unnoticed or culturally unconscious ways. Such transfers of power may also both constrain and/or enable the emergence of possible futures. This is a reason why a discerning engagement with history is so crucial to critical sociological approaches to culture and power. History may represent what C. Wright Mills called "the organized memory" of a given culture (1959: 145). But an effective history of the present is also capable of disrupting hegemonic and commonsensical understandings of the relation between past, present, and future. This it accomplishes by opening the doors of interpretive social action to the recognition of new facts, new perspectives, and possible new formations of power.

In Mills' terms, this is why a critical sociological imagination requires a "continual rewriting" of history (1959: 145). Otherwise, the organized memory of our culture will be written by those who dominate our hierarchical present, such that "even the dead will not be safe from the enemy [of justice] if he wins. And this enemy has not ceased to be victorious" (Benjamin, 1968: 255). We are here quoting Walter Benjamin. Like Foucault and Mills, Benjamin dreamt of a form of effective history that would constructively "brush . . . against the grain" of dominant cultural understandings of the past and, in so doing, open up flash-points in the present that will "constantly call into question every victory, past and present, of the rulers" (1968: 255). In Benjamin's analysis, this produces a different kind of history – a redemptive form of history, capable of exploding the false continuum between past and present, while paving the road for future actions better able to guide us in the direction of social justice. This is also a notion of history that resonates with each of the chapters included in this volume.

"Black Belts and Ivory Towers," the opening essay in this section by Davarian Baldwin, reopens the dominant organized memory of the early "Chicago School" of sociology led by Robert Park and his associates. This Baldwin does by examining how racialized forms of social power limited what Chicago sociologists were able to see and not see about the historical actualities of such matters as civilization, assimilation, social organization and the meaning of urban social life. As Baldwin carefully argues, this is not simply a story about how sociologists constructed "race" as an analytic category, but about how collective anxieties about race permeating early 20th century America facilitated the construction of the "Chicago School" and US sociology as a whole. In this, Baldwin dislodges dominant institutional memories of Chicago sociology reproduced within our discipline and replaces them with a critical interpretation of how early sociological thought was itself shaped by the racialized economy of industrializing capitalist America.

Baldwin also introduces readers to an important "second wave" of Black social scientists schooled within, while brushing against the grain of the Chicago tradition championed by Park. Examining the contributions and struggles of Charles Johnson, E. Franklin Frazier, St. Clair Drake, Horace Cayton, and other prominent Black Chicago sociologists, Baldwin both resurrects a commonly unrecognized history of Black sociological thought and explores the limits placed upon such thought by the epistemological blinders of the objectifying social science framework that early African American sociologists inherited from their white institutional mentors. Then, to remind us that critical social thought is hardly the same thing as disciplinary sociological thought, Baldwin concludes his analysis by drawing upon the voices of Black Chicago residents, who often interpreted the cultural, political, and economic exigencies of their own lives in ways that differed significantly from the social scientific viewpoints of both Black and White professional sociologists.

A relatively unacknowledged history of dominant social science complicities with power is also a central feature of Jackie Orr's "The Militarization of Inner Space." Orr weaves a cautionary sociological story of how a fateful convergence of US social science, media, technology, and strategic governmental interests resulted in the fearful militarization of the collective cultural sensibilities of the US civilian population during World War II, the Cold War, and again today in what appears as if a seemingly endless and terroristic war against terror. At the core of Orr's analysis is an examination of a series of strategic psychological manipulations of civil society aimed at both producing support for war and instilling a sense of fear within the public at large. If this strikes you as relevant for an understanding of our contemporary historical situation, Orr reminds us that the systematic targeting of the psychic and emotional lives of civilians has long been a strategic aspect of the management of "total war" from the mid-twentieth century to the present. This is what Orr means by the militarization of inner space – the collective psychological organization of civil society for the production of violence.

Orr reviews and interprets a wide range of public documents, as well as previously classified government reports, the records of quasi-experimental interventions perpetrated upon the American public, and the annals of social science research, as each bears upon a strategic set of psychological border operations aimed at preparing the civilian population to accept, and even embrace, the seeming inevitability of war. Among the materials examined by Orr are a special 1941 issue of the American Journal of Sociology devoted to the problem of managing civilian morale during wartime, a series of Cold War government pamphlets, newsreels, and film produced to alert a fearful public about how to survive nuclear war without panicking, the 1952 Report of Project East River, the so-called "Bible" of civil defense preparedness, arguing that true national security rests on the psychological fortitude of the civilian population, and the project known as Operation Alert, a series of simulated exercises in the mid-1950s aimed at familiarizing people with what it would be like to experience a "real" nuclear attack. "The Militarization of Inner Space" begins and ends with President George W. Bush's declaration that after September 11, 2001, "every American is a soldier, "a troublesome blurring of the line between the "civilian" and the "soldier," a distinction upon which popular understanding of the term "terrorism" typically depends. This is a sociological history of the present. It challenges us to grapple with the meaning of terrorism in the ritual organization of everyday American life and culture.

While Orr's chapter attends to how powerful governmental agencies deploy calculated media campaigns to instill a collective sense of fear and, thereby, mobilize the public to accept the inevitability of war, Charlotte Ryan's analysis of the strategic use of media during a successful labor strike demonstrates the potential for counter-hegemonic uses of the media as a tool for social justice. Ryan's "It Takes a Movement to Raise an Issue" is a case study of media activism during the 1997 Teamsters strike against United Parcel Service (U.P.S.) As Ryan shows, a major element in the union's organizing strategy involved a careful analysis of media culture and the effective framing of key ingredients of the story it wished to communicate to the public. While this strategy ultimately proved successful, with the union winning significant gains in the areas of additional full-time jobs with benefits, pay raises, control of pension funds, and various "quality of life" concerns, these gains did not occur without a concerted effort to analyze and counter negative stereotypes about unions that had become part of the everyday culture of journalists employed by market-drive mass media systems. So, too, did media activists have to package their stories in ways that would gain positive attention in the media, creating "hooks" for reports to cover, while working to secure influential sponsors for the way they sought to frame issues pertaining to the injustices of being denied full-time work and threats to workers' health and safety.

Ryan's work situates union efforts at mobilization in terms of both the historical specificity of organized labor's late twentieth-century struggles within the US and the particular type of corporate media culture that union activists attempted to work within and strategically appropriate. As Ryan's case study demonstrates, this level of analytic and strategic specificity is required if union organizers and other justice-oriented activists are to effectively mobilize the power of media in leveraging public support, particularly in today's context of market-driven corporate media, where what is typically reported is simply what sells the best. In this regard, Ryan depicts how the Teamsters' communications staff labored to frame their central messages in clear, well documented, and strategically sponsored ways. So, also, was the union successful in gaining sympathetic media attention, not only through the use of carefully crafted press releases, but also by mobilizing events such as a highly visible "die-in" for Worker's Memorial Day. Ryan's analysis of these strategies carries important lessons for those who would seek to undermine the power of the dominant cultural economies of our day. Of particular note is Ryan's insistence on both the strategic importance of constructing "collective actors" and on the need for a site-specific and historically informed analysis of power dynamics on the part of activists.

William Wood's "(Virtual) Myths," crafts a spiraling series of poignant sociological meditations on power at the intersections of two distinct but related forms of mythic spatialization – the imperial mapping of supposedly "discovered" geographical territories and the clinical-scientific mapping of the human body. While different, the parallel histories between these two modes of spatialization are considerable. Each begins in the early modern capitalist-colonialist period with the production of visual spatial images (the explorer's map and the anatomist's diagram), which at once objectify and "naturalize" the socially situated reams of physicality they claim to represent. Each does so, moreover, not as gestures of intimate or immanent knowledge but as distancing gestures performed in the service of conquest and commerce. In this sense, early modern cartographers constructed supposed neutral maps of homogenous land devoid of ecological, cultural, and spiritual significance to those whom, like the Amerindian peoples of the "New World," belonged to or with such land, while anatomists diagramed the human body devoid of holistic connections to lived relations to others and the environment by which it finds sustenance. In this, the body of the earth as well as the human body itself became relationally unanchored and set adrift, only to be reterritorialized on discursive terms that speak the languages of profit and endless self-preservation. In this the earth is transformed into property to be possessed, while human bodiliness becomes the dissected object of the clinical gaze.

The restrictive economic containment of both the earth and our bodies are, in Wood's critical sociological allegory, magnified exponentially with the historical invention of digital technologies in the late twentieth-century. This is a story of how the abstractions of high-speed digital imaging systems virtually supplant earlier modes of technological objectification and the exploitative profits they promise. Here, the resistive physicality of land fades before the bright lights of boundary defying cybernetic simulations, just as the fleshy body disappears before the electronic lightning of coded bioinformatics and the discourse of genetic manipulations. With nearly every aspect of spatiality today wed to the relentless global circulation of finance capital, Wood's disturbing history of our collective cultural present leaves us with no easy-to-read map of how to exit from the powerful technological confines in which so much of contemporary society is ensnarled. It leaves us instead with a critical sociological challenge concerning how to urgently reconstruct cultural senses of space that optimize, rather than subordinate, our natural historical relations to the vicissitudes of the earth, the flesh and a sustainable relation between these two.

The final chapter in *Culture, Power, and History*, Ramón Grosfoguel's "Geopolitics of Knowledge and Coloniality of Power" reads the history of Puerto Rico's colonial present. In this piece, Grosfoguel debunks the myth of the decolonization of the Caribbean through an analysis of Puerto Rico as a modern colony. Puerto Rico's official status as a colony of the United States is peripheral to Grosfoguel's argument; more central in Grosfoguel's analysis is an exposition of the coloniality of power at work for Puerto Rican migrants and residents as they live under racial/colonial ideology. Anibal Quiano's concept of global coloniality informs Grosfoguel's essay. In global coloniality, or "independence without decolonization," old hierarchies of West/non-West produce new consequences: an international division of labor, the production of subaltern postcolonial resistance strategies, and the inscription of third world migrants into (American) racial/ethnic hierarchies of power. Grosfoguel's exposition of the Puerto Rican case further draws out and illuminates this concept.

Grosfoguel's debunking of the myth of decolonization brings him to a call for dialogue between postcolonial theory and world systems theory. While Grosfoguel finds important critiques in both theoretical systems of thought – with world systems analysis providing important critique of Eurocentric developmentalist ideologies and postcolonial theory providing important critique of Orientalist constructions of non-Europeans as inferior Others – he finds that each perspective misses the strengths of the other. World systems theory finds causal explanation in the economy (global capitalist accumulation) while postcolonial thought finds explanation in cultural determinants (colonial culture). The opposition of these two causal explanations provides a false dilemma for those that seek an understanding of and resistance to the workings of power in the modern/colonial world system. As a way out of this false dilemma, Grosfoguel seeks and sketches a new language to bring these two perspectives together and closes his essay with an application of this new language to illuminate the racist discourse that underlies neoculture of poverty and new economic sociology explanations of poverty.

Our Collective Editorial Process

Culture, Power, and History originated as and expands upon a special issue of the journal, *Critical Sociology* (volume 30, number 2, 2004). The special issue and edited book highlight recent scholarship emerging out of the Boston College Sociology Department. The sociology graduate program at Boston College is organized around the theme "Social Economy and Social Justice: Gender, Race and Class in a Global Context." This theme and our faculty attracts a diverse array of justice-oriented scholars to our department and university, each typically combining a commitment to analytic rigor with a passionate concern for how sociological knowledge might best contribute to the construction of more just social world. These dual commitments – to critical sociological inquiry and the pursuit of social justice – led many BC graduate students and alumni to participate in a symposium on "The Future of Critical Sociology" in the summer of 2001. This symposium was sponsored jointly by this journal and the Society for the Study of Social Problems and took place during the annual SSSP Meetings. The invitation by the journal for a collective of faculty and graduate students at Boston College to edit this special issue of *Critical Sociology* stemmed from our participation in and contributions to that engaging symposium. This book brings together expanded and revised versions of articles from the special issue along with several new pieces.

The final versions of the chapters contained in this anthology are each the result of over two years of sustained labor on the part of the collective of faculty and graduate students working together on this project at Boston College. Meeting frequently on a regular basis, we began our work by a lengthy discussion of possible themes for the special issue we had been invited to prepare. Soon thereafter we solicited proposals for article-length papers and reviews of recent books authored by alumni from our graduate program. Other aspects of early conversations included a discussion of the organizational structures and editorial decision-making processes that we would adopt. The collective organized itself into three small editorial groups, each composed of a faculty member and several graduate students. These groups took responsibility for coordinating the discussion of submitted works by the collective as a whole. The small editorial groups also took the lead in communicating with authors and guiding manuscripts through proposed revisions. All members of the collective typically read and discussed all articles and book reviews submitted for consideration and, later, discussed revised manuscripts.

We also committed ourselves to facilitating the development of papers that showed a genuine promise of making a strong and engaging contribution to the special issue. Typically this meant providing prospective authors with detailed written comments about the substance, style, theoretical framework, methods, and social-political implications of their work. We also often conversed with authors at length in person or over the phone, discussing issues raised by their papers and providing suggestions for strengthening and revision. Some papers went through several rounds of review until arriving at the version you will find here. We are confident that the result of our labor has been fruitful and hope that you find this collection of critical sociological writings of interest and value. We believe that each addresses important sociological topics and provides an inviting angle of inquiry into justice-oriented concerns with the relations between culture, power, and history.

On behalf of the Boston College Editorial Collective, we wish to thank Editor David Fasenfest for the invitation for us to develop the special issue of *Critical Sociology* and this book and for his ongoing support of this project. We also wish to thank the Sociology Department at Boston College for its support and for providing modest summer research stipends to the graduate students working on the collective. While many individuals contributed to the work of the Editorial Collective over the last two and one-half years the following people represent the nucleus of our group, most working tirelessly from beginning to end. These included Patricia Arend, Abigail Brooks, Denise Leckenby, Stephen Pfohl, Juliet Schor, Aimee Van Wagenen and William Wood. Other individuals who participated in the Collective for extended periods of time included William Gamson, Idolina Hernandez, Kelly Joyce, Patricia Leavy, and Jeffery Littenberg. At various points Aimee Van Wagenen, Patricia

Arend, William Wood, and Jeffery Littenberg, who took turns in serving as the group's Managing Editor, also served the Collective. We also wish to thank Blair Kanis for constructing the index to this book and BC Sociology Department staff members Jessica Bickley, Jessica Geier, Toni Vicari, and Jean Lovett for providing assistance and support.

Culture

Abigail Brooks

"Under the Knife and Proud of It:"[1]
An Analysis of the Normalization of
Cosmetic Surgery*

As a child, I often dreamt of living among fembots.
My entire family had become fembots except for me.
Fembots, creatures in my favorite television series
"The Bionic Woman,"[2] were exact external copies of
human beings, down to every freckle, every scar, and
yet, when you pulled at their faces, their skin would
peel off to reveal whirring gears and motors – they
were only machines, evil machines, that had replaced
the unique humanness of each being. The Bionic
Woman soon found a method of deciphering fembots
from humans: fembots had, at the nape of their necks,
a small egg-shaped nodule, easily concealed by cloth-
ing. In my dream I discovered that each of my fam-
ily members had such a nodule and, with growing
anxiety, I peeled back their faces one by one, finding
myself alone amongst a sea of whirring gears.

AUTHOR'S NOTE: *I would like to thank Stephen Pfohl, Juliet Schor, and all members of*
the editorial collective at the Boston College Sociology Department for their helpful comments
on earlier drafts of this article.
[1] This phrase is taken from an article on cosmetic surgery in the May 20th, 2002
issue of *US Weekly* magazine, page 29.
* An earlier version of this essay appeared in *Critical Sociology*, vol. 30, no. 2 (2004).
[2] "The Bionic Woman" television series aired from January 1976 to May 1978 on
ABC and NBC television networks. Actress Lindsay Wagner played the lead role of
the bionic woman.

Introduction

In the United States, 6.9 million cosmetic procedures were performed in 2002, a 203% increase since 1997 (American Society for Aesthetic Plastic Surgery 2003).[3] This expansion may be attributed, in part, to growing approval rates of cosmetic surgery. Recent survey data indicate that 38.8% of men and 46.8% of women have more favorable attitudes towards cosmetic surgery than they did ten years ago (American Society for Plastic Surgery 2002). Survey data collected from 1000 American households in February of 2003 reveal that over half (54%) of Americans approve of cosmetic surgery and nearly 1/4 (24%) are considering cosmetic alteration for themselves now or in the future (Synovate [Marketing Facts] 2003; American Society for Aesthetic Plastic Surgery 2003). Americans' increasing comfort level with cosmetic surgery may indicate a lessening of stigma associated with cosmetic surgery. In a recent survey, 77% of women and 74% of men said that if they had cosmetic surgery they "would not be embarrassed" if people knew about it (American Society for Aesthetic Plastic Surgery 2003).

Within feminist scholarship, cosmetic surgery often surfaces in discussions of the cultural and aesthetic dictates of femininity, where it is identified as a mechanism that promotes compliance, but also resistance against, such dictates. Some feminist scholars argue that cosmetic surgery works as a coercive device that, overtly and covertly, pushes women to conform to feminine ideals of youth and beauty (Wolf 1991; Morgan 1991; Bordo 1993; Gillespie

---

[3] The figure of 6.9 million, and the increase of 203% since 1997, includes surgical and non-surgical cosmetic procedures. Surgical procedures account for 1.9 million of the total procedures performed in 2002 and non-surgical procedures make up the remaining 5.3 million. According to ASAPS data, the most popular surgical procedures for 2002 were liposuction (372, 831), breast augmentation (259, 641), and eyelid surgery (229, 092). Botox injections ranked highest for non-surgical procedures (1, 658, 667) followed by microdermabrasion (1, 032, 417), collagen injections (783, 120), laser resurfacing (736, 458) and chemical peels (495, 415). My analysis of cosmetic surgery includes both surgical and non-surgical procedures. When I am not discussing specific cosmetic procedures by name, I use the term "cosmetic surgery" as a general referent that applies to surgical and non-surgical procedures. Thus "cosmetic surgery" includes the following non-surgical procedures: Botox injections, collagen injections, Perlane injections, microdermabrasion, microlipo, dermaplanning, mesotheraphy, Artecoll, Isolagan, Intense Pulsed Light Therapy, Silver Ion Facials and the Lift 6. It should also be noted that the two plastic surgery organizations, The American Society for Plastic Surgery (ASPS) and the American Society for Aesthetic Plastic Surgery (ASAPS), that serve as primary sources of statistical data throughout this paragraph, consist of board-certified plastic surgeons and are certified by the American Board of Plastic Surgery.

1996; Brush 1998).[4] Others explore the ways in which cosmetic surgery, and the achievement of bodily or facial compliance with aesthetic ideals, empowers women (Davis 1995; 1997; 1999).[5] Still others emphasize cosmetic surgery's effectiveness as a resistive strategy against feminine norms that restrict bodily expression to attracting and pleasing men (Balsamo 1992; Orlan 1991, 1997).[6] From this perspective, cosmetic surgery enables women to move beyond a body reduced to the function of reproduction, a body "passively victimized," to one that becomes a site for "staging" new identities (Balsamo 1992: 23).

Feminist scholarship on cosmetic surgery reveals a multiplicity of perspectives, including cosmetic surgery as oppressive, empowering, and resistive, coercive, choice-based, and both.[7] Across these perspectives, many feminist

---

[4] Feminist philosopher Kathryn Pauly Morgan argues, for example, that cosmetic surgery creates a kind of "technological beauty imperative" – by making feminine ideals of youth and beauty "technologically achievable" cosmetic surgery also makes "obligatory the appearance of youth and the reality of 'beauty' for every woman who can afford it" (Morgan 1991: 40, 41).

[5] Kathy Davis argues that women experience cosmetic surgery (and their post-surgery faces and bodies) as self-esteem building and empowering. One woman Davis interviewed described her decision to attain cosmetic surgery as follows: "I'm doing it for myself and not for someone else. I guess it was pretty brave of me to take this step" while another enthusiastically recounted her experience of breast augmentation surgery: "I am really *proud!* It was just great, I felt about ten feet tall" (Davis 1995: 128, 139, 140).

[6] French performance artist Orlan, whose cosmetic surgeries have been filmed and performed live in front of an audience, uses cosmetic surgery to construct and re-construct her face and body in ways that disrupt dominant beauty norms. Orlan had silicone implants injected into her forehead, giving her an "extraterrestrial" appearance and plans to have the "biggest nose physically possible" constructed and implanted mid-way up her forehead (Orlan as cited in Reitmaier, 1995; Davis 1997: 174). Kathryn Pauly Morgan also highlights cosmetic surgery's potential as a mode of resistance against feminine norms of youth and beauty. She calls upon women to have their faces and breasts "surgically pulled down" rather than lifted, to have "wrinkles sewn and carved" into their skin, and to hold Ms. Ugly pageants (Morgan 1991: 46).

[7] Susan Bordo (1993) and Rosemary Gillespie (1996) provide sophisticated readings of cosmetic surgery as at once coercive and choice based, oppressive and agentic. For Bordo (1993) the oppressive power of the contemporary norm of feminine beauty is such that, in the Foucauldian sense, "it produces effects at the level of desire" (Foucault 1980a: 59). It follows that women may experience their compliance with contemporary beauty norms as desire, as "choice," with cosmetic surgery becoming one more mechanism by which women are able to "chose" to fulfill their desires (Bordo 1993: 247). For Gillespie, a woman's decision to attain cosmetic surgery is an "individual choice" that is also "enmeshed in social and cultural norms" or "choice socially and culturally constrained" (Gillespie 1996: 79). Cosmetic surgery may be "liberating at the individual level" but also reinforce "oppressive images of female beauty, whereby women are valued for their looks, and as physical capital to be displayed by men in the public sphere and consumed by them in the private sphere" (Gillespie 1996: 82, 83).

scholars continue to interpret cosmetic surgery as a means to achieve or rebel against dominant norms of femininity, and to frame their analyses around this interpretation. While the feminist contributions to date help us to understand motives and pressure to obtain cosmetic surgery in the context of particular desired outcomes (such as the achievement of feminine beauty ideals), they do not, I argue, fully explain Americans' increasing comfort with the actual practice of having their faces and bodies surgically altered.

In this article, I extend feminist scholarship, or shift the feminist lens, towards an analysis of the normalization of cosmetic surgery. Why do Americans increasingly accept and approve of cosmetic surgery, and why are they more comfortable with its practices? I investigate several characteristics and factors that are contributing to this trend of normalization and analyze some of its repercussions. The first section locates the normalization of cosmetic surgery within the larger context of the de-regulation and commercialization of American medicine. After noting an increase in volume and frequency of media coverage and advertising of cosmetic surgery, the second section describes my content analysis of articles in *Vogue, Harper's Bazaar, US Weekly* and *People* magazines from October 2001 to June 2003. Paying close attention to associations between cosmetic surgery and technology and to portrayals of the body undergoing cosmetic surgery, I identify two dominant narrative frames and analyze several normalizing themes within each. Finally, in the last section, I draw upon a combination of personal reflection and contemporary theory to investigate potential after-effects and consequences of the normalization of cosmetic surgery: new and insidious forms of mental and bodily social control, losses in aesthetic diversity (or what I term an encroaching aesthetic homogenization), and a disruption in mind-body reflexivity, or a loss of embodied knowledge.

Cosmetic Surgery in an Era of De-Regulation

In the post World War II era of "leisure and unbridled consumption" cosmetic surgery, in its new and accessible form (an accessibility due, in large part, to new surgical techniques and technologies), first began to be marketed (Turner 1984; Haiken 1997).[8] Marketing campaigns targeted not only the phys-

---

[8] The American Board of Plastic and Re-constructive Surgeons established a budget and a full time director of public relations in 1950.

ically deformed or psychologically suffering, but all individuals who could afford cosmetic surgery.[9] The payoff of mainstream marketing was soon evident: in 1958, 130,000 Americans had plastic surgery compared to just 15,000 a decade earlier (Haiken 1997: 136).

While public relations within the field of plastic surgery began in the 1950s, plastic surgeons continued to comply with the American Medical Association's ban on direct advertising and patient solicitation until the late 1970s (Sullivan 2001). In 1975 the Federal Trade Commission filed an antitrust complaint against the American Medical Association. By 1978 the FTC declared that the AMA ban against "'soliciting business, by advertising or otherwise'" was in violation of the Sherman Act of 1890, which deems any restraint of trade by combination illegal. In 1982 the Supreme Court, despite its long standing precedent of interpreting the Sherman Act as applying to private entities only, upheld the FTC's ruling. The FTC and Supreme Court rulings mark the beginning of a new era of de-regulation and commercialization within American medicine – the first paid advertisements for cosmetic surgery appeared in the late 1970s (Sullivan 2001).

Marketing became a major priority for William Porterfield, the president of the American Society of Plastic and Re-constructive Surgeons from 1981–1982. With input from marketing consultants, Porterfield developed a new logo, patient financing plans, and a public information program that included outreach to broadcast media and a series of brochures on cosmetic procedures (Sullivan 2001: 86). In June of 1982, the ASPRS was mentioned in 250 press clips. Outreach to broadcast media yielded 320 requests for interviews with plastic surgeons from television and radio program directors (Hugo 1982b as cited in Sullivan 2001: 87). By the mid-1980s, the ASPRS grossed over

---

[9] In the WWI and depression eras of the 1920s and 1930s, plastic surgery was deemed most appropriate for so-called physically "abnormal" individuals and applied as a tool to facilitate the integration of these individuals back into society. In the late 1930s and 1940s, cosmetic surgery was placed in a clinical context and framed as mechanism for psychologically suffering patients to attain mental health and to improve their self-esteem. In the post WWII era of "the modern" however, the development of anesthesia and antibiotics (the "wonder drugs"), new cosmetic technologies, widespread abundance and consumerism, the advent of television and mass media, the modern ideal of youth-beauty, and an overwhelming fascination with science and technology, with all that was new and innovative, proved fertile ground for the marketing of cosmetic surgery to so called "normal" individuals. My summary of these periods is drawn largely from Elizabeth Haiken (1997) – see Haiken's work for more on these periods and for an excellent social and historical analysis of cosmetic surgery throughout the 20th century.

1 million in sales of brochures to members (Sullivan 2001: 87). The society also began to sponsor seminars and workshops for members on how to market their practices.[10] In 1988, a survey published in *Plastic Surgery News* indicated that 48% of board certified plastic surgeons advertised in the Yellow Pages, newspapers, magazines, direct mail, television or radio.

Since the 1990s, public relations, marketing, and advertising have expanded tremendously. Information sessions and presentations on cosmetic surgery, often sponsored by national plastic surgery societies or local hospitals, are held in local television studios, retail stores, and in hospital settings (Sullivan 2001: 150). The ASPRS recently sponsored advertising segments that ran in five women's magazines, two men's magazines, in USA Today and on Lifetime and CNN (Sullivan 2001: 140). Special advertising sections run in prestigious papers such as the Washington Post and the New York Times. Increasing numbers of plastic surgeons hire private marketing firms to help with the selling of their services and products.

Finally, plastic surgeons are benefiting from the de-regulation of the pharmaceutical industry. In 1992, Congress enacted legislation that mandated reductions in the time allotted to the FDA for the testing and approval of new drugs. Drug approval times have been reduced by 50% as a result (Cohen 2001: 192). The FDA's ability to regulate the advertising and marketing of drugs has been sharply curtailed due to Federal Trade Commission rulings and increasing pressure from pharmaceutical companies.[11] In 1998, pharmaceuticals began to be advertised in print media, on television, and on the internet.[12] The FDA is no longer legally mandated, nor does it have the legal jurisdiction, to review and assess the accuracy of advertisements before they reach the public (Cohen 2001: 157). The FDA sends over a hundred letters a year to various drug companies citing overstated benefits, inaccurate safety claims, and minimized side effect risks, but most letters are not received by the drug companies until after the advertisements have run. Furthermore, on account of the restricted legal and regulatory power of the FDA, the companies face no significant penalties (Cohen 2001: 157).

Plastic surgeons make use of the fast track approval process for an array

---

[10] *Plastic Surgery News*, 1985.
[11] Pharmaceutical companies employ hundreds of lobbyists and donated a total of 44 million dollars to major political parties in the last decade (Cohen 2001).
[12] *Advertising Age*, 1998.

of biochemical compounds and synthetic materials such as silicones, imitation collagen substances, and diluted toxins. The legalization of pharmaceutical advertising proves advantageous as well. Consider the example of Botox, a diluted form of botulinum toxin. 1.6 million cosmetic Botox procedures (in which Botox is injected into the face and neck to reduce wrinkles) were performed in 2001 for a total sales value of $310 million. The FDA approved Botox in April of 2002 and television and print advertisements began the following month. Botox advertisements ran in *People*, *The New Yorker*, *Vogue* and *In Style* magazines in May 2002. With advertising and the FDA's approval, analysts project that Botox sales will reach 1 billion within the next several years.[13]

Media Content

In this section, with expanding media coverage and advertising as a backdrop, I investigate media content. What are the common themes in recent media coverage of cosmetic surgery? Do they promote normalized understandings of cosmetic surgery? To answer these questions, I analyzed articles on cosmetic surgery in *Vogue, Harper's Bazaar, US Weekly* and *People* magazines from October 2001 to June 2003.[14] I found large numbers of articles on cosmetic surgery in all four magazines, with *Harper's Bazaar* carrying one or more article on cosmetic surgery in nearly half, and *Vogue* in more than half, of the total number of issues reviewed.[15] Most articles, in all four magazines,

---

[13] Noonan, David and Jerry Adler, "The Botox Boom," *Newsweek*, May 13, 2002, pp. 50–58.

[14] I selected these four magazines because they reflect a range of magazine "types", from women's fashion, to Hollywood lifestyles, to personal interest stories. Further, taken together these magazines encompass a wide and diverse readership. *Vogue* and *Harper's Bazaar* draw predominantly upon middle and upper middle class women while *US Weekly* and *People* appeal to a broader audience, inclusive of women and men and greater socioeconomic and racial diversity.

[15] In *Vogue*, for example, out of 21 issues reviewed, 13 contain at least one article on cosmetic surgery, with some issues carrying up to three articles. *Harper's Bazaar* contains at least one article on cosmetic surgery in 9 out of 21 issues reviewed. *People* and US Weekly contain fewer articles on cosmetic surgery when compared with Vogue and Harper's Bazaar (for example, out of 84 *People* issues reviewed, 12 contain at least one article on cosmetic surgery) the articles in *People* and *US Weekly* are often cover stories (for example, 6 out the 12 articles in *People* are cover stories) whereas the articles in *Vogue* and *Harper's Bazaar* are less frequently previewed on the cover (*Vogue* offers 4 previews, *Harper's Bazaar*, none).

depict cosmetic surgery in a favorable light.[16] I identify two dominant narrative frames that encourage the acceptance and approval of cosmetic surgery: cosmetic surgery as new technology and the candid, first person account of the experience of cosmetic surgery.[17] The majority of articles fit into one of these two narrative frames and some articles combine elements of each. For example, a recent *Vogue* article titled "Face Lift of the Future" introduces readers to the benefits of "cosmetic surgery's new most promising technique," the ThermaLift, through recounting an actual patient's experience of the procedure and recovery process in quasi-ethnographic detail.[18]

Not all articles fit into a variation of these two narrative frames, nor are they exclusively positive in tone. For example, out of twelve articles on cosmetic surgery in *People* magazine, nine provide affirmative views of cosmetic surgery but two focus on cosmetic surgery "mishaps" – Botox shots inducing nausea and fatigue and gastric bypass surgery leading to a life-threatening illness.[19] While many of the articles I characterize as favorable contain no mention of adverse side effects or cosmetic surgery-induced health risks, some contain one or more references (albeit brief) to such effects and risks.[20] In

---

[16] Out of 13 issues of *Vogue* that carry one or more articles on cosmetic surgery, 11 contain at least one article that is overwhelminglly favorable. In *Harper Bazaar*, out of 9 issues that carry one or more article on cosmetic surgery, 7 issues contain at least one article that is overwhelmingly favorable.

[17] In a content analysis of women's magazines from 1980–1995, based on an index compiled by the Reader's Guide to Periodical Literature, Deborah Sullivan (2001: 161, 162) identifies three principle types of articles on cosmetic surgery: 1) The instructional guide (two fifths of articles) 2) autobiographical accounts (one-fifth of articles) and 3) instructional guides with personalized descriptions of patients' experiences (one-fifth of articles). My categorization of articles compliments and contradicts Sullivan's findings. Like Sullivan, I found the candid, first person account to be a prevalent narrative frame. However, unlike Sullivan, I found the cosmetic surgery as new technology narrative frame to be more prevalent than the instructional guide. Some articles I reviewed did include physician's descriptions of procedures and advice about ideal candidates for particular procedures. For example, two articles in the July 2002 and February 2003 issues of *Harper's Bazaar*, titled "Plastic Surgery At What Age?" and "The Truth About Lipo", easily fit Sullivan's descriptions of "how too" advice or the "instructional guide". But overall, my findings indicate that the cosmetic surgery as new technology narrative frame is more prevalent than that of the instructional guide.

[18] Kazanjian, Dodie, "Face Lift of the Future," *Vogue*, May 2003, pp. 258–261.

[19] The article on the adverse effects of Botox is titled "A New Wrinkle" (*People*, February 24, 2003, p. 59) and the "serious – even deadly – complications" of gastric bypass surgery are reported on in an article titled "Weighing the Risks" (Adato, Allison and Galina Espinoza, *People*, March 10, 2003, pp. 137–140).

[20] In later sections of my paper, I present a discussion and analysis of the framing of side effects in these articles.

addition to a steady stream of articles that profile non-cosmetic surgery methods of changing and improving one's face and body, such as diets and exercise,[21] I also found several articles that offer alternatives to dominant youth-beauty-thinness norms – "Older women Younger Men,"[22] "Sexy at Any Size,"[23] "Living Large,"[24] and "Relationships can be more honest, more equal and yes – more sexual – after 50."[25] Finally, a handful of articles highlight examples of resistance to the practice of cosmetic surgery. For example, "Respect Your Own Beauty" is a narrative of a woman who celebrates her non-cosmetically altered body.[26] With these anomalous articles noted, I turn now to a discussion of the two narrative frames outlined above, (cosmetic surgery as new technology and candid, first person accounts of cosmetic surgery), and analyze several themes that surface within each.

Cosmetic Surgery as New Technology

More than half of the articles on cosmetic surgery fit into the narrative frame of cosmetic surgery as new technology.[27] In these articles, new cosmetic tech-

---

[21] A *People* article on Yoga and Pilates urges readers to "Ready, Set, Glow" (*People*, May 27, 2002). A recent *People* cover story reads "Half Their Size!! Real Life Diet Success Stories and Hollywood's Shape Up Secrets" (*People*, January 2003) whereas a recent *US Weekly* cover reports "Fighting Weight. Stars talk about their struggles. Plus one sensible diet that works" (*US Weekly*, November 2001). An article in *Harper's Bazaar* (Nicholas, Perricone, M.D., August 2002, pp. 76–78) explores an alternative to cosmetic surgery in the ongoing battle with wrinkles: "The Wrinkle Free Diet: Can you Get Younger-Looking, Glowing Skin Just by Eating Certain Foods?"

[22] *US Weekly*, January 2002.

[23] Unidentified Author, "Sexy at Any Size: Whose Sexy Now?", *People*, October 21, 2002, pp. 117–122.

[24] *People*, June 2002.

[25] *Vogue*, August 2002.

[26] Grody, Katherine, "Respect Your Own Beauty," *Harper's Bazaar*, March 2002, pp. 163–164.

[27] Of the 13 issues of *Vogue* magazine that contain one or more article on cosmetic surgery, 11 contain at least one article highlighting new cosmetic technologies. Of the 9 issues of *Harper's Bazaar* that contain one or more article on cosmetic surgery, 5 have at least one article on new cosmetic technologies. In *People* and *Us Weekly* magazines the narrative frame of the candid account is more prevalent than the narrative frame of new technology. However, many of the articles on cosmetic surgery in *People* and *US Weekly* magazines combine elements of both narrative frames. For example, none of the 12 *People* magazine articles fit exclusively within the cosmetic surgery as new technology frame, but over half of these articles combine the frames of new technology and the candid account. A typical example is the January 20, 2003 issue of *People* magazine which contains an article that introduces readers to the new cosmetic technology of mesotherapy through providing a candid account of singer Roberta Flack's use of it.

nologies are linked with the following themes: scientific wonder, innovation, and progress; casual accessibility; medical expertise and health. Cosmetic surgery, accessible and healthful, forward-looking and medically legitimate, may become increasingly appealing – even difficult to refuse.

Scientific Wonder, Innovation, and Progress

Articles often emphasize the sheer capacity of new cosmetic technologies and equate their capacity with the almost unthinkable power of science. After admitting to a short-scar face lift, a forehead lift, under-eye peels, a permanent nose job and lip and eye lining, Stephanie Miller, the television host of *Pure Oxygen*, exclaims: "As it turns out you *can* fool Mother Nature!! She's not that bright."[28] The catch phrase in print and television advertisements for Botox, "It's not Magic, it's Botox Cosmetic," clearly identifies Botox as a scientific marvel, one that can "dramatically reduce even your toughest wrinkle in days." Singer Roberta Flack extols the feats of mesotherapy, a procedure that consists of multiple injections (filled with drugs that "break down fat") into the mesoderm, the middle layer of the skin: "I saw my chins disappear! The fat dissolved in front of my eyes!"[29] Indeed, doctors who perform microdermabrasion are described as using a "wand like device" as they gently "shoot superfine aluminum oxide crystals across the face, sanding away dead skin cells."[30]

Detailed descriptions of cosmetic technologies, in their new and improved capacity, conjure up associations with scientific progress and innovation. Articles with titles such as "Artificial Intelligence," "Face Forward" and "Beyond Botox" feature new technologies like Intense Pulsed Light therapy, or IPL, and the Lift 6, a "skin kneading" machine that encourages lymphatic drainage, increases oxygen content, and "jump starts collagen and elastin production." Dr. Jean Louis Sebagh touts the advanced qualities of Perlane, a biosynthetic form of hyaluronic acid: "It can add volume to the drooping and melting that comes with aging" and "fewer people are allergic to it than

---

[28] Miller, Nancy, "Forever Young: Some Women will Stop at Nothing to Ward off— and Reverse—the Signs of Aging," *Harper's Bazaar*, January 2002, p. 44.

[29] Adato, Alison, "Scaling Down. Singer Roberta Flack Sheds 32 lbs. with an Unusual Injection Therapy," *People*, January 20, 2003, p. 110.

[30] Diamond, Kerry, "Shaving Face. The New Secret to Soft, Wrinkle-Free Skin," *Harper's Bazaar*, September 2002, p. 182.

collagen, which comes from the hide of cows."[31] Readers are introduced to the innovative capacities of Artecoll, a collagen "infused with plexiglass particles to increase bulk and longevity" and Isolagen, a "skin harvesting" technique that enables a patient to grow her own collagen. Skin is harvested, "a pencil-eraser-size chunk from, say, the crack behind the ear", and then sent to a lab where "fibroblasts —collagen- producing sites – are grown in a petri dish."[32]

Casual, Unthreatening, and Accessible

Articles that frame cosmetic surgery as new technology often highlight its casual ease and accessibility. In recent print advertisements, Botox is described as a "simple, non-surgical procedure" which consists of "one ten-minute treatment – a few tiny injections." Cosmetic technologies are described as relatively hassle-free methods for upkeep that consist of "meticulous tweaking" in contrast to "painstaking means for serious repair."[33] Cosmetic surgery has become a "matter of maintenance" like hair coloring or dental work due to safer, easier techniques that require "no downtime" and yield real results.[34] As Ann Marie Gardner reports of her Perlane treatment (in which a biosynthetic form of hyaluronic acid was injected into her cheeks): "I injected freshness and life into my face with less time and effort than a visit to the hairdresser!"[35]

The casual, unthreatening appeal of new cosmetic technologies is strikingly evident in the recent phenomena of plastic surgery parties. Women turn cosmetic surgery into a "fun, lighthearted pastime" as they gather at the doctor's office for an "an evening of mixing girlfriends, gossip, and Botox shots."[36] SkinKlinic, one of a growing number of cosmetic technology chains, or "face factories," offers "dermatology's greatest hits," such as Botox and collagen, on a casual, walk-in basis.[37] New, unthreatening technologies may soothe and

---

[31] Gardner, Ann Marie, "Beyond Botox: Imagine looking younger in an instant, with no surgery and no side effects," *Harper's Bazaar,* April 2002, p. 78.

[32] Snowden, Lynn, "Face Forward," *Vogue,* August 2002, p. 256.

[33] Ibid., pp. 255–257.

[34] Brown, Sarah, "Scratching the Surface," *Vogue,* January 2002, pp. 110–112.

[35] Gardner, Anne Marie, "Beyond Botox: Imagine Looking Younger in an Instant with no Surgery and no Side Effects," *Harper's Bazaar,* April 2002, p. 77.

[36] Robinovitz, Karen, "The New Lipo: Does it Really Melt Away Your Fat?" *Harper's Bazaar,* November 2001, pp. 180–184.

[37] Astley, Amy, "Face Factory," *Vogue,* October 2001, p. 316.

tempt otherwise anxious and wary potential clientele. Veronica, a graphic designer in her late twenties, reveals that "the thought of just walking in and walking out afterward with hardly any down time is really tempting."[38] A new liposuction procedure, called microlipo, succinctly illustrates the capacity of new technology to increase people's ease and comfort with cosmetic surgery. Dr. Patricia Wexler explains that thanks to microlipo, "People aren't intimidated anymore by the word *liposuction*."[39] New microlipo technology, in contrast to the "painful, less precise" macro, or large volume, liposuction procedure, consists of a cannula the diameter of a pencil lead which, when inserted like a needle, creates several "quick-healing puncture holes" and moves back and forth in a "fanlike pattern to remove fat." While Dr. Debra Luftman concedes that her patients are "treated to local anesthetic" and "admittedly a valium or two," all and all microlipo is described as a dignified, non-invasive procedure: "They watch a movie; we chat. It's civilized."[40]

Health and Medicine

New cosmetic technologies are increasingly associated with health and medical expertise. Advertisements for Botox are sprinkled with phrases such as "ask your plastic surgeon about Botox Cosmetic," "FDA approved" and "call 1–800–Botox MD." Medi-spas[41] provide face and body services supervised by doctors that combine results-oriented treatments packed with what Dr. Scott Wells describes as "medically active substances that can actually heal the skin."[42] The silver ion facial reestablishes the "normal electrical surface terrain of healthy skin" as clients, hooked up to electrodes, wear a "leather mask with an adjustable frequency."[43] Biosculpt facials create a "regenerative" effect – skin specific serums ranging from collagen and elastin to "animal derived amniotic fluid and tissue extracts" are "micronized by an electric

---

[38] Brown, Sarah, "Addicted to Lipo: Thanks to the Latest Advances in Microliposuction, Perfection is Easier to Achieve than Ever. But, Asks Sarah Brown, is America's New Crash Diet of Choice Really a Good Idea?" *Vogue*, October 2002, p. 370.

[39] Ibid., p. 368.

[40] Ibid., p. 370.

[41] This term was coined by Dr. Bruce Katz, clinical professor of dermatology at Columbia University, who opened the first official Medi Spa in 1999.

[42] Lamont, Elizabeth, "Complexion Perfection. Can a Facial Deliver Flawless Skin?" *Vogue*, January 2003, pp. 184–185.

[43] Brown, Sarah, "Scratching the Surface: Spa Services of the Future," *Vogue*, January 2002, p. 112.

microcurrent in order to increase penetration."[44] Dr. Bruce Katz, a dermatologist who runs the Juva Skin & Laser Center and Medi-Spa in Manhattan, adds 5 fluorouracil, a prescription-strength cancer chemotherapeutic agent that targets pre-cancerous and sun-damaged cells, to his full-body hydrating masks. As Dr. Katz explains: "5 fluorouracil is like a smart bomb. It goes in and destroys abnormal cells but leaves healthy cells alone."[45]

Surgeons and dermatologists often equate new cosmetic technologies with healthful exercise. The Skin Master Plus stimulates facial muscles, alpha beta peels provide a facial workout, and the Lift 6 is described as a "cardio for your face."[46] Sonya Dakar, owner of the Sonya Dakar Skin Care Clinic, provides what she terms "skin care boot camp" for her clients: "This is not a luxury that feels good. This is meant to get your skin in shape, just like going to the gym does for your body."[47] Plastic surgeons also promote cosmetic technologies as a healthful alternative to excessive exercise. As an article in *Vogue* magazine explains, people who have been working out for a year but still "cannot lose the fat" make "ideal candidates" for microlipo.[48] According to Dr. Bellin: "The solution is modest lipo, true body sculpting used as an add-on to a healthy lifestyle."[49] Indeed, surgeons and patients both frequently claim that cosmetic technologies produce a healthy radiance, skin with a "rosy hue": "nothing has made my skin glow quite like this!" a woman exclaims, referring to her dermaplanning treatments.[50]

The narrative frame of cosmetic surgery as new technology encourages normalization in several respects. As new cosmetic technologies are touted as fantastical and wondrous, innovative and progressive, these same characteristics are equated with the people who use them. Praised for their courage, daring and forward-looking sensibilities, women who embrace new technologies without fear or hesitation become living symbols of scientific advancement and innovation. News anchor Greta Van Susteran's eye-lift is admired

---

[44] Lamont, Elizabeth, "Complexion Perfection. Can a Facial Deliver Flawless Skin?" *Vogue*, January 2003, p. 184.

[45] Brown, Sarah, "Scratching the Surface: Spa Services of the Future," *Vogue*, January 2002, 112.

[46] Ibid.

[47] Byrd, Veronica, "Face to Face," *People*, February 4, 2002, pp. 69–70.

[48] Brown, Sarah, "Artificial Intelligence: Can Features be Fashionable? Sarah Brown Reports on the Rise of the Somewhat Natural Woman," *Vogue*, April 2002, pp. 242–247.

[49] Ibid., p. 247.

[50] Diamond, Kerry, "Shaving Face. The New Secret to Soft, Wrinkle-Free Skin", *Harper's Bazaar*, September, 2002, p. 180.

as a "bold look"[51] and television star Patricia Heaton proudly describes her decision to have a tummy tuck and breast lift as a forward leap: "the future is here!"[52]

It may be difficult to justify the refusal of new cosmetic technologies that are increasingly casual and easy to obtain. Saying no to an arduous and invasive operation is easier than refusing a short treatment. Advertisements for Botox read: "It took forty years to get it. And ten minutes to do something about it." After all, it makes good, rational sense do something about that forty-year old frown line, especially if it only takes ten minutes. Technologically-produced accessibility also enables the framing of cosmetic alternation within a "rhetoric of choice" (Bordo 1993) – a rhetoric clearly projected in Botox print advertisements: "It's really up to you. You can choose to live with wrinkles. Or you can choose to live without them." Writer Elizabeth Hayt asks: "The technology is available . . . so why on earth would I choose to age gracefully?"[53] Finally, cosmetic technologies, increasingly associated with health and medical expertise, gain legitimacy. As Dr. Seth Martin, a San Francisco-based dermatologist explains: the FDA's approval of Botox "gives those people who were on the fence that extra initiative and comfort level."[54]

The Candid Account

A large number of articles consist of individuals' personal stories of their cosmetic surgeries and fit within the narrative frame I call the candid account.[55] Some examples of articles in *People* and *US Weekly* that fall within this narrative frame include: "Plastic Surgery: The Real Low Down From Real People"; "Patricia Heaton on Kids, *Raymond*, and her Plastic Surgery"; "Carnie Wilson's Plastic Surgery Diary – Liposuction, Breast Lift, and Tummy Tuck: Finishing Touches"; "Stars and Implants: Who Has Them and Who Doesn't"; and "A

---

[51] Smolowe, Jill, Macon Morehouse, Colleen O'Connor, et al., "Nipped, Tucked, and Talking," *People*, February 18, 2002, p. 47.

[52] Heaton, Patricia, "Belly Laughs," *People*, September 30, 2002, p. 110.

[53] Hayt, Elizabeth, "Addicted to Plastic Surgery," *Harper's Bazaar*, February 2002, p. 76.

[54] Shea, Christine, "Beyond Botox: With Doctors Extolling the Wonders of a Frozen Forehead, the Fountain of Youth has Never been Quite so Tantalizingly Accessible," *Vogue*, August 2002, p. 260.

[55] Deborhah Sullivan (2001: 160) refers to "autobiographical accounts" as an increasingly popular format among articles on cosmetic surgery in women's magazines. Indeed, out of the twelve articles on cosmetic surgery I reviewed in *People*, ten are characterized by first person, candid accounts.

New Day Dawns for *Today's* Al Roker who Speaks Candidly About the Gastric Bypass Surgery that Transformed his Life."[56] Within the candid account I found associations between cosmetic surgery and the following themes: courage and virtue; a gift or treat; independence and rebellion; common sense and pro-activity.

Courage and Virtue

Individuals who honestly admit to having cosmetic surgery, like those who embrace cosmetic surgery without hesitation, are praised for their boldness and courage. Before-and- after surgery photographs of TV newswoman Greta Van Susteren grace the February 18, 2002 cover of *People* magazine which reads: "Why I had Plastic Surgery: With Refreshing Candor, the 47-Year-Old Anchor Tells All About the New Look That is The Talk of TV." The article's heading salutes Van Susteren's courage to speak openly about her surgery: "Nipped, Tucked, and Talking: Greta Van Susteren debuts a bold look on her new show – and breaks TV news taboo by spilling the beans on her cosmetic surgery." Van Susteren explains: "I'm not the first woman on TV to do it. But here's where I'm different, I fess up."[57] After all, as she sensibly states, "Why was I doing it if it wasn't going to be noticeable?" A cover story on cosmetic surgery in *US Weekly* magazine includes "The No Shame Hall of Fame."[58] while a recent headline in *Harper's Bazaar* rings with honest defiance: "Why age? At 40, writer Elizabeth Hayt is proud to say she's done it all – an eye-lift, Botox injections, fat transplants, a breast augmentation, liposuction. And she doesn't plan to stop."[59]

In these articles of "full disclosure," honest admissions are often equated with virtue. Individuals who admit to cosmetic surgery provide an "ethical service" to others. Greta Van Susteren hopes that her own honest portrayal will help promote more widespread acceptance of cosmetic surgery, dispel

---

[56] Magazine articles are not the only forum for the candid account. "Extreme Makeover," a weekly ABC television series that began in December 2002 and continues through the 2003–2004 year, profiles everyday individuals getting cosmetic surgery. These individuals' cosmetic surgeries are filmed live and camera crews follow them throughout their recoveries.

[57] Smolowe, Jill, Macon Morehouse Macon, Colleen O'Conner, et al., "Nipped, Tucked, and Talking," *People*, February 18, 2002, p. 46.

[58] Sawyer, Beth, "How Far Stars Go to Get-and Stay-Gorgeous," *US Weekly*, May 20, 2002, p. 39.

[59] Hayt, Elizabeth, "Addicted to Plastic Surgery," *Harper's Bazaar*, February 2002, p. 76.

the need for secrecy, and make it easier for others to engage in it without fear. "I've made it safe for other people to have plastic surgery. It's no longer a bad word."[60] Indeed, Van Susteren, who was profiled in the December issue of *People* magazine entitled "25 Most Intriguing People of 2002," is hailed as the woman who, by "unveiling her still swollen eye lift on air – and then proceeding to talk about it," has "helped erase the stigma of plastic surgery."[61] *Today* television host Al Roker's gastric bypass surgery was filmed and shown on NBC's *Dateline* on November 12, 2002. Country music singer Carnie Wilson's surgery was broadcast live on the internet. Wilson, who gives bi-monthly lectures on gastric bypass surgery and plastic surgeries such as liposuction and tummy tucks, offers her own experience as an "educational service" to others: "I went public. I love to assist people. It makes me feel good."[62] The American Society for Bariatric Surgery credits Wilson with helping to popularize gastric bypass surgery. In 2001, 62,400 gastric bypass surgeries were performed, a seventy-percent increase from the 36,700 performed in 2000.[63]

A Gift or Treat
Within the narrative frame of the candid account, cosmetic surgery is often justified as a much-deserved treat or self-reward. Greta Van Susteren's eye-lift surgery, which she had while on vacation, is described as a deserved indulgence, something "just for her." As Van Susteren herself explains, "I just did it on a whim. It's the first time since I was 17 that I had a month off and no responsibilities."[64] Writer Elizabeth Hayt's multiple (and continuing) cosmetic alterations serve purely as gifts to herself: "I have no expectations of looking like a Hollywood siren, finding my dream guy, or giving up my shrink simply because I've been dipped, stripped, and nipped." Instead, through erasing "damage caused by an adolescence spent with sun reflectors and *Hawaiian Tropic*," Hayt simply hopes to face the world as a "less shriveled, more radiant forty year old."[65] Carnie Wilson's husband describes

[60] Smolowe, Jill, Macon Morehouse Macon, Colleen O'Conner, et al., "Nipped, Tucked, and Talking,"*People*, February 18, 2002, p. 51.
[61] *People*, December 30, 2002, p. 132.
[62] Tauber, Michele, "Weigh to Go," *People*, January 15, 2001, p. 90; Scott, Sophronia and Ulrica Wihlborg, "Finishing Touches," *People*, June 17, 2002, p. 102.
[63] *People*, June 17, 2002, 102.
[64] Smolowe, Jill, Morehouse, Macon, O'Conner, Colleen et al. "Nipped, Tucked, and Talking," *People*, February 18, 2002, p. 47.
[65] Hayt, Elizabeth, "Addicted to Plastic Surgery," *Harper's Bazaar,* February 2002, p. 78.

her last round of plastic surgeries as a hard earned, well-deserved, treat: it was a "celebratory thing for her. It was the topper."[66] Wilson herself is exuberant: "I feel younger, I feel more alive, I feel more vibrant!"; "I'm always smiling out of no-where!"; "I'm noticing men staring at me and you know what? They're not just staring at my face; they're looking at my entire body. It feels wonderful"; "I've never looked down and not had a belly my entire life! It feels incredible."[67]

Independence and Rebellion

The narrative frame of the candid account frequently contains heroic stories of struggle, independence, and rebellion.[68] Greta Van Susteren's decision to engage in cosmetic alteration was made in the face of reservations and even opposition from her husband, co-workers, and boss at Fox news. As *People* reports, Fox news chairman Roger Ailes, concerned about adequate healing time before she was due to be on air, actively discouraged Van Susteren from having surgery. Van Susteren went ahead with the surgery anyway: "I'm an independent type. No one tells me what to do."[69] Carnie Wilson's decision to have cosmetic surgery has given her a sense of autonomous strength and self-defiance: "I feel like I can do anything. I took control."[70]

Common Sense and Pro-Activity

Finally, the decision to have cosmetic surgery is praised as a rational, proactive step towards self-improvement or economic success. For Tom DeBonis, a businessman profiled in the October 2002 issue of *People* magazine, having cosmetic surgery symbolizes practical action and refutes passivity: "Some people never do anything about it – and some people go for it."[71] Greta Van Susteren's decision to have cosmetic surgery proves her willingness to take

---

[66] Scott, Sophronia and Ulrica Wihlborg, "Finishing Touches," *People*, June 17, 2002, p. 102.
[67] Tauber, Michele, "Weigh to Go," *People*, January 15, 2001, pp. 87, 93; Scott, Sophronia and Ulrica Wihlborg, "Finishing Touches," *People*, June 17, 2002, p. 98.
[68] In her interviews Kathy Davis (1995) found that many of her subjects decided to have surgery in spite of objections from loved ones and, in this respect, felt empowered, courageous, and even rebellious.
[69] Smolowe, Jill, Macon Morehouse, Colleen O'Conner, et al. "Nipped, Tucked, and Talking," *People*, February 18, 2002, p. 48.
[70] Tauber, Michele, "Weigh to Go," *People*, January 15, 2001, p. 87.
[71] Espinoza, Galina and Mike Neill, "About Face," *People*, October 28, 2002, p. 53.

a pro-active step towards self-improvement and maintaining a successful television career. According to Marcia Brand-wynne, a former Los Angeles news anchor and current station executive, "Women who are on TV know they have to look good. It's all about youth."[72] Van Susteren's eye-lift shows Kelly Lange, a former KNBC anchor, that she understands the unwritten rules of the game: "The pressure is there, period. It's not a part of the job description but women are savvy."[73] From NBC reporter Lisa Myers' perspective, Van's Susteren's eye-lift is clearly a rational move: "If the way we look gets in the way of how well we communicate then I don't mind the suggestion that we do something about it."[74]

Cosmetic Surgery and the Body

The two narrative frames discussed above contain several distinct portrayals of the body undergoing cosmetic surgery. These portrayals range from graphic, to straightforward, to casual, to upbeat, and often occur simultaneously within one article. I argue below that these portrayals contribute to the normalizing impact of media coverage, and help explain Americans' growing comfort with cosmetic surgery.[75]

An article in *Harper's Bazaar* offers readers contradictory accounts of the body undergoing new liposuction technologies and the potential side effects of these technologies. After being warned that new liposuction technologies can lead to "excessive bleeding," "permanent nerve damage," and "shock" readers are reassured that these risks can be avoided by "choosing an experienced doctor."[76] Dr. Pittman enthusiastically praises "tumescent" or "wet lipo" as the "new gold standard."[77] Despite "seeping fluid from the incision areas," "swelling for up to six months" and the need to wear a "tight girdle to re-drape the skin to the muscle," it causes "less blood loss" and helps

---

[72] Smolowe, Jill, Macon Morehouse, Colleen O'Conner, et al. "Nipped, Tucked, and Talking," *People*, February 18, 2002, p. 51.

[73] Ibid., p. 51.

[74] Ibid., p. 51.

[75] My discussion of body portrayals here is limited to the two narrative frames discussed above – cosmetic surgery as new technology and the candid account – both of which tend to be overwhelmingly positive in tone. It is also important to note however, that there are some (albeit few), articles that focus exclusively on the potentially dangerous and risky effects of cosmetic surgery. These articles will be discussed in the "Social Control" section below.

[76] Foss, Melissa, "The Truth About Lipo," *Harper's Bazaar*, February 2003, p. 122.

[77] Ibid., p. 120.

patients "heal quickly."[78] In an article in *People* magazine, Patricia Heaton, star of the television show *Everybody Loves Raymond*, describes her body undergoing cosmetic surgery with a combination of graphic realism, enthusiasm, and cheerful exclamation: "I got to take Percocet, Valium, and Ambien all at the same time! That's right! Who knew? It was as if cutting me open, creating a new belly button and scraping out seven years of scar tissue never happened!"[79] Similarly, writer Elizabeth Hayt punctuates her no-frills description of the immediate after- effects of cosmetic alteration on her body with ironic humor:

> It does seem as if I spend more time in hiding, recovering from my procedures and treating my ink-blue bruises, than I do flaunting the benefits. "No I can't go out tonight," I tell my friends, "I have a date with a pair of ice packs." When I walk down the street – my face dotted with scabs and glistening ointment – I do feel like an object of public ridicule. Crossing my path, small children have been known to point. And don't believe the crap the doctors tell you, that you'll feel no pain and be up and at Man Ray for dinner in no time. Needles, scalpels, lasers, chemicals – it all hurts like hell.[80]

Despite her candid admission of pain and side effects such as ink-blue bruises and scabs, Hayt cheerfully reassures readers of her ultimate satisfaction and comfort with her technologically altered self: "So far I have no regrets!"[81]

People's account of Greta Van Susteren's face undergoing eye-lift surgery, and the side effects of the surgery, alternates between straightforward candor and comic relief:

> Although Van Susteren felt no reservations when the doctor warned she would suffer bad swelling for three weeks, she says that when "I was told I couldn't have coffee that morning that was almost a deal breaker." At the outpatient clinic she was given a painkiller, which was enough to block all memory of the operation, but no general anesthesia. Four hours after the surgery, Coale found his groggy wife in the recovery room, her eyes partly sewn shut. "There was surprisingly no pain" says Van Susteren.[82]

---

[78] Ibid., p. 120.

[79] "Belly Laughs," *People*, September 30, 2002, 110.

[80] Hayt, Elizabeth, "Addicted to Plastic Surgery," *Harper's Bazaar*, February 2002, p. 78.

[81] Ibid.

[82] Smolowe, Jill, Macon Morehouse, Colleen O'Conner, et al., "Nipped, Tucked, and Talking," *People*, February 18, 2002, p. 50.

An honest portrayal of potential side effects is followed by a light quip about her morning's coffee. Van Susteren's eyes were "sewn shut" but readers are reassured that she felt "no pain." Van Susteren's own frank descriptions of her face, post eye-lift surgery, are tempered by tongue and cheek humor. After admitting that "I looked like hell," she recounts an anecdote about how her husband teased her about not recognizing her and suggested she wear a nametag. Van Susteren also confesses that she continues to put on "makeup and sunglasses" before she leaves the house "so I don't look like a victim of spousal abuse."[83]

Finally, *People's* second cover story on country music singer Carnie Wilson's plastic surgeries includes a combination of light and chillingly straightforward descriptions of her body undergoing cosmetic surgery. The article begins with a blow-by-blow account of Wilson's body parts as altered by Dr. Steven Jax:

> In an eight hour operation she had the skin on her tummy tucked (leaving her lighter by 7 pounds), her belly button repositioned, breasts lifted, and minor liposuction on her torso and hips. Zax also cut away half a pound of skin from under each armpit.[84]

Honest admissions of Wilson's post surgery side effects follow: "stiffness," a stomach "pulled so tight I could barely walk at first" and wearing a "tight girdle for eight weeks and a support bra day and night." But readers are also reassured by Wilson's exposure to oxygen therapy treatment: "Luckily the eight hour long sessions of hyberbaric oxygen therapy prescribed by Dr. Zax and administered (at 250$ each) in a cylindrical plexiglass chamber, kept bruising to a minimum."[85] While oxygen therapy does not help with scarring, Wilson remains thrilled with the overall results of her surgeries:

> Though her abdomen, breasts, and armpits were marred with dark brown scars that will take 10 months to fade, by mid-April Wilson was exultant. "It's so fun to be proud when you're stripped down" she says. "Now I can wear so many things!"[86]

These portrayals of the body undergoing cosmetic surgery, combined with descriptions of the effects of surgery on the body, encourage new, cosmetic

---

[83] Ibid.
[84] Scott, Sophronia and Ulrica Wihlborg, "Finishing Touches," *People*, June 17, 2002, p. 98.
[85] Ibid., p. 99.
[86] Ibid., p. 98.

surgery-friendly understandings of the body. Chillingly matter-of-fact accounts of the body undergoing surgery – "half a pound of skin cut away from under each armpit" – combined with straightforward descriptions of side effects – "small bowel obstructions and potentially deadly blood clots" – demystify cosmetic surgery.[87] Graphic details of surgery and side effects – "cutting me open," "scraping out seven years of scar tissue," "marred with dark brown scars" – can de-sensitize readers.[88] Upbeat descriptions – the excess skin was "snipped away," coupled with outright enthusiasm – "I got to take Percocet, Valium and Ambien all at the same time!" – casualize cosmetic surgery.[89] Finally, light, even humorous accounts of side effects – "bruising kept to a minimum" and "small children have been known to point!" – downplay side effects.[90]

Taken together, these portrayals of the body can discourage readers and viewers from listening and paying attention to bodily pain, cutting, bruising, swelling, and bleeding, as potential warning signals or indicators of distress. An aspect of bodily knowledge, wherein pain and bleeding are respected as meaningful, informative signals, recedes and an intervention-receptive, side effect-tolerant, understanding of the body takes its place.

Cosmetic Surgery as Social Control

Aesthetic Conformity

Kathryn Pauly Morgan argues that cosmetic surgery fuels a "pathological inversion of the normal" – as more women obtain "surgically created, beautiful faces and bodies" the naturally given will be labeled the "technologically primitive" while the "'ordinary' will be perceived and evaluated as the 'ugly'" (Morgan 1991: 41). But I am convinced that we are slipping deeper into that pathological inversion. Beyond making beauty "technologically

---

[87] Scott, Sophronia and Ulrica Wihlborg, "Finishing Touches," *People*, June 17, 2002, p. 98; Tauber, Michele, "Weigh to Go," *People*, January 15, 2001, p. 90.

[88] Heaton, Patricia, "Belly Laughs," *People,* September 30, 2002, p. 110; Tauber, Michelle, "Finishing Touches," *People*, June 17, 2002, p. 99.

[89] Espinoza, Galina and Mike Neill, "About Face," *People*, October 28, 2002, p. 54; Heaton, Patricia, "Belly Laughs," *People*, September 30, 2002, p. 110.

[90] Hayt, Elizabeth, "Addicted to Plastic Surgery," *Harper's Bazaar*, February 2002, p. 78; Scott, Sophronia and Ulrica Wihlborg, "Finishing Touches, *People,* June 17, 2002, p. 99.

achievable" and creating a "technological beauty imperative" (Morgan 1990: 40, 41), beyond creating increasingly stringent understandings of beauty and liberal understandings of ugliness, cosmetic surgery also produces a fundamental story of sameness versus difference, a story of encroaching aesthetic conformity.

A woman explains her reason for having cosmetic surgery as wanting to "look ordinary," to "fit in" (Davis 1995). Actress Carrie Fisher reports that at her mother's 70th birthday party the only woman who "stood out" was an old school friend of her mother's "who had had nothing done."[91] As increasing numbers of women engage in eye lifts, forehead lifts, mini and macro face-lifts, Botox and Perlane injections, liposuction, breast lifts and implants, beyond looking more "beautiful," or "younger," they also may begin to look *more alike.* Indeed, the erosion of women's "natural diversity and difference" (Gillespie 1996: 70) begins to reconstruct our understanding of difference. If difference is defined as "degrees of deviation" from a growing contingent of technologically altered faces and bodies, those with "naturally diverse" faces and bodies may "stand out" and feel "different"—in short, abnormal (Brush 1998: 35).

Health and Normalcy

Cosmetic surgery promises aesthetic conformity. It also offers the potential to achieve mental and physical health. In fact, saying "no" to cosmetic technologies, increasingly accessible and easy to use, may risk ill health and irrationality. According to Dr. Patricia Wexler, liposuction improves physical and mental health while refusal may lead to compulsive over exercise and neurosis:

> A woman who is ultrathin but has a body part she doesn't like is better off having lipo than continuing to exercise three hours a day and starve herself in hopes of reducing an area that is genetically impossible to change. The hope is that she will become a little less neurotic.[92]

Proponents of cosmetic surgery continue to promote it as an accessible, rational, and practical tool to *improve* physical and mental health. Increasingly however, plastic surgeons identify their ideal clients as *already* "normal,"

---

[91] Fisher, Carrie, "The Truth About Renee," *Harper's Bazaar*, July 26, 2002, pp. 22–26.
[92] Brown, Sarah, "Addicted to Lipo, Thanks to the Latest Advances in Microliposuction, Perfection is Easier to Achieve Than Ever. But, Asks Sarah Brown, is America's New Crash Diet of Choice Really a Good Idea?" *Vogue*, October 2002, p. 370.

"healthy" individuals.[93] An article in *Vogue* identifies the ideal candidate for liposuction as follows: "she has a fit, yoga-toned body; she eats healthfully."[94] A recent feature in *Harper's Bazaar* explains that "being fit helps ensure a great result, because the doctor can see your best silhouette, and your skin will be more resilient."[95] Dr. Z. Paul Lorenc refuses to operate on physically unfit individuals: "I won't take a patient who is overweight."[96] Dr. Jarrod Frank, master of ceremonies at a Botox party, praises his clients' rationality and practical initiative: "My clientele is predominantly young women who understand the importance of starting a maintenance program before their faces start sagging down to their knees."[97]

Over-users and Adverse Effects

So-called "mentally ill," "unfit," and "unhealthy" individuals receive little attention in the majority of articles on cosmetic surgery, except as examples of non-preferred clients. On the other hand, these individuals are often used as case studies in articles with an exclusive focus on the adverse side effects and health risks of cosmetic surgery. While only two out of *Vogue*'s eighteen articles on cosmetic surgery contain in-depth discussions of potential health risks, both explicitly associate the risks with individuals who misuse and overuse cosmetic technologies. Women with "mottled, irritated, de-hydrated" skin are described as "skin care junkies" and "addicts." Kate's "over-processed," "pre-maturely aged" skin is the result of her "compulsive over-use" of glycolic-acid cleaners, Botox injections, and her insatiable appetite for untested, non-FDA approved products. "If the treatment is somehow forbidden – the frisson of knowing that the Perlane injected into her forehead is non-FDA-

---

[93] This is a striking example of normalization, especially when one compares the contemporary notion of the ideal cosmetic surgery client (normal, healthy individual) with previous conceptions throughout the 20th century. As Elizabeth Haiken (1997) documents, these conceptions included individuals with physical deformities, those suffering from economic hardship (particularly throughout the depression era) and, in the late 1930s and 1940s, individuals with mental illness and low self-esteem.

[94] Brown, Sarah, "Addicted to Lipo: Thanks to the Latest Advances in Microliposuction, Perfection is Easier to Achieve Than Ever. But, Asks Sarah Brown, is America's New Crash Diet of Choice Really a Good Idea?" *Vogue,* October, 2002, p. 368.

[95] Foss, Melissa, "The Truth About Lipo," *Harper's Bazaar*, February 2003, pp. 119–122.

[96] Ibid., p. 120.

[97] Robinovitz, Karen, "Plastic Surgery Parties," *Harper's Bazaar*, November 2001, pp. 180–184.

approved – she's ecstatic."[98]* In "Addicted to Lipo," the harmful effects of liposuction are discussed in the context of over-use (termed "serial lipo"), with over-users identified as anorexics, bulimics, and individuals suffering from BDD (Body Dysmorphic Disorder). These mentally ill individuals often have too much fat removed from a certain spot, creating "future weight gain in the nearest area of fatty disposition," or a distribution of fat that is "abnormal-looking."[99] Not only are the symptoms of serial lipo "unattractive," but the consequences can be physically dangerous. As Dr. Wexler describes: "At a certain point, you'll start gaining weight intra-abdominally, around your organs – the classic beer belly. It's unhealthy fat, and as a result, it is these people who are more prone to have heart attacks and different systemic diseases."[100]

Perhaps the most detrimental consequence serial lipo users suffer however, particularly from the loss of too much natural fat, is a serious reduction in the potential for successful surgical alteration of the body later on in life. According to Dr. Frileck: "If I'm doing a make over, I need that fat in order to add highlights and angles. And it's not just any fat. It's fat that's going to survive, it's your own fat."[101] Over-users, unable to correct their "loose, hanging skin" with a face-lift, will lose out on that "healthy, youthful look" achieved by their normal and well-adjusted counterparts. As Dr. Wexler succinctly puts it: "if you've removed too many fat cells you can't do anything to fix it."[102]

---

[98] Urquhart, Rachel, "Damage Control. Is Your Skin-Care Regimen Making You Look Older – Faster?" *Vogue*, November 2002, p. 463.

* Highlighting the dangers of using of untested, non FDA approved cosmetic technologies is unusual, and contradicts the many articles I found that contain positive examples of the use of untested, non-FDA cosmetic technologies. For example, the April and October 2002 issues of *Harper's Bazaar* feature positive reviews of Perlane and LipoDissolve and the January 20, 2003 issue of *People* contains a positive autobiographical account of mesotheapy. All of these procedures are untested and non-FDA approved. Further, the use of non-FDA approved and untested cosmetic technologies is often portrayed as exciting, cheerful, and fun. As Dr. Seth Matarasso enthusiastically observes in a recent *Vogue* feature: "'People are injecting everything but the kitchen sink into their faces!'" Finally, the embrace of new and untested technologies is often praised as bold and courageous. Writer Elizabth Hayt explains: "When people ask 'Aren't you afraid of having a foreign substance injected into your body?' I invariably answer, 'Which one?'"

[99] Brown, Sarah, "Addicted to Lipo: Thanks to the Latest Advances in Microliposuction, Perfection is Easier to Achieve Than Ever. But, Asks Sarah Brown, is America's New Crash Diet of Choice Really a Good Idea?" *Vogue*, October 2002, p. 371.

[100] Ibid.

[101] Ibid.

[102] Ibid.

In this way, over-users become non-preferred clients, punished for their failure to utilize cosmetic technology rationally and effectively.

The Body Re-Visited

In some respects, cosmetic surgery promotes the body as a site of creative self-formation and re-formation, a malleable material through which new identities are forged. French performance artist Orlan utilizes cosmetic surgery as a tool for self-expression, as a way to reveal her "true self," a self that consists of multiple and shifting identities, through her body. As she puts it "by wanting to become another I become myself. I am a bulldozer: dominant, aggressive . . . but if that becomes fixed it is a handicap. I, therefore, renew myself by becoming timid and tender" (Orlan as cited in Actuel 1991: 78). Indeed, for some, cosmetic surgery enables freedom of expression and improves the body's capacity for accurate self-representation. One woman describes her post cosmetically altered body as follows: "It was such freedom. I could finally just move around in my body. I felt so free" (Davis 1995: 82) – And for Barbara Leight, a manager at the Maryland Port Authority, it is her post-face lifted, post-laser surgeried look "that fits with how I feel on the inside."[103] A recent *Vogue* article promises the potential for true self-expression through the use of new cosmetic technologies: by "stripping down the skin" and "starting fresh," by peeling away layers of sediment the real you is revealed.[104]

Individuals often experience their cosmetically altered bodies as expressive of their "true" selves (Kathy Davis describes cosmetic surgery as "reducing the distance between the external and the internal"), and many feel comfortable, "at home," and *embodied* in their cosmetically altered bodies. Without contradicting the validity of these experiences, I suggest below that cosmetic surgery can also disrupt the potential for reflexive communication between self and body. On the one hand, cosmetic surgery can produce a body of limited capacity, lacking in physical sensation and responsiveness – a body less able to reflect the full range and complexity of subjective experience. On the other hand, cosmetic surgery, and the tolerance or dismissal of bodily responses such as pain, blood and bruising that often accompany

[103] Espinoza, Galina and Mike Neill, "About Face," *People*, October 28, 2002, p. 55.
[104] Brown, Sarah, "Face Time," *Vogue*, May 2002, pp. 200–202.

it, may begin to discredit the body's role as a knowledge source and self-informant. Whether through rendering a mistrust of bodily signals, or the production of a body of reduced sensation and expressiveness, cosmetic surgery can restrict interactive relations between self and body, or put differently, invoke a loss of *embodied knowledge*.

The Cold, Still Body

Cosmetically altered bodies can fail to adjust to environmental temperature fluctuations. For example, a woman in Davis' study explains that when she goes running or biking her post-implant breasts feel "like ice cubes" and that when she enters a warm room after being out in the cold they are "completely stiff" (Davis 1995: 144). Women with breast implants sometimes experience numbness, reduced pleasure sensations, and capacity to breast-feed. Finally, cosmetic procedures often restrict muscle movement. Botox "paralyzes" facial muscles, while D-contraxol, "a complexion smoothing cocktail" that contains manganese gluconate, prevents the contraction of "contractile fibers," or "fibroblasts."[105]

Those with cosmetically altered faces can, albeit to varying degrees, experience a reduced capacity to emit emotion and to respond and interact with the world around them. A non-altered face engages in about 15,000 expressive responses (or muscle movements) a day, including "smiling, laughing, frowning, and eye brow arching," all of which are "wrinkle causing."[106] Technologically altered skin, on the other hand, or "dream skin" as top aesthetician Cornelia Zicu puts it, "looks like marble."[107] In addition to a limited capacity for expressiveness and responsiveness (a recent *Vogue* article profiling new cosmetic technologies is titled "Freeze Frame"), cosmetic surgery may erase physical evidence of past expressive activity. Botox "wipes out lines of expression."[108] while Dr. Lisa Airan describes the post-cosmetic surgery face as a "smooth, blank canvas."[109]

By restricting muscle movement and erasing the physical evidence of lived

---

[105] Brown, Sarah, "Freeze Frame," *Vogue*, February 2003, p. 282.
[106] Ibid.
[107] Urquhart, Rachel, "Damage Control. Is Your Skin-Care Regimen Making You Look Older Faster?" *Vogue*, November, 2002, p. 494.
[108] Brown, Sarah, "Freeze Frame," *Vogue*, February 2003, p. 282.
[109] Urquhart, Rachel, "Damage Control. Is Your Skin-Care Regimen Making You Look Older – Faster?" *Vogue*, November 2002, p. 494.

experience, cosmetic surgery reduces the body's capacity to express knowledge. Susan Griffin's profound phrase, *"From the body of the old woman we can tell you something of the life she lived"* (Griffin 1978: 210), loses some of its meaning in light of the cosmetically altered body. What can we learn and remember from a body that has been cosmetically altered? Other than technological residue – some scarring perhaps, reduced muscle movement and a lack of facial lines – the cosmetically altered face and body bears less trace of a unique lived history, of the complexity of subjective experience, than an unaltered one. Instead, one technologically altered face can be difficult to decipher from another.[110] A recent headline in *Vogue* magazine reads: "Are we fast approaching an ageless society? With the latest innovations in plastic surgery, it at least *looks* like it."[111] The author of the article goes on to describe that, due to rapid increases in facial plastic surgery, "We are now hard-pressed to say what a 35-year old or a 43-year old looks like."[112]*

The Discredited Body

Performance artist Orlan offers audiences live performances of cosmetic surgery. We bear witness to the technological cutting and severing of Orlan's flesh and watch her body respond to the technology. Her blood pours and her skin bruises and swells. At the same time, we witness her making light of, and ignoring, these bodily signs of protest. Her mood is often playful and she talks animatedly while her face is being jabbed with needles or cut (Davis 1997; Reitmaier 1995). By exposing her audience to the graphic technological invasion of the human body, revealing the fleshy protest to that invasion,

---

[110] I am hauntingly reminded here of the world of blankness and mechanized homogenization envisioned by Madeleine L'Engle in her 1962 children's novel, *A Wrinkle in Time*. In this world, each child looks exactly like the next child and at the same time everyday, all the children go out onto the sidewalk and bounce a ball, the same red ball, for the same amount of minutes (L'Engle 1962).

[111] Shea, Christine, "Beyond Botox: With Doctors and Patients Extolling the Wonders of a Frozen Forehead, the Fountain of Youth has Never Been Quite so Tantalizingly Accessible," *Vogue*, August 2002, p. 254.

[112] Ibid.

* Soap operas provide rich sites for viewing this phenomenon of aesthetic homogenization. Actresses such as Melody Scott Thomas ("Nicki" on the "Young and the Restless") and Susan Lucci ("Erica" on "All my Children") both of whom have worked on their respective soap operas for over twenty years, have blank smooth faces, faces with limited expressive ranges, unchanging over time. Indeed, on soap operas, mothers, daughters, and granddaughters are increasingly undistinguishable from each other in age.

and ignoring and making fun of that fleshly protest, Orlan evokes an unworthy body, a body as a source of unreliable knowledge.

Country singer Carnie Wilson's body, post-gastric bypass surgery, is plagued with recurring physical discomfort. Gastric bypass surgery "short circuited" her digestive system, producing an increased vulnerability to sugar intake.[113] Too much sugar sends Wilson's body into an insulin reaction, a reaction that she describes as "the worst feeling in the world," one characterized by a "cold sweat," "heart racing," and "nausea."[114] And yet, for Wilson, the potentially life-threatening symptoms she encounters whenever she eats certain foods, or more than a certain amount, are tolerated, even welcomed. They are "a blessing" because they "keep me from eating foods that are not good for me."[115] While bodily protests to cosmetic surgery are often met with matter of fact tolerance or upbeat dismissal, those responses that signal outright rejection of cosmetic technology may invoke impatience and anger. For example, several women in Kathy Davis' study expressed frustration with their bodies' resistive responses to breast implants – fever and infection – as these responses required the implants' removal (Davis 1995).

The body's innate capacity for knowledge has been widely articulated by feminist scholars. Helen Longino describes the body as a "cognitive resource" that directs our attention to features that "we would otherwise overlook" (Longino 1999: 335). Alison Jaggar teaches us to pay attention to bodily signals that prompt us to "caress or cuddle" and to "fight or flee" (Jaggar 1997: 190). Cosmetic surgery, by contrast, appears to engender a growing mistrust of bodily signals. Pain, blood, bruising, swelling, and infection are ignored, made light of, and even provoke feelings of anger and frustration. In this respect, cosmetic surgery challenges feminist interpretations of the body as a legitimate, innate source of knowledge and may undermine the body's capacity to serve as a vital self-informant and protector.[116]

---

[113] Tauber, Michelle, "Weigh to Go," *People*, January 15, 2001, p. 93.
[114] Ibid.
[115] Ibid.
[116] Curiously, feminist scholarship on cosmetic surgery offers little analysis of how cosmetic surgery may disrupt reflexive communication between self and body, or undermine the body's legitimacy as a source of knowledge. Instead, feminist analyses of cosmetic surgery and the body appear to be limited to two positions. First, some feminist scholars critique cosmetic surgery as a form of material violence on the body and argue that cosmetic surgery pathologizes the non-cosmetically altered body – the unaltered body becomes "ugly" and "deformed" with body parts described as "symptoms" in need of repair (Morgan 1991; Brush 1998: 30). Second, some fem-

Concluding Thoughts

First, cosmetic surgery may discredit the body as a worthy knowledge source and self-informant. Second, cosmetic surgery can limit the body's potential to reflect and respond to unique, lived experience. Third, cosmetic surgery can also serve as a tool to re-construct bodies in compliance with shifting identities – a device that improves the body's capacity for self-representation. In each of these readings, cosmetic surgery promotes the assumption of an inner self apart from, or superior to, the body. In the first instance, the dichotomy between self and body is most pronounced. The body, perceived as an "unreliable knowledge source" and potential "contaminant" to the realization of pure self, may be discarded altogether.[117] In the second instance, cosmetic surgery endangers the relationship between self and body such that the body's capacity to respond to, and express, the full range of subjective experience, erodes.[118] In the third instance, the body's utility is acknowledged

inist scholars argue that cosmetic surgery offers women an escape hatch from fixed, essentialist notions of the female body (Balsamo, 1992; Orlan 1995, 1997). Examples of the second position are revealed in the opening paragraphs of the "Body Revisited" section. (The statement from performance artist Orlan, in which she refers to cosmetic surgery as an enabler of free, bodily self-expression, provides a particularly striking example). These two positions, cosmetic surgery as oppressive (doing violence to the female body), or liberating (freeing women from an essentialized female body, a body limited to the function of reproduction), leave questions regarding cosmetic surgery's effect on the body's capacity to offer knowledge unanswered.

[117] Here I am reminded of the repudiated Cartesian body, a body prone to "deceptions and entanglements", a contaminant of the real self, the "seat of reason and will, cognition and action" – the mind. Indeed, for Decartes, the body must be "shorn away from the essential self" such that the self can perform acts of pure reason (Longino 1999: 332). This disassociation between self and body is evident in television actress Patricia Heaton's dismissal of her natural, pre-cosmetically altered breasts as bothersome appendages, "two empty flesh sacs plaintively whap-whap-whapping against my chest on my morning jog" (*People*, September 2002), and in another woman's description of her pre-implant breasts as "those things" (Davis 1995). Finally, performance artist Orlan's work also invokes a distancing between self and body. At a multimedia festival in Amsterdam in 1995 Orlan delivered a lecture while continuous film of her latest cosmetic surgeries (film that included her lips being sliced open and her ear being severed from her face with a scalpel) played on a large screen behind her. As Kathy Davis recounts, Orlan, though visibly irritated by audience noise and agitation (she asked the audience whether it was "absolutely necessary to talk about the pictures *now* or whether she could proceed with her talk"), appeared "unmoved by these images." One audience member stood up and said "You act as though it were not *you* up there on the screen" (Davis 1997: 168).

[118] In an article entitled "Respect Your Own Beauty" a woman celebrates her non-cosmetically altered body's reflection of her unique lived experience and refuses to get cosmetic surgery for fear of losing her bodily capacity for self-expression. She proudly describes standing out among a crowd of cosmetically altered bodies: *In a*

only as "brute matter" (Grosz 1987: 5), a mere mechanism bonded in a hierarchical relationship with the self, and molded and re-molded in accordance with self-expression.[119] Whether dismissed or discredited, restricted in capacity for self-expression, or like Plato's *chora*, treated as a passive receptacle that only gives forth "further versions" (Butler 1993: 42) of the self that enters it, the body fades as a contributory element to self creation. I suggest that, in this respect, cosmetic surgery denies the body as a "formative principle" (Butler 1993: 42) of the self.

Writer Elizabeth Hayt cherishes her technological origins and proves herself an eager Platonic receptacle. "I celebrate the fact that my glow doesn't come from within but has been manufactured by the Michelangelos of modern medicine."[120] Like the "phallic Form" that Butler describes as reproducing itself through the feminine, but "with no assistance from her" (Butler 1993: 42), Hayt's glow is produced through her body, but with no assistance from it. Hayt's technological self may present us with a real-life manifestation of what Teresa Brennan calls the "foundational fantasy." This fantasy, a symptom of western, Protestant, liberal, humanist, capitalist, patriarchal dominance, invokes an egoistic, individualist subject, a subject "without ties, dependent on no-one" who objectifies and denies the agency of nature (the body) (Brennan 2000: 160). Indeed, as technological efficiency increases, so too does the "capability of satisfying the desires in the foundational fantasy with more precision" and, with that, nature is more easily "denied as a source" (Brennan 2000: 161).

*   *   *

Waking up from my recurring dream of being surrounded by my family who had become fembots, I felt hauntingly alone. But I also felt relieved that I was not

---

room of identical bodies, factory made shapes that not much had ever happened to (except the knife and the surgeon's suction machine), I wanted to whip off my coat and put on a belt. No one in that room had my body, and mine is a body that has been places. It's been loved, it's given birth, it's strutted in glee and been brought to its knees by grief. It's uniquely mine (*Harper's Bazaar*, March 2002). This article provides one of the few examples of resistance against cosmetic surgery I came across in my sample, and certainly it is the most explicit one. The only other article from *Harper's Bazaar* that provides an alternative to cosmetic surgery is titled "Growing Old Gracefully" (April 2003).

[119] Orlan describes her body while undergoing cosmetic surgery, as "just an inert piece of meat, lying on the table " (Davis 1997: 175; Reitmaier 1995: 8).

[120] Hayt, Elizabeth, "Addicted to Plastic Surgery," *Harper's Bazaar*, February 2002, p. 78.

a fembot, I was still my human self. I went downstairs and frantically searched
each of my family members for the fembot nodule, finding none. More relief flowed
over me.

While fembots resemble humans almost perfectly, they do have a technological indicator, a distinguishing nodule that gives away their non-human-
ness. I fear being the only human among a crowd of fembots. But I am more
afraid of not being able to distinguish my humanness from technology, of
failing to decipher a technological glow from a human one. Indeed, plastic
surgeons are perfecting their skill at "covering their tracks." A recent *Vogue*
article subtitled the "The Evolution of Plastic Surgery and the Rise of the
'Somewhat Natural Woman'" reports that the plastic surgery community has
"witnessed a backlash against looking 'done.'"[121] Breast implant design inno-
vations in "profile shapes" have replaced the "hemispherical or semicircular
shape" of past eras. As Dr. Scott Wells explains, "it used to be that you could
always spot implants in a plunging neckline or bikini" but, with the new
teardrop shape, "If they're well done, you really shouldn't be able to tell
they're there."[122]

We may be growing nearer to that world envisioned by Isaac Asimov, a
world that is populated by humans and humanoid robots, robots identical
to humans in appearance, with no distinguishing nodule or technological
indicator. In Asimov's story, "Evidence," a man named Stephen Byerley, who
is suspected of being a robot, eventually becomes the first "World Coordinator."
Many years later, the humanity of Bryerley remains in doubt:

> "I stared at her with a sort of horror. 'Is that true?'
>
> 'All of it' she said.
>
> 'And the great Byerley was simply a robot.'
>
> 'Oh there's no way of ever finding out. I think he was. But when he decided
> to die, he had himself atomized, so that there will never be any legal
> proof.
>
> Besides – what difference would it make?'"[123]

---

[121] Brown, Sarah, "Artificial Intelligence: Can Features Be Fashionable?" *Vogue*,
April 2002, p. 247.
[122] Ibid.
[123] This excerpt is taken from Ellen Ullman's article entitled "Programming the Post-
Human: Computer Science Redefines Life" in the October 2002 issue of *Harper's
Magazine*.

What difference would it make? For the most part, we march onward, cheerfully embracing the technological replacements of human, plant and animal forms.[124]

* * *

But technological copies often fall short of the original. As Teresa Brennan puts it: "Take the giant, airy American strawberry. Genetically recombined for improved size, and grown in degraded soil, it looks great and tastes . . . like nothing" (Brennan 2000: 120). Scientists have found that genetically cloned sheep and pigs, in addition to suffering other health problems, age prematurely. Technological replacements also produce symptoms. These symptoms, while often ignored, "do not disappear" and can appear elsewhere, perhaps in "more virulent forms" (Romanyshyn 1988: 30). Some scientists believe that the consumption of genetically modified and hormone-treated foods explain, at least in part, the earlier onset of menstruation and breast development among girls. Pesticides, used extensively in agriculture and on lawns, along with wide spread use of other synthetic chemicals, including plastics, contribute to growing rates of cancer.[125] Hormone Replacement Therapy (HRT), commonly administered to women to treat menopause, has been found to increase the risk of breast cancer, heart disease, and dementia.

Perhaps the most "deadening effect" (Brennan 2000: 187) of technological replacements is a loss of biological complexity and diversity.[126] The spread of

---

[124] Computer and cognitive scientists, mathematicians, and cryptographers gathered in June of 2002 for the first workshop on "human interactive proofs" where the goal was the creation of CAPTCHA or "Completely Automated Probabilistic Public Turning Test to tell Computers and Humans Apart." But, as Ellen Ullman, a writer and former software engineer who attended the workshop, points out, the primary concern addressed by scientists was not one of "human dignity and worth." Instead scientists focused on the development of automated methods to prevent software robots, or "bots" from invading chat rooms and barraging email systems with unwanted "spam" messages (*Harper's Magazine*, October 2002, pp. 60–71).

[125] According the EPA, approximately 165 of the active ingredients approved for use in U.S. pesticide products are known or suspected human carcinogens. According to studies conducted by the National Academy of Sciences, exposure to pesticide residues in food causes 4000–20,000 cases of cancer per year in the United States (Miller 2004: 234, 518).

[126] According to Harvard biologist E.O. Wilson we are losing twenty-seven thousand plant and animal species each year, or seventy-four species every day (Raeburn 1995). The Rural Advancement Foundation International reports, for example, that of the seventy-five kinds of vegetables grown in the United States, 97% of all varieties are now extinct. Of the 7,098 apple varieties grown in the United States between 1804–1905, 6,121 have become extinct (RAFI report as cited in Rifkin 1998). In India,

modern agricultural practices, such genetically engineered crops and mono-cultures, are contributing to genetic uniformity within the plant and animal worlds (Rifkin 1998: 108).[127] Just as technological replacements produce a "dulled" earth (Brennan 2000: 179), they also risk a deadening effect upon the human body. Cosmetic surgery can inhibit the body's capacity for move-ment, animation, and for intricate and complex functions. With the ongoing production of "dulled bodies," the unique physical reflection of each human being's life erodes.

As we attempt to "know" the human body, the natural world of plants and animals, the earth, to improve it and control it, we succeed in creating a world of depleted knowledge and complexity. But, despite the consequences, such as living among a crowd of inferior copies, we continue to indulge in that "illusion of self-containment," to deny our dependence upon the body and the earth, and to dismember and destroy it (Brennan 2000: 160, 189).

Afterward

Since the publication of this essay, I've begun an ethnographic investigation of the normalization of plastic surgery, interviewing women who engage in surgery, those who resist, and interviewing and observing the work of some cosmetic surgeons. My initial investigations are proving that the narrative themes I discuss here are not at all limited to the pages of women's maga-zines. These themes, and others that I will elaborate in forthcoming work, populate my interviews with women who have had cosmetic surgery. They are also found in the words of surgeons themselves. I was particularly struck by the resonance between the component themes of the normalization of cos-metic surgery found in women's magazines and the narrative framing of a cosmetic surgeon whose "plastic surgery information session" I recently attended.

---

farmers grew more than thirty thousand traditional rice varieties just fifty years ago. Today ten modern varieties account for more than 75% of the rice grown in India (Rhoades 1991).

[127] Garrison Wilkes, a professor of botany at the University of Massachusetts, explains that the spread of modern agricultural practice is destroying the "genetic resources upon which it is built" and likens the situation to "taking stones from the foundation to repair the roof" (Wilkes as cited in Rifkin 1998: 111). Paul Raeburn, author of *The Last Harvest* and science editor for *Business Week* agrees: "No breakthrough in funda-mental research can compensate for the loss of genetic material crop breeders depend on" (Raeburn 1995).

I sat in a sea of women. Faces strained with concentration and pens scratched. Dr. Peter Wyler[128] spoke and gestured energetically towards women's necks, noses, breasts, arms, stomachs and buttocks that flashed on the power point screen. His voice and arm movements alternately critiqued and praised, critiqued and praised, as the power point slides shifted from un-altered to surgically altered body part. The whirlwind power point presentation stopped momentarily, an image of a woman's surgically altered neck frozen on the screen. Dr Wyler leaned forward over his lectern, looked directly into the faces of his female audience, and said:

> You need to understand that plastic surgery is *serious business*. Women think that they can just "squeeze it in" – no – this is absolutely not the case. In fact, I recommend serious planning and putting aside at least six months – preferably up to a year – for the surgery and recovery. If you are serious about surgery you are going to have to make some *serious sacrifices* with regards to your schedules.

Two women sitting next to me exchanged anxious looks. Did their anxiety stem from a genuine fear of having "serious surgery" I wondered? Or were they worried that they might not have what it takes?

Dr. Wyler continued. And the "side effects," he said, can be "quite painful" and last "for months to a year after surgery." After a neck lift, "you'll feel like someone is pressing their thumb into your neck." This pressure, combined with "numbness and sensitivity," can last for months. With a nose job you'll experience "difficulty breathing and dull aches" and the "swelling usually lasts for a year." The list went on – face lifts, breast augmentations, breast reductions, tummy tucks, arm lifts, eye lifts, and liposuction among others – the side effects for each were carefully reviewed. "The ones who are in denial about the pain and seriousness of plastic surgery are the ones I worry about," said Dr. Wyler, concluding the side effect portion of his presentation.

The two women sitting next to me appeared to be reassuring each other. "It's good to know"; "this is serious business"; "I want to go in with my eyes open," I heard them say. Dr. Wyler's discussion of side effects was thorough and informative – he was a responsible doctor doing his job. But an expanding sub-text, part-challenge, part-demand, part- warning, continued to haunt

---

[128] The actual name of the doctor has been changed. "Peter Wyler" is a pseudonym.

the audience: *Plastic surgery is for serious, dedicated, strong, brave women – women who are willing to take the time needed and to accept the pain and suffering that surgery entails.*

Next, Dr. Wyler moved to a more overt, more stringent, review of a viable woman's characteristics. He would only work with patients who were "physically healthy," "do not smoke, " and have *"reasonable expectations"* about plastic surgery. "First of all," Dr. Wyler confided to his audience, "liposuction *does not make you lose weight*." Those "vats of fat" from liposuction are a "myth, " he explained. That is why the best patients for liposuction are "healthy, fit individuals," who "despite serious exercise, just cannot get rid of one particular area of dimpling or fat pocketing."

"Many women don't know this," Dr. Wyler continued, but breast augmentation surgery "is *not a one time surgery*." Because of the "high risk of deflation," you're "signing up for repeated surgery – every ten years or so." Dr. Wyler also worried about women "who think that I can give them perfect C-cup breasts." "Instead," he explained, "I try and match the breast size to the woman's shape and her breast weight to her body mass."

Dr. Wyler made clear to his audience the serious nature of surgery, the reality of side effects, and the need for reasonable, rational expectations. And these realities and requirements may have discouraged some women from having plastic surgery. But Dr. Wyler did not stop there. He told the audience that women who were able to accept the seriousness and side effects of surgery, and who exhibited reasonable and rational expectations, were better off than those who couldn't. They were better off because, in the end, having plastic surgery was a better choice than not having it.

To illustrate this point, Dr. Wyler returned to his power point presentation. First, the example of a tummy tuck. He pointed to a slide of a woman's stomach before she had surgery and said, with a smile, "with all that skin and fat hanging off her she looks like a Shar-Pei dog!" Several audience members giggled in response. Next, he flipped to a slide of the woman's stomach after the tummy tuck. She was "pretty sore," and had to "walk hunched over for a while," he said as he traced the raised scars, running across and up and down her abdomen, with his pointer. The last slide showed the woman's stomach from the side view. "See," he said, "the stomach is almost entirely flat, which makes it look great in clothes." You're "trading fat and hanging skin for a scar. And looking great in clothes and in a bathing suit matters a lot more to women than how they look without clothes – am I right?"

Appreciative laughter surfaced from several women in the audience. *Dr. Wyler really gets what women want.* "The women I perform tummy tucks on are my happiest and most grateful patients," Dr. Wyler confirmed.

Dr. Wyler moved on to the example of breast reduction surgery. The first slide showed a woman's breasts pre-surgery. "Her breasts hang down below her belly button," Dr. Wyler said, emphasizing the width and length of her breasts with his pointer. The next slide revealed the woman's post-surgery breasts (Dr. Wyler removed a "total of four pounds – two from each breast"), complete with scars. "These scars cause numbness and reduced physical sensation," and can "restrict the capacity to breast feed by up to fifty percent," Dr. Wyler explained. In the final slide, we saw the woman's reconstructed breasts, clothed. Several women sitting next to me oohed and aahed over his handiwork. "Now remember," Dr. Wyler said, "I cannot guarantee a perfect bra cup size – but we all know that no woman actually has such a thing anyway, right? Every woman's size and shape is different, after all." The women sitting next to me nodded and murmured in appreciative agreement. And, said Dr. Wyler, her breasts now look "great in clothes."

An hour and a half had passed and Dr. Peter Wyler's official "plastic surgery information session" came to end. But the audience still wanted more from him. "Are there any surgeons that specialize in necks?"; "Is there any age that's too old for having plastic surgery?"; "I'm afraid of going under the knife, should I be?"; "Do breast implants interfere with mammography?" Dr. Wyler didn't rush any woman, answered every single question, waited, and asked if there were any more, before he thanked everyone for coming and began to gather his materials. Before he left however, he had to contend with the line of women forming in front of his lectern. Women with questions who were too shy to speak out in front of the audience, or women wondering about the availability of his services perhaps? As I left the auditorium, he was handing out his business card.

Steven D. Farough

"What Are You Lookin' At?" The Oppositional Gaze, Intersectionality, and the Social Geographies of White Masculinities*

I use the metaphors of "mapping" and "intersectionality" to understand the dynamic process of identity transformation of white men as they move from feeling "nonracial" in mostly white environments to "racial" in urban spaces with primarily black/white racial dynamics.[1] The result of this movement highlights how class and gender are deeply embedded in this process of racialized identity transformation. The concepts mapping and intersectionality will demonstrate how white men's movement across urban space is more than geographical; it will signify how racial identity formation fundamentally intersects with class and gender dynamics within specific social contexts. This allows one to better envision how white masculinity is not a thing but a dynamic and unfolding process of construction across

AUTHOR'S NOTE: *I would like to thank Heidi Bachmann, Julie Childers, and the editors of* Critical Sociology *for their excellent editorial advice and helpful support in writing this article.*

* An earlier version of this essay appeared in *Critical Sociology*, vol. 30, no. 2 (2004).

[1] Although the United States is becoming an increasingly multi-racial nation based on progressively more hybrid notions of race and ethnicity that are highlighted in such states as California and Florida (Patterson 2002), black/white racial dynamics in the Northeast and Midwest regions of the US still continue to be significant in areas like Detroit, Chicago, Boston, and New York (Patterson 2002, Hartigan 1999, Farough 2001). The narratives discussed throughout this article refer to experiences in Boston, Chicago, and another east coast city that an interviewee asked to remain anonymous.

time, space, and different landscapes of knowledge and power. Use of the concepts of mapping and intersectionality also illuminates the interconnections of context-specific micro interactions and macro level forms of structural power.

Through a set of semi-structured intensive interviews with white men currently residing in the Boston metropolitan area, I consistently found that the movement of white men between mostly white and mostly black social geographies produced a transformation in how they see themselves. In white social geographies the overwhelming majority of the respondents felt "nonracial" in their everyday life experiences. However, in mostly black urban locations almost seventy percent of the interviewees noted that they either explicitly felt "white" or interpreted their urban experience as distinctly racialized.[2] Such experiences were rooted in politics of masculinity and class. This reveals an important dynamic in the intersectionality of race, class and gender identity formation. Race, class, and gender may indeed "intersect" but for the respondents, race serves as an initial entry point into these systems of privilege and oppression. In their narratives, the respondents documented a phenomenological shift in how they came to see themselves in a racialized manner. But class and gender dynamics are revealed as a constitutive element of their racialized discussions.

This process is not merely a cognitive sense of identity change. In some cases the movement produced emotionally powerful feelings such as fear, discomfort, or anger. Although the majority of white men often discussed concern over crime or personal harm when they entered these urban areas, it was also evident that they had a sense of being interpreted as privileged. The feelings discussed in the narratives of the respondents appeared to be so powerful in some cases that even the most liberal among them could not help but feel fear or discomfort when entering mostly black social geographies.

I begin with the research methodology of this study. I then provide an overview of what I believe to be the dominant standpoint of white men, sovereign individuality. Next, with the use of postcolonialism, social cartography, psychoanalysis, intersectionality, and poststructuralism, I demonstrate

---

[2] Eighteen out of the twenty-six interviewees felt "white" or marked their urban experiences as racialized. Three of the white men claimed that they did not notice racial difference between urban and suburban space. Four of the interviewees did not frame their racialized experiences in an explicit urban/suburban context.

how the movement of white men in racially diverse urban environments highlights how white male racial identity is bound up in the historically specific set of power relations in the post-Civil Rights era in the United States.

Methodology

The data came from a set of semi-structured intensive interviews with twenty-six white men, all twenty years and older, ranging from different class, political, and geographical backgrounds. Using a purposive/snowball sampling technique, I selected respondents who ranged from working class to wealthy, liberal to conservative, and who lived in racially diverse urban areas to mostly white suburbs. I conceptualized the respondents' class position by obtaining their income and educational background. I then used this data to put the respondents into a class position by using Gilbert and Kahl's (1993) socio-economic measurement of class. My conceptualization of the respondents' political beliefs and the extent of diversity in their neighborhood was defined by the respondents themselves.

In our initial contact I explained to the interviewee that we would discuss a range of issues relating to race and gender, as well as how he felt about being perceived as a white man. In using a semi-structured interview format I had a set of general areas that I explored with each interviewee, but I also left the interview process open ended with the hope of allowing the respondent the freedom to discuss specific racial and gender issues that concerned him. In each interview I addressed the following areas with the respondents: (1) racial and gender identity, (2) perception of race and gender relations in general, (3) degree and types of interaction with people of color and women, (4) views on white male privilege and affirmative action, (5) experiences with whiteness and race and masculinity and gender, and (6), their thoughts on racism and sexism.

Much of the data on white men's experiences in mostly black urban areas came from a set of conversations that addressed their actual thoughts with feeling "white" and/or experiences that they interpreted as distinctly "racial." Like Frankenberg's (1993) research on white women, I found that the respondents often felt "racial" in areas where whites are in the numerical minority. As the respondents discussed their experiences in mostly black social geographies, many would talk about the possibility of being singled out or harmed because they would be viewed as wealthy and/or benefactors of racial privilege. Feeling privileged also brought forth issues that were embedded in the dynamics of masculinity and class. Thus, the feeling of being racialized signified a dynamic process of movement between two different identities or "subject positions": it was this dynamic process of movement that exposed the respondents to the possibility of being interpreted as privileged. Although these questions addressed race, the dynamics in the respondents' experiences suggested class and gender were fundamental components of feeling singled out as privileged.

Sovereign Individuality & White Masculinities

In order to understand the dynamics of feeling "white" in a mostly black urban area, it is important to obtain an understanding of how the "nonracial" identity, or sovereign individuality, operates in the respondents' lives. Here, I rework Andrew Herman's (1999) use of *sovereign individuality* to situate this seemingly individualistic identity formation in a context of discourse and power.[3] In *The American Heritage Dictionary* "sovereign" means:

> **Sovereign** *adj.* **1.** Paramount; supreme. **2.** Having supreme rank or power . . .
> **3.** Self-governing; independent . . . **4. a.** Of superlative strength or efficacy . . .
> **b.** Unmitigated . . .

By combining the different meanings of the definition of "sovereign," one effectively connects a sense of individualism to having a disproportionate amount of power. To be sovereign, or free, means that only those who are in positions of privilege or "supreme rank or power" may posses a consistent sense of self-determination. The outcome of sovereignty is a subjective sense of "complete independence," a distinct separation between the individual and the social world, where the person is self-governing and autonomous. I chose the term *sovereign individuality* as an explanatory metaphor to theorize the connections between a sense of individuality that white men often experience and their privileged location in race, class, and gender institutions.

---

[3] Andrew Herman (1999) uses the term sovereign individuality in his research on wealth to discuss how affluent men achieve a sense of individuality through masculine discourses on wealth accumulation. However, unlike Herman (1999), I am using the term to address how white men achieve a sense of individuality in the context of white male privilege.

Achieving Sovereign Individuality Among White Men

In the interviews respondents were asked whether on not they identify with being a "white male." The overwhelming majority of the respondents did not associate with this category and positioned themselves as "individuals" or used generic categories that did not contextualize them as privileged. They provided explanations like:

> Bob:[4] *I don't know*, just another *guy* on the street, I guess. Yes, that's tough [re-the question on defining identity].
>
> John: I think of myself as being a good kid . . .
>
> Sam: I don't think that I would. . . . And maybe that's because I am a white male. . . . I don't think of myself in terms of my whiteness or my maleness unless I'm, you know, radical feminism, which you know, as a male I'm going to take issue with or something like Affirmative Action, which as a white person, I would take issue with because it is directed against me. But, other than that, it wouldn't be my normal point of reference.
>
> Fred: I think they're [re – white and male identity] so obvious I probably wouldn't articulate them. But I might speak as being a father which is a masculine role, *but no*, I don't think I would speak in terms of race or gender. (emphasis added)
>
> David: Well, actually just posing the question is interesting for me, because I don't think of myself as a white male. So, it's interesting. I mean, I just don't generally think about race very much consciously in terms of how I'm interacting with people or about myself.
>
> George: I don't usually think about it. . . . Well, I think of myself more as a being *fun* than as being a white male. (emphasis added)
>
> Daniel: I definitely have identified myself as being Italian. . . . It's such a fascinating question. I've never actually said, 'yeah, I'm a white male and I can identify [with that].'

As the above quotes clearly highlight, the respondents do not identify with *white masculinity*, or if they do, it is only in certain contexts and not as a consistent marker of identity formation. Nevertheless, in most of their everyday

---

[4] The respondents' names are pseudonyms.

life experiences, the interviewees did not *feel* like white men. Instead they defined themselves through concepts such as personality characteristics, employment, ethnicity, and humanness – all standpoints where they are positioned as active agents in the social world and in control of their own destiny.[5] For most of the respondents sovereign individuality was the dominant, comprehensive identity that they inhabited in their everyday life experiences.

It is also important to note that most of the respondents argued that they were against racism and sexism and realized that white men as a group were in generally more powerful positions. In addition, many pointed out that they were in favor of diversity and equal opportunity for people of all races and genders. However, the respondents were also *resistant* to the idea that they received unearned advantages because of their racial and gender standpoint or that white men as group benefited from whiteness and masculinity.[6]

Postcolonialism: Discursive & Structural Mapping

The achievement of sovereign individuality comes through a particular standpoint in liberal humanist discourse. In this section, I use the concept "the good citizen/subject" from postcolonial theory (Sandoval 1997) and the poststructuralist critique of liberal humanist discourse on individualism to demonstrate the epistemological foundations of the identity of sovereign individuality (Foucault 1979, Weedon 1997, Herman 1999). In Chela Sandoval's (1997) theorization of white consciousness, she uses Roland Barthes' concept "good citizen/subject" to explore a new form of awareness among whites in the emerging postcolonial world. The "good citizen/subject" to Barthes refers to individuals who espouse a liberal standpoint characterized by anti-racist and individualistic rhetoric to signify how racism is bad and that race no longer matters in society. However, despite the good citizen/subject's use of more progressive rhetoric on race, Barthes argues that the individual in this stand-

---

[5] Waters (1990), Gans (1980), & Brodkin Sachs (1993) have noted that ethnic identities among whites are largely "symbolic," or a standpoint that has no real material consequences in their life opportunities.

[6] I am using the term resistant to highlight the ambivalence that white men felt toward seeing themselves or other white men as privileged. In many cases white men would acknowledge that white men as a group were disproportionately in positions of power, but became dismissive of critiques of where they were seen as receiving unearned advantages in contemporary US society.

point is incapable of seeing the persistence of exploitative relations between the colonizer and the colonized. The good citizen/subject is "inoculated" from such unpleasant realities. This inoculation occurs through the investment in liberal humanist discourse that shields the subject from the exploitative social relations. Thus, the good citizen/subject takes on a position that appears liberal or open minded while still being complicit in reproducing the structures of racial inequality (Sandoval 1997).

Liberal humanist discourse emerged during the rise of modernity (Foucault 1979). This discourse has enormous breadth and many epistemological underpinnings. Although it is beyond the scope of this chapter to provide an extensive genealogy of the liberal humanist discourse, the following sets of assumptions operate within this discursive field. First, liberal humanist discourse constitutes the self as inherent, meaning that it exists ontologically prior to society (Herman 1999). Second, liberal humanist discourse interprets language as reflecting the intentions, thoughts, and feeling of the inner self, not producing them (Weedon 1997). Therefore, this discourse positions the individual as primary in producing both themselves and acting in the social world.

Those who employ liberal humanist discourse often take on the subject position of the good citizen/subject when discussing race and gender. Through the use of liberal humanist discourse, the good citizen/subject views him or her self as separate from the social world and not participating in racial or gender inequalities (unless they consciously act against people of color or women). Thus, liberal humanist discourse, allows the good citizen/subject to take on a standpoint that is accepting of diversity but unable to comprehend how he or she could be privileged by race and gender. According to this subject position, unless white men consciously act against women or people of color they cannot be interpreted as privileged. In fact, Omi and Winant (1994), Feagin (2001), Frankenberg (1993) and Gallagher (2003) have argued that this more seemingly egalitarian standpoint has resulted in a color-blind view to the world, one where race does not exist unless it is explicitly stated. The standpoint of the good citizen/subject has become the dominant way of interpreting race in the post-Civil Rights era within the discursive field of liberal humanism (Feagin 2001). In a similar vein, Deborah Rhode's (1997) research on the persistence of institutionalized gender inequality in the post-Civil Rights era finds a similar discourse on gender: it is no longer a significant issue in the workplace and domestic life unless plainly declared. Therefore, the good citizen/subject should be understood as the standpoint or subject position in liberal humanist discourse that allows white men to take on a perceived identity of sovereign individuality.

The good citizen/subject position and sovereign individuality were pervasive throughout the majority of the interviews. However, as previously mentioned, the standpoint of feeling like an "individual" is not a constant experience. I found that in certain social contexts white men's sense of sovereign individuality was challenged, particularly in mostly black urban areas. The result is an unfolding process of identity transformation in the context of race, class and gender hierarchies.

Social Cartography

In this analysis of the identity transformation of white men, I employ the metaphor of "mapping" from social cartography to understand how the shift in identity for white men in mostly black social geographies is a movement across physical, psychological, discursive, and structural space in the context of power. Social cartographers take seriously the notion that geographical space becomes symbolically meaningful through the effects of power and knowledge (Herman 1999). Social cartography widens the purview of the process of mapping to include a "map" of the interaction between physical, historical, discursive, and psychic space. For instance, in Ruth Frankenberg's (1993) *White Women, Race Matters*, she employs the term "social geography" to connote how physical landscapes are mediated by regimes of racialized power and knowledge. Frankenberg (1993) notes the importance of space as a context-specific element of white racial identity formation. Depending on the geographical context, being "racial" came to the forefront of white women's lives. Like Frankenberg (1993) I found that most of the respondents felt racialized in mostly black urban spaces but in a manner that was deeply linked to masculinity and class. The "embeddedness" of masculinity and class in these racialized experiences also evoked further questions about how race, class, and gender intersect in identity formation.

The Social Geography of Mostly Black Urban Spaces

In this process of identity transformation as white men moved into mostly black social geographies, one of the consistent elements of their narratives was the documentation of a sense of feeling "white" or marking the experience as racialized.[7] This occurred for the respondents who lived in both white social geographies and areas that were interpreted by white men as mostly black or "diverse." For instance, growing up in a multiracial urban environment Frank, a twenty-one year old undergraduate from an upper middle class background, notes, ". . . but around people just walking down the street I *felt* . . . very white."[8] (emphasis added) Being a long time resident of Boston, George points out that he periodically felt white in certain urban areas. "I felt recently in [Boston] that I was the only white person in Caldor, the only white person more or less in Bed and Bath where I was. I thought, 'Well, here I am. You know? I'm the little minority guy.'" Moving from a mostly white New England town to Boston to work for the Department of Social Services, Daniel describes his initial reaction working with mostly black co-workers and clientele in an economically depressed section of Boston.

> I can remember when I first got there, because I'm believing all that stuff I heard about it. [violence in a mostly black urban environment] Had *anxiety attacks* going into Roxbury and Dorchester to visit my clients. . . . It was almost to the point where – the perception is, as soon as I got out of my car, I was going to get clubbed and dragged away and never seen again.

Daniel's anxiety subsided, noting how his experiences in mostly black and Latino spaces were not filled with danger or hostility but friendliness. Daniel's initial "crossing" from a mostly white to a mostly black and Latino social geography had a powerful effect on his identity. Daniel felt not only fearful but also white. Therefore his physical movement also transformed his identity of sovereign individuality to being a "white male."

Anxiety, fearfulness, and feeling like one "sticks out" racially are powerful emotional responses that almost seem beyond the control of many of the respondents. For instance, David, an upper middle class white men who lives in a mostly white suburb of Boston, points out how a mostly black social geography can make him suddenly feel white and subsequently fearful.

---

[7] Again, almost 70% of the white men interviewed felt this way.
[8] Frank noted that he lived in an area of Chicago where African Americans, Asian Americans, Latinos, and whites lived in close proximity. Despite the multiracial social geography most of Frank's narratives in the interview addressed black/white racial dynamics.

Well, I do notice – I mean, when I kind of go into a black neighborhood, then I'm very aware of being white, and that's when I start to feel fearful. So, I mean, sometimes when I'm like it doesn't happen too often, but like if I'm having to drive through Dorchester to get to Route 93, there's like a part of the drive that goes through kind of a bad area. It's like Route 203 or something, and it crosses Blue Hill Avenue and it's like – it's not like a great neighborhood, and I know that at those times it's like I'm feeling some fear; I'm very aware that most people there are black and I'm white, and I'm a little bit scared. So, I guess that's an experience. [Int: Well, what about the fear? Why do you think you had those feelings of fear when you're driving through?]

Why I ever had that? Yes. Well, I'm afraid – there's some fear that I would be shot or that something might happen to me, or that there might be some – whatever, like I don't know. Some bad people – some gang or something that would want to do something bad to me. [Int: Because you're white, you think? Is that a fear?] Yes. Maybe because I'm white, although I know those kinds of gangs, they don't just pick on white people, they attack black people, too. But I do have a fear of that, and I do associate in my mind being in a poor, black neighborhood with being unsafe.

In moving between different racial social geographies, David experiences a sense of being interpreted differently than he normally sees himself. David links urban space to race and the potential for personal harm. Bill makes the connection more explicit, "Ah, most of the crime is done, you know, by blacks. OK? These kids, ah – basically they wrecked that, [referring to three black men who mugged him outside of his urban school] so it was just like, you know, be leery. You know, the kid's radar is up and mine is too now if I see a group of black guys. It's also up when there is a group of white guys, but you know, I'm just watching things a little more closely, the black guys . . ." Bill comes from a major East Coast city where he is often aware of black men on the street.

Whether directly experiencing crime or not, at the most general level such fear seemed to be produced through a racialized calculus – mostly black urban environments have "high" rates of crime committed by African American men. Therefore, according to this calculus, it is more likely that white men will be robbed and/or beaten up. Such discourses are also seen within mass media contexts, giving this racialized calculus wide-ranging circulation. For instance, in a 1992 *Wall Street Journal* editorial political science professor James

Q. Wilson argued that white fear of black and Latino men is justified because black and Latino men have high crime rates (Russell 1998). Wilson concludes it is not that whites have racist perceptions of men of color; it is that they have a legitimate fear of being harmed. Wilson suggests that the fear of men of color by whites would drop if the crime rate of men of color would decline.

However, Wilson's argument that blacks commit most of the crime is not supported by governmental statistical evidence (Russell 1998). Although African Americans are over-represented among offenders of violent and property crime, the majority of these types of crime are committed by whites (Messner & Rosenfeld 1997, Conklin 1998, Russell 1998). African Americans have higher victimization rates than whites for rape and sexual assault, robbery, and aggravated assault (Conklin 1998). It is also far more likely for a white person to be attacked by another white person than an African American or a person of another racial background (Russell 1998). In spite of this, the fear of crime among many whites is often associated with black men in urban settings, creating a racialized and gendered dynamic.

Such powerful reactions can also be produced by more than the threat of physical harm. Being in mostly black urban environments can also signify to white men that they are privileged and possibly going to be subjected to revenge for racial injustices of the past. Criminologist Katherine Russell's (1998) work on the white fear of black crime supports this view. In a critique of James Q. Wilson's controversial *Wall Street Journal* editorial she notes, Wilson "provides neither theoretical nor empirical support for this sweeping assertion [re – that white fear will drop as the black crime rate drops]. In fact, he could not, as there are no such data available" (Russell 1998: 125). Indeed, Russell (1998) argues that Wilson assumes that white fear of blacks is only produced through crime. Although white fear of crime in urban areas is not entirely illusionary or insincere, Russell (1998) points out this theory cannot entirely explain why whites fear black men. She notes that white fear of black men should be understood as multi-dimensional. Russell (1998) argues that white fear has at least four dimensions – the fear of crime, the fear of losing jobs, the fear of cultural demise, and the fear of "Black Revolt."

In particular, the last three dimensions point to the persistence of noticeable inequalities between whites and people of color; that whites at a certain level know that they are seen as privileged and fear some form of retaliation. In mostly black urban spaces the sense of sovereign individuality is challenged, as many of the respondents noted their distinct sense of being racialized.

Thus, the sense of autonomous individuality is never a constant feeling or identity among the interviewees.

My data supports both Russell's (1998) multi-dimensional explanation of white fear and Teresa Brennan's (1993) theorization of the exploitative relations that surround the production of the ego, as I will demonstrate momentarily. The respondents not only mentioned fear of crime in urban contexts, but also noted how people of color could interpret them as "privileged" and "oppressors." Bill, the interviewee who is "leery" of black men in urban areas, believes firmly that "I'm just looked at because I'm white, that, ah, you know, that I'm the oppressor." David is more ambivalent about the feelings of African Americans perceptions of whites but notes, ". . . I would think that some black people might feel resentful or feel like – or feel misunderstood, or feel in some way oppressed by white men; that they've been their oppressors. And historically that's true." Frank argues that blacks consciously act hostile toward whites in urban contexts – "'cause it's – a lot of times it's not just white people being racist toward blacks. A lot of times it's the other way around." Consistent with Russell's (1998) conceptualization of white fear of black revolt, the belief as being perceived as unfairly privileged is a strong undercurrent in numerous interactions with African Americans.

At a more immediate, context specific level, this sense of privilege and fear comes from the possibility of being *looked at* by people of color. Indeed, the link between social geography, race and the transformation in identity is so powerful that it is not necessary for the respondents to be literally looked at by African Americans in urban environments. Simply by entering mostly black social geographies, some of the white men noted that they literally felt "white" or as Frank says, "sticking out like a sore thumb." Clearly, this experience of feeling racialized and gendered is produced through sight. Yet this fear is not evoked through face-to-face contact alone. Although African Americans are clearly not in the same positions of power as whites in general, the fear is in a sense panoptic – white people regulate themselves to avoid direct forms of contact with the predominately black urban space (Foucault 1980).

These feelings appeared to be so powerful that they even overwhelmed some of the respondents' good/citizen subject positions that are key to achieving sovereign individuality. For instance William notes,

> Well, I think I had an intellectual opinion and an emotional opinion. My
> intellectual opinion was very supportive of, at that time, Martin Luther King

and civil rights and all that, and started participating in demonstrations and things in the middle-late sixties. So, on that level, I though of myself as very liberal. Emotionally, I was terrified of black males, because I had had some bad experiences growing up, I'd been robbed and beaten up a couple of times. Of course, I also knew that white kids [did] the same things to black kids, and because it was a racially mixed neighborhood there was that kind of warfare going on, and I just happened to be the victim of it a couple of times. And because of that, I think, at an emotional level my emotions around it were different than my intellect around it. And at that time, I never really resolved it – it was like two separate lives. On the one hand, I could be passionately supportive of civil rights, but if I saw three black kids walking down the street, I'd cross the street, out of fear. So I had both of those things going on in parallel with one another.

William's narrative highlights an intellectual and emotional split, where to this day he feels a disjuncture between being supportive of civil rights and yet still finds him self, in certain urban contexts, fearful of black men. Such a transformation in one's sense of self, no matter how brief or context specific, is a significant sociological event that addresses the movement between geographical, historical, discursive, and structural space. By entering into such spaces it was as though some of the respondents experienced what Avery Gordon (1997) would call a haunting – experiencing a force normally rendered invisible by the discourses and practices in one's everyday life that becomes inexplicably present. The movement between different social geographies proves to be a difficult and often unresolved experience for the respondents, as such movement also forces them to confront uncomfortable situations about being privileged by racialized and gendered social power.

Psychoanalysis & Mapping of the Psyche

As demonstrated above in mostly black urban contexts the standpoint of the sovereign individual can be severely challenged, regardless of political stances on race. To avoid this unpleasant experience where one must potentially face being seen as privileged, psychoanalytic theorist Teresa Brennan (1993) argues that those in privileged positions attempt to remove themselves from the other through spatial distancing. This ultimately creates an unresolved space in the psyche where periodic confrontation with the other directly challenges the sense of sovereign individuality. Brennan (1993) theorizes that those in

privileged standpoints who take on the discursive logic of sovereign individuality are never entirely successful. She notes that this autonomous state
is ultimately in relation to racialized and gendered others. Brennan (1993: 43)
believes that in order for this self to exist it must ultimately "[close] off . . .
the truth about itself." To do so, it must control both discursive and physical space to achieve its structural privileges and produce a sense of individuality that appears unrelated to the other. Unsurprisingly, Brennan (1993)
argues that urban space is particularly threatening to the privileged sense of
sovereignty individuality. The city is bustling with movement, diversity, and
a sense of unpredictability, all phenomena that can disrupt the standpoint of
the good citizen/subject in liberal humanist discourse.

Still, the respondents consciously acknowledged this seemingly uncontrollable sense of fear. For instance, Daniel was able to overcome such worries
of working in a mostly African American neighborhood. Despite William's
seemingly inevitable fear of walking down the street in mostly black social
geographies, he is conscious of this intellectual and emotional split. According
to psychoanalytic theory, William should be unaware of such a distinction.
Indeed, not all white men reacted defensively in mostly black contexts, nor
were they necessarily unable to resolve such experiences to their own satisfaction. Thus, psychoanalysis is useful in theorizing how powerful emotions
become inexplicably present due to the unresolved standpoint of privilege,
but one needs to take into account the agency of individual actors in privileged positions as well.

The Oppositional Gaze & the Agency of the Oppressed

It is also important to consider the agency of those marginalized by racial
inequality. In *Black Looks*, bell hooks (1992) notes the racialized politics of
looking back to those in position of power. This seemingly innocuous act
highlights the exploitative relations of power for those in privileged standpoints.
To gaze upon someone constitutes an interrogation, a right for the gazer to
survey the gazed. Hooks (1992) points out that the entitlement of whites to
gaze upon blacks is a deeply structured practice throughout U.S. history.
However, when African Americans gaze back this produces violent or defensive reactions among whites because their privileged standpoint is exposed.
Such a gaze is deeply gendered as well. John Berger (1972) notes the gendered
structure of sight where men are allowed to look at women as objects; between

men the gaze is structured through rituals intended to mark dominance and deference (Connell 1987). The right to gaze also plays out in a spatial context where the public sphere is more often occupied by men and structured by the male gaze (Connell 1987). However, the structure of racialized and gendered sight that positions white men as those who posses the "right" to gaze can fail in certain contexts. In geographies where whites are the numerical minority, the power to gaze can be reversed by the traditionally oppressed group. This reversal of the gaze can have the effect of transforming the sense of self of those in privileged positions. bell hooks calls this the oppositional gaze. She notes:

> That all attempts to repress our black peoples' right to gaze had produced in us an overwhelming longing to look, a rebellious desire, an oppositional gaze. By courageously looking, we defiantly declared: 'Not only will I stare. *I want my look to change reality.*' Even in the worse circumstances of domination, the ability to manipulate one's gaze in the face of structures of domination that would contain it, opens up the possibility of agency. (hooks 1992: 116; emphasis added)

It is this possibility of looking back that marks white male bodies in a way that produces anxiety, fear, and anger among those in positions of privilege. The structures of power work through the oppositional gaze, exposing what is more readily invisible or repressed in the spaces of the everyday life of some white men, and thus "changing reality." Those within positions of domination can feel disoriented.

> . . . [T]he movements, the attitudes, the glances of the Other fixed me there, in the sense in which a chemical solution is fixed by a dye. I was indignant; I demanded an explanation. Nothing happened. I burst apart. Now the fragments have been put together again by another self. This 'look,' from – so to speak – the place of the Other, fixes us, not only in its violence, hostility and aggression, but in the ambivalence of its desire. (Fanon; quoted from hooks 1992: 116)

In this field of vision, Fanon provides a reading of the paranoia of counter surveillance; that white men can feel fear that the others might look back and retaliate. Fanon's quote addresses a Lacanian understanding of the limits of a sense of self in relation to the other – that there are conditions where the production of a sovereign sense of self comes into a context where it must address the privileged production of its own existence (Brennan 1993). Yet the political economy of this visual form of exchange is deeply rooted in the specifics of spatial context, social interaction and the dynamics of intersectionality.

Intersectionality

The particular dynamics of the oppositional gaze created narratives that signified the respondents as racialized but in ways that also intersected with gender and class. Invoking the metaphor of "intersectionality" with "mapping" helps to demonstrate how gender and class connect to an identity formation that initially appears to be only about race. Patricia Hill Collins' (2000) introduced the concept of "intersectionality" in her elaboration of her theory of the matrix of domination. As Collins' (2000) notes, race, class, gender, and sexuality should not be seen as autonomous variables, but as social forces that intersect to provide a varying amount of privilege and oppression. Depending on where one is located in race, class, gender and sexuality institutions, he or she will receive a varying amount of privilege and oppression.

In the second edition of *Black Feminist Thought*, Collins (2000) expands on how power operates within the matrix of domination. She argues that power needs to be understood across a range of different contexts. First, Collins (2000) conceptualizes power at the structural level, where different interlocking institutions provide a varying amount privilege and/or oppression. The second domain of power – called the disciplinary domain – lies at the level of bureaucracy. Here, power is enacted through a myriad of regulations and laws in government and industry. The third area of power is called the hegemonic domain; power is enacted through discourse, constituting social relations and identities in different ways. Finally, there is the interpersonal domain of power. At the interpersonal level, individuals can use their own agency to resist or alter coercive practices. Collins' (2000) expansion of the matrix of domination to include a more complex theorization of power is important because it helps in understanding how race, class, gender, and sexuality not only intersect but also combine across a range of different contexts.

However, the respondents' narratives suggest that the intersection of race, class, and gender operate in what I call "the prism effect of intersectionality:" In certain social contexts, either race, class or gender is most immediately salient but then unfolds outward in a manner that reveals how the others are connected to the situation. The prism effect of intersectionality also unfolds across the macro and micro levels, creating a portrait of power that connects a range of different power domains. For example, in mostly black social geographies the respondents' feeling of being racialized is most prominent, but as will be demonstrated below, this feeling is fundamentally connected to class location and masculinity. The prism effect of intersectionality also highlights how power operates in specific contexts, ranging from the micro to macro level. This creates an unfolding portrait of power that connects specific experiences at the micro level to discursive and structural concerns at the macro level. For instance, while white men often feel at a momentary disadvantage in mostly black social geographies, they remain in a structural context that provides them greater access to resources and social status than most people of color and women.

Urban Space as a Gendered Racial Formation of Economic Decline

As a racial formation, urban spaces with a black/white racial dynamic are structured by discourses that make cities intelligible as having more crime and violence than suburban areas (Russell 1998). The result of this fear produces and reproduces a highly segregated space (Massey & Denton 1993). When white men enter or think about urban spaces they attempt to make sense of geographical and structural space with these discourses on crime and economic decline (Anderson 1991, 2000, Wilson 1987). As hooks (1992) would suggest such a position allows white men the possibility to be gazed upon.

Elijah Anderson's (1990) *Streetwise* demonstrates both the gendered racial formation of urban space and the power of the oppositional gaze upon whites in mostly black areas of economic decline. He notes that black men have what he calls the peculiar ability to alter physical space. Anderson (1990) points out that much of the daily patterns of white people on the street are produced through an implicit understanding of avoiding black men. "[B]lack males exercise a peculiar hegemony over the public spaces, particularly at night or when two or more are together" (Anderson 1990: 164). The fear of black men is a powerful representation in public discourses, particularly among white people. The fear of physical violence and robbery are, of course, key elements of how such "power" is enacted. Nevertheless, most black men do not commit violent acts and robbery (Russell 1998). "Incapable of making distinctions between law-abiding black males and others, [most whites] rely for protection broad stereotypes based on color and gender, if not outright racism. They are likely to misread many of the signs displayed by law-abiding black men, thus becoming apprehensive of almost any black male they spot in public" (Anderson 1990: 165). According to Anderson (1990) whites use a rationalistic framework of cause and effect when walking urban streets. Through discourses that mark black men as criminals, some whites use this correlation between blackness, masculinity, and crime to avoid contact with just about any black man. The poverty-stricken and mostly black urban space where the respondents feel racialized creates the context for experiences that are relevant to identity formation and questions of power.

Oppositional Gaze & the Prism Effect of Intersectionality

Consistent with hooks' (1992) oppositional gaze, I found that it is not just that some of the respondents are afraid of robbery or being beaten up in urban spaces, it is also the experience of *being looked at* that exposes them as privileged. In this section I will specifically explore the narratives of three white men to highlight the inter-relationship between the oppositional gaze, social geography, identity transformation and the intersectionality of race, class and gender.

For instance, consider Jesse, an urban raised, working class white man who offers his interpretation of being stared at. "You know, when I go into the ghetto and I see them, you know, in the morning hanging out, ten people . . . and I honestly felt that they hated us more than we hated them, you know." Jesse specifies this perceived hate though staring.

> I mean, I mean, I was on the bus a couple weeks ago. You know, and this black kid was *looking* at me. Younger kid, 19 or 20. So he is staring at me. And I – you know how you just know that someone is looking at you. [Int: Right, yeah] He is staring at me, *he's looking at me in the eyes*. So I looked at him, and I'm saying to myself 'if I turn away from them, he's going to think, like, you know, he punked me.' You do know what I'm saying? [Int: Right.] So, I'm staring at him, staring at him, staring at him. So he says, 'what are you looking at'? I said, 'nothing.' I said, 'I'm not looking at anything.' And I just wanted – I just wanted to say something to him. Because I just wanted to take it out on him. [Int: umm hmm.] But he was just smart enough and walked away. But I've had other run ins. *They are defiant. They are defiant people*. I mean, you know – I don't allow other people to do this. Racist how I look at it. But I see it, man, all the time, you know?

Jesse notes that the stare was rooted in a context of "defiance." In this narrative he argues that the young black man on the bus engaged in a scrutinizing stare. Jesse believes that this stare is "racist," a look of contempt toward a white man. Also rooted in this staring contest was the production of masculinity in an urban context. As Connell (1987) notes, hegemonic forms of masculinity are not only defined in relation to femininities, but is also produced by marginalizing other men. According to Connell (1987) the prolonged stares and verbal exchange are produced by the historical connection between public space and the entitlement of being a man. Eye contact between men can evoke a sense of defending one's right to the public sphere. In this ritual, who ever looks away first is interpreted as deferring to the other man. Yet in the context of staring Jesse's interpretation makes references to racialized and gendered social power. Jesse notes that he could not stop staring, otherwise he would "lose" in the visual exchange. The narrative ends with anger – "They are defiant. They are defiant people. . . . Racist is how I look at it."

Jesse's ending comments of African Americans being "defiant" and "racist" in this narrative are important because it moves his specific experience with a young black man on a bus to a more general account of racialized and gendered social power. Jesse interprets the gaze as a stare that is sending a message of hatred toward white people, an oppositional gaze. The stare clearly makes Jesse angry. In this context the stare implicitly reminds him of his white masculinity, and thus makes it impossible to feel as if separate from racialized and gendered forms of social power. Subsequently Jesse's narrative maps an emotionally frustrating experience, one that not only addresses the potential for physical conflict but one that lays the foundation of how he positions himself as a white man in structural and discursive space as well.

As a result, Jesse's racialized and gendered narrative leads him into a subsequent story where he provides an implicit class-based analysis, one that places his biography in relation to the context he lives and his standpoint as a white man. Geographically, Jesse lives in a part of Boston that he feels has a large population of African Americans. He also believes that whites are not privileged in this area. In fact whites are the new recipients of discrimination. In another part of the interview, Jesse notes that whites have been helping out blacks for too long. The following narrative makes the point more apparent.

> I was on the bus one day. A black woman got on with her two kids. And I
> was sitting there . . . and the whole back of the bus was all blacks . . . and I

mean . . . and she said to me, you know, 'Do you think I could have the seat.' And, and I looked straight at her and I said, 'Oh, why should I. Why don't you ask your own people?' And this was like an uproar on the bus – 'oh, you racist!' [Int: OH, you said that?] They heard me. And – 'you racist!' I'm not the racist. Why don't you guys get up for a white lady? You won't get up for your own kind. Why should I? Oh, they were pissed. You should – they were bull shittin'. [Int: Umm hmm, did the whole bus hear that too?] Oh, I made sure they heard it. You know, the bus was quiet. I mean, everyone from the back door heard it. [Int: umm hmm.] It – she was like and, and, and she said something about God or something. And ahh, that's just the way I felt. You know, I speak my mind. I have no problem. I say what is my mind. I say what's on my mind. I'm not going to hide it or hold – I'm going to tell you how I feel. And well what I did that day. . . . You know, you do something, a part of me felt bad. Of course, a part of me felt bad. *You know, we have been getting up and moving for them for far too long.* And I ain't moving. That's the way it is. (emphasis added)

Jesse's story also positions him in a counter discourse that marks white men as privileged. Jesse believes that white men are continually seen as advantaged in the public sphere. However, he sees himself as a victim of reverse discrimination, busing, and racist actions from African Americans. In the interview Jesse argues that he was denied employment at the post office and the Boston mass transit system because he is white. Jesse also believes the he was unable to get a grant to go to college because his whiteness. As Jesse states, "We [sic] have been getting up and moving for them for far too long." Jesse also notes in another part of the interview that there are many white men who are in positions of power and blames some of his marginal economic condition on himself. After high school Jesse was sent to jail for selling drugs. Yet he feels that he has been prohibited from obtaining a decent education because of busing and denied employment opportunities because of affirmative action. In the above narratives Jesse's anger seems in part produced out of the tension between those discourses that view white men as privileged and his own economically marginal experiences that he attributes to race. Jesse feels that he is not in a position of economic privilege. Jesse earns approximately $32,000 a year as a tiller and lives with his mother. Jesse's narrative of his experiences living in a diverse social geography highlight a set of competing discourses on racialized social power that also relate to class.

Jesse's anger over race appears largely rooted in his lack of access to decent employment and income.

In using the metaphor of "mapping" and "the prism effect of intersectionality," Jesse's narrative highlights a tension and feeling of being oppressed in the context that he lives. Jesse is aware that white men as a group are seen as privileged, but attempts to produce a narrative that demonstrates he is the victim of "black racism." It is also important to understand that the competing set of discourses that Jesse is basing his narrative upon occurs within a specific geographical context and where he is located in the class structure as a working class white man. He blames part of his marginal economic position on what he sees as unfair benefits given to African Americans. The anger that Jesse feels from being stared at by the young black man and the black women asking him for his seat on the bus highlights the complex ways race, class, and gender operates in Jesse's life. The oppositional gaze marks Jesse as racialized and gendered benefactor of white male privilege, something he strongly disagrees with. However, his narratives also unfold across his immediate experiences in the city to broader structural and discursive concerns at the macro level. By mapping Jesse's narratives across time, space, discourse and social structure, the portrait highlights a prism effect of race, class, and gender interaction within his lived experiences.

In another example of the politics of the gaze, Bill, a twenty one year old lower middle class college student who grew up in a racially diverse urban area, explains the ritualized dynamics of eye contact in urban contexts among men.

> One – something that I realized last year. Um, I'm walking, I'm passing this black kid. [Int: Um hmm.] And, you know, I just, you know, I try to look people in the eye, and I don't do it a lot so I try help out – so I try to help the guy. So I'm lookin' him in the eye. And usually, um, in [the city] . . . ah . . . I'm – it, it, it's kinda strange. This is how it is. You go down the street. [Int: Um hmm.] And if you don't want any trouble with whatever race, you know, you catch somebody's eye and you glance away. OK? [Int: Um hmm.] And whoever glances away first . . . ah, you know, they're backing down. OK? That's the mentality. [Int: OK.] It's stupid, but you know if you want to stay out of trouble, you know, you don't sit there and look at somebody in the eye. [Int: OK.] Ah, so . . . back home black guys all the time . . . because there's usually more of them . . . Ah, like I like to do things on my own . . .

[Int: Um hmm.] And I definitely look down, you know, I don't want any trouble. [Int: Um hmm.]

I come here. [To college at a mostly white university] And this black guy who has the same kind of mentality. We're passing each other. We looking in the eye . . . and he looks down. And he just keeps walkin'. And like I felt, you know, ah, ah, ah, I didn't feel like 'yes, I won' as I might in [Big East Coast city]. [Int: Um hmm.] But I was just like, I wonder how this guy feels, ah . . . you know, going to a school that's like 95 or whatever the percentage of white is, you know, at [this school]? [Int: Um hmm.] How that must be. So, ah, that was one specific incident.

Here, Bill is aware of the politics of the gaze between white men and men of color. When engaged in eye-to-eye contact this brings up questions of how power relations are mediated by the particular geographical context. Bill argues that as a white man he must defer in eye-to-eye contact with African American men in mostly black social geographies. However, in the mostly white university he attends, Bill is attentive changes of the relations of power by race and masculinity through eye-to-eye contact. In this context whiteness is dominant. The ritual of eye contact evokes a set of power dynamics along race and gender lines, where Bill is reminded of his standpoint as a white man. He feels empathy for the African American man, but also feels that he has been unfairly singled out by people of color as an oppressor.

Frank, an urban raised upper middle class white man, has a similar experience to Jesse's and Bill's frustration with feeling singled out as a white male. Although Frank comes from a racially diverse urban area in the Midwest, his time at a mostly white private college on the East Coast has diminished his sense of having a racial identity. However, this was not always the case. Frank notes that he often "felt white" in the racially diverse Midwest city he lived in while growing up. In the following narrative Frank recalls an experience where he felt racialized in a mostly black area of his home city. Frank argues that he was prevented from driving at a green traffic light because an African American man intentionally waited to cross the street with his girl friend to make him wait longer. In this confrontation, Frank muttered the racist slur, "nigger," under his breath.

But I do have – probably the last time I said nigger was, um . . . I think it was last year . . . and, ah, I was waiting for, the – I was at a red light in my car. [Int: Umm Hmm.] And there's a black kid and his girl friend. They were waiting to cross the street. And I had the red light they, they had the right of way, and so, they're – I thought they would cross the street, but, you know, his girlfriend he went – she went to go cross the street, and the boyfriend grabbed her and pulled her back, and, ah, then they just waited for me to have the green light for them to cross in front of me. Just so, you know, I have to wait longer. And, you know, I was, I was pissed off and . . . [Int: Umm Hmm.] And I didn't go screaming at 'em or anything, but I remember saying that and then a couple of seconds later I was like, you know, I was stupid for saying that but . . . umm, just weird things like that, that happen everyday. [Int: Umm Hmm.] They like build up and it kinda ticks me off when people who never had to experience that . . . [Int: Umm Hmm.] Ahh, they, they get up on their high horse and talk about how racism is wrong or . . . [Int: OK.] And, and when they've never had to confront it, 'cause it's a lot of times it's not just white people being racist toward blacks. A lot of times it's the other way around.

By being delayed at the traffic light, Frank believes this was an explicit attempt to make him wait longer because he is white. "Racism" works both ways, according to Frank. The moral of this story is that he was seen as a white male and was subsequently punished for it. Yet Frank's anger also is experienced in the context of racialized power and privilege. By observing this narrative through the metaphors of mapping and the prism effect of intersectionality, we can see how Frank is attempting to make sense of his particular geographical location in a mostly black urban space. However, to make sense of this experience he must make sense of his particular experience with the discourses available on racism and his own structural location as an upper middle class white man. In the Midwest city he grew up in Frank notes that white privilege is not experienced while walking or driving the streets. Frank feels this the lack of white privilege in mostly black urban areas is an essential element that is lost within discourses on white male privilege. In the mapping of Frank's narrative, we see that he has difficulty resolving his own experience with the African American couple at a streetlight and those discourses that mark him as a privileged white man. Frank insinuates that the actions of the young black man and his girl friend are racist.

In liberal humanist discourses that privilege the individual, as self-governing and autonomous, racism is understood as a conscious action against a person of another race. Frank appears to be reacting to those discourses that mark whites as privileged and primary producers of racism. As he notes, "'Cause a lot of times it is not just white people being racist toward blacks.

A lot of times it is the other way around." Thus, in this narrative Frank is trying to make sense of this geographically specific incident by orienting his story to white racism discourses. Frank is aware that white men as a group are privileged but in his narrative Frank is traumatized by the actions of the couple. He feels unfairly singled out because he was white and the experience evokes anger.

Although not explicitly stated in the interview, the actions of the young black man and his girl friend also became intelligible through the visual field. Frank did not mention any form of direct conversation. In this exchange, we again see how the action of a young black man in a geographical space where whiteness is not the norm produces a powerful feeling in Frank. His anger suggests that his masculinity was challenged as well. This opens up a constellation of race and gender dynamics ranging from the micro to macro level that force Frank to relate questions of privilege to his own life to the experiences of the African American couple in the city.

This emotionally traumatic experience highlights Brennan's (1993) psychoanalytic argument that confrontation with the other can expose the subject to his or her privileged position. It also highlights Russell's (1998) conceptualization of white fear as rooted in the possibility of revenge by blacks. In fact, Frank's narrative suggests a certain degree of trauma over using the word "nigger." Earlier in the interview he starts out his narrative by noting that the last time he said "nigger" was during his freshman year but latter in the narrative he remarks that he also used the slur "nigger" during his junior year. Thus, it appears that Frank contradicts himself, which again highlights the especially traumatic aspects of relatively privileged subjects' encounters with African Americans in mostly black social geographies.

Daniel recounts a confrontation with an impoverished African American man asking for money outside a convenience store in Boston.

> About two years I was coming out of a – I was down by Kenmore Square. I don't know if it was a Red Sox game or it was after. I had gone into the *Store 24* and they had two guys who were, they opened the door and they beg when they open the door.[9]
>
> So I went in, and I said, 'I'll catch you on the way out.' And I usually

---

[9] Latter in the interview I asked Daniel about the race of the men outside of the convenience store. He informed me that they were African American.

don't give them money, but usually ask if they want something to eat. But this time I just threw a dollar in the first cup I saw. Well, apparently it was the wrong cup, because the guy opened the door, and I turned and he was right there in my face. He's like, 'What the fuck, man? You were supposed to give me a dollar.' I opened the door. 'What the fuck is your problem?' He's going off on me, going off on me. And I can remember going through my head, it's like, 'Well when was the last time you were ever unpleasant?' And okay, I'm like 'I don't know if this guy is going to back down, what [am I going to] do?' So what I came up with is, I gave him a dollar. And that was fine. Like no problem; I'll give you a dollar. But that old stuff, saying 'Screw you, pal, man. Part with my money?? No way [I'm] doing that.' I'm not sure if that's ever going to go away. I'll be able to process it, and say, 'Wait a minute, you did the right thing.' But if that was me maybe in college, if that was me with my friends around me in college, I probably would have done something different. [INT: Been more confrontational?] Yeah.

In this example, Daniel's interaction with a confrontational African American man who is poor also demonstrates the differences in power between men as they vary along class and racial lines. Daniel also feels that he has to carefully negotiate this situation, as he is being challenged. "That old stuff" refers to a gendered challenge centered on masculinity. At a certain level, Daniel did not want to defer to the confrontational man. He ultimately decides to give the man a dollar to defuse the situation, but this again demonstrates how the politics and performances of masculinity also open up the possibility of unequal access to power along class racialized lines as well.

Frank, Jesse, Bill and Daniel all feel that they are gazed upon by people of color and treated negatively because they are seen as privileged white men. This creates a paradox in the their understanding of racialized social power – white men are often seen as privileged in critical discourses on white masculinity but they have had experiences where they feel they are victims of a racist act.[10] They see themselves as innocent and as victims. Following the metaphors of mapping and prism effect of intersectionality, these narratives create a complex and dynamic portrait of the operation of race, class, and

[10] Although not highlighted in this article Bill also had negative experiences with African American men in urban contexts.

gender dynamics that unfold across time and space and vary from the micro to macro level. This also demonstrates that privilege and oppression operates simultaneously at the macro level of social structure to the micro level of individual interactions with others.

Thus, in the narratives of the respondents it is important to be attentive to the production of privilege and oppression at both the macro and micro level. In the above narratives, accounts of white men moving between mostly white to mostly black social geographies imply that white privilege is non-existent in that context. However, even though some of the white men above may have lived in areas where whiteness is not the norm, their access to walking the streets is privileged by their standpoint as men in the gender order (Anderson 1991, Connell 1987). Class also is crucial to the understanding of how social geography mediates a sense of context specific identity formation. Jesse may be structurally positioned as man in a way that allows him to walk the streets with greater comfort than women; still his working class economic status does not afford him the economic privileges often associated with whiteness. However, Frank comes from an upper middle class background that provides him a certain amount of economic privilege. Although Bill inhabits a more economically modest position than many of the students at the mostly white university he attends, his whiteness allows him to take on a more nonracial, individualistic position at the school. Using the prism effect of intersectionality, one can place the identity movement across geographic space in a broader context of power relations. Indeed, even though in some cases whiteness might not be the norm and thus fail to provide privileges in specific geographic settings, the prism effect of intersectionality helps us to consider how in other contexts white men may in fact receive forms of privilege that are longer lasting and more significant to a life of comfort.

Conclusion

In this article, I demonstrated how social geography is a key element in the transformation of white men's identity from "nonracial" to "racial." The narratives of the respondents also demonstrate how such an identity transformation can be difficult because such a movement forces white men to confront issues of racialized privilege and power as they intersect with class and gender. Part of this difficulty lies within the investment in liberal humanist discourses and the standpoint of sovereign individuality. For some of the respondents, the difficulty in part stemmed from making sense of living in an area where whiteness is not the norm and those critical discourses that mark white men as privileged. By incorporating the equalizing logic of liberal humanist discourse, some of the white men had difficulty in resolving experiences where the benefit of whiteness was not operating with discourses that argue white men are privileged. The result is an emotional reaction of frustration and an argument that racism can operate both ways, thus making it difficult to accept that white men are structurally privileged. By incorporating this method one can provide a map of how movement between and within distinct social geographies operates in relation to the discourses available and where one is located in the hierarchies of race, class, and gender.

I argue that if institutionalized racism, sexism and classism are to be overcome both liberal humanist discourse and the standpoint of sovereign individuality need to be challenged. Although the production of the sovereign individual through liberal humanist discourse has the utopian qualities of people who are self-governing and free, it also denies the co-constructed character of human existence and the structural aspects of privilege and oppression. To deny the co-constructed qualities of human existence can lead to massive structural inequalities. In the twenty-first century, I believe it is essential for white men to move beyond the verbal acknowledgement that they have been privileged by the institutions of race and gender. It is also vital for white men as group to engage in social action that alters the structures of racism, sexism, and economic inequality.

Thus, if the investment in sovereign individualism can create barriers to understanding how race and gender power operate in the post-Civil Rights era, I argue that there must be a movement to both deconstruct sovereign individuality and reconstruct an identity that is capable of acknowledging how identities are always produced out of power and knowledge. Obviously such a project is daunting but by paying attention to how power operates at the level of consciousness and identity, I believe that new forms of identity can emerge. This process must work both at the level of the individual and at the level of social structure, for it is the consistent relationship between the two that produces both regimes of power and forms of consciousness.

Afterward

In the opening chapter, Stephen Pfohl (2004: 191) argues, ". . . no cultural meanings or practices are ever truly understandable without making discerning connections to the historical landscapes of power out of which such meanings and practices arise, are challenged, and change." Indeed, Pfohl (2004) is calling for developing a more complex understanding of the materiality of culture in sociology, as it should be understood as being constituted through knowledge and power. This forces a reevaluation of how one approaches the micro/macro divide: micro and macro arenas are not discrete parts but different phases of social processes in the context of power and knowledge. When done well, understanding the materiality of culture demystifies the realm of common sense and mundane cultural practices. Culture is moved from its apolitical domain into a site where everyday cultural practices become part of reproducing or resisting systematic forms of inequality.

In this afterward, I relate Pfohl's (2004) call for the understanding of the materiality of culture to the study of whiteness and other privileged identities. I believe that understanding privileged identities and practices in the context of power and knowledge continues to be one of the most important areas that 21st century sociology can study. In the early 1990s scholars of color such as Toni Morrison (1991) and bell hooks (1992), called for whites to examine their own privileged position. The result was an explosion of literature on whiteness, culminating in brief mass media attention in the late 1990s (Talbot 1997). However, with the growth of critical whiteness studies came a range of different criticisms. Some worried that the study of whiteness would displace Ethnic Studies programs or the study of other racial and ethnic groups (Grillo & Wildman 1995; Hill 2004). Others worried that the study of whiteness would reinforce the system of white privilege by not being attentive to how white racial identity, or "white culture," is connected to racialized systems of power. As Fine et al. (1997: xi–xii) note, ". . . [I]n our desire to create spaces to speak intellectually and empirically about whiteness, we may have reified whiteness as a fixed category of experience and identity; that we have allowed it to be treated as a monolith, in the singular, as an 'essential something.'" The concern of Fine (1997) and her colleagues lies in part on the emphasis of understanding the discursive construction of whiteness without contextualizing it in local practices. Much of the literature on whiteness has been oriented to theoretical analysis of the key discourses that constitute whiteness. Without understanding the distinct and local processes of white racial formation, whiteness becomes reified. This has even caused some scholars to wonder if the study of whiteness should be aborted (Fine et al. 1997).

Although I agree that the study of whiteness has been at times done poorly, the increasing number of empirical studies on whiteness gives hope to the goal that whiteness can be studied as a process of construction in the context of knowledge and power (Frankenberg 1993; Hartigan 1999; Perry 2002; Gallagher 2003; Bonilla-Silva 2001). In this chapter, I further document the dynamic and unfolding process of white racial identity as it moves across time, space, and different landscapes of knowledge and power. The result allows one to see white masculinity in the context of lived experience and power relations and as a process that is unfolding and dynamic. This chapter also demonstrates how the study of the materiality of white racial identity formation is embedded in masculinity and class dynamics. The understanding of the specific aspects of privileged identity formation develops a materiality of culture that reconceptualizes micro and macro levels as merely different areas of emphasis in the formation of power. This helps contribute to the demystification of how racialized, classed, and gendered power operates in the lives of the privileged. Therefore, if the study of whiteness or other privileged positions is to continue, it should done in a manner consistent with Pfohl's (2004) call for a material understanding of culture. This will allow for a continued deconstruction of privileged identities in a manner that demonstrates how they become complicit in reproducing oppressive systems.

Juliet B. Schor

The Commodification of Childhood: Tales from the Advertising Front Lines*

Introduction

In the last ten years, the academic literature has taken note of the growth of commercial influences on childhood, with contributions such as Joe Kincheloe and Shirley Steinberg's *Kinderculture: The Corporate Construction of Childhood*, Stephen Kline's *Out of the Garden*, Ellen Seiter's *Sold Separately*, Henry Giroux's *Channel Surfing*, Elizabeth Chin's *Purchasing Power*, Henry Jenkins' *The Children's Culture Reader,* and Daniel Cook's *The Commodification of Childhood.* Some of these texts explicitly address the question of the commodification of childhood, although the literature has yet to settle on a precise definition, and meanings and uses vary widely. Among marketers, the term commodification implies a process in which brand value is disappearing, and the product, increasingly unable to command a price premium, is degraded to the level of an unbranded commodity. In the academic literature, the term is sometimes used almost synonymously with commercialization, as in the notion that children are increasingly involved in consumer, or commercial, culture.

AUTHOR'S NOTE: *I would like to thank the Advertising Education Foundation and the many professionals within the advertising industry who gave generously of their time and expertise. For research assistance, I am grateful to Chiwen Bao. I would also like to acknowledge the support of the Philanthropic Collaborative for this project.*
* This essay originally appeared in *The Hedgehog Review*, vol. 5, no. 2 (2003).

I have in mind a more specific meaning, which comes from classical Marxian theory. For Marx, a commodity is not only bought and sold (as in the commercialization meaning), but also produced specifically for the purpose of exchange. Therefore, the status of commodity is not inherent in any characteristics of the good itself, but emanates from the social relations that govern its production and exchange. Is my sweater a commodity? If it is produced in a factory to be sold on a market, it most certainly is. If I knit it at home for myself, it most certainly is not. But if I knit the sweater at home for the purpose of selling it, it becomes commodified. (Labor power, readers of *Capital* will remember, is a peculiar commodity, because under capitalist social relations, it is sold on a market, but not necessarily produced for that purpose.)[1]

According to this notion, the commodification of childhood refers to a process in which the cultural category childhood is itself produced for the purpose of being sold. And while the notion that a cultural concept can be a product may involve an intellectual stretch, I would argue that this formulation is an insightful illumination of processes now at work in the field of marketing and advertising to children – what industry insiders call the "kidspace." These industry professionals have become increasingly influential in the social, cultural, and economic construction of childhood. They affect children's sense of identity and self, as well as their values, behaviors, relationships with others, and daily activities. They help shape the normative vision of childhood that is held by both children and adults. In this sense, they are creating, transforming, and packaging childhood as a productive cultural concept that they then sell to the companies who make the actual products that children buy.

When we conceptualize marketing to children in this way, it becomes apparent that marketers and advertisers are also involved in the commodification of children. This phrase ordinarily refers to a process in which children are literally bought and sold, for example, into a state of sexual bondage or other forms of productive labor, such as plantation or factory work. But it is increasingly the case that advertisers and marketers are also involved in a different type of commodification: they are influential in actually producing children – that is, in raising, educating, forming, and shaping them. And they

---

[1] Labor power is peculiar for other reasons as well, such as the fact that it is only a capacity to work. Once the labor process commences, labor itself is the relevant input.

do this in a commodified form; that is, they produce children in order to sell them back to their clients. They create in-depth research that they then sell. They provide children with cultural products such as television programming, movies, and web content. They sponsor museum exhibits, school curricula, and leisure activities for children, all of which help to create children as social beings. Advertisers have even gotten into the business of structuring the form and content of social interaction and conversation among children, a phenomenon they benignly term peer-to-peer marketing. In the last fifteen years, advertisers and marketers have been extraordinarily successful in these endeavors. They have profited from an explosion of expenditures for, and, even more importantly, by children.

I have reached these conclusions on the basis of research carried out during 2001, 2002, and early 2003 in the advertising industry. I conducted interviews, attended industry conferences, shadowed marketers, participated in client meetings, and spent about two weeks as a visiting professor at an agency where I was attached to a group that handled a major children's account. I read selectively in the trade literature. My aim in this research was to identify and understand how children are being marketed to and how that has changed over time. I took a broad-brush approach, looking across product groups, including toys and food. I investigated conventional advertising (e.g., television, print, radio, and web ads), looking specifically for the major thematic approaches in the messages. I also catalogued the wide variety of marketing and promotional activities that currently comprise the bulk of total marketing expenditures, including sponsorships and viral, stealth, peer-to-peer, and school-based marketing. I studied the transformation and expansion of research about children. In addition to conventional survey, interview, and focus group techniques, new methodologies such as ethnography, videotaping, diaries, and in-home and in-situ observation have become popular.[2] Three trends in the field of marketing to children help reveal the processes of commodification that are now occurring on a wide scale: the rise of naturalistic research, peer-to-peer marketing, and the new discourse on kid empowerment. These three

---

[2] As a complement to this work, I conducted a survey of 300 fifth-, sixth-, and seventh-grade children. The survey data was used in the creation of a new scale that measures children's level of involvement in consumer culture. The consumer involvement scale was included in a structural equation model that tested the impacts of consumer culture on a variety of measures of psychological and social well-being. See Schor (2004).

trends represent only a few of the developments that are re-shaping childhood, and this account is more illustrative than complete. Nevertheless, they are key factors in the transformation of children's lives.

Accessing the Advertising Industry

As is well known, advertising is a field in which confidentiality is extremely important. Clients are typically very concerned about secrecy, and agencies are careful about sharing information with outsiders. Compared to other sites of market production, such as factories and offices, conducting academic research inside advertising agencies is relatively infrequent. Most research and findings about children are proprietary in order to protect the economic return that this information yields. The presence of controversy and debate about the entire enterprise of marketing to children also contributes to the secrecy that surrounds research on children. During the period of my research, various groups were actively protesting and organizing against the people I was attempting to study. Industry participants had good reason to be cautious about outside researchers.

Despite these factors, I did get inside a number of agencies and was able to arrange interviews with many practitioners. At times I was given confidential information. I gained access to a couple of client meetings and focus groups. I believe that my initial entrée, which occurred in part because of my affiliation with a highly prestigious academic institution, led others to believe I was safe to talk to. I employed a snowball sampling technique, using the names of people I had previously interviewed in order to convince others to meet with me. This method proved reasonably successful. I also believe that I benefited from a generally positive and at times enthusiastic attitude toward academic researchers. This is especially true in cases where industry people hold Ph.D.s in liberal arts disciplines. Although I had considerable success in gaining access, it was not complete. Two of the firms I tried to penetrate, Channel One and MTV Networks, were relatively closed, explicitly citing their desire to avoid criticism. I was also unable to arrange first-hand experiences of certain research practices that I was interested in. I did not typically ask to see confidential material, knowing that it might raise red flags about my presence and that I would probably be unable to write about it in any case.[3]

---

[3] Unless otherwise noted, all quotations in this paper are from interviews conducted by the author in 2001, 2002, or 2003.

The Rise of the Children's Market

During the last two decades, children have increasingly taken on the role of independent consumers with considerable purchasing power of their own. No official statistics on the volume of children's independent purchases exist. This is not surprising, given that children do not have legal rights over their "own" money. However, the field of marketing to children has relied heavily on soft estimates from practitioners. Paul Kurnit, one of the deans of children's marketing, with extensive experience in toys, food, and other children's categories, identifies two factors in the field's expansion: [What's new] has been the recognition over the last 20 years that kids are a powerful, very influential market and that they are very brand-aware. . . . One of the fundamental changes has been the quantification of kid buying power, which back in the '60s and even in the early '70s nobody was quantifying until guys like Jim McNeal came along.

As Kurnit notes, James McNeal, Emeritus Professor of Marketing at Texas A&M University, has been the field's most influential quantifier of children's purchasing power. McNeal believes that in 2002, children aged four to twelve made an estimated thirty billion dollars in purchases using their own money. (McNeal 1999, and private communication with author, July 12, 2002). His calculations suggest that direct expenditures rose from $6.1 billion in 1989, to $23.4 in 1997, to their current level (McNeal 1999: 17). Teen spending is far greater. According to survey data from TRU, a market research company specializing in teens, the average 12–19 year old spent $104 per week in 2001.[4] Teen spending is important because the children's market has been growing alongside it, and because trends and styles now migrate quickly from adolescents to kids.

In addition to possessing greater purchasing power, children are becoming more autonomous and involved consumers. Six to twelve year olds are reported to visit stores 2–3 times per week (White-Sax 1999). Time spent shopping by children has risen significantly in the last 20 years as they accompany parents to stores (Hofferth and Sandberg 2001) and they are also shopping without adults. McNeal estimates that one in four make trips to stores alone before they enter elementary school and that the median age for independent trips is eight (McNeal 1999: 96). The growth of youth shopping is leading

[4] Teen Research Unlimited, "Teens Spend $172 Billion in 2001," www.teenresearch.com, January 25, 2002.

to changes in retail environments, as merchants cater to younger patrons. Teen- and child-themed malls have begun appearing around the country.

Children have also become far more influential in family purchase decisions. According to McNeal, children aged four to twelve directly influenced $300 billion of adult purchasing in 2002 and "evoked" another $300 billion.[5] He estimates that this "influence market" is currently growing at 20% per year. Kurnit believes that the origins of children's influence are more than 20 years old: "I would say the real watershed was in the eighties: the recognition that the influence chain between parent and child worked extremely well, that it was effective, that a direct message to a child could empower the child if the message was clear, simple and well-branded."

Since that time, children have been understood as important influencers of brand choice for a variety of adult products, including automobiles, hotels, tourist destinations, fast food, consumer electronics, and a majority of the in-home foodstuffs that are eaten by children. In response to this increased influence, manufacturers of these products have begun to advertise directly to kids. Research done by Nickelodeon finds that 89% of parents of 8–14 year olds report that they ask their children's opinions about products they are about to buy for them.[6] Children's technological savvy and avid consumer information-seeking is another reason for their increased influence over parental spending. Market researchers report that many parents now believe that their children know more about products and brands than they do, and the parents rely on that knowledge.

Constructing the Kid Consumer

Companies' successes in both direct and influence marketing to children are partly due to a vastly expanded research effort. In the early days of children's marketing, most of the people who made commercials or crafted branding strategies relied on personal experience. They were parents and considered their own children to be good representations of the target audience. Today, most of the how-to books on children's marketing explicitly condemn such

---

[5] Norris, Michelle, "Buy, Buy, Baby: Companies Taking the Fight for Consumer Loyalty to Kids," www.abcnews.com, May 10, 2002.
[6] Penn, Schoen and Berland Associates Inc., 2001, Untitled Proprietary Nickelodeon Study.

an approach and warn that it will lead to failure. Instead, they counsel, extensive research is necessary to succeed in this competitive market. The experience of Nickelodeon bears out this advice. The fabulously profitable Nickelodeon and the larger MTV Networks of which it is a part base their work on extraordinarily detailed, expansive, varied, and careful research. As Donna Sabino, a Nickelodeon executive who supervises research, explained to me, the network studies thousands of children every year, using every conceivable type of research – surveys, mall intercepts, intensive videotaping, focus groups, in-home observation, internet research, and online panels, to name a few of the types of research they conduct.

Perhaps the fastest growing component of research on children is naturalistic, in-situ ethnographic videotaping and observation. Detailed naturalistic research began with adults in the 1980s, as anthropologists migrated out from the university into advertising agencies. Ethnography is popular partly because it is able to go beyond the now-exhausted insights of the large-scale quantitative research that was done in the 1950s and 60s and partly because it is far less expensive. The popularity of naturalistic research is also due to the shortcomings of traditional interviews and surveys, which are conducted in artificial settings, are subject to various types of artefactual response biases, and do not examine how consumers actually live with or interact with products. Advocates for this daily life research also argue that they can uncover insights that consumers cannot or prefer not to articulate. This is an especially compelling rationale for children, whose ability to articulate their reasons for liking or disliking products is more limited than that of adults. Emma Gilding, the researcher behind AT&T's mlife campaign, and a leading practitioner of naturalistic research in New York, contends that this method is far superior to traditional approaches: "It's not research, we live with them . . . not anthropology, we're in the frame."

The pioneer agency in applying such techniques to children was Saatchi and Saatchi, who, in 1998, circulated an influential report on children's computer use entitled "Digital Kids." That study stationed anthropologists inside children's homes to watch them as they used computers; altogether, they taped about 500 hours of children's online use. Since that time, the use of intensive naturalistic observation has grown dramatically, and the range of observed activities has expanded markedly. Marketers are scrutinizing virtually every activity kids now engage in – from playing, eating, and grooming, to bathing – and virtually every aspect of their lives – from what's inside their closets to how kids interact in the classroom and what really goes on at a tween girl's slumber party. They are probing how kids talk about, and even how they use, drugs. Naturalistic research, with cameras, notebooks, and videotapes, is also occurring in retail environments, such as toy stores, clothing shops, and supermarkets. It is going on in public spaces, such as in playgrounds and on the streets. Noggin, a joint venture of Nickelodeon and PBS, set up shop for six months in an elementary school in Watchung, New Jersey to do preparatory research prior to launching its joint cable station.

Children are also being drawn into the process as researchers themselves. Levi-Strauss, the company that pioneered closet-peeping, was also one of the earliest to use children as consultants. In the 1980s, they hired Manhattanite Josh Koplewicz, who was ten at the time. Josh accompanied executives into stores to give his opinions on the clothes; he vetted styles that were in various stages of production and design and was periodically asked to comb the city for cool styles, which he recorded through photographs, interviews, and other documentary methods. Such practices have now taken root at market research firms all around the country. For example, The Strottman Group of Southern California hires "kid engineers on staff" and estimates that they maintain an ongoing relationship with about 750 kids, ages 6 to 17. Doyle Research in Chicago has an extensive kid consultant program, in which children are used for brainstorming "Kideation" sessions to help with product development. Most of the other major research firms and many of the "producing" firms, such as Nickelodeon and Microsoft, run some type of kid consultant program, using children extensively in research, product design, and evaluation.

With these types of methods, researchers can make the claim that they know children in ways that are far deeper, more sophisticated, and more profound than a past generation that relied on focus groups and standard surveys did. Today's researchers "construct" children for their clients, who then use that construction as the basis of their strategies of communicating with children.

Peer-to-Peer Marketing

A second development is the development of what is alternately called "viral," "buzz," "stealth," "street," or "peer-to-peer" marketing. This strategy relies on creating a word-of-mouth advertising campaign that creates buzz, which in turn enhances the effectiveness of conventional ad campaigns. Buzz marketing has become standard for a large number of youth products, especially apparel, footwear, music, and consumer electronics. In a typical buzz campaign, the manufacturer will give or "seed" products with individuals. Converse was one of the first companies to begin product seeding, giving its shoes to inner-city athletes in the 1970s. Since then the process has intensified and expanded to other trendsetters, such as actors, performers, musicians, and a wider range of athletes. There are now whole agencies that specialize in this practice of "real life product placement" with celebrities and other influential people.

Product seeding has also migrated out to non-celebrities. In these campaigns, companies typically identify people they consider to be "trend-setting" individuals, give them samples of a product, and ask them to recruit friends. There are even agencies that specialize in finding these kinds of trend-setting (or "alpha") individuals. One practice is to pay people to pose as ordinary consumers. For example, alcohol brands pay people to sit in bars and order their drinks, and then to talk to other patrons about them. Chat rooms are seeded with paid representatives to promote brands. The internet and email are full of these paid communications. Movie, book, and music reviews are increasingly written by paid representatives of marketing companies.

While teens and young adults were the targets of many of the early viral campaigns, these techniques have filtered down to children. An example of peer marketing among children is the Girl's Intelligence Agency. In 2002, its first year of operation, the company had already developed a network of 40,000 girls who assist the company in testing and marketing products for its clients. GIA was founded by Laura Groppe, a former film producer and a feminist advocate for girls within commercial culture. (She's one of the few experienced feminists for girls that I encountered in my research.) Girls as young as six are recruited to become GIA "agents." Once accepted they become part of an online and daily life network. Profiles of agents are posted on GIA's website. Six-year-old "swimmergirl" lives in San Diego and loves swimming, cats, and chatrooms. Eleven-year-old "singsalot" loves fashion. The girls report going to Agent Kiki, a fictitious "older sister" type whose answers are written by GIA staffers, three to four times a week for style and fashion advice.

The GIA's trademark product is the Slumber Party in a Box, which takes place in what the company calls the "inner sanctum," that is, the girl's bedroom. GIA runs both "insight" (i.e., research) and marketing parties. Parties feature toys, films, television shows, health and beauty aids, and other products. The host girl (a GIA agent) invites up to eleven of her friends to the party, where they are given a sample of the product, which is then used (or watched) during the party. The party becomes an informal, intimate sales session. Sometimes parties are videotaped, and sometimes GIA staff attend, but many of the parties are run by the agent herself. GIA claims that each of the agents reaches an average of 512 other girls, in virtually every area of daily life. With their network of 40,000 agents, the company claims it can reach 20 million girls nationwide.

One piece of evidence for how far these kinds of efforts have infiltrated the mainstream of U.S. society is the kinds of institutions that are now participating in these marketing ventures. In my research, I uncovered recruiting programs for children to become market consultants through Boys and Girls Clubs. Laura Groppe explained to me that she makes contacts with major organizations, which then "evangelize" for GIA. Groppe was unwilling to name these organizations, explaining only that they are "regional and national organizations that are pro-girl." When I suggested Girl Scouts and national church organizations, Groppe did not disagree.

Buzz and peer-to-peer marketing are important examples of commodification because they rely on children to use their friends for the purposes of gaining information or selling products. (GIA's network is called BFF – Best Friends Forever.) Similar practices include organizing kids into "friendship pairs," where researchers tape conversations between friends, or the use of e-mail buddy lists for marketing. Throughout the world of kids marketing, using kids to recruit other kids is a rapidly growing practice. Indeed, a viral or peer-to-peer "rollout" has become a standard element of marketing plans for many children's products, with especially elaborate programs aimed at tweens.

A major reason that peer-to-peer marketing is so widely used is that word-of-mouth from friends is one of the few remaining sources of credibility in a world over-saturated by commercial messages. It is assumed to be disinterested, objective, and pure, unlike ads, which carry the taint of deceptiveness or manipulation. But if the trend toward more word-of-mouth advertising continues, it is likely that people will learn to be more skeptical of it, recognizing that the purveyor of the advice may well be acting instrumentally. One result will be that this valuable type of consumer information will be corrupted. Another, more serious consequence is the corruption of the friendships themselves. Marketers are teaching children that their friends are a lucrative resource that they can exploit to gain products or money. But what we cherish most about good friendships is often their insulation from those types of pressures. Friendships are commonly thought to be one of the last bastions of non-instrumentality in our society, as money and market values have become ever more transcendent and important. And that's precisely why the marketers are so keenly interested in them.

The New Discourse of Kid Empowerment

Intrusive research and peer marketing are practices that have the potential to become highly controversial, as are a number of other trends in children's marketing that I do not have the space to elaborate on here.[7] These include the marketing of "cool," tweening or age compression, the anti-adult bias in commercial messages, in-school marketing, and the marketing of addictive products. Advertisers and their clients are aware of the potential for an anti-marketing backlash from parents and child advocates. Many know that in the last few years, the Annual Golden Marbles Award (a children's version of the industry's CLIO award) has drawn protests and that debate about the enterprise of marketing to children has been growing. Serious opposition to the promotion of violence, junk food, and in-school marketing has already surfaced. In response, industry insiders have attempted to create a defense of their activities based on a new discourse of "kid empowerment." One indication of how the critique of marketing has begun to gather force is that the 2003 Annual Kidpower conference included two sessions on how to respond to this opposition.

The notion of empowerment is a considerable departure from previous industry practice, which was to market to children mainly through mothers. Of course, there have always been some exceptions to this practice, particularly in candy and toy marketing, but they were the exception, rather than the norm. Marketing through mothers, which is called the "gatekeeper" model, holds that parents (in theory), but mothers (in practice), are responsible for ensuring children's well-being in the face of the consumer market. The gatekeeper era began in the 1920s and started to weaken in the 1950s, with the advent of the first television programming exclusively for children, but it was only in the mid-1980s or so that marketers consciously rejected a gatekeeping

---

[7] For a full accounting, see Schor (2004).

strategy in favor of direct marketing to children. Kurnit has been one of the industry's most vocal proponents of the decline of the gatekeeper model and the benefits of directly targeting children:

> The expression in marketing was always "mom is gatekeeper." And I've spoken recently that the "mom is gatekeeper" thing is over. A decade ago I called it "the unmanned tollbooth." Today I call it "Easy Pass." And to a large extent that analogy is really true. And it does relate to the fact that in dual-income families – and in 67% of families with kids, mom and dad are working – you've got kids who are increasingly home alone, latchkey kids. You've got the after-school day part, which is the fourth meal, and kids rule the kitchen, and all that kind of stuff. So there's a level of kid independence today that is unprecedented. And so on some level the parent cannot have the level of control either over the TV dial or food that she once had because she's literally not there.

Relying on these social trends, marketers are now arguing that children do not need protection from advertising. For example, the industry claims that earlier findings about children's inability to understand and resist commercial messages are no longer relevant. This was a debate that raged in the 1970s and to a lesser extent in the 1980s. Marketers describe today's children as savvy, not able to be manipulated, sophisticated, and worldly, with built-in "truth meters." Child advocates pushing for stricter regulations are put down as know-nothings.

Indeed, some advertisers have argued that current industry practice is *too* protective of children. The anti-adult themes in kid marketing are justified as ways to empower children against an overly authoritarian adult presence. Commercial spots that portray adults as buffoons, out of touch, or objects of ridicule are pervasive. Industry proponents defend these messages as examples of "kid mastery," which "level the playing field" and "empower kids." Conservative cultural critics see them as treasonous. Of course, when things go wrong, advertisers continue to blame parents, and especially absent mothers. Food marketing has become an especially contentious topic, as rates of overweight and obesity among children have skyrocketed, amidst a torrent of junk food marketing and deteriorating diets. Marketers point their fingers at parents, who they fault for buying junk food, not patrolling the kitchen, and taking their children too frequently to fast food outlets. "Just say no," they counsel. At the same time, many of their most sophisticated approaches, they have explained to me, involve breaking down parental resistance.

Conclusion

The trends I have discussed (new research forms, peer marketing, and the new discourse of empowerment) are part of a new relationship between child consumers and the people who make a living taking money from them. On the one hand, kids are increasingly constituted as a market of *empowered subjects*: they have money, exert influence, and navigate consumer culture on their own. Marketers argue that we should treat them as functionally equivalent to adults in the liberal discourse of laissez-faire consumer policy, that is, as rational, knowing subjects who can act in their long-term interest. At the same time, these same people are constructing children as *marketable objects*, dissected and classified, and then served up to client companies. This knowledge enhances the power of those client companies to affect children's everyday lives, by making their products and experiences ever more irresistible. Together, marketers and manufacturers are creating a powerful experience of commodified childhood.

Of course, that formulation is too simple. We are no longer living in a world of one-way interaction between producer and consumer in which, to use Douglas Holt's words, marketers retain "cultural authority" (Holt 2002). The relationship goes two ways. And after years of refinement, processes of naturalistic research such as cool-hunting, the advent of peer-to-peer and street marketing, and the discourse of consumer empowerment have not only become very sophisticated, but have also led to a dynamic back and forth between marketers and their target audiences. This dialectical movement, or feedback loop, has been noted by Thomas Frank (1997) and Douglas Holt, who trace its origins to the decline of "cultural authority" in the 1950s (Holt 2002), and by other analysts of popular culture. As Douglas Rushkoff observes in his plea to marketers to cease and desist: It's turned into a giant feedback loop: you watch kids to find out what trend is "in," but the kids are watching you watching them in order to figure out how to act. They are exhibitionists, aware of corporate America's fascination with their every move, and delighting in your obsession with their tastes.[8]

In the end, we are not only commodifying our children, which is the standard critique of consumer culture, but, even more powerfully, we are recruiting them to commodify themselves.

---

[8] Undated, available at www.rushkoff.com/essay/sportswearinternational.html.

William A. Gamson

Movement Impact on Cultural Change*

> *"I shall not attempt further to define it . . .; and perhaps I could never succeed in intelligibly doing so. But I know it when I see it."* (Justice Potter Stewart, struggling with the problems of a legal definition of obscenity, in Jacobellis v. Ohio, 1964.)

Is cultural change the latest candidate for the "it" in the above quote? How can we possibly assess the impact of social movements when we can't answer the question of impact on *what*? Various writers call upon us to consider changes at the level of personal identity and consciousness, in the lifeworld of the household and neighborhood, in our daily life in the workplace, in making the unthinkable thinkable, in the supplanting of one "moral-intellectual" universe with another. In fact, the referents for cultural change are all around us, diffused through the civil society in a thousand ways, but this doesn't tell us where to look to assess impact. If the changes are everywhere, then one can look anywhere. One is left to wonder whether, in observing the cultural changes around us through the myriad ways in which people in different social locations live their lives, we will have any common referent at all by which we can assess movement impact.

---

* An earlier version of this paper, titled "Social Movements and Cultural Change," appeared as a chapter in Guigni, McAdam, and Tilly (1998).

Perhaps this is one reason why, to quote McAdam, McCarthy, and Zald (1996: 6), "the literature is long on ringing programmatic statements regarding the necessity for 'bringing culture back in,' but short on the kind of cumulative scholarship that we now have on political opportunities or mobilizing structures in the emergence and development of movements." Furthermore, this weakness seems most acute on the issue of impact. In contrast, there has been detailed specification of cultural processes in movement mobilization which helps us to understand why symbolic processes and identity processes are central. But, as Polletta (1996: 483–4) observes in reviewing a recent collection of essays on cultural politics and social movements, there is considerably less success "in demonstrating the *impacts* of cultural challenge."

Fortunately, a solution is at hand and is already well begun – *assess movement impact on cultural change through public discourse*. This has several advantages. For one, it differentiates a cultural level of analysis from social psychological processes such as personal identity, political cognition, public opinion, and political socialization. The conflation of these levels of analysis invites the-culture-is-everywhere-so-look-anywhere confusion. If we want to know whether one moral-intellectual universe has been supplanted by another, we look at particular forums of public discourse to see if it has been supplanted in that forum. Whether it has been supplanted in the hearts and minds of citizens is a separable issue involving the complex ways in which people use public discourse in combination with other resources in making sense of issues raised by social movements.

A second advantage is the way in which the study of public discourse lends itself to the Swidlerian view of culture as a tool kit (Swidler 1986). We ask what has happened to the tool kit available to people through public discourse and whether any changes reflect an input from social movements that is in some sense distinguishable from that of other social actors. By not making culture everything – and by recognizing the ways in which people use their personal experience and popular wisdom as well as public discourse – one can specify the referent and make manageable the assessment of cultural impact.

Finally, it enables us to extend the well-known typology of outcomes used in *The Strategy of Social Protest* (Gamson 1990, herein referred to as *Strategy*). In doing so, it highlights the problems of using the outcome measures in *Strategy* for assessing *cultural* change. But by looking to public discourse to find outcome measures, we can use the same typology, thereby helping to integrate cultural change into studies of movement impact on social policy and power alignments.

Constructing Public Discourse: A Working Model

The focus on public discourse also has some limits, as I hope to make clear in proposing a working model of the construction of public discourse.[1] Public discourse means public communications about topics and actors related to either some specified policy domain or to the broader symbolic interests of some constituency. It includes images as well as information and argumentation. The production of images rather than information or argumentation is worth emphasizing because this more subtle form of meaning construction is at the heart of measuring cultural impact. It is useful in reminding us to attend to the visual, to verbal imagery, and other modes of conveying a broader frame – through music, for example. It encourages us to look beyond conventional discussion of public affairs to advertising and entertainment as additional sites where images are communicated. But the distinction between images and factual information can be overdrawn: facts as much as images take on their meaning by being embedded in some larger system of meaning or frame.

Public discourse is carried out in various forums. A forum includes a site or arena in which meaning is being contested plus an active audience or gallery. The contributors or players in any given forum are aware of the gallery, some of whose members may themselves become active players at

---

[1] This working model is a collective one, shaped by numerous discussions with my partners in research on the construction of abortion discourse in Germany and the United States: Myra Marx Ferree (University of Wisconsin), Friedhelm Neidhardt and Dieter Rucht (Wissenschaftszentrum Berlin für Sozialforschung) and Jürgen Gerhards (University of Leipzig) and by the participants in the Media Research and Action Project (MRAP) at Boston College. It is informed by a broad and eclectic literature and developed most fully in Ferree et al. (2002). On the role of the mass media in framing issues, it draws especially on Tuchman (1978), Gans (1979), Gamson and Modigliani (1989), and Gamson (1992). On the interaction of movements and media, it draws on Gitlin (1980), Ryan (1991), and Snow and Benford (1988, 1992). On the role of public discourse in a democracy, it draws on Dahlgren and Sparks (1991), Entman (1989), Fraser (1995), Garnham (1986), Gerhards (1996), Habermas (1987, 1989), and Keane (1991). On the mediation of discursive interests, it draws on Rucht (1995). On movements as a field of organizations, it draws on Melucci (1989) and Klandermans (1992).

other times or in other arenas. We define the public sphere as the set of all forums in which public discourse takes place.

Every forum has its own norms and practices governing both the form and content of expression and who has standing to participate. The model does not assume that any given forum is "fair" in the sense of providing a level playing field for all participants. On the contrary, the rules and practices of the gatekeepers in any forum are part of the explanation of cultural impact or its absence. Not only do the assemblers of discourse provide opportunities and constraints for cultural challengers, especially around issues of access, but they actively participate as important sponsors of meaning in their own right.

The *mass media* are the most important forum for understanding cultural impact since they provide the major site in which contests over meaning must succeed politically. First, they provide a master forum in the sense that the players in every other forum also use the media forum, either as players or as part of the gallery. Among the various forums of public discourse, it provides the most generally available and shared set of cultural tools. Social movements must assume that their own constituents are part of the mass media gallery and the messages their would-be supporters hear cannot be ignored, no matter how extensive the movement's own alternative media may be.

Second, the mass media forum is *the* major site of contest politically in part because all of the would-be or actual sponsors of meaning – be they authorities, members, or challengers – *assume* pervasive influence (whether justified or not). The mass media often become the critical gallery for discourse carried on in other forums, with success measured by whether a speech in the legislative forum, for example, is featured prominently in the *New York Times* or the *Frankfurter Allgemeine Zeitung*.

Finally, the mass media forum is not simply a site where one can read relative success in cultural contests. It is not merely an indicator of broader cultural changes in the civil society but influences them, spreading changes in language use and political consciousness to the workplace and other settings in which people go about the public part of their daily lives. When a cultural code is being challenged, a change in the media forum both signals and spreads the change. To have one's preferred framing of an issue increase significantly in the mass media forum is both an important outcome in itself and carries a strong promise of a ripple effect.

Political Interest Mediation

This dual role of the mass media as both sponsor of meaning and site of a meaning contest emphasizes its role in a complex system of what Schmitter (1977) and Rucht (1995) call "political interest mediation." Various actors in this system – political parties, corporations, associations, and social movements – attempt to generate, aggregate, transform, and articulate the interests of some underlying constituency. Social movements are only one of several potential *carriers* of the interests of a given constituency in this larger system of interest mediation. To assess their impact on any kind of change – be it cultural or institutional – one must consider their relationship to the other carriers.

To call this a mediation system, as Rucht (1995) reminds us, implies the linking of at least two external elements which, for a variety of reasons, can not or do not communicate directly. They "obey conflicting logic and principles which permit no direct link" (Rucht 1995: 105) or, more metaphorically, they don't speak the same language. But the mediation system discussed here does much more than simply translate inputs and outputs into a common language. It takes on a life of its own with its own operating logic and interests and transforms and shapes what is being communicated; indeed, its processes often override the intentions of actors in the external systems being linked.

If social movements are part of a complex mediation system, what are the external systems being linked? On the one hand, we have constituencies. One may think of these as solidarity groups or, to borrow Anderson's (1991) useful concept, "imagined communities." Examples would include women, workers, Christians, greens, conservatives, Latinos, the "left" and many others. Since people have multiple identities, they are potentially part of many constituencies. A given solidarity group may provide a lead identity for some people that they use on all or most issues while for others, it may be one of several which vary in salience from issue to issue. The degree of solidarity or personal identification with a particular imagined community is an empirical question, with the operation of the interest mediation system providing most of the explanation.

The other end of the mediation system is more problematic and forces us to take a closer look at what is meant by "interests." Consider, for example, that the constituency whose interests are being mediated is "farmers." The term "interests" conjures up images of crop subsidies, regulations, and other agricultural policies that will operate to the advantage or disadvantage of this group. Or perhaps of power arrangements that will increase or decrease the political influence of those who carry the political interests of farmers. In this narrow sense of policy interests, the other end of the mediation system is the system of authorities who are able to make binding decisions on policies and how they are implemented.

In considering cultural change, however, the term "interests" seems too narrow and restrictive. Farmers also have certain "interests" in the nature of public discourse and these include both interests in promoting desired policy frames in various forums, but also more subtle ones that do not relate to any specific policy contests. As an example of the former, support for policies favoring farmers is likely to be greater if the image of farmers in public discourse emphasizes the small, independent family farm rather than the agribusiness that is, in fact, the dominant "farmer" in the production and distribution of most crops. But aside from this instrumental and strategic use of public discourse to further policy interests, some groups of farmers may have concerns about the degree of respect they receive in the broader culture – for example, about the disparaging depiction of white farmers in the South as "rednecks" or "hillbillies" in movies and in television entertainment forums. In short, the various constituencies whose interests are being mediated have *symbolic interests* and these should be the focus of an assessment of cultural impact.

For the mediation of symbolic interests, the other end of the mediation system is less clear. Authorities do not make binding decisions about language use nor does anyone else. Their decisions about usage may or may not be adopted by others and often authorities may simply follow the lead of various parts of the mediation system – especially the dominant usage in mass media discourse. Hence, for symbolic interests, it is the outputs of the mass media system, rather than the decisions of authorities, that are being linked to constituencies via the mediation system.

Both authorities and the mass media, then, play a dual role in the system of interest mediation. For power and policy interests, authorities function as the external system being linked – that is, as the target of the carriers in the mediation system. But at an organizational level, some official agencies may function as carriers of the interests of some constituency – as an inside voice for these interests in the internal discussions of decision-making bodies. In this role, they are part of the mediation system rather than the external system being linked. The Department of Agriculture, for example, may be less a producer of binding decisions than a carrier of a particular definition of farmers' interests within internal government forums.

To complicate matters further, we can not assume that the state is merely a target system that produces outputs but must recognize that it has system-wide interests of its own. These may or may not be engaged on a given issue but can not be ignored. On abortion, for example, state interests may involve the maintenance of a given population level, thereby providing a link to the abortion issue and reproductive policies more generally. Certain carriers in the mediation system may also be carrying these state interests. Clearly, those who do will enjoy advantages in any contest with rival carriers.

Similarly, when the media are a site in which various carriers compete to further the symbolic interests of their constituencies, they are the external end of the mediation system. But when we examine how their structure and practices shape the outputs and how journalists articulate the symbolic interests of particular constituencies, we are considering them as part of the mediation system in their own right.

The mass media system, like the state, can also be assumed to have autonomous interests of its own, beyond the varying organizational interests of the field of actors that comprise it. Again, these system wide interests may or may not be engaged on a given issue but cannot be ignored. We do not assume that the mass media system is neutral among different types of carriers – for example, between members and challengers – but that the openness varies from issue to issue and must therefore be part of any assessment of cultural impact.

Nature of the Mediation System

The political parties, corporations, associations, and social movements in the interest mediation system are each *fields of actors* that may overlap. Green interests, for example, may be mediated by a movement/party that is simultaneously part of the political party and movement sub-systems and is variously linked with associations as well. One cannot assess the impact of movements independently of their role in this broader system. The symbolic interests of a given constituency may be shared by a field of actors who pursue them in different ways – including a movement sector.

If we find an improvement in the salience of preferred frames in public discourse, we can not attribute it to the movement component in particular unless we can differentiate the symbolic interests it emphasizes from those that are common to the network of carriers. Since the internal decisions of this network are typically the site of a contest about what are the best frames and policies to pursue, one can often use this internal discourse to distinguish the particular symbolic interests being articulated by social movement organizations and advocacy networks.

The mediation system as a whole structures the opportunities and constraints in which carriers of particular interests must operate. Different opportunity structures may make it easier or more difficult to mediate a given set of interests. Movements, parties and associations each may have more or less opportunity for influence within the mediation system . . . For cultural change, we should focus on the *media opportunity structure* – that is, the linkage between the mass media subsystem and the various carriers of symbolic interests. In addition to internal norms and practices, the political economy of the mass media also affects the rules of access for whose and which ideas ideas are taken seriously. Any comparative assessment of the success of movement symbolic strategies must reflect differences in media opportunity structure lest we underrate success in movements challenging more fundamental aspects of cultural codes and, hence, face more formidable obstacles to change.

Public Discourse and Public Policy

Success in having an impact on public discourse is important but it does not necessarily translate into impact on either public policy or a broader set of practices in everyday life. With respect to public policy, decision makers in the political system are clearly an attentive part of the gallery and may be directly influenced by the metaphors, images, and arguments that they watch and read. But other forums may be more important – including a policy forum where the gallery is less the general public and more those with professional work interests and responsibilities in the policy domain.

Most of the impact of the media forum on public policy is indirect – mediated by the perceived or actual impact of media discourse on the distribution of individual opinion among voters. To the extent that media discourse shapes these opinions on issues that are electorally relevant, it will constrain political decision makers or induce them to follow dominant tendencies to avoid defeat at the next election. This argument can be seen as a version of the two step flow of influence – in this case, from the media to voters to policy-makers. But the opinions of voters – whether in the form of sample surveys or the words of one's taxi driver – are open to interpretation with various carriers competing to give their spin on what the "public" really thinks. For advocates in the policy arena, media discourse may be primarily a cultural tool whose content they can use in their own efforts to garner support rather than something by which they are influenced directly.

Policy processes, however, are not driven only or even primarily by ideas. Decision makers may be influenced by many other factors that operate with substantial insulation from public discourse – for example, the exchange relationships and deal-making of political insiders, the maintenance of support from influential political supporters who may have substantial material interests engaged, and the demands of party discipline. It is quite possible to win the battle of public discourse without being able to convert this into the new advantages that flow from actually changing public policy.

But doing badly in mass media discourse creates vulnerability in pursuing policy interests. Political parties and individual politicians looking for issues that will attract voters for themselves and embarrass or divide their opponents may make the issue electorally relevant. For supporters of existing policies, the success of challengers in the mass media forum puts supporters on the defensive and complicates their work. They are left consistently vulnerable when their would-be allies are worried that their policy choices will become an issue that opponents are likely to use against them in the next election. If challengers are sufficiently successful in defining the terms of debate in media discourse, the support of a powerful but discredited interest group may stigmatize those who carry its water in policy disputes.

The link between cultural success and policy outcome is further mediated by the complicated relationship of media discourse to public opinion. In their attempts to make sense of the world of public affairs, ordinary people are only partially dependent on media discourse and dependency varies widely among different issue domains. *Talking Politics* (Gamson 1992: 179) likens people's efforts to make sense of issues to finding their way through a forest. "The various frames offered in media discourse provide maps indicating useful points of entry, and signposts at various crossroads highlight the significant landmarks and warn of the perils of other paths."

On certain issues, media discourse may be a first resort and the primary resource for making meaning but even on such issues, ordinary people typically will find multiple frames available. The openness of the media text requires that they use other resources as well to complete the task. People control their media dependence, in part, through their willingness and ability to draw on popular wisdom and experiential knowledge to supplement what they are offered. If media dependence is only partial when media discourse serves as the starting point, it is even less so where experiential knowledge is the primary resource for finding a path through the forest.

However, lack of dependence does not imply lack of use or influence. Most people on most issues construct meaning by different combinations of media discourse, experiential knowledge, and popular wisdom. They integrate these sources of meaning with varying degrees of success into a coherent cognitive schema for those issues that are important to them; for many policy domains, they may never have thought or talked about it, or ever felt the need to have any opinions about it. The flow of influence from media discourse to public opinion is itself heavily mediated, indirect, and partial, further diluting the impact of success in the mass media forum on policy outcomes.

Finally, success in public discourse also fails to guarantee that broader cultural and institutional practices will necessarily change. One may win the battle of words while practices remain unchanged or even change for the worse. Here, the abortion issue will serve well as an illustration. Most studies of media discourse on abortion suggest that – in the United States, at least – the proponents of frames emphasizing rights of individual privacy and women's self determination do very well. At the same time, access to abortion is not increasing and has significantly declined in some areas. Some states have only a single abortion provider, requiring women to travel great distances. The symbolic contest over the framing of abortion may be very far from the minds of potential abortion providers who are deterred by the fear that they may become the target of anti-abortion violence – regardless of whether the violence is roundly condemned in media discourse.

Nevertheless, there is solid evidence that abortion access is heavily influenced by public support for abortion rights. In Wetstein's (1996) quantitative study of abortion rates in the 50 American states, he examines the percentage of counties within a state which have one or more abortion providers. Using a multi-variate LISREL analysis to estimate a path model, he finds that two primary factors can account for 63% of the variation in abortion access. "Greater support in the mass public translates directly into greater levels of access to abortion (B = .32). The only other significant variable to influence the level of providers is the socio-economic variable [a combined measure using median income, median education, and other similar indices] (B = .53)"

(Wetstein 1996: 120). Wetstein included no measures of media discourse in his analysis but his results certainly suggest that the cultural climate on the issue in a given state is one of the most important predictors of abortion practices.

Measuring Success

Cultural social movements are sustained with conscious challenges to cultural codes by a field of actors, some of whom employ extra-institutional means of influence. Extra-institutional refers to everything other than the use of the electoral system, the judicial system and the peaceful petitioning of public officials (lobbying, testifying at public hearings, presentations, letters, petitions). In the case of cultural challengers, the extra-institutional means may include guerrilla theater or other dramatic displays, demonstrations, vigils, marches, burning of effigies, graffiti, "culture jamming," and other norm violating symbolic politics.

ACT UP, an AIDS activist organization, has been especially inventive in this regard, using such venues as a Mets game at Shea Stadium to denormalize taken-for-granted codes. J. Gamson (1989: 351) describes their slogans, using baseball themes: "No glove, no love," "Don't balk at safer sex," and "AIDS is not a ballgame." He quotes a straight fan who complains, "AIDS is a fearful topic. This is totally inappropriate," suggesting that the fan has inadvertently summed up the point of the action. The opportunity to challenge invisibility and the taken-for-granted is there for challengers willing to use unconventional forms of collective action.

Many movements seeking structural change also challenge cultural codes. The civil rights movement, the women's movement and the environmental movement, for example, are cultural movements by the above definition. Rather than classifying movements, it seems more useful to ask how any movement that has a cultural challenge as one component, can measure success in this realm, even if it is not their primary emphasis.

The Strategy of Social Protest (Gamson 1990) offers an approach to measuring success which can be adapted to measuring cultural impact as well. *Strategy* suggests that we think of success as a *set* of outcomes, recognizing that a given challenging group may score differently on equally valid measures. However, it divides the outcome measures into two basic clusters: one concerned with the fate of the challenging group as an organization and one

		Acceptance	
		Full	None
	Many	**Full Response**	**Preemption**
New			
Advantages			
	None	**Cooptation**	**Collapse**

Source: Gamson 1990: 29

Figure 1: Outcomes of Challenges

with the distribution of new advantages to the group's beneficiary. The central issue in the first cluster focuses on the *acceptance* of a challenging group by its targets as a valid representative for a legitimate set of interests. The central issue in the second cluster focuses on whether a group's constituents gain *new advantages* during the challenge and its aftermath.

By combining these two questions, as in Figure 1 above, we can specify four possible outcomes: full response, co-optation, preemption, and collapse. The full response and collapse categories are relatively unambiguous successes and failures – in the one case the achievement of both acceptance and new advantages; in the other, the achievement of neither. The remaining are mixed success categories: co-optation refers to acceptance without new advantages and preemption to new advantages without acceptance. *Strategy* operationalizes these variables with a strong structural bias, inadequately meeting the challenge of measuring cultural impact. But with appropriate modification, the same outcomes can be used.

Acceptance

Acceptance in *Strategy* assumes the existence of a visible antagonist or set of them. "This antagonist necessarily begins with a relationship of active or passive hostility toward the challenging group or, at best, indifference. Acceptance involves a change from hostility or indifference to a more positive relationship" (Gamson 1990: 31). As indicators of a more positive relationship, *Strategy* focuses on consultation, negotiations, formal recognition, and inclusion in positions of authority in the antagonist's organizational structure.

This operationalization of acceptance ignores the fundamental dilemma of those who challenge cultural codes – the invisibility of the antagonist. Much of what ACT UP is fighting, for example, "is abstract, disembodied, invisible: control through the creation of abnormality" (J. Gamson 1989: 352). The premise of a visible antagonist who can grant acceptance is violated, requiring a different type of operationalization. But by focusing on media discourse, there is a ready solution to a cultural definition of acceptance.

Acceptance, for cultural challengers, can be measured by media *standing*. In legal discourse, standing refers to the right of a person or group to challenge in a judicial forum the conduct of another, especially with respect to governmental conduct. The rules for according legal standing have been anything but fixed and clear. Former Chief Justice Earl Warren, in Flast v. Cohen (1968), referred to it as "one of the most amorphous concepts in the entire domain of public law." Rather than a matter of clear definition, legal standing is a battleground and the environmental movement, in particular, has had considerable success in expanding who has standing to sue the government.

By analogy, media standing is also contested terrain. In news accounts, it refers to gaining the status of a regular media source whose interpretations are directly quoted. Note that standing is not the same as being covered or mentioned in the news; a group may be in the news in the sense that it is described or criticized but has no opportunity to provide interpretation and meaning to the events in which it is involved. Standing refers to a group being treated as an agent, not merely as an object being discussed by others.

From the standpoint of most journalists who are attempting to be "objective," the granting of standing is anything but arbitrary. Sources are selected, in this view, because they speak as or for serious players in any given policy domain: individuals or groups who have enough political power to make a potential difference in what happens. Most journalists would insist that their choice of sources to quote has nothing at all to do with their personal attitudes toward those sources. If they choose to call Operation Rescue and quote its erstwhile spokesman, Randall Terry, on his reactions to a Supreme Court decision on abortion, this has nothing to do with whether they like or dislike Operation Rescue or Terry. They are simply reflecting a reality that is out there – for better or worse, the group has enough power that it needs to be taken into account and Terry is able and willing to speak for them.

Croteau and Hoynes (1994) conducted studies of the guests on *Nightline* and identified some apparently significant sources who did not appear. Host Ted Koppel and his associates defended their choices. The authors quote

Nightline executive producer Richard Kaplan who argued, "We're a news show, not a public-affairs show. Our job is to bring on guests who make the news – the players, in other words."[2] News, in this world view, is about those powerful enough to make a difference – this objective reality is the basis of standing for a news show.

Of course, sophisticated journalists such as a Ted Koppel or a David Brinkley are aware that an appearance on their show also enhances the claims of players to be taken seriously. Presumably, they are both flattered by their ability to influence who has standing with other journalists and made uncomfortable by the unwanted responsibility. They would like it to be true that they merely reflect rather than create standing and their awareness that this is only half true is disquieting. In the end, they content themselves with trying to pursue the ideal of objectivity as best they can in an imperfect world.

In the model offered here, media standing is the endpoint of a contest over which sponsors of meaning will have an opportunity to appear in a mass media forum *that defines membership in terms of political power*. Defining *acceptance* in these terms, emphasizes standing as a measure of achieved cultural power. The model here assumes that journalists operating in a news forum try to reflect their perceptions of who the key players are but that, in practice, they are influenced by various other factors in choosing sources and quotes. Choice of sources – at least in the U.S. media – is often driven by the need for spectacle and drama; the sources who are used are those who give good sound bite or provide footage of people with fire in the belly. In cultural contests, sources are often chosen because they are seen as representing a particular perspective. Rather than being seen as representative in the sense of typical, they are chosen as prototypes who represent a particular cultural tendency in a compelling and dramatic way. In this sense, standing still reflects a journalistic political judgment about which cultural movements make a difference or are players.

Note that this discussion of standing operationalizes the concept for policy discourse; to assess some broader cultural acceptance, one needs to look beyond news forums to include such mass media forums as television entertainment, movies, talk shows, and advertising. It is especially problematic to

---

[2] In the case of *Nightline*, this defense fails to deal with one of Croteau and Hoynes (1994) principal findings – that the most frequent appearing guests were often *former* players, not those who were presently active.

ignore these when talking about cultural change because they may be more sensitive indicators. Standing, measured as who gets quoted in news accounts, does not capture this broader form of cultural acceptance. It does not deal, for example, with the portrayal of gay and lesbian characters in a sympathetic or matter of fact way in entertainment forums which may say more about the acceptance of the homosexual constituency than quoting a person from ACT-UP or the National Gay and Lesbian Task Force.

New Advantages

Much of the discussion of this variable in *Strategy* is relevant here in spite of the structural bias in operationalizing it. Did the potential beneficiaries of the challenge receive what the group sought for them? The challenger's perspective and aspirations are the starting point for assessment. We are left to judge whether the benefits sought were or would have been "real" benefits; they are benefits as defined by the challenger. On the issue of whether the benefits actually happened, *Strategy* supplemented the group's own assessment of success with that of the antagonist and professional historians, looking for consensus.

By using media discourse as the measure of new cultural advantages, we have a simpler and more quantifiable measure of success than perceived outcome by observers in different social locations. Challengers to cultural codes have an alternative way of framing the issues in some normative domain. Their preferred alternative frame calls into question the taken-for-granted assumptions of the code being challenged – for example, about the nature of what is normal and abnormal, visible or invisible, or what is appropriate behavior in work and family settings. Often such challenges focus on visual images, language and labels – whether on the abortion issue, for example, one uses the term "fetus" or "baby."

If one charts mass media coverage of some issue domain over time, frames and their associated idea elements and symbols will ebb and flow in prominence. Success in gaining new advantages in cultural terms is measured by changes in the relative prominence of the challenger's preferred frames compared to antagonistic or rival frames. Take, for example, a specific cultural practice challenged by the women's movement – the use of the generic "he" in English, to be replaced by various alternative forms of gender inclusive language. To assess success, one compares media samples from today with those before the second wave of the women's movement began in the late

1960s. If gender exclusive language is reduced or has disappeared, here is a clear measure of success.

Extending this measure of success to other non-news forums is less problematic than it is for standing. Frames can be extracted from cartoons, films, advertising, and entertainment as readily as from news accounts. The prominence of preferred movement frames can be assessed over time in such forums in the same way as in news forums.

Using these two measures, the four outcomes above are redefined for cultural challengers. *Full response* means that a challenger receives both media standing and a significant increase in the prominence of its preferred frame. *Collapse* means it receives neither standing nor increased prominence for its preferred frame. *Cooptation* means that the group receives media standing but no significant increase in its preferred frames; finally, *preemption* means that the challenger's preferred frame has significantly increased in media prominence in spite of the absence of media standing for its sponsor.

Explaining Success

Cultural movements face a number of daunting obstacles in competing with public officials, corporations, political parties, organized interest groups and other more resource-laden sponsors of meaning. Some do well in spite of the uneven playing field. Why do they succeed? To answer this, we'll examine each of the four major factors in determining the success of a frame in the mass media forum: sponsor activities, media norms and practices, cultural resonances and narrative fit.

Sponsor Activities

Frames succeed, in part, because of sponsors who promote them through such tangible activities as speech making, interviews with journalists, advertising, article and pamphlet writing, and the like. Many of these sponsors are organizations who employ professional specialists whose daily jobs bring them into contact with journalists. The sponsor of a package is typically an agent who can draw on the resources of an organization to prepare materials in a form that lends itself to ready use. Professionalism abets sophistication about the news needs of the media and the norms and habits of working journalists.

Cultural challengers can rarely hope to compete with the full array of production assets that defenders of cultural codes can muster but they can compete successfully in some realms. Production assets include not only material resources such as personnel and money that are available for sponsoring preferred frames in the media but also sophistication and know-how about how the mass media work in a practical way. Many cultural challengers can and do acquire this know-how.

The abortion issue in the U.S. is a ready illustration. Both pro-choice and pro-life movement groups have highly skilled professionals with a sophisticated understanding of what works in the mass media forum. They concede nothing in this respect to organized religious groups or political parties, for example. Many of the actors in the movement organizational fields have a relatively stable flow of resources although some, of course, struggle to survive. In this case, the general disadvantages movements face in production assets have been neutralized to the point at which they can compete on more or less equal terms with non-movement sponsors.

The importance of production assets is mitigated by what Gamson, Fireman, and Rytina (1982: 87–88) call the *threshold hypothesis*. They suggest that the simple linear hypothesis – the greater the production assets, the higher the probability of success – is inadequate. It is more useful to specify a desirable threshold for different kinds of assets. "Those groups of potential challengers that fail to meet this threshold have a deficit with negative consequences [for success]. But enough is enough. Once a group has sufficient assets, no further advantage accrues from having more." By this argument, cultural challengers must overcome any deficits in production assets to succeed but having achieved a certain threshold, increasing production assets will only add marginally to the probability of success.

Media Norms and Practices

Hallin and Mancini (1984, p. 841), building on Habermas' arguments about the structural transformation of the public sphere, note the replacement of a participatory, decentralized bourgeois public sphere "by a process of political communication dominated by large scale institutions: political parties, unions, and other organized associations of the private sector, and the mass media." This public sphere is structured quite differently in the U.S. and in Germany, for example. Political interpretation in Germany is provided by the institutions that have traditionally dominated the modern public sphere: political parties, unions, industrial associations and organized religion. In such a situation, the journalist does not need to play a very active role as an interpreter of meaning.

In the U.S., in contrast, the institutions of the public sphere are weak. Political parties are loose coalitions organized to compete for public office, not for expressing unified frames. The meaning of events is often a matter of internal party contention; to sponsor any given frame is to risk a potentially costly internal division which may weaken the party in competing for electoral success. As a result of this relative institutional vacuum, the mass media become *the* primary institution of the American public sphere in performing the function of providing political interpretation.

Partly because of this function of giving meaning to the events of public life, certain journalistic conventions have developed in the United States that are unusual in Europe. These include, Hallin and Mancini (1984) argue, a greater tendency to frame and interpret, and to use narrative structures and images. The result of these differences in journalistic conventions and the nature of the public sphere is a greater opportunity for social movements to shape media discourse in the United States. The relatively smaller importance of institutional actors leads journalists to seek other interpreters, including social movement spokespeople. The consequence is that movement actors are generally more likely to be given standing in the media as interpreters of meaning even though they must compete with rival movement actors, public officials, corporations, and private interest groups to get their ideas across.

The operation of the journalistic *balance norm* also opens opportunities for challengers, albeit in a complicated way. In news accounts, interpretation is generally provided through quotations and balance is provided by quoting spokespersons with competing views. The balance norm is vague and the practices that it gives rise to favor certain frames over others. Organized opposition to official views is necessary to activate the norm which, once invoked, tends to reduce controversy to two competing positions – an official one and the alternative sponsored by the most vested member of the polity.

The balance norm is not generally interpreted to include challengers unless they have already achieved standing. But even challengers without standing can open doors for allies. In the U.S. antinuclear movement, for example, access to the media was greatly enhanced by the 1977 site occupation of the Seabrook, New Hampshire reactor by the Clamshell Alliance. This action helped to define nuclear power as controversial, thereby invoking the media's balance norm. The chief beneficiary in terms of enhanced media standing was not the Clam but the Union of Concerned Scientists (UCS). As Gamson (1988: 235) puts it, "When demonstrators are arrested at Seabrook, phones ring at UCS." Preemption is one likely outcome for cultural challengers who use extra-institutional means to draw the attention of the media – their preferred frame increases in prominence through the words of others even though they do not themselves receive standing.

Of course, internal rivalries between movement actors can undermine such convenient divisions of labor. Gamson and Wolfsfeld (1993: 123) point out that movements frequently offer multiple frames, each identified with different actors. Those who increase movement standing through their unconventional actions may find that their particular preferred frame is poorly represented by those who become the media-designated spokespersons. They may attack and attempt to undercut these spokespersons.

The internal movement contest can easily become the media's story, distracting attention from the issue and blurring the preferred frame. There is an underlying tension between the more pragmatic and cynical culture of journalism and the more idealistic and righteous culture of movements. Movements, of course, do not have a monopoly on self-righteousness, moralizing, piety, and the like. Conventional politicians frequently exhibit these traits as well but they often privately share the journalists' culture of cynicism in off the record contacts. They are playing a public role with a wink to journalists – although this does not make them immune to discrediting accounts when their private behavior blatantly seems to contradict their public persona.

Only those who are true believers are operating counter to the culture of journalism but they are also operating counter to the culture of conventional politics. Most movement participants believe in an injustice frame and *are* indignant rather than faking it for public consumption. Movements hector people, including journalists, and call them to account. This righteousness is unappealing to those who are living with the inevitable compromises of daily life. Gamson and Wolfsfeld (1993: 120) suggest that this means "that internal movement conflicts and peccadilloes will have a special fascination for journalists, giving them an opportunity to even the score from their standpoint. The fall of the righteous is a favored media story wherever it can be found and movements offer a happy hunting ground." Hence, a division of labor is likely to work only if there is a common frame and a willingness to subordinate concerns about who gets credit for being the messenger.

Cultural Resonances

Not all symbols are equally potent. Some metaphors soar, others fall flat; some visual images linger in the mind, others are quickly forgotten. Some frames have a natural advantage because their ideas and language resonate with a broader political culture. Resonances increase the appeal of a frame by making it appear natural and familiar. Those who respond to the larger cultural theme will find it easier to respond to a frame with the same sonorities. Snow and Benford (1988: 210) make a similar point in discussing the "narrative fidelity" of a frame. Some frames, they write, "resonate with cultural narrations, that is, with stories, myths, and folk tales that are part and parcel of one's cultural heritage."

Talking Politics (Gamson 1992) suggests that this level of analysis can best be captured by focusing on the dialectic between cultural themes and counterthemes. Themes are safe, conventional, and normative; one can invoke them as pieties on ceremonial occasions with the assumption of general social approval, albeit some private cynicism. Counterthemes typically share many of the same taken-for-granted assumptions but challenge some specific aspect of the mainstream culture; they are adversarial, contentious, oppositional. Themes and counterthemes are linked with each other so that whenever one is invoked, the other is always present in latent form, ready to be activated with the proper cue.

Discursive strategies, for challengers as well as for other players, center on the use of language, symbols, and images that resonate with cultural themes and counterthemes. The basic strategy is to invoke the resonances of themes and counterthemes on behalf of one's preferred frame and to neutralize the potential resonances of the most important rival frames. Framing contests often involve competition over a particular theme.

The battle over the symbol of "equal opportunity" in the United States is a good illustration. In the civil rights movement of the early 1960s, demonstrators carried signs demanding "Equal Opportunity for all Americans." The demand was that every individual be given a fair chance to succeed, regardless of skin color. The symbol of equal opportunity utilizes the resonances of the powerful self-reliance theme which invokes a world in which with resourcefulness, pluck, and a few breaks, even a poor bootblack can become a millionaire. Rival frames, far from competing for the resonances of this theme, were vulnerable to the charge that they denied individuals the opportunity to succeed on the basis of their efforts and talents.

But during the 1970s, as policy controversy centered on affirmative action programs, the power of these resonances was effectively challenged and neutralized. The major vehicle, a *reverse discrimination* package sponsored by a neo-conservative advocacy network, fought over the same resonances. Advocates embraced equality of opportunity and colorblindness claiming that this is what they sought while opposing only those programs in which "some are more equal than others." The power of the original resonances was effectively neutralized since there is no effective resonance when discordant frames play the same note.

When dominant frames that are being challenged rely heavily on resonances with certain themes, challengers can sometimes compete by invoking the countertheme. The antinuclear movement, for example, found themselves confronting a dominant frame that invoked the theme of progress through technology. Existing alongside this theme is a countertheme that emphasizes harmony with nature rather than mastery over it and suggests that technology can sometimes develop a life of its own. To quote Emerson, "Things are in the saddle and ride mankind." The more we try to control nature through our technology, the more we disrupt the natural order and threaten the quality of our lives. Much popular culture reflects the countertheme: Chaplin's *Modern Times*, Huxley's *Brave New World*, Kubrick's *2001*, and countless other films and books about mad scientists and technology gone wild, out of control, a Frankenstein's monster turned on its creator.

Before there was an antinuclear movement, supporters of nuclear power handled the potential tension between nuclear energy as a symbol of technological progress and as a symbol of ultimate destruction by a strategy of nuclear dualism. Atoms for Peace invoked the progress theme and the countertheme was safely compartmentalized in the nuclear weapons discourse. By invoking the resonances of this countertheme, the antinuclear movement was able to interpret events in ways that helped to destroy nuclear dualism and, with it, the resonances of nuclear power as a technofix for America's energy problems.

Narrative Fit

A theory explaining the success of frames must be based on an epistemology that recognizes facts as social constructions and evidence as taking on its meaning from the master frames in which it is embedded. The essence of frame contests is competition about what evidence is seen as relevant and what gets ignored. Does this social construction model force us to abandon all attempts to evaluate the implications of empirical evidence for the claims of competing frames? Does it reduce us to what Goodman (1978) calls a "flabby relativism" in which all frames have an equal claim in interpreting the world?

Clearly, there is an important and complicated relationship between the characteristics of events and the success of certain frames. The accidents at Three Mile Island and Chernobyl did not make life easy for those who frame nuclear power as technological progress. But neither did they provide empirical refutation of this frame. As its advocates will point out, Three Mile Island "proved" the "defense in depth" safety system works; even in this most serious of nuclear accidents, no one was killed and no significant amounts of radiation were released. And Chernobyl "proved" the wisdom of the American nuclear industry in building reactors with the reinforced concrete containment structures that the Chernobyl plant lacked.

Frames provide a narrative structure which leads one to expect certain kinds of future events. No spin control is necessary when the frame already suggested that such events were likely. But when the narrative confronts unexpected events, some ad hoc explanation and special effort is required by advocates to sustain the frame. A poor narrative fit with unfolding events that cannot be ignored places the burden of proof on those frames that must make sense of them; with a good narrative fit, unfolding events carry the much easier message: "I told you so."

Conclusion

To assess cultural impact, this paper urges a focus on mass media discourse. This is the most important forum for understanding cultural impact because it is the major site in which contests over meaning must succeed politically. One can use the outcomes at this site to read relative success in cultural contests. More specifically, one can use it to define acceptance and new advantages in cultural terms – where acceptance is measured by standing and new advantages by relative success in having ones preferred frame and its idea elements displayed there. This allows one to redefine the outcome categories of full response, co-optation, preemption, and collapse in cultural terms.

Cultural challengers operate on a playing field that is rarely level and is tilted against them to various degrees, depending on the issue domain.

However, even an uneven contest does not prevent some challengers from success. The ones who succeed, do so by overcoming deficits in production assets and acquiring the necessary know-how; by using media norms and practices to their advantage; by the use of discursive strategies that resonate with broader cultural themes and counter themes and by providing an expected scenario that can anticipate and include unfolding events easily and comfortably in its narrative structure. Of course, challengers may still perform as skillfully as possible and fail because their rivals are equally skilled and have additional structural advantages as defenders of the status quo.

Cultural success is important but winning the battle of words does not guarantee success in other realms. It is a necessary condition for success in changing policies and practices and one major factor in the set of sufficient conditions. But policy processes are political processes and political influence does not operate primarily through persuasion with words and symbols. Nor are broader institutional and cultural practices determined merely by the outcomes in the mass media forum. Nevertheless, there is much evidence for ripple effects.

Success in media discourse is one important influence on public opinion and on which issues will be relevant for electoral politics. Losing the battle of words certainly adds to the difficulties of those who rely on other means of influence to shape public policy. Cultural and institutional practices are influenced by other factors as well but the climate created by media discourse plays an important role in maintaining or changing them. Cultural impact is not everything but it is a significant goal in its own right for cultural challengers.

Charles Sarno

On the Place of Allegory in the Methodological Conventions of a Critical Sociology:
A Case Study of Max Weber's *Protestant Ethic**

> *The Researcher stepped forward, acting supremely con-*
> *fident and well intentioned, ready to greet the demands*
> *of the day.*[1] *Meanwhile the Ethnographer hung back in*
> *the shadows.*
>
> A scientific ethnography normally establishes a
> privileged allegorical register it identifies as
> "theory," "interpretation," or "explanation." But
> once all meaningful levels in a text, including
> theories and interpretations, are recognized as
> allegorical, it becomes difficult to view one of
> them as privileged, accounting for the rest. Once
> this anchor is dislodged, the staging and valu-
> ing of multiple allegorical registers, or "voices,"
> becomes an important area of concern for ethno-
> graphic writers. . . . Much ethnography, taking
> its distance from totalizing anthropology, seeks
> to evoke multiple (but not limitless) allegories.
> – James Clifford (1986: 103), "On Ethnographic
> Allegory."

* An earlier version of this essay appeared in *Critical Sociology*, vol. 30, no. 2 (2004).
[1] I would like to thank the members of the editorial collective of *Critical Sociology*
at Boston College for their helpful comments on several drafts of this paper. An earlier version of this manuscript was published in *Critical Sociology*, Volume 30, No. 2
(2004).

Over the course of the past two decades a number of researchers situated on the borders of a more conventional sociology have begun to explore the place of allegory within the social sciences. Critical methodologists such as James Clifford (1986, 1988), Donna Haraway (1989, 1997), Stephen Pfohl (1992), Laurel Richardson (1994, 1997), Avery Gordon (1996), and Patricia Clough (1998) have examined the allegorical elements and "fictive" devices found within the ethnographic practices of the social sciences. This diverse body of writing has drawn attention to the often unconscious literary and narrative conventions employed in ethnographic work, the uses of metaphor and story telling in the construction of even the most rigorous theoretical and descriptive accounts, and the qualitatively different methodological and political implications that such awareness of allegory has across a range of scientific disciplines.

This resurgence of the allegorical within the social sciences has opened up broader possibilities for critical and power-reflexive interpretations of culture and history. In particular, an awareness of allegory shifts the more conventional tones of cultural and historical interpretation, creating fissures in the landscape that allow for previously repressed knowledge – both in terms of the form as well as the content of evidence – to emerge and reshape the lay of sometimes narrowly specialized and repressed disciplinary fields. In key ways allegory furnishes not only substantively different details about how culture and history unfold, but a different categorical sense of that culture and history as well. It is this peculiar capability available within allegorical modes of expression, one which understands power not only in the presence or absence of material and symbolic resources, but in the shifting configurations of force which makes the presence or absence of such elements recognizable in the first place, which gives this interpretative approach its own transformative ability. As a result, allegory can help to generate new vistas and imaginary spaces. It promotes more complex, generous and reciprocal notions of culture and history, wherein the very material struggles for social justice and social change can take place. Thus, within the context of a discussion surrounding the themes of culture, power and history, allegory comes forth with provocative offerings and exchanges.

Often this impulse towards allegory has come from, or been inspired by, people in movement, both personal and social, on the periphery of more conventional formations of power/knowledge within social science ethnography. It is a part of the practical and theoretical experience of subjugated individuals and groups who do not stand on the shoulders of giants, but rather on the margins of a given order of things. These others – women, people of color, prisoners under the rule of law, and political and cultural dissidents of various stripes – have found allegory to be an important critical tool for countering hegemonic and disciplined discourses of power/knowledge, particularly those discourses predicated on exclusionary standards of hierarchy and domination.

This point can be taken quite literally. It has been pointed out that allegory conceals as much as it reveals. Allegory has often been employed within and under situations of physical imprisonment and material deprivation, where speaking freely is severely constrained or forbidden. It is technique suited to escaping or evading a censorious intent, at least when read against and past the straightforward and some what blank gaze of the censor's eye. Consider, for example, figures like John Bunyan, or Antonio Gramsci, or African American slaves, who during the course of their captivity used allegory (in the case of slaves stories that have been labeled "folktales") as a way of talking past the authorities, resisting dominant narratives, and countering with stories of emancipation. For those on the margins, allegory serves as a mode of knowledge production that demands to be taken seriously even while it tries to skirt the more formal demands of *certain*[2] disciplinary styles, styles which have become analytically tired, socially stagnant, politically oppressive and sometimes downright depressing.

In order to avoid this stifling sense of depression that is privately felt even as it is being publicly generated and instituted, many feminist and anti-racist social researchers, engaged with post-structuralist social theory, have attempted to reintroduce elements of allegory and story telling – already implicitly present but unconsciously buried in the dominant narratives of social science – back into their analysis of major social institutions. For instance, Donna Haraway, in her work on *Primate Visions*, employs the concept of "constrained and contested story telling" in order to explore how both natural and social scientific practices in the United States during 20th century have constructed changing narrative images of apes, monkeys and humans in the developing field of primatology. Because Haraway's work takes place across the contested

---

[2] These disciplinary styles are *certain* in the multiple sense of being particular, partial, and imperially self-assured in the very same instant.

terrain of several narrative fields – including the powerfully productive field of science *per se*, her position does not succumb to the singular temptation of reducing these scientific accounts of primate behavior to *merely* a form of story telling. Nonetheless, according to Haraway (1989: 8), "the lens of story telling defines a thin line between realism and nominalism," and it is by playing along the course of this thin line that alternatives between these two positions are worked out. Furthermore, Haraway discusses the different aesthetic and ethical dimensions built into thinking about scientific practice as a form of story telling. This ethic and aesthetic moves beyond the narrow choices of believing that knowledge is simply a passive reflection of what is "out there" on the one hand, or the ironic skepticism that things are just "made up" on the other. As Haraway (1989: 8) tells it, "the aesthetic and ethic latent in the examination of story telling might be pleasure and responsibility in the weaving of tales. Stories are means to ways of living. Stories are technologies for primate embodiment."

Similarly, as a sociologist, Laurel Richardson has elaborated upon the narrative structures and devices upon which social scientific writing, as a technology, depends. For Richardson (1997: 27), it is not a question of whether or not "sociology should use the narrative, but which narrative will be provided to the reader," and how conscious and explicit this provision will be. In her work entitled *Fields of Play*, Richardson demonstrates the importance of deeply meditating on the presence of things like narrative voice, the use of extended metaphor, and shifting senses of audience, in the construction of sociological literature. She further explores how the disciplinary distinctions between social science and literature first arose and how it is maintained by policing the borders between fact and fiction, the same concerns which animate the labors of sociologists like Clough (1998), Gordon (1996) and Pfohl (1992). Finally, Richardson experiments with a variety of writing forms in the course of doing sociology. These forms, which are a way of breaking the grip of unconscious disciplinary traditions that cover up as much as they reveal, include poetry, dialogue, fictive reconstructions, parable and other story telling modes. As Richardson (1997: 18–9) explains,

> the reasons for experimenting with literary style and genre are not simply to deal with the false dichotomization of subject and object; these writing experiment[s] are raising political and ethical questions as well. Separating the researcher's story from the people's story implies that the researcher's voice is the authoritative one, a voice that stands above the rest. But because

people have differential access to the use of the authoritative voice – and for the most part the people we study have less access than we do – we may unwittingly colonize, overgeneralize, or distort. Furthermore, by objectifying ourselves out of existence, we void our own experiences. We separate our humanity from ourselves as well. We create the conditions of our own alienation.

The point of these writers is to not take the authoritative workings of these literary and narrative conventions for granted, nor to overlook the powerful functions of rhetoric in the process of creating powerful forms of knowledge via such conventions. Moreover, far from wishing to purge allegorical elements as extraneous, much of this recent work positively embraces these elements of the "fictive" by actively deconstructing the absolute distinctions between fact and fiction as a way of methodologically opening up the field of qualitative research.

But, for the sake of a certain conventional sensibility sociologically speaking, let me give a slightly more disciplined account than this, and in the process conjure up some other memories.

The recognition and avocation of allegory as an alternative mode of representation in the context of an ethnographic social science may at first appear to be a novel impulse, but the move does have a rich – albeit less than fully conscious history – in what is now considered the classic tradition of sociology. As one case study and example, I will look specifically at the figure of Max Weber and the elements of allegory that can be found in his work on *The Protestant Ethic and the Spirit of Capitalism*. While a similar recourse to allegorical practices can be located in the writings of sociology's other "founding fathers,"[3] they are especially replete in Weber's work. Thus, one of the key sources for this recent allegorical impulse can be traced not only to the newer theoretical and methodological movements – which to their credit have

---

[3] For instance, check out the "Mr. Moneybags" section of *Capital*, and how the figures of "Capitalist and Proletariat" are mobilized by Marx; Simmel's motif of "the Stranger"; Durkheim's images in the *Elementary Forms* of "the aborigine" during the corrobbori; Marcel Mauss general metaphor of *The Gift*. Nor should one overlook some of the founding "mothers" and their use of allegory. Charlotte Perkins Gilman, whose "fictionalized" accounts of late 19th/early 20th century gender relations in the *Yellow Wallpaper Paper,* and later on her utopian writing *Herland,* provides one of the earliest examples of this movement in modern social theory.

been explicit about what is often an implicit and unconscious movement – but to the very classic heart of sociology itself.

* * *

The Researcher, with his well-trimmed beard and studious good looks, went searching for an old mule to which he could hitch his star and go to market. But first there was the task of plowing the field.

Before turning specifically to Weber's work it is necessary to provide a provisional sense of what allegory is and how it might operate in the social sciences. There are a number of competing definitions and descriptions of allegory available from across the field of literary studies. These range from broad characterizations of allegory as simply "an extended metaphor" to more specialized and strict usages of the term.[4] When using the term allegory I have a couple of distinct but interrelated meanings in mind. One sense is suggested by the etymology of the word from its Greek antecedents, *allos* (other) + *agorein* (to speak publicly). Allegory is literally a forum or medium (practically and imaginarily) where *the other is able to speak publicly.* It is a mode of expression which is well-suited to allow differences and alternatives to speak forcefully in situations that were formerly and formally marked off as repressive and oppressive, to make objectives statements – public and political – about experiences and things that were once ghettoized as purely personal, private, and subjective. This is, I imagine, what some of those old slave folktales featuring "Mules and Men" – to reference the work by Zora Neale Hurston – had in heart and mind. As such, allegory is a mode of testimony that serves to conjure connections between various levels of human thought and experience, as well as between various levels of analysis: between the conscious and unconscious; between the particular and the general; between form and content; and between those *things* which sociologists designate as biography, milieu (or situation) and structure. This, at least, is one possible way of connecting something called "allegory" to something called "the sociological imagination."[5]

---

[4] James Clifford (1986: 98), in a footnote in his essay on "Ethnographic Allegory" reviews several of these definitions, including Angus Fletcher's loose characterization ("in the simplest terms, allegory says one thing and means another") to Tzvettan Todorov's more precise formulation ("First of all, allegory implies the existence of at least two meanings for the same words; according to some critics, the first meaning must disappear, while others require the two be present together.")

[5] Or as Mills (1959: 7) puts it: "It is the capacity to range from the most impersonal

James Clifford, who has examined in detail some of the allegorical features found in various ethnographic accounts, provides a second significant sense of the term. Clifford's own work as an anthropological writer is situated in reaction against ethnographic styles based on the unproblematized "truthful" and "representational" accounts of the conventional researcher. Clifford is especially interested in the subtle presence of allegory in those accounts given by the human sciences. Again, this presence is more consciously and explicitly acknowledged in some of these accounts more than others. Following Clifford's usage of the term (1986: 99), "[a]llegory usually denotes a practice in which a narrative fiction continuously refers to another pattern of ideas or events." Allegory tells a story in which figures, places, actions and events enact doubled or secondary meanings. As Clifford (1986: 98) describes it, "[e]thnographic writing is allegorical at the level both of its content (what it says about cultures and their histories) and of its form (what is implied by its mode of textualization)."

For the purposes of this essay allegory may be viewed as a continuous and ongoing metaphor, elaborated and developed in the course of a story, containing different levels of meaning, sometimes convergent and sometimes not; sometimes consciously explicit and sometimes not. Understanding these multiple levels of meaning – including those encoded in the form and content of the ethnography – is the key to understanding an ethnographic text as a work of allegory. Within literary theory there is an important debate as to how explicit, guided and corresponding the meanings of these different levels and the relation of the One level to the Other will be. On the one hand, for an allegory to be recognized as such, there has to be some degree of convergence and correspondence between figures and their underlying referent or meaning. On the other hand, for an allegory to work its alchemy and magic, there must be some playful divergence between the One and the Other in order for more structurally buried possibilities of meaning to emerge in a process of free association. Nonetheless, there is general agreement that one figure is interpreted as a type of an other (or perhaps several others simultaneously in more complex and "headless" forms). As Craig Owen (1982:

---

and remote transformations to the most intimate features of the human self – and to see the relations between the two. Back of its use there is always the urge to know the social and historical meaning of the individual in the society and in the period in which he [or she] has his [or her] quality and his [or her] being."

203) has described it, "let us say for the moment that allegory occurs whenever one text is doubled by another: the Old Testament, for example, becomes allegorical when it is read as a prefiguration of the New. . . . in allegorical structure, then, one text is read through another, however fragmentary, intermittent, or chaotic their relationship may be: the paradigm for the allegorical work is thus the palimpsest." This type of writing (and the reading it provokes or calls forth) thereby allows for the doubleness (and more) of the cultural form (as in a double crossing of the sociological field) to pour forth.

* * *

But the Ethnographer was more timid and skeptical by measure. For one thing, he knew how stubborn and recalcitrant old mules could be. Zora Neale Hurston had told him so, and he trusted her, even if she never got that Ph.D. in anthropology . . . . Moreover, he was suspicious of plowing too deeply, because he remembered – however dimly – where the bodies were buried.

Section 1. . . . A-mazing Art-ifice . . .

> [For writers in the mandarin-like tradition of German literary humanism,] ideas are synchronized rather than serialized. At their best, they erect a grammatical artifice in which the mental balconies and watch towers, as well as bridges and recesses, decorate the main structure. Their sentences are gothic castles. And Max Weber's style is definitely in their tradition. – Gerth and Mills, "From Max Weber," p. vi.

The context for the above passage is the preface by H.H. Gerth and C. Wright Mills to their edited translation *From Max Weber: Essays in Sociology*. At the outset Gerth and Mills are attempting to explain some of the difficulties involved in translating Weber's work from German to English, and some of the questions of style involved in trying to read through such a translation. This passage, in discussing the elaborate literary style which marked much of Weber's social scientific writing in particular (and the tradition of German literary humanism in general), itself operates by a series of extended metaphors, central of which is the gothic castle, with its balconies and watchtowers, recesses and bridges. If this metaphor were sustained throughout it would rise to the status of an allegory. Perhaps a few pages later, when presenting a biographical over view of Weber's work and tracing its modes of defenses, identifications and subterranean Victorian impulses, Gerth and Mill's analysis unconsciously does so. In any case, this particular passage is a small but nice bit of writing. It provides a useful place to begin thinking about the tradition of humanistic social science (*Kulturewissenschaft*) that Weber was working within and against. It calls to mind questions not only about the explicit content of Weber's work, but also about the manner and method – simultaneously probing, cautious and passionate – which animates his writing. Moreover, this passage provides a telling model of the subject it is talking about. Like any good metaphor, and even more so in the case of allegory, it demonstrates while it explains, something appreciated by the literal minded amongst us.

I start here because I want to point out how elements of a literary sensibility, including metaphor and allegory, were involved in some of the earlier "classical" attempts at doing social science. And despite the best attempts by some to purge the sociological field of such, this sensibility – imagined as a structure of feeling – remains an active presence in sociological writing today. I also want to use Gerth and Mills, and Weber, in turn, as authorities of a sort in the case of my own authorship. For this too is part of a tradition of social science literature, an invocation of ghosts past which endow the present writing effort with an aura of respectability and responsibility, a homage to ancestors. But is this really how social science works? What about supercession and transcendence in science?

Max Weber's own methodological objective may be read as a complex attempt to navigate between the now distinctively emerged fields recognized as either pure literature or pure science, and to work towards a "humanistically-oriented social science." Weber wished to give equal emphasis to each element of the term "human science." This was to provide an objective *and* interpretative accounting of the subjective dispositions that allow social action to take the possible directions it takes. In many quarters nowadays Weber's interpretative performance is found wanting, save for its evocative value. For one thing it is not always easy to read as literature. And it is even more difficult to clearly operationalize as science. It often digresses from main points with exceptions to the rule, nuances, qualifications, and editorial comments. It is ambiguous and equivocal in its statements of causality and determination. For my own part, this ambiguity is refreshing, for it suggests the tensions inherent in social reality and a corresponding reluctance to reduce the world of social facts purely to things. Moreover, it betrays its relevancies more clearly and more passionately than much contemporary mainstream sociology.

But this betrayal is not always conscious. If there is a critique of Weber's work, it lies not so much in its lack of parsimony or its difficulty to operationalize, important as these methodological standards might be. Rather, what I find wanting is the lack of explicit comment and reflection by Weber on his own positioning within the scheme of things and the evident tensions this leads to in his work. This doesn't mean I want him to become central to his own work, but I would like to see some greater reflexivity as to how his "subject position" impinges on what he can and cannot know, the science he can and cannot do. Though he possesses an awareness of the literary, and thereby moves to relativize the field of science as an ultimate value, he sometimes wants to imagine that his own sociological work can exist purely on the field of social science and not have to explicitly wander here and there in the process of its own evaluative searching. On the contrary, in the end, Weber imagines that he has no choice but to follow the way and the vocation of scientist. And this, paradoxically for him, is the more heroic path. In the final analysis, he tries to position his work above or beyond it all. As such, elements of the allegorical enter his work in more disguised ways than are necessary. It would have been better had he made them apparent, even at the risk to his "scientific authority."

Allegory enters into Weber's writing in a couple of ways. First, Weber's work generally relies on written texts as documentary sources of information and evidence.[6] This, for instance, is very much the case for his comparative work in the sociology of world religions. His typifications (i.e. ideal types) for the ethics of the world religions are derived primarily from the textual remains of adepts within the tradition he is examining (or else from secondary source renditions of a tradition's history)[7] and not from any method-

---

[6] More generally speaking things like allegory, metaphor, parable and other "fictive" modes of expression, written or spoken, often provides the documentary evidence upon which a social scientific analysis is based. In the course of their work social scientists are typically dealing with the stories of others. It is the stuff of cultural analysis. Some perspectives in social theory, such as behaviorism, attempt to empty human activity of its meaning and significance by ignoring this sense of story – and consequently their own implicit sense of story. But a critical interpretative social science cannot allow itself this luxury. It is the approach to these stories, and the story that is in turn told, as dead fact or live fiction, that makes a lot of difference.

[7] There are clear and important differences between those ethnographies based on solely on historical documents and written records, and those developed in the course of face to face encounters where differences of interpretation are more likely to be in one's face.

ologically systematic or sustained encounter with living participants within those religious movements.[8] In many instances the documentary sources Weber employs and emplots are quite "literary" in nature. This can especially be seen his seminal essay on the *Protestant Ethic,* which includes an outright allegory as a main evidential source (i.e. John Bunyan's *The Pilgrim's Progress*), as well as other literary forms which utilize metaphor and allegory more indirectly: the sermons, tracts, and journal entries of Richard Baxter and other Puritan divines; Ben Franklin's adages and maxims; biblical proverbs and other sacred wisdom literature; German satire and poetry (e.g. Ferdinand Kurnberger and Goethe's *Faust* respectively); operatic lyrics (from Richard Wagner); theological reflections (from Luther, Calvin, and Zwingili); and ecclesiastical creeds (e.g. the Westminster and Augsburg Confessions). These sources – themselves artificial if not fictional constructs – are all used to construct ideal types of cultural figures upon which his study rests: "the protestant ethic" borne by the generic figure of the Calvinist saint; the "spirit of capitalism" which infuses the "us" of today, modern man [sic]. Indeed, the haunting conceptual image of modernity as an "iron cage" found at the conclusion of his work, is nothing if not a literary metaphor, derived from a particularly torturing section of Bunyan's Christian allegory.[9]

---

[8] This is not to say that Weber had no experience of "participant-observation," at least in terms of the Protestant sects. Several friends and family members were involved with these groups, and Weber comments on his observations of them in several places, especially his essay on "The Protestant Sects and the Spirit of Capitalism." However, this enters his work primarily in the form of illustrative anecdote rather than a systematic accumulation of evidence.

[9] "Now," said Christian, "let me go hence." "Nay, stay," said the Interpreter, "till I have showed thee a little more, and after that, thou shalt go on they way." So he took him by the hand again and led him into a very dark room, where there sat a man in an iron cage. [A footnote by Bunyan in the text indicates that "Despair is like an iron cage."]

Now the man to look on seemed very sad. He sat with his eyes looking down to the ground, his hands folded together, and he sighed as if he would break his heart. Then said Christian, "What means this?" At which point the Interpreter bid him talk with the man.

CHR[ISTIAN]. Then Christian said to the man, "What art thou?" The man answered, "I am what I was not once."

"What was thou once?"

MAN. The man said, "I was once a fair and flourishing professor [i.e. a professing Christian], both in mine own eyes and also in the eyes of others. I once was, as I thought, fair for the Celestial City, and had then even joy at the thoughts that I should get thither."

CHR. "Well, but what art thou now?"

MAN. "I am now a man of despair and am shut up in it, as in this iron cage. I cannot get out. O, now I cannot."

Secondly, the methodological process of typification (i.e. constructing the "ideal type") is itself a mode of literary analysis derived in particular from the reading of allegory. Admittedly, this process of "reading" and typifying is now much more rigorously controlled by the disciplinary methods of sampling and discrete operationalization found in sociology. It is no longer a purely "literary" endeavor, if it ever fully was. Nonetheless, allegory in some instances provides not only the evidences upon which Weber's sociological typifications are based, but it also constitutes a "typical" mode of reading, where one thing stands in a relationship of prefiguration to an other (e.g. "the Protestant Ethic" prefigures the "spirit of Capitalism"). This peculiar mode of making connections between the One through the Other is itself the product of an allegorical imagination. The implied historical relation between two typifications in allegory represents a foreshadowing rather than a directly causal relation; this, at least, is what claims to separate the necessary determinations of social science from the literary dimension of free association. In science this cause is considered "real" in a distinctively material sense and it is subject to certain evidential rules. A further comparison and contrast of the meaning of the "type" found in literature and social science is the subject for another discussion, but for now it is important to note that they shared a common ancestor in allegory and were not as rigidly segregated as they may now appear to be.

Section 2. . . . Amazing Grace . . .

If the main body of Weber's work on the world religions, and particularly the *Protestant Ethic*, relies for its construction on sources and interpretative techniques that are in part allegorical, in what sense may this work itself be seen as an allegory? What are the multiple levels of story it tells? Weber (1958b: 13) explains the question that animates his work in the following manner:

CHR. "But how camest though in this condition?"

MAN. "I left off to watch, and be sober. I laid the reins upon the neck of my lusts. I sinned against the light of the word, and the goodness of God. I have grieved the Spirit and he is gone. I tempted the Devil, and he is come to me. I have provoked God to anger, and he has left me. I have so hardened my heart that I cannot repent."

Then said Christian to the Interpreter, "But is there no hopes for a man as this?"

"Ask him," said the Interpreter.

CHR. Then said Christian, "Is there no hope but you must be kept in this iron cage of despair?" – excerpted from *The Pilgrim's Progress* by John Bunyan (1981: 38–9).

A product of modern European civilization, studying any problem of universal history, is bound to ask himself to what combination of circumstances
the fact should be attributed that in Western civilization, and in Western
civilization only, cultural phenomena have appeared which (as we like to
think) lie in a line of development having *universal* significance and value.
[Emphasis in the original translation]

This is an important and fruitful problem, albeit one that is stated in a pretty
tortured and convoluted way. Weber is both curiously detached and value
neutral in asking this question of universal significance and value (i.e. first
posing himself as a "product of modern European civilization") and yet somehow intimately involved in asking the question in ways that are compelling
but not explicitly stated (i.e. as a person who "is bound to ask himself"). One
can read this passage as a symptomatic text involving a couple of subtexts.

The manifest story he tells is a socio-historical one, and as such it belongs
properly to the field of the cultural sciences, including history and sociology.
It is also a story of origins and becoming. Weber is concerned with what factors were involved in the unique development of the modern West, and the
central (though by no means solely sufficient) place of religion in that now-
becoming-universal development. A historical-comparative interpretation of
the ethical structures of the world religions is the main method for solving
this problem and telling this story. And in the course of his telling examination, Weber finds that while each of the world religions contain elements
of beauty, majesty and value, they are all – except for a variety of sectarian
Protestantism – found wanting in terms of providing the distinctive social
psychological orientation which leads to the modern industrial West.[10] For in
Weber's eyes the modern West represents a world distinguished by the systematic adjustment of means to ends and a continuous process of rationalization
in all spheres of social life: this includes an increasingly technically efficient
form of capitalist development marked by the relentless quest for profitable
accumulation in the economic realm; the development of bureaucracy and

---

[10] To repeat a point which Weber does at numerous points throughout his essay in
order to avoid a misunderstanding: This is not to substitute a one-sided idealism for
a one-sided materialism. Neither ideal nor material factors are sufficient in themselves
to "cause" capitalism. But given that some of the necessary material preconditions
for capitalism existed in other civilizations, what made the West different in its constitution and development? Hence the recourse to the importance of religious factors,
amongst other things.

democracy (and their attendant tensions) in the political realm; and the development of science, with its increasing secularization and disenchantment of the world, in the cultural realm.

The manifest sociological story of the *Protestant Ethic* is focused primarily on the internal religious disposition of a generalized figure named "the Calvinist" – not any particular Calvinist – but one who represents the ideal typical ethos or disposition of a this-worldly asceticism, which in turn constitutes the cultural foundations for the spirit of capitalism. Like any good story, this one contains elements of mystery and even has a twist at the end. It is a story laced with paradox, irony and unintended consequences. In the quest for a religious sign of eternal life in this world, the peculiar Protestant ethic of the Calvinist has paradoxically led to the transformation of this world in a cultural direction that no longer possesses any profound sense of transcendent meaning (generally speaking and in Weber's estimation). It is this religious ethic that ironically provides the disciplined motivation towards work and the experience of relentless accumulation necessary for the modern capitalist cosmos to "take off." But once this new cosmos has taken off it will profoundly undermine and displace any dominant religious sensibility and lead to the disenchantment of the world.

This manifest story is, in and of itself, an interesting one sociologically speaking, and there is some evidence to recommend it. But even more interesting and ironic are the ways the manifest story interacts with the various subtexts found in Weber's writing. By reading the manifest story too quickly and in too literal a sense one may miss some of its more subtle and cutting points brought about by the acute tension between the text and its subtexts. For there is another story being told here involving a stance and an outlook, in part methodological, in part prophetic evaluation. These two parts can be read as two latent narratives that are nonetheless intertwined, despite Weberian claims to the contrary for the necessity of an absolute separation between "fact" and "value." These two subtexts to the manifest story only become apparent for a fleeting and breathless moment in the last few pages of the *Protestant Ethic*. But this brief presence, and the haunting absence it evokes, lingers throughout much of his work.

The methodological subtext involves the man of science[11] who has a duty

---

[11] Given that this represents a methodological stance rather than an actual person, I will use the masculine pronoun to refer to this figure who, from my reading of fem-

to tell the story of the origin and development of this thing called the modern West, no matter where it (the story and the thing) will lead. And in the course of his very specialized accounting of the matter he is to be a modest witness.[12] On the one hand, this is a properly academic story, a model as to how methodologically one is to proceed in a focused manner in the social sciences, and this level of story is implicitly present (perhaps occasionally more reflected upon in the course of a methodological appendix) whenever the claims of a conventional science are being raised. The manifest story is made more powerfully and credibly present by this subtext, which involves the apparent absence of an interest or a desire on the part of the researcher, save for these purely scientific ones: 1) proceed in a workman-like fashion; 2) proceed with intellectual integrity and recognize those facts that are personally uncomfortable, and 3) repress the impulse to exhibit personal tastes or other sentiments unnecessarily (Weber, 1949: 5).

But there are evident tensions in Weber's methodological framework, and other things – not fully speakable in the terms of science – creep in towards the end of the *Protestant Ethic*. These tensions are laid out to a greater degree in some of Weber's other essays, particularly "Science as a Vocation" and "The Meaning of Ethical Neutrality," though never in an explicitly situated manner. Thus, on the one side, there is the figure of the detached scientist who is engaged in a very specialized process of clarification and abstraction, subjecting these things of science to the analytic necessity of cause and determinism. At the same time, for Weber at least, this image of the determined scientist also represents several other elements: a vocation and a calling, a distinctive value choice, a sense of personal identity, including a heroic commitment to the discovery of truth – along with the inevitable supercession of this truth that scientific progress will bring. There are many elements of a self and his subject position deeply at stake in this image, separate from a rarified claim of disinterest and dispassion, but they must go unmentioned in order for science *to work*. There is a Kantian sense of obligation throughout this all in Weber's (1958a: 156) refrain for scientific man to meet "the demands of the day." Moreover, in the case of the social sciences, this stance

---

inist critiques of science, generally represents "masculine qualities." Nonetheless, in its particular embodiment, these days at least, it is possible for the man of science to be a woman, and perhaps vis a versa, though more uneasily.

[12] For more on the relation of the modest witness to the testimony of science, see Haraway (1997: 23–28).

represents an attempt to objectively unpack the subjective dispositions and meanings of a cultural development possessing a "universal history and significance." (Weber 1958b: 13)

But where will his story lead?

Paradoxically, for Weber, it leads to the modern world of science itself, passionately disenchanted, through whose method the story is told "as a matter of fact," but now emptied of any ultimate or transcendent meaning, only the possibility of technical or instrumental mastery of the world. This is a science all dressed up with no where to go. As Weber writes (1958b: 180), invoking a literary hero no longer relevant to this modern world of science: "Limitation to specialized work, with a renunciation of the Faustian universality of man which it involves, is a condition of any valuable work in the modern world; hence deeds and renunciation inevitably condition each other today." There is in this lament, of course, no explicit telling of Weber's own profound biographical experience of despondence and despair around the turn of the 20th century, a depression so profound that he could not write or speak publicly on "purely" academic matters for several years. (Bendix, 1977: 2ff.)

Section 3. . . . All along the Watchtower . . .

At this point it should be noted how Weber shows a tendency to displace his more existential burdens in the subtext of a digression or literary detour.[13] It often appears that the heart of his study – the very problems of modernity that personally agonized and antagonized him – are found in these places of textual displacement, beyond the spaces of his purely scientific focus, specialization, and determined determination. These prophetic digressions appear almost as "metaphoric asides," but when read as a whole they form a narrative in their own right. They suggest a second subtext buried within and intertwined, a haunting and haunted story about how the ascetic "idea of duty in one's calling prowls about in our lives like the ghost of dead religious beliefs."(Weber 1958b: 182) In the modern world this is a way of life that is often marked by the absence of a way of life. In fact Weber acknowl-

---

[13] For more on the methodological opening to a historically repressed materiality that the conscious use of a "detour" can provide for sociologists, see Avery Gordon's (1996) *Ghostly Matters: Haunting and the Sociological Imagination.*

edges the problem more explicitly in his work on "Science as a Vocation." In this essay he laments – albeit "like a man" – the "disenchantment" and loss of "magic and mystery" that occurs in conjunction with western, scientific, rational "'progress.'" (Weber, 1958a: 139ff.) Weber's own quotations around the word "progress" suggest this is advancement only in a technical sense, but not in any ultimate sense. On the contrary, such technical progress, of which science is a part, has the effect of "making life tired" and emptying death of its meaning.

But in the *Protestant Ethic* this problem is latent and buried. It can only by discerned by paying attention to the evaluative metaphors which begin to appear towards the end of the text, when Weber's lets down his "scientific guard" for a brief while. The critique trickles out subtly enough when he describes how "asceticism descended like a frost on the life of 'Merrie Old England.'" (Weber 1958b: 168) But the trickle soon turns into a torrent. Despite its immense and undeniable productivity, the tremendous cosmos of the modern economic order represents a place of loss for Weber, and the romantic metaphors and phrases he uses towards the end of the *Protestant Ethic* to describe the changes which have occurred are both symptomatic and telling: "renunciation," "a departure from an age of full and beautiful humanity," "an iron cage," all culminating in the final Faustian lament: "Specialists without spirit, sensualists without heart; this nullity imagines that it has attained a level of civilization never before achieved." (Weber 1958b: 182) This sounds like plaintive cry of an Old Testament prophet as much as anything else.

Yet to the degree that this cry is explicitly acknowledged as such it works to subvert the specialized knowledge of the scientist, which is both practically useful in terms of technique but ultimately useless in terms of providing meaningful judgment. For as Weber (1958a: 146) contends elsewhere in "Science as a Vocation," "I am ready to prove from the works of our historians that whenever the man of science introduces his personal value judgment, a full understanding of the facts *ceases*." Consequently, even while Weber relativizes science as an ultimate value, he modestly believes it as the only credible game in town. Given the logic of its own progressions, the scientific enterprise has no ultimate meaning, but it can aid in the generation of inconvenient facts and in the clarification of values and the relations of means to ends. This is neither a very easy nor very comforting stance to maintain, but it at least represents a "manly" posture. For Weber it requires a heroic effort, even as he must repress his more "sentimental" impulses. And overall (t)his scientific posture necessarily involves a certain messiness and digression, in one moment if not the next.

But again, being a man in the realm of science, this is all impossible to admit in the *Protestant Ethic*, because it suggests a value judgment and undermines the necessary clarity of things which science most forcefully brings. Consequently, at this end of that work, after invoking the spirit of Goethe, Weber (1958b: 182) tries to step back and once again assume a more scientific voice and tone: "But this brings us to the world of judgments of value and faith, with which this purely historical discussion need not be burdened."[14] Nonetheless he has already intimated in the framework of a subtext what this world of pure fact means to him, and it is not a particularly comforting or joyful place. Elsewhere Weber (1958a: 155) suggests that if these qualities of missing meaning are what one is looking for, church – and not academia – might then be the place to be:

> To the person who cannot bear the fate of the times like a man, one must say: may he rather return silently, without the usual publicity build-up of renegades, but simply and plainly. The arms of the old churches are opened widely and compassionately for him. After all, they do not make it hard for him. One way or another he has to bring his "intellectual sacrifice" – that is inevitable. For such an intellectual sacrifice in favor of an unconditional religious devotion is ethically quite a different matter than the evasion of

---

[14] For elsewhere, in another remarkable passage (in "Science as a Vocation") Weber writes (1958a: 134–35): "All work that overlaps neighboring fields, such as we occasionally undertake and which the sociologists must necessarily undertake again and again, is burdened with the resigned realization that at best one provides the specialist with useful questions upon which he would not so easily hit from his specialized point of view. One's own work must inevitably remain highly imperfect. Only by strict specialization can the scientific worker become fully conscious, for once and perhaps never again in his lifetime, that he has achieved something that will endure. A really definitive and good accomplishment is today always a specialized accomplishment. And whoever lacks the capacity to put on blinders, so to speak, and to come up to the idea that the fate of his soul depends upon whether or not he makes the correct conjecture at this passage of this manuscript may as well stay away from science. He will never have what one may call the 'personal experience' of science. Without this strange intoxication, ridiculed by every outsider; without this passion, this 'thousands of years must pass before you enter into life and thousands more wait in silence' – according to whether or not you succeed in making this conjecture; without this, you have *no* calling for science and you should do something else. For nothing is worthy of man as man unless he can pursue it with passionate devotion." [Emphasis in the original translation]

the plain duty of intellectual integrity, which sets in if one lacks the courage
to clarify one's own ultimate standpoint and rather facilitates this duty by
feeble relative judgment.

And so the prophetic subtext is buried once more beneath the concern for
the manifest story. The voice of the scientist reemerges from the whirlwind
of the concluding pages of his essay. In the final two paragraphs of the
Protestant Ethic there is shift from a story about origins and development
towards something resembling an eschatology, but only as far as science can
imagine the future: this is not a story of the final culmination of history and
the end things in the traditional religious sense of that term, but it is a story
of overcoming and transcendence nonetheless. These last couple of paragraphs make suggestions about the future course of the research and ways
of overcoming the limitations of the current study, which after all is only a
part of a much greater whole that Weber has in mind, the progress of science.
And so the heroic scientist is poised once more as a modest witness who
must, as a matter of manly duty following an ethic of responsibility, confront
the ultimate meaningless of his work, and become part of a workable tradition. . . . standing on the shoulders of giants . . . as he posits his progress . . .
though never ultimately . . . working solely in the interest of historical truth.
Even while something else whispers out of the silenced whirlwind in the
background.

There are no doubt other stories being told here as well. The story that an
Ethnographer – displaced once more in the course of his own discourse – is
now telling about Weber's work. This is different from a Researcher's more
optimistic story of *verstehan*, but still full of complex identifications and transferences. And there is also the story a reader is now retelling him or herself,
different from whatever original story may have been, but still full of complex identifications and transferences. As one was warned at the beginning,
"[i]n the end the reader must make them over into one by rereading and
recapitulation. The writer is no speaker and the reader is no listener . . ."
(Gerth and Mills in Weber, 1958: v) For this too is a matter of allegory.

* * *

*"Standing on the shoulders of Giants leaves me cold" the Ethnographer mused to
himself, when suddenly the plow went "thump, thump, thump" against several
unknown and unknowable objects. Then, out of the dark brown ground, one corpse
after another became unearthed. The Ethnographer was both terrified and fascinated*

by the evident decomposition before him, while an old mule brayed in horror. Meanwhile the Researcher carried on – undisturbed and work/man/like – as if nothing had really happened.

Let me add a concluding comment and provocation here. Meaning in allegory is more condensed and overdetermined than other modes of expression. Allegorical stories work at multiple levels, in terms of both form and content, and in relating instances of the particular to the general. Moreover, the density and layering of meaning which allegory possesses is supplementary and value added, involving a dynamic relation between the performer and the reader. This important dimension of multiple layers of meaning usually involves provocatively transmitting some sort of moral or evaluative desire, even if this is not a fully conscious intent on the part of the author (at least in the case of allegory found in ethnographic social science. In the case of more traditional religious forms of allegory this evaluative dimension of the work is itself more explicit and apparent). As such, allegory does not represent a neutral space of cultural representation and interpretation. It betrays its own desires and thus makes its relevancies clear. This is part of its irony and this is its power, and it can be used to great effect depending on the reader's (and writer's) awareness of the matter. Unlike the sense of closure found in the conventional realistic narrative – the narrative form which varieties of positivistic social science usually partake – allegory subverts a singular reading of things. It is a place of reconfiguration. As a result, allegory can allow for relatively unrestricted play in a relationally open field of different voices, voices which are never purely self-sufficient. Obviously I speak metaphorically here. There is no such thing as a pure reading and play going on. Limits and partiality necessarily indicate some interests at work. But there is something else as well which is allowed to emerge in the recognition of such partialities. The awareness of this is a reaction against the compulsive singularity and self-sufficiency that marks so much of social science today, even in its qualitative forms. The allegorical dimension found in contemporary ethnographic accounts have a plot in mind, one that is usually buried after the fact, but which helps to constitute the very authority of such facts in the process of writing. Thus allegory insinuates itself within the literature of social science in subtle and often hidden ways, often working through a process of demonstration rather than explanation. As Clifford (1986: 99) has remarked, "[e]thnographic texts are inescapably allegorical, and a serious acceptance of this fact changes the ways they can be written and read." The desire here is to make all this more apparent, within and across the necessary limits of a social scientific field. In this way, other previously repressed cultural voices and histories may speak forth, and in their stead new possibilities for a reciprocal sharing of power may emerge.

This is not to say that ethnography is solely allegorical in nature. Such a claim would stray too far into the field of Literature and simply get stuck there. And very certainly fellow participants within the conventions of sociology will help keep things in check here. But it is to say that any field that calls itself scientific can only ignore its literary dimensions and disavow its written tenses and pretenses at its own peril. Some varieties of social science ethnography make the claim or wish to remove (i.e. purge) the literary elements through the use of "a plain narrative style" in an attempt to get at the "truth" of the matter. This appears to me to imply an impoverished notion of how representational truth works, namely the effective power of rituals always behind the constitution of such a truth, as well as the disciplinary distinctions between fact and fiction resting on categorical impositions which language itself often betrays. Can you *see* the distinction I am plainly making here?[15] Clifford (1986: 100) comments on how "[a] recognition of allegory emphasizes that realistic portraits, to the extent that they are 'convincing' or 'rich,' are extended metaphors, patterns of associations that point to coherent (theoretical, esthetic, moral) additional meanings. Allegory (more strongly than 'interpretation') calls to mind the poetic, traditional, cosmological nature of such writing processes." While one thing refers to another, it doesn't simply or innocently stand for the other. Representation is a process of invention and imposition even while attempting a correspondence of (or co-responses from) the other being represented. A specific ethnographic account is never simply a pure scientific description – a one to one correspondence between the (imagined) word and the (seemingly) objective event that displays some Other. Rather, ethnography attempts to make that which is strange appear as familiar and comprehensible within some other (already recognized) field of thought.[16] Thus a casual identification and symmetry between other and self, difference and similarity, cannot be easily made, even though a "good"

---

[15] See, for instance, Clough's (1998) critique of the writing style of Blumer.

[16] As Clifford (1986: 101) observes, "To say that exotic behavior and symbols make sense either in "human" or "cultural" terms is to supply the same sorts of allegorical added meanings that appears in older narratives that saw actions as "spiritually" significant."

or well done ethnography will promise and create such a sense, and will make sense as such. But those ethnographies that are more consciously allegorical create a necessary degree of displacement away from the literal and self-identical that troubles easy identifications and certainties. The suggestion here is that this is precisely what social science ethnography needs to do if it is to remain reflexive about the power of cultural forms in the world in which it works.

Whilst from somewhere else on high, or rather deep down below, Zora Neale . . . with Max by her side . . . gave a coy and compassionate smile. But that's another story . . .

A Postscript: Some Stories on the Margins

> *. . . and in the ellipses of a sentence the dead can be made alive . . .*

"I'm cracking but I'm facking."[17] – Zora Neale Hurston (quoted in Watson 1995: 68).

Subtext and context are obviously important to the preceding text, as well as the words that follow. The bodily situation and situatedness by which a *certain* knowledge is produced or made absent are crucial to its understanding. Consequently, it may help the reader to know that the words above were excerpted from a dissertation work that really had very little to do with Max Weber. Instead, it had much more to do with the workings of the Holy Ghost in a Black (Apostolic) Pentecostal church located in Boston, which was the substantive subject of the research. The problem I faced as a researcher, and as an ethnographer, was how to furnish a just and accurate representation of a dynamic religious worldview and experience that was dramatically different from my own. It was in the course of thinking and writing about this problem that I stumbled upon the idea and practice of allegory – or better yet "story telling" – and later on decided to use Weber as my authority. His ghost was evoked to show how matters of literary form and allegorical language shape the writing of even the most esteemed of classical sociologists.

So let me tell a couple more stories related to these matters of "Culture, Power and History," ones with an overtly moral desire, which will help to raise some of those things buried just below the surface.

---

[17] Rough translation: "I'm wisecracking, but I'm also telling the truth."

As was suggested above, there are several other sources that inform this allegorical impulse, albeit not as respectably accepted within the confines of sociology as Max Weber's work. Historically, this impulse has come from or been inspired by people in movement, both personal and social, on the periphery of conventional formations of power/knowledge. It is a part of the practical and theoretical experience of subjugated individuals and groups who do not stand on the shoulders of giants, but rather on the margins of a given order of things.

The spirit work of African American women, particularly those associated with the sanctified church tradition, has also provided crucial impetus for critical theorists of allegory. These voices originally did not have much of an effect on the course of the classic sociology, but their powerful senses of story telling are now beginning to move the discipline in different ways. And in thinking through the place of allegory in the course of social science, as an ethnographer, I have been moved by the words of black women (and some men), many who have labored within relationship to the church and sometimes beyond it. Some of these folks have had formal academic training, though usually outside the field of sociology proper. Still others have had no relation to academia, but were tending their own fields of culture. And then there were a few who were caught in between. It is no coincidence that these women have found themselves as part of a broader African American cultural tradition which has placed a strong emphasis on allegory, fable, parable and story telling as a means of conjure and creativity.

At this point one could conjure up the spirit of Zora Neale Hurston, mentioned only in passing by the Researcher, as another early practitioner of, and inspiration for, the allegorical form within and without social science. Hurston's own story is a complicated and highly situated one. She attended Barnard College in the mid 20's where she studied anthropology under the guidance of Franz Boas. Later on, in 1935, she made an abortive attempt to get a Ph.D. at Columbia in that same field, though the rumor is "she seldom attend[ed] classes" and was not well disciplined in her work (Watson 1995: 69). During this period, Hurston spent much time collecting and recounting the religious and magical lore of African Americans in the South. Shortly thereafter she tracked the folktales and practices of former slaves in Haiti and Jamaica. This rich ethnographic material is presented in her books *Mules & Men*, *Tell My Horse*, and *The Sanctified Church*. All this was in addition to her own avowedly fictional writing produced during the same time frame, including *Jonah's*

Gourd Vine and *Their Eyes Were Watching God*, now considered minor classics of American literature.

Through the sympathetic magic of her own practice of story telling, Hurston was able to movingly retell the stories and practices of nameless black others. In *Mules and Men*, for instance, she relates the African American tradition of folktales from her field experience in Eatonville, Florida. These tales often involve trickster figures – usually relatively powerless animals like the briar rabbit or a stubborn old mule – who by the dint of their cleverness and wit, are able to avoid ensnarement and celebrate their freedom. These fables, parables and folktales provided a common language for Southern black folk, opaque to those outside the tradition, but a rich source of cultural strength and expression for those in the know. In fact part of the tradition's strength relied on this play between being opaque and being in the know. Hurston's own field method is presentational and demonstrative; she does not overtly impose theory on the reader, but instead conjures a situation of story from which something like a "social theory" can emerge and be discussed. Her method of story telling involved a mode of discourse or performance which has been termed "mythomania." According to Houston Baker Jr. (1991: 74, 76), this is the sign of an Afro American fabricating performance in which the storyteller embroiders the truth (or sometimes even "lies") in order "to forward the cultural anima's always already impulse towards freedom or liberation." Here, the line between performance and sincerity is a thin one. There is a "will to adorn," rather than "the will to power," in the telling of these seemingly simple stories. Hurston's ethnography, supported by the white patronage of a paternalistic dowager named Mrs. R. Osgood Mason, attempted to embody this conjuring spirit in her own representation of Southern black life heading into the twentieth century.

But why not just say these things straight out? Why rely and relie on quaint little stories instead of articulating matters in clearer and more disciplined terms? Holding aside for a moment important questions of formal education, cultural capital and all that this implies, in a period when there wasn't even the minimum legal consensus amongst whites that lynching black folks was to be considered a crime, when theories of racial hygiene were still quite in vogue if not all the rage, when Jim Crow laws were firmly in place and all major areas of social life were highly segregated – and not just in the South – then one must proceed delicately even while possessing an effusive sense of soul. This, at least, is one of the ways of reading Zora Neale Hurston's story. Moreover, if there is something that haunts her story, it is this: despite numerous publications of merit within and outside the field of anthropology – and an earned acclaim over the course of the last twenty five years – Hurston died penniless and in obscurity in 1960, never having earned that Ph.D.

No doubt this will be attributed as her own fault for not "playing by the rules," for not being too well disciplined, and for perhaps being a bit lazy to boot. But one wonders if at the heart of even the most humanistically oriented of social scientific disciplines, there exists a certain unconscious brutality that should leave even the most unbiased observer feeling somewhat disturbed. And one also wonders if Hurston was aware and playfully suspicious about all this. Particularly when she was standing on the street corners of Harlem in the late twenties . . . measuring the heads of black folks with cranial calipers under the tutelage of Boas . . . in order to prove that black folks were the intellectual equals of whites. All the while knowing things that most white folks – including her fellow ethnographers – would never know (See Watson 1995).

But excuse me if this last paragraph is much too tendentious and inflamed. It brings us to the world of judgments of value and of faith, with which this purely historical discussion need not be burdened. For social science does progress, along with changing disciplinary standards, dispensing with the fictional and absurd, and knowledge predicated on the vagaries of skin color. Too bad this did not happen quickly enough for Zora Neale Hurston to enjoy these changes in the flesh.

But here's another story. Approximately 30 years before Hurston's brief matriculation at Columbia University, F.M. Davenport, a Professor of Sociology at Hamilton College, wrote a book entitled *The Primitive Traits in Religious Revivals*. More than coincidently, this was written in 1905, just as Max Weber was finishing his work on the *Protestant Ethic*; just two years after the publication of *The Souls of Black Folk* by one of Weber's more famous students, W.E.B. Dubois; and one year before the Azusa Street Revival of Pentecost hit Los Angeles. Davenport's work, however, is unaware of these important theoretical and cultural developments. Instead, his book was an expansion of his earlier Ph.D. dissertation in the discipline of political science earned at Columbia University. And he appears to have been well disciplined at the time. In his preface, and in the tradition of standing on the shoulders of giants, Davenport (1905: ix) makes special mention of the helpfulness he received from his "honored preceptor, Professor Franklin H. Giddings, whose splendid constructive thinking in the "Inductive Sociology" has avowedly furnished important principles for the prosecution of this study." He further thanks Professor Livingston Farand of the Department of Ethnology at Columbia for his direction to the "facts of recent investigation" and other evidences "that nervous instability must have been the normal characteristic of primitive man" (1905: x). In the opening paragraph of a chapter entitled "The Religion of the American Negro," Davenport (1905: 55) writes, without white blush, the following:

> No one doubts, I suppose, that in the Negro people, whether in Africa or America, we have another child race. The old slave system of the Southland snatched the ancestors of this race from savagery only one or two hundred years ago. A century or two is not a long period in the social evolution of any people, especially one whose early abode was in the African jungle beneath a tropic sun.

This paragraph continues on in the same vein for *two* more pages; in fact it goes downhill from here. And you can imagine that the preceding chapter on "the Indian Ghost dance" is not much more insightful. One also suspects that Davenport probably was not much interested in the Harlem Renaissance which was about to begin a few streets uptown from his alma mater just a few years later. Again, he was no doubt "well-disciplined" and avoided such places. The point is that if "no one" doubted the reliability and validity of Davenport's anthropological knowledge, and at the time many if not most proper Anglo-Saxon folks probably did not – ratified as it was by the Ivy covered walls of Columbia University – there is less wonder as to why Hurston proceeded in a more circumspect fashion, relying on the very same tools that her informants did to fend off the stupid gaze of white eyes.

Again, I grow tendentious. And the more conventional Researcher will probably object that things have advanced much in the area of race relations and in the study of race since the Progressive Era when Davenport wrote. After all, Davenport is long forgotten while Hurston, along with a number of other black social scientists like Dubois and Ida B. Wells, have been resurrected and live on, albeit in spirit and in republication. This is true, though it is too bad they couldn't have done as well when their bodies were alive and such acclamation could have physically mattered. This is not to deny that some things have improved for large segments of the African American community, and that in the meanwhile some social scientific techniques and methods have come a long way as well. But it has been precisely because of activist critiques of the dynamics of power/knowledge that these positive changes – political and intellectual – have taken place; and they cannot be complacently accepted as complete with the advent of the latest technique or the continuous seizures of material progress upon our collective imaginations. Moreover, when in the 1990s *The Bell Curve* is one of the most renowned pieces of "real" social science reviewed on the front pages of the popular press, one has to wonder about the nature of such progress, as well as the continuing maintenance of the fact/fiction divide in the social sciences today. For somehow, the very detailed scientific critiques of that book just didn't come across as quite so newsworthy, buried on the back pages as they were. Thus, this is not just a story about the formations of an exclusionary racist knowledge found in the distant past, but formations which continue into the present, despite the evident progress that has been made.

So let me conclude, once more with a reference to the situation within which I write. I type these words on All Souls Day on the eve of a Presidential election where cryptic events are likely to be unfolding in the swampy lands around Eatonville, Florida, as well as further north near the terminus of the underground railroad in Cincinnati, Ohio. And when doing so I wonder about whose bodies matter and count, and whose are buried and left behind. But again, why not say things "straight out" and present the evidence in a more convention format? This is because what counts for "evidence" is itself part of a story – the story – and part of a relation of power to knowledge. For instance, there's a horrible and fascinating story being told just this week in one of the premier medical journals in Britain, *the Lancet*. The article entitled "Mortality before and after the 2003 invasion of Iraq: cluster sample survey," wherein this story unfolds, is quite methodologically rigorous. It describes how "the risk of death from violence in the period after the [U.S. led] invasion was 58 times higher (95% CI 8.1–419) than in the period before the war." (Roberts et al., 2004: 1) The story – and there's really little that is "allegorical" about it – concludes that "making conservative assumptions, . . . about 100,000 excess deaths, or more have happened since the 2003 invasion of Iraq" (Roberts et al., 2004: 1). Again note that the sampling techniques and statistical methods used to tell the story are impeccably crafted. Note too that the British government has simply dismissed the story as "wrong" without substantively engaging its argument or evidence, while the U.S. government and most of the U.S. public has apparently ignored it completely. This, on the eve of a US presidential election in which the public has been repeatedly told that "freedom is on the march," although where freedom is actually marching to or from remains somewhat of mystery. So the questions remain and confront us: what stories do we tell as social scientists? What stories can we tell? And what stories can we tell before it's too late?

Aimee Van Wagenen

An Epistemology of Haunting*

> *Nothing, neither among the elements nor within the*
> *system, is anywhere ever simply present or absent.*
> *There are only, everywhere, differences and traces of*
> *traces . . .*
>
> — Jacques Derrida

The dialectics of presence and absence, of inclusion
and exclusion, and of the visible and invisible, are
deeply woven into modern and postmodern lived
social experience. If sometime in our recent history,
it seemed that the notion of a *dialectics of presence and*
absence was mere academic parlance, far removed
from actual lived social experiences, its relevance is
now undeniable. With the collapse of the World Trade
Center, the presence of its absence has become the
definitive reality of the two towers. People speak
about the loss of the towers like the loss of a limb.
And as the last of the ghostly white dust of steel,
glass, concrete, computers, paper and bodies is wiped
away from New York windows and sidewalks, the
presence of the absence of the Towers remains. We

AUTHOR'S NOTE: *I extend my sincere thanks to all of the members of the Editorial Collective*
for their very thoughtful comments; in particular I would like to thank Denise Leckenby and
William Wood for giving this essay their special attention and critical insights.
  * An earlier version of this essay appeared in *Critical Sociology* vol. 30, no. 2 (2004).
The main work under consideration in this review essay is *Ghostly Matters: Haunting*
and the Sociological Imagination, by Avery Gordon (Minneapolis: University of Minnesota
Press, 1997).

are reminded on 24 hour cable news, in the multiplication of anniversaries and television specials, with ongoing debate over plans for reconstruction of the Trade Center site and with peeling and faded "United We Stand" stickers on bumpers of cars. Throughout the nation, the televisual image along with the material reality of the collapse of the World Trade Center towers brings a shared, if complex, dynamic of presence and absence to us all and powerfully reasserts the importance of the dialectics of presence and absence in lived experience.

In her 1997 work, *Ghostly Matters: Haunting and the Sociological Imagination*, Avery Gordon follows the lead of present absences to investigate global ghostly matters. Gordon challenges sociology to take seriously the material reality – the matter – of ghosts. The book is an ethnographic re-telling of three ghost stories: the story of Sabina Spielren's work and relationships in the early history of psychoanalysis; the story of the disappeared in Argentina; and the story of the ghosts of slavery in the United States. But more than a telling of ghost stories, the book is about the phenomenon and way of knowing that is haunting.

> *Ghostly Matters* is about haunting, a paradigmatic way in which life is more complicated than those of us who study it have usually granted. Haunting is a constituent element of modern social life. It is neither pre-modern superstition nor individual psychosis; it is a generalizable social phenomenon of great import. To study social life one must confront the ghostly aspects of it. This confrontation requires (or produces) a fundamental change in the way we know and make knowledge, in our mode of production (7).

Gordon's endeavor to study the complexity of social life brings her to investigate ghostly matters. These are the matters that have been and continue to be excluded from rational conscious memory and from the historical record. Ghostly matters are those matters made marginal through the structured historical violences of modernity. For the cases Gordon takes up, the violences are of gender oppression, imperialism, state terror and slavery. Ghostly matters reside in the shadows, in the margins, in the barely visible and they are never simply absent. The very impact of the ghostly is made through its exclusion and the exclusion is never total. Ghosts return to haunt.

The work, however, is not simply a collection of academic ghost stories. Though the book is centered around *ghostly matters*, the ghosts themselves are not the center of study. Instead, haunting is at the center. It is through haunting that ghostly matters move out of the shadows and are felt as a *seething presence*. "Seething, it makes a striking impression; seething, it makes everything we do see just as it is, charged with the occluded and forgotten past. [To perceive haunting is to] comprehend the living effects, seething and lingering, of what seems over and done with, the endings that are not over" (195). An investigation of haunting is a history of the present. This is the nature of a haunting; it makes the absent past present in structuring the here and now. Investigating a haunting is a matter of following the figure of the ghost, between the present and absent, the excluded and included and the visible and invisible, to *that dense site where history and subjectivity make social life* (8).

Confronting the presence of ghostly matters in social life demands a change in knowledge production. Gordon's work introduces such a change in her epistemology for making sense of that interconnection of history and subjectivity. She finds herself dissatisfied with the conventions of social science that erase the complexity of social life and in its place substitute disembodied, objective, and factual accounts of one-dimensional subjects. Gordon demands an epistemology that can reckon with *the fact that life is complicated* and can comprehend the complex and often contradictory dynamics of subjectivity. She demands an epistemology that recognizes "that even those called 'other' are never never that" (4) and that recognizes that those who haunt are also themselves haunted. This is an epistemology that can manage contradictions in hierarchies of power, knowledge and subjectivity without minimizing their importance to the constitution of social life.

In elaborating this epistemology, Gordon finds and draws upon insights in psychoanalysis and literature that both deal with hauntings, but she is unwilling to give up what sociology offers as the study of social life. Haunting is not a psychological phenomenon to be explained in the exploration of the inner workers of the haunted subject's psyche. To be haunted is to be in a social relation with those made remainders through the violences of modernity. Her epistemology demands that sociology rethink its object of study, its methods of telling stories, the kinds of data it allows to count as such, its relationship to history and the relations of power around its representations.

Gordon's concept of haunting and the epistemology from which it arises are both densely theoretical. For Gordon, haunting is a generalizeable social phenomenon on a large scale. She draws out a theory of haunting that is sufficiently broad to encompass a variety of empirical investigations of this overlooked dimension of social life. Given that Gordon's proposal is a rethinking of the practices of sociological investigation and writing, the specific directions that future empirical analyses of haunting will take promise to be diverse. But Gordon gives us one kind of map for making use of this epistemology of haunting as she takes these dense theoretical concepts to her three cases. Just what kind of shape of this epistemology can take unfolds in the course of the book.

Gordon's project is deeply connected with contemporary movements that question modern conventions for the production of knowledge. Gordon identifies her connection to epistemological ruptures produced by poststructuralist, postcolonialist, postmodernist, post-Marxist and post-feminist movements across disciplines. She finds a crossroads in these movements and, unlike many scholars from these traditions, not only elaborates a dense, theoretically complex critique but also finds a way to simultaneously do ethnography differently and thereby put into practice a sociology that *enters through a different door* (65).

The epistemology of haunting takes us to a number of these crossroads. One crucial crossroad brings the "crisis of representation" and the problematized place of the researcher to bear upon the doing of sociological truthtelling. Postcolonial critic Gayatri Spivak alerts us to the dangerous trap of the "first-world intellectual masquerading as the absent nonrepresenter who lets the oppressed speak for themselves" (Spivak 1988: 292). Chandra Mohanty (1991) outlines some of the dangers of this trap that Western feminists have often found themselves in by speaking for the third world woman: the feminist investigator assumes the possibility of speaking for the subaltern, thereby ignoring the politics and power involved in this representation of subjectivity; the feminist investigator assumes a universal structure in the struggle of women against patriarchy, thereby producing a blind spot in the analysis to the particular, local specificities of third world women's struggles; the feminist investigator assumes a homogeneity of third world women, thereby creating a typical and universalized subaltern subject who is destitute, illiterate, backward and primitive in contrast to the complexity and heterogeneity of the liberated Western woman. Mohanty also speaks to the limits of speaking of subaltern subjects. She notes that the subjectivity of the subaltern woman is constructed by its very exclusion from, and inability to be assimilated under, Western hegemonic discourse and practice. Understood as such, recovering "the voice" of this subaltern subject within Western discourse is impossible.

A facile use of Gordon's concept of haunting might fall into this dangerous trap. The epistemology of haunting is about following marks and traces to tell the story of absences felt as presences. The epistemology of haunting is about conjuring subjects who have been excluded, their histories and subjectivities repressed. A vulgar use of this epistemology carries the danger of figuring the ghost as subaltern from beyond the grave, speaking on her own through the clear channel of the researcher. Gordon averts this danger by placing the phenomenon of haunting at the center of analysis. The channel between the ghost and the researcher is not at all clear for Gordon. That channel is the problematic of study as a mediation between the ghost and the haunted researcher. Thus, "we are part of the story, for better or worse" (24) and "the ghost is nothing without you" (179).

It is in Chapter Two of *Ghostly Matters*, titled "Distractions," where Gordon best considers the mediation between herself as researcher and the ghost at the center of the story. The ghost here is the figure of Sabina Spielren, a patient of Carl Jung's and a psychoanalyst in her own right. Gordon tells some of the story of the transferential love triangle between Spielren, Jung and Freud. She also tells a story of Spielren's relationship to the uncanny in contradistinction to Freud's ultimate repudiation of its reality. While Spielren allows for a reckoning with the ghostly, Freud explains it away as either an individualized psychic phenomenon (repressed infantile complexes) or merely lingering superstition (carried over from an earlier era of primitive animism). Experimenting with literary form and repetition, Gordon conjures these stories in the mediation between this complex history and subjectivity and her own. Avoiding the pitfalls of a vulgar epistemology of haunting, Gordon makes her relation to this haunted history as much a part of the story as the facts of Spielren's unacknowledged influence on Freud.

Sabina Spielren's story comes to Gordon as a distraction from her path to a conference to give a talk on ethnography and problems of representation. She finds a book on Spielren and a photograph that evidences Spielren's absence at a 1911 conference of psychoanalysts in Weimer. "Remarkable, yet familiar, an uncanny recognition of her story called out my desire to know more" (32). As Gordon spins the story of Spielren, psychoanalysis, transference and the uncanny, she spins her own transference into the story. The reader never gets a window to the ghosts apart from the window of Gordon's own haunting.

Heeding Spivak's warning, Gordon never performs the masquerade as a nonrepresenter who lets the oppressed Spielren speak for herself. She does want to listen to what the ghost has to say, *as it speaks, barely, in the interstices of the visible and invisible* (24). But she also speaks *to* the ghost and in doing so, follows Spivak's prescription for the postcolonial intellectual: "In learning to speak to (rather than listen to or speak for) the historically muted subject of the subaltern . . . the postcolonial intellectual systematically 'unlearns' . . . privilege. This systematic unlearning involves learning to critique postcolonial discourse with the best tools it can provide and not simply substituting the lost figure" (295). Struck by Spielren's recounting in her diary of facing a ghostly image of a wolf in the mirror, speaking to it, and hearing it answer back, Gordon follows Spielren's lead and speaks to her ghost:

> Dear Sabina, I'm uneasy about using your story, or the story of the places you were between, as a pretext for speaking about methodology and other matters, about needing or seeming to need a dead woman to enliven matters, to make them have some material force. *Subjects repose in the archives, always inconsolable, never having the right to speak . . .* But I have not really told the story of your "decisive influence" and significant contributions, or what happened to you when you returned to Rostov-on-Don in 1923 to write, teach, and raise your daughters . . . I could not write that story, not because it cannot be recounted, but because you led me beyond yourself . . . I admit that I may have gotten only so far as to insist on our need to reckon with hauntings and to ponder the paradox of providing a hospitable memory for ghosts *out of a concern for justice.* Perhaps this is not nearly enough (59).

Speaking *to* instead of speaking *for* the ghost respects the ghost and the intersubjective nature of a haunting. Speaking to the ghost is a recognition that the subjects in the archive can't speak without passing through the mediation of the investigator.

Spivak asks, "Can the subaltern speak?" and her answer is resolutely: No, it cannot. But this is not Spivak's only thesis as the last few sentences of her piece make clear: "The subaltern cannot speak . . . [But] the female intellectual as intellectual has a circumscribed task which she must not disown with a flourish" (308). Though the investigator cannot speak for the subaltern, she does have an important – if circumscribed – task. That task requires a systematic unlearning of the privileges that allow for the fallacy of speaking for the subaltern. Spivak's prescription: *speak to* and not *for* the subaltern. What does this *speaking to* entail? What is this circumscribed task of the critical investigator? Spivak gives us some answers to these questions in "Can the Subaltern Speak?"

As an alternative, Spivak suggests a study of "the *mechanics* of the constitution of the Other" (294). This is a study of how the absence of the subaltern is also a study of the construction of the subaltern subject in Western discourse. This kind of a study rejects the notion that the Other – the subaltern, excluded, the ghostly – is fully outside the Western discourse. This move rejects the reality of an authentic subaltern that exists "over there" and instead interrogates the reality of the constituted Other that exists "right here," inside Western discourse. This move further recognizes that Western discourse knows the Western subject only in relation to an excluded subaltern Other. The excluded subaltern Other can never speak in its own authentic voice, but the critical investigator can speak to the subaltern by tracing the mechanics of its constitution. This *speaking to* is not necessarily always about writing a letter to a subaltern ghost. It can also be a *speaking to* the issue of the constitution of the other. The critical investigator *speaks to* the issue by finding the Other in the presence of its absences. One method that Spivak suggests is to make the object of investigation the measurement of silences in the historical record. Gordon, in speaking to the issue of ghostly matters and the mechanics of their constitution, gives us a specific model of how such a measurement might work. This model is a sociology of haunting, a sociology that enters through a different door.

In Chapter Four of *Ghostly Matters*, Gordon takes on slavery and Reconstruction by entering through a different door and treating Toni Morrison's novel, *Beloved*, as sociological data. Gordon makes the case that *Beloved* does a much better job at getting at the complexity of social life and the unfinished reckoning with "the problem of the twentieth century" than do other realist forms of representation (slave narratives, engravings of cross sections of slave ships) of the subaltern subjects of slavery. *Beloved* does a better job by problematizing the retrieval of the excluded subjects and substituting in the place of a realist description of life under slavery a "ghost story, a story of enchantment, of 'knowing the things behind things', as Morrison says. A story that is no longer located in the vice of the morality of verisimilitude, which the abolitionist, with honorable motivations, nonetheless demanded [from the slave narrative]" (164).

Gordon also reads Morrison's novel as a study in the mechanics of the constitution of the Other. The ghosts of slavery are never intrinsically Other, but always a part of the constitution of ourselves. Gordon quotes Morrison:

"Whitepeople believed that whatever the manners, under every dark skin was a jungle . . . But it wasn't the jungle blacks brought with them to this place from the other (livable) place. It was the jungle white folks planted in them. And it grew. It spread. In, through and after life, it spread, until it invaded the whites who had made it. Touched them everyone" (189). Gordon implores white readers to allow themselves "to be in the seemingly old story now scared and not wishing to be there" (190). This is to allow white readers to be haunted and to examine the mechanics of the constitution of the Other. This is the only way that the ghosts can be collectively exorcised and another world can be made.

As Gordon makes her way through the historical archive in search of Margaret Garner, the basis for the fictionalized central character, Sethe, in Morrison's novel. Margaret Garner is a woman who becomes known as "the slave mother who killed her child rather than see it taken back to slavery." According to pieced together accounts, Garner fled slavery in Kentucky with her husband and children, headed for Cincinnati. Empowered by the Fugitive Slave Act and carrying warrants for the Garners arrest, United States marshals found the family barricaded inside a Cincinnati abolitionist's house. With the marshals at the door, Margaret Garner apparently chose to kill her children rather than see them returned to slavery. It seems she was disarmed after only successfully killing one of the children – a three year old girl. This pieced together narrative of Garner is not all together clear in the archive. Garner doesn't write a slave narrative for herself and even if she had, Gordon's position is that this representational form is not a clear window to the reality of slave life, but a form constrained by the demands of the abolitionists who sponsor and consume such texts. Garner's story is found in Cincinnati newspapers and in the "authoritative account" written by abolitionist Levi Coffin. Garner's story is then taken up as an argument against slavery by many prominent abolitionists.

Gordon finds Margaret Garner's absence in all these stories, and in the dehumanizing engraving of a slave ship she finds as she searches for more traces of Garner in the archive. The novel *Beloved* registers her absence and follows this as a notice of a haunting – perhaps *the* haunting of the twentieth century. As avowed fiction and not sponsored or vouched for by white authority (as is the slave narrative), *Beloved* better represents Garner. As such, *Beloved* is a novel that disrupts the distinction between fictional and real representation. Morrison profers "a different type of sociological realism, one that encompasses haunting and the complexity of power and personhood that inheres in its work" (147). This disruption of the factual and the fictional, this new sociological realism, opens a different door for sociological analysis and for an epistemology of haunting.

Chapter Three, written around Luisa Valenzuela's novel *He Who Searches*, also enters this different door. Here Gordon argues that activists in Argentina like Amnesty International who trade only in "the facts" of disappearance – the numbers, descriptions and locations of the illegal abductions, detentions, interrogations, tortures and murders – belie the nature of disappearance. Such activists argue that disappearance is a misnomer and should be called what it "really" is, torture and murder. They argue that no one is "really" disappeared because someone somewhere knows where the disappeared person is and if he or she is alive or dead. Gordon is sympathetic to Amnesty's need to represent the phenomenon of disappearance and to make visible the actions of the Argentinean state in order to engage in political action towards justice. But Gordon argues that disappearance is not merely a synonym for the actions that have been taken by real people against other real people.

Disappearance is not, for Gordon, torture and murder by a different name. It is also a form of state terror that works by producing the disappeared as a missing but felt presence.

> If there is one point to be learned from the investigation of ghostly matters, it is that you cannot encounter this kind of disappearance as a grand historical fact, as a mass of data adding up to an event, marking itself straight in empty time, settling the ground for a future cleansed of its spirit. In these matters, you can only experience a haunting, confirming in such an experience the nature of the thing itself: disappearance is real only when it is apparitional. A disappearance is real only when it is apparitional because the ghost or the apparition is the principle form by which something lost or invisible or seemingly not there makes itself known to us through haunting and pulls us affectively into the structure of feeling of reality we come to experience as a recognition (63).

Disappearance produces epistemological doubt that "is specifically designed to break down the distinctions between visibility and invisibility, certainty and doubt, life and death that we normally use to sustain an ongoing and more or less dependable existence" (126). Gordon argues that these elements of disappearance are a kind of haunting, represented as such in Luisa

Valenzuela's haunted, fragmented novel of a Lacanian psychoanalyst's discoveries, losses, journeys and encounters through and with disappearance and the disappeared, with political surreality and violence, through the unconscious and conscious and the in-between. It is a novel fraught with omissions, silences and present absences. For Gordon, haunting better represents both the history of violent state terror and the basis for a politics for today that levers a reckoning with the ghost. In the ongoing work of the Mothers of the Plaza de Mayo Gordon finds a forward-looking concern for justice that reckons with the ghost.

Gordon makes a strong case that the fiction of Valenzuela and Morrison do better to represent haunting. Her use of fiction as sociological data is provocative. But in both of the chapters that center around novels, Gordon does much less of an examination of the mediation between herself as investigator and her ghostly subjects. Valenzuela and Morrison stand in as mediators. They are the haunted researchers who follow the ghosts. This move lets Gordon off the hook in the examination of that mediation and as such removes much of the force of her epistemology of haunting. In all three substantive chapters, Gordon looks at the material phenomenon of haunting by examining haunted histories that push into the present. But it is only in the second chapter on Spielren that Gordon fully makes use of this epistemology of haunting by examining herself as haunted by her subject of study.

In each of the chapters, Gordon isn't interested in telling a realist story of the facts. She's not interested in the true history of Spielren or early psychoanalysis, of the definitive account of those terrorized, tortured and murdered in Argentina or retelling the autobiography of Margaret Garner. She *is* interested in throwing off the conventions of ethnographic authenticity and following where the ghosts lead. Her interest in history is in the history that makes present the ghostly matters of the past. Gordon seeks "the willingness to follow ghosts, neither to memorialize nor to slay, but to follow where they lead, in the present, head turned backwards and forwards at the same time. To be haunted in the name of a will to heal is to help you imagine what was lost that never existed, really" (57).

Critical ethnographies of the present follow ghosts in a number of ways. Abigail Brooks brings the fictive and an uncanny sense that the loss of humanness does make a difference in her research and critique of the normalization of cosmetic plastic surgery (2004 and this volume). Scenes from science fiction where the human body is taken over by technology haunted Brooks as child. These scenes animated her dreams and worked themselves into her waking life as she found herself compelled to search for evidence of the humanness of those around her. Rather than dismissing these memories as childhood foolishness or fantasy – or the simple effect of too much TV-watching – Brooks takes seriously what these uncanny sensations had to tell her about the workings of culture, power, technology and the body in the present. Brooks follows the leads of fictive human replicants to investigate the absence in media representations of the deleterious effects of cosmetic plastic surgery on the bodies of women (and, increasingly, men). She finds that these representations normalize plastic surgery and do not account for the differences such surgeries may make to women as (dis)embodied subjects. Cosmetic surgery, she argues, denies the agency of nature and the body as a formative principle of the self. Nature is denied as a source and the foundational fantasy of the individual as an autonomous subject without ties is reinforced.

Brooks' haunting fear of a hypertechnologized future for the body alerts her to what is lost with the normalization of cosmetic surgery. Respect for the body's signals (like pain, fear, attraction or connection to another) as sources of knowledge that protect and guide is lost. Reverence for the body as an archive and expression of lived experience is lost. Recognition of the interdependence and mutual construction of our selves, our bodies and the earth is lost. These are devastating losses, even as they are losses of what has never existed. We've not had – not on any large scale, really – respect for the body's signals, or reverence for the lived bodily experience or recognition of the interconnection of the body, the self and the earth. But Brooks follows her ghosts to a critique of plastic surgery and, with a will to heal, she imagines these losses of what never existed. These losses turn her toward an imagined future where the technological replacement of human form is rejected in favor of a renewal of respect and reverence for the body.

In her subsequent ethnographic research, Brooks interviews consumers of cosmetic surgery and those who resist surgery and engage in alternative practices that connect the self and body. In this research, Brooks traces these haunted themes in her conversations with and in the narratives of her research subjects. Steve Farough (1994 and this volume) similarly looks for the ghostly in the narratives of his subjects. Farough, through intensive interviewing and photo ethnography with white men, traces the present absence of the recognition of race and gender privilege among his subjects. Yet privilege doesn't remain simply absent for his subjects. Their race and gender privilege seems to haunt them and makes itself unexpectedly felt when they move across racial geographies from mixed race or primarily white geographies to primarily non-white social spaces. It is then that these men feel themselves to be white or "racial." Gordon's epistemology of haunting is a rich and promising resource for alerting researchers to the theoretical and political importance of such present absences in the narratives of their subjects.

These critical ethnographies of the present – ethnographies that engage with the ghostly in the narratives and practices of contemporary actors rather those in the archive or in fiction – make clear the relevance of the ghostly for a critique and a will to transform the politics of the present. We see in Brooks' work a critique of the contemporary politics of the cosmetic surgery and a will to transform bodily relations of power. Similarly in Farough's work we see a critique of white privilege *and a will* towards transformation of the racial order. But Gordon makes her work in the archive relevant for critique and transformation of the present too. Gordon's stories of haunting are powerful fictions of the real that allow for the head turned forwards, towards a utopian transformation of the present. Working through haunting is "to make this past come alive as the lever for the work of the present" (66) to reckon with the ghost and the call for action it makes. This sort of fiction of the real connects Gordon's work with that of Michel Foucault. Foucault in an interview tackles this "problem of fiction":

> I am well aware that I have never written anything but fictions. I do not mean to say, however, that truth is therefore absent. It seems to me that the possibility exists for fiction to function in truth, for a fictional discourse to induce effects of truth, and for bringing it about that a true discourse engenders or 'manufactures' something that does not as yet exist, that is, 'fictions' it. One 'fictions' history on the basis of a political reality that makes it true, one 'fictions' a politics not yet in existence on the basis of a historical truth (Foucault 1980: 193).

Dorothy Smith in her review of *Ghostly Matters* (1999) is uncomfortable with all of the layers of mediation of the epistemology of haunting and finds a political desperation in Gordon's work. "If we follow Gordon, there is nowhere to go from here other than to treasure the ghost and the intimations of utopia that arise in the reader" (121). But there is a place to go from here – to *fiction a politics not yet in existence*. For Gordon, this politics is about a reckoning with ghosts. This requires moving with the ghosts beyond resistance to dominant hegemony towards "the something to be done [that] their arrival announces" (194).

The first step in this politics is to recognize the ghostly and to reckon "with the fundamentally animistic mode by which worldly power is making itself felt in our lives" (202). Gordon suggests we follow Spielren's rejection of Freud's approach to the uncanny where this animistic mode is merely a left-over of a primitive time that the educated and civilized man has surpassed and transcended. Gordon suggests instead that we, like Spielren, recognize the very real and transformative force of the uncanny. Spielren, despite her status as educated and civilized, believes in spirits. Gordon recounts a story in Spielren's diary: one day, she looks into the mirror and finds a wolf staring back. She speaks to the wolf, asking it what it wants. The wolf speaks back. Spielren wakes the next morning, feeling transformed. Freud in his work, *The Uncanny*, describes a similar experience. Riding in a train, the door of his compartment swings open. He jumps up when in front of him appears an intruder – an elderly, unpleasant looking man. Freud, a rational man, then realizes this intruder is not an intruder at all. He had simply failed to recognize his double reflected in the mirror.

Spielren reckons with the ghostly; Freud repudiates it. Freud explains away the uncanny as a wholly individualized phenomenon whereby repressed infantile complexes return to appear in conscious life as uncanny experiences. Freud does, however, leave open one door to a possible social, rather than individual, reality of the uncanny in his second explanation of the uncanny. Here Freud explains the uncanny as a kind of left over "primitive animism." While Gordon takes issue with this term and its connection to colonialist ideology, she does find potential in its assumption of a connection of the uncanny with the "world of common reality.' Gordon quotes Freud: "Is it not possible, though, that [my] dislike of [my double] was a vestigal trace of the archaic reaction which feels the 'double' to be something uncanny." She continues: "What Freud called the archaic here is the recognition of himself as another, as a stranger, the arrival of the person from elsewhere, from the world outside himself, from what we call the social" (54). Ultimately, however, Freud dismisses this possibility and reverts to a second, individualized explanation of the uncanny as an affair of reality-testing for the ego. The mature man has, in Freud's words, "surmounted these modes of thought" where spirits are real; the mature, civilized man receives a ghost as a mere test of the material reality of the phenomenon. For Freud, the only correct answer to the reality-test is the realization of uncanny as superstition, as a psychic wish, as an illusion. For Spielren, it is something more: "she talks to the wolf, listens to its answer, and believes in the transformative power of the encounter" (55).

Spielren's recognition of the transformative power of the ghost is only the first step in reckoning with the ghost. Her recognition of the uncanny is a small, but critical opening. Gordon finds the second step, transformation, in her engagement with Valenzuela's and with Morrison's work. Transformation is a crucial step in Gordon's fictioning of a politics not yet in existence. Transformation requires a transition from the knowledge of the ghostly that reckoning produces to *doing something about it*. The transformation that Valenzuela's work highlights is the possibility of a *social* psychoanalysis that engages with the ghostly. Gordon also finds transformation in the activism of the Mothers of the Plaza de Mayo whose organized demonstration became a force in protest of the government's policies of disappearance. The Mothers began their weekly illegal public demonstrations in April 1977, walking quietly in a circle around the Plaza de Mayo wearing photographs of their children pinned to their clothes and white shawls embroidered with the names of their children and the dates of their disappearance. As material evidence of their children's present absence, the photographs punctuate the silence of disappearance and bring a haunting into relief. The Mothers insist, "Aparicion con Vida" – in English, "Bring Them back Alive." For Gordon, this is not a denial of the likelihood of the death of those who have been disappeared. Instead the slogan is a reaction to the government policy of searching for the bones of the disappeared, sending them to the families and then asserting that the government owes no more to the families. For the Mothers, this is not enough. They insist on a reckoning with disappearance as what has happened to their children, not the reduction of disappearance to death. While disappearance remains a phenomenon of the present, the sending of bones denies its present and haunting nature.

Dorothy Smith was correct in noting that reading *Ghostly Matters* produces "intimations of utopia" in the reader. This is a utopia where sociology can represent the dialectics of absence and presence, complex personhood and that dense site where history and subjectivity make social life. *Ghostly Matters* is a beautifully written, evocative book that enacts a powerful critique of sociological epistemology while simultaneously advancing an epistemological innovation in the concept of haunting. This is a book that sociologists should take seriously as we endeavor both to represent social life *and* to transform it.

Eva Marie Garroutte

Defining "Radical Indigenism" and Creating an American Indian Scholarship*

In their influential book *Writing Culture*, James Clifford and George E. Marcus (1986) probed the challenges and limits of anthropological work. Rejecting the assumption that conventional research methods supplied tools for the neutral description, classification, and analysis of data drawn from the objective observation of other cultures, they argued instead that such methods often functioned as mechanisms of control and domination. The critique easily generalized to related disciplines, and the resulting loss of social scientific innocence helped create a space for members of subordinated and colonized groups, including indigenous peoples around the world, to call for new models of research that better reflected *their* interests, perspectives, goals, and voices (Rigney 2001).

In the intervening decades, indigenous scholars have begun the important work of articulating the values that might motivate such research and the general goals it must reflect (e.g., Rigney 1997; Warrior 1995; Weaver 1997; Alfred 1999; Smith 1999). They commonly express interest in the community-based or "participatory" research models that are increasingly finding currency in the academy, but they also set their sights on a more distant horizon. They call, as well, for a "new intellectual

* This essay is an abbreviated version of an argument that has been developed more fully elsewhere (Garroutte 2003).

agenda" – one that embodies truly distinctive perspectives and enables genuinely different types of interactions between researchers and indigenous peoples (Warrior 1999). Indigenous scholars hope for a vision of scholarship that they can call truly their own.

The distinctive theories and methodologies that might undergird such undertakings have been slow to emerge, however. In this essay, I make an early attempt at this daunting project. I define a new theoretical perspective that brings together the goal of contributing to the health, survival, and growth of indigenous communities with the goal of the academy to cultivate knowledge. I consider some methods of inquiry that might be appropriate to this new perspective, and I give it a name: Radical Indigenism. I then develop this perspective by applying its theoretical and methodological assumptions to a specific question of concern to indigenous communities in the Americas: the issue of American Indian identity. My specific and overarching goal is to demonstrate that it is possible to create distinctive bodies of thought and practice that can properly be called an *American Indian scholarship*.

Radical Indigenism: Theoretical Predecessors

I will begin by briefly describing my understanding of the theoretical perspective that I am calling Radical Indigenism and pointing out the features that distinguish it from ideas that have preceded it, particularly ideas in the domain of post-colonial theory. The name Radical Indigenism reflects the Latin derivation of the word "radical": *radix*, meaning "root." Radical Indigenism, as I define it, illuminates differences in assumptions about knowledge that are at the root of the dominant culture's misunderstanding and subordination of indigenous knowledge. It argues for the reassertion and rebuilding of knowledge from those roots.

The kernel of a revolutionary American Indian scholarship, as I imagine it, is a rejection of the academy's long-standing assumption that the main reason to examine Indian cultures is to learn something about the *people* who practice them – their beliefs and values, their "worldviews," their psychological health or illness, the social structures they create. Radical Indigenism dares to suggest, as its fundamental theoretical premise, that American Indian peoples possess philosophies of knowledge that can be understood as rationalities – articulable, coherent logics for ordering and knowing the world. This assumption permits us to understand these philosophies not merely as objects of curiosity (unusual things that people have *believed*) but as tools for discovery and for the generation of *knowledge*.

In crafting this new scholarship we have much to learn from the work of the postcolonial theorists.[1] These thinkers have taught us that non-Western peoples all over the world had – and *have* – viable intellectual traditions. They have showed us how those intellectual traditions have, nevertheless, often been overwhelmed, deformed, and rendered invisible by what Walter Mignolo (1994) calls "academic colonialism" – the attempt of Amer-European thinkers to construe them through foreign categories of thought. The postcolonial theorists have also pointed the way to a rediscovery of "alternative ways of knowing that may impinge on our current conception of knowledge, understanding, and the politics of intellectual inquiry" (Ibid.: 310). It is such a way of knowing that a new, American Indian scholarship must also seek.

But postcolonial theory may be limited in its ability to inform an American Indian scholarship. A persistent complaint directed at postcolonial theorists is that they have had difficulty really separating themselves from the categories of knowledge provided by the "academic colonialists."[2] The most serious criticism in this category concerns the postcolonialists' failure to grapple with very fundamental assumptions regulating the conduct of inquiry, and the difficulty is especially apparent when one considers indigenous philosophies of knowledge.

Kwame Anthony Appiah (1993), drawing heavily on the work of anthropologist Robin Horton, observes that models of inquiry that dominate the academy (which he calls "scientific," but are alternatively referred to as "modern" or "post-Renaissance") distinguish themselves from indigenous models in many ways. These include their pronounced experimental emphasis, their orientation to narrowly-defined sensory information, their value on the acquisition of new knowledge strictly for its own sake, their "adversarial" approach in which knowledge emerges from the competition of precisely-articulated theories, their value on the universal dissemination of knowledge, their preference for explanations in terms of material forces rather than personal agents, and their willingness to eschew questions of ultimate meaning. Many of these

---

[1] The field of postcolonial theory is extremely diverse. For a useful overview, see Childs and Williams (1999).

[2] There are various versions of this critique (e.g., Prakash 1992, McClintock 1993). Efforts to assess the utility of postcolonial theory specifically in regard to American Indian concerns include Stover (2001), Weaver (1998), and Vizenor (1994).

differences derive from the modern interest in creating a thoroughly secular means of seeking knowledge.

The cultural ascendancy of scientific models of inquiry means that indigenous knowledge can be integrated into academic discourse only if it is pared down, sanitized of the spiritual elements pervading the models that birthed it. The sanitizing process typically means one of two things: either indigenous knowledge is presented as a set of "primitive beliefs" that have been superseded by modern "factual knowledge," or it is reconstructed (without reference to the contrary assertions of the indigenous carriers) as symbolically rather than literally truthful. The first strategy portrays indigenous claims as simply wrong (although possibly interesting), while the second strategy allows them to be right only by "deny[ing] that traditional people mean what they say" (Appiah 1993: 116).

While postcolonialists have observed differences between conventional academic and indigenous models of inquiry, they have yet to work through their meaning for the practice of scholarship. What Appiah writes about indigenous African peoples is more broadly applicable. Their frequent conviction that the world cannot be approached with a model of inquiry that excludes assumptions about a spiritual reality, he observes,

> means that most Africans cannot fully accept those scientific theories in the West that are inconsistent with such assumptions. . . . If modernization is conceived of in, part, as the acceptance of science, we have to decide whether we think the evidence obliges us to give up the invisible ontology [that is, belief in spiritual agencies]. . . . The question [of] how much of the world of spirits we intellectuals must give up (or translate into something ceremonial without the old literal ontology) is one we must face: and I do not think the answer is obvious (1993: 135).

The new, American Indian scholarship that I propose must confront exactly this latter question, and formulate an answer. Radical Indigenism urges resistance to the pressure upon indigenous scholars to participate in academic discourses that strip Native intellectual traditions of their spiritual and sacred elements. It takes this stand on the ground that sacred elements are absolutely central to the coherence of our knowledge traditions and that if we surrender them there is little left in our philosophies that makes any sense.

Perhaps we should say that the postcolonial theorists have led us to a high plane from which we may glimpse the landscape of a radically different scholarship. But they have not yet led us into the new country. We American Indian scholars, it seems, must find our own way. With the help of our tribal communities and those others in the academy who will join with us, we must find perspectives that respect and reflect distinctly American Indian ways of knowing the world.

Radical Indigenism: Assumptions and Methods for an Inquiry

Radical Indigenism requires that the researcher work within assumptions drawn from American Indian philosophies. Where can these assumptions be discovered? A common premise of indigenous philosophies is that the seeker looks to tribal traditions for guidance. American Indian speakers frequently refer to these traditions as embodied in their people's "Original Instructions" – the body of teachings about the nature of the world and how humans are to live in it. There are, I would suggest, at least three sources to which a researcher working within the perspective of Radical Indigenism may turn to discover Original Instructions on a specific subject. The first obvious place one must seek these traditions is in the statements of elders and others who know community lifeways from their own long experience. Second, we will want to see how (and if) those statements are grounded in larger bodies of teachings – stories, oral narratives, songs, dances, and other records. Finally, we might look to the ways that our ancestors created forms of community life that made flesh the teachings our traditions set forth. The examination of what sociologists call social structures may allow us to deduce traditional principles not only from what the ancestors *said* but also from what they actually *did*.

Having specified these three sources of knowledge, we have defined a simple methodology by which to proceed. We shall see, however, that this methodology can lead to genuine departures from the conclusions of more conventional scholarly approaches – that this methodology can properly be included under the rubric of Radical Indigenism.

Radical Indigenism and The Question of American Indian Identity

In the pages that follow, I illustrate and develop the methodology just described by applying it to an extremely tendentious question of considerable concern to contemporary American Indian communities: the question of tribal "identity."

Since the 1960s, a significant subset of the U.S. population has become interested in American Indian ancestry, and many people have begun to formally
identify themselves as Indians even though they had previously identified
themselves as some other race. The trend in racial identification is nowhere
more obvious than on the U.S. decennial census, which has shown very large
gains in the number of people identifying themselves as Indians every decade
since 1960. The increases are far too large simply to reflect a high birth rate,
and such trends have raised serious tensions in American Indian communities regarding the legitimacy of many people's claims to a tribal identity
(Snipp 1986; Nagel 1996; Thornton 1997).

Indeed, today's identity conflicts are severe enough to be sometimes characterized as "race baiting" and "ethnic cleansing." A published letter to the
newspaper *Indian Country Today*, in which one well-known activist attacks
another, illustrates the animosity seething through discussions about who is
a "real Indian." His object is not an Indian, the writer asserts, but "a former
redhead, a 'white' female radio personality in New York who made an abrupt
transition to Lady Clairol black hair-dye and a career as a professional
Washington Indian some fifteen years before she was ever enrolled in anything other than night school."[3] In other recent examples, entire tribes have
been indicted of inauthentic Indian-ness, and legal struggles have challenged
their right to exercise the prerogatives of tribal nations (Benedict 2000; Clifford
1988).

The problem central to the identity conflicts is that individuals and groups
who successfully lay claim to an American Indian identity may gain access
to legal, political, economic, and cultural resources. At the individual level,
these may include tax advantages, treaty rights, federal or tribal entitlement
programs, specific legal protections, as well the privilege of voting in tribal
elections, running for tribal office, or participating in community events. At
the collective level, a group that receives federal acknowledgement as an
Indian tribe establishes itself as a "domestic dependent nation" that is exempt
from state laws and takes on a special relationship with the United States
government (Canby 2004).

---

[3] "Enrollment" refers to the process by which Indian people formally establish citizenship in a tribal nation, the implication being that the individual only sought relationship with her tribe late in life. I have deliberately omitted publication information
for this quotation, so as to discourage circulation of such rumors.

These benefits are sufficiently substantial that it is important that they be distributed appropriately, and this reality motivates careful contemplation of individual and collective claims to Indian-ness. At the same time, tensions about identity have also stifled useful discussion on a variety of subjects by creating an aura of suspicion, anxiety, and rage in many Indian communities (Garroutte 2003).

I believe that there is a way for American Indian communities to address identity issues with the seriousness they deserve, yet without being destroyed by them. I also believe that there is a way to bring together this project with the project of the academy to cultivate knowledge. That is why I have chosen the identity debates as a way to illustrate a methodology by which an approach within the perspective that I call Radical Indigenism might proceed. However, I conceive my remarks not as a prescription for how tribes should think, but as a way to encourage Native scholars and communities in their *own* conversations. I conceive it, as well, as a way to stimulate Native and non-Native scholars toward a conversation about the meaning of scholarship in a pluralistic world. In other words, the reader should understand that, in what follows, I speak only for myself, reflecting on my own interactions as an American Indian person in tribal communities and on my own scholarly work.

If we apply the methodology that I have proposed above – a model of inquiry that draws upon evidence collected from elders, sacred teachings, and records of historic social structures – to the task of building up (or recovering) a definition of tribal identity, what might we discover? The only way for a community really to arrive at an answer to this question is to seek, *as a community*, within its own knowledge traditions. But for the purposes of illustration, I will start the conversation down a specific pathway: I propose that a definition of identity that is available within many American Indian knowledge traditions is what I call a definition of *kinship*. As I see it, a definition of identity founded in kinship responds to at least two themes that one encounters across a range of tribal philosophies. One of these reflects a condition of *being*, which I call *relationship to ancestry*. The second involves a condition of *doing*, which I call *a responsibility to reciprocity*. I will begin by considering examples of how each theme is expressed in the philosophies of specific tribes, following the methodology I have laid out. That is, I draw first on the published and unpublished remarks of Indian people themselves, then on tribal stories that deal with this theme, a finally on a consideration of social structures that suggest specific principles related to it. I then consider the ways that the conclusions that suggest themselves differ from the conclusions that have followed from investigations carried out within more conventional intellectual perspectives.

A First Kinship Principle: Relationship to Ancestry

The significance of relationship to ancestry for determining inclusion in Native communities is readily apparent in the published remarks by and about Indian people. Ella Deloria (1994), that monumental scholar of Lakota (Sioux) culture, wrote that the genealogical connections of her people were "assiduously traced and remembered, no matter how far back" (27). Scholar of Native American literature Elizabeth Cook-Lynn explains this genealogical preoccupation:

> One cannot be a Lakota unless one is related by the lineage (blood) rules
> of the *tiospaye* [tribal community]. . . . [B]iology is *never* dismissed categor-
> ically. On the contrary, it is the overriding concern of the people who assid-
> uously trace their blood ties throughout the generations (1996: 94).

Nor have ideas about the importance of ancestry disappeared. Sentiments about the significance of familial relationship for determining identity were frequently repeated by American Indian people with whom I spoke on this subject between 1999 and 2000.[4] For instance, Julie Moss, a Cherokee grandmother, described the significance of family relationship this way:

> [i]n Cherokee culture, [relationship to ancestry] is *very* important. . . . It's *all-*
> important in Cherokee culture. Without it, it's like you're a person without

---

[4] As I have noted, this essay presents an argument that has been condensed and adapted from a larger project. That project drew on a range of published and unpublished sources, both contemporary and historical. Unpublished sources included interviews with twenty-two American Indian and non-Indian people who are, in one way or another, caught up in conversations, controversies, and conflicts about Native identity. The sample of research participants from which I selected illustrative quotations for this essay is more fully described in Garroutte (2003). Here it suffices to note that I conducted in-depth interviews with these individuals, mainly in person, between the summers of 1999 and 2000. Three interviews, however, were conducted by telephone, and one respondent answered interview questions in writing. Respondents were selected by me because of their diversity of individual characteristics and personal opinions. The small size of the sample forbids any claims to generalizability of the respondents' remarks. Instead, I use this material only to illustrate some of the many ways that Indian and non-Indian people today speak about their identity claims and those of others.

a ... country. It's actually even worse than that. ... I think Cherokee culture operated on that [kinship principle] from ancient times, and it still does to this day. Because of the clan system and because of the extended family. ... It's part of being Cherokee. ... It's what we're *about*.

Other American Indian people that I consulted added that relationship to ancestry provided not only an organizing principle recognized by tribal communities, but also the conviction of tribal belonging for the individual. Melvin Bevenue, honorary chief of the Creek Nation observed that, if a person is born with tribal ancestry,

> that [tribal] identity is *in* you from the day you're born. The *day* you're born. If you're an Indian, it's *there*. What ... a Indian person has the hardest time [with] is *losin'* it, gettin' rid of it. Because it's *there*. Like a tiger or a lion has an instinct to kill to live. And that's *born* in them. Born in that tiger or the lion. The same way with a *human* being. The day you're born, if you're an Indian, whether you, you pet it [one's identity] and grow up with it [or not], it's there. ... It's [present from] the day you was born. It's *in* you. It *comes* that way. ...

This speaker's statement is reminiscent of the published remarks of N. Scott Momaday, a Kiowa-Cherokee author. Momaday hints at the significance of the intimate, physical connection shared among tribal people in his repetitive and oft-quoted statements about "memory in the blood" and "a racial memory that leaps across generations," linking him to his ancestors (Momaday 1997: 40). "I think that each of us bears in his genes or in his blood or wherever a recollection of the past. Even the very distant past. I just think that's the way it is" (Momaday 1989: 21). For Momaday, the people of a tribe share a powerful connection because of their genealogical relatedness. It is something heritable, fundamental and effectual.

Statements that privilege physical relationship as a determinant of tribal belonging have received scornful treatment in the scholarly literature, where they are dismissed under the rubric of "primordialism" or "essentialism." Prominent postcolonial theorists argue that essentialist ideas are colonial impositions – "the respectable child of old-fashioned exoticism," as Salman Rushdie asserts (1991: 67). Similarly, in a representative sociological critique, Jack Eller and Reed Coughlan (1993) lament the "poverty of primordialism," while Eugeen Roosens, in his study of Native ethnicity in Canada, invests essentialism with distinctly threatening associations:

The less critical can be led to believe that the "ethnic feeling" is a primordial, essential dimension of every human being, that it is inborn in the blood, that one can almost feel it physically, that one must fight to safeguard this "high value," that one is indebted to the ancestors from whom one has received life and "everything." Political leaders can create stereotypes that give almost religious exaltedness to ethnic identity and, via stereotypes, lead to economic and cultural wars with other groups and even to genocide (1989: 18).

Scholar of Native American literature Arnold Krupat (1989) is more succinct. He angrily labels Momaday's claims to "memory in the blood" as "absurdly racist" (14).

In such assessments, essentialist ideas – ideas presupposing a tribal connection inherent to the individual's fundamental nature – are displayed as the property of the intellectually deficient and the politically rabid. That leaves American Indian speakers and authors who have articulated ideas about the centrality of genealogical relationship in determining tribal identity in unfortunate company. But before rushing to the judgment that this is where they belong, let us proceed as a research program attentive to the perspective of Radical Indigenism might direct.

Is there evidence that these claims have a foundation in tribal philosophies of knowledge? If so, can they be understood *there* in more sophisticated ways than academic criticisms of essentialism propose?

Even a cursory examination reveals that sacred stories about the importance of kinship defined in terms of genealogical descent abound in tribal oral traditions. But to suggest the distinctiveness of American Indian ideas about kinship, let us examine only one type of story. Narratives of this general type appear in a number of different tribes and describe the birth and life of great mythological figures.[5]

In these stories, the hero is frequently born from a miraculous union of a spirit being and a human woman. His mother may not know the father's identity, but the child knows, or sets out to discover it. Thus, when Water Jar Boy of the Tewa-speaking Pueblos in New Mexico questions his mother about

---

[5] Other stories might illustrate a similar point, but the type of story that I have chosen recommends itself both for the central focus on issues of kinship and also because of its distribution across many different tribes.

his miraculous paternity, "somehow [he] . . . knew the answer to his own question. He announced to his mother, 'I know where my father is, and tomorrow I will go and find him!'" On his ensuing quest, Water Jar Boy discovers a man sitting near a spring (within which the man lives) and recognizes him. The father joyfully leads Water Jar Boy into the spring to meet his other paternal relatives. "Water Jar Boy stayed in the spring and lives there to this day" (Cajete 1994). Although Water Jar Boy has never previously met these relatives, he shares a powerful and meaningful bond with them: a bond of common ancestry.[6]

In a thematically similar story told by the Cherokee of North Carolina and Oklahoma, the offspring of the thunder being and a human woman seeks his unknown father and is restored to his paternal family after a series of ordeals. Through his journey, he is cured of physical affliction and discovers the powers that are his birthright: he learns that he is the lightning being, with the power to rend the sky with his deadly bolts and strike down his opponents in battle. Lightning begins his quest physically disfigured and ignorant of who he is; he does not realize that he is a powerful spirit being. Healing and self-knowledge follow reunion with those previously unknown others with whom the hero shares a relationship of ancestry and, with it, an essential nature.[7]

Still another story, this one from the Hopi of Arizona, features a child conceived of the sun who seeks and finds his father. In the interactions that follow, he discovers extraordinary abilities that belong to him as the child of his father; he then returns to earth transformed from an object of village contempt into a radiantly attired teacher of how the people should live. As in the Cherokee story, a child's genealogical relationship has real consequences for who he fundamentally is and for what he becomes.[8]

My remarks here can only be suggestive. A proper interpretation of sacred stories requires that they be considered in the context of tribal languages, cultures, and community life. These interpretative tasks belong to those with very special competencies and, importantly, to tribal communities who take on such tasks *as* communities. But these examples of a story theme found across various tribes show evidence – not only in what contemporary elders

---

[6] For the full text of this story, see Cajete (1994: 125–27).
[7] For the text, see Mooney (1992: 311–15).
[8] For the text, see Erdoes and Ortiz (1984: 145–50).

say but in what sacred stories relate – for a kind of traditionally-grounded essentialism (or, more likely, essentialisms) among at least some American Indian peoples. In so doing, they provide a context for remarks such as those of Momaday and other elders about the importance for tribal identity of genealogical relationship in and of itself. They invite tribal communities to explore these ideas further, by examining their own stories about tribal belonging.

The existence of essentialist themes in tribal sacred stories suggests that their academic dismissal as racist incitements or as colonial artifacts must be inspected carefully. Do the versions of essentialism that Native communities may discover in their traditional stories differ from the essentialist claims that arise in academic contexts and that have been so roundly criticized there? Do all essentialist definitions of identity come from the same intellectual place? Do they all function in the same way? Social scientific studies of kinship provide a context in which to explore such questions.

Whereas contemporary social scientists explicitly reject essentialist assumptions, anthropologist David Schneider (1984) shows that their work has often implicitly depended upon such assumptions. In his analysis of nineteenth- and twentieth-century studies of kinship, he concludes:

> There is an assumption that is . . . widely held and necessary to the study of kinship. . . . It is the assumption that Blood Is Thicker Than Water.
>
> Without this assumption much that has been written [by social scientists] about kinship simply does not make sense. . . . [This assumption posits that] *kinship is a strong solidary bond that is largely innate, a quality of human nature, biologically determined, however much social or cultural overlay may also be present* (original emphasis) (165–66).

The consistent orientation of kinship studies, Schneider summarizes, has understood "true" kinship as founded exclusively on biological relationship. Such an assumption clearly implies a kind of essentialism in that it posits a fundamental substance connecting relatives. This substance is conceived as a physical material – "blood" – that can, like other physical materials, be attenuated and eventually exhausted. The corollary of what Schneider calls this "biologistic" assumption is that the significance of kin relationship depends absolutely on the proximity of the ancestral connection: "Primary relatives are closer than secondary, secondary are closer than tertiary, and so on . . . [W]hat has been called 'genealogical distance' . . . is a measure of the magnitude of the biological component and hence the strength of the [kinship] bond" (173).

How do these prevalent social scientific ideas compare to the essentialisms that might be expected to emerge from indigenous communities' contemplation of their philosophies of kinship? Certainly some modern American Indian people embrace a similarly biologistic construction of identity. But others suggest the very different idea that Indian identity is a discrete, not a continuous variable. Momaday, for instance, makes no indication that his tribal "memory in the blood" is in any way compromised by being mingled with his European ancestry, and several of the American Indian people with whom I spoke went out of their way to reject such a conclusion. For instance, Anishnabe artist, teacher, and grandmother Kathleen Westcott argued that the simple *fact* of physical relationship is significant in a way that overwhelms any ideas about what the federal government refers to as "blood quantum," or degree of relationship:

> When a person says they're Native, it's very important to me that they *are* Native. . . . It's *not* important to me what their blood quantum is. I really – honest to God – do believe that the teensiest, tinsiest – in order to use the language of blood quantum – blood degree is nevertheless the most powerful presence of ancestry. And I know that I'm not alone in that. I know that elders who I really, really respect see it that way.

From the perspective that such sentiments imply, one either belongs to the ancestors or one does not; the notion of fractionating one's essential substance is untenable. A discussion offered by Powhatan/Lenape/Saponi anthropologist Jack Forbes supports this contention and provides further insight into tribal versions of essentialism. In certain tribes, Forbes writes,

> persons are descended in the female line from a "first" ancestor, usually a being with an animal or plant name. If, for example, one is a member of the "turtle" matrilineal lineage, one might find this situation: 500 generations ago the first "turtle" woman lived, and in each subsequent generation her female descendants [in order to respect incest prohibitions] had to marry men who were non-turtles, i.e., with other lineages in their female lines. A modern-day "turtle" person, then, might well be, in quantitative terms, one-five-hundredth "turtle" and four-hundred-ninety-nine-five-hundredths non-"turtle," and yet, at the same time, be completely and totally a turtle person (1990: 38–39).

This example elegantly demonstrates that the essentialism of tribal philosophies can be founded on a different logic than that of Schneider's social scientists: a sacred logic to which quantification is irrelevant.

A second significant difference in the way Native and non-Native philosophies may construct essentialist ideas concerns assumptions about how the identity-conferring substance is transmitted. The biologistic theories underpinning social scientific studies of kinship assume the essential substance is inherited through birth. In a number of Native philosophies, however, it appears that essential nature *can* be, but does not necessarily *have* to be, so transmitted. Alternatively, it can also be created ceremonially. We learn this from an examination of social patterns related to adoption practices in specific tribes.

Although some tribes, at certain historical moments, were very bounded and closed societies, others had strong, incorporative traditions. In the wake of disruptions introduced by European arrivals, for instance, "interethnic cooperation and acceptance of new members into the group to achieve a numerical advantage over other groups became an important strategy. . . . Some groups added outsiders who were captives, slaves, orphans, outlaws, social outcasts, mixed-bloods, trading partners, or fictive kin" (Miller 1994: 226–27).

Various American Indian individuals whom I interviewed gave examples of "outsiders" being incorporated into the tribe in ways that cause them to take on relationships that are understood in essentialist terms and that may even be spoken of as physical or "blood" relationships. For instance, retired educator Archie Mason told me that, along with Osage and Cherokee ancestry he,

> can claim [to be] Ponca because of a relationship of two women long ago
> [in the nineteenth century]. A Ponca woman and an Osage woman, who
> was my relation, took each other as sisters. There are few people today who
> still acknowledge that relationship. Those of us that do, we are blood-related
> because of that. It [the adoption ceremony] was a very *special* ceremony held
> on the Arkansas River, between the Osages and the Poncas, a very special,
> spiritual thing way back there. . . . When that happened, there was a . . . con-
> nection between families. And today, I have Ponca people who are my *fam-
> ily*. . . . [W]e recognize each other as *blood*. We're the *same*. . . . I know that
> and it affects *me*. I tell my children and my grandchildren these kinds of
> things.

Archie suggests an understanding of ceremony as the vehicle for a powerful transformation by which the object becomes a different *kind* of person – in his case, a person related to other Ponca people in fundamentally the same way that those born with Ponca ancestry are related.

There is a long tradition, at least in certain tribes, of the kinds of practices that this contemporary speaker suggests. The tribes of the Iroquois Confederacy, for example, were at times very active in adopting outsiders (Calloway 1983: 194). Evidence suggests that, among the Iroquois, adoption rituals did not merely alter people's formal citizenship status; rather, they ceremonially *recreated* the individual, changing her essential nature in accordance with what I am calling a definition of kinship. For instance, Frederick Webb Hodge (1968), in his *Handbook of American Indians North of Mexico*, tells the story of two white sisters who were captured by the Seneca (a member tribe within the Iroquois confederacy) and prepared for tribal adoption. However, Hodge writes, "instead of both being adopted into one clan, one [sister] was adopted by the Deer Clan and the other by the Heron clan, and thus the blood of the sisters was changed by the rite of adoption in such wise that their children could intermarry" (15).

Had these sisters been born Senecas, they would have belonged to the same clan. All their children would have belonged to that clan as well and would have been restrained from intermarriage by incest prohibitions. But the Seneca ceremonial procedures permanently transformed the sisters' fundamental nature and being. The choice of wording – that their very "blood . . . was changed" – may, of course, reflect an outside observer's interpretation. Yet the consequences of the act are clear. The adoption ceremony made the sisters different from each other at a level that transcended straightforward biological relationship. It caused a *sacred* transformation that brought into being what nature had originally wrought otherwise. It seems to have bestowed, quite literally, a connection of fundamental substance to other members of the tribal body.

These new Seneca relatives are not properly described as "fictive kin" – the category to which anthropological studies of kinship since the nineteenth-century writings of Henry Maine would relegate them. They entered the ceremony as one kind of being and emerged as another. The kinship substance thus acquired is real and consequential, enabling new relationships – both social and physical. But it does not behave like the strictly material kinship substance assumed by social scientific theories because it can be created in ceremony. Given the limitations of the English language and of Amer-European conceptual categories, perhaps we can only say that the kinship substance implied here is both physical *and* more-than-physical.[9]

These observations, like the themes explored in tribal sacred stories, challenge the postcolonialists' claim that any embrace of essentialism necessarily represents surrender to non-indigenous ideas and values. These examples suggest that there are indigenous essentialisms quite different from the biologistic, social scientific varieties. They also challenge the accusation that essentialist claims are necessarily racist: the essentialisms explored here have nothing to do with the idea of race, a concept rooted in the same biologistic assumptions that have driven social scientific studies of kinship. Instead, the identity definitions that I have explored emphasize the unique importance of genealogical relatedness to tribal communities while also allowing, at least in principle, for people of *any* race to be brought into kinship relations through the transformative mechanism of ceremony.

A Second Kinship Principle: Responsibility to Reciprocity

The definition of kinship that I think may be recoverable in at least some American Indian philosophical traditions comprises not only the significance of relationship to ancestry, but also the way that individuals behave. In this vein, Julie Moss described the life of small, Cherokee communities in Oklahoma:

> I grew up in a . . . huge, extended family. And you never had to worry about anything. You always knew that you had help. If you needed food, that whole community helped you. . . . So I know what that kinship system does for you. . . . You know that if you venture out into the world, you don't have to do it by yourself. . . . And that whole idea of individuality and compet-

---

[9] Hartland's (1909–1910) extensive study of kinship philosophies argues that similar ideas have characterized many indigenous cultures:

> Descent is . . . the typical cause of kinship and a common blood. . . . But kinship may also be acquired; and when once it is acquired by a stranger he ranks thenceforth for all purposes as one descended from a common ancestor. To acquire kinship a ceremony must be undergone: the blood of the candidate must be mingled with that of the kin. The ceremony, no less than the words made use of in various languages to describe the members of the kind and their common bond, renders it clear that the bond is the bond of blood (258).

itiveness wasn't really in our [Cherokee] culture, in that kinship culture . . .
because it was all about helping one another and sharing everything. . . . There
are communities that still practice that [way of life] to this day.

In tribe after tribe, one finds a conviction that The People – those who understand themselves as bound together in spiritually faithful community – are
responsible to live with each other in particular ways. These ways of relationship constitute what I am calling a responsibility to reciprocity. It is likewise suggested by Christopher Jocks (1997) when he writes of "the ability to
participate in kinship" (original emphasis). He regards kinship as an ongoing
practice or skill, an active relationship that must be maintained, and that is
not invariably tied to one's genealogical connections: "In every Indian community I am aware of there are a few non-Indians who have gained [entry
into kinship relations]. . . . Generosity of time and spirit, respect and polite-
ness, willingness to help out, and openness to learn, are what our elders seem
to value most; and all of us who pursue this work [in American Indian Studies]
know non-Indians who have succeeded in it." The same logic also works in
reverse: "There are full-blood Indians who have lost this ability to participate in kinship. . . ." (172).

The foregoing observations suggest an emphasis on *behavior* in defining
tribal identity that is quite different than the ideas that have dominated social
scientific studies of kinship. Schneider's critique, discussed earlier, argues
that the biologistic preoccupation of such studies has long motivated social
scientists to consider any kind of behavior as merely a "social and cultural
overlay" upon the fundamental fact of physical descendancy. Accordingly, it
makes little sense within social scientific frameworks to speak of kinship as
a venue of willful participation.

Can a consideration of tribal sacred stories and social structures challenge
the dismissal of behavior as an element of tribal identity? As in the preceding discussion of essentialist ideas, I propose to look at a single story theme
that appears across many tribes and invite communities to consider its implications. All over North and South America, tribal traditions include a theme
of humans who marry animals, sometimes going to live in the animal village (Harrod 2000, Thompson 1929).

One illustrative story expressing such a theme is found among the Thompson
River (Ntlakyapamuk) Indians of British Columbia. In it, a hunter takes a
deer woman for a wife and goes to live with her people in their underground
village. He learns to follow their way of life, and the hunter and his new

relatives quickly take on their proper roles, each making an appropriate gift to the other: whenever the people become hungry, one of the deer people offers itself and the hunter kills it. Everyone eats, and the hunter performs the ritual that allows the dead deer to return to life. Thus there is a full circle of reciprocity: the deer people share their flesh, each in turn for the others, while the hunter shares his skill with weapons and his attentiveness to ceremonial requirements.

In this particular story, the hunter is fully and permanently transformed: "The hunter never returned to the people. He became a deer." But stories of animal-human marriages do not always work out this way. In many stories, even if the human spouse temporarily takes on animal form, he or she may be unable or unwilling to entirely adapt to the requirements of living with the new community. Ultimately there comes a moment in which people make a choice, by their behavior, about the community to which they truly belong. Many times they end up back with human relatives.

The children of human-animal unions may also have to decide their place, and again their actions determine the answer. Thus, in the Thompson River story, the hunter's son makes a choice that is the opposite of his father's. Although in his youth he is a deer, when he grows older he decides to return to his father's village and live as a human: "He became an Indian and a great hunter" (Thompson 1929: 173). Although this child's ancestry – partly human and partly deer – gives him a potential claim on two communities of relatives, he eventually chooses to bring the gift of hunting skills to the human village. Thus, it is with humans that he belongs, and it is a human that he finally becomes. The story theme about marriages that link human and non-human communities provides a provocative starting point for a discussion of kinship conceived as an act of *doing* as well as an act of *being*.

Traditional social structures in a number of tribes likewise suggest an explicit recognition that tribal belonging could manifest itself as a kind of behavior, a relationship that was proven over time. Thus, among the tribes of the Iroquois confederacy, a trial period was required of adoptees, during which the new relatives proved themselves. After a ritual of initiation, "captives embarked on a period of probation – it might end months or years later or never – during which new relatives and fellow villagers judged whether they had truly become Iroquois" (Richter 1992: 69). Ultimate acceptance was contingent on what adoptees did:

Captives became one people with the Iroquois by *acting* like Iroquois. . . . For some adoptees, especially potentially dangerous adult warriors, the behavioral test might entail such a dramatic act as participation in a raid against one's former people. For women and children, however, the requirements were more mundane: doing one's share of the work, fulfilling one's kinship obligations, marrying one's new relatives' choice of a spouse. Usually that was enough. . . . A newcomer could secure a permanent place in the family by adequately performing the duties of the person she replaced (72).

The historic social structures of various tribes reveal the opposite situation as well; if some behaviors earned individuals a place in the tribal circle, certain acts could place one outside it. Sorcery was such an offense in some tribes; so was the murder of another tribal member. But seemingly lesser failures of reciprocity might cause others at least to question one's place in the tribal society. Ella Deloria's work explaining the importance of generosity in traditional Lakota (Sioux) society provides an example. A significant part of tribal life, she writes, was to participate in reciprocal exchange: to share one's possessions and to accept help from others whenever necessary. Further, those who sought the accumulation of wealth were met with distrust. "A man who showed that tendency was suspect, as if he were not quite human. *Tak-tanin-sni* they said of him; meaning 'what kind of thing (he may be) is not plain'" (73). In other words, those who did not participate through reciprocal behavior in the kinship system could even bring into question their place in the classification of humans. Although the relatives of such an individual might still try to protect him, their task would not be easy. He did not act like a Lakota.

What might one learn about tribal identity by taking an emphasis on reciprocal behavior more seriously than social scientific studies of kinship have done? One limitation of any strictly biologistic model of kinship becomes clear when considering the extended nature of the reciprocating community typically presupposed in indigenous philosophies. That is, social scientific analyses have concerned themselves primarily with the relationships of *humans* to one another, presenting elaborate diagrams and analyses of kinship terminology and detailed discussions of the behaviors that individuals expect from different categories of relatives.

By contrast, in tribal philosophies, people take their place, or find their identity, within a kinship network that includes not only other humans, but also animals, plants, minerals, geographic features, the earth itself, celestial bodies, and spirit beings. They owe certain things to, and expect things from, all these entities. Acts of reciprocity in this extended community occur not solely – perhaps not even *primarily* – to benefit humans. As is richly illustrated in the story of the hunter who became a deer, reciprocity serves humans no better – and no worse – than any other member of the natural world. Humans are simply one set of participants in the vast cycles of giving and receiving, of covenant and celebration, that constitute kinship relations.

Indigenous perspectives on tribal belonging not only draw attention to more actors than conventional academic scholarship has recognized. They also reveal a different way to think about the behaviors by which humans establish and maintain kinship relations. Especially in the case of nonhuman relatives, these activities likely include ritual action.

Twentieth-century literature in the social scientific study of ritual activity – work by such disciplinary founders as Malinowski, Radcliffe-Brown, Homans, Parsons, Kluckohn, Geertz, and others – centrally concerns itself with the *functions* of ritual, particularly its role in channeling anxiety. A central claim is that humans resort to ritual where rational contemplation and utilitarian technological intervention fail to produce a certain outcome – as in the hunting of game animals that may not show themselves. Ritual, as Bronislaw Malinowski writes, "is . . . generally to be found whenever man comes to an unbridgeable gap . . . in his knowledge or in his powers of practical control, and yet has to continue in his pursuit" (1979: 43).

The foregoing construction of the ritual reciprocation characterizing the relationships between human and nonhuman kin differs substantially from understandings that are more likely to emerge from tribal philosophies. Relationships with nonhuman kin are often characterized, in indigenous philosophies, by awe and respect, as well as by emotions much more positive than the social scientific concentration on anxiety suggests. In particular, many indigenous people speak of ritual reciprocation as a means of enjoying and expressing loving communion. Thus Herbert John Benally, writing from within Navajo philosophy, refers to "establishing an intimate relationship with nature" (1994: 28). Elsewhere, the same author characterizes this relationship as thanksgiving: "gratitude is directed to the water, the trees, the plants and animals that nourish and shelter, and especially to the creators, that their blessings would never diminish" (1998: 244).

Julio Valladolid and Frédérique Apffel-Marglin (2001) likewise describe the understanding, among the Andean indigenous people, of ritual as a means of establishing profound emotional relationships. In preparing the fields for planting, the Aymara of Conima, Peru offer coca leaves and deep reverence: "'Pachamamma, Holy Earth, please pardon us, please excuse us. . . . Thus saying, we kiss her on our knees'" (656). The relationship continues as new life emerges and matures:

> The plants . . . that [the Andean indigenous people] nurture with dedication and love are members of their families. When the small shoots emerge in the *chacra* [small field], they are their children; when they flower, they are companions with whom they dance and to whom they sing; and when they give fruit at the time of harvest, they are their mothers. Andean peasant agriculture is this nurturance, full of feelings as for their own family (660).

The sentiments described here can only be spoken of as love. They suggest the possibility of ritual relationships as a vehicle enabling people to experience the sheer joy of connectedness, the pleasure that comes from making and having relatives, the satisfaction of acting like a relative oneself. It is a perspective that makes the social scientific reduction of ritual behavior to a means for channeling anxiety feel considerably less satisfying – or at least less complete.

The foregoing observations about the importance for tribal identity of a responsibility to reciprocity, and the distinctive ways that this idea may be developed within indigenous philosophies, add another dimension to our understanding of what I am calling a definition of tribal identity founded in kinship. They show us that even strongly essentialist definitions of identity do not necessarily reduce to determinations of one's fundamentally-given nature: the ideas about tribal belonging just suggested imply that one must not only *be* a relative (in a genealogical sense), but that one must also *act* like one.

Radical Indigenism, Tribal Identity, and Tradition

The definition of identity that I have explored sets some conditions for the compassionate incorporation, into tribal communities, of Indian persons whom other definitions can exclude. At the same time, being grounded in the value of reciprocity, it provides for protection of Indian communities from the abuse that can result from loosened boundaries, particularly the behavior of would-be "free riders" who attempt to exploit the privileges and resources associated with tribal membership without contributing anything to the community

(See further Garroutte 2003). This is true because the themes of the sacred stories provide models of community life in which all members are held to a rigorous standard of responsible participation. The definition I have explored may let Indian people be more gentle with one another than we are now in discussions about tribal belonging.

Nevertheless, the particular ideas about tribal identity that I have proposed are less important than the larger perspective upon which I drew to generate them. The process I have attempted might be labeled a tentative exploration of the meaning and promise of the theoretical approach that I have called Radical Indigenism. This exploration responds to a common principle of traditional tribal philosophies by orienting itself to an expressly practical goal. It tries to assist tribal communities in conversations about identity, inviting them to their own work of creating new definitions by displaying themes about tribal belonging found in particular contexts. At the same time, it reflects another common principle of tribal philosophies by refusing to separate practical pursuits from spiritual ones. It is expressly oriented towards Original Instructions, and it looks to elders, sacred stories, and traditional practices in the attempt to uncover these. It draws upon these sources – ones that the academy has neglected or used in a different way – to generate ideas about a question that is important to Indian peoples today. It proposes a place in the conversations for those who live and move in Indian communities, in scholarly communities, or in both.

Of course I anticipate an urgent protest from my academic colleagues. The foregoing discussions urge recovery of "traditional" ideas about tribal belonging – an endeavor that will generate little scholarly enthusiasm. Salman Rushdie echoes a common sentiment when he asserts: "it is completely fallacious to suppose that there is such a thing as a pure, unalloyed tradition from which to draw. The only people who believe this are religious extremists" (1991: 67). Other scholars will certainly ask me what I can possibly mean by "tradition" – a word so slippery that most scholars have abandoned it. Happily, the answer elucidates the central premise of Radical Indigenism.

I am pleased to agree that "tradition" does not equate to some petrified pattern of life – to what The People have unchangingly done. American Indian communities have found such varied solutions to the problems of survival that individuals living in different historic periods might have difficulty even recognizing their ancestors. Even in relatively recent times, Indian people have continued to adapt and change, and their practices in relation to kinship are no exception. Neither does "tradition," by my understanding, equate to ancient practice: to whatever The People did, at the most distant historical moment of which we have knowledge. Certainly, Indian people must take seriously our ancestors' struggles and solutions. But that does not mean that we enshrine a single moment as the enduring touchstone. As an old family friend, a Navajo ceremonialist, once said to me, "not *everything* people did a long time ago was 'traditional.'"

What then *is* tradition? Joyce Johnson, a Cherokee great-grandmother, makes a significant distinction:

> Nowadays we [Indian people] have "culture" and we have "tradition," and they can be separate. . . . Culture has to do with outward things that let other people see that you are Indian: what we eat, what we wear, the things we make. Those can be *part* of our teachings from the past; some parts of culture come from spiritual teachings. But some things that have become a part of culture might even be bad.

By contrast, she says,

> tradition is what is passed on orally, and it tells you the way you are *supposed* to be. It has to give us *good*. It has to give us *growth*. It is the lessons that were taught us by the ancient ones and the elders to help [each of] us be a better person, and closer to the Creator. And we have to use it in the way it is intended. . . . It's spiritual.

My approach to defining "tradition" is consistent with the goal of Radical Indigenism to respect the tenets of indigenous philosophies of knowledge; this approach accepts that tradition is fundamentally a *sacred* concept. As such, it is inextricably bound up with the idea of Original Instructions: the spiritual teachings that describe the way that The People must live. It designates the modes of thinking and acting that correspond to the fundamental principles of those teachings.

This definition of tradition has several implications. One is that we should not expect that our ancestors always chose to live in the light of their sacred teachings (any more than we do). Nevertheless, time cannot transform behavior into tradition if it departs from those teachings. Another implication is that many different ways of organizing tribal life may be equally traditional – though, to the extent that our ancestors responded to their Original Instructions, we may expect to find certain threads of continuity reflecting similar principles. We can expect that what Mohawk professor of political science Gerald Alfred writes, in his study of political life among the Kahnawake Mohawks of Quebec, is generalizable beyond that sphere:

> There is no simple answer to the question: "Do ideologies/peoples/ nations/cultures change or not?" They of course change – and they do not. . . . In Native cultures at least there exists a stable core which forms the basis of the political culture and nationalist ideology. There are also peripheral elements within the culture which are malleable and which do shift and transform, rise and fall in importance and relevance according to shifts in the political context and according to the exigencies of the general political and economic climate (1995: 188).

A third implication of the foregoing definition of "tradition" is that claims about it are ultimately validated through processes of inquiry that include a spiritual dimension, including such activities as dancing, singing, praying, dreaming, joining in ritual, and interacting with the natural world. Tradition, by my understanding, was first received in these ways, and indigenous philosophies allow for knowledge to continue to be so received. This means that, when communities seek knowledge in the context of their traditional philosophies, there is another place to look, in addition to those I have discussed. Tribal communities can validate what they learn from elders, stories, and their own histories by comparing their conclusions to what they learn through individual and collective ceremonial participation.

My definition of tradition is, of course, completely indefensible from the perspective of the social sciences, or for that matter, any other science. The same is true for its implications. This is precisely the point of the theoretical perspective that I call Radical Indigenism. Radical Indigenism respects the definitions and assumptions that characterize the philosophies of knowledge carried by tribal peoples. The rules of conventional academic inquiry relegate the types of explorations I describe here to the realm of faith and belief, rather than the realm of scholarship and knowledge. But there is a heavy price for following these rules. By excluding information derived from inquiries that include (or are infused by) spiritual elements, the academy also will never *really* encounter Indian people. Certainly it will not encounter them as equal participants in a common enterprise. It is simply not possible to split off or ignore the spiritual aspects of tribal philosophies and make any sense of them or the people who carry them. Radical Indigenism is an intellectual perspective that embraces this academically inconvenient truth.

American Indian Communities and Radical Indigenism

There is a great deal that the academy might learn – not just *about* but also *from* American Indian peoples. Native communities have great traditions of knowledge that have not been appreciated or respected and Radical Indigenism insists that this situation change. But it is not only the academy that could benefit from the development of Racial Indigenism; modern Indian communities also have an investment in the creation of distinctively American Indian forms of scholarship. As Mohawk scholar Gerald Alfred (1999) has argued, part of the process of making American Indian communities whole and fully functional again is to recreate our institutions, including the institutions of scholarship and learning.

In addition, Radical Indigenism allows Indian people to settle their claims on the academy, and even the larger society, upon a different foundation. For many years Indian people and their allies have asked universities to invest in the study and teaching of Indian languages, to recognize their histories and cultures, to divest themselves of stock holdings in corporations that are destroying the ecology of Indian homelands, to refuse funding for scientific research projects that entail the desecration of tribal sacred sites, and so on. Indian people have had very limited success in pressing such agendas because, to date, they have been unable to frame them as anything but *political* goals. They are subsequently relegated to the wish list dedicated to all the other campus "special interest" groups – the disabled, gays, bisexuals, foreign students, women faculty, Italian American students, college Republicans, and so on. The minimal resources universities dedicate to claimants on this list are divided among them all.

But from the perspective of Radical Indigenism, arguments that universities must protect American Indian land, languages, history, and cultures are not political claims at all, nor even religious or legal ones; they are *epistemological* claims. Radical Indigenism supports the assumption enshrined in tribal philosophies throughout the Americas: that relationships with all these things are rich sources of knowledge. Thus when scholars pursuing Radical Indigenism ask universities to protect sacred lands and our ability to be in relationship with them, when we ask them to support the teaching of our history, when we ask them to invest in the protection of our languages and cultures, we will be asking them to protect *the conditions under which we carry out our scholarship*. We ask for these things for the same reason that scholars ask for laboratory equipment, or books, or the protection of tenure: because they are the wellspring of what scholars working within the perspective of Radical Indigenism can *know* and *discover* through the means laid out in traditional philosophies of knowledge and of inquiry. Radical Indigenism offers Indian people a means to help the academy understand what we need in order to pursue a new, and distinctively American Indian, kind of scholarship.

Radical Indigenism and the Academy

To accept Radical Indigenism will require the academy to make itself open to entirely new models of inquiry. I have argued that explorations within this perspective can properly be based upon the teachings of tribal elders, upon sacred stories, and upon knowledge of the ways that healthy Native communities functioned historically. In so doing, I hope that I have offered some suggestions that tribal communities might investigate further. But Radical Indigenism will ask the academy to accept a great deal more than this.

A fully developed Radical Indigenism presupposes that Indian peoples possess complete philosophies of knowledge that include not only the sources just named, but also knowledge that is received through ceremonial means: through dreams; through communication with the non-human relatives that inhabit the universe; through the collective, ritual seeking of spiritually faithful communities; and through interactions with land and language for which the conventionally-defined academic disciplines have no names and no place. It will likely ask the academy to allow for different constructions of the "observable," of the relationship between mind and body, of the nature and powers of language, of the meaning and utility of "subjective" knowledge and of unique (nonrepeatable) events – and much more. It will require, in other words, not discarding or replacing fundamental tenets of scientific models of inquiry, but a willingness to allow other, very different models to stand alongside them. These models of inquiry posit a very different order in the world than the one that academic disciplines generally assume, but a world that is nevertheless not *dis*orderly. Radical Indigenism will ask the academy to allow scholars to demonstrate that the diverse philosophies of knowledge carried by many different tribal peoples can be the basis for genuine, worthwhile scholarship.

These are truly monumental requests. It is therefore appropriate to consider *why* the academy should be motivated to expand its boundaries in such a way as to include Radical Indigenism under the rubric of scholarship. The most compelling reason is that, by accepting indigenous perspectives on knowledge, conventional scholars might discover things that they presently do not know, and have no means to know, because of the limitations of the intellectual frameworks within which they operate. American Indian (and other indigenous) philosophies present whole new ways of thinking about the world and the relationships within it. And new frameworks do not come along very often. Karl Marx gave the social sciences one such framework. Sigmund Freud provided another. The academy never saw the world in the same way again after the work of these scholars. This is the reason that even those who do not think they were *right* still think they were *brilliant*. I submit that Radical Indigenism, properly pursued, has the potential to elucidate ways of thinking that would reorder our understanding of the world and everything in it even more substantially than these two modern "Western" thinkers did.

Conclusion

If Radical Indigenism is to advance, and if it is to avoid exploiting Indian communities, it will require the participation of scholars who find ways to embed themselves in those communities as contributing members, who can look to traditional knowledge from a position of personal commitment, who can profoundly encounter the sacred stories and songs in the language that generated them, who contribute to conversations that the communities themselves understand to be important, and who make themselves answerable to the rules of conduct and inquiry that govern those communities. If the academy is willing to make a safe place for such people and the perspectives they carry, it will have to broaden conventional assumptions about what it means to do scholarship. The perspective of Radical Indigenism suggests a means by which such a process might begin, and by which it might inform conversations about American Indian identity, or anything else. Some American Indian (and non-Indian) scholars have already begun to enter into the ceremonial ways of knowing that belong to indigenous peoples, and to write and think about the implications of spiritual practice for their scholarship. I have discussed some of this work in my book *Real Indians,* and I believe that more will follow. It falls to the academy to make itself ready to hear the voices of these emerging scholars.

Power

R. Danielle Egan

Eyeing the Scene: The Uses and (RE)uses of Surveillance Cameras in an Exotic Dance Club*

Introduction

Exotic dance is a form of sex work where women sell erotic fantasy for money.[1] Exotic dance emerged from burlesque theater and involved strip-tease, wherein dancers teased audiences with fans or feathers, very rarely showing their fully nude bodies (Cooper 1929; Aldridge 1971). With the dissolution of Burlesque theaters, exotic dance went through a transition moving from small bars and carnival tents to urban clubs which were devoted to exotic dance (Boles and Garbin 1974). With the emergence of video-graphic pornography, which allowed men to view sex acts with ease in the privacy of their own home, and with the formation of adult material on the inter-net, exotic dance was transformed – in order to keep its customer base and maintain profit (Williams 1999; Liepe-Levinson 2002). In its present state, exotic dance involves more physical contact between dancer and customer (i.e., lap dances) and has shifted its clientele

* An earlier version of this essay appeared in *Critical Sociology*, vol. 30, no. 2 (2004).
[1] My research specifically deals with female exotic dancers – women who take off their clothes and perform lap dances (which involve sitting on a male customer's lap either topless or fully nude and erotically grinding on their laps for the length of a song) for male customers for monetary compensation. As more women perform this type of labor than men and have far less access to other forms of labor (particularly working class women) that are as lucrative I view exotic dance as a site of "women's work." For more information on male exotic dancers see Liepe-Levinson 2002.

with the formation of expensive "four star" gentlemen's clubs that serve expensive dinners and cater to businessmen (Frank 1998). As a result of these shifts the emotional labor of the exotic dancer has also increased (Barton 2002; Frank 1998; Ronai-Rambo 1993). Moreover, the gentrification of many former urban zones where sex work flourished led to the rise of exotic dance clubs in suburban settings. These range from "four-star" gentlemen's clubs to "neighborhood" bars that most often cater to locals and have far fewer women employees.

The primary question that guides this chapter is: how does the space in which exotic dance takes place shape the experiences of it for exotic dancers and regular customers?[2] Moreover, how do modes of social control, particularly work rules and surveillance technologies, employed in these spaces affect the labor and consumption of exotic dance? Lastly, I question the ways in which power and resistance are used by dancers in a space that is saturated with social control mechanisms. In order to illuminate issues of space, social control and surveillance I focus on "Flame," a club in the New England area where I conducted ethnographic research[3] as a dancer/researcher for 18 months.[4] I map the ways in which surveillance and social control operated in the club, what the owner's intentions were with respect to this social control, and how this generated both docility and resistance in dancers within the walls of Flame.

There has been an explosion of academic interest in exotic dance (Rambo-Ronai 1992; Rambo-Ronai 1993; Forsyth & Deshotels 1997; Erikson and

---

[2] Regular customers are men who come to a particular dance club repeatedly to see the same dancer and often develop strong emotional bonds with her. Occasional customers are men who frequent exotic dance clubs for "special occasions" such as bachelor parties or birthday parties or when they visit a particular place known for its sex work but have no recurring relationship with the club or the dancers.

[3] This article emerges from a much larger ethnographic account of two clubs in the New England area. Between 1997–1999 I conducted research in two clubs – Glitters, an urban club where I was a full observer, and Flame, a suburban club where I was a full participant. My research centered on the intersubjective relationships between dancers and their regular customers to explore how desire, fantasy and power as well as space, subjectivity and feminism operate in these interactions. The data in this article come from extensive field notes, informal and formal interviews and personal experience. Flame is a middle-range club, meaning that it is in between a four star club and a 'dive club' and it primarily services middle to upper-middle class white men. Moreover, most dancers in the club were predominantly white.

[4] Flame is a pseudonym used to protect the identities of the people used in the club in which I both danced and did my research. For more on my research on Flame, please see Egan 2000, Egan 2003.

Tewksbury 2000; Liepe-Levinson 2002; Brucket 2002; Brewster 2003; Murphy 2003); mainly focusing on exotic dancers themselves and on the cursory customer (For an exception see Frank 2002). For example, Carol Rambo-Ronai (1992) explores the performance of feigned authenticity as part of the emotional labor performed by exotic dancers and the challenges this produces for the dancer. Craig Forsyth and Tina Deshotels (1997) examine the ways in which women give meaning to their work and the symbolic interactions with customers that form dancers' experiences of their work. Katherine Liepe-Levinson (2002) investigates the performance of self of male and female exotic dancers, the ways in which these performances are subject to the objectifying gaze of the customer, and how dancers resist these gazes. She finds that exotic dance is not simply a site of exploitation of women and men, but is a site of agency and resistance. The importance of understanding the labor of women who work as exotic dancers is crucial to a further enumeration of women's work and emotional labor in multiple settings. However, the topic of spatiality and surveillance and how this functions to shape both dancers' and regular customers' experiences within an exotic dance club has yet to be addressed in a systematic fashion.[5]

Issues of spatiality and the surveillance technologies that mark the spaces of exotic dance clubs are essential to the understanding of exotic dance. These mechanisms create forms of power such as the regulation and control of dancers in the club by the owners and management – which in turn affect both dancers and customers within this space. According to Lisa Law (2001), "[t]he spaces through which bodies move are far from innocent; they are landscapes of power that also mould and police subjectivity" (2001: 24). Thus the space in which the gendered labor and the gendered consumption of exotic dance takes place is not neutral. The space of the club is a place where both power and resistance operate on a continual basis, and as such the space of the club is a site of contestation (Pile 1996, 1997).

Foucault (1980) theorizes power as both productive and repressive in its mechanisms. Power can coalesce in certain ways to produce exploitative or repressive regimes; however, it is this same productive function that produces resistance to forms of exploitation (Foucault 1980). Thus, power produces the

---

[5] For current research on exotic dance see Ronai-Rambo 1992, 1993; Law 2000; Liepe-Levinson 2002.

social order and produces its own resistance (Foucault 1980). There are no social interactions that can take place outside of power. Foucault's theory of power shifts previous frameworks of power from dialectics to iteration. It is iterative because power can only garner its position through repetition. Power relations depend "on a multiplicity of points of resistance: these play the role of adversary, target, support or handle in power relations. These points of resistance are present everywhere in the power network" (Foucault 1977: 95). By incorporating a Foucauldian framework I explore how the space of the club and the subjectivities found therein are intertwined in a network of power and resistance. Dancers and regulars are subject to restrictive mechanisms set forth by the owner and managers of the club, and they also subvert these mechanisms through strategies of resistance. As such, space and the influence of spatiality for understanding mechanisms of the social and subjectivity are crucial.

Exotic dance differs from other forms of gendered labor (i.e., waitressing or nursing) due to the informal economic sphere in which it takes place. In exotic dance clubs official records (i.e., tax forms) of workers are rarely, if ever, kept; women work as independent contractors and are often unaware of their rights as laborers (Liepe-Levinson 2002).[6] The ways in which social control and space function in exotic dance clubs differ from their operation in more formal economic sites (e.g., hospitals, restaurants), making exotic dance more like other informal gendered labor such as brothel based prostitution or domestic labor.[7]

Lisa Law (2001), in her discussion of prostitution in Asia, argues that prostitutes "are surveyed, regulated and controlled – usually but not exclusively through the machinery and technologies of the state – and this exertion of power creates much knowledge about a pathologized subject ('prostitution')"

---

[6] Most exotic dance clubs function in a similar manner. In the United States there is only one club that has successfully unionized, The Lusty Lady in San Francisco.

[7] Exotic dance as a cultural practice is often subject to moralizing discourses from communities and churches under the rubric of secondary harmful effects. These often poorly researched arguments claim that exotic dance clubs lead to community degradation by attracting other illegal elements such as drugs and violence as well as associating exotic dancers and prostitutes (Frank 2002). These claims have led to strict zoning laws in several cities and towns across the United States, which aim to stop the growth of exotic dance clubs. However, the popularity of exotic dance has not declined and since 1987 the number of exotic dance clubs in the United States has doubled.

(2001: 24). Hausbeck and Brent (2001) discuss the ways in which prostitutes in Nevada brothels are subject to continual surveillance by both brothel owners and the state. When prostitutes go to work in a brothel they are required to stay "in house" for approximately 21 days at a time, during which they are permitted little, if any, movement off the premises. When prostitutes leave they are forced by the state to obtain health exams in order to obtain a state health card clearing them of any diseases (Hausbeck and Brent 2001). Although exotic dance is not prostitution in terms of its function (exotic dancers do not have sexual intercourse for money) or legal status (at least in the United States – with the exception of Nevada), both types of work are considered deviant on account of their sexual nature. Moreover, both are subject to high levels of surveillance in the work place.[8] However, prostitution is subject to surveillance by the state whereas state intervention in exotic dance is far less pervasive.

Surveillance in the exotic dance club is carried out by the owners and management. Owners seek to form an atmosphere that protects their interests by creating a space in which dancers feel the need to watch themselves, and in which they succumb to the social control of the owner.

Surveillance and the Space of the Club

Imagine a room flooded with black/red light as semi-nude women dance on stage while the music blares and the deejay urges men to "take their special lady" to the back/lap dance room for the "ride of their lives." See men, with hands in their pockets some fishing for money, some watching with no intention of paying, and some reaching for something else. Mirrors cover the walls where dancers watch themselves, being watched and watching back – hoping the gaze leads to something more lucrative later. Fantasy, desire and power saturate this space as fantasy objects twirl on poles and laps bringing customers to satisfaction that always fades. Far above the mirrors surveillance cameras scan the room, observing, surveying and classifying – classifying productivity, behavior and the following and breaking of the "rules" that seem to change on a weekly basis. Unlike the human gazes that circulate in this space, the gaze of the camera seems more encompassing . . . taking in different angles,

---

[8] For more on surveillance and prostitution see Hausebeck and Brent 2001; O'Connell 1998 and Kempadoo and Doezema 1998.

shooting all the rooms at the same time and transmitting these videographic images to small screens which are monitored by owners and managers. As we make our schedules or get a "talking to" in the office . . . these glowing green televisual images remind us that we are being watched. The message being sent is reminiscent of a 1980's song, which proclaimed, "Every breath you take. Every step you take. Every move you make . . . I'll be watching you."[9]

The geography of exotic dance clubs has significant impacts on the ways dancers come to understand their work. Through the physical layout of a club (i.e., stage placement, chair and table arrangement, and semi-private rooms such as lap dance rooms) and the social structuring practices of space, owners construct a club atmosphere for dancers and customers (Pile 1996, Kirby 1996). In doing so, owners also attempt to create particular kinds of experience. The facet of space that serves as the focus of this article is the ways in which owners use surveillance cameras and rules to enforce social control over dancers and how dancers are subject to and subvert this form of social control. My investigation of the surveillance mechanisms at Flame traces the ways in which surveillance maps/situates/coordinates the experiences of "exotic dance" within a particular club. In addition, I examine how surveillance technologies function to organize this space, operating as a form of social control by the owner and management, in order to create more productive and docile workers. Moreover, I map how dancers resist the ways in which the owner of Flame constructed the spaces of the club.[10] Vision, or the use of the gaze, has been a frequent topic of examination on exotic dance; however, "looking" has usually referred to the ways customers gaze at dancers (Ronai-Rambo 1992; Liepe-Levinson 2002). Watching dancers' every step, breath and move was a strategy often couched in terms of "protection" by owners and managers. While at times surveillance can operate as a form of protection when customers get out of hand, most often surveillance cameras serve as a strategy of social control for owners and managers over dancers in clubs.

---

[9] All italicized portions of this article are excerpts from field notes and research memos during my field work at Flame.
[10] All names in this text are pseudonyms to protect the identities of the people with whom I conducted my research.

The Oscillating Eye of the Camera

Protection, Profit and Possession/Policing

On stage I round the pole, sliding down to the floor to make my way over to a cus-
tomer . . . as I strut over to the dollar waving, I see the camera rotating in the cor-
ner. Focusing its gaze throughout the club – the eye of the owner takes in the scene.
My body captured on a digital feedback loop flickers in black and white in his office.
I always heard that it was the men at the stage that sought to objectify us, but I
think it is the man in the office, who seeks to make us the objects of his profit, who
is far more dangerous. As I do my dance for a dollar I look up and wink at the cam-
era – all the while worrying more about the manager's classifications of my behav-
ior than the fleshy customer in front of me.

Michel Foucault (1977), in *Discipline and Punish*, states that the panopticon
was designed to be a "marvelous machine, which, whatever use one may
wish to put it to, produces homogenous effects of power" (1977: 202). The
panopticon functions as a mechanism of hyper-visibility, making those under
its gaze continuously visible. Panoptic surveillance diffuses the locus of super-
vision from the individual who can not be everywhere at once to a roaming
gaze that can capture subjects and analyze their movements in multiple places
at once. Providing a means to document, analyze and control the movements
of those under its watchful eye – the panopticon produces a far more effective mode of social control.

Cameras are placed in a circular fashion around the main room of Flame.
At every corner rotating surveillance cameras are mounted on the walls.
In this way, the cameras are organized like the seating plan on the main
floor – they see from every direction and can hone in on the center of the
room where the stage is located. Moreover, the cameras can pan out to the
dancers performing table dances in the rest of the room.[11] Surveillance cameras are mounted in a similar fashion in both the lap dance room and the
champagne room on the lower level of the club. There were several instances
during my time at Flame when a dancer in the lap dance room was "breaking the rules" (e.g., letting a customer touch her breasts) and another dancer

---

[11] A table dance involves dancers going to a customer's table and performing a
mini-lap dance for $2.00 per dance (lasting approximately a minute) in the hopes of
getting customers to pay for longer lap dances.

would get her attention, by pointing to the camera, so the dancer would immediately stop what she was doing. In this way the cameras served not only as a way for the manager's and owner's gaze to be everywhere at once, but also functioned as reminders for dancers to police each other's actions.

In exotic dance clubs, social control is actualized in three distinct ways: owner and manager surveillance, self surveillance and peer surveillance. This hyper-visibility allows the owner's and the manager's gaze to be almost everywhere in a non-physical form and allows the owners and managers to watch without ever being seen. In this way, surveillance reinforces managerial authority, which becomes saturated throughout the club through the owner's or manager's ability to call dancers back to the office to show them their transgressions. This form of surveillance is successful precisely because of its lack of physical presence; dancers start to watch themselves because they never know when the camera is watching. It is the oscillation of the gaze – in this sense, the lack of coordinates or its omniscience – that imposes the authority of the owner and management over the dancers who never know when the camera is focusing on them and thus fear that the eye is always on them.

The owner of the club stated that the use of cameras was for the protection of dancers, that is, to keep dancers safe from unruly customers and help him see a problem before it gets out of control. However, in reality, surveillance systems were used as a way to protect investment, in both the legal and economic sense, at Flame. Surveillance often served to keep dancers "in line," stopping them from either "going too far with a customer" (i.e., performing fellatio, hand jobs, or allowing customers to touch their breasts and/or vaginas) or from "cheating the club" (i.e., not paying the club a 15% portion of each lap dance performed, or sitting with a customer who was not paying). Therefore, while the gaze of the customer focused on dancers on stage or in closer contact, the management's panoptic gaze surveyed the space. This surveillance enforced a form of social control that, when breached, resulted in fines or firings of dancers and expulsion from the club for customers. It was never clear exactly when the cameras were on and observing; however, the camera's presence produced a mode of self-discipline in dancers. According to Foucault the panopticon produces an individual

> who is subjected to a field of visibility and knows it, assumes responsibility for the constraints of power; he makes them play spontaneously upon himself [sic]; he inscribes in himself the power relation in which he simul-

taneously plays both roles; he becomes the principle of his own subjection. By this very fact, the external power may throw off its physical weight; it tends to the non-corporal; and, the more it approaches this limit, the more constant, profound and permanent its effects: it is a perpetual victory that avoids any physical confrontation and which is always decided in advance (1977: 202).

Uninscribed Rules

During my first few shifts I met Jacquelyn, a thin woman with long black hair and a dancer of many years. She took me aside and informed me about the rules of the game. "Trust no one." "Never leave your money anywhere." "Never stop working the room." "They are always watching." Confused, I asked, "Who is watching, the customers?" I had not really paid attention to the ceilings and had not spent much time in the manager's office. Exasperated with my ignorance, Jacquelyn replied, "The owners and bouncers! They are always watching and they will fire your ass if you don't follow the rules." The rules of the house were still unclear to me because the owners never posted them and so each time I went to work I asked dancers to tell me about the rules. So far I knew that the customers were not allowed to feel your vagina or lick you, and that you would be fired if you poked a hole in the leather couches with your high heels in the lap dance room. Understanding the rules in their entirety seemed particularly crucial now that Jacquelyn informed me that the elec-tronic gaze of the owners was watching and that I could be expelled from the club if any of them were broken. "So what are they looking for?" I asked, "What shouldn't I do?" "Well," she replied, "the rules are always changing, but don't do drugs here, don't do anything that you're not supposed to in the back room. A girl got fired for giving a blowjob back there. And don't agree to see customers outside the club or it can be considered solicitation." I looked around noticing the cameras and the bouncers everywhere and looked back at Jacquelyn and said, "Thanks." "No problem," she replied as she got up and continued to "work the room for customers."

After this interaction, I began to notice how pervasive the cameras were and how, when I went into the office, the televisions with surveillance footage served as a reminder of the management's gaze permeating our workspace. Moreover, because the rules of the house were unwritten, and thus always changing, watching my own actions in the club became paramount. For exam-ple, during my first few months at the club any type of music could be played by dancers when they were on stage; however, one Friday night I received a warning for playing rap music and was told that I would be fined if I did it again.[12] Additionally, the rules regarding the amount dancers had to pay the club to work,[13] the number of mandatory work days[14] and the percentage dancers had to pay the club owners for lap dances shifted several times during my research. Dancers came to understand the rules from other dancers or by violating them, which usually resulted in being "talked to by management" or fined.

One dancer, Marie, spoke about the cameras in this way,

> You always see them [the cameras] on and most of the time I think twice before doing something I shouldn't, but it pisses me off. I feel like we are treated like children. I know they are there to protect us, but I feel like they are mostly there to keep us in line.

Marie points to the contradictions of the surveillance that circulates through the club and articulates the effectivity of the social control employed by the owner of Flame. The ever present gaze of the cameras serves to make Marie survey herself and monitor her own actions lest she be caught by the feedback loop which sends her image into the manager's office. Trena discussed a similar type of self surveillance:

> Sometimes I feel like I am a fucking rat in a cage here with these damn cameras. I feel so self-conscious. I don't know, I think Vincent [the owner] gets off on watching us. God knows he's too fucking ugly to get anyone himself.

Trena's feelings of being a "fucking rat in a cage" and feeling "self-conscious" point towards the entrapment women feel working in the club. Taking her sense of freedom, these cameras employ a form of specifically male surveillance reminiscent of sweatshop labor when women performed with the shift

---

[12] The owner, in an attempt to make Flame a "more classy" club, decided that the use of songs which had profanity were offensive and thus less appealing for the customers. However, this shift in rules did not last long, as dancers continually broke it. The owner eventually decided that we could use any music we wanted.

[13] Exotic dancers at the club in which I conducted my research, as well as many clubs across the country, have to pay the club when they make a work schedule and have to pay the club each night when they come into work. When I started my research there was no scheduling fee; however, this changed during my time in the club, as did the amount paid per shift (from $7.00 to $10.00).

[14] A mandatory work day is a shift that all dancers must fulfill at least once a month. This day usually falls on a Sunday which is the slowest, and thus least popular day to work.

boss continuously looking over their shoulders. This form of surveillance creates self-policing in women who, in internalizing the "eye of the boss," begin to watch their own actions and mold their behavior to the rules set out by the boss and his omnipresent focus on their bodies. This form of docility gets reaffirmed when the cameras capture a transgression on tape and dancers see the consequences of getting out of line.

Intervention

During my third month on the job Maggie and I were sitting having a drink. It had been a good night so far, and we were taking a rest. After ordering our second, a bouncer approached Maggie and asked her to come to the office. A nervous commotion erupted in my stomach as she left. The authority in the club, when it made itself present, was powerful. After watching the door for about five minutes, I saw Maggie emerge. She was visibly angry. She sat down and called for the cocktail waitress to bring her another drink, at which point she said "fucking cameras." I asked her what was wrong. She said, "I just got fined $50 because I told Bruce I had done two dances, when I actually did four." I realized then that I had to take the cameras even more seriously than before.

Surveillance reinstantiates authority and reminds dancers that they are being watched. The gaze of the owner and management secures its presence by its variability: a dancer can never be sure if the cameras are on or if her actions are being watched. If the camera cannot be everywhere at once, its presence continuously makes her suspect its focus and therefore compels her to assume that it is always watching. Social control is effective because of its simultaneous presence and absence. For example, if a police car is parked on the freeway, many drivers will slow down – we assume that there is an officer in the car and that he or she is tracking our speed, taking down our license plate number and will pursue and ticket any transgressions. Whether or not an actual police officer is in the car is irrelevant. Why? Because it is the presence of the car that makes us slow down, and the visibility of the actual corporeal police body is irrelevant. It is the symbol that functions as the authority and not the actual person (Bogart 1996).

Like the police car, the cameras in the club stand in as symbols or simulations of the actual owner or manager's presence. Simulation replaces "actual" events or objects with their virtual electronic signs and image counterparts (Bogart 1996). According to Baudrillard (1993), simulation is different from a lie or fiction, because it not only presents an absence as presence, the representation as the real, but also undermines the contrasts with the real through its absorption of the real. As such, through simulation the camera comes to serve as the owner or manager, and in this sense embodies his existence. In effect the camera becomes more real than the reality of the owner himself. It is for this reason that surveillance operates so effectively in Flame. The cameras could be off or malfunctioning and the effect would be the same. Similarly, anyone could occupy the seat of the surveyor, watching and recording the scene of the club, and the surveillance in the club would function in the same way. The presence of the management is not essential. The cameras do the work for them. It is the random quality of the presence or absence of fleshy bodies that makes surveillance technology such an effective form of social control.[15]

This is not to say that surveillance could function seamlessly without the presence of the owner or manager, but it is to say that actual punishment only needed to be given out sporadically to make it known to dancers that they were being watched. Therefore, for surveillance to function effectively it needs to be omnipresent and there has to be occasional punishment. The fact that Maggie got caught served to create a form of docility or passivity in her and other dancers, making them watch their own actions. Once someone gets caught, the presence of authority makes itself known and authority reinstates itself through the use of its technological eye. To this extent, the cameras simulate the owner, replacing his real body.

The simulation of the owner's gaze, in the omnipresent eye of the camera, is a field of power that dancers must negotiate, and it serves to mark their bodies in significant ways. Pacification, docility, command and control are the main objectives for this type of surveillance (Foucault 1977). In imposing this form of control owners are able to enforce both their position of power and secure the highest level of productivity and profit within a club. Accord-

---

[15] Although it has been argued that we are all involved in surveillance as both surveyors (take for instance the show *Cops* where we watch the police apprehend suspects) and the surveyed, it is important to note that some people are under surveillance much more than others. Similarly some have much more access to simulated surveillance technologies than others. As such the gendered component of who is surveying and who is being surveyed must not be forgotten in this scene. Surveillance is never neutral in its function or practice. Williams (1993), for example, theorizes that poor women and women of color have not had the privilege, historically, of a private life and many have faced the continuous scrutiny of classist, sexist and racist governmental polices.

ingly, owners insure that their profit-oriented financial interests are looked after and dancers become like factory workers, losing even more control over their own labor practices than in the past.[16] Nonetheless, to assume that this form of surveillance is totalizing or seamless in its reproduction would be short sighted.

Social control needs continual reenactment or repetition in order to be successful (Butler 1990, Foucault 1980). It is precisely the need for power to continually reassert itself in a reiterative fashion that enables forms of resistance to social control. As stated earlier, resistance, according to Foucault, "depends on a multiplicity of points of resistance; these play the role of adversary, target, support or handle in power relations. These points of resistance are present everywhere in the power network" (1977: 95). Through the necessity of its own repetition, social control and thus power is inherently open to contestation. If people subvert its authority and engage in acts of resistance cracks in its authority begin to form. This does not mean that social control is any less material in its effects; however, it does mean that contestation and resistance is inherent in its operation. In the next section, I will discuss how dancers at Flame resisted the social control mechanism of surveillance, and how dancers produced fissures in the authority of the owner of the club to protect themselves from both the gaze of management as well the owner and from their regular customers.

Refusing the Gaze of the Owner: The Uses of Resistance

Resistance

The music was blaring and I was in the back/lap dance room when Angel was doing a lap dance and had her back to the camera . . . she had figured out a way to get extra money without reporting it. With her back turned she slipped her hand down her stomach to her knee and bent to get a twenty placed underneath her regular's leg.

---

[16] Although independent contract work is not an empowering source of labor in and of itself, due to a dancer's lack of security and lack of benefits, this form of surveillance creates an even more inequitable situation. Dancers are placed under a microscope and have little privacy in their work and are more vulnerable to management's scrutiny – a scrutiny that very rarely has dancer's best interest at heart. For more information on the conditions of work for exotic dancers in the past see Scott 1996 and Peterson and Sharpe 1974.

Angel in this move was able to escape the gaze – she refused to succumb to its authority. Watching her later on I saw her do it again. I took in this knowledge and decided to use it later . . . so that I might have some type of privacy in the club. Talking to Angel in the dressing room, I asked how she did it. She said, "well I am sick and tired of having to pay out so much to the club . . . so I just tell my regulars to slip extra money when they sit down and that way Vincent [the owner] doesn't know that I am charging extra for my dances and that way I don't lose 10% of every dance to the club. You can't do it with every customer, but my regulars understand."[17]

Dancers subverted the control of the owner and managers on a regular basis, by hiding their actions from the eyes of the cameras and bouncers. For instance, dancers at Flame were only supposed to get money while performing on stage or for doing lap dances; receiving money from customers on the floor is strictly forbidden. However, I saw many dancers using tables strategically to get money from their regular customers, an act that would be cause for dismissal. Some dancers used their backs as a shield to the cameras allowing customers to touch their breasts. Moreover, dancers at Flame used the bathroom, which had no cameras, for other prohibited actions such as drug use.

In order to create a space for themselves, dancers must learn strategic forms of resistance that disrupt the omnipresent vision of the cameras. Dancers must learn actions that fracture the gaze of the owner and management to demarcate spaces of (in)visibility for themselves. For instance, by moving to

---

[17] The economy of the club functions according to the rules set out by the owner to protect his profit. For example, dancers do not give any portion of the tips that they make on stage or in cabaret dances (mini lap dances on the main floor) to the owners – because this is not the place where dancers make the most money. Lap dancing is the place from which dancers make the majority of their incomes. A topless lap dance costs $20.00 per song – $5.00 of which goes to the owners. A fully nude lap dance costs $40.00 per song – $10.00 of which goes to the owners. Dancers are required to track every lap dance they do and a bouncer has a sheet to record each time a dancer goes to the lap dance room. Dancers are also supposed to give the owners 15% of what they earn in the champagne room (which costs approximately $100.00 per 30 minutes). Dancers are also required to pay the deejay $10.00 per shift. It is rare for an occasional or non-regular customer to give dancers any extra money in the lap dance room as they have no emotional investment in the dancers and do not know how much money dancers must pay to the owner of the club. By contrast, it is common for regulars to give dancers extra tips as they are emotionally interested in the dancers and thus want to help them as much as they can. They also understand the economics of the club.

the shadows of the club – those spaces that evade the owner's gaze – dancers are able to secure a space for themselves within the walls of Flame. Tammy, a dancer at the club, describes this process as follows:

> Whenever I really need some privacy with a customer I either try to go to the champagne room where there are really dark corners or I try to exchange stuff (money) under the table. I think it is stupid that we can't get money on the floor. If one of my regulars wants to give me extra money . . . fuck that I am taking it.

In this statement, Tammy articulates her resistance to the camera – her disruption of both the rules and the mechanisms of social control (surveillance) that are used to reinforce the rules. In doing so, she is able to construct a space for herself in the club where she has a form of agency in her own labor as an exotic dancer. In addition, Tammy disrupts the role of the consumer in the club as well. By making her regulars complicit in her subversion, she engages in a form of contestation with the owner. Dancers who use their regulars as a way to take money out of the owner's pocket and place it into their own subvert the owner's intentions. It is through these forms of resistance that dancers begin to control how they interact with customers and subvert the rules.

Gina, another dancer at Flame, discusses the importance of resistance:

> Look Vincent isn't the one out here dealing with people . . . he fucking makes a shit load here (at Flame). So if I can make extra money there is no fucking way I am going to not do it. I have a kid and I am going to school and I need the money. I already pay him to make my schedule and pay him for my dances where I use my body and I refuse to not make extra when I can. The rules here are ridiculous! I am careful . . . you know, but I still do it.

Gina is cognizant of the dangers in breaking the rules; she is "careful," but she is also ready to break them because they are "ridiculous." Gina recognizes that the main concern for the owner is not her safety, but the profit that the club makes from her labor and her body. As such she is more than willing to resist the exploitative forms of social control in order to take care of her "kid" and "go to school." In effect, Gina is constructing a space where she has more control over the means of her production – where she comes to undercut the intention of the owner to use her body to turn a profit.

Serenity, a dancer for six years, makes a similar point:

> It sounds childish, but shit he is not the boss of me! He has it easy back there raking it in, while we work our asses off. And you know, I have gotten in trouble before here with those fucking cameras, but since he is not my father and there are a lot of other clubs, I am going to keep doing what I am doing (taking extra money from customers), I am just more careful about it.

Serenity refused to be treated like a child or to validate the presence of the owner's authority via his use of surveillance cameras. She is going to "keep on doing what [she] is doing" in order to make the space of the club a place where she has agency. Although Serenity and other dancers have to be "careful about it," resistance to the field of power and social control remains a continuous possibility. Therefore, the ways in which people in power construct the social cartographies of particular places are fragile, as social cartographies are always subject to reinterpretation and resistance (Pile 1996, Pile 1997).

In rejecting the atmosphere set forth by the owner, dancers at Flame found savvy ways to fracture the hypervisibility of surveillance by hovering in its shadows and finding places of (in)visibility for themselves to transform the space of the club to a site in which dancers had a sense of agency with regard to their labor practices. In doing so, they were able to disrupt the repetitive function of social control, illuminating its fragility through their subversion and resistance (Butler 1990). By either using their bodies as shields – the bodies owners sought to control and use for profit in the club – or by conducting business "under the tables," dancers found creative ways to earn extra income and subvert the rules. Dancers also used the owner's surveillance technology as a tool through which to interact with regular customers who wanted more than a regular lap dance.

Re(f)using the Camera: Or Using the Master's Tools to Construct a Dancer's House Reinscription

One night Marcus wanted something special. He was a regular who came in weekly. He always brought gifts . . . sliding extra money to me under the table and felt that he was in "love." He wanted to "know more of (me)." I felt I was in the midst of a quagmire . . . not wanting to lose him as a customer, but not necessarily wanting him to feel my breast and/or vagina, I did not know what to do. As we went into the back/lap dance room I looked at the cameras. It was then that I figured out what to do . . . crooning to him softly I said, "Marcus, I would love to, but the cameras are watching and I could get fired." Although I knew that there were ways around the gaze, I used the eye of the camera for my own uses. It was then I knew that the power of the camera's gaze could be used for our own purposes.

Surveillance cameras usually go unnoticed by customers, although most customers cognizant of the bouncers do not do anything in an obvious manner (such as trying to grab a dancer's vagina on the main floor) that would get them kicked out. Cameras serve as a strategy for dancers when customers get out of hand. Unlike the owners who prescribe the camera as a social control mechanism for dancers to protect both their legal and economic investment, dancers use the camera as a convenient way to secure their income without having to break their performances of feigned intimacy.[18] In so doing, dancers reinscribe the owner's intentions for their own purposes. De Certeau (1984) theorizes how individuals are able to subvert or play with dominant readings of texts such as the law:

> [w]e should try to rediscover the movements of this reading within the body itself, which seems to stay docile and silent but mines the reading in its own way: from the nooks of all sorts of "reading rooms" (including lavatories) emerge subconscious gestures, grumblings, tics, stretchings, rustlings, unexpected noises, in short a wild orchestration of the body (1984: 175).

De Certeau argues that although dominant meanings are issued by authors (usually the social elite) of the law their interpretations and thus authority can never be completely guaranteed. Through reading, new interpretations emerge – as people play, rustle, stretch or reinscribe its meaning. The same could be said with the atmosphere of the dance club. Although owners set up specific rules, dancers do not always work the ways in which owners proscribe.

Dancers rustle with the rules to reinscribe their meanings for their own purposes. Through these reinscriptions dancers blame the owner and management for their inability to have increased physical contact with a customer. In so doing, dancers are able to create a space of shared disappointment with the customer and create a relationship against the management to the chagrin of the owner who relies on patriarchal solidarity to insure his profits in the club. The atmosphere of patriarchal pleasure and patriarchal profit is subverted by dancers who blame the management for their inability to be more

---

[18] For more on feigned intimacy see Ronai-Rambo 1992.

intimate with a customer. I have seen and talked to several dancers who use the surveillance cameras as a safe excuse to not do things that customers want them to. Gina, for example, told me about an incident that resonated with my own:

> There was this customer and he wanted to touch my tits and my cooche[19] and he was a good guy and a regular, so to put him off gently I told him, 'Hey sweetie, I would love it, but those cameras are watching and I don't want to get in trouble.' He totally got it, but didn't think that I would rather puke than have him touch me like that.

Gina and other dancers take the owner's form of social control and use it to their advantage to ward off the wandering hands of customers without having to break the fantasy of intimacy and sexual attraction they perform in order to keep regulars. Dancers invert the purpose of the panoptic gaze – implementing the tools of social control meant to control their actions in order to control customers and protect themselves.

Trena also used the camera for her own purposes:

> You know Harry, he is always wanting to feel more of me than I necessarily want him to . . . and who could blame him, I mean the guy drops $300 every time he is in here, but luckily he also feels protective of me. And so, I always use the cameras as an excuse. You know . . . saying stuff like, 'yeah of course I want to, but . . .' stuff like that, I mean . . . like . . . I do enough grinding their cock and all and I don't really want their hand on my crotch so I just use the camera as an excuse.

Trena is able to use the camera as an excuse taking the tools that are supposed to manipulate her behavior and instead use them to manipulate the behavior of her customers. As such she is able to maintain the feigned intimacy and interest in the interaction, while not losing a good paying regular – one who drops $300 every time he is in the club. In addition, by using Harry's protective feelings for her, Trena constructs an alternative notion of protection – one that competes with and subverts the owner's protection. Trena problematizes the owner's authority by disrupting his excuse for surveillance and uses Harry's feelings to her advantage.

---

[19] "Cooche" means vagina.

Re(f)using the camera is not an uncommon strategy among dancers. Marie discussed it this way:

> I know that its [the camera] supposed to be big brother and all, but I use that thing [the camera] all the time. I swear I use that shit all the time with customers. Because it never pisses them off or if it does they are pissed at the club and not at me.

Marie is able to reverse the intention of the owner – gaze of "big brother" – for her own purposes and thus is able to pacify an angry customer who wants more for his money than the typical lap dance. She redirects the frustrations of her customers to the owner, and is able to subvert the owner's position while maintaining the relationships with her customers.

Dancers reinscribe the tools used by the owners for their own purposes to create a safe barrier between their bodies and the customer's hands without having to tell the customer they are not interested. In doing so, they reformulate the intended use of surveillance and resignify its meaning (De Certeau 1984). This undercuts the management's authority showing that social control and the ways in which social control seeks to secure its own power are open to reformulation by those who are subject to it. Because the circuits of social control are most effective when individuals reinstantiate it by succumbing to its wishes or demands, when dancers seek to reuse it and in effect refuse its purpose, they disrupt the circuits of power in their acts of subversion.

Power is therefore not unilateral in its function (Foucault 1980). It is not something that only flows in one direction; rather it is a field or matrix dancers traverse in their everyday lives and thus are both subject to it and actively resist it. It is for this reason that owners cannot guarantee the success of their efforts to control the space of the club. Therefore, the power that the owner of Flame tried to instill in the club and the mechanisms he used to do so functioned through the reinscriptions of dancers to be used against him. Surveillance functioned to open up the possibilities of its resistance to it. The multiplicity of power relations in the club served as a palpable form of social control dancers felt in the space, and was simultaneously a site of resistance dancers used to forge a space for themselves within the walls of Flame.

Conclusion

Social cartographies are not unitary; they are contextual, multiple, and complex, mapping and marking us differently, producing resonances and resistances. The social cartographies of exotic dance clubs are neither seamless nor totalizing; dancers often resist the rules set out by the owners in their use of surveillance as a strategy to control customers "who are getting out of hand," by understanding how to avoid the eye of the owners, and by using their bodies or other objects to take money or "go too far with a customer." Thus, dancers purposely reinscribe the owners' intentions as to how these spaces should operate. Through their resistance, dancers operate both within and beyond the dominant cartographies, inscribing the space and creating fissures in the dominant cartographies.

The space of exotic dance clubs is a field of contestation in which the struggles among dancers, managers and owners are played out. The space of the club is never static, and the ways in which individuals are complicit, submit to or subvert it is complex to say the least. The owner, by never making the rules explicit, enforces a flexible and omnipresent form of social control. Through surveillance technologies dancers learn self surveillance and become a docile workforce. However, dancers in their interactions with one another and with customers find ways to disrupt the ever-present gaze of the cameras in order to protect themselves and subvert the control of the owner. Dancers in their strategies of resistance enlist the complicity of their regular customers as a way to disrupt the management's authority in order to continue making money and find agency in the club. Regulars, as customers who frequent the club often and bring in large amounts of money, are privy to the unwritten rules of both the owner and dancers. Regular customers become sites of contestation in the struggles between dancers and the owner. Both seeking regulars' loyalty, both trying to enlist them for their profit making – dancers and the owner use strategies with the hope of garnering more money for their labor. As such, the owner tries to construct a space for male pleasure and privilege to secure his profits, and dancers use fantasy and feigned intimacy to secure the bonds between them and their regulars. It is in this way that the regular becomes a pivotal site for dancers' resistance.

It is through the use of resistance that dancers construct an alternative atmosphere – one that problematizes the intentions of the owner and produces a more inhabitable space for themselves. By doing so, dancers construct an alternative organization of space in a site of work which all too often does not have their interest at heart. Through examining the complexity of women's sex work as a site of both social control and subversion, a site which is often viewed as only oppressive, we can begin to sociologically expand our vision of gendered resistance. In so doing, we can explore how women in other work sites may resist male authority in subtle and not so subtle ways. Authors such as Kempadoo and Doezema (1998) in their work on global prostitution examine how female prostitutes are anything but pliant in their work – how they subvert customer and brothel control via microforms of resistance. For example, prostitutes refuse to perform certain sexual acts and employ macro forms of resistance such as political organizing for prostitutes' rights. By using female agency and acts of subversion in seemingly oppressive sites, such as sex work, we can view women's work in other domains more critically to deconstruct patriarchal authority and the many ways in which women encounter and may or may not subvert its mechanisms of social control. To do so would aid theorists in moving beyond the theoretical stalwart of false consciousness (which necessitates a vanguard's expertise) and provide a sociological vision of the ways in which working class women workers negotiate the social cartographies of their work on an everyday basis. Through listening to women's struggles and subversions we can use their experiences and visions to broaden the sociological study of resistance and its effectiveness in an ever-expanding service economy.

Afterward

On this warm fall day in October 2004, I am contemplating the implications of my analysis of exotic dance for larger issues of culture, power, and history in relation to the events that have transpired since I completed my ethnographic research. In the midst of homeland security measures, color coded warnings of potential terror attacks, skyrocketing gun sales, home security systems and "nanny cams" – discourses of "protection" about ourselves, our children, and our country have proliferated in new forms across a variety of institutions in the United States. The attacks as well as the ever present iconography of twin towers falling illuminate how our concern for welfare has been superceded for our government's desire for warfare (Hardt and Negri 2004). Orwellian nightmares seem to be a reality in a culture consumed with the perceived necessity of preemptive strikes and homeland security. Part and parcel of our security state is the omnipresence of surveillance (see Lindsay, this volume). With the Patriot Act and new technological systems such as Echelon (an international system to monitor global communication technologies) the distinctions between public and private spheres become hazy at best (Hardt and Negri 2004). Surveillance, a cultural pellicle, normalizes the social control of the state making it seem as if it is for our own good. With the ubiquity of such mechanisms and the proliferation of high speed technologies we have moved beyond the modern panoptic to a postmodern form of hyper-surveillance (Bogart 1996). Given these shifts, what can we learn from the strategies, both covert and overt, employed by the dancers with whom I worked?

Exotic dancers enacted resistance on a daily basis. The manner in which women in the clubs found savvy ways to subvert managerial surveillance illuminates how techniques of power can not guarantee their own outcome (Foucault 1977). According to Foucault (1977), power produces both oppressive as well as resistive possibilities. Aleatory in their operation, even the most totalitarian modes of power are not seamless and shed light on how resistance is anything but futile. As such, "dominance, no matter how multidimensional, can never be complete and is always contradicted by resistance" (Hardt and Negri 2004: 54).

Dancers contests with surveillance demonstrate the tug and pull of power and resistance in the midst of their everyday lives at work. In their use of covert (i.e., slipping money under the table) as well as overt (i.e., using their regulars) practices, dancers show gaps in the authority and control of the owners. Moreover, through their reinscription of the discourses of legitimation used by owners for surveillance, they show how the logic and practice of surveillance is open to subversion. What dancers render visible is how resistance can jam the mechanisms of social control in small, but important ways. This is not to say that the resistance dancers employ is always efficacious, but it does show how those who are in marginal positions can negotiate and reinscribe hegemony on a repeated basis. To investigate how resistance operates in both micro and macro fashions across the social landscape is particularly crucial in our contemporary cultural milieu. Moreover, it may enable us to explore how resistance is made manifest in the most unexpected ways.

It is of course important to remain cognizant of how surveillance is not uniform in its operation and marks some bodies more violently than others.

While the materiality of surveillance does not function in the same way for everyone, the strategies of subversion (in their various manifestations) are possible even within our contemporary culture – and exploring the strategies of those in marginal positions may offer new models for us to consider in this particularly challenging time.

Delario Lindsey

To Build a More *Perfect Discipline*:[1] Ideologies of the Normative and the Social Control of the Criminal Innocent in the Policing of New York City[1a]

An Introduction

Since the tragic events of September 11, 2001, we have seen here in the U.S. (indeed, in many quarters of the world) an ever-increasing obsession amongst government leaders with safety and security. This ascending Cult of Security has led to the implementation of a range of new defensive measures (both policies and practices) that include: the registering of foreign nationals from 'hostile' nation-states;

---

[1] This is an allusion to Michel Foucault and his work *Discipline and Punish* (1979). While detailing Bentham's concept of "The Panopticon," Foucault describes a reality wherein social control is complete and the rationale for the control is unquestioned. A medieval city under siege by the plague serves as an ideal illustration of social control as the everyday norm as well the *consent* to discipline that is implied when the effort is to bring a disorderly situation (however constructed) back under control. Foucault writes:

> *The plague-stricken town, traversed throughout with hierarchy, surveillance, observation, writing; the town immobilized by the functioning of an extensive power that bears in a distinct way over all individuals bodies – this is the utopia of the perfectly governed city. The plague (envisaged as a possibility at least) is the trial in the course of which one may define ideally the exercise of disciplinary power. In order to make rights and laws function according to pure theory, the jurists place themselves in imagination in the state of nature; in order to see perfect discipline functioning, rulers dreamt of plague.*
>
> *(Foucault 1979: 198).*

[1a] An earlier version of this essay appeared in *Critical Sociology* , vol. 30, no. 2 (2004). It is taken from a larger project dealing with the issues of social control and world city formation.

data-mining and information gathering on U.S. citizens;[2] stricter controls of the nations borders and airports, all with the expressed goal of waging the war against terrorism. September 11th represented a significant rupture in both the material and rhetorical exigencies of safety and national security, as they may have existed prior to the attack. Within the space of a few months Americans have had to become accustomed to ever increasing levels of surveillance and social control. The seemingly omnipresent threat of terrorism represents a moral panic[3] that has gripped the nation, and has emboldened national leaders to take unprecedented actions in waging "The War on Terror."

It is not my intention to assess the value or to detail at a national or international level the unforeseen consequences associated with the initiatives

---

[2] Here is a brief encapsulation of the Bush Administrations proposed Terrorism Information Awareness Program:

> How TIA Would Work
> For an understanding of the potential benefits that DoD believes may be achieved with TIA, it is important to understand how DoD envisions it would work if implemented. Teams of very experienced analysts and other experts (a red team) would imagine the types of terrorist attacks that might be carried out against the United States at home or abroad. They would develop scenarios for these attacks and determine what kind of planning and preparation activities would have to be carried out in order to conduct these attacks. These scenarios (models) would be based on historical examples, estimated capabilities, and imagination about how these tactics might be adapted to take into account preventive measures the United States has in place. The red team would determine the types of transactions that would have to be carried out to perform these activities. Examples of these transactions are the purchase of airlines tickets for travel to potential attack sites for reconnaissance purposes, payment for some kind of specialized training, or the purchase of materials for a bomb. These transactions would form a pattern that may be discernable in certain databases to which the U.S Government would have lawful access. Specific patterns would be identified that are related to potential terrorist planning. It is not a matter of looking for unusual patterns, but instead searching for patterns that are related to predicted terrorist activities ("Report to Congress regarding the Terrorism Information Awareness Program, in response to Consolidated Appropriations Resolution", 2003, Pub. L. No. 108-7, Division M, § 111(b)).

This proposed program of the Bush administration was formerly known as the Total Information Awareness Program.

[3] See Stuart Hall et al., *Policing the Crisis* (1978). In this text Hall and his collaborators make the connection between mugging panic that occurred in London in 1970–71, the subsequent implementation of restrictive social control practices and burgeoning crisis in British hegemony and traditional English values. The issue of a hegemonic crisis may have particular relevance in the discussion of the "War on Terrorism" given the Bush administration's rhetorical use of a civilizational "Us against Them" discourse which has proved to be very effective in rallying support from constituents, allies and even one-time enemies (like Iran) for waging the international "War on Terror."

described above. Nor will this paper serve as an argument in favor of protecting individual liberties in a time when we are being asked to trade some of our liberty for a greater sense of security. What the "War on Terror" and its associative social control measures illustrates is the willingness on the part of those charged with securing the nation to resort to any means necessary in accomplishing that task. The goal is security; the reality is one of control.[4] With the 'reality of control' serving as the context and backdrop, this paper describes a continuity of practice with respect to control and security of a given space. The particular space in question is that of the urban metroplex (specifically) New York City.

Preceding the September 11 terrorist attacks, the city of New York experienced its own moral panic during the early 1990s centering on the issues of crime and safety. Like September 11th had done for the nation as a whole, the issues of crime and public safety captured the imagination of the inhabitants New York City in the early 1990s. Also like September 11th, those charged with the task of guaranteeing public safety (the NYPD and Mayor Giuliani) seemed willing to employ a range of policies and practices as a means of bringing the problem of crime under control in a city that was out-of-control. This period in New York City history began with a tale of crime and the city. This was a story that was deployed by (then) candidate Rudolph Giuliani and his supporters to influence the New York voting public during the 1993 mayoral campaign. The story told was of New York becoming a deteriorating city, and it was this framing of the city that served as the rhetorical justification for sweeping changes in the means and methods used to keep the city safe. This is a story that concluded with one unfortunate African immigrant – Amadou Diallo – whose violent death demonstrates the unforeseen consequences of what had become a reality of control in New York City.

My analysis of the reality of control and its consequences has three central components, the first of which sets forth the framework and structure of what I call *Ideologies of the Normative*. The second component involves the use of

---

[4] The reality perhaps even exceeds control to approach a situation of *over-control* where the social cost of security and safety is out of proportion with the contextual need for security and safety. Over-control takes on particular salience when dealing with the consequences of social control on specific communities, social classes or ethnicities.

Frame Critical Analysis[5] as a method to explicate the narrative that constructs the crime crisis in New York City and the counter-narrative that critiques that construction and what becomes a reality of control in New York City – a reality where, for certain groups of individuals in certain spaces, social control *is* the norm. The third and final component illustrates the consequences of Ideologies of the Normative instituted as social control practice in New York City by examining the relationship between the resultant reality of control and the slaying of African immigrant Amadou Diallo at the hands of four white New York City police officers.

Ideologies of the Normative

My discussion of Ideologies of the Normative begins with making the fundamental distinction between ideas about the normative and *norms*. Norms are understood simply as rules that govern behavior in a given social context. Norms are typically considered to be a part of our cultural inheritance, passed through the various social institutions and organizations that are an integral part of lifelong social development. Norms are also shaped by the landscapes of power in which they are situated. By contrast, ideologies of the normative are the explicit outcomes of historically specific conflicts between differing perspectives and/or worldviews. Ideologies of the Normative are the outcomes of discursive contests, or ideological battles, waged by interested parties to make their particular perspective (on a given issue) the dominant or given perspective.[6] Ideologies of the Normative are made applicable

---

[5] Frames are moralistic narratives constructed around particular issues or events (and I also include spaces) that may be used to shape and influence policy. Frames can include diagnostic and prescriptive narratives about a given issue. Interested groups (known as sponsors in the literature) frame issues within a given policy controversy in terms of a particular vision of what the issues are (or how they should be viewed) and what should be done about them (Schon and Rein 1996). There are two types of frames, both of which are relevant to an analysis of framing of the issue of crime/social control in New York City. *Rhetorical frames* appear in publicly available texts and promote or otherwise denote advocacy of one view of an issue over all others, or seek to persuade an audience to accept a given narrative regarding the issue at hand. *Action frames* are narratives deployed by policy-makers and practitioners to justify or rationalize policy decisions and strategies. This type of frame is central to the story-building process and acts as a kind of cover story or front, which conceals the true intentions of policy makers (Ibid.).

[6] Frame Critical Analysis is a particularly salient research method for analysis of Ideologies of the Normative because is allows researchers to identify these discursive

to particular issues, or social contexts, and not only prescribe the content and limits of appropriateness, but exemplify the general interpretation of those same issues and social contexts. The construction of Ideologies of the Normative is a willful act, and both its content and design are purposeful. In Ideologies of the Normative the goal is to universalize the particular by disguising the particular as the universal. To be successful, framers of Ideologies of the Normative must create exclusive perspectives on given issues that are held as the norm, shared and agreed upon by all.

Ideologies of the Normative are persuasive as worldviews because of the relatively simple dichotomous structure of the ideologies themselves. Ideologies of the Normative are predicated on commonly accepted *moralistic* dualities. Framers of these ideologies associate their particular vision of the problem and the solution with widely held beliefs and values. Good vs. evil, in-group vs. out-group, boom vs. bust and vitality vs. decay for example, exist in a contentious relationship of opposites within the structure of an Ideology of the Normative. The tone of an Ideology of the Normative is essentially polemical, minimizing the possibilities of rendering a complicated interpretation of a given issue. All that lies within the scope of the ideology is interpreted via the binary framework of the ideology.[7] The Ideologies of the Normative create both that which is affirmed and that which is denied. Within the context of the ideology, images of the 'denied' implicitly call forth that which the ideology seeks to affirm, and it is that which is affirmed by the ideology that is to be inscribed as the *norm*. Action is advocated not on the basis of halting normative transgressions, but as a requirement of upholding the deeply held beliefs and values associated with the moralistic constructs of the ideology.[8]

Inasmuch as Ideologies of the Normative play to simple moral dualities, the construction of an in-group/out-group dynamic is implicit. As a function of the moralistic dualities, Ideologies of the Normative designate both privileged and discredited subjectivities.[9] With the idea of the "normal" or the

---

contests as struggles for the hearts and minds of a given community. Frame Critical Analysis dismantles the everyday assumption that normative constructs (such as laws, regulations practices etc.) are timeless and naturally given.

[7] Similarly, in Michel Foucault's analysis of the Panopticon (1979), efforts to control a space and the subjects that inhabit it rely upon the construction and labeling of binaries.

[8] Similarly, an appeal to principle (Gamson and Lasch 1983) advocates the frame or narrative through the use of commonly held moral precepts.

[9] My usage of the term 'discredited subjectivity' is not borrowed from Erving Goffman (1962) who used the term, "discredited person" to designate a person for

"norm" as given, Ideologies of the Normative create and separate out those subjects who are presumed to be in normative compliance from those who are not. These privileged subjects are (within the structure of the ideology) automatically affirmed, as they are the 'moral' subjects par excellence. If the ideological context is one concerning employment (for example), these are the people whose jobs should be protected. If the context involves health and wellness, these are the people who should have healthcare. If the context deals with crime and violence (as is the case in this article), these are the people to be protected and made to feel safe. The discredited, on the other-hand, are denied affirmation and privilege. The discredited are without legitimacy within the context of the ideology, which makes the denial of these subjects nearly incontestable. The discredited subjects are not merely deviant (as transgressors of the boundaries of the normative), they are implicitly immoral as determined by the particular Ideology of the Normative. In an ideological context involving crime and violence, the discredited are deemed perpetrators and are subject to control.

Methodological Briefing

Frame Critical Analysis allows for examination of the telling of a crime crisis (as opposed to the description of a crime crisis). For the purposes of decoding the Ideology of the Normative that informs New York City's crime crisis, I have chosen to sample from four New York based news serials. These four publications, The New York Times, The New York Post, The Village Voice, and The New York Amsterdam News, are themselves a relatively small sample of the total universe of New York based publications, but were chosen because they represent a range of spatial and economic (class) locations of the New York body politic. Also, each of these papers has provided significant coverage of the Diallo incident, social control policy implementation during the Giuliani administration and the 1993 the mayoral campaign.

---

whom stigma – "the discrepancy between an individual's actual social identity and his virtual one" – is evident or has been made known to others interacting with the individual. Goffman's concept is situational in context and micro in orientation. I use the term here to refer to more general discursive outcome that goes beyond the situation context. The ultimate source and cause of an individual's illegitimacy and invalidation lies outside of the individual sphere of influence. Entire groups, communities and even spaces can be discredited.

By focusing on the print media forum, one is able to examine the issue of crime/social control in New York City by reviewing the "public record" on the subject. Using print media one can piece together the history of a given narrative (or frame), and document the ways in which a narrative has evolved over time, in, through, and between critical discourse moments. Two narrative frame categories were uncovered – the deteriorating city the repressive city (a counter-narrative to the 'deteriorating city'). The data was coded by frame and further sub-coded to note an advocacy or rebuttal of the frame. The 'deteriorating city' narrative frame told the story of New York City as a city in decline due to spiraling rates of crime and ineffective social control. The repressive city narrative frame told the story of the city's transformation into a space of over-control. The discursive evidence (which amounted to approximately 100 examples) included op-ed pieces, news-stories and political cartoons from the four source publications.

Each of the four publications takes a different political inflection or tone on the issue of crime/social control. The serials are each generally reflective of political leanings to the right or left and, as such, one might hypothesize a differential advocacy by a publication of one of narrative frames concerning the issue of crime and social control over the other (Sasson, 1995). For instance, the publications (and their audiences) can be arranged from right to left (or conservative to liberal) with respect to the type of inflections built into editorials or feature stories dealing with the issue of crime/social control and the Diallo incident. It is commonly held that The New York Post is conservative with a local readership that is mostly working class to lower middle class and predominately white; The New York Times is moderate/ liberal with a local, regional and international readership that is middle class and predominately white; The Village Voice is liberal with a local and regional readership that is middle class and predominately white; The New York Amsterdam News is very liberal with a local and regional readership that is working class-lower middle class and predominately black. Positions supported by the four sources (pro or con) in relation to the narrative frames were both explicitly and implicitly stated. I found that The New York Post and The New York Amsterdam News were more willing to take expressed position vis-à-vis certain narratives (examples give below), than were The New York Times or The Village Voice.

The sampled discursive data can be broken into four time periods that begin with the election period (circa 1991–1994), the policy implementation period (1994–1997), the period of alterative discourse of crime and social control (1997–1999) and the moment of Amadou Diallo (1999–2000). By following the narratives through the different periods one sees the ways in which the narrative frames developed and evolved. The discursive analysis begins with a focus on the narrative most associated with what would become a reality of control in New York City. This narrative told the story of a crime crisis in the city and was sponsored by Rudolph Giuliani.

Crime Crisis in a New York minute

The discussion of New York City's 'crime crisis' begins with then mayoral candidate Rudolph Giuliani's 1993 New York campaign. At the center of this campaign was a narrative response to the state of crime and safety in the city under the administration of then Mayor David Dinkins. This narrative was designed to undermine support for the incumbent Mayor David Dinkins while at the same time building a support base for Giuliani centered on one of the most central issues in any New York City election: crime. During the electoral campaign, the reality of control began to take shape and an Ideology of the Normative was created.

But even before the 1993 campaign for mayor, Giuliani and his supporters used the 1991 Crown Heights riot as the centerpiece of their crime narrative.[10] Images of the riot, with bands of angry Black and Latino youths terrorizing the crown Heights neighborhood, served as the quintessential metaphor for crime and disorder in New York City. In commenting on the use of the sensational events of the Crown Heights Riot as a media spectacle and mayoral campaign issue, Carl Bloice of the New York Amsterdam News writes:

---

[10] The Crown Heights riot was ignited when a Hasidic Jewish man (Yosef Lifah) accidentally ran down two black children (Angela and Gavin Cato), killing young Gavin. After the incident three days of rioting ensued during which time Lemrick Nelson (a young black male from the neighborhood in which the accident took place), allegedly stabbed and killed Yankel Rosenbaum. Though there were many arrests made related to the riot (including Robert Wesley who was charged with first degree riot and Lemrick Nelson who was charged and tried with manslaughter, but was later acquitted), the media and later independent investigations of the event lay blame squarely on the delayed response of police and the "ineffectiveness" of Mayor Dinkins' office in dealing quickly and decisively with the situation. Mayor Dinkins was perceived as 'soft on crime,' a flaw that led to the death of Yankel Rosenbaum and the destruction of millions of dollars in property.

The editors of The New York Times are probably to be commended for deciding the time has come for "Containing the Crown Heights Fire." But, they might take another look at who's fanning the flames.

The paper says Republican mayoral candidate Rudolph Giuliani "worsened matters by calling the disturbances that involved the reprehensible fatal attack on Yankel Rosenbaum a 'pogrom.'"

Guiliani didn't invent recklessness.

Times former editor A.M. Rosenthal wrote Nov. 20 about a three-day "anti-Semitic pogrom" in Brooklyn last summer. Demonstrating he's not cowed by current editors' admonitions, he's back Dec. 11 writing about a "neighborhood pogrom" carried out by African-American "pogromists."

The dictionary describes a pogrom as an "organized massacre." No such thing has taken place in New York for a long time.[11]

The question of the persistence of crime in New York City (or any large world city for that matter) is not a subject for debate. Crime and public safety was then and is now a major issue for both administrators and inhabitants of major cities all over the country.[12] But, it is also true that the most violent crimes (murder, rape, and armed robbery) are relatively rare even in big cities like New York. Nationwide the number of victimizations reported between 1973 and 1995 has decreased by 5%.[13] The purposeful promotion of the idea of a crime crisis in the city served the dual function of discrediting incumbent Mayor David Dinkins, while at the same time greatly legitimizing Giuliani's run for mayor by putting him on the leading edge of an issue (crime and safety) that he himself put front and center in the minds of the New York voting public.[14] With the Crown Heights Riot as centerpiece,

---

[11] "Reading the major White press with a critical eye," *New York Amsterdam News*, January 9, 1993, p. 16.

[12] There is currently a crime spike occurring in Los Angeles involving gang violence. Los Angeles Chief of Police William Bratton (a familiar notable from the Giuliani administration and former Commissioner of the NYPD) hopes to implement a New York style crime control program.

[13] According to the two major crime indices (the Uniform Crime Report Data or the National Criminal Victimization Survey Data) incidence of violent crime (like murder, rape, and armed robbery) have remained rather steady and in some cases have declined since the early 1970s. Furthermore, most of the crime committed in the US is against property and non-violent. The period between 1973 and 1992 saw 116% increase in the number of reported crimes, but this has been argued to be a consequence of better criminal recording methods on the part of police officials. (Beckett and Sasson 2000)

[14] Though criticisms of Dinkins' came from all sides during and after the riot in

Giuliani's framing of New York City was that of a city in the midst of crime crisis due in large part to the ineffectiveness of incumbent Mayor Dinkins to control the city. I argue that Giuliani created and promoted a narrative frame of New York City as a 'deteriorating city,' deteriorating due to uncontrollable rates of crime and violence.[15] A New York Times article discusses the centrality of crime in the city as a campaign issue, and the rhetoric used in a Giuliani campaign commercial. Note the nostalgic references to how the city "used to be":

> As the race for mayor moves into the decisive final weeks, Rudolph W. Giuliani has gone on the airwaves with a new set of radio and television commercials that feature the frustrated testimonials of crime-weary New Yorkers – and also speak volumes about the campaign strategy of the Republican-Liberal challenger.
>
> In one commercial, a restaurant worker, with a voice with the nasal essence of Brooklyn, stares straight into a video camera and punctuates wistful reminiscences by slamming his hands down in emphasis on a metal sink. "I remember when I was a kid," he says. "Avenue N used to be lined with people sitting out in front of their houses or in front of their apartments at night to cool off, and you don't see that in New York because everybody's afraid to come out at night.[16]

Crown Heights (for example, "Crown Heights study finds Dinkins and police at fault in letting unrest escalate," *The New York Times,* July 21, 1993, p. A1), it was Giuliani (guided by political ambition) who solidified the argument that Dinkins was unfit to occupy the office Mayor.

[15] Politicization of fear and crime has been discussed elsewhere. The effective usage of the issue of crime as a political strategy may be reflective of broad trends in crime policy of the past 30 years. In describing the shift away from what he calls 'penal welfarism' toward a post-modern 'Crime-Complex,' David Garland (2001) writes:

> In another significant break with past practice, crime policy has ceased to be a bipartisan matter that can be devolved to professional experts and has become a prominent issue in electoral competition. A highly charged political discourse now surrounds all crime control issues, so that every decision is taken in the glare of publicity and political contention and every mistake becomes a scandal. Policy measures are constructed in ways that appear to value political advantage and public opinion over the views of experts and the evidence of research. The professional groups (social scientists) who once dominated the policy-making process are increasingly disenfranchised as policy comes to be formulated by political action committees and political advisers. (13)

[16] Alison Mitchell, "Giuliani Zeroing In on Crime Issue; New Commercials Are Focusing on Fears of New Yorkers," *The New York Times*, September 20, 1993, p. B3.

The construction of the 'deteriorating city' narrative frame begins with Giuliani's particular narrative about the city (or the overall health of the city) and its relationship to crime. This is a narrative that tells the story of how the city has changed because of crime and the fear of crime. The 'deteriorating city' narrative frame was first and foremost a 'law and order' narrative designed to (re)construct the image of New York City through the issue of crime/social control. Imbedded within the 'deteriorating city' narrative frame was an Ideology of the Normative that refers to an ongoing state of moral decay as well as increasing rates of crime. Images of degradation and rot (which include the city's infamous "squeegee-men" public urinators, and the perpetually 'unclean' Times Square) spoke not only to the effects of crime in the city, but to the moral character of the city as well. In an attempt to rebut this narrative position, a New York Amsterdam News editorial questions the idea of the city as suffering from a declining quality of life:

> In the third century of the American civilization, we see similar patterns begin to emerge in the cradle of this civilization, New York City. It began with the vague cry that the city must be cleaned up, with the warning that the quality of life is being destroyed and that "those people" are responsible for it.
>
> We know who "those people" are. They are the squeegee entrepreneur, the bicycle messenger, the derelict, the homeless, the mentally ill, the lame, the halt, the elderly, the AIDS victim, the vagrant, the illiterate and the poor.
>
> It begins with a drumbeat and a slogan, a flag and an anthem, and a conviction that the clean-up mission has been ordained by God.[17]

This piece also identifies those groups that are responsible for the city's deterioration. These are segments of the population that are discredited by the 'deteriorating city' narrative frame as an Ideology of the Normative.

As an Ideology of the Normative the 'deteriorating city' narrative frame constructed an implicit comparison between some New York that Giuliani had imagined (possibly from memories of his childhood) – a cleaner, safer city where crime was nearly non-existent – and the space New York had

---

The piece points out Giuliani's implicit use of nostalgic imagery when describing what he views as the city's current state of decline under the leadership of Mayor Dinkins.

[17] "Totalitarianism Begins Here," *New York Amsterdam News*, January 15, 1994, p. 12.

become under the stewardship of the David Dinkins. The 'romanticized city' that New York once was (if only in Rudolph Giuliani's mind), served as the moral ideal for New York City as this excerpt from his inaugural address illustrates. After promising to "reverse the trend of ever increasing tolerance of crime," Giuliani goes on to say:

> "It's time to enhance or relationship with the United Nations, and build on it. Think of this," he says "Albany, the capital of New York State. Washington, DC, the capital of the nation. And New York City will again be the capital of the world."[18]

This speech also references the eras of Fiorello LaGuardia and Ed Koch, evoking a time in the city before David Dinkins, rejecting what New York City had become in the form of the deteriorating city, and affirming the ideal of the *'safe space'* – the idea of what New York could, and should be. The construction of New York City as a 'safe space' is meant to evoke images of a vital, clean and prosperous city, which was a far cry from the 'unlawful' and 'unsafe' deteriorated space New York had become by 1993.[19] Those imagined morals and values that once kept families and communities together, and would otherwise keep the city at-large relatively safe, had withered away. Because of the moral precepts of the 'deteriorating city,' the space of New York City had effectively been 'othered.' The goal of this particular Ideology

---

[18] Quoted by Sam Roberts, "Giuliani's no-frills speech evokes an earlier era," *The New York Times*, January 3, 1994, p. A17.

[19] "Freedom is About Authority: Excerpts From Giuliani Speech on Crime," *The New York Times*, March 20, 1994, p. 35, provides short excerpts from a speech Giuliani delivered to a forum on crime. The excerpt was taken from a speech Giuliani gave at crime forum sponsored by *The New York Post*, (a publication that is arguably a co-sponsor of the 'deteriorating city' narrative). In his own words Giuliani links rising tide of criminality in New York City streets to a decline in collective community values, and the diminishing roll of family and religious institutions play in the instilling on values over the past 30 years. For Giuliani, these missing values, and morals are *"the basics upon which a lawful and a decent society are based."* Morality is equivalent to 'lawfulness,' which is the true missing element with respect to crime/social control in the city. With this speech, it can be seen early on in his career as Mayor that Giuliani intended to transform New York City into a modern police-state, and here he uses his own construction of a "moral" imperative based on the responsibilities of citizenship to justify this, as Giuliani says:

> We see only the oppressive side of authority . . . What we don't see is that freedom is not a concept in which people can do anything they want, be anything they can be. Freedom is about authority. Freedom is about willingness of every single human being to cede lawful authority a great deal of discretion about what you do.

of the Normative was to normalize the 'safe space' ideal. The vision of New York City affirmed by Giuliani lay at the moral center of the Ideology of the Normative. Though it did not yet exist, rhetorically the vision of the city represented the standard that *should be*. The 'deteriorating city,' by contrast, is the space that *is*, but should not be. The 'deteriorating city' is an alien space, devoid of anything resembling the familiar and the sacred, and for this, it is worthy of disdain.

There is evidence of a racial 'othering' of the city as well. The process of racial 'Othering' can be linked to historic relationships of domination and oppression. These historic relationships are continually manifested in and through contemporary social relations rooted in race/ethnicity and class that comprise the everyday reality of urban life in New York City. Grosfoguel and Georas (2003) use the concept of the 'coloniality of power' (defined as the "cultural, political, and economic oppression of subordinate racialized/ethnic groups by dominant racial/ethnic groups with or without the existence of colonial") [20] in their study of the racial/ethnic hierarchies that have come to characterize race relations in major metropolitan areas like New York City. The concept proves useful for examining the relationship between fear of crime and the historic criminalization of minority groups in our society. Coloniality of power helps to explain the persistence of in-group/out-group

---

[20] The concept of coloniality of power seeks to explain the persistence of colonial relations in the absence of a formal colonial apparatus. Anibal Quijano describes how relations of inequality formed during the colonial area permeate a society's cultural and social institutions, and serve to keep in place a racialized social order, Quijano writes:

> Racism and ethnicism were initially produced in the Americas and then expanded to the rest of the colonial world as the foundation of the specific power relations between Europe and the populations of the rest of the world. After five hundred years, they still are the basic components of power relations across the world. Once colonialism becomes extinct as a formal political system, social power is still constituted on criteria originated in colonial relations. In other words, coloniality has not ceased to be the central character of today's social power . . . With the formation of the Americas a new social category was established. This is the idea of "race" . . . Since then, in the intersubjective relations and in the social practices of power, there emerged, on the one hand, the idea that non-Europeans have a biological structure not only different from Europeans, but, above all belonging to an "inferior" level or type. On the other hand, the idea that cultural differences are associated with such biological inequalities . . . These ideas have configured a deep and persistent cultural formation, a matrix of ideas, images, values, attitudes, and social practices, even when colonial political relations have been eradicated. (Quijano 1993: 167; translation by Grosfoguel and Georas 2003: 155).

dynamics that have become spatialized in metropoles like New York, and can be said to inform the ideology of the normative with respect to the construction of privileged and discredited subjects. Grosfoguel and Georas (2003) describe the colonial relationship between the privileged and the discredited in this way:

> The global coloniality of power from colonial to postcolonial times helps us understand the ongoing power of the white male elites to classify populations and exclude people of color from the categories of citizenship and from the "imagined community" called the "nation." The civil, political, and social rights that citizenship provided to members of the "nation" were selectively expanded over time "white" working classes and "white" middle-class women. However, "internal" colonial groups remained "second-class citizens," never having full access to the rights of citizens and to the "imagined community" called the nation (Gilroy 1987). "Coloniality of power" is constitutive of the metropolitan nation-states' narrative frames of the nation. Who belongs and who does not belong to the "nation" is informed by the historical power relations between Europeans and non-Europeans. The persistence of a colonial culture in the present informs and constitutes social power today (156).

Those who benefited from historical colonial relationships are considered to be among the privileged, and within the context of public safety and social control, these are the subjects that should be protected and made to feel safe. In the same instance, those who were once colonial subjects find themselves among the discredited, and are denied full and equal protection. As the New York City's first African-American mayor, David Dinkins is one such discredited subject. Dinkins was not only confronted with a narrative that sought to construct him as 'soft' on crime, but his 'blackness' and his ability to empower other blacks in his administration were constructed as factors that promoted crime in the city as evidenced by Dinkins' inability or unwillingness to go into Brooklyn hard and fast and protect the white citizens of Crown Heights from rampaging black youths.

One of the reasons the 'deteriorating city' narrative frame was so successful in re-casting the image of the city, and in attacking Mayor Dinkins, lies with the receptiveness of its target audience. The 'deteriorating city' narrative frame may have tapped into latent resentment and fear within the larger white community that 'blacks were taking over the city,' – a fear magnified by the occupation of the most important political office in the city by an

African-American man.[21] The 'deteriorating city' frame gained strength in this racialized 'othering' of a city under the control of a member of the discredited and his cohorts. The Crown Heights Riot served to amplified the racial distrust and animus already present in some quarters of the city. A New York Amsterdam News piece responds to the New York state report on the Crown Heights Riot, and the way Giuliani managed to turn the Riot into a racialized campaign issue:

> First of all, I was happy that the report finally puts to rest the inflammatory claim that the mayor sanctioned a pogrom. The word "pogrom" implies the active involvement of the government in organizing a slaughter. This word, which has been invoked by the mayor's political rivals, such as Rudy Guliani, conjures up images of the Holocaust and corresponds to the worst fears of many Jews.

Patterson goes on to write:

> I was also disturbed by the fact that this report also perpetuates two dangerous myths: One, that African-Americans were the only initiators of violence; and two, that the police only held back from arresting African-American perpetrators of violence. Leading up to the riots, bad blood between elements within these communities ran both ways; and eyewitnesses say there were some elements within the Hasidic community that also initiated violence.[22]

At the time of the Crown Heights Riot, New York City was experiencing a spate of racialized violent incidents. From the December 1986 attack of three black youths by a group of young white men, to the infamous 'wilding' incident in April of 1989 where four black youths were falsely accused of beating and raping a white women while she was jogging in Central Park, to the brutal beating death of Yusef Hawkins by a group of white youths in Bensonhurst Brooklyn in August of 1989, the Crown Heights Riot seemed the latest in a series of high-profile racialized or racially motivated acts of violence in the city. The 'deteriorating city' narrative frame managed to take

---

[21] In his analysis of racialized violence in New York City Howard Pinderhughes (1993) points to the reaction of some New York's white inhabitants to the political power wielded by people of color (specifically African-Americas) as a contributing to the general racial malaise present in the city around the time of the Crown Heights Riot.

[22] "Patterson responds to Whites on Crown Heights," *New York Amsterdam News*, August 7, 1993, p. 12.

the anxieties associated with safety and security and combine them with a diffuse sense of general racial discord in the city to generate a new image of a the city. In this new image, the city is portrayed as unsafe for the law-abiding and as haven for the violent and the criminally inclined.

The 'deteriorating city' narrative frame had the effect of racializing victimization, further politicizing the issue of crime and social control. This is not to say that the city's white residents were led to believe that they would fall victim to crime because they were white. Rather, due to the state of crime and social control in the city (as illustrated by the violence of the Crown Heights Riot), whites were being told the story that their victimization was likely to be at the hands of young and black perpetrators, and that their black mayor was likely to hold back (as he had purportedly done as the Crown Heights Riot began) on the policing of criminally violent African-Americans.[23] The Ideology of the Normative created a dichotomous situation for New York City voters: the continuance of a crime-ridden, morally decayed space that the city had become under Dinkins, or a safer, cleaner, more family-friendly ideal under a newly installed Giuliani administration.[24]

---

[23] The New York State Report on the Crown Heights Riot does not say that there was any statement, directive or order from the mayor or anyone in the administration directing the police to "hold back" during the unrest in Crown Heights. This is important, because many leaders in the Hasidic community (and their supporters, including Rudolph Giuliani, have stated explicitly and implicitly that as a matter of fact that such an order was given (Wallace Ford, "Crown Heights – The Aftermath," *New York Amsterdam News*, July 31, 1993, p. 13). On the issue of criminal victimization and race Beckett and Sasson (2000) write:

> In the news, when crime victims are depicted, they are typically white, female, and affluent. One content analysis of national and local television newscasts, for example, found that when race and gender of crime victims could be identified, white females were the most common category of victims. In fact, young men of color-especially those living in poor and urban areas- experience the highest rates of victimization, and white females report the lowest. (79)

[24] In a November 13, 1993 *New York Amsterdam News* editorial (p. 12), "This election wasn't won: It was stolen and bought," Wilbert A. Tatum argues that the 1993 election was lost by Dinkins due the influences of anti-black, anti-Dinkins media in New York City. Tatum seems to refer to a conspiracy fostered by the white dominated media to de-fame in the eyes of the voting public New York's first black mayor from the moment he was elected, as he writes "It was an immediate assault, often untrue, misstated, overstated or not stated at all of his every day designed to inflame Whites and Jews and to undermine the confidence that Blacks had over time developed in him." The editorial calls Giuliani a "tool" of the media forces, as his message became their message. Tatum asserts that the New York Times (an official Dinkins ally) held

Along with constructing the crime crisis, the deteriorating city narrative frame also designates those subjects to be privileged by the narrative of "the average law-abiding citizen," or what I will call 'the average New Yorker.' Not so much representing an actual group, 'the average New Yorker' should be thought of as a composite of desirable traits made whole by the images associated with and inspired by the narrative frame of the deteriorating city. Aside from obvious qualities like 'law abiding' and 'productive,' the primary trait associated with the privileged 'average New Yorker' was that of victimization. As part of simple moral duality created by an ideology deployed around the issue of crime, the designation "victim" is vitally important. Here the label of "victim" is generalized to include not just actual victims of crime in that city, but those victimized by the fear of crime as well. The average New Yorker represents that group that is put upon by the aggressive panhandlers, squeegee-men and the other quality of life infractions as described in this New York Times article:

> In contrast to David Dinkins, who focused on expanding the Police Department, the Giuliani-Bratton team seems intent on changing the department's tactics . . . More street-level drug busts. More protection for schools. More accountability from police commanders. And more attention paid to quality-of-life intrusions, like uninvited windshield washing.
>
> In line with Mr. Giuliani's concerns, Mr. Bratton signaled last week that he wanted to attack low-level infractions, like the "squeegee men" washing windshields. He believes a squeegee crackdown is not petty, says Mr. Bratton, because "it's that type of activity that is generating fear."

If such tactics fit in a comprehensive strategy that attacks both the demand and supply side of serious crime, emphasizes more police doing real police work and includes an unrelenting gun control effort, the Giuliani-Bratton team may succeed in reclaiming New York's many sad streets.[25]

'The average New Yorker' also refers to that portion of the extended gallery (extended because it includes non-residents like tourists) that is privileged and thereby protected. The 'safe space' narrative sub-theme promotes the liberty of the 'average New Yorker' for these are the subjects who should feel

---

a position similar to that of anti-Dinkins media: ". . . they (the New York Times), set the stage for the Dinkins loss in their news and editorial pages, notwithstanding the fact that they endorsed him."

[25] "A Broad Plan for Safe Streets," *The New York Times*, December 7, 1993, p. A26.

free to move about and consume the space of the city. These are the subjects for whom the city is to be made safe. To get a fuller understanding of characteristics of those who found themselves discredited by the 'deteriorating city' narrative frame it is necessary pick up the story after Giuliani's successful run for the Mayor's office; at a time when the ideal of safety was made manifest in the reality of control.

The policy implementation period began in 1994. Giuliani went to work transforming what had become crime-ridden 'deteriorating city' under the Dinkins administration into the world-class 'safe space' the city was reputed to be up until September 11th. A top-notch crime-fighter (in the from of police commissioner William Bratton) was assigned the task of re-organizing the NYPD and implementing new "get-tough" crime policies.

After unifying the three major police agencies (NYPD, transit police and the public housing police), one of the first policy measures undertaken by the newly installed Giuliani administration was the highly publicized "quality of life" measures. The "quality of life" measures were less about the creation of new laws to combat street crime than about the 'aggressive enforcement' of laws already on the books. The logic of the "quality of life" measures was not without its merits in that the 'average New Yorker' experienced Giuliani's 'deteriorating city' in the form of the petty offenses listed above, offenses which would be subject to the "zero tolerance" strategy of Commissioner Bratton. The "quality of life" measures also spoke directly to the moral degradation aspect of the 'deteriorating city.'[26] "Quality of life" offenses encompassed crimes that could contribute to *an image* of moral depravity in New York City. In this regard, the "quality of life" measures implicitly refer to the ideal imagined by the narrative of the 'safe space,' and with this, the 'safe space' as an Ideology of the Normative had become law.

Giuliani's "quality of life" measures proved most effective at ridding the streets of those crimes and criminal agents that most impacted the daily lives

---

[26] The 'Broken Windows' hypothesis is the theoretical criminological basis for the 'quality of life measures'. The 'Broken Windows' hypothesis states simply that appearances matter with respect to crime control and prevention. In this hypothesis, a neighborhood with many abandoned dwellings, trash in the streets, and a high degree of loitering is supposed to draw criminal elements and activities to the area due to the appearance of lawlessness. The 'quality of life' measures seek to counter the appearance of lawlessness by vigorously prosecuting the less severe nuisance offenses in an effort to reinforce the appearance of control over a space. See Kelling 1996 and McArdle 2001.

of "average New Yorkers," and whom contributed most to the perception of New York as a 'deteriorating city.' Everyone from the notorious squeegee men to public urinators and subway turn-style hoppers to the homeless (many of whom suffered from mental illness) were either ticketed or jailed. A comprehensive anti-graffiti program was implemented to rid city buildings, buses and subways of vandalism. The same fate was in store for the sex trade that made its home on historic 42nd street. The Giuliani administration cleaned up Times Square by shouting down or displacing the district's long-standing adult entertainment industry with the new 60/40 laws (which means adult businesses must reduce the amount of adult related products to 40% of their total business). This New York Times editorial piece points to the Giuliani administration's rationale for cleaning up Times Square:

> [Giuliani's] plan to regulate the location and concentration of adult video stores, topless bars and other such establishments is a response to legitimate community anger. That anger has grown as these businesses have spread into residential areas from Rego Park in Queens to Manhattan's Upper East Side, provoking realistic concerns about neighborhood ambiance, property values and crime.
>
> . . . The city's present zoning laws treat adult businesses like any other businesses, allowing them to open in areas zoned for commercial or manufacturing uses. But both the New York City Planning Commission and the Times Square Business Improvement District, of which this newspaper is a member, cite evidence that such establishments can discourage economic growth, lower property values and exacerbate crime.[27]

Once the adult entertainment businesses were out, the family entertainment corporations (like Disney) quickly moved in (Zukin 1995). These changes and the perceived increase in safety led to an increase in tourism (one of New York's leading industries), which spurred a new wave of consumption of the city. But, the 'quality of life' measures were not simply about the control of crime; they were also about the control of access to the city. The new crime control efforts not only kept the streets clean (in a very literal sense), but also kept the city (particularly the core of the city heavily consumed by tourists and other formal business concerns) free from undesirable subjects. As squeegee-men and other segments of the poor in New York City become the

---

[27] "Zoning, Sex, and Videotape," *The New York Times*, September 15, 1994, p. A22.

targets of social control, the 'deteriorating city' narrative frame incorporates class privileging in protecting 'the average New Yorker.' The New York Amsterdam News rebuttal references this class privileging:

> Consider New York Mayor Rudolph Giuliani's horrific revelation of the past week. When asked by a reported from WNYC during a budget briefing if the unspoken strategy behind his budget cuts was to push poor people out of the city, Giuliani replied, "That's not unspoken strategy; that's the strategy. We just can't afford it. Those left out will have the option of moving elsewhere. That will help make New York City like the rest of the country. That population shift may be a good thing for the city."[28]

These undesirables – the discredited – not only included the homeless, panhandlers, graffiti vandals and those who would urinate in public, but also groups of young people (especially Blacks and Latinos). These 'types' of subjects were those discredited by the 'deteriorating city' narrative frame as these are the subjects whose presence within the city was rhetorically responsible for its deteriorating status. If the 'safe space' ideal guarantees the liberty of the privileged 'average New Yorker,' the 'deteriorating city' narrative frame simultaneously calls for the control and containment of New York City's 'undesirables' (whether these subjects are deserving of the designation or not). In reporting on a law suit levied against the NYPD, Mayor Giuliani, Police Commissioner Bratton, the Civilian Complaint Review Board and several police officers from the 33rd precinct for unlawful arrest of a Harlem man, the New York Amsterdam News comments on this practice as a type of social control:

> The suit said New York City and the Police Department permitted, tolerated and encouraged a pattern and practice of unjustified, unreasonable and illegal arrests and assaults of black and Hispanics by New York City police officers.
>
> . . . In his suit (Raymond) Wells pointed out that arrests and abuses like he experienced against Blacks and Hispanics are commonplace in the city and that the city's top brass, including the mayor and police commissioner, knew and turn a blind eye and deaf ear to them.

---

[28] Abiola Sinclair, "Media Watch: Giuliani's Shameful Strategy; Export the Poor," *New York Amsterdam News*, May 6, 1995, p. 26.

"As a result the police officers of the New York City Police Department," Wells charges "were caused and encouraged to believe that Black and Hispanic persons could be falsely arrested and/or illegally assaulted, and that such acts would be tolerated and permitted by the City New York and the Police Department."[29]

Social Control as the Norm[29b]

For the most part the 'quality of life' measures were enacted to combat nuisance offenses most of which were non-violent misdemeanors. For those more major transgressions like drug-dealing, armed robbery, homicide and the like, Giuliani and Bratton turned to a veteran Street Crimes Unit to "own the night." The Street Crimes Unit was originally formed in 1971 and focused on ridding the city of illegal guns. It consisted of 100 or so specially trained officers, and had long been regarded as a tough elite group. Under commissioners Bratton (and later Howard Safir), the unit increased to over 350 officers, and was given the expanded mission of fighting more serious crimes. The Street Crimes Unit (hereafter referred to as the SCU) exemplified Giuliani's "zero-tolerance" philosophy. The unit patrolled those neighborhoods that were deemed high-crime areas and swooped down on individuals or groups of individuals who were presumed to be engaging in criminal activity, sometimes stopping crimes while in progress. The SCU did not make routine traffic stops, nor did they respond to domestic violence calls. This unit wore plain (street) clothes, drove city streets in un-marked cars and focused on the removal of illegal guns and narcotics (and the people found carrying these articles) from the streets. To do this the SCU was empowered by the mayor to detain and interrogate (stop and frisk),[30] any individual or group of individuals they deemed "reasonably suspicious."

The re-organization of the NYPD (along with the formation of the SCU) went a long way in reversing the perception of an ineffectual police force.

---

[29] William Egyir, "Harlem man sues city, Mayor, cops, for unlawful arrest, humiliation," *New York Amsterdam News*, November 11, 1995, p. 4.

[29b] Portions of the section are taken Lindsey, Delario, *Of Crime and Violence in the World City: A Case Study of the Amadou Diallo Incident*. Boston College GYRO Colloquium Papers, vol. VII, 2003.

[30] "Stop and frisk" is defined as "the lawful practice of temporarily detaining, questioning, and, at times searching civilians on the street" (Spitzer 1999). The legal precedent for the practice was set with Terry vs. Ohio 1968.

And the "success" of the crime/social control policies did not go unheralded, particularly by Giuliani and police officials. The Giuliani administration actively worked to make New York's increasing security part of the city's identity. From 1994 to 1997, regular updating of crime statistics for the city showed a steady decline in everything from serious violent felonies (like rape and murder), to petty offenses (See table 1 below).[31]

Historical Perspective

(Historical perspective is a complete calendar year of data)

	1993	1997	% Chg vs. '93	2002	% Chg vs. '93
Murder	1,927	767	-60.2	584	-69.6
Rape	3,225	2,783	-13.7	2,024	-37.2
Robbery	85,892	44,335	-48.3	27,129	-68.4
Fel. Assault	41,121	30,259	-26.4	20,716	-49.6
Burglary	100,936	54,866	-45.6	31,308	-68.9
Gr. Larceny	85,737	55,686	-35.0	45,74	-46.6
G.L.A.	111,622	51,312	-54.0	26,343	-76.4
TOTAL	*430,460*	*240,008*	-44.24	*153,844*	-64.26

Source: NYPD website. Notice the comparison in crime rates between the period ending the Dinkins era and first four years of the Giuliani era.

Giuliani's use of crime data served to provide New Yorkers definitive proof that their city was becoming safer (as this excerpt illustrates):[32]

---

[31] CompStat figures are preliminary and subject to further analysis and revision. Crime statistics reflect New York State Penal Law definitions and differ from the crime categories reported to the F.B.I. Uniform Crime Reporting System. All degrees of rape are included in the rape category. Prepared by NYPD CompStat Unit.

[32] Giuliani's use of statistics served more than the public good; the political benefits of broadcasting what would seem to be constantly falling crime rates are obvious. The use of crime statistics in the case of New York City during the 1990s takes on greater complexity when considering the decline in rates of crime and violence nationwide. The reasons for this period of relative calm around the nation have been associated with the economic boom of the mid to late 1990s and (ironically) the 1994 Clinton Crime bill. Stuart Hall discusses the political nature of crime statistics:

> Statistics – whether crime rates or opinion polls – have an ideological function: they appear to ground free floating and controversial impressions in the hard, incontrovertible soil of numbers. Both the media and the public

Announcing the yearly crime statistics with full fanfare at City Hall, Mr. Giuliani said the declines at least in part reflected his administration's efforts to focus on "quality of life" annoyances from aggressive panhandlers to squeegee pests, even as the police undertook new strategies to combat more serious crimes. "We've had an improvement in most, if not every area of the city in quality of life and a sense that these so-called smaller things are being paid attention to," he said of the "quality of life" issues that bedevil many New Yorkers. "At the same time, you've had substantial declines in most serious crimes, in some cases in historic proportions.[33]

The gesture of regularly updating New York City's crime statistics had the effect of perpetually re-iterating the 'deteriorating city' narrative frame. Implicit comparisons between the safety of the city under the Giuliani's management and the relative disarray in the city during the tenure of David Dinkins were reflected in the crime data. Giuliani's use of statistics to reinforce his claims about the safety of the city under his management did not go uncontested as this excerpt from The New York Amsterdam News illustrates:

The Rev. Al Sharpton said the removal of Capt. Louis Vega (police commander at the 41st Precinct) makes one clearly question if other statistics taken by police officers elsewhere are accurate. "This is why we need an independent citizens' review board to oversee the behavior of cops on all matters," he added.

Sharpton further said that as long as cops are left to police themselves, the public wouldn't get a fair and truthful analysis on any level. This sentiment was also shared by another activist.

Attorney Colin Moore said it's not surprising that a police captain would be accused of fabricating figures to show an unprecedented decrease in crime because the Giuliani administration is trying to put pressure on the NYPD to come up with favorable statistics.

---

have enormous respect for 'facts' – hard facts. And there is no fact so 'hard' as a number – unless it is the percentage difference between two numbers. With regard to criminal statistics, these are not – as one might suppose – sure indicators of the volume of crime committed, or very meaningful ones. This has long been recognized even by those who make most use of them, the police

(Hall, et al. 1978: 9).

[33] Steven Lee Myers, "Mayor Says Crime Data Affirm Strategies," *The New York Times*, January 8, 1995, p. A26.

"Mayor Giuliani intends to use this as a main theme for his re-election campaign," according to Moore. He said that very few people will deny that there is a decrease in crime, but the credit cannot be given to Giuliani.

"If there is any contribution Giuliani can take credit for, it would be the increase in police brutality and creating the impression that police officers are above the law," Moore declared.[34]

But, greater than the combined effects the 'quality of life' measures, the newly empowered SCU on crime, and the perception of safety in the city were the consequences of an ever-intensifying reality of control for the groups constructed as 'undesirable'. As an Ideology of the Normative, the 'deteriorating city' narrative frame did not truly propose making the 'safe space' ideal the 'norm'; rather, it was a 'reality of control' that was being normalized. Because of the spatialized relationship between this particular Ideology of the Normative and New York City, social control is not a response to transgression of shared norms, nor the mandatory reaction to deviance (criminal or otherwise). Social control is not a means to an end, because within the logic of the ideology, social control is the end itself. The normative ideal is safety, but the norm in the everyday is social control.

The crime and social control practices implemented during this era were fully informed by the Ideology of the Normative. The ideology served as an organizational paradigm that allowed the NYPD (as social control agents) to expeditiously determine those to be controlled within the city.[35] The 'deteriorating city' narrative frame that designated the 'undesirables,' combined with the quality of life measures (along with 'stop and frisk'), normalized the practice of controlling these subjects. It is my contention that as part of the process of normalizing social control and the actualizing of a 'reality of

---

[34] Zamgba J. Browne, "Fudged crime statistics no surprise, says Al Sharpton," *New York Amsterdam News*, November 11, 1996, p. 33.

[35] An organizational paradigm serves as a 'working ideology' (also known as a theory of office (Kelly 2003) that in a given space of control enables those charged with the task of social control (law enforcement) to quickly and easily sort through a range of criminal types for the purposes of diagnosis and action implementation. In referring to the use of this practice in settings as varied as social control to education Kelly (2003) writes:

> . . . each agency can be analyzed relative to its prevailing theory of the office, diagnostic stereotypes, career lines, staff socializing procedures (both the formal and informal aspects), client selection and assignment routines (i.e., the application of diagnostic stereotypes to actors), and the like (303).

control' the 'deteriorating city' narrative frame had two associative gazes that served to inform police practice as officers went about the business of patrolling the city. The gaze of protection is reserved for those who have been affirmed by the 'deteriorating city' narrative frame and designated the 'victims' of crime in the city. The gaze of suspicion casts the assumption of guilt on those discredited by the 'deteriorating city' narrative frame. The SCU became notorious for its racialized application of 'stop and frisk.' In the year leading up to the slaying of Amadou Diallo, Blacks comprised 62% of the individuals subjected to 'stop and frisk' at the hands of the SCU and 50.6% of all NYPD stops while making up only 25.6% of the city's population (Spitzer 1999).[36] This not only exemplifies the institutionalization of the gaze of suspicion, but this is also a situation of 'over control' where the Black and Latino communities disproportionately bore the cost of safety in the city. In the process of imagining the ideal New York City, the 'deteriorating city' narrative frame created the ideal subjects to control – Blacks and Latinos – as part of the process of actualizing that ideal scenario. As a component of an Ideology of the normative, any and all agents that fall into the category of 'discredited' (despite whatever else they might be in their everyday lives) are understood by law enforcement in terms wholly inscribed by the 'deteriorating city' narrative frame. The discredited are the 'undesirables' who serve as the source of crime and moral decay in the city. As a consequence, they are subject to the gaze of suspicion and ultimately, control.

Practices associated with the reality of control fall into a continuum of control that sees common occurrences like homeless removal on the same line of control as the relatively rare police shooting of a suspect. This New York Amsterdam News piece alludes to the trend of racialized policing culminating with the brutalization of Abner Louima:

> When Mayor Giuliani decided to create a task force on police brutality, he said that "sometimes it takes tragic and difficult events to create openings and opportunities to change things." Apparently the mayor has been out of touch with the relationship that exists between the police and communities of color. Rather than merely looking at the Abner Louima case, he should have referred to some past and recent cases. Examples include the

---

[36] The Office of the Attorney General's report drew from data collected using 175,000 "UF-250" forms (forms that are filed each time an officer makes a stop) provided by NYPD precincts from all over the city.

tragic killing of Eleanor Bumpurs, the beating death of Michael Stewart, and recently, the shooting death of 15–year-old Kevin Cedeno, and the shooting death of Nathaniel Gaines. The community's response to these tragic events (demonstrations) sent a signal to past administrations and the Giuliani administration that something is terribly wrong with the relationship between the police and the neighborhoods they patrol. Are these not tragedies?

Last year's report by the Amnesty International, which cited the NYPD with human rights abuses in its 1996 report, was completely ignored by the mayor and the police commissioner. In response to calls from community groups and from individuals from around the nation, the Center for Constitutional Rights convened the first National Emergency Conference on Police Brutality and Misconduct this past April. The event was attended by over 700 people from 50 cities and 16 states. This, too, was ignored by the current administration.[37]

The creation of the reality of control demonstrates the dominance of the 'deteriorating city' narrative frame and its associative imagery. Though the 'deteriorating city' narrative frame proved compelling enough to normalize discriminatory forms of social control for a great portion of the city's population, an alterative discourse of crime and social control practices did accompany the 'deteriorating city' narrative frame. Early in the policy implementation period, two personal practices of Mayor Giuliani were heavily commented on throughout the discursive record. Giuliani became well known for his staunch support of his police officers (whether they were right in their actions or wrong),[38] and refusing to meet and recognize leaders from the Black and

---

[37] Torres, Gabriel and David Love, "Is a task force the answer?" *New York Amsterdam News*, September 10, 1997, p. 44.

[38] In "Rudy Insults Cop: Giuliani praises Del Debbio for shooting Robinson in the back," A *New York Amsterdam News* (October 15, 1994, p. 1) piece comments on the Giuliani practice of supporting his police officers using an example of cop on cop violence:

Mayor Giuliani has come under sharp criticism for joining his Italian brothers and sisters in an all-out salute to the police officer who shot a Black transit cop in the back nearly two months ago, in what was described as "friendly fire."

Hizzoner reportedly participated in a vigorous applause during an annual party given on Columbus Day for Italian-Americans on the city police force. Giuliani was quoted as saying that Officer Del Debbio, who actually pulled the trigger, hasn't been accused of any crime.

In his further support of Del Debbio's shooting of Officer Desmond

Latino communities. The latter practice was commented on in this 1994 *New York Amsterdam News* editorial:

> Mr. Giuliani's attempt to isolate Blacks one from another by piously decid-ing who our leaders are is sure to fail. It is not so stupid of him to try to do this. This method has been used by White politicians for years and has succeeded very well.
>
> . . . Mr. Giuliani's continuing refusal to meet with those Black leaders who he has decided are not worthy of a meeting with him is a basic error in judgment that will not redound to the benefit of the city.
>
> It only serves to harden attitudes against him that already exist in some sectors of the Black community, and that has other Blacks who are willing to give him a chance, as he has asked, begin to harden for he appears to be arrogant and unreasonable. Giuliani may well be able to do this to salve his ego, but he cannot run a city running on this kind of political and moral "empty."[39]

These personal practices were consistent with the content of the 'deteriorat-ing city' narrative frame. Guiliani's strong support of police officers when-ever an incident called into question the actions of the police reinforces the law and order underpinnings of the 'deteriorating city' narrative frame by legitimizing the actions of the law enforcement officers (no matter how extreme) while discrediting claims of complainants or victims. Guiliani's refusal to meet with black and Latino community leaders reinforces the status of their respective communities as 'undesirable.' These practices would later add validity to the claims of those who sponsored an alternative narrative frame of crime and social control in the city. Only against this social backdrop can a thoroughgoing analysis of the Diallo incident can be made.

Robinson, he expressed deep concern and said Del Debbio must be given every possible support as he goes through an investigation. But Giuliani's action didn't set too well with a number of Black leaders.

[39] "Giuliani must change if he hopes to lead city," *New York Amsterdam News*, January 22, 1994, p. 12.

Discipline of the Criminal Innocent

"Giuliani Time" and Place of the Louima Incident

In the summer of 1997, the brutalizing of Haitian immigrant Abner Louima at the hands of the NYPD became the critical discourse moment that would open a space in the media forum for counter narratives of crime/social control in New York. The incident occurred August 9, in the Brooklyn police station where Louima was taken after having been arrested for assaulting a police officer and resisting arrest outside of a local night-club. Back at the station restroom Louima was beaten and brutally sodomized with what was said to the wooden handle of a plunger by officer Justin Volpe. The Louima incident opened a space in the media forum for the development of a critical counter-narrative of crime/social control in New York City in the era of Giuliani. The 'repressive city' narrative frame spoke directly to the reality of control that had become the norm in New York City. The 'deteriorating city' and the 'repressive city' frames existed in a dialectical relationship. That which was affirmed by one narrative frame, was denied by the other narrative frame. Where the 'deteriorating city' frame told the story of the city's decline because of crime, the 'repressive city' frame argued that the security of the city had been founded upon the repression of those groups implicitly designated criminal agents by the 'deteriorating city' frame.

The 'repressive city' narrative frame is one that affirms an inclusive urban space, and denies restricted access to the city and racialized policing. The 'repressive city' narrative frame views crime/social control policies of the Giuliani administration and the aggressive crime-fighting posturing of his police force less as the strategies for promoting public safety, and more as the day to day means of keeping the discredited – that is, populations of color, always already criminalized – in check. Sponsors of the 'repressive city' narrative frame (who included Reverend Al Sharpton's National Action Network, and the New York Amsterdam News) saw the torture of Abner Louima as a perfect example of racialized policing despite the fact that Giuliani (after coming to terms with the fact that the incident actually occurred), condemned the brutality and dismissed its occurrence as the actions of one rogue officer who should not be taken to represent the NYPD as a whole. Here is an example of the some of the discourse associated with the "repressive city' narrative frame:

From Grand Army Plaza – between Park Slope and Prospect Heights – the marchers began assembling early Friday morning.

. . . (M)archers with multicolored flags of practically every Caribbean island, the red, black, and green Black liberation flags and a plethora of Haitian flags were evident along with placards reading: "It's Stop Giuliani Time," "Guliani Time, Brutality Time" and "Criminals, Perverts, Racists," a play on the NYPD's adopted courtesy, professionalism, respect slogan.

"We are going to march until the police are accountable," the Rev. Al Sharpton said on a platform at the south end of Grand Army Plaza, minutes before the march began. "We are going to march until . . . the people have the right to live without fear of the cops or robbers."[40]

As an affirmation of the 'deteriorating city' narrative frame (as well as an implicit rebuttal of the repressive city narrative frame) a New York Post editorial draws comparison between the Giuliani and Dinkins eras:

"Giuliani Time." While it is patently unfair to hold a mayor personally responsible for isolated acts by individual police officers, it is beyond argument that the chief executive calls the cadence to which any administration marches. So maybe it is "Giuliani Time" in New York City regarding public safety and the New York Police Department. If so, we find it vastly preferable to "Dinkins Time."

Remember the Crown Heights riot? Anti-Semitic mobs surged through the streets for three days while cops – dodging rocks and bottles – watched impotently. While murder was being committed – as a gubernatorial commission subsequently determined – City Hall sat on its hands. It was a critical moment for the Dinkins administration – but it was by no means a defining event. That occurred earlier – during the racist boycott of a Korean-owned grocery, when the NYPD declined to enforce a series of restraining orders meant to apply reasonable limits to picketing and related activities. Which is to say, when the Dinkins-appointed police commissioner declined to direct that the court orders be enforced. Meanwhile, the city's streets were chaotic; aggressive panhandling, in particular, contributed to a pervasive sense that New York was out of control. And violent crime was rampant.

---

[40] "Marchers blast police barbarism at City Hall," *New York Amsterdam News*, 1997, vol. 88, p. 8.

> . . . Giuliani's response to the (Louima) incident has been swift and force-
> ful. There will be no cover-up. His appointment of an ideologically diverse
> task force to study the nature of police-civilian relations in the city certainly
> will spark dialogue – if not substantially greater understanding. Does any-
> body really want to return to "Dinkins Time?" Of course not.[41]

The Louima incident served as an important critical discourse moment, forcing comment from all sides of the crime and social control issue in New York
City. In fact, I argue that this was the greatest significance of the Louima incident as it served to complicate the discursive battleground of crime and social
control in the city. In a forum that had come to be dominated by one particular perspective on crime and social control in the city, the gruesome details
of the Louima incident forced the public to deal with an alternative vision
of what it meant to live in a 'safe-space.' The social cost of safety for those
communities discredited by the 'deteriorating city' narrative frame was placed
front and center in the public imagination by the Louima case.

Without denying that the Louima incident served as a powerful rallying-
cry for those seeking to redefine the nature of crime and social control policy in New York City – those who wished to disrupt the 'deteriorating city'
narrative frame – it is my contention that the brutalization of Abner Louima
was not an act of social control consistent with the 'deteriorating city' narrative frame as an Ideology of the Normative. The Louima incident took place
behind closed doors, and outside of official NYPD practice. Abner Louima
was not subject to the 'gaze of suspicion,' and the sexual nature of the attack
points more toward the individual psychology of office Volpe than to institutional police practice. And as such, the Louima case lies just outside of the
bounds and cannot easily be explained in terms of the 'repressive city' narrative frame. While the Louima incident was arguably racially motivated, it
can also be argued that this was not a case of 'policing' or crime and social
control. The Louima case was not indicative of social control as the norm,
nor is illustrative of the consequences of racialized policing. The Diallo case,
on the other-hand, served as the metaphor par excellence for both the 'deteriorating city' narrative frame and the 'repressive city.'

---

[41] "Giuliani Time," *The New York Post*, August 21, 1997, p. 56.

The Place of the Diallo Shooting

On February 4, 1999, four New York City police officers (officers Sean Carroll, Edward Mcmellon, Kenneth Boss, and Richard Murphy) fired 41 shots at an unarmed African immigrant named Amadou Diallo, while he stood in the vestibule of his Bronx apartment building and hit him 19 times, killing him instantly. More than a tragic set of events, the Diallo incident illustrates the normative power of an ideology rooted in the control of space and the bodies that occupy that space. The Diallo slaying is an example of police procedures and social control policies (as shaped by the influence of 'deteriorating city' narrative frame) working in the just the ways in which they were intended. This is not to say that the shooting of Amadou Diallo was in any way justified. Rather, the shooting falls neatly into what had become a normalized continuum of control. For instance, according to NYPD officials, Officers Sean Carroll, Edward Mcmellon, Kenneth Boss and Richard Murphy (all of whom were white) claimed to have been patrolling the area of Bronx where the shooting occurred "hoping to make arrests and, in the process turn up information about a serial rapist in the area."[42] But the story of the serial rapist seemed to have come from nowhere. The fact that there was a rapist prowling the Bronx neighborhood where Diallo happened to live received media attention only after Diallo had been shot. In regards to the media coverage of the serial rapist story, three of the four articles describing the rapist referred to the same statement made by an un-named police officials (cited above) with no further corroboration. These articles tacitly justified the shooting, intimating that Diallo (being black) could have easily been mistaken for a black rape suspect by police.[43] The racist inference, of course, is that all black people look alike. Another article questioned the serial rapist story, quoting residents of the neighborhood where the rapist allegedly stalked his victims who asked why the NYPD had not informed them of the rapists activities prior to the Diallo shooting.[44]

---

[42] "Officers in Bronx Fire 41 Shots, and an Unarmed Man Is Killed," *The New York Times*, February 5, 1999, p. A1.

[43] For example, "Safir: I Know What Kind Of Pressure Diallo Cops Faced," *New York Post*, November 21, 1999, p. 6, went so far as to describe Amadou Diallo as "a twin of the (rape) suspect."

[44] "Publicity About Rapes Met With Fear And Suspicion," *The New York Times*, February 17, 1999, p. B3.
One article did, however, corroborate the serial rapist story. A suspect was indeed captured in the area of the Bronx where the shooting took place, but there was no mention of the suspect's resemblance to Amadou Diallo.

These four members of the SCU were in Diallo's neighborhood, performing duties that they were empowered by the NYPD and the Mayor's office to perform. They were safeguarding the city from violent criminals who would otherwise run amuck and contribute to the city's decay. The 'quality of life' measures, the practice of 'stop and frisk,' and the newly empowered SCU were all part of the effort to transform New York City from a 'deteriorating city' into a city more in-line with the 'safe space' ideal.

When the four SCU officers encountered Amadou Diallo, the outcome was not dictated by the personal motivations of the officers or by "criminal" actions of Diallo; the only items found on his bullet riddled body were a wallet and a pager. The events that night were manufactured (in part) by the 'deteriorating city' narrative frame that guided the four officers in the determination of Amadou Diallo as "reasonably suspicious."[45] I argue that Amadou Diallo suffered the consequences of a *criminalized presence,* which is to say that the effect of the racialized 'deteriorating city' narrative frame was to render his occupancy – his very existence as a black male – in certain spaces of New York City and at certain moments as suspicious, worthy of further investigation and even criminal.[46] Though Amadou Diallo committed no crime that

---

Issaac Jones was charged last night with four rapes and detectives were grilling him about the lengthy string of serial rapes and robbers *that began in 1993,* police said [Emphasis added].

Jones' apartment on Story Avenue in the Soundview section is just a mile from the wheeler Avenue building where four Street Crime Unit cops patrolling for the serial rapist shot and killed African immigrant Amadou Diallo in February.

"There is no more heinous crime than a serial rapist," Safir said, charging that Jones once raped a mother in front of her child ("BX. Rapist Toll at 51: Cops," *The New York Post,* April 8, 1999, p. 16).

[45] "Reasonable suspicion" is defined as "a reasonable belief on the part of the officer – based on experience, observations, and/or information from others – that criminal activity is 'afoot' sufficient to warrant police intervention" (Spitzer 1999).

[46] In describing the broad discretion allowed police officers when making what are referred to as "Terry stops" (as in Terry vs. Ohio 1968), and the use of the doctrine of reasonable suspicion Frank Cooper (2002) writes:

The precise quantumness of evidence required for a Terry stop as opposed to a probable cause arrest is indefinable. As the (Supreme) Court puts it, reasonable suspicion is "not readily, or even usefully, reduced to a neat set of legal rules." Moreover, a court hearing a motion to exclude evidence based on a Terry stop must scour the "totality of the circumstances" to see if it can find a basis for reasonable suspicion. The "totality of the circumstances" is inherently difficult to define negatively. Thai is, what would not be included in the "totality of the circumstances"? Consequently, reason-

night, the normative power of the 'deteriorating city' narrative frame permitted the four members of the SCU to subject him to the 'gaze of suspicion' and to imagine that he was probably a serial rapist. In the end, the unarmed Diallo was deemed an eminent threat to the lives of the four officers and was consequently, and based on NYPD procedure justifiably, shot and killed.

The fact that it was reported the that four members of the SCU were searching for a serial rape suspect when they encountered Amadou Diallo added another dimension to the criminalized presence of the slain immigrant. When read in the newspapers that Diallo was shot by police who were looking for a serial rapist, the shock of an innocent man shot 19 times was somewhat lessened because rationally one could interpret the event as a tragic case of mistaken identity. Even if one does not question the convenience of NYPD's contention of there having been a serial rapist at work in the same area where Amadou Diallo lived, the idea of mistaken identity, combined with notion of criminal presence, has profound explanatory power in the mind of the 'average New Yorker.' Mistaken identity coupled with the criminal presence of persons of color (as determined by the 'deteriorating city' narrative frame) implies interchangeability amongst and between the criminalized subjectivities designated as 'undesirables.' Thusly, it need not have been Amadou Diallo shot 19 times that night. Any number of young black males (fitting Diallo's description) could have easily played the role of the slain innocent.

But what if it was the elusive rape suspect in the vestibule of the apartment building that night? All else being equal, the NYPD may not have known they had their man until after he had been shot and killed. The SCU was not looking for an individual "suspicious" of the serial raping case. As underwriters of the narrative frame that associates crime in the New York City with populations of color, the SCU were looking for a "suspicious" type – he imagined criminal agent par excellence as created by the 'deteriorating city' narrative frame. To that end, the SCU found the man they were looking for in Amadou Diallo. A spokesperson for Police Commissioner Safir tried

---

able suspicion is a fluid concept that takes its content from the particular contexts in which [it is] being assessed. The very terminology of the reasonable suspicion doctrine, therefore, prevents meaningful review of an officer's decision to stop or frisk a suspect. (885)

to use statistics to justify the over-control of persons of color like Amadou Diallo while reinforcing the racialized nature of the 'deteriorating city' narrative frame:

> The majority of people who were stopped and frisked in recent years in areas where the Street Crime Unit were indeed black, said a senior police official with knowledge of the department's preliminary analysis. But Mr. Safir will argue that the percentage of people stopped and frisked who were black is similar to the percentage of suspects identified by crime victims as black, and to the percentage of people arrested who are black, the official said.
>
> "The numbers are remarkably consistent," the official said.[47]

This excerpt from The Village Voice comments on Giuliani's use of statistics to counter claims of increasing police brutality in New York City:

> When pressured by Congressman Gregory Meeks during his recent House testimony, Giuliani put his hand up in the air and swore that there'd been 50 percent fewer "police shootings" in 1998 than in 1993, the final year of his predecessor, David Dinkins. Since the Diallo incident was more than a mere "police shooting" defined as the number of incidents in which police fire at a perpetrator, whether they hit him or not it was a curious statistical choice. Presumably the mayor picked it, rather than the much more parallel stat of "police fatal fire," because the numbers worked better for him.[48]

The Diallo incident exemplifies the 'safe space' affirmed by the 'deteriorating city' narrative frame. The 'safe space' New York City is not one where

---

[47] "Safir may use Data on Frisks to back Unit", *The New York Times*, April 19, 1999, p. A23.

[48] The article continues:

> ... Shots fired by cops in each of the first three Giuliani years exceeded Dinkins's last year, reaching a 1995 high of 535 more than 1993, even though shots fired by perps fell by almost 50 percent in the first Giuliani year and stayed near that low level. As with police killings, shots fired by cops did not begin to dip until 1997.
>
> ... the slight decline in police killings between 1993 and 1998 is hardly a mark of Giuliani-NYPD restraint when juxtaposed with the murder rate, a statistical correlation that held, in broad terms, for decades prior to the Rise of Rudy. Take 1985 for example. In the middle of the Koch years, murders suddenly fell to a decade and a half low of 1392, and police killings hit 11, a modern record. Yet, while murders last year were a mere 629, less than half the 1985 total, the 19 cop killings almost doubled the '85 figure (Wayne Barrett, "Ducking Diallo," *The Village Voice*, March 3–9, 1999, p. 23).

blacks and Latinos are summarily executed by police for standing in their apartment doorways, but one where crime and criminality are synonymous with the presence of persons of color. This is a city where safety was maintained through the criminal-legal control of populations of color. This *Village Voice* piece comments on the Diallo incident and what the city had become under the Giuliani administration:

> The mayor and Police Commissioner Howard Safir will no longer be able to summarily dismiss their critics as malcontents, the usual suspects out to defile City Hall. Despite the increasingly coarse nature of New York City's political life, City Hall can no longer afford its poisonous us-versus-them mentality. Because after Diallo, the city will never be the same. No matter how often Giuliani invokes the warm images of his Brooklyn youth and a bygone New York, this is not that city. In his sixth year as mayor, Giuliani's winning streak has ended. The Republican's miscalculations in the wake of the Diallo killing were so monumental that they have served to galvanize a remarkable cross-section of New Yorkers – rabbis, teachers, social workers, and even some Giuliani allies.[49]

In this excerpt we also see reference to Guliani's implicit comparison made between an idealized "bygone" New York City associated with the 'safe-space' ideal, and the 'deteriorating city' of 'Dinkins Times.' The space New York City became was one where communities of color bore the cost of creating the 'safe space.' This is the New York City created by policies of the racialized 'deteriorating city' narrative frame. This was the narrative that sought to normalize the criminalization of persons of color for the purposes of controlling and constraining their presence within the city. And it is this control of the presence of populations of color that lies at the heart of the 'repressive city.'

The 'repressive city' discredits not only the normalization of repressive crime and social control practices. It also denies the criminalization of communities of color that served the purpose of justifying or rationalizing the violence (ranging from undeserved 'stop and frisk' encounters to police shootings), committed against members of these communities by law enforcement. The death of Amadou Diallo embodies the most excessive form of this state

---

[49] "The City Will Never be the Same," *The Village Voice*, March 31, 1999, p. 38.

sanctioned violence. This case represents a quintessential example of 'over-control.' If the Crown Height Riot served as the premiere metaphor for the 'deteriorating city,' it follows that the slaying of a criminalized innocent in the person of Amadou Diallo serves as the most extreme consequence of the reality of control.

Conclusions and Implications

Perhaps the greatest indication of the normality of control in New York City came after the four SCU officers were put on trial for the killing of Amadou Diallo. Because of claims that it would be impossible for the four officers to receive a fair trial in New York City, the case was moved to Albany, New York. This outcome was due in large part to a defense argument that made the claim that the four officers shot Amadou Diallo in the process of carrying out their duties – though the outcome was tragic, it was a good 'stop' and proper police procedure. The defense's tactic proved to be effective as the four officers were acquitted on all counts. How does it make sense that four men after having been tried for 2nd degree murder, (of which all had fully admitted to taking part), should then be judged 'not guilty' of having committed any crime? It makes sense only within the context of a 'reality of control.' The 'reality of control' is a situation wherein social control (of even the extreme variety) is not only normalized but is in fact the norm.

This context wherein social control becomes the norm is the greatest consequence of the 'reality of control'. As an Ideology of the Normative, the 'deteriorating city' narrative frame set forth the proposition of creating the ideal 'safe space' predicated on the control of 'undesirables' (included among this group are persons of color and the poor). In such a context the phrase 'quality of life' takes on dialectical significance as an increase in the 'quality of life' for the 'average New Yorker' inevitably means a corresponding decrease in the 'quality of life' for those labeled 'undesirables.' The greatest social harm comes from the combination of social control practices inspired by such an ideology, and the 'reality of control' created by the normalization of these practices. Like those who would argue that one of the detrimental effects of an excessively violent media culture (film, television, video games) is the phenomenon of 'desensitization' to violence, it is my contention that in a society wherein social control is the norm, it is possible to become desensitized to 'over-control.' In post-September 11th America the possibilities of a nationwide 'reality of control' are becoming ever more real. The 'war or terror' has become an 'Ideology of the Normative' in its own right. It may be a simple matter of time before the 'war on terror' narrative, in an effort to create the ideal 'safe America' claims the life of yet another criminal innocent.

Karen McCormack

Resisting the Welfare Mother: The Power of Welfare Discourse and Tactics of Resistance*

> *". . . Guys, they used to call you welfare b's, you know?"*
>
> *"B's?" I ask.*
>
> *"B*I*T*C*H's, you know, call you names and say you need to get a job. Sit around waiting on welfare, that's worse than them embarrassing questions."[1]*

The words of welfare are powerful. Powerful in a double sense: the putative 'welfare mother', ever present in the political discourse of the 1990s, served clear political interests as a scapegoat for enormous economic and social changes threatening to undermine the comfort and stability of the middle and working classes. But the discourse is also powerful as it affects the everyday lives of those who engage with it, perhaps most clearly the women receiving public assistance themselves.

One remarkable product of this set of dominant discursive practices is the common sense meanings of welfare that became, by the early 1990s, so powerful as to seemingly silence alternative voices. Consider the following three quotes:

AUTHOR'S NOTE: Thank you to Stephen Pfohl for his helpful comments on all of the iterations of this work, and to the editorial collective at Boston College for comments on earlier drafts.
* An earlier version of this essay appeared in *Critical Sociology*, vol. 30, no. 2 (2004).
[1] Renee Davis, 26-year-old black woman, welfare recipient, Middle County.

The Chicago welfare queen has eighty names, thirty addresses, twelve social security cards and is collecting veteran's benefits on four nonexisting deceased husbands. . . . Her tax-free cash income alone is over $150,000. (Ronald Reagan)[2]

Miss Young, you're so full of shit. Why don't you get off your fat, lazy ass and get a job. You know, taxpayers like me really resent the shit out of you. What makes you so special that you don't have to get up and go to work? You just work the system and take and take and take. Why don't you get a life, get a job, and quit taking from people who do have lives and jobs. (Excerpt from a message left on the answering machine of Mara Anna Young, a California resident by the county's Department of Social Services. Transcript appears in *Harper's*, June 1997, p. 16)

I know a girl that used to have (children) so that she wouldn't have to work, because they had started this thing where once your child starts school, you got to go get a job. She would have a baby, and I am dead serious, this girl wound up with about seven or eight babies, and she's no older than I am. She wind up with about seven or eight babies because she didn't want to go out and work. She had gotten so lazy and so stuck on social service that that's all she wanted to do. [Alice Brown, 40-year-old black woman receiving welfare]

The three people quoted above, one a former President of the United States, the second a caseworker at the Department of Social Services, and the last a woman receiving welfare represent surprisingly consistent understandings of welfare. Each of these quotes suggests an understanding of welfare recipients as manipulative and undeserving, as a particular type of person, one who is less honest, less hardworking than the rest of us. While these three individuals do not share a singular, consistent understanding of welfare, these quotes display some commonality that exists despite their different social locations, revealing a "common sense" understanding of welfare that had solidified by the mid-1990s.

The discursive practices surrounding welfare and its recipients are part of "the moral economy",[3] a particular understanding of the relationship between morality and wealth.

---

[2] Quoted in Lou Cannon. 1991. *President Reagan: The Role of a Lifetime*. New York: Simon & Schuster, p. 518 (cited in Albelda et al., p. 92).

[3] Andrew Herman, in his study of philanthropy and the meanings of wealth, exam-

> Simply stated, the *moral economy of wealth* involves the discursive produc-
> tion and circulation of symbolic representations of wealth that serve to invest
> the behavior of the wealthy with a certain moral identity . . . through the
> moral economy of wealth, financial wealth is transformed into moral worth,
> and so-called redundant or excess resources are accounted for as signs
> of the bountiful surplus moral value and virtue of the wealthy. (Herman
> 1999: 7)

The Protestant ethic of hard work and ascetic living, coupled with the widely
accepted achievement ideology (of a fair and just meritocracy), celebrate the
achievements of the wealthy while deriding the shiftlessness of the poor (cf.
Weber 1930; MacLeod 1997). This specifically American equation of morality
and wealth provides for little acknowledgement of structural determinants
of opportunity and economic well being, relying instead upon explanations
for economic success or failure located clearly with the efforts and abilities
of the individual.

Programs to aid the poor in the U.S. have historically accepted the values
of this moral economy by attempting to separate the deserving poor from
the undeserving. The content of these categories has changed over time,
though the assumption remains that poverty represents a failing of the individual except in unusual circumstance (which have varied historically from
disability, death of a spouse, etc.). With large numbers of women with children moving into the workforce in the 1980s, the decline of married-couple
households, and the increasing number of African American women receiving assistance (following the Civil Rights Movement), poor single mothers
joined the "undeserving" category in what can only be understood as a backlash against feminist and civil rights gains (cf. Quadagno 1996; Sidel 1996;
Fraser and Gordon 1994). Within this moral economy, particular discursive
practices frame the welfare mother as undeserving: lazy, dependent, irresponsible, oversexed; she came to be seen as responsible for her own fate and
marked as an outsider. This image, the flip side of the image of the wealthy
philanthropist, clearly serves to maintain the status quo. The practices that
frame the welfare mother in such a way represent a dominant discourse, they
". . . are granted the status of truth, the agreed-upon frameworks of language
and meaning." (Maracek 1999 cited in Hollander 2002).

---

ines the ways in which the wealthy have come to be seen as the "better angels of
capitalism".

That this image represents the real character of poor women receiving assistance becomes taken for granted, apparently needing no substantive evidence. Ronald Reagan's welfare queen was shown to be a fabrication[4] and yet the image of the welfare queen lived on, long past Reagan's presidency. That women receiving welfare payments echo the judgments made against them (in particular ways to be discussed below) speaks to the power of discourse. Governmental assistance does not provide enough money for families to get by, nor does the minimum wage provide enough to support families. Edin and Lein (1997) have demonstrated the relative costs of work vis-à-vis public assistance for poor women with children, showing clearly that neither provides enough and that low-wage work leaves women worse off than welfare. Women on welfare understand this reality; they see the shortage of jobs, the impossibility of survival on a low-wage job while attempting to pay for rent and childcare. And yet even they often echo the sentiments about the lazy, manipulative welfare mother.

Herman proposes about the wealthy men that he studied that the ". . . moral economy provides these men with the basic discursive categories, linguistic repertoires, and vocabularies of motive with which they give rhetorical shape to their self-identity." Throughout his work he explores the relationship between the moral economy and the identity of wealthy men. The moral economy, particularly the specific dominant discourse about welfare constructs these categories for women receiving assistance as well. The particular discursive practices surrounding welfare are stigmatizing to women receiving assistance. That is, they mark these women as less deserving, more dangerous, even less human than the "rest of us."

By naming welfare mothers as others – dependent, immoral, and irresponsible – the dominant discourse allows for little positive identification as persons receiving assistance. Yet the understandings produced by the recipients themselves may run counter to the dominant construction. Lisa Dodson's (1999: 189) exploration of the lives of poor women and girls suggests that many alternative strategies exist in the margins, that women construct a range of responses to dominant constructions, ways that they ". . . tried to make sense of their place in the world and to hold on to themselves."

---

[4] When reporters finally found Reagan's 'welfare queen', she used 2 aliases to collect 23 public assistance checks totaling a whopping $8000 (Albelda 1996: 92).

Previous examinations of stigma among welfare recipients suggest that negative effects of the moralizing discourse are pervasive. Kingfisher (1996: 33) writes that the experience of stigma was so pervasive among her sample that "all recipients who participated in [her] study were aware of the stigma associated with being on welfare and felt compelled to address it in one way or another". Yet what I found in interviewing women receiving welfare was not a monolithic "welfare discourse" or "welfare stigma", a clear field within which women lived, but rather a more varied materialization of these dominant practices that was dependent upon the communities in which they lived. For women residing in mixed-class communities, interacting with the working poor, working and middle classes, Kingfisher's assessment rang true. These women were palpably aware of the dominant imagery and took steps to distance themselves from the putative welfare mother. On the other hand, women living in the inner city, surrounded by other poor people, appeared to be partially immune from the pernicious associations with the welfare mother. While they were not wholly unaware of the dominant practices, they were also operating upon a different field, one in which poverty and welfare receipt were understood quite differently.

In this paper, I explore how physical and social location shape and mediate the powerful, dominant discursive practices that serve to stigmatize those women receiving assistance. I will demonstrate how women in the inner city in some ways defy the previous studies of welfare stigma and construct, instead, a more structural interpretation of their life chances. And yet they do not escape the web of dominant practices completely unscathed. All welfare recipients in this study discursively acknowledged the power of the welfare mother and employed various tactics to escape from the damaging effects of this putative Other.

The tactics that people employ to negotiate the dominant categories and meanings are often ignored, since they may not produce an immediate challenge to structures of power. Yet these tactics are critically important in forming identity and in foreshadowing the cracks within which future strategy may be devised. As Ewick and Silbey (1992: 749) write, "To ignore . . . (these) tactics because they are momentary and private is to reinscribe the relations of power they oppose . . . To dismiss these momentary feints and ruses is to deny the dimensions of . . . identity forged in the cracks . . ." For women receiving welfare in the mid-1990s, these tactics were often all that was available to them as a means of resisting the powerful moral discourse on welfare.

Foucault has suggested that discourse, as a powerful material force, operates in a complicated way.

> We must make allowances for the complex and unstable processes whereby
> discourse can be both an instrument and an effect of power, but also a hin-
> drance, a stumbling-block, a point of resistance and a starting point for an
> opposing strategy. Discourse transmits and produces power; it reinforces it,
> but also undermines and exposes it, renders it fragile and makes it possi-
> ble to thwart it (Foucault 1990: 101).[5]

In this paper, I explore the relationship between dominant discursive practices and the possibilities for resistance. The ways in which poor women respond to such powerful practices tells us much about the operations of discourse and its relation to power.

Method

Armed with these questions, I interviewed 36 women receiving welfare in 1997, one year after the passage of the Personal Responsibility and Work Reconciliation Act of 1996, or welfare reform. I began the interviews in the inner city neighborhoods of an older, industrial, mid-sized city, Harbor City.[6] These were neighborhoods that had been devastated by the loss of manufacturing jobs, dramatic increases in rates of incarceration, and the rather fast deterioration of their neighborhoods over the past two decades.[7] Drawing from the literature on welfare stigma, I expected to hear from women of the

---

[5] Foucault does little to explain where resistance comes from. More traditional sociologists of power, such as Peter Blau and Richard Emerson argue that resistance results from the pain of the loss of other opportunities that have been denied, the loss of life's chances. From these interviews, it seems likely to be the case that resistance results from anger, though the anger seems to be directed not so much at the structural inequalities that produce their life chances but toward others that seem not to understand the rift between the lives of the poor and 'the rich'. When they meet up with others, in the welfare office, for example, who seem to locate the cause of poverty in the character or actions of the individual, they are angered. The resistance results from gap between the barriers that they see and feel in their own structural positions and the expectations that if only they worked hard enough they could make it without welfare.

[6] I have changed the location name as many more specific examples of encounters with caseworkers are discussed elsewhere.

[7] For a thorough discussion of the devastation of inner city neighborhoods, see Wilson 1996.

shame and pain of welfare receipt. While I heard much of the economic strain and challenge of raising children with so few resources, I heard very little to suggest that welfare receipt was stigmatizing. Instead, women described living in communities where welfare receipt was taken for granted, and seemed to expect that most other communities in the United States resembled their own. I suspected that the concentration of poverty in these areas was mitigating the effects of the dominant discourse, though I wanted to understand the mechanisms through which this occurred. To explore this, I decided to stratify my sample on the basis of place, and interviewed half of the 36 women in a rural/suburban county outside of the city, in areas where the poor, working, and middle classes lived in close proximity.

The majority of women interviewed for this study were participating in educational programs, primarily designed to prepare them to receive their GED. After distributing fliers to many community centers and educational facilities, several women elected to participate in the study, and from there I used a snowball sampling technique to locate other potential interviewees. The sample overrepresents women involved in educational and job training programs, which likely has an effect on the results presented here. However, it is important to note that this sampling bias existed in both locations, Harbor City and Middle County, so the differences between the two cannot be explained by the sampling technique.

Race also plays a very important factor in the construction of welfare discourse. The dominant image of a welfare mother is of a young, black woman, living in the inner city with a large family. While white recipients represented 39% of AFDC recipients in 1993, Blacks 37%, and Latinos (of any race) 18%, the imaginary welfare mother is black.[8] Ideally, my sample would have included equal numbers of black and white women, with some representation of Hispanic women as well. However, in Harbor City I was able to interview only 2 white women out of 17. Due in part to the heavily segregated neighborhoods of Harbor City, I had a very difficult time finding white respondents (64% of the population of Harbor City was African American in 2000). The white women that I was able to interview had children with black men. In Middle County, my sample was more racially diverse, although still included more black than white respondents despite the fact that the population of

---

[8] Data from 1994 Green Book, used in Albelda et al. 1996.

Middle County was 90% white. This difficulty in finding white women willing to discuss their experiences of welfare may be specific to the location, or may perhaps be related to the dominant imagery. As one woman in Harbor City put it, "when you live in the city, most people will see you because of the area you live in, that you're on it anyway." In the same sense that a woman's address might signal their welfare status, race may operate in such a way that others assume that it symbolizes welfare receipt, and thus the stigma exists regardless of self-disclosure or truth.

The Importance of Location

Living in areas of concentrated poverty, many poor people lack the networks of friends and family with access to jobs, transportation, and cultural capital (cf. Wilson 1996; Ferguson 2001). Those living in such spaces are left behind, with little way out of the poverty in which they live. The interviews that I have conducted suggest that there are other effects, perhaps not so pernicious, to living amongst people with equally scarce resources. With the exception of interactions with caseworkers and other employees of the Department of Social Services, daily interactions with members of their communities, in the neighborhood, at the medical clinic, and in the grocery store tended to be characterized by less stigma and ill-treatment for those in poor communities than for those in mixed-class communities.

Carolyn Barnes and Ayana Richards provide good examples of the differences created by location. Carolyn Barnes is a 26-year-old black woman who lives with her two children, ages 2 and 4, in an apartment complex in Harbor City. Her rent is subsidized; she had lived in her apartment for 18 months. The year and a half prior to the interview had provided a much needed stability for Caroline and her family, who had spent the 3 prior years moving between the houses of various relatives and friends. She lived in a "very nice neighborhood", though around the corner "they shoot like almost every other night." If she didn't have a window air conditioner, she says, she would hear the gunfire in the night.

Carolyn grew up with her father and paternal grandmother, while her siblings were raised by her mother. When she was 17, her grandmother died. At this point she was on her own, moving between the houses of relatives and friends. When her grandmother died, the welfare benefits were transferred over to Carolyn who then began to receive assistance for herself. Her grandmother had been strongly affected by her encounters with caseworkers at the Department of Social Services. Carolyn describes how her grandmother would come home from appointments, lay her head down on the table, and cry. Her grandmother was treated poorly, but was particularly upset at the inability of caseworkers to distinguish between the 'deserving' and 'undeserving', those who spent their money wisely and those who used it for themselves rather than their children. Carolyn says, "It seems like the people that's not really takin' care of their responsibilities getting more than the people who are."

While the workers at the Department of Social Services have treated Carolyn and her grandmother disrespectfully, this has not been her experience outside of the DSS. Using her Independence Card (electronic Food Stamps in the form of a debit card) in the grocery store has not, she says, led to poor treatment by the clerks at the store or by other customers. She has experienced no negative treatment using her Medicaid card, cashing her checks, or at any of the other places where her status as a recipient of aid would become evident.

Carolyn understands the struggle of single mothers in poverty well, as her own mother and grandmother as well as her boyfriend's mother and grandmother found themselves in the same situation. Carolyn describes the struggle of raising children alone with little money, and she connects her experience to those of her extended family.

> I can understand how some people feel because my grandmother used to struggle with me, then my mother was struggling with my sisters, so I mean I seen on both halves. And his family, my children's father family, his mother used to struggle with him all the time, so I can understand.

In Carolyn's words we can read more than a history of persistent poverty; Carolyn identifies herself as a member of a group – perhaps even of a class. Her own poverty relates to that of others, and through the experience of her family, Carolyn can connect her personal biography to larger forces, even if she is unable to name them clearly.

Carolyn describes herself as a worker, not dependent, despite the fact that she has received social services since she turned 18 with a short (several month) night job when she stopped receiving benefits. Her self-image, however, is more consistent with a working person.

> It's cool sometimes to be on it but sometimes you, you know, you want your check. Just like a person who worked want theirs every two weeks . . . I'm used to a paycheck, cause before I had my children I was workin'. From 14 on up, so I'm used to my paycheck.

She has no moral qualms about being on welfare and seems to be able to locate her welfare receipt within a history of her family. Despite the hassle, Carolyn sees the money that she is receiving as helpful since it enables her to be with her children until they are a little older. She takes great pride in the time and energy she spends on her children, taking them "somewhere they can have fun" and teaching them the things that they need to know. She is currently teaching her daughter "her address and her phone number before she goes to school." She identifies primarily as a mother and a worker, and she does not see her status as the result of individual actions, but rather of being born into a poor family. Carolyn does not see welfare as a measure of dependence.

Ayana Richards is a 19-year-old single black woman, who, on the surface, shares a great deal in common with Carolyn. Ayana was raised by her father and grandparents while her mother raised her four sisters and brothers in the same town. Yet Ayana has grown up in a predominantly white, middle class neighborhood in Middle County. She describes her neighborhood as safe, familial, and friendly, though she was "just like the only little black kid on the block . . ." Ayana continues to live with her grandparents while she is on the waiting list for public housing and attends school at the Family Friends Center (FFC), located in one of the Middle County High Schools.

After leaving school, Ayana came to FFC to continue her education in the hopes of getting her GED. For several months after her son's birth, she took classes and worked to earn money to support him, but was unable to continue the rigorous schedule. She found that she did not have enough time with her son, was unable to complete homework, and was chronically tired. After being supported by her grandparents for a short time, Ayana applied for social services.

> . . . That's when I signed up here . . . I mean, just for the time bein' while I'm in school, tryin' to get myself together, I decided . . . it'd be okay to get on social services for a little help . . . I don't need to be dependent on my grandfather all the time . . . it's just money 'til I get myself together, my education together.

Ayana hid the fact the she was receiving social services because she was ashamed and embarrassed. While her friends had encouraged her to get a check once she had the baby, her grandparents had never received assistance and she was especially embarrassed about telling them. "I was embarrassed about it for the longest time, I wouldn't even tell my grandparents that I got it . . . It makes you feel embarrassed inside, you know." Despite the fact that her mother had received assistance for her younger siblings when they were young, she didn't share the information with her mother, either, choosing to go to apply by herself: "I just told her watch the baby (while) I was walkin' to the store real fast."

Applying for social services was embarrassing as well. Ayana's spirits were buoyed only by the thought that she was doing what was best for her son.

> I was nervous, embarrassed, scared that somebody would see me. There was a lotta different emotions I went through that day. But I knew I had to do it for me, I mean for my son actually . . . But while we go to school full time he still needs Pampers, he still needs clothing, still needs shoes, needs coat. So I had to do what I had to do.

Like Carolyn, Ayana describes her welfare receipt in terms of her children and her ability to mother – welfare enables her to spend time with her son and is a sacrifice that she is making for his benefit. Welfare affords both young women a degree of autonomy and independence (a central concern fueling the welfare queen ideology), allowing both more time with their children. While both young women see welfare as enabling them to take better care of their children and to be better mothers, Ayana is still far more vulnerable to the stigmatizing effects of welfare discourse.

Ayana has a clear and present image of the way others view women receiving assistance. She describes the way that she imagines other people think of those on welfare:

> You're dirty, you're stupid, you have no education, you're not doin' nothing with yourself, you're layin' on the couch with a bag of potato chips and your kids just running around, rollers in your hair and a robe on, and you're watchin' your talk shows.

Ayana's experiences, in the grocery store, with her family, and in her community are in part shaped by the embarrassment that she feels about receiving assistance. While she is somewhat more comfortable with the idea now, when she first began receiving AFDC, she would try to conceal the symbols that marked her as a welfare recipient. Ayana recalls that she would quickly swipe her Independence Card through the machine and get it back into her pocket as quickly as possible so that no one would notice what she was using. While she has not encountered as much direct negative treatment as some of the other women interviewed, her shame about "sitting on social service" was significant.

Despite the stigma that she sees associated with welfare and her belief that the stereotypes are true for many women receiving assistance, she sees herself differently:

> I don't see myself like that. . . . I don't see myself as that type of person, I do do something with myself, even though it may not seem nothing, like nothing to them, it's a whole lot to me . . .

Ayana reinforces the deserving/undeserving distinction: while she sees her efforts to get her GED and develop the skills she will need to support her son as creating a reasonable justification for receiving benefits for a short period of time, she paints others as less deserving and in fact points to the undeserving to explain the stigma of welfare receipt. Ayana displays a very individualist orientation toward poverty and welfare; individual effort ranks highest in understanding poverty; this contrasts sharply with Carolyn's family and class orientation that exposes persistent poverty with structural underpinnings.

A group of friends from high school that did not have children figures prominently in Ayana's assessment of who she is and what she could be.

> I see them but they all in college, they all have cars, they all have jobs. And then with my friends who have the babies and they'll, you know, they'll stop pick up our babies and give them a kiss and then they're off on their merry little ways. And I just . . . I don't think my other friends realize but I just say look at us, you know, that could've been us. We could've been somebody. But *we chose the wrong life to live for a minute*. And that's really sad . . . we used to play with them in school. We wasn't no . . . worse or no better than them . . . I think about it everyday.

Ayana's language differs significantly here from Carolyn's; while both recognize some of the structural issues underlying poverty and welfare receipt, Ayana explains her own position in the system in the language of choice: "we chose the wrong life to live for a minute." Carolyn's explanation for her welfare receipt suggests that there was little choice involved, only survival. Ayana engages with the deserving/undeserving distinction by comparing herself with friends who have made it, who seem little different from her except for the choices that they've made and the success that they've found.

Carolyn and Ayana are both young, black women. Their fathers and grandparents raised both, while their mothers raised their siblings.[9] The similarities in the life history of these two young women are somewhat striking, yet the effects of 'welfare discourse' on the two are quite different. Carolyn does not associate negative imagery, stereotype, or poor treatment with welfare receipt. In fact, she is somewhat surprised by my questions, clearly seeing the lack of money, not welfare receipt, as the issue. Ayana, on the other hand, is quite familiar with the discursive construction fueling my concerns. She is embarrassed to apply for AFDC, to use her food stamps, even to tell her family that she has begun to receive aid. Ayana blames herself for her poverty, and because of her individualist orientation and self-blame, welfare receipt, even in the service of her son, is stigmatizing. Carolyn understands her situation as connected to that of her extended family and other members of her community. Her poverty is not the result of bad choices or lack of individual effort, but rather persistent poverty, lack of jobs and child care, and low wages. These different orientations shape and are shaped by the welfare mother discourse; they are not simply individual aberrations.

The differences to which these two women give voice follow patterns that emerged from the interviews conducted. The social location of these two women differ in at least two significant ways in explaining their different orientations toward social service receipt: community/location and family history. In this paper I will focus on differences in the communities in which these women live, though it is important to note that family background matters

---

[9] Only a few of the women in this sample had fathers that were present in the household while they were growing up. Many of the fathers of their own children are involved, though the involvement ranged from frequent contact to phone calls and visits from prison (quite a large number of fathers were incarcerated). The involvement of family members, whether fathers, grandmothers, siblings, aunts and uncles, is very important for these women in making a life for themselves and their children, though it appears to matter less who is providing the emotional and material support than that there is someone else that might be relied upon in times of crisis. Many of the women report that they feel quite sorry for other women receiving aid who have no outside help.

a great deal.[10] In both locations, women whose families had not received public assistance were much more conscious of the stigma of welfare than women whose families had received assistance. Comparing the two locations, women living in Harbor City, all of whom lived in areas of concentrated poverty, experienced much less stigma than women in Middle County.

Community and Location

The two communities in which I conducted interviews were markedly different in several respects. Harbor City is a mid-sized, older industrial city south of the Mason-Dixon line. Employment in Harbor City is scarce, with many of the jobs available for those with high school or less education moving outside of the city, yet 38% of households have no access to a car.[11] Employment is concentrated in retail sales and service industries, jobs that traditionally offer little stability, few benefits, and low pay.

In 2000, 12.4% of the U.S. population had an income under the poverty line. In Harbor City, however, 22.9% of individuals had incomes under the poverty line. As in most cities, poverty was concentrated in specific though large geographic regions of the city. There were many more residents of Harbor City who, while not under the poverty line, struggled to make ends meet. In fact, 44% of the population of Harbor City earned less than 200% of the poverty line.

The poor in Harbor City largely live in areas of concentrated poverty. Their neighbors and friends may have jobs, but they are often temporary, low-paid, and part-time. The factory jobs that had previously employed several of the women over 30 in my sample had relocated to the south or overseas. In their wake are left fast food, telemarketing, and other service work such as cleaning and taking care of the elderly. Many of those who are working are still eligible for Food Stamps, making Food Stamp use extremely common in the grocery stores in many areas of Harbor City.

Middle County lies about 60 miles west of Harbor City. In that 60 miles are many small towns, some farmland, apple orchards, farm stands, and typ-

---

[10] Less than 15% of my sample, only 5 women, grew up in households. that had never received assistance. None of these women grew up solidly middle class, though they were better off than the women whose families had received aid.

[11] 1990 US Census (http://homer.ssd.census.gov/cdrom/lookup/).

ical rural sights. One small city, Middletown, with a population of approximately 53,000, accounts for more than a quarter of the population of Middle County. The rest of the county is quite rural with many small towns, open spaces, and a number of farms.

The residents of Middle County are, on the whole, much better off financially than those in Harbor City. The poverty rate for individuals in Middle County was 4.5%, in 2000, far below the national average. Less than 14% of persons fell below 200% of the poverty line, compared with 44%, of Harbor City residents. There are far fewer desperately poor persons in Middle County compared with Harbor City; however, there is still a sizable population of persons who are near poor, vulnerable to the same economic shifts that have left so many behind. The poor of Middle County, surrounded by those doing a bit better, nonetheless live in communities that are diverse economically. Even those living in public housing projects go to school, church, grocery stores and laundromats with their working and middle class neighbors. They do not live in the underclass ghettoes that William J. Wilson has so clearly described.

The effects of location

The literature on welfare stigma suggests that women experience negative treatment in several locations when they are on public assistance, including the grocery store and medical clinic as well as the Department of Social Services (Kingfisher 1996; Rogers-Dillon 1995; Jarrett 1996). Women receiving assistance in Middle County experience much of the stigma reported in the literature. In interactions with community members and customer service representatives in area businesses, women on welfare reported frequent poor treatment, being marked as less desirable, as an outsider; as one young woman described, "... when you're on welfare, you're like an outcast..." [Annette Johnson]. An experience that all women receiving Food Stamps share is the visit, most often monthly, to the grocery store. Among the women interviewed in Middle County, most reported feeling uncomfortable and being treated as an outsider while they were at the grocery store. One young mother of three describes the situation this way:

> When I'm in the line and I have a lotta groceries on the counter, and I've
> got my two little kids in the cart and my older son standing there holdin'
> up candy bars, I want this and I want that. And then they, it's like they're

already mad enough as it is because I'm standing there with these three
screamin' kids, and then when I pull out my Independence Card I hear 'em
(breathes loudly), now we're gonna be standin' here all day. [Barbara Miles,
23-year-old black woman, Middle County]

While her children's behavior may be cause for some of the reactions she
recounts, the frustration that others express toward her increases when they
recognize that she is paying with an Independence Card.

Processing Independence Card transactions is little different from credit
and debit cards, yet women are frequently shopping monthly, and therefore
often have more than one cart full of food. Cashiers and customers alike
appear frustrated to deal with these women.

When you in the grocery store and you in line and stuff and you pop out
your Independence Card . . . they look at you, my god, cause you know,
when we go to the grocery store . . . I be getting like carts of food. You know,
I'm not comin' back out, once I get my food stamps . . . I go out to the grocery store that morning and I . . . spend all my food stamps so I don't have
to come out no more. . . .The clerks get mad sometimes because they don't
like pushin' all them buttons . . . It's not like a lotta buttons . . . They be actin
like it's a lotta trouble . . . [Annette Johnson, 20-year-old black woman from
Middle County]

Many women reported that clerks frequently drew attention to persons paying with food stamps.

I've noticed, with like the WIC program, now they have to get a manger to
sign each check and get it approved. . . . People look at that as a part of welfare too. And I've noticed people sayin' "We got a WIC approval over
heeeeere", or they'll say, really, really loud, "we got a problem with a
Independence Card", you know, and I think that's just drawin' unneces-
sary attention to the customer. [Jenny Mitchell, 23-year-old white woman,
Middle County]

Several (though not the majority of) women in Middle County explicitly
account for the differential treatment that they received by explaining that
cashiers and other customers saw them as less worthy since they received
welfare. Two women described the following encounters:

. . . today I was in the store and I wanted to make a food stamp . . . transaction and then a cash transaction. Well, I made the food stamp transaction,

then when I told her I wanted cigarettes off of my cash card, she just gave
me a real dirty look. And I'm like, 'excuse me, do you have a problem with
me usin' my card?' And she didn't answer me, she just started pushing buttons and stuff . . . [Jenny Mitchell, 23-year-old white woman, Middle County]

We get out to meetings outta here every Monday night and . . . we stop at
a store to get like sodas and stuff to take to the meetings with us, and I had
a Independence Card and I was in line one day, and . . . these guys had been
waiting for a long time, behind us, and they said . . . something like . . . 'they
need to let us get up there, we're people that work for our money, you know
what I mean?' . . . and they were really offended that we were in there buying stuff, on the card . . . [LaVonne Wells, 30-year-old black woman, Middle
County]

In Middle County, women's accounts of interaction in the grocery store mimic
those found in other studies of welfare stigma. Their accounts are not surprising. They are, however, markedly different from those of women residing in Harbor City.

Recipients in Harbor City tell a very different story about using their
Independence Cards. They experience few problems in stores and, with little exception, feel that there is little stigma associated with Food Stamp use.
When asked about the experience, women responded in ways similar to the
following:

I get my food and I pay for it with my Independence Card and that's that
(laughs). [Sharon Jones, 26-year-old black woman, Harbor City]

. . . you just . . . get what you gonna get, take the card to the machine, they
ring up your stuff and punch out, punch the amount that you need and
that you spent and then they, um, slide the card through the machine and
punch it, see if you got that amount on your card. . . and it pays . . . [Shavonne
Perry, 26-year-old black woman, Harbor City]

The questions that I asked about stigma experience were most often met with
surprise in Harbor City. The idea that they might be looked down upon for
receiving social services and using Food Stamps was novel to several of the
women, surprising given the amount of media attention that conservative
politicians bashing 'dependency' were receiving.

The women that I interviewed accounted for the neutrality of the interactions in the grocery store in two ways. Both of these explanations refer back
to the concentration of poverty in these areas. First, some women believed

that they were already pegged as welfare mothers because of their residence in the inner city, so using Food Stamps would not change the treatment they received.

> ... when you live in the city, most people will see you because of the area you live in, that you're on it anyway. So you really don't have to worry about it. [Shantrise Jackson, 23-year-old black woman, Harbor City]

The more common account, however, was that Food Stamp use was so common that everyone was affected. Because their lives and their communities were so poor, their social networks and extended families, in fact, entire neighborhoods were living so close to the edge that if they were not now relying on Food Stamps, they could be at any moment.

> I don't think, wherever you go it doesn't matter, you know, you use the card everybody's gonna yield to you because you have to use the card. And I don't think they gonna treat you differently. Cause everybody's using it. [Donna Oakley, 33-year-old black woman, Harbor City]

For those managing to get by without food stamps, most were likely to have used a friend or relative's stamps in the past. As Carolyn Barnes remarked, "... people who don't have 'em use 'em, cause they use their cousin's or ... somebody else's." The common experiences of poverty and recognition of the constant threat of poverty in Harbor City seem to strengthen the group identification described by Carolyn above. Perhaps because all residents recognize, as Donna suggests, their own material closeness to poverty, there is less moral judgment of these poor women. Their neighbors, families, and friends can largely understand their situations and see their poverty not as the result of individual moral failing, but as bad luck or structural constraint that they might well share, if they do not presently.

For these women in Harbor City, the economic landscape looks bleak. Their reality is one in which the vast majority are poor and few are wealthy. In their descriptions of the city and state, they recognize that there are working poor, but they see virtually no middle class. Their language that "everybody's using it" extends beyond their descriptions of their own neighborhoods to the country at large. They envision that the state and the country look much like the city in which they live, one in which everyone is vulnerable at any moment. The women in Harbor City locate themselves as members of a group, the poor, and while they overestimate the amount of poverty in the country, they understand poverty as a condition of their social group rather than a primarily individual affliction. They understand the welfare mother discourse as wrong, not only because of the conditions of Harbor City but because they imagine that the vast majority of Americans face similar conditions.

Shantrise Jackson is one of the few women living in Harbor City whose vision of the economic landscape differed. She was raised by her parents in a suburb of Harbor City, attended a middle class school, and moved into the city when her parents divorced when she was in middle school. Having experienced life in a working and middle class community, she thought that the stigma would be much greater receiving welfare in such an area.

> If I lived in another area . . . I think I'd probably be treated more different. Because the people there mostly work, and they buy new cars, and they assume that because you're on social services that you're a bad person, that you're blastin' music, that you're loud and things like that. . . . I think that I would be treated worse, that I would have more problems. [Shantrise Jackson, 23-year-old black woman, Harbor City]

Unlike Shantrise, most of the women in Harbor City had never left the city. Some had never even been to the Harbor, renovated 10 years earlier, a tourist destination for many from other states and less than 10 miles from their homes. Since their social worlds were so circumscribed, they understood the poverty of their communities as representative of the country.

In other community locations such as banks, hospitals, and neighborhoods, interactions mimic the difference that exists between Middle County and Harbor City in the grocery stores. While women have very few problems in the city using Medicaid or getting money from their cards, those in the county experience a much more negative response. Annette Johnson, a 20-year old black woman living in the housing projects in Middle County, describes her experiences this way:

> You go to the doctor's, you pop up your medical assistance card and, I mean, they act like they don't wanna give you the best care they can. You know, I just feel like I'm the outcast. I mean, people and their little remarks, like cab companies, they be like, we stay busy when it's check day because everybody get their checks and they wanna go out to the mall and they call the cabs. And then you get people that's at the stores, I mean, people I know that work at the malls used to say it, you know, everybody in here around . . . they say mother's day . . .

The mall employees call it Mother's Day when checks come, suggesting an image of women waiting to spend their money on new clothes and jewelry while their children go without.

Even in interactions with neighbors, women in Middle County face stigma as welfare recipients. Surprisingly, it is not only from those that work but from poor men as well, using the epithet of 'welfare bitch' to attempt to discipline women who dare speak out against the drug dealing going on in the housing projects in which they live. Renee Davis, a 26-year-old black woman from Middle County, told me that in the housing projects "... guys, they used to call you welfare b's, you know, all that ..." I ask, confused, "b's?". "B-I-T-C-H's, you know, call you names and say you need to get a job, sit around waiting on welfare, that's worse than them embarrassing questions." Surprised that she had encountered this in a public housing project where presumably everyone was receiving some help, I asked who had said this to her: "... it came from drug dealers, they say go in the house welfare bitch ..." Other women reported similar encounters with men in the housing projects in Middle County. I heard no similar accounts from the women in Harbor City.

For the women in Middle County, the stigma of welfare was an everyday, face-to-face, lived reality. For the women of Harbor City, even those who read the newspapers and were aware of the public discourse going on nationally, welfare stigma was not the reality of their daily lives. Aside from their experiences in the offices of the Department of Social Services, many had only seen the spectacles of women fighting with one another about welfare on the daytime talk shows. Their other experiences suggested nothing of the level of rancor marking the public discourse. The explanation for this lies in the concentration of poverty within which the poor of Harbor City live.

The effects of the stigma associated with public assistance are not direct or clear. Discourse works in and through the specific contexts and histories in which these women live. The discursive field that is created through the public debate around welfare turns out to be a somewhat different discursive space than that which organizes the lives of the women in Harbor City. These women still experience some of the fallout from the dominant discursive practices, particularly in the ways that they are treated in the welfare offices. Their daily life practices in their communities, with their families, and with their peers, however, are not conducted in the same discursive space. While they must negotiate their identities in the welfare office (as well as other institutional spaces), they do not internalize the stigma of welfare nearly as much as do the women in Middle County. If they are constituted outside of, and in opposition to, the 'normal' adult citizen, they are surrounded by others who are outside, if not because of welfare receipt then because of out-of-wedlock childbearing, relationship to the criminal justice system, race, and the devastating effects of long-term poverty. Their identities are shaped by their group, or class, affiliation more than by their welfare receipt. Welfare matters less for their identity than it does for the women in Middle County, except when they have a point of reference outside of their immediate neighborhood and circumstance.

This difference in the impact of the dominant construction of the welfare mother for the everyday lives and identities of women based on location has another effect: women whose identities were least harmed, who experienced the least amount of stigma in their daily lives, were most able to enact strategies of resistance, demonstrating the hypocrisy of the dominant discourse and its practitioners. These alternative practices, those that do not echo and reinscribe the dominant discursive practices, are not available to all women receiving assistance, even though they are all aware that the money received from the state is a paltry sum, enabling no one to live well.

Possibilities for Resistance

> A society is thus composed of certain foregrounded practices organizing its normative institutions and of innumerable other practices that remain 'minor', always there but not organizing discourse and preserving the beginnings or remains of different (institutional, scientific) hypotheses for that society or for others. (Michel de Certeau 1984: 48)

The *remains of different hypotheses* can be heard in the meanings attributed to welfare by many of the recipients, whose understandings of the administration of social services to the poor contain within them a challenge to the universality of the dominant construction. To a certain extent, strategies that accommodate the dominant discourse, that reinforce the common sense understanding of welfare receipt, also resist by challenging the application of such an understanding to themselves. All of the women that I interviewed rejected some part of the welfare mother discourse. For some women, this was an active process of separating themselves from the putative welfare mother while discursively reinforcing her existence, while for others resistance took the form of direct discursive challenge to the underlying assumptions about poverty and value that bolster the ideology.

Scott (1985, 1990) uses the phrases "everyday forms of resistance" and "hidden transcripts" to describe those discursive practices that resist dominant constructions. Everyday forms of resistance are those mundane practices that occur as recipients participate in their daily lives, challenging in an unorganized and often invisible way the meanings that render them powerless objects. None of the women interviewed belonged to any type of welfare rights organizations, and while they may have discussed their rights with lawyers at legal aid offices or their teachers at various educational sites, they weren't involved in any organized effort to change the policies or meanings of welfare. The types of resistance in which they were engaged were all a part of their everyday lives. As one recipient put it, they are "just livin' life".

Engagement with the dominant discourse may in fact make possible these "reverse" discursive forms. Foucault (1990: 101–102) writes that:

> There is not, on the one side, a discourse of power, and opposite it, another discourse that runs counter to it. Discourses are tactical elements or blocks operating in the field of force relations; there can be different and even contradictory discourses within the same strategy . . .

By recognizing the category of the welfare recipient or welfare mother, by naming poverty and deservingness, these women are also able to construct their response and, sometimes, their resistance. The forms of their resistance are not arbitrary but are patterned clearly by the level of stigma and surveillance that they experience.

The tactics that my respondents employed might be divided into two types or categories, discursive and instrumental. Instrumental tactics were designed to secure for them the best possible treatment in a variety of situations, particularly in the welfare office. At the same time, recipients deployed a number of discursive tactics designed to counteract the negative effects on their identity of the dominant discursive construction of the welfare mother. Many of these tactics accommodated the welfare mother discourse while protecting the identity of the particular woman speaking. They were able to do this by emphasizing their own commitment to work, to mothering, to thrift while juxtaposing their own values and practices with those of the putative welfare mother. This tactic of accommodation employed the distinction between the deserving and the undeserving poor, using this dualism to at once justify their welfare receipt and embrace the putative welfare mother of the dominant discourse. Women in both Harbor City and Middle County employed these accommodating tactics to protect their identity in a variety of ways.

Women living in Harbor City, and to a lesser extent those in Middle County with a family history of welfare receipt, were often able to directly challenge the American Dream ideology, a belief that by working hard and playing by the rules, anyone can be successful. The poverty experienced by many of the parents and grandparents of these women provided an example of the limited mobility available to most poor people, particularly those in regions of concentrated poverty. These women also came into adulthood during the deindustrialization of Harbor City and witnessed not only the loss of factory jobs but also a rapid increase in the imprisonment of men in their communities. While most are hopeful for their individual futures, their aspirations are tempered by the world that they see around them. Most aspire to be day care providers, beauticians, hospital and nursing home aids, and other low-paying service sector employees. Many expressed an understanding that poverty was persistent, structural, and intergenerational, and while they frequently tempered that belief in their hopes for their children's futures, they viewed the criticisms of welfare recipients as arising from a class privilege that they would never enjoy. In other words, they had a certain degree of class consciousness, understanding that they had similar interests with others in their same situation.

For these residents, the stigma associated with welfare receipt appears to come from those who were born with more: wealth, status, and educational opportunities. The recipients express what I found to be surprisingly little resentment toward those who were born with so much more than they. At the same time, they suggest that those who see welfare in moral terms lack an understanding of their structural positioning.

> It's really hard. People don't understand, not the people who was born, you know, with money in their pocket. Some people aren't born like that. Some people born struggling and gonna stay struggling. [Ayana Richards, resident of Middle County]

Those who were not born struggling simply cannot understand life at the bottom of the economic hierarchy. Those who were born with more are often seen as less capable, since they would find it very hard to manage in the conditions that recipients of welfare face everyday.

This understanding of life from the bottom includes a critique of the structure of the economy, not with regard to corporate excess or CEO pay, but rather of what they see: the paucity of jobs that pay a living wage. These women are especially hard hit by the restructuring of the economy; they are most in need of health insurance and family friendly policies, yet they are the least likely to have access to jobs that offer such benefits. They are subject to increasing pressures to work, yet they see few good options for childcare. They will require larger apartments than a single person along with money to pay for daycare, yet they are faced with rising rents and less help from the state. They understand these contradictions in terms of their daily lives.

> There's no jobs. Or if there is jobs, they don't pay enough . . . Even if I do have a job, where am I gonna stay so that I can keep this job, know what I mean? Or if I do get a job, I'm not gonna be able to pay the rent, let alone put food on the table. [Carmen Diego, resident of Middle County]

The lack of good jobs, insurance, educational opportunities, affordable housing – all of the structural conditions that keep them from working and moving out of poverty – are apparent. The stigmatization of welfare mothers must, they conclude, come from a failure to see these conditions on the part of those born "with money in their pocket".

While some resistive tactics were available to women from both areas, some tactics were almost exclusively employed by Harbor City residents, tactics that challenged the underlying assumption of the achievement ideology, the belief in a clear and just meritocracy. These acts are similar to what de Certeau calls tactics. Tactics are actions that take place "in the space of the other. [They] must play on and with a terrain imposed on . . . [them] and organized by the law of a foreign power" (de Certeau 1984: 37). The tactics engaged in by recipients were often not calculated in a direct and clear way. However, in recreating those interactions in narrative form for me, an amount of deliberation appears. Consider the following discursive reversals of the dominant understandings of welfare:

> I feel as though if we wasn't on social service, they wouldn't have a job
> [Carolyn Barnes, Harbor City]

Referring to negative treatment by caseworkers, many women in Harbor City employed a customer model of social services to reverse the trajectory of dependency. The following represents another take on dependency,

> I ain't feelin' like they're takin' care of me. They ain't even give me enough
> money for all that. That's to pay a bill, one bill, and that be the whole check.
> Please. [Nakeia Ellis, Harbor City]

And finally, many Harbor City residents juxtaposed their supposed dependency with their independence from others:

> Long as I got my own I can say leave, get out, do whatever you gotta do.
> I just like mine. I like having my own. [Carolyn Barnes, Harbor City]

Residents of Harbor City much more commonly reversed the notions of welfare dependency in their discursive practices. While these practices may not have been calculated actions, as they are continually repeated, they may begin to move from tactic to strategy. While nearly all of the women use some accommodation tactics, those on the resistance end of the continuum are employed almost exclusively by women who experience low levels of stigma and less surveillance than their counterparts, primarily residents of Harbor City.

Along with an understanding of the structural underpinnings of poverty, some women were able to engage in a structural critique involving the system of values of the dominant society that equate money and the things that money can buy with success, happiness, and moral rectitude. In other words, they challenged the moral economy. In the midst of a culture focused on economic success, poverty and welfare mark those, even the hardworking poor, as failures. Some women challenged the value system on which these judgments are made.

> The people in my complex, all of us have two bedroom apartments and
> some of them working, you know. Their apartments are cute, but still, I
> mean I tell them in a minute, you ain't no better than me. Because you ain't
> in a big house. [Carolyn Barnes, resident of Harbor City]

Carolyn challenges the distinctions between working and nonworking, arguing that she cannot be judged as inferior to women who are working, and yet at the same time reinforces the cultural value on economic success in claiming that the other women better because they aren't "in a big house".

Others substitute an alternate set of values, oftentimes based on religious or spiritual beliefs, to suggest that their economic status is not the most important thing and does not reflect a personal lack.

> When we die, God don't look at how much you had in life. He don't look at, well, this person had a mansion and a car and graduated on time, so we'll put her in the highest category, you know. [Annette Johnson, resident of Middle County]

By asserting a seemingly more just set of values, based upon kinship and reciprocity or on religious doctrine, the stigma of welfare is effectively rendered powerless. This use of religious values to challenge the moral economy was one resistive strategy that appeared equally open to women from Harbor City and Middle County, suggesting that religious discourse carried power for these women that politico-economic practices did not. References to religious beliefs and values were prevalent in the majority of interviews conducted, suggesting that religious belief is an integral part of the sense-making practices of these women. Even those women that most internalized the stigma of welfare receipt were able to imagine themselves as worthy in a more spiritual sense.

Each of these structural strategies of explanation provides a greater challenge, a more systematic critique, of our economic system and cultural values. They do not, in their most complete form, accommodate the dominant discourse on welfare. In fact, they do not accommodate dominant cultural understandings of worth and value. While these critiques are less common than the accommodating strategies of claiming deservingness, they nonetheless serve an important role in challenging the dominant understandings of poverty and welfare.

The ability to articulate resistive definitions is tied to the location (both social and geographical) of the individual. Using focus groups, Hollander (2002: 490) examined the ability of women and men to articulate alternative visions of gender that deemphasized or refuted the notion of female vulnerability. She found that "resistance is more common in contexts where those who are disadvantaged by existing hierarchical structures can interact freely." Safe spaces facilitated challenges to the dominant construction of vulnerable femininity; women in all-female focus groups were much more likely to articulate a resistant view of women and to have that view upheld by the group. While the women in Harbor City live in some of the most physically dangerous neighborhoods in the United States, the concentration of poverty may create a "safe space", a discursive space where alternative understandings of welfare and poverty and challenges to the moral economy might be able to flourish. This safe space may be made possible by the lesser degree of surveillance to which the women in Harbor City are subject. Foucault (1977) and Staples (1997) argue that surveillance has become a prevalent form of discipline in modern society. While we are all subject to surveillance, women on welfare are the object of more explicit and demeaning surveillance, from the questioning by social workers to the examination of items in their grocery cart at the check out. While Harbor City women are subject to the surveillance of the Department of Social Services, they are protected somewhat from community surveillance by virtue of their shared material conditions and group identification in Harbor City. This partial protection created a safe space in which alternative and resistant practices could emerge.

Discourse, Stigma, and Resistance

A clear pattern emerges if we map the deployment of resistant and accommodating tactics against the levels of stigma, the discursive context, that welfare mothers experience. What we find is that respondents in Harbor City and Middle County participate almost equally in accommodating strategies, with nearly every woman claiming deservingness and separating herself from the imagined 'welfare mother'. This suggests that, counter to the almost total lack of stigma associated with welfare use in inner-city poor communities, women in these contexts still live out their lives in relation to the same discursive field that positions them outside of the boundaries of the acceptable. Perhaps they don't live within it in the same way that women in Middle County or women from working class families do, but they, nonetheless, constitute their identity in relation to that dominant discourse.

On the other hand, as oppositional tactics become more resistant, their use becomes more clearly restricted to women experiencing low levels of stigma, namely those respondents living in Harbor City. Women that experience high levels of stigma, represented by those respondents from Middle County, seldom employ the most oppositional, resistant tactics. This does suggest that the discursive field strongly effects the constitution of the self, rendering some women more 'docile', in Foucault's language, than others. The truly resistant voices are those located furthest from the center of the discursive field. Hollander (2002), in the study discussed above, finds that "successful gender resistance was almost always collaborative; it required multiple voices to challenge the status quo." Harbor City represents one place where poor women of color discursively challenge the status quo quite openly; the irony (and arguably the reason) of this is that they are the least able to launch material or symbolic challenges that might truly threaten the moral economy.

Reading further into the data, it appears that two sets of stories emerge about welfare and what it means to be a welfare mother, and the differences between these two stories are in part structured by women's relationships to welfare discourse. Women experiencing high levels of stigma, those in Middle County, tend to talk about their welfare use as the consequence of bad choices, to compare themselves with others that may have been more financially successful, and in general to approach these issues with an individualist orientation. These individuals appear to have internalized the American Dream ideology – if they work hard enough, stay on the straight and narrow, they too will make it. They reinforce the distinction between the deserving and undeserving poor, and while they often see themselves as deserving, they do not extend this judgement to other poor women.

We can compare with this the women living in areas of concentrated poverty – areas less penetrated by the dominant discursive practices. These women frequently explain that everyone is vulnerable to poverty, and that those making judgments about the welfare poor ought to be careful. No one is immune, from this point of view, from the constant risk of poverty. This group of women tends to overestimate the number of poor in the country, while the other group tends to underestimate it. Seeing poverty as persistent and structural, these women understand that their personal choices, good or bad, are not wholly responsible for their situation in life. They see themselves as members of a group, a class, that has largely shaped their opportunities in life. While they have aspirations for the future, they are quite modest.

Both groups of women want to leave the welfare rolls, yet their desire to leave welfare seems to be fueled by different concerns. From these interviews it would seem that the high stigma group, the respondents from Middle County, want to leave because welfare is ethically problematic, leads to poor choices, poor morals, and is a bad example for children. These seem self-evident truths in their accounts of future plans and expectations. On the other hand, the respondents from Harbor City appear to be more concerned with the material conditions of welfare receipt. For the respondents from Harbor City, welfare appears primarily undesirable because it does not provide enough money, is unreliable, and is unpleasant. Welfare appears in the accounts of the Harbor City respondents to be primarily a practical issue rather than a moral one.

Conclusions

Welfare and the 'welfare mother' are constituted in and through discourse, and yet mothers receiving welfare are hardly docile bodies; while the dominant discursive construct of welfare mothers touches their lives in myriad ways, from the policies that flow from it to the treatment that they receive, they also employ a set of oppositional discursive and instrumental practices that allow them to forge alternative meanings and identities in the cracks of dominant institutional and discursive practices. The specific communities in which they live structure their understandings of welfare at least as much as does the dominant discourse. Women in Harbor City, embedded in poor communities, implicitly understand their connection to other poor people, their location in the economy, and the larger structural forces at work, even if they are not able to articulate them or understand their origins. We might say that they have better developed sociological imaginations, that they recognize the relationship between their own biographies and history. Women in Middle County, disconnected from this sense of class or group consciousness, are more vulnerable to the dominant practices, both materially and internally. Family history of welfare receipt mitigates the effects for Middle County women, but it does not erase the impact of the dominant practices.

The words of welfare are powerful; they shape identities as well as policies. They shape interactions at the Department of Social Services. They shape interactions at the medical clinic, the grocery store, on the nightly news, and in the living rooms of welfare recipients. And yet while they appear powerful enough to render politicians silent, they have not completely silenced those most at the mercy of the intertwining systems that produce this discourse.

Afterward

In the intervening years between the collection of this data and the present, welfare has moved from center stage in domestic policy issues to the back burner. The welfare rolls were decreased dramatically by welfare reform and a strong economy, from 4.4 million families in 1996 to 2.1 million by 2001 (Hays 2003). However, many of these working families were still poor and struggling despite the strong economy and governmental surplus in the late 1990s. In the early years of the new millenium, economic recession narrowed the options that poor working families had even further and intensified their struggle to make ends meet. Even in the current period of struggle, however, the issues of poverty and welfare reform rarely break through the surface of the media to call public attention to the issue.

Given the current political climate and lack of overt attention to problems of welfare and poverty, it may seem as if the central problem addressed by this paper – the effects of the discursive construction of the welfare mother on poor women – are no longer relevant. It may appear as if the image of the welfare mother has retreated into history, or at least into the archives of newspaper and television reporting. I would like to suggest two reasons why lack of media attention to welfare issues has not likely relieved the pressure from women receiving governmental assistance.

First, the one-to-one correspondence between mass-mediated public discourse and the everyday lives of women receiving welfare is challenged by what these women tell us in the main section of this paper. Specific communities and institutions can reinforce or subvert these dominant understandings. For example, it is in the welfare office that women frequently met with the most difficulty dealing with negative assessments of their worth. In the current system, welfare seekers are met with additional bureaucratic measures to determine eligibility and fitness. Most of the rules that existed before the 1996 reforms stayed in place, with new rules simply added (Hays 2003). The bureaucratic arrangements within welfare offices appear to be premised upon the assumption that welfare applicants and recipients are deceptive and likely to commit fraud, and while the public displeasure is tempered by shrinking welfare rolls and little media attention, the daily lives of women receiving assistance may in fact be subject to even more surveillance and stigma than in the past.

Second, while welfare and poverty assistance programs have receded from the headlines, issues of sexual morality are moving to the center of political dialogue. In the past several years, we have seen very public debates about the role of the state in regulating sexual behavior, from the proposed federal constitutional amendment banning same-sex marriage to the shift to teaching abstinence-only sex education in schools. Nonmarital sexual activity appears to have taken a central position in the public debates of morality. This is highlighted by the fact that a candidate for the United States Senate from South Carolina won his 2004 race despite suggesting that single mothers not be allowed to teach in the public schools. This same election saw eleven states pass anti-gay marriage amendments. Given that many welfare recipients are single mothers (always a central concern in the 'welfare queen' rhetoric), I would suggest that their behaviors and values are scrutinized as much today as they were ten years ago, only with the focus of this scrutiny shifted toward their reproductive rather than their productive lives

These recent changes suggest that rather than see the data here as simply historical artifact, we examine how these processes are at work in the current climate and examine the specific contexts in which daily lives are lived. While the 'welfare mother' was constructed through a national discourse in the 1990s, the effects of this on women's day-to-day lives were specific to local communities. Similarly, the recent disappearance of welfare from newspaper headlines raises important questions about the impact of this shift on local communities and individual women today.

Leslie Salzinger

From Gender as Object to Gender as Verb: Rethinking how Global Restructuring Happens*

It has been clear for some time that global restructuring processes integrate women and men in distinct ways and that young women are preferentially hired to assemble the products which flow from third world to first. For at least two decades, scholars have struggled over the impact of these processes on women's overall wellbeing (Fuentes and Ehrenreich 1983; Lim 1983; Wolf 1990; Pearson 1991; Gibson-Graham 1996) or explored their impact on the situation of export processing work on workers overall (Frobel et al. 1980; Standing 1989; Sklair 1993). These are, of course, significant issues. However it is time to flip the question: to ask not how global processes affect "women," or even "men," but how gendered understandings, assumptions and subjectivities structure global production itself. Thus, in the following pages I will explore the consequences for global restructuring of its gendered form.

There has been no shortage of scholars looking at the role of gender in globalization in recent years, but much of this work has focused on questions of

AUTHOR'S NOTE: *The research upon which this paper was based was done during my affiliation with El Colegio de la Frontera Norte (COLEF) in Juárez and was funded by the Fulbright-Hays Doctoral Dissertation Research. Abroad and the OAS Regular Training Program Fellowships. My thanks to all. Thanks also to Joan Acker for perceptive and helpful comments on an earlier draft.*

* The original version of this paper appeared in *Critical Sociology*, vol. 30, no. 1 (2004).

consumption, citizenship and transnational identity (Grewal and Kaplan 1994; Sassen 1998; Appadurai 1996). Here I want to look more closely at how the economic dynamics of global restructuring themselves happen in and through gendered tropes. More concretely, I will argue that managerial decisions about the legitimate, possible and desirable uses of labor are structured through their gendered senses of self, other and object. Decisions about what can conceivably be asked and expected of a worker are both enabled and limited by managers' sense of who workers are, and this sense is fully imbued with gendered understandings and assumptions. Thus, I claim that global restructuring is gendered not as a metaphor and not as an assertion about the dismal fate of women within it, although both these assessments would, in my view, be accurate. Instead, I am arguing that, within transnational production, the creation and allocation of labor power is organized around and in terms of tropes of gendered personhood, and this has consequences for the way production works in general, above and beyond its impact on gendered selves *per se*.

This exploration is part of a larger genre of feminist criticism which has emerged in recent years to challenge the ways in which "the left" (often figured through the work of David Harvey) has theorized globalization (Gibson-Graham 1996; Massey 1994; Freeman 2001; Bergeron 2001; Bhavnani et al. 2003). Feminist scholars working in this vein have noted these theorists' tenacious disregard, both of the contributions of feminist theory and of the empirical role of women (not to speak of gender!) in constituting global economic processes. They have gone on to delineate the consequences of these omissions for the picture these theorists present of globalization overall – arguing that such depictions make globalization appear to be far more linear, obdurate and inevitable than is in fact the case. Ultimately, they argue, such partial accounts are not only inaccurate, but function to undermine our capacity to imagine and thus to work for change.

In this essay, I aim to take their work a step further, laying out what such an alternate story about global "economic" processes might actually look like. Focusing on Mexico's largest export-processing (*maquila*) labor market in Ciudad Juárez on the country's northern border, I will trace the ways in which the notion that women are inherently malleable, supplementary earners – innately suited to the repetitive and tedious work characteristic of export-processing – actively shapes the on-the-ground work of transnational production, with contradictory effects for shop-floor control. Thus, I will follow the empirical process whereby gendered meanings and subjectivities – crystallized both in global conversations and in (often linked) local arenas of discussion – shape the embodiment, incarnation and development of transnational production on the ground. The narrative demonstrates not only that gendered meanings shape how transnational production is accomplished, but that the impact of this process is potentially contradictory, not only for women and men, but for capital itself. This in turn fruitfully disrupts images of the inexorably "efficient" drive of "rational managers" or "competitive markets." Global restructuring is shaped and limited by the way those who make it see the world, and these ways of seeing may or may not be ultimately in the interests of capital as such.

The Juárez maquila industry is a particularly rich field in which to think about these issues because it makes visible not only **that** gender shapes export-processing labor markets, but **how** it does so. In this region, externally generated, globally extensive and historically tenacious narratives about "cheap, docile and dexterous" third world women workers have had the ironic consequence of producing precisely their opposite on the shop floor.[1] The city's maquila managers, members of social networks that span the globe, entered the plants with deeply embedded expectations about the intrinsic "femininity" of "assembly" work. When the demand for feminine workers – that is workers who are as definitively cheap and malleable as they are sexed – produced a shortage of all these characteristics in the local labor market, these men – ongoing participants in larger transnational discussions – were unwilling and unable to shift frameworks. As a result, by the late eighties, women maquila workers were less and less "womanly" and men made up almost half of a labor force that continued to be understood and employed **as** women. All these contradictions makes Juárez an ideal place in which to catch a glimpse of gendered tropes at work and see the complex and unpredictable ways in which they structure production.[2]

---

[1] See Lown (1990) for a historical analysis of women's use as cheap labor in the first centuries of silk manufacture in Britain. See Benería and Roldán (1987), Milkman (1987), Safa (1986), Enloe (1989, especially Chapter 7), Pearson (1986), Gordon et al. (1982) for general discussions of women's use as cheap labor in early industrialization.

[2] I am not arguing here that the Juárez labor market is "typical" of all export-processing labor markets. To the contrary, it is precisely in understanding what makes it unusual that it becomes an instructive case study, as its very idiosyncrasies illuminate processes that otherwise might remain opaque. Where managers' gendered expectations are easily put into practice, the difference between hiring women and feminizing

In looking at the omnipresence of young women in export-processing plants scattered across the third world, it is easy to assume that transnational assembly is feminized in the crudest sense – women's social position outside the factory makes them the "right" labor force for plants dependent on cheap, malleable labor. The Juárez labor market's idiosyncrasies make it possible to see the flaws in assuming social process from a demographic snapshot. It is not that "women" fit some autonomously created structure, but that what I call the trope of productive femininity shapes managers' desires, expectations and plans, and thus shapes production itself. In this context, even in the absence of women, femininity continues to structure production. Thus, what the Juárez history makes visible is not only the impact of "globalization" on a particular group of women, although it does do this, but the impact of gendered tropes on the process of globalization overall.

Engendering an Export-Processing Labor Market

When the program which established Mexico's maquilas was put into place in 1965,[3] it was already framed in public, gendered rhetorics, although not those one might expect today. For decades, the U.S. government *bracero* program had imported Mexican men to work in the fields of the southwestern United States. Domestic pressures in the U.S. brought this to a halt in 1965, leaving both countries worried about the impact of 200,000 returning – and jobless – *braceros* on Mexico's border states (Baird and McCaughan 1979; Van Waas 1981). The guarantee of tax-free entree into the U.S. for the products of Mexican export-processing factories was intended to alleviate this problem by encouraging the establishment of businesses that could hire returning male farmworkers. On the face of it, the program was a phenomenal success. In 1975, a decade after it was established, maquilas employed more than 67,000 workers (INEGI 1990), almost entirely at the border. By early 1992, when I began my research in the area, they provided work for seven and a half times that number (INEGI 1996). Unfortunately for this scheme however, the jobs were not going to returning *braceros*; in fact they were not going to men at

---

jobs is obscured, hence the social process whereby the market itself is engendered becomes difficult to see. In the case of Juárez, the disruptions created by discursively produced labor "shortages" make gender's operations visible.

[3] The Border Industrialization Program (BIP).

all. From the outset, young women made up over eighty percent of maquila workers (Fernandez-Kelly 1983; Carrillo and Hernández 1982). Investors, while increasingly willing to participate in the program as the years progressed, had arrived with their own ideas about whom to hire.

By the time the maquila program was established, free trade zones were already operating in East Asia, explicitly advertising the virtues of their feminine labor force.[4] Managers coming into Mexico had visited or heard reports of these East Asian plants and took for granted that they would hire women (Pearson 1991). A 1966 report by the consulting firm Arthur D. Little (Fernandez-Kelly 1983; Carrillo and Hernández 1982; Van Waas 1982), oft-cited as a "smoking gun" in discussions of the exploitative dimensions of maquila hiring practices, explicitly suggested hiring women in order to increase the number of potential workers and thereby increase employer leverage. More telling, however, is an early treatise for prospective maquiladora investors which simply assumed the workforce would be female and went on to enumerate Mexican women's many attractions: "From their earlier conditioning, they show respect and obedience to persons in authority, especially men. The women follow orders willingly . . ." (Baerresen 1971: 36). This set of assumptions operated on the shop floor as well as in public relations. In a particularly fascinating example of this managerial common sense in the program's early years, we find managers looking to hire gay men when women were unavailable. Thus, when women were still prohibited from doing night-work, Van Waas reports a manager requesting gay men "as queer and effeminate as possible," commenting "if I can't have women, I'll get as close to them as I can" (Van Waas 1981: 346). Similarly, in another local plant, a manager with a long history in the industry describes his experience supervising "the pink line." "They worked well, like women. It was very famous, that line."

Such rhetorics were particularly believable in a labor market such as that faced by the maquilas in the early years. In response to ads seeking "*damitas*," unemployed young women flocked enthusiastically to maquila jobs. A

---

[4] The reason for women's initial predominance in East Asian assembly work is the subject of an extensive literature. Analysts generally attribute it to women's "cheapness" and attribute this in turn to their position in the family (Safa 1986, Pearson 1991, Standing 1989). Melissa Lutz (1988) focuses instead on the circulation of images of women's docility. Although I am not attempting to explain this larger historical phenomenon here, the data suggest that such explanations are less distinct than they appear, and that women's disproportionate share of low-wage assembly is due to the way in which their familial situation is understood, used and reconstructed by capitalist processes.

woman who managed to get work in one of the first plants recalled stringent entrance requirements, the thrill of entrance given the "gigantic line of people trying to enter," and the amazing sensation of being paid in dollars without having to cross the border.[5] In 1979, a union spokesman still described the many "little ladies" who "aspired" to work in the maquilas, adding that the quantity of female labor in the area was "inexhaustible."[6] In the same period, the manager of a General Electric plant in Juárez explained at a conference that, given the twenty-five percent unemployment rate, they were able to hire two or three of every twenty-five applicants (Baird and McCaughan 1979: 146–7).

In the early eighties however, the industry romance with its workers began to fade. The U.S. economy went into a downward spiral, and maquila workers immediately began to feel the effects, not only in decreased hiring, but in mass layoffs and enforced "time off." After years of double-digit growth, the number of workers employed by the plants in Juárez fell by six percent between 1981 and 1982. By 1982, formerly "docile" workers were losing patience. The years 1981 to 1983 saw a burst of worker "demands" against their employers before the labor board (the Junta de Conciliación y Arbitraje) (Carrillo 1985). Local papers reported in June 1982 that there had already been more formal strike threats in six months than there had ever been before in a full year – .8 per maquila.[7]

In 1980 and 1981, two strikes became the focus of dramatic media coverage. In mid-1980, a conflict between two unions[8] erupted at "Andro-

---

[5] Interview with ex-worker. One of Iglesias' (1985) interviewees also discusses the maquilas as an alternative to working illegally on the other side of the border and similarly comments on the significance of being paid in dollars for this decision. The practice of paying in dollars ended as the utility of peso devaluations became clear to maquila investors after the peso devaluation of the late seventies.

[6] El Fronterizo, June 13, 1979. All newspaper articles cited here dated between 1974 and 1985 come from the COMO archives.

[7] El Diario de Juárez, June 3, 1982.

[8] Through the mid-eighties, the Juárez maquila industry was the scene of union conflicts over who would represent workers. Conflicts took place both between the two largest national unions, the CTM (Confederation of Mexican Workers) and the CROC (Regional Confederation of Workers and Peasants), and between them and the CRT (Revolutionary Confederation of Workers), the smallest of the three. The conflict at Andromex was between the CTM and one of its recently ousted leaders. He had established a local CRT branch and was attempting to reinsert himself into the Juárez union scene in this era by taking over CTM contracts. Roughly a third of Juárez maquilas were unionized in 1987 (Carrillo and Ramírez 1990). In those that were unionized, workers generally saw little benefit, as all three union locals operated as company unions.

mex,"[9] and for seven months, the public was treated to the sight of women workers yelling at their bosses, barricading themselves into the plant and forcefully asserting their right to be heard. The following year, at "Fashionmex," workers legitimately concerned that the company would close down without paying the legally required worker indemnizations took their complaints to local authorities, to the streets and to the media. They marched through downtown handing out leaflets calling "For the union of all maquila workers!!" and forcibly stopped a truck full of company products from leaving the city before workers were paid.[10] At the same time, a newly radicalized COMO (Center for the Orientation of Women Workers)[11] weighed in on the side of "working women" in general, supporting both the Fashionmex and Andromex struggles and loudly proclaiming working women's right to self-determination.

The maquilas responded to these challenges either by leaving town[12] – or more commonly by threatening to do so – or with highly-publicized blacklists intended to keep out "conflictive people."[13] Although they complained loudly of worker intransigence, they showed no sign of reevaluating the gendering of their hiring strategies.

Amid this charged context, 1982 brought a drastic peso devaluation – the first of a series that would follow over the upcoming decade. Between 1981 and 1982, the dollar value of the peso was cut in half, and average maquila wages fell from US$234.30 weekly to US$105.60 (Jiménez 1989: 417). The following year, maquila employment in Juárez jumped twenty-six percent. Nineteen-eighty-six and 1987 saw even more dramatic devaluations. By the end of the decade, in dollar terms the peso was worth a mere fraction of its value at the outset of the maquila program (Sklair 1993: 40), and maquila employment in Juárez had tripled (INEGI 1991 and 1996).

The soaring demand for workers had immediate consequences. In December 1982, the first sarcastic headline appeared: "Two companies seek 120 workers;

---

[9] Company names used here are pseudonyms.

[10] For a detailed chronology of the conflict at Fashionmex as seen by COMO, see Beatriz Vera (n.d.). For an analysis of the "contract" see de la Rosa Hickerson (1979). Also see Carrillo and Hernández (1985: 158–164).

[11] For detailed histories of COMO, see Young and Vera (1984), Yudelman (1987), Kopinak (1989) and Peña (1997).

[12] Fashionmex, for instance, did ultimately flee the city, typically leaving wages unpaid.

[13] El Correo, Nov. 17, 1980.

but ... the CROC[14] 'doesn't have anyone free.'"[15] Four months and a half-dozen articles later, the tone was anything but sarcastic. "Marked absence of female labor for the maquiladoras: In the unions controlled by the CROC they need 500 young people; Yesterday only one hundred showed up."[16] By May the tone was frankly hysterical: "'DEFICIT' OF LABOR FOR THE MAQUILADORAS: With Sound Systems They Look for Workers in the Shantytowns."[17] The union leader who only four years earlier had claimed that the female labor force was "inexhaustible" now announced that it was "obvious that all the women of Ciudad Juárez are already employed"[18] and began suggesting importing labor from rural areas further south.[19] Personnel managers who worked during the early eighties communicate the mood of their departments at the time through the black humor of the period: "In personnel in those days, all we needed was a mirror. If they were breathing, they were hired"; or "We'd hire anyone with ten fingers ..."[20]

Despite the sudden scarcity of young women workers willing to work at maquila salaries, after its initial collapse, pay stagnated (Jiménez 1989: 422–3; Sklair 1993: 72), with real wages falling throughout a decade legendary among managers for the severity of its "labor shortages" (see Rosenbaum 1994; Santiago and Almada 1991). In 1983, the plants began offering benefits such as free lunches, transportation to and from work and credits at nearby chain stores, but base pay remained low.[21] Industry representatives made much of the external factors which prevented them from raising wages, including pressures from the Mexican state, which was concerned with protecting international competitiveness,[22] and pressures from domestic capital, unable to

---

[14] In the first decades of the maquiladora industry, workers seeking maquila jobs could go to the union hiring halls, from which they were sent to maquilas that requested workers. This system fell apart as the demand for workers outstripped supply. Until 1982, union complaints about insufficient employment were a fixture of Juárez public discussion, hence this headline's sarcastic tone.

[15] *El Universal*, Dec. 22, 1982.

[16] *El Universal*, April 20, 1983.

[17] *El Diario de Juárez*, May 24, 1983.

[18] *El Universal*, April 6, 1983.

[19] *El Universal*, April 20, 1983 and *El Fronterizo*, July 27, 1983. In fact, some companies did eventually seek out and hire women workers from nearby villages to avoid hiring men (see *El Universal*, June 18, 1983). As far as I can ascertain however, no one ever traveled to the southern states to import migrant laborers.

[20] Managerial interviews, 1992–93.

[21] Catanzarite and Strober (1993). *El Universal*, April 11 and February 17, 1984. Managerial interviews.

[22] In the Nov. 3, 1983 *El Universal*, AMAC (the maquiladora industry association)

afford wage inflation computed in dollars.[23] However, local maquila management was also limited by the image of assembly labor elaborated in home offices and accepted as common sense in their border outposts, which took the linked characteristics of femininity, supplementary earners and extreme cheapness as defining features of appropriate export-processing labor.[24] Thus, discussion of raises in pesos, even if their costs were constant in dollars, remained taboo, even as labor shortages and turnover played havoc with productivity on the line. Instead, in interviews, managers frequently referenced the (feminine) "irrationality" of workers, who, they said, were not that focused on money, and thus could be assuaged by benefits and shows of appreciation, but not by wage increases.

As a result of these transnationally generated assumptions about who assembly workers should be, the maquilas in 1984 paid less than half what they had just a few years earlier and far less than comparable national industries in Mexico City (Jiménez 1989: 424). Although by 1988, even the industry's English-language newsletter was remarking that "earning $3.50 or less for a full day's work simply doesn't seem attractive to many people,"[25] managers in plants where I did fieldwork in the early nineties continued to reassure themselves about the ethics and efficacy of paying low wages with ongoing references to the fact that these were appropriately women's jobs (see Salzinger 2003, Chapter 7).

Managerial bromides notwithstanding, as the value of maquila wages fell, women workers who had become reliant on higher salaries indeed began to

---

[23] complained publicly that the state wouldn't permit the maquiladora industry to raise wages. Shaiken (1994: 58) reports similar pressures on the plants he studies. Nonetheless, industry complaints about this pressure are somewhat disingenuous, as they frequently note that labor is cheaper elsewhere when pushing to keep local wages down.. For instance, Baird and McCaughan (1979: 144–6) and Van Waas (1981) describe the tremendous (if unsuccessful) maquila campaign to lower the minimum wage in the inflationary mid-seventies and the plants' explicit references to "the loss of international competitiveness' of the BIP" (Van Waas: 245) in the service of this goal. Sklair (1993: 179) argues that the reasons for low maquila wages are less byzantine than the industry claims, and that ultimately the maquilas have simply found turnover to be cheaper than wage increases.

[24] In an industry conference in 1990, industry representatives claimed that they did not raise base salaries so as not to undercut other economic sectors in the city (*El Diario de Juárez*, March 28, 1990).

[24] Home offices generally insist that their third-world outposts pay "prevailing wages" (managerial interviews). Shaiken (1994: 58) also reports such requirements.

[25] *Twin Plant News* 3:10, May 1988.

look elsewhere. Local newspapers reported them moving into better-paying "men's jobs"[26] and crossing the border to earn dollars.[27] It was this set of decisions which, in tandem with management's inflexibility on wages, produced the "shortage" so dramatically presented in personnel department accounts. This was occasionally recognized at the time. In May 1988, the industry newsletter tartly lectured its readers. "Many companies believe that (because of) the large number of maquila plants that have been started in the last few years . . . there aren't enough people to go around . . . We would like to point out . . . that the number of 'employable' operators is still larger than the number of vacancies."[28]

Transnational managers expected "feminine" workers. However, cheapness and pliancy are at least in part market products, and tight labor markets rarely produce them. Thus, despite maquila managers' experience of the grueling labor shortage of the eighties as something like a natural disaster, it was substantially of their own making. In defining the paradigmatic maquila worker as simultaneously cheap, female and docile, they created a market which eventually undercut the conditions of existence for such a creature. Many young women were still willing to work in the plants of course, but there were no longer enough of them to run the assembly lines without other workers as well. Ultimately the demand for cheapness made some shift in the demographics of maquila assembly lines inevitable.

The rigidity of transnational management's image of an appropriate maquila worker not only created a bona fide labor shortage, but it also eroded the "docility" of those women workers who were available. The alarmism of the early eighties notwithstanding, maquila lines did not come to a halt for lack of workers. However, in the context of high labor demand, idiosyncratic benefit packages virtually invited workers to shop around. Thus, although maquila wage policies did not stop production, they did produce turnover.[29]

---

[26] *El Diario de Juárez*, July 2, 1985; *El Diario de Juárez*, June 8, 1986.
[27] *El Diario de Juárez*, April 20, 1988.
[28] *Twin Plant News* 3:10, May 1988, p. 8.
[29] Shaiken (1990: 99) reports that although maquilas "would clearly like to reduce turnover, they have structured work in a way where transience in the production work force has a minimal negative impact." The highly fragmented labor process to which he is referring here is visible throughout the maquilas. Just as complaints about labor shortages must be understood within the context of the decision not to raise wages, so complaints about turnover must be understood within the of context of the decision not to introduce seniority systems.

In February 1984, the head of AMAC (the maquiladora industry association) said as much when he "dismissed the version that there is a labor shortage on our border, what is going on in these moments . . . is that there are seven thousand unstable workers . . . (who) go from one industry to another to where it's most convenient that they offer their services, and this is reflected in the plants that don't bring their benefits up to the level of their competitors."[30]

Women's growing leverage in the labor market produced a similar phenomenon on the line, and after years of calling the shots, managers found themselves at a disadvantage. A supervisor who had been a worker in the seventies lamented the new order: "In the beginning it was marvelous, when the maquilas started, because you looked out for your work, you knew there were 200,000 more willing to do it."[31] This comment, and others like it, were encapsulated in tropes that, like the labor shortage jokes, were repeated throughout the interviews I conducted with personnel managers who had been in the industry during this period:[32] "They always knew they could get work on the other side of the street"; or "All a supervisor needed to do was look at her crosswise and she was out the door." Newspaper reports of the period took the same exasperated tone. Early in 1983, one complained: "Due to the current scarcity of women workers in the maquiladoras . . . the women change employment when they feel like it . . ."[33] A year later, the same paper reported:

> Yesterday, maquila operators were found enjoying the labor shortage facing the plants; they don't worry about arriving early or being fired. At the Juárez Monument, Guadalupe Cárdenas and Laura Lozano were interviewed when they commented that they were already late; both said that, because of the labor shortage, they couldn't fire them, and that's the way it is, because the one thing there's plenty of is work in all the factories.[34]

Women workers' "bad behavior" was directed at new male workers as well as at their bosses. A frustrated union boss complained that the few men who entered the plants were forced out by catcalling women coworkers, who were gleefully taking advantage of their unusual numerical superiority.[35]

---

[30] *El Diario de Juárez*, Feb. 5, 1984.
[31] "Panoptimex" supervisor, 1992.
[32] Managerial interviews, 1992–1993.
[33] *El Universal*, Nov. 10, 1983.
[34] *El Universal*, Feb. 17, 1984.
[35] *El Fronterizo*, Aug. 31, 1983. Senior women workers in Andromex also told me they had teased new male workers during this period.

On the heels of women workers' increasing assertiveness, a few cracks in the maquila managers' implacable image of the "docile woman worker" emerged in the spring of 1983. Fresh from a year of shop-floor militancy, and in the midst of soaring male unemployment rates,[36] Andromex's new Mexican plant manager was among the first to recognize that "docile" was as scarce as "female" in its current workforce, and to announce that he was hiring men.[37] By March of 1983, a few others were quietly following, although they were reluctant to admit publicly that they were breaking with tradition. The head of the CROC announced that several companies the union worked with "had seen themselves obliged to hire men." He refused to name them, commenting that if he did so "afterwards they wouldn't hire them anymore."[38] Obviously, these companies were not the only ones. In June, men made up three of every five workers hired,[39] although they would not make up this high a percentage of the total workforce until the end of the decade.

Despite the burst of men hired in 1983, management remained skeptical about the utility of men for assembly work. In a typical statement from the first uptick in hiring men, the union boss responsible for hiring for a group of maquilas commented:

> The hiring of men is done with more rigorous selective criteria, given that they are more disobedient, irresponsible and prone to absences; distressingly, in Juárez, the men already got used to not working.[40]

Newspaper ads from the first half of the decade reflected this attitude, continuing to request women.[41] Nonetheless, by the end of the eighties, industry representatives were frantic. Turnover was well over a hundred percent annually,[42] and industry complaints about shortages and increasing training costs had reached a fever pitch.[43] Still focused on getting their hands on fem-

---

[36] On Sept. 5, 1983, amid the maquila "labor shortage," Banamex announced that unemployment was soaring in the city as a whole (*El Fronterizo*).

[37] *El Diario de Juárez*, June 11, 1983.

[38] *El Diario de Juárez*, March 30, 1983.

[39] *El Diario de Juárez*, Aug. 23, 1983.

[40] *El Diario de Juárez*, March 30, 1983.

[41] Review of COMO archives.

[42] By 1989, AMAC statistics were showing an average of a hundred and forty-four percent turnover annually AMAC (1989).

[43] *El Diario de Juárez*, September 14, 1987; *El Diario de Juárez*, January 25, 1988; *El Diario de Juárez*, June 17, 1989; *El Diario de Juárez*, March 28, 1990; *El Diario de Juárez*, October 20, 1990.

ininity, however embodied, a few plants hired transvestites. One manager recalled, "The need for people was so great that we had men who walked around the plant dressed as women." Maquilas began paying workers to bring in friends,[44] established "gentleman's agreements" not to hire workers who'd left previous jobs "without clear reasons,"[45] and even considered setting a single salary and benefit structure for the industry as a whole.[46] In this context, they began to publicly discuss broadening their worker profile for the first time, acknowledging the possibility of hiring men, albeit in the most disrespectful terms. Their first public statements on the subject coincided with assessments of the feasibility of contracting senior citizens and the handicapped,[47] and although discussions of these latter two groups were pitched in the most self congratulatory terms,[48] the possibility of hiring men was consistently framed as a compromise. Although women are "more careful and responsible," commented the head of AMAC in 1988, men had also been found "acceptable."[49]

Not surprisingly, men responding to these mixed messages were slow to enter maquila doors. In the spring of 1983, amid reports of the first labor crisis in the maquilas, their pace drew the ire of the editors of a local paper. A picture of men sitting under the trees was glossed by the caption: "Despite the many maquiladora factory announcements soliciting male workers, it seems that the *juarenses* have declared war against work and prefer to face the heat in the shade of a tree."[50] In 1988, the head of AMAC reiterated these complaints, commenting that "despite the invitations to take positions, there are very few (men) who are interested in working." Managerial ambivalence and male workers' responses meant that the proportion of women in the maquila workforce did not go into free fall. Rather, between 1982 and the end of the decade, the percentage of men increased between two and six percent yearly. It was not until 1988, in the third year of over ten percent growth in the city's maquiladora workforce, that there was finally a surge of adver-

---

[44] *El Diario de Juárez*, April 1, 1989; *El Diario de Juárez*, November 29, 1989.
[45] *El Diario de Juárez*, September 18, 1990.
[46] *El Diario de Juárez*, October 11, 1990.
[47] Not surprisingly, there is little evidence that either group was ever hired in large numbers.
[48] *El Diario de Juárez*, May 27, 1989; *El Diario de Juárez*, November 29, 1989; *El Diario de Juárez*, August 27, 1990.
[49] *El Diario de Juárez*, May 14, 1988.
[50] *El Fronterizo*, May 31, 1983.

tisements directed at men as well as women.[51] Not until the end of the decade did men constitute a stable forty-five percent of the industry's direct local workforce, and even then, on the great majority of shop floors, neither the language, the labor control practices nor the pay schemes implemented by management acknowledged the shift.[52] Despite the thousands of men working in the maquilas, there was still no trope, no structure of meaning, within which "male maquila worker" made sense. At nearly fifty percent, they remained the ubiquitous exception.

As cheap, docile and female became an increasingly difficult combination to find among flesh-and-blood job applicants, one might have expected that the tenacious feminization of maquila work would erode. As thousands of men filled shop floors with no noticeable impact on industry productivity, this would appear foreordained. However, this was not the case.[53] The trope of productive femininity, nourished by ongoing links to a larger transnational imaginary, remained in place. In the fantasy world of "offshore production," docile women continue to hold the microscope and thread the needle. Maquila managers, ongoing participants in a larger, transnational system of meanings and taken-for-granteds, continued to cite the "maquila-grade female"[54] as a standard against which to measure maquila labor. As a result, for the most part men were hired, but marked upon entry as lacking, sometimes with disastrous consequences for managerial control.[55]

Managers facing this situation – simultaneously constrained by transnational frameworks and local recalcitrance – implemented a variety of shop-floor compromises and innovations. Some continued to insist on women workers, importing them from rural areas outside the city at extra cost or even relocating further from the border. A minority consciously shifted both demographics and shop-floor expectations, reframing maquila jobs as "men's

---

[51] Review of *El Diario de Juárez* archives.

[52] INEGI, 1991. These levels remained stable throughout the years of my fieldwork in the industry (INEGI 1996).

[53] Catanzarite and Strober (1993) assert that maquila work no longer was feminized by the late-eighties. My own research shows no support for this conclusion. In interviews, managers constantly expressed their preference for women workers, generally referencing women's purportedly greater patience, tolerance for boredom and shop-floor malleability.

[54] Sklair (1993: 177) reports that this phrase was used by a speaker in an industry seminar in 1984 who discussed the scarcity of "maquila-grade females."

[55] Andromex was to become a fascinating and suggestive exception to this pattern (see Salzinger 2003).

work" by changing labor control mechanisms on the job floor and even marginally improving wages. And many faced ongoing turnover and shop-floor disruption, as neither prized women (with other options) nor insulted men (never addressed in terms they could accept on the shop floor) made for ideal workers.[56] However engaged, these problems were not inherent in the fact of production in Juárez. They were produced by the gendered structure of the labor market itself. Women were no longer the only ones at work in the Juárez maquilas, but for the most part, femininity continued its contradictory reign.

The evolution and development of the Juárez maquila industry has been shaped by a myriad of understandings and assumptions – frameworks constituted in many locales and invoked internally in the service of distinctive strategies. Gender is clearly not the only, or even necessarily the primary, referent here. Nonetheless, the narrative above suggests the crucial role of the trope of productive femininity in this context – evoking and, perhaps more crucially for this historical period, stabilizing, a particular set of pay, hiring and labor control practices, with consequences not only for workers, but for the productivity and efficiency of the industry itself.

Opening Accounts

So, why might this matter? Gendered meanings and selves organize and structure the development of transnational production. Why should we care? What are the implications of this argument for how we might reckon with what is and imagine possibilities for change?

Many accounts of global restructuring – including those written by feminists – picture globalization as a whirlwind descending upon us. In such an image, the local is always-already constituted, never acting, always acted upon. In the same narrative, the global (often conflated with "capitalism" itself) bears down inexorably: linear, focused, with a logic of its own.[57] Despite the grim seductions of such an image, the narrative above suggests such stories are partial and misleading. The managers I describe above certainly

---

[56] See Salzinger (2003) for ethnographic accounts of these varying shop-floor responses and of the role of gender in producing export-processing work and workers in the arena of production itself.

[57] This is beautifully captured by J.K. Gibson-Graham (1996) in her analysis of globalization as a "rape script."

make "rational" and "efficient" decisions in their own experience. However, seen outside their (empirically erroneous) assumption that "woman" is a fixed subject and therefore a highly specific kind of labor, their strategies appear to be neither of those things. Instead, weighed down by a set of taken-for-granted assumptions about gender, about legitimate manliness as well as womanliness, they make choices which directly produce the labor shortages and chaotic shop floors which go on to plague their daily work lives.

I am not suggesting here that capitalism has no logics of its own, simply that the relationship between those logics and what actually happens on the ground may be more tenuous than such naming suggests. Actors' on-the-ground intentions and strategies are necessarily framed, grasped and practiced through particular lenses. Gender of course is only one among many of these, but the history of "cheap labor" makes it a highly salient one in this context. Each optic distinguishes what is possible, desirable, and legitimate from what is not, thus shaping the organization of production itself. Among other things, this illuminates one of the many ways in which managers' considered decisions may undermine as well as support their conscious intentions. Certainly, in Juárez, the attempt to employ what was understood to be women's natural docility fractured on the shoals of the new gendered selves these very strategies had created.

It is compelling to picture global restructuring as an unyielding, superhuman force, remaking everything in its path for its own purposes. Part of what makes this narrative so credible is that it matches individual experience as well as theory. Nonetheless, to read this experience back into explanation is a mistake. The fact that no one of us can shift history alone does not mean that it is created by "forces" that lie outside the process of meaning and subject-making we engage in on a daily basis. If this is the case however, then it is important analytic work to delineate how this works, and thus to make concrete how ways of seeing are linked to what is made and thus to what enables and constrains us in the next iteration. In this context, gender's links to our conscious sense of self make it particularly helpful to us as analysts, as its insistent presence disrupts too-elegant images of capitalism's relentless linearity.

William Wood

Viral Power: Arthur and Marilouise Kroker Interviewed by William Wood*

Forward

Looking back on this interview, actually a series of extended email exchanges that occurred in the fall of 2002 and the Spring of 2003, it is difficult to understate the degree to which the Krokers accurately depict the emergence of a new global logic subsumed under the so called "war on terror." For readers not familiar with the writings of the Krokers, this interview is an accessible and profound starting point into the work of two theorists genuinely concerned with the relationship among technology, politics, and culture, particularly as they relate to the radical transformation of the global landscape following September 11.

Although the interview is presented unabridged, a few of the Krokers observations merit further comment. This is especially the case in regards to knowledge that has come to light since the interview regarding the adoption of "rouge" tactics by the United States and its allies: the sheer number of "disappeared" persons both foreign and domestic; Abu Ghraib and the apparent legalization of systematic torture as a weapon; the growing dependency of the United States on "private contractors" (i.e. mercenaries) accountable only to the corporations

---

* This interview originally appeared in *Critical Sociology*, vol. 30, no. 2 (2004).

which employ them; and the reemergence of civilian surveillance and counter-intelligence programs rivaling and perhaps surpassing those such as COIN-TELPRO in the late 60s and early 70s.

If many of these tactics appear to be old wine in new wineskins however, the Krokers are insistent that technology has altered the ability of the United States to wage war on its enemies and its own population in substantial ways. Viral logic demands technologies able to function at the micro-level, able to trace and identify single individuals, able to sift rapidly through billions of global communications, able to nuke single caves instead of entire countries. Real-time communication, not mere brute force, becomes imperative in a logic that circulates both invisibly (as in the case of real time attacks on so-called terrorist havens) and publicly (as in the case of real-time media terrorist warnings).

Viral logic is more than the indiscriminate use of sophisticated technology, however. "Confronted by a direct challenge to its symbolic power," note the Krokers, "the empire of the global American state itself adopts the logic of terrorism." It is a logic of torture, of imminent violence and indiscriminate suffering. It is a logic of "us against them," an apocalyptic and fundamentalist position derisive of history, opposition or ambiguity. It is no mistake that the discourse surrounding the "war on terror" has been expanded to include the academy, as well as to scientists who dare side against the current administration. Unto itself, this is an age-old tactic, used effectively by the Church and various despotic governments for hundreds of years. What is peculiar, and chilling, in the Krokers' work is the degree to which technology becomes increasingly instrumental in an apocalyptic cosmology of sin and salvation.

The Empire of Infinity and the Twin Towers of Light

William Wood: Not long after September 11, in an article written by the both of you, you noted that with the attack on New York, "The triumphant era of the last superpower suddenly gave way to the contagious logic of viral power. In place of the certainty principle of nuclear stalemate, there emerges now the radical uncertainty of the terrorism of micro-power."[1] On one level there

---

[1] Arthur and Marilouise Kroker, "The Terror of Viral Power" *CTHEORY,* September 16, 2001. Internet resource <http://www.ctheory.net/text_file.asp?pick=296>

is a deceptive simplicity to this statement. For the past few months, we have been turning on our televisions and watching the reality of "cells" and "networks" trickle into our living rooms. But are you also speaking about something much more ubiquitous than rogue terrorism?

Krokers: The theory of viral power was written within weeks of the terror. Since then, the theory of viral power has become *the* political reality of power, with rogue terrorism quickly evolving into the viral logic of the rogue state. Confronted by a direct challenge to its symbolic power, the empire of the global American state itself adopts the logic of terrorism. Through a new light-based system of military communication, the "war on terrorism" circulates at accelerated speed through an expanding network of so-called terrorist havens. Through a binary rhetoric of "friend or enemy," the war *meme* of the empire is imprinted on the political skin of the world. Through a logic of apprehended threats to the internal security of the American "homeland," state security forces "disappear" always suspected "aliens" and mute most domestic political dissent into silence.

Unconventional, circulating, parasitical, the rogue state that is the essence of American empire enters the political bloodstream of world terrorism, studying its codes, its methods of operation, its weapons of financing. Like a virus hidden deep inside the terrorist attack of 9/11, state terrorism is itself triggered by the attack. Certainly not weakened by the terror, definitely not fragile because of its global (financial) virtuality, the hegemony of American empire is clearly strengthened, indeed reanimated, by the events of last September. Breaking with the rules of the now superceded empire of normalized inter-national relations, the new empire of the viral state goes it alone.

For example, consider the highly charged symbolism of the twin towers of light that memorialized the six-month anniversary of the terror. A monument of cold blue light. 88 spotlights were used: double symbols of infinity. The industrial age of the mechanical skyscraper is over. The electronic age of light-based power is about to begin. America is about to move from an empire based on steel and glass to an empire moving at the speed of light. The empire of steel and glass is destructible, combustible, pierceable, reachable. The empire of (electronic) light rises triumphantly from the ruins, firewalled from the terror, reaching to the heavens and beyond the stars. This is a double ceremony: the ending of one form of empire, and the beginning of another. An empire of light, speed, and violence.

That viral power is based on light, not matter, is confirmed by the recent Pentagon position paper on a new "Nuclear Posture" recommending a basic change in American nuclear strategy. Breaking with the logic of deterrence and mutually assured destruction, the Pentagon now promotes the idea of the "conventional use" of nuclear weaponry for "precise strikes" against enemy forces. Nuking caves. As reported in *The New York Times*, Ivo Daalder, an analyst at the Brookings Institution, noted: "The policy has been turned upside down. It is to keep nuclear weapons as a tool of war-fighting rather than a tool of deterrence."[2]

However, in the way of all media, remember Marshall McLuhan's famous thesis that the final act of old media is to serve as content for the invisible form of new media. Consequently, if the Pentagon wishes now to conventionalize nuclear weapons, it probably indicates that in reality we are already living in a post-nuclear age: an era of viral power not nuclear power; bio-power not the power of physics; circulation not deterrence; parasiting the language of terrorism not dissuasion. Ironically, the stage may be finally set for global nuclear holocaust as the final "accident" of a declining form of power. Or perhaps something different. In its futurist scenario, Space War 2020, American military strategic planners, acknowledging that the United States will likely experience no credible military threats in the next two decades, have already created the conceptual framework for a coming age of galactic warfare: extra-terrestrial, satellite-based, warfare in the darkness of space.

The New Cold War Will be a "Dirty War"

WW: In light of your observation above, it does seem apparent, however, that the U.S. is simultaneously trying to position itself back into the age of the superpower. This certainly seems to be the case when we look at the continued justification for missile defense. In a strange way, the Cold War is now being rearticulated in the media as something romantic and even desirable – I have recently seen an interview on cable news where the guest was speaking longingly about the doctrine of mutually assured destruction.

Krokers: In terms of international relations, global politics has suddenly flipped: the Cold War has come finally home to America, and the hot war

---

[2] Michael R. Gordon, "Nuclear Arms: For Deterrence or Fighting?" *New York Times*, March 11, 2002.

is the world offshore: uncertain, threatening, intensely local, potentially uncontainable.

The domestication of the Cold War? That's the instant convergence of a televised Pearl Harbor-style "sneak attack" on the American homeland with an always prepared, off-the-shelf right wing agenda to instill a new cold regime of loyalty oaths in the American mind. President Bush might be caricatured for speaking of "you are either with us or you are with the terrorists" but he is only staying one step ahead of the raging parade of the American war spirit. Here, a strong and deeply emotionally felt will to revenge combines with the necessary mechanics of the war machine to produce a new fifty-year cycle of domestic repression. The evidence is everywhere: the deafening silence of many citizens in the face of juridical and legislative limitations on traditional civil liberties; the immediate mobilization of the owners of the organs of mass culture – cinema, television, radio, newspapers – into a Kafkaesque repetition machine of the rhetoric of propaganda; relentless assaults against the environmental/anti-globalization movement as an apprehended threat to "national security;" massive, unquestioned increases in the armaments budget; deploying armies of secret police against the Muslim population; the Lieberman/Lynn Cheney attack on dissenting opinions in American universities.[3]

The new Cold War will be a "dirty war."

And the hot war? That's the "alien" world outside: from the bunkered down perspective of fortress America: unknowable, volatile, threatening. A hot world that can never really be engaged in terms of cultural understanding, but only pacified by means of the global projection onto Afghanistan, Georgia, Yemen, Indonesia, Sudan, Iraq of the futurist war scenarios of what Pentagon planners have dubbed America's "space war strategy." Here, the hot war will be fought by a twofold strategy: first, the use primarily of colonial mercenary forces (Britain) on the ground; and the deployment in space of unmanned predator drones equipped with Hell-Fire missiles, all this networked with a smooth semiurgy of real-time communications – satellites,

---

[3] The Krokers are referring here to a report published in February, 2002, by the American Council of Trustees and Alumni entitled "Defending Civilization: How Our Universities Are Failing America and What Can Be Done About It." The authors of the report are Jerry L. Martin and Anne D. Neal. Lynn Cheney is Chairman Emeritus and Co-Founder of the ACTA. Senator Joseph Lieberman is also a founding member of the ACTA.

GPS's, and always observing video displays of world "troublespots" in the war rooms of the American panoptic.[4]

America's Technological Future: Protestant Ressentiment and Catholic Transcendence

WW: Indeed, we hear now that in this new age, the "war on terrorism," will likely extend throughout and beyond our lifetimes. And, in a sense, the image of America as reborn – both with a president that has purged himself of his past through his newfound faith, and with the reinvention of American apocalypticism in general – predominates throughout this new discourse of what you call viral power. I know that you, Arthur, spent time in a seminary. Also, in your writing, you have spoken on the theme of a new eschatology of "the interfacing of cybernetics and flesh as the (post)-human good."[5] My interest as a sociologist is where and how this new eschatology, something I find peculiar to American culture, plays into what you have called the "will to technology" and specifically into the emergence of a post-cold war viral logic.

Arthur Kroker: In America, viral power clips itself to the political bloodstream in two ways: first, biblically by continually reanimating the Book of Revelations with its images bleak and desolate of parasites, pestilence, and the wrath of God to come as the motor-force of right-wing fundamentalism; and second, by emotionally merging this wrathful biblical image of America as the "fifth seal" with a transcendent technological vision of the disappearance of the body into its wireless prosthetics. The Old Testament cut with the speed of Pentium Double-Track Chip is the ever reversible logic of American empire. Which is why I think the story of America is always read best through

---

[4] Ed. Note. Semiurgy, originally *sémiurgie*, arises out of French postmodern thought, possibly the writings of Jean Baudrillard. The word denotes the work involved in the endless production and proliferation of signs. For Baudrillard such signs do more than represent, they simulate the real while concurrently masking their simulation, a condition Baudrillard calls *hyperreality* – more real than real. Etymologically, the word comes from the prefix semi[o]-, meaning sign, and the suffix -urg, meaning work or a type of work.

[5] Arthur Kroker and Michael A. Weinstein, "The Political Economy Of Virtual Reality: Pan-Capitalism," *CTHEORY*, 3/15/1994. Internet resource <http://www.ctheory.net/text_file.asp?pick=49>

the screen of the Old Testament: through stories always on the (cinematic) mind of Jeremiah's "Babylon;" of the war on terrorism as an instant myth in which the United States is religiously cast as Job smitten unjustly by his enemies, by the numerology of Deuteronomy, by stories recoded directly from the bible of secret cults, strange conspiracies, and the signs of apocalypse. But if America's animus is biblical in its origins, its destiny is the technological imagination. The reason for this: in America, the utopian vision of technology as emancipation links directly to another deep current in religious antiquity, to Catholic theology which since Augustine has worshipped at the altar of the will to virtuality. Of course, in the language of Catholicism, virtuality is spoken of in the vernacular language of "grace," but if we were to go back again to that primary semiological text of Western (technological) mythology, Augustine's *De Trinitate*, we would find in the transcendent, apocalyptic image of God the Father, the Son, and the Holy Ghost, the basic code of the technological imagination: a continuing struggle amongst the antinomies of Will, Intelligence and Affect as the specular logic by which we are promised deliverance from "corrupted" flesh. Today, the classics might be worn bare by the desert winds, but the ruling code of *De Trinitate* still horizons the technological mind. Between Christianity and technology, the struggle for the transcendence of (digital) grace over the "meat" of the always dying flesh is exactly the same. In this case, Negroponte's *Being Digital* simply recodes in wireless terms the yearning for religious epiphany through the disappearance of flesh that was always the basis of post-Augustinian Catholic theology. Ironically, now that we live in the aftermath of Nietzsche's pronouncement of the death of God, the spirit of Christianity may have found its successor in the technological imagination. The digital matrix recapitulates Christian confessionality.

Curious isn't it? American technological imagination is a brilliant morality play between Catholicism and Protestantism: both separate, both necessary to complete the terms of the imminently techno-religious compact that is the American dream. Perhaps this is why the war on terror can be streamed so easily in the bile called network news. Islam is the threatening other, the presence of which both destabilizes the reversible binary of the American mind, but on behalf of which the war on terrorism can so deeply unify American purpose in an otherwise universe of random meanings.

Pushed from behind by ancient Protestant dreams of Old Testament revenge and pulled from ahead by Catholic yearnings towards the technological sublime, American hegemony is unbeatable, unstoppable, and perhaps even unthinkable.

Surplus, But Definitely Not Superfluous

WW: You have spoken about the degree to which the so called third world, and perhaps increasingly parts of the industrial world, are becoming "surplus to the continued functioning of technological culture."[6] In what way do you mean surplus? I say this because, reflecting on the degree to which the third world has become the unwitting market for the expenditure of military technology, it seems to me that many of these countries are hardly superfluous. I think the new war on terrorism epitomizes this, but we see it as well with South America and the war on drugs.

Krokers: This is not what we mean by surplus. We are not equating surplus with superfluous, but the fact that in contemporary culture, predatory strategies of global colonial oppression exist with such intensity that they render whole societies as useable at will, and then abandoned. The empire then moves on to another country, another continent. We are speaking here of Heidegger's language of "harvesting" as the reality-principle of the politics of domination.[7]

Hegemonic control of technological culture is firmly vested in the geographical center of the empire of the virtual, nominally the United States and the European Community, but in (hyper)reality, the vector of pan-capitalism that is the actually existent framework determining capital flows, rates of consumption, labor discipline, the marketing of the signs of power, from the culture of military weapons to the militarization of cultural images. In this strict sense of power, the third world is abjectly "surplus" to virtual capital. Its place in the framework of technological culture is to be harvested of its labor, bodies, desires, economy. An always vicious market of guns for drugs appears everywhere. A so-called "underground" economy emerges that on closer inspection reveals itself simply to be the truth principle of normal economy. Use and Abandon is the regnant political principle of the empire of the

---

[6] Interview with Arthur Kroker, *Canadian Broadcasting Corporation*, "Sunday Morning," July 23, 1995.

[7] See Martin Heidegger, *The Question Concerning Technology, and Other Essays* (New York: Harper and Row, 1977).

virtual. Ultimately, everybody and everyplace will prove to be fundamentally surplus to its will to mastery of the social and non-social universe.

The Empire (Always) Strikes Back

WW: This distinction, between surplus and superfluous, is useful. It is also ironic in the sense that, when you say the Cold War has finally come home to America, we are seeing the effects of countries and regions which have been harvested. Afghanistan, as a remnant of the Cold War, of course comes to mind here. But the truly frightening thing about your proposal of a viral power is the idea that, on a global scale, this nefarious process has been repeatedly enacted. Baudrillard's article recently published in *Le Monde* makes this point clear when he says, "the entire world without exception had dreamed of this event . . . nobody could help but dream the destruction of so powerful a hegemon. . ."[8]

Arthur Kroker: Baudrillard's thesis elaborated in his book, *L'esprit du terrorisme* is a truly brilliant account of the seduction of terrorism. With one exception: following his classic formulations about the "terrorism of the code" versus the "death of symbolic exchange," Baudrillard analyses 9/11 in terms of the apparent instability of a globalized hegemonic power that is always weakened by its loss of a sustaining symbolic myth. 9/11 then, has about it the fascination of the "wrecked windshield," the delirium of always anticipated apocalypse. Maybe so, but perhaps something else is at work. Maybe the real secret of American power is that the language of empire has never been passive, but an active reader of the cultures it harvests. And so, perhaps one day rummaging through the texts of French theory – reflecting in passing on Virilio's theory of "electropolitics" and Barthes' eloquent meditations on the "empire of the sign" – the eyes of the empire stumbled upon Baudrillard's earlier texts: *The Death of Symbolic Exchange, Simulacra and Simulations, The Perfect Crime*. Alarmed by this prophecy of its apprehended doom, the "empire struck back." Refusing to be the lumbering patsy in the game of "terrorism of code" versus the lost language of "symbolic exchange," the empire flipped

---

[8] Originally published in the French newspaper *Le Monde* as "L'esprit du terrorisme," November 11, 2001. An English translation appeared in *Harper's Magazine* and more recently as a book, *The Spirit of Terrorism* (New York: Verso, 2002).

the political binary by injecting itself with its own spasms of symbolic exchange. Nietzsche understood this first. In *Zarathustra*, he said that power reanimates itself by injecting itself with poisons, mild at first but then as the effects of the injection wear off, stronger and stronger doses of self-administered poison. Nietzsche's "poison" is Baudrillard's "symbolic exchange" is America's "9/11." A poison whose ironic effect has been to immediately *strengthen* the empire.

Collecting DNA Traces from the Bodies of . . .

WW: In terms of strengthening the empire, while we have been hearing for some time now about the "end of innocence," I have come to think of September 11th more as the beginning (or at least rearticulation) of American sanctification. In a way, we are seeing a very peculiar "end of history," or at least the beginning of a new ahistorical terrain. What seems paramount in this is the scale to which the Human Genome Project and bio-technology in general, which have received virtually no coverage since September 11th, assume and even necessitate a particular break from the past. To what degree do you see the debates about these technologies becoming usurped into the larger conversations of security and market-necessity? Can we separate America the free from America the virtual?

Krokers: Biotechnology is fundamental to the new security state. Consider, for example, the swift emergence of new forms of biotechnologies in the service of stricter surveillance of the domestic American population: the use of optical scanners at airports that ID the retinas of the traveling public; the freewheeling deployment of swipe card technologies in order to feed private information into massive security databases; demands by intelligence agencies for the DNA "fingerprinting" of immigrants.

Offshore, the American military machine is now actively involved in gathering DNA from the corpses of members of the so-called al Qaida network, from prisoners in Guantanamo Bay, and, of course, from the Bin Laden family. According to military officials, the purpose of this DNA databank is to provide instantly accessible genetic markers for identifying terrorists when they attempt to infiltrate the American homeland.[9] However, given the intense

---

[9] The *Boston Globe*, for example, reported on May 14, 2002, "The United States is

debates now underway in areas ranging from sports and entertainment to the military about the possibility of developing genetically-streamed artificial beings – part-flesh/part super-clone – the collection of DNA from members of Al Queda may be in support of new forms of futurist forensics: forensics not aimed as much at identifying potential threats to the security state, but at isolating the specific genetic traits that later "express" themselves in terrorism. In the biotech state of the future, the "warrior gene" will probably be used simultaneously for purposes of genetic surveillance of the domestic and global populations, but also developed in the new recombinant DNA factories of the future as the prototype of the ideal American soldier. The militarization of biotechnology combined with radical forms of futurist space war are the dual basis for American military hegemony during the 21st century.

The War on Terrorism as Script

WW: Recently CNN ran a segment about journalism in Afghanistan. It seems the network was unhappy that Hollywood producers are being allowed more freedom and access to U.S troops than the reporters themselves. The military is apparently working with these producers for a new reality television program, providing them with transport, props and the like. In the segment, CNN noted that, "The backdrop itself is funded to the tune of about a billion dollars a day by U.S. taxpayers."[10]

I don't think CNN meant to imply that the purpose of the war is to serve as a backdrop for reality television, although this sentence should at the least warrant another look at Baudrillard's writings on the Gulf War. However, Paul Virilio's notion of the war machine, and how the state first and foremost always commits war against its own population, seems right on target here. Certainly, we are seeing a war against civil liberties, as well as an articulated propaganda effort. Is this what you are referring to, or something more?

Arthur Kroker: The "war on terrorism" is a classic simulacrum. A global political script written by secret elites is now running on automatic. Triggered by the events of 9/11, reenergized by periodic injections of media "poison"

---

compiling a DNA database as part of its global campaign against terrorism and has gathered blood, tissue, and hair samples from hundreds of suspected Al Qaeda and Taliban members, dead and alive, government officials said."
[10] CNN, *American Morning With Paula Zahn*, Feb. 22, 2002.

into the circulatory system of American public opinion, from anthrax scarces traceable to US Army testing laboratories to Tom Clancy scenarios of nuclear weapons in suitcases delivered to New York City by viral terrorists, the simulacrum of the "war on terrorism" is already a new form of hyperreality, understandable only in relationship to its internal signifiers. A closed system of meaning, the war on terrorism declares war most of all on perception. That is why the "theatre of war" is literally transformed into a cinematic bluescreen for projecting a global right-wing script back into the screenal consciousness of America. A new form of hyperreal TV in which war itself becomes a "staged communication," the object of the "script" is the constant enervation of always-flagging American attention. Very much a politics of conspiracy, the war on terrorism as simulacrum combines the best political efforts of what has been publicly acknowledged as America's "Shadow Government," with the zealous cooperation of Hollywood cinema which resequences the popular diet of cinema to feed psychological war scenarios of betrayal and blood-revenge. But, of course, as in the nature of all great conspiracies, everybody is in the know: political, economic, entertainment and academic elites most of all, but certainly the masses in "mass society" as well who grant the changing scenarios of the war on terrorism a special place of honor in a mediascape that is also populated by basketball, Britney Spears, and TV trials of "Mothers Who Kill their Children" and "Attack Dogs that Eat the Neighbours."

The "war on terrorism" is equal parts Virilio's war machine, Baudrillard's simulacrum and Kathy Acker's "empire of the senseless."[11]

Canadian Political Pragmatism

WW: Finally, I am curious as to your view on where Canada fits both into this new war on terrorism, and more generally within the framework of global politics after September 11th. In the American media, news on Canada has been particularly silent, except for the coverage of the border. In a way, the intense scrutiny of this "border porous-ness" fits well into your notion of viral power.

---

[11] Paul Virilio and *Sylvère* Lotringer, *Pure War* (Semiotext(e), 1998); Jean Baudrillard, *Simulacra and Simulation* (Ann Arbor: University of Michigan Press, 1994); Kathy Acker, *Empire of the Senseless* (New York: Grove Press, 1988).

Krokers: As a relatively small culture on the northern tier of American empire, Canada is playing a pragmatic stalling game.

In the "war on terrorism" Canada has been assigned three immediate roles: first, to be a convenient "scapegoat" for relatively tolerant immigration practices; second, to be a source of relatively small deployments of highly secret commando units in support of American military objectives in Afghanistan; and third, to make critical concessions in the domestic security area in order to be included within the "shield" of fortress America. While Canadians were deeply affected by the tragedy of 9/11, the Canadian government remains deeply pragmatic in its security policy. Thus, Canada will continue to tack in the direction of the prevailing winds of the war on terrorism only to the point that it receives strategic compromises in trade relations. Thus, for example, it seems to be a fact of the real world of international politics that Canada committed troops to Afghanistan only after the Bush administration agreed to exempt Canadian steel-makers from a punitive increase in tariff duties that was subsequently imposed on the European Union. The fact that four Canadian soldiers died as a result of so-called "friendly fire" by an overzealous US Air Force lent a real air of tragedy to Canada's involvement.

As usual, while America runs the emotional extremes of revenge and redemption, Canada survives.

WW: I want to add here, that as a graduate student working on shareholder activism and militarism, I was surprised to learn the degree to which Canada and Canadian companies play a role in the U.S. military industrial complex. Military exports in late 1990s totaled almost 1 billion a year, and Canadian defense contractors play a vital role in both the Canadian economy and also in the U.S military industrial complex. It is interesting to juxtapose this with your assertion of political negotiations between the U.S and Canada that "generally run against the grain of Canadian popular culture which traditionally has deeply embraced the earlier liberal vision of Canada as a peaceful force in the world." It seems as if Canadian survival is closely linked to American extremes of revenge and redemption in this sense as well.

Arthur Kroker: In the realm of political economy, Canada has pursued for many decades a continentalist economic strategy, culminating with the North America Free Trade Agreement which sought to harmonize the natural resource base and technology output of the Canadian economy with the globalizing imperatives of American empire. Politically, it is only in the underground culture of music, comedy and writing that Canadian popular culture finds its most authentic expression. As opposed to the continentalism of its political economy, Canadian popular culture runs on a separate track: fiercely nationalistic, strongly regionalist, generally anti-war, earthy in its politics, and scatological in its humor. As the historian W.L Morton intimated in his book, *The Canadian Identity*, to live on a hard northern landscape, with the Laurentian Shield for ground and the Northern Lights for horizon, a sense of humor is necessary for survival, with satire being the cultural position of choice. Of course, Harold Innis, Canada's preeminent political economist, responded, that the peculiar fate of Canadians living on the northern edge of American Empire is to have consciousness of much, but the (political) incapacity to do much about it.[12] So then, two perspectives from the Canadian north: economic elites accommodating their interests to the operational logic of a now rearmed globalization; and the suppressed sounds of discontent from a working culture whose politics involves questions of social justice. None of this is clear-cut: an uneasy compromise between accommodation with globalized consumption and a very active vision of world peace are uncomfortable partners in Canada's cultural imagination. But then, every culture has its saving illusions. For the future, it is certainly noteworthy, and hopeful, that Canadian social movements have long played a leading role in popular campaigns against globalization and that, at the present juncture, Canada sides with the European Union in opposition to more military adventures in the name of the "war on terrorism."

---

[12] The quote is a variation of Herodotus' statement: "The ultimate bitterness is this: to have consciousness of much; but control over nothing."

History

Davarian L. Baldwin

Black Belts and Ivory Towers: The Place of Race in U.S. Social Thought, 1892–1948*

. . . it was not until I stumbled upon science that I discovered some of the meanings of the environment that battered and taunted me. I encountered the work of men who were studying the Negro community, amassing facts about urban Negro life, and I found that sincere art and honest science were not far apart, and that each could enrich the other. The huge mountains of fact piled up by the Department of Sociology at the University of Chicago gave me my first concrete vision of the forces that molded the urban Negro's body and soul.

Richard Wright

The migration of Negroes to the metropolitan areas of the North had destroyed the accommodation that had been achieved to some extent following the racial conflict during and following Reconstruction . . . The new impact of the Negro problem on American life undoubtedly helped Park as much as his experience in the South in the formulation of a sociological theory.

E. Franklin Frazier

In the above passage, Black writer and migrant, Richard Wright expressed a deep gratitude for the "huge mountains of fact" generated by the "Chicago School" of sociology and their impact on his literary

---

* An earlier version of this essay appeared in *Critical Sociology*, vol. 30, no. 2 (2004).

(re)presentations of Black life (Drake and Cayton 1945: xvii–xviii). Within African American arts and letters, Wright's observations and writings sparked a debate as to whether such nods to social science indicated a moment of liberation *or* colonization. One argument is that the concepts and categories of the "Chicago School" encouraged over generalized and negative representations of the Black community. Others contend it was precisely the utilization of social scientific facts and methods that gave scholars and writers the necessary tools to better "make sense" of the Black experience and offer more "objective" and comparative representations. This conversation within African American studies continues and there has been important work that has attempted to create a valuable middle space between Black representations and social theory (Reilly 1982; Cappetti 1985, 1993).[1]

Yet, the above tension also draws notice to debates about the legacy of the "Chicago School" itself, which is equally centered on representations of racial experience. Noting the Chicago School's "liberal" denouncement of Social Darwinism, alternative to authoritarian strategies of "Americanization," liberal critique of capitalism, and landmark training of African and Asian American social scientists, some have posited it as progressive. Others have argued that the "Chicago School" simply replaced a biological with a cultural determinism, served the interests of capitalism, excluded primarily women reformers under the guise of professionalism, and used scholars of color as "native informants" in communities where White scholars could not research.

The complexity of positions and figures within the dynamic relationship between the "Chicago School" and the racial worlds it hoped to (re)present, force me to say that to some degree all of the arguments are in some way correct. But, whether the "Chicago School" was cultural determinist or constructionist, reformist or scientific, politically progressive or conservative, is not the point. Bringing the debates within African American arts and letters and sociology together allows this essay to explore something a bit different. This is not simply a discussion about how sociology constructed racial cate-

---

[1] I want to thank my many students for struggling over these ideas with me and especially Katherine Lummis and Leah Tseronis for their rigorous archival research and reading. I also want to express extreme gratitude to my colleague Deborah Levenson-Estrada and especially Bridgette Baldwin for looking over numerous drafts. Finally, I want to thank the Boston College *Critical Sociology* Collective for their invitation to write this essay, particularly Stephen Pfohl, Juliet Schor and Patricia Arend for their personal correspondence.

gories, but how anxieties about racial difference in the early 20th century *constructed* the "Chicago School" and U.S. sociology more generally. The well-worn road from the ivory towers of the University of Chicago (U of C) down to, for example, its Black Belt outposts, has been well documented. However, little has been said about how the "Chicago School" appropriated dynamic events within the racial economy of industrializing capitalist America and quantified them under social "scientific" categories. There are profound ways in which Black life, even in gross misrepresentations, influenced what Black sociologist E. Franklin Frazier called "the formulation of [a] sociological theory" at the U of C (1947: 37). The question at hand is: how have the racial experiences of the "Jim Crow" south, the Great Migration, immigration and urban culture etc. pervaded the most seemingly neutral social theories about civilization, assimilation, social organization, and the city? To begin answering this question, we must pay more attention to Black people, the urban Black Belt where they lived even in their most inaccurate depictions, and eventually the Black "native informant" sociologists trained at the U of C.

Sociology at the U of C was obsessed with Black people, Black behaviors and Black neighborhoods and this opened the door to Black sociologists who both critiqued and reinforced that same obsession. Critical scholarship rightly places this intellectual period within the context of the "Progressive Era," or "The Age of Professionalization." At the same time, Black experiences informed, worked within, transformed and even directly challenged many of the fundamental organizing principles of sociological theory, method and interpretation. This period of social and intellectual development could easily be termed the "Era of Race Relations." The racial contacts and conflicts between White residents and Black migrants but also non-White and White immigrants, profoundly shaped the U.S. social sciences (Tchen ed., Siu 1987; Wilson 1996; Scott 1997; Baker 1998; Yu 2001).

The "Chicago School's" theories of race consciousness, cultural assimilation, and urban organization are integral to what is called a sociological outlook and celebrated as challenges to the dominant biological theories of social difference at the turn of the last century. The institutionalization of these ideas emerged with the rise of Harvard and German trained, White scholar Robert Park, the "father" of urban sociology and race relations in the U.S. He challenged fixed genetic visions of social relations with a theory of cultural evolution informed by the idea that race is a dynamic and changing product of socio-historical conditions. However, Park's discussions of Black people in this critical period reveal a "cultural turn" that was infused with equally rigid categories of identity and distinction. The dynamic events of Black migration, urban racial violence and "New Negro" resistance posed direct threats to his paradigm of cultural cohesion and order. To maintain scientific certainty, Park incorporated race conflict and racial traits into his overarching social system, as natural elements to be overcome by the inevitable force of cultural assimilation.

Frustrated with a strict Parkian vision of cultural determinism, Chicago trained Black sociologists variably countered their mentor with studies investigating the socio-economic "facts" of race and class struggle. The social context of protest and resistance during the "Age of the New Negro" in the 1910's and 20's and the "Popular Front" period of the 1930's and 40's heavily informed the Black sociological critique. However, Black sociologists were equally beholden to the sociological tendency to measure and evaluate group behaviors according to an overarching social system of, at this point, industrial relations. Whether dysfunction was found within the social group or the social system the indicator, even in the most progressive work, remained Black behavioral deviation from a pre-defined norm. This essay ends with a stripping away of this overarching, over-determining sociological framework and re-contextualizing the "data" derived from race relations scholarship within its Black migrant and urban context. Doing this reveals how people in Chicago's Black Belt theorized their immediate conditions, constructed their neighborhood and situated themselves within the larger social world in ways that challenged both White and Black sociologists at the U of C.

To paraphrase historian Henry Yu, the centrality of the "Negro Problem" to sociological studies at Chicago does not deny the relatively progressive work done there. But at the same time, this very same focus institutionalized a sociological knowledge that was profoundly racialist. At the end of the day, or the beginning of a new century, the intentions of individual progressive thinkers cannot be divorced from the "structural effects of their practices" (Yu 2001: 10). More directly, our at best partial eye to the relationship between Black experience and social theory at the U of C, has allowed scholars to divorce themselves from notions of "assimilation," "deviance," "dysfunction" and the "inner city" that continue to creep up in both academic and popular writings to this day. In the quest to develop more dynamic, collaborative and contextualized sociological imagination(s), we must continue to revisit our disciplinary pasts to dismantle static, stable and overly systemic or even individualistic categories. To understand the resilient connection between Black behaviors and "inner city" life, we must examine the racial contexts from which the University of Chicago, arguably the most influential department in the field, emerged. Both the university and the city of Chicago were direct products of the socio-historical processes of an industrializing America in the early 20th century that, important for this study, brought "foreign" races and their cultures to U.S. urban centers. This period of social contact and contestation would transform the political economy and the professional social sciences.

Disjuncture and Difference in the Urban Racial Economy

The turn of the century marked the early years of both the "professional" intellectual and the development of industrial capitalism as the dominant economic and cultural force in the United States. The US became a world power through the application of science and technology to production, which encouraged the concentration and centralization of capital into monopoly corporations. The merging of bank capital and industrial capital signified a new stage in the national and international reach of capital accumulation. Americans "believed that industrial technology and the factory system would serve as a historic instrument of republican values, diffusing civic virtue and enlightenment along with material wealth. Factories, railroads and telegraph wires seemed the very engines of a democratic future" (Trachtenberg: 38). For many, Chicago became the emblematic symbol of a new industrial vision of the U.S. as a democratic civilization. As a phoenix rising out of the Great Fire of 1871, the "City of Big Shoulders" (Spiney 2000) became the physical manifestation of a transforming American modernity. This claim was solidified by the national reach of the Illinois Central Railroad and their locally made Pullman cars; the productive force of International Harvester, Swift, Armour, nearby U.S. Steel and the cultural reach of Sears and Roebuck and the *Chicago Tribune* (Cronon 1991). While industrialization and mechanization became symbols of infinite progress and abundance, they also brought disastrous effects to social groups newly arriving to the city.

Industrialization and subsequent (im)migrations made visible the cohabitation and sharpening contrast between urban prosperity and poverty directly along racial lines. Chicago's rapid growth and accumulation of wealth most notably celebrated itself with the World Columbian Exposition of 1893 and its prized "White City." But before the pristine plaster could barely dry on this not-so-subtle racialized spectacle of Americanization, the "off White" working "hordes," within the Chicago machine, took to the streets in the bloody Pullman strikes of 1894. Neo-classical preserves, like the Opera House, the Art Institute of Chicago and Lincoln Park had been built to signify the opulence of an urban aristocracy. Not far away, the growing "towns" and "belts" of cramped and unsanitary shanties, shacks and slums arose to pen in the rising tide of European, Asian and Black (im)migrants. A serious disjuncture (Appadurai 1990) emerged as older forms of human "incorporation" were replaced with their capitalist variant (ideally the corporation as a person). Muckraking journalists and crusading reformers like Sophonisba Breckenridge and Jane Addams at Hull House (Deegan 1988, 2002)[2] made direct links between the wealth generated by capitalist expansion and exploitation and the growing threats of disease, vice and crime in the neighborhoods of working-class racial groups (Burg 1976; Harris 1978; Kasson 1978; Lewis 1983; Rydell 1985; Trachtenberg 1991).

Ever-expanding networks of railroads and wire services both brought communities together and loosened the tight grip of provincial standards on social behavior. The local gentry could no longer govern their residents' lives in the same way and city fathers were confronted not just with new people but "foreign" cultural values that challenged definitions of America. This set of circumstances, summarized as a "crisis of cultural authority" (Lears 1981), encouraged a strong desire to reconstitute some sense of a normative social order. The advances in technology and the centralization of industry opened up the possibilities for long term planning and calculated management to assist in the development of industrial productivity and cultural authority.

Many colleges and universities moved away from a "classical" education and re-designed their curricula to support the scientific and technical needs of the growing industrial economy (Bledstein 1976). The professionalization of science and its knowledge systems of planning also encouraged private monopolies of "expert information" that separated mental from manual labor (Haskell 1984). As the status of technical education rose, older crafts and

---

[2] In fact, philosopher George Herbert Mead, one of the prominent scholars who was later associated with the "Chicago School" and most known for his theories of symbolic interactionism, served for years as the secretary of Hull House (Lewis and Smith 1980).

guilds were phased out for the "universal" standards of certification and status (Taylor 1912). By professionalizing certain forms of information, knowledge was converted into a form of property. Legitimacy was maintained by claiming that these new fields could define human need and supply the services for a highly technological society. National standards of scientific competence paved the way for a new technical intelligentsia.

For industry, the development of a managing class served a dual purpose; it presided over both machine and labor (Gouldner 1979). The instability of a social and cultural authority (Boyer 1984; Levine 1988) and the promises of an industrial civilization brought new interest to the stabilizing possibilities of the American *social* sciences (Vyesey 1965; Furner 1975; Haskell 1977; Olsen and Voss 1979; Ross 1991). The captains of the industrial metropolis were forced to realize that the rapid rationalization and uniformity of resource and land use was quite different than homogenizing or "Americanizing" the outlook and use of workers (Hartman 1948; Horsman 1981; Pedraza and Rumbaut ed. 1996; Gerstle and Mollenkopf 2001). These dynamic changes would find orthodox Social Darwinism too rigid and progressive reformers too radical. Sociologists, and the U of C in particular, positioned themselves as an objective middle ground solving the social "problem" of racial incorporation without bias, but scientifically (Pfohl 1994).

Colonial Outpost on the Racial Frontier

The discipline of sociology in the U.S. was a direct product of America's struggles over the "race" problem. Sociology, with its roots in post-Enlightenment and industrializing France, England and Germany, was first introduced to the U.S. through the training of individual scholars abroad who studied under leading figures like Georg Simmel and Max Weber or read Emile Durkheim and Herbert Spencer (Rodgers 1998). However, in 1892, the two-year-old University of Chicago opened its doors to the equally young field of sociology to become the flagship department in the U.S. (Madge 1962; Kurtz 1984; Harvey 1987; Rochberg-Halton 1989; Abbott 1999). The "Chicago School" is often heralded as instigating a shift in sociology from a politically charged version of social reform and uplift in the later 19th century, towards a more neutral and empirically minded discipline directed by a "scientific" observation and measurement of social life (Small 1907; Hinkle and Hinkle 1954). Yet, regardless of outlook, the larger racial economy would continue to influence sociology's institutional development at the U of C. Spatially, the suburb of Hyde Park, where the U of C was located, was surrounded by White people fleeing to northern suburbs and growing Black Belts, Chinatowns and "off-White" communities to the near northwest.

These changing demographic shifts left the university as one of the few "pure white" preserves on the south side, making it a colonial outpost on the racial frontier. Ideally, the U of C had a prime seat from which to offer solutions to the problems caused by the social differences amongst arriving populations and the department would develop an array of institutions to substantiate their particular vision. Quickly, department founder, Albion Small, established the U of C's hegemony over social thought with his heavy hand in establishing the American Sociological Society (now Association), the *American Journal of Sociology*, the University of Chicago Press and publishing an early sociology textbook (Dibble 1975; Martindale 1976; Lengerman 1979; Persons 1987). The U of C took its social scientific gospel to the streets through these institutions while the social problem of assimilation or "race relations," was a central anxiety in the city (Wacker 1983; Bulmer 1984). The most common organizing principle for understanding social differences was "race." At this time, any group with a specific ancestry and geographical origin in common, such as Irish, Polish or Jewish, was referred to as a "race" (Omi and Winant 1986; Persons 1987).[3] As "foreign" races exploded onto the urban landscape, social scientists turned to the most familiar "laboratory" (Small and Vincent 1894; Park 1921) of contact between distinct social groups at their disposal: the Jim Crow south (Stanfield 1982).

---

[3] Stowe Persons points out that the distinction between "race" and "ethnicity" is quite recent. The Chicago sociologists under discussion often used "race" where we would now use "ethnicity." Persons prefers to use "ethnicity" as the comprehensive term, whereas, the subject of this essay encourages me to use "race." Just to highlight, I will be using race in the same way that it was deployed by "Chicago School" social scientists, which exposes both the conceptual instability and social resiliency of the term. So again, race is understood as any group with a specific ancestry and geographical origin in common, such as Irish, Polish, Jewish, or Negro. Furthermore "race relations" are studies of contact, conflict and possible assimilation between racial groupings. Racial economy refers to an economic system influenced or even determined by racial identity or difference. A racial or racist division of labor speaks to the distribution of tasks, compensation etc. according to racial groups and possibly even their presupposed traits or characteristics. Furthermore, terms like racial discrimination, racial exploitation etc. are composite phrases that combine the aforementioned definition of race with another term.

Race was clearly not the only theme discussed within Small's *American Journal of Sociology* (AJS). However, it is between the covers of the *AJS* that we get a sense of the published and hence institutionalized ideas about racial assimilation/incorporation within the field. Institutionalization must be understood as a technique of standardization and hence power by marking what stands inside and outside those standards. The innovative Black scholarship on race relations was different enough from most ideas within the traditional organizational structure of *AJS* and hence the larger field, that the work was systematically illegible, illogical and hence invisible (Reed 1988; Goddard 1999). For example, if the journal wanted to study the Jim Crow South as a model, it had at its disposal, *Southern Horrors*, the groundbreaking 1892 study of lynching by Ida B. Wells (1892), herself a Black migrant that fled to Chicago in the face of a lynch mob (Duster 1970; Broschart 1991) or the work of Black Chicago scholar/activist, Fannie Barrier Williams (1905; Deegan 2002). If certification was a problem they could have turned to U of C trained Black social scientists Richard R. Wright (1901, 1911, 1965) and Monroe Work (1901, 1903; McMurray 1991). Of course, the sociological profession could have also easily accessed the insights of Harvard and German trained social scientist W.E.B. DuBois and his 1899 text *Philadelphia Negro*, or one of his many studies on race relations conducted at Atlanta University (Katz and Sugrue 1998).[4]

All points seem to suggest the issue of racism but at the same time, there is no "smoking gun," – archival letter, mission statement etc. – that explains the marginalization of these preeminent Black scholars from the *AJS* or sociological legitimacy. Based on the case of Monroe Work, the inclusion/exclusion of Black social scientists seemed predicated on both the representation of racial realities in scholarship and the race of the scholar. Monroe Work's essay, "Crime Among Negroes in Chicago," was published in the *AJS* in 1901. This essay exposed extreme levels of segregation within local housing patterns but also reinforced many of the popular assumptions that linked that very neighborhood vice and restriction to Black behavior. To get a sense of institutional policies on "race" it is important to recognize that Work's essay was published in the *AJS*, but also that the journal went on to most prominently

---

[4] In fact, most of the early secondary scholarship on Black sociology scholars and DuBois in particular, came out of the journal DuBois founded at Atlanta University, *Phylon*, because of the marginalization of Black sociological knowledge in mainstream institutions.

showcase and celebrate the "Negro Problem" scholarship of a White Mississippi planter, Alfred Holt Stone, and hence an entirely different legacy of expertise on "racial relations."

Many early White sociologists were significantly influenced by the genetically determined explanations of racial difference found in the Social Darwinist (Hofstadter 1944; Banister 1979) thought of British scholar, Herbert Spencer and applied then to race relations in the U.S. South (Frazier 1947; Martindale 1976). Henry Hughes' *Treatise on Sociology* (1854) and George Fitzhugh's *Sociology of the South* (1854) both defended slavery as natural and economically beneficial long before the more recognized "Social Darwinism" of W.G. Summer and the relatively more progressive work of Lester Ward. Even the U of C head and *AJS* founder Albion Small spent some time in his textbook *An Introduction to the Study of Society* (1894) discussing the possibility of combining distinct races into an organic unity, with the union of the United States as the social scientific laboratory. While Small seemed to fear the reduction of the Indian to destruction and the Negro to servitude he understood these groups as "weaker elements" that had to be amalgamated into a "single civilization." The question of incorporation was especially acute as both industrial capitalism and Black resistance transported the "Negro Problem" beyond the physical and conceptual boundaries of a "peculiar" southern institution (Small and Vincent 1894: 179). At the same time the migration of "Black Belts" north made southern interactions between Black and White races the perfect raw data for more general, and highly ahistorical, theories on social interaction and race relations in particular. It is in this context that Alfred Stone's *Studies in the American Race Problem* (1908) was celebrated by the *AJS* as the "most valuable contribution yet appearing on the race problems of the United States" (Blackmar 1909: 837). Stone argued that "white blood alone made black intelligence possible" and the savagery inherent in Black people could only be repressed by White controls (Lewis 1993: 368). This book length project was not the first time social scientists had been privy or even celebrated the arguments of this southern planter "expert" on race relations.

The ideas in *Studies* were an extension of Stone's paper, "Is Race Friction in the United States Growing and Inevitable" (1908), read one year earlier at the meetings of the American Sociological Society. He posited that racial friction resulted from pressure felt by White people, "almost instinctively in the presence of a mass of people of a different race" (680). Stone argued that the level of racial contact was not the cause of racial friction but the dismantling of social relationships, like slavery, that held Black demands for equality at bay. Out of the many northern academic discussants that engaged Stone's work (820–840), only W.E.B. DuBois rose to disagree with the idea that racial antipathy was a natural response to Black demands for social equality. DuBois' critique of Stone and call for scientific study of the race problem were universally ignored by the society of social science (821–40, Lewis 1993). Moreover, when Robert Park and Ernest Burgess later collected essays on race relations for their important sociological textbook, *Introduction to the Science of Sociology* (1921), they again did not include an excerpt from *Philadelphia Negro* (1899) or *Southern Horrors* (1892). Instead, they printed a revised version of Stone's essay "Race Friction," under the heading "Conflict and Accommodation" (1921). These related choices of inclusion/exclusion, made clear the early racial, and hence sociological, vision of these Chicago sponsored institutions.

Albion Small's journal implicitly endorsed Stone and suggested the inferiority of different races. But Small's work also began a shift in sociological outlook from a consensus to conflict model that broke from the strict genetic fixity found in the work of Stone. Chicago sociology would then make a more pronounced move to caste (culture) over biological explanations of social difference when W.I. Thomas replaced Small as chair of the Chicago department. He found that despite the "inferiority" of primitive racial cultures the problem was not genetic. Foreign races could be uplifted, reformed and brought into American civilization. Thomas posited that distinct historical experiences produced race while racism designated a primitive stage of social relations. He linked race prejudice to the tribal stage of social relations when group solidarity was necessary for survival and posited this form of antagonism would decrease with improved education, communications and contact (Persons 1987). He marked industrial American culture (read White) as having reached this normative state of civilization while also challenging authoritarian solutions to Americanization. Through *The Polish Peasant in Europe and America* (with Znaniecki 1918–1920), Thomas introduced the idea of primary (face-to-face and familial, group contacts) and secondary (rational, individual interests with political or intellectual objectives) relations. The evolution to the urban industrial and more civilized secondary relations took place along a spectrum of organization and disorganization.

Thomas importantly rejected cultural homogeneity as the solution to social incorporation for what he termed the "ethnicity paradox" (with Znaniecki 1918–1920). Within the "paradox," ethnic organizations in the city like newspapers, political groups and schools, best maximized the industrial and hence civilized traits of efficiency and individualization. Thomas argued that ethnic institutions helped facilitate the socio-historical evolution from immigrant to ethnic American to "American." This basic idea about the historical and dynamic construction of race came from his earlier work comparing the immigrant and "Negro Problem" (1904, 1912). The logical extension of Thomas' argument was that all races, even with different physical traits, must be mixed in order to stimulate individualization. However, even in the city, the mixing of White with non-White races was still a taboo subject outside of producing slave labor (Mumford 1997). But to help work through this problem, Thomas brought Robert Park to Chicago (Wacker 1995); an emerging scholar who was most recently executive secretary to Booker T. Washington at the all Black Tuskegee Institute in Alabama (Lyman 1992). Park's first hand experience, as another southern, White "race expert" on the Negro Problem would help Thomas develop his own ideas about assimilation. As eventual chair of the department, it is through the lens of Park's writings that we see the intimate relationship between the realities of race relations in the early 20th century and their challenges to social theories of an inevitable cultural cohesion. The institutional and conceptual vision and the basic organizing concepts of what was becoming the "Chicago School" of urban sociology emerged directly from this dialectic of racial contradiction and struggle.

Race(ing) into Urban Sociology: Temperaments, Cycles, Zones and Mentalities

Robert Park had quite a diverse set of learning experiences that profoundly influenced the direction of the "Chicago School." He attended the University of Michigan during the tenure of pragmatist John Dewey, and worked as an investigative and crime reporter, before completing graduate studies with William James at Harvard and Georg Simmel at Berlin. After completing his doctorate degree in Germany, Park first worked for the Congo Reform Association, where he penned numerous articles about the detrimental affects of European colonialism on Belgian outposts in Africa. Then in 1905, he accepted a position as executive secretary to Booker T. Washington at Tuskegee Institute. Within these contexts, Park developed the deep belief that the Protestant ethic would bring morality and efficiency to the children of Africa in a rapidly industrializing world. At Tuskegee, Park was able to study Black rural settlements in the south and witness Washington's ethic of industrial progress in motion. Radical integrationists like W.E.B. DuBois labeled Washington an "accommodationist," because he argued that Blacks must first work to uplift themselves in the spheres of labor and morality before demanding political equality (Washington 1901; Harlan 1972). It has been argued that Park was a ghostwriter for Washington, but we find in early articles by Robert Park that the ideological influences ran both ways. Park's writings on Black rural settlements consistently espoused the idea of self-betterment and offer some insights into the building blocks of basic social theories later developed at the U of C (Farris 1967; Wacker 1976, 1983; Mathews 1977; Raushenbush 1979; Smith 1988; Lal 1990; Lyman 1992; Lindner 1996).

In 1905, Park wrote about his race relations study of Winston-Salem, North Carolina, for the popular magazine *World To-Day*. He found that in Winston-Salem, Black residents created a community with various enterprises without antipathy from their White neighbors. Accordingly, the principles of the Protestant work ethic, instilled by the White Moravian missionary founders of the community, combined with a "bi-racial" system of interaction were credited with fostering the state of "Racial Peace." Park and Washington argued that the separate race neighborhood of Columbia Heights, within Winston Salem, helped Black people "find a freer expression to their native energies and ambitions" (Washington 1909: 119). At the same time, industrial education and Black employment at the R.J. Reynolds Tobacco Company civilized Black residents with lessons from the Protestant ethic of life and labor.

Park's developing theory of race relations measured social interactions and groups along a scale from savagery or primitivism to civilization. In this theory, civilization was consistently equated with a personal identity of individualization where all interactions and behaviors were rationalized within a marketplace system and mediated through some form of "contractual" exchange. For the *World To-Day* Park later suggested that instruction from Christian leaders on "moral abstemiousness, personal hygiene, domestic simplicity, hard work and vocational instruction" had moved Black people forward on the civilization scale (1908, 1913, Lyman 1992: 103). Park identified "domestic slavery" as the "most striking illustration" of the assimilation of Black people where the intimate relationships between slaves and "the language, religion, and the technique of the civilization of his master," removed any remaining primitive African characteristics (1913 (1950): 209). While they were "not citizens," slavery helped make the transition from an "alien people" to domestication (211). In order to substantiate his theory, Park had to ignore the entire history of slave revolts and rebellion. But he could no longer ignore the form of resistance created by African American movement North and away from "cities of peace" in the Jim Crow South.

The literal complexion of urban and rural landscapes changed in the early 1900's with the beginning trickles of the larger tidal wave of the Great Black Migration North looming on the horizon (Henri 1975; Marks 1989; Grossman 1989; Trotter 1991; Griffin 1995). This movement limited the successful application of static theories like Social Darwinism and even Park's concept of bi-racial accommodation. Yet, his "scientific studies" of Christian tolerance, and industrial education within a bi-racial system of capitalist relations, still made Park an attractive expert on race relations in Chicago. His ideas did not advance a strict Social Darwinist notion of social relations, but incorporated a level of dynamic change within a racially ordered system of urban assimilation. Park recognized that unlike immigrant groups, the "Negro has had his separateness and consequent race consciousness thrust upon him because of his exclusion and forcible isolation from White society" (1913 (1950): 218). The physically changing landscape of White violence and Black resistance, combined with the alluring quest for "scientific" legitimacy, required Park to replace rural, religious with more urban, "rational" metaphors of cultural cohesion.[5] However, he would develop explanations of urbanization that naturalized rather than historicized and politicized the processes of social change and Black discontent.

Park clearly was not African American, but the phrase used to describe the early migration of the Black elite, "the professional man, himself [is] migrating to recapture his constituency . . . (Locke xxvii)" could be directly applied to his move in 1913 (Phelps 1919: 12).[6] The U of C needed an "expert" on race relations and Park also realized that not staying abreast of his "subjects" and their changing social relations could quickly make his theories irrelevant. The rapid increase in the Black populous of 6,480 in 1880, to 30,150 in 1900 to 109,850 by 1920, made Chicago the perfect new "laboratory" of social

---

[5] This essay is included in an edited collection of twenty-nine of Park's many essays committed to his obsession with "race relations" (1950).

[6] Alain Locke is most popularly credited with this phrase. However, I have found that Chicago Black writer Howard Phelps uttered the phrase, "professional men are leaving the South on the trail of their clients and patients who have settled in Chicago," six years earlier (See Phelps 1919, Locke 1925).

forces that are still being felt (Drake and Cayton 1945; Spear 1967; Grossman 1989). Once settled, Park immediately became a student of the city teaching one course at the U of C (not receiving a full-time position until 1919). He also served as president of Chicago's new Urban League that formed to help rural Black migrants in their adjustment and incorporation into urban life (Strickland 1966).

The issue of racial incorporation would come to an acute head in 1919 when the entire nation, and Chicago in particular, was rocked by what has been called the "Red Summer" (Sandburg 1919; Tuttle 1970). Direct resistance to Black competition for jobs and housing by working-class immigrants coupled with legal restrictions on and benign neglect of Black communities by city fathers, had been on-going and finally erupted into race riots all over the country. The Urban League was brought in to direct the Chicago Commission on Race Relations' study of the riot (1922). Black researcher and future student of Park, Charles Johnson, literally conducted most of the work on the project while letting Park come along to observe (Bulmer 1981). More attention will be given to Charles Johnson in the next section. But in the capacity of observer with Johnson, Park produced a number of articles and with Ernest Burgess, *the* textbook for sociologists, *Introduction to the Science of Sociology* (1921). In this context, Park's general theories about the urban experience were driven by his attempt to reconcile the contradictions between social "scientific" systems of order and organization and the very real events of conflict, contestation and racial violence.

An important element in Park's work was his argument that physical differences – hair, facial features, skin color etc, were not indicators of racial traits. Racial conflict arose from people's awareness, or what he called, "race consciousness" about these physical differences and not in one's biological makeup. So in the case of Winston-Salem, the (White) Protestant ethic became the glue between disparate groups and altered their qualitative views of visible social distinction. This idea of cultural cohesiveness or scientific faith in a "moral order" found its way into two early and important U of C projects. In 1921, Park and Herbert Miller published *Old World Traits Transplanted* as part of a Carnegie sponsored series on Americanization.[7] This was an early

---

[7] *Old War Traits Transplanted* was funded by the Carnegie Corporation as part of a larger series on Americanization. Most of the work was done by Thomas who had to leave the university under a controversial scandal (See Rashenbush 1979: 88).

attempt to make generalizable comparisons between all racial groups in the movement from a rural, agrarian and traditional to an urban, industrial and cosmopolitan social system. They contended that the above struggles could be found among both European immigrants and non-White races. Therefore, Thomas' theory of disorganization and organization mediated by the "ethnicity paradox," was an objective process. When Park and Ernest Burgess published, *Introduction to the Science of Sociology* the same year, it forcefully institutionalized the above ideas as social scientific. This standard textbook within the field, called the "green bible" because of its green cover, was a wide-ranging and eclectic mix of approaches to social relations that most formally introduced the significant "interaction cycles" paradigm. The "interaction cycles" posited a universal system of contact between social groups through a series of progressive steps from competition to conflict to accommodation and finally, assimilation. This theory built conflict, like the 1919 riots, directly into the system as a "natural" element on the way to an eventual state of equilibrium.

The interaction cycle allowed Park, in many ways, to reconcile his thoughts on a southern bi-racial peace with the events of Black migration and racial violence. Conflict and violence became a natural part of an inevitable process. However, Chicago's race riots also proved to Park that the incorporation of "non-White" racial groups into a cultural whole would not occur solely through a change in consciousness. He recognized that the Negro and "Oriental," unlike the Irish or Russian, wore a "racial uniform" (1913 (1950): 208). Park argued that physical traits were not an indicator of social difference, but also had to reconcile the very real resistance to assimilation with his argument about an inevitable cultural cohesion. He turned to a theory of "racial characteristics" that imposed bio-cultural explanations on social conditions and groups. Within this new outlook, genetic codes did not immobilize group assimilation but *cultural* traits determined the present state and speed at which racial groups became "mere individuals" (read White). Park's developing theory rationalized race, without letting racism undermine social cohesion. The turn to biology secured coherency for his theory, within a scientific language of apparent rational predictability and inevitability. As early as 1918, Park's article for *American Sociological Society*, "Education in its Relation to the Conflict and Fusion of Cultures," used biological metaphors to legitimate sociology as a science and at the same time naturalize not just social processes but the groups involved. The experience of the Negro constantly undermined, and so became the primary subject of, his general theories about the cycles of social interaction. Park then posited what seemed to be a defense of anthropological arguments about the relative parity of intelligence among races. However, he quickly shifted to a comparison of the "innate and characteristic differences of temperament" (261) from the "most primitive" Negro and Jew to the "most sophisticated Teuton and Latin" (264).

In this essay, Negro traits became the focus of discussion to determine whether racial difference was a product of biology or culture and how particular racial characteristics aided or impeded assimilation. Park rhetorically asked: "Is the Negro's undoubted interest in music and taste for bright colors, commonly attributed to the race, to be regarded as inherent and racial traits or are they merely the characteristics of primitive people" (Park 1918 (1950): 264)? In the final analysis he answered both: "the individual man is the bearer of a double inheritance. As a member of society or social group, on the other hand, he transmits by interbreeding a *biological* inheritance" (Park 1918 (1950): 264). The double inheritance became a way to argue that social incorporation was a consequence of nature and nurture, that it depended on both culture and biology. This was a process applicable to all races, but the distinct "temperaments" of each group placed them at different stages of development:

> The Negro is, by natural disposition, neither an intellectual nor an idealist, like the Jew; nor a brooding introspective, like the East African; nor a pioneer and frontiersman, like the Anglo-Saxon. He is primarily an artist, loving life for its own sake. His *métier* is expression rather than action. He is, so to speak, the lady among the races (Park 1918 (1950): 282).

So if the industrial symbols of "enterprise and action" (282) designated a culture of civilization, the Negro's "genial, sunny and social disposition, in an interest and attachment to external, physical things rather than to subjective states and objects of introspection" (282) were the "natural" explanation for their slow advance. He recognized racial inequality, but the metaphor of "racial temperament" fixed the Negro as the negation of civilization. This fixity of racial difference is what radical psychiatrist Franz Fanon later described as the Black subject's imprisonment into a state of "crushing objecthood" (1952).

At the same time, it is important to acknowledge the various explanations that have been deployed to account for Robert Park's ideas on racial temperaments. Sociologist Morris Janowitz reminds us that Park later regretted his infamous "lady among the races" comment, "again and again" (1965: 733). However, Janowitz's further explanation that Park's notion of temperaments was an attempt to challenge more biological notions of race, seem to justify Park's use of the very term he apologized for using. Scholar of the "Chicago School" Barbara Ballis Lal even more forcefully states that because Park rarely mentioned racial temperament, the subject is "of little consequence" within his full body of work (1990: 154). But it seems the number of times he mentioned "racial temperaments" doesn't compare to where he said it. A version of Park's infamous essay, with that comment in tact, was published as "Temperament, Tradition and Nationality," in the aforementioned and highly influential textbook, *Introduction to the Science of Sociology*, which was taught in most introductory sociology courses throughout the country. Lal also counters that Park's deep investigation and published celebration of Harlem Renaissance work also displays his continued belief that race traits were dynamic and not static (1990). In a series of understudied essays, Park saw in "the sophisticated singers of the Harlem cabarets and the radical poetry of the so-called Harlem Renaissance" race-conscious acts of "rebellion and self–assertion" (1923 (1950): 294). Park believed that the Negro's interest in art and entertainment would push them as a group further along the interaction cycle (1926, 1928). For him, the location of the Black content of folktales, spiritual hymns, dialect etc. within the civilizing European forms of literacy, composition and verse became a Black version of the "ethnicity paradox."

However, under closer examination this is not as dynamic a process as it appears. In fact, as a response to the work of Lal, sociologist Stanford Lyman points out that Park's interest in the Harlem Renaissance did not dispute his earlier work on racial temperaments. It sought to "respecify" the manner in which the Negro race would absorb civilization (Lyman 1992: 108). The cultural forms of "New Negro" art appealed to Park precisely because they were in accordance with the prescribed racial temperament of the Negro. In one of the very same essays that Lal cites, Park announced that the work of the Harlem Renaissance was a, "natural expression of the Negro temperament under all the conditions of modern life" (1923 (1950): 294). Unlike DuBois, who argued that the Negro Spirituals were the repository for a Black moral vision that was coercively resisted everywhere else (1903, Allen 2001), Park defined art and culture as *the* natural forms of expression in accordance with the Negro's racial character. But in actuality, Park's discussion of racial temperaments was not as influential as his racially determined construction of urban space. Park's co-edited volume, *The City* (1925), would most prominently become the canonical prose of urban sociology and policy.

According to cultural critic Andrew Ross, the guiding theory of "human ecology" within *The City* was completely "infused with assumptions about the pathology of the racial and class compositions of neighborhoods and their populations" (117). This collaborative text by Park, Ernest Burgess, and Roderick D. McKenzie, replaced Victorian terms like "civilization" and "temperament" with the more scientific categories of equilibrium, order and mentality. However, this linguistic shift occurred without excising the now proper "mental" traits of thrift, industriousness and objectivity as normative and racially "White." These scholars applied the metaphor of plant ecology, as a habitat of various species competing for finite resources, to the state of flux in cities instigated by the high turnover of (im)migrant populations and land reallocation in the 1920's. In his introductory essay to the volume Park announced, "the city is not, in other words, merely a physical mechanism and an artificial construction. It is involved in the vital processes of the people who compose it; it is a product of nature, and particularly of human nature" (Park 1925: 1). Park's earlier ideas about civilization, cycles of interaction and racial temperaments were combined in a way that created an urban form of naturally fixed evolution.

This biological framework afforded "private enterprise" with the traits of a natural force determining the "city's residential and industrial districts" (Park 1925: 5). This observation co-existed with claims that "the city acquires an organization and distribution of population which is neither designed or controlled" but segregated by "personal tastes and convenience" (Park 1925: 5). Accordingly, Chicago's vice district was the perfect example of this natural selection of space by "tastes" or "temperaments" (Park 1925: 43). Park recognized that the poor and delinquent lived in vicious, unhealthy conditions but concluded that these people would not live there "unless they were perfectly fit for the environment in which they are condemned to exist" (1925: 45). He suggested that each "moral region" contained a "common temperamental difference[s]" where "the original nature of the individual" and that social environment coalesce (1925: 45). Park does not discuss the unequal access to residential spaces or the incidents of vice, crime etc. that existed in affluent moral zones. Instead he describes the slum and its naturally vicious environs as simply one example of a diversity of places with spatially tailored "moral codes" that had little to do with history or power. In this essay, Park also continued W.I. Thomas' ideas about primary and secondary relationships. Accordingly, the civilizing effects of the city moved individuals from the personal sentiments of intimate contacts within family and community to the rational interests of vocation, labor union and individuation. Industrial capitalism replaced the tight bonds of survival with the more impersonal networks of interest mediated by telephone and transportation. The mobility of individuals within more dynamic social interactions produced "the civilized man" inside the moral order of the marketplace. This human ecology theory was extremely powerful and dangerous. Yet, it took on a whole new level of significance when Park's colleague, Ernest Burgess, literally mapped out these so-called tastes and temperaments again on racialized bodies and now their communities. The visual connection between group behavior and neighborhood district "reinforced and developed popularized spatial understandings of culture and race. People's stereotypes, mythologies and pre-conceived notions were now embedded in the physical landscape" (Yu 2001: 47).

The competitive struggle between organization and disorganization in the city was materialized through Burgess' famous diagram of four concentric circles or zones. Within the natural expansion and invasion between the first region of downtown business and the second zone of factory and light business, he identified a "moral region" of "deterioration." This area included the "so-called 'slums' and 'bad lands,'" with their submerged regions of poverty, degradation and disease, and their underworlds of crime and vice" (Burgess 1925: 54–5). Based on the description, this is the same area that Park generally referenced as an example of the natural attachment of cultural traits to the appropriate spaces. However, Burgess goes on to describe in more detail *who* actually lived there and why:

> The slums are also crowded to overflowing with immigrant colonies – The Ghetto, Little Sicily, Greektown, Chinatown – fascinatingly combining old world heritages and American adaptations. Wedging out from here is the Black Belt with its free and disorderly life (1925: 56).

Burgess made it clear that the groups most equipped to handle slum living were those most visibly racial. He also suggested that occupational choices as "Irish policeman, Greek ice-cream parlors, Chinese laundries, Negro porters, [and] Belgian janitors," were a result of "racial temperament" and not "economic background" (1925: 57).

Yet Burgess reserved special distinction for residents of the Black Belt. Based on his syntax, their "disorderly life" was different than the "American adaptations" of other immigrant groups. As a visual compliment, the White map of concentric circles was punctured from zones II through IV by the Black Belt; represented as an intrusive and monolithic black strip disrupting the natural order. Burgess added textual weight to this visual image by making Black people the naturalized standard in measuring disorganization: "the natural rate of growth may be used to measure the disturbances of metabolism caused by any excessive increase, as those which followed the great influx of southern Negroes into northern cities since the war" (Burgess 1925: 54). These accounts of Black migrants and their place in this neat circulatory system of progression, physically mapped them as "disturbing," "disorderly" and so dysfunctional in accordance with nature. For Burgess and Park, Black people's impenetrable racial consciousness would seem to never move them to zone III of working class homes and definitely not the commuter zones of IV and V with their luxury apartments and suburban living. Park concluded that resistance to Black assimilation, for him spurned on more by Black nationalist "sentiments" than White supremacist "interests," would not be breeched.

By the late 1920's, Park foresaw miscegenation or racial hybridization[8] as one of few possible answers to the Negro's now triple "inheritance" of the racial uniform, temperament and space. These ideas coalesced between Park's final essay in The City, "Magic, Mentality and City Life," and his 1931 essay "Mentality and Racial Hybrids." Reading these two essays together reveals a transition from the term "temperament" to the more generally applicable "mentality" without excising the link between civilization, organization and "whiteness." In the first essay, Park disputed that rationality is a racial attribute. He forcefully posited that the Negro's association with magic, versus science, did not indicate racial inferiority but a "savage" mentality at an early stage on the universal scale of evolution (126). That the so-called scientific fields of medicine and religion had still not "been fully rationalized" proved to Park that "mentality" was objective and not a racial measure (140). At the same time, while Park understood the transition from a folk magical to a modern scientific mentality as a universal process, his case study for the primitive stage was "Negro magic" (123). Negro magic on American soil was

---

[8] While the term miscegenation is usually associated with white supremacists, Park used the terms miscegenation, racial hybridization and the stridently biological phrase "mixed-bloods" interchangeably (Park 1931).

identified as a "primitive mentality" with African origins that has eroded "under the influence of contact with the White man's culture" (136). Moreover, while the primitive magic mentality is supposedly found in all rural, folk societies governed by what Park called primary relations, the civilization of reason and science is distinctively racialized as a preserve of White culture with their origins in "European[s]" societies (125). This implicit tension between race, culture and biology came full circle in his 1931 essay.

In "Mentality of Racial Hybrids," Park spent ample time using World War I intelligence tests to prove mental capacity was not an innate property but determined by freedom, education and status. Then Park made the assertion that these same tests proved the intellectual superiority of the "mixed blood" over the "Negro" (1931 (1950): 387). He forcefully argued that mulatto superiority is a product of tradition out of slave conditions but also came, again, from racial temperament. Park showcased Black leaders like Frederick Douglass, W.E.B. DuBois and others of mixed-race to prove the mulatto's superiority because of their education, freedom *and* infusion of White blood making them, "more restless, aggressive and ambitious" (387). Park then quoted, of all people, White planter Alfred Stone, to describe the full-blooded Negro as, "'docile, tractable and unambitious and invariably contended and happy' when free from the influence of the mulatto and White man" (387). This essay offers a detailed investigation of the social construction of racial difference but it could not excise suggestions, especially through the term "mixed bloods," that mulatto superiority was also "the product of a double inheritance, biological and cultural" (389). Those of mixed-race were superior because combined, their marginalization from two racial worlds and their White temperamental inheritance, encouraged a restless self-consciousness propelling them further toward civilization. The mulatto then did not just become an example of successful incorporation but a solution to the Negro's specific deterrents to assimilation and progress, while keeping "White" standards intact through a blood contract.

The very clear racial foundation of urban sociology is not important simply for our reconstruction of social thought but because it left a lasting impact on how the nation conceived of community development and instituted urban policy. Students of Park, like Louis Wirth and Harvey Zorbaugh, continued to argue that city planning and regulation would only be successful to the degree that urban areas were recognized as products "of growth rather than of deliberate design" (Wirth 1928: 285). Like "private enterprise" zones in *The*

City, the areas of the White elite, in Zorbaugh's *The Gold Coast and the Slum* were imbued with a natural right to cultivate and control. Using the biological metaphor of the "nerve center[s]," the "Gold Coast" and "Central Business District," were the only areas with the appropriate "mentalities" of "expert ability and leadership" to see the "city as whole" and the imagination to "play[s] with the city as a living thing." Whereas, in "little Sicily or the world of furnished rooms the city is merely part of the landscape" (1929: 274–75).

By 1940, the work of Park and his students became the expert knowledge that helped put Chicago at the cutting edge of state sponsored slum clearance, urban renewal and development. The boundaries of White anger and benign neglect, that had always surrounded the Black Belt, became the city's infamous public housing constructed out of brick and steel (Carey 1975; Philpott 1978; Diner 1980; Kucklick 1980; Breslau 1990). The works of these students note an important legacy of the "Chicago School," but they are not the only legacy to be recognized. Within a strange, yet common, dialectic of racism and progressivism, the "Chicago School" did not just create a body of work on race relations. It also generated a body of Black scholars that, like Wirth and Zorbaugh, reproduced over-generalizations about race relations and urbanization. At the same time, Black scholars brought new eyes to the study of race to offer some of the first and still unrecognized critiques of the very sociological systems that the U of C used to quantify sociology as a usable commodity.

The "Chicago School" and the "Second Wave" of Black Social Scientists

The already mentioned social studies of lynching by Jessie Daniel Ames and Ida B. Wells were excluded from conversations about the field. But, as scholars have pointed out, sociology erected a gendered division of labor between reform oriented appeals and disinterested observation and description in the bid for scientific legitimacy (Deegan 1981, 1988, 2002). This strategy even denied genealogical connections between Burgess' "pioneering" mapping work and its roots in Jane Addams' study *Hull House Maps and Papers* and her work at The Chicago School of Civics and Philanthropy (Fish 1985; Sklar 1991). But the fact that German educated Black scholars, like W.E.B. DuBois and Chicago trained Black social scientists like Richard R. Wright, Monroe Work and Lorraine Greene were also marginalized, prophetically breathes life into the "lady among the races" phrase as both race and gender always shaped the construction of sociological knowledge. DuBois' work in, what he described as "would have been called sociology," at Harvard, took place before there was even a department at the U of C (1940: 39). Moreover, his 1899 study *The Philadelphia Negro* (1899) and his series of social studies at Atlanta University are undoubtedly the formal institutional origins of race relations within sociology (Hine 1996). However, it is not until White scholar Robert Park stewarded Black students that we witness a begrudging acceptance of not just a sociology of race relations but Black scholars as producers of sociological knowledge.

Most of the world is just now beginning to recognize pioneers like DuBois, but Black scholars at the U of C understood that "progressive" race relations scholarship preceded Robert Park. U of C sociologist E. Franklin Frazier, dedicated *The Negro in the United States* to DuBois marking his work as "the first attempt to study in a scientific spirit the problems of the Negro in American life" (1957: 503). St. Clair Drake and Horace Cayton dedicated *Black Metropolis* to their direct mentor Robert Park, but they also noted that *Philadelphia Negro* was the "first important sociological study of a Negro community in the United States" (1945: 787). These comments are important for a couple of reasons. The work of these U of C scholars could not have been financially supported at a place like Atlanta. That the U of C opened their doors to these great minds in the field is quite significant. However, the U of C's racial liberalism occurred at the very moment they were marginalizing sociological giants like DuBois from the center of the field. Our celebration of their open door policy to Black people as subjects or as students was predicated on the very exclusion of Black people as peers. This helps explain why even Chicago trained Black scholars like Frazier, Drake, Cayton, among many others, are still at best recognized for their presence in the field but rarely for their work (Frazier 1947; Bracey, Meier and Rudwick 1973; Blackwell and Janowitz 1974).

The "second wave" of Black sociologists at the U of C emerged from the dual inheritance of Robert Park and W.E.B. DuBois and the competing histories of race and science these two signified. The forces that conspired to make possible the "second wave" of Black sociologists were complex and are still being revealed (Key 1978; Bowser 1981; Watts 1983). The Chicago School's vision of race was so dominant that despite their strong critiques, the Black students of Park had to contend with his sociological framework in some ways that reinforced the paradigm. What follows is not a comprehensive analysis of U of C trained Black "native informants" but an examination of their collective and complicated struggles with the pre-existing fields of race relations and urban sociology.[9]

Like their mentor Park, but in a much more direct way, Charles Johnson and E. Franklin Frazier were products of the age of the "New Negro." According to cultural critic Alain Locke the New Negro represented a new generation of masses coming out of the Jim Crow South "with a new psychology" that, in direct response to positivist sociology, no longer wanted to be seen as a "formula . . . to be argued about, condemned, or defended" (3–4). Locke's edited anthology *The New Negro: Voices of the Harlem Renaissance* announced this new spirit with a tenor that intentionally shied away from general statistics by concentrating on the individual expressions of artists and intellectuals as symbols of Black personality and humanity. His showcasing of artistic and essay work by and not about Black people offered a direct challenge to the predominance of "Negro Problem" studies generated primarily by social scientists at the beginning of the twentieth century. While Locke's selective anthology of Negro personhood offered a necessary intervention, even he recognized that the broader Black modern experience of the "New Negro" (Carby 1987; Gates 1988), far exceeded his cultural vanguard of the petty bourgeoisie in 1920's Harlem (Huggins 1971; Bontemps 1972; Lewis 1981; Baker 1987; Hutchinson 1995; Wintz 1996, 1997; Wall 1997; Johnson 1997; Helbling 1999; Balshaw 2000).

The New Negro was a product and producer of the global economic, political and cultural transformations that generated "Modern Times" (Washington, Williams and Wood 1901). More than an aesthetic metaphor the New Negro was a movement, in both senses of the word, most directly emerging between the Great Migration of over 1 million African Americans north, beginning in the 1890's and the convergence of proletarian and Black radical internationalisms in the mid-thirties. The interwar movement of at least 200,000 "new" settlers to Chicago's "Black Belt" was part of the larger workers movement from the colonial poles of southern/eastern Europe, Asia and the Caribbean to U.S. industrial metropoles (Drake and Cayton 1945; Spear 1967; Grossman

---

[9] The most glaring absence from this study is a detailed examination of the work of Lorraine Richardson Greene. However, this is not a matter of disinterest but a result of her pioneering work just recently being brought to my attention. There will be a full treatment of her work in the larger project (See Greene 1919).

1989). This migration was a symbol of larger processes including the growth and expansion of industrial capitalism searching for new labor and markets and the long march of Black resistance to subservience continually offering new definitions of freedom and enlightenment. These two inextricably tied forces came to the apocalyptic head of World War I. Cultural critics, activists and laborers interpreted the war as a direct product of the conditions that brought them to the now multi-hued and stridently stratified cosmopolitan cities. Moreover, as many were migrants themselves, they also saw in the war a violent struggle between European industrial nations over colonial markets. One of the unintended consequences of global capitalism was that White on White violence on the world stage exposed the dark underside of patriarchy and progress and undermined a blind faith in the racial supremacy of rational-industrial nations (Moses 1978; Lewis 1987). Post-war disillusionment with "the west" solidified visions of resistance that pulled from the Great Migration, "third world" nationalisms in Ireland and Mexico and the Bolshevik Revolution of 1917. The general sense of angst, uncertainty and even excitement found expression in various intellectual and cultural collectives (Douglas 1995), including the Harlem Renaissance, cubism, the Association for the Study of Negro Life and History (Goggins 1993; Conyers 2000), surrealism and the "Chicago School" of sociology.

This demographic shift troubled the harsh distinctions between capital and labor, producer and consumer, representatives and represented, as the "private" lives of an urban proletariat spilled out on the streets and onto the world stage. The post-migration centrality of Black people and their culture to the American consciousness and cityscapes intersected with a moral ambivalence about the future of Western civilization. On one side, Black soldiers returned home with a Pan-African sense of race militancy against long standing White restrictions on Black labor, leisure and living that erupted into the race riots of 1919 as far away as Liverpool, England (Sandburg 1919; Tuttle 1970; de Quattro 2003). In direct response, the "New Negro" spirit manifest itself through old and newer nationalist/radical organizations like the National Association for the Advancement of Colored People (Reed 1988, 1997) the Universal Negro Improvement Association (Hill 1983), the African Blood Brotherhood (Taylor 1981; Beekman 1998) the Brotherhood of Sleeping Car Porters (Bates 2001), the Moorish Science Temple (Nance 2002), the Negro Sanhedrin Movement (Hughes 1984) and a general feeling of Negro entitlement in factories, nightclubs and on streetcars (Binder 1927; Robb 1927).[10] On the other side, White artists, intellectuals and consumers turned to the, in their minds, pre-modern vitality, spirit, rhythm and communalism of Africa and its now urban descendants as an alternative to and critique of the over-industrialized, atomized modernity of the western world (Osofsky, Huggins, 1971; Lewis 1981; Kenney 1993; Hutchinson 1995; Douglas 1995). Everyone from the visual artist Pablo Picasso (Powell and Bailey 1997), classical com-poser Antonin Dvorak (Floyd 1990), gangster Al Capone (Kenney 1993) to social scientists Franz Boaz (Baker 1998) and Robert Park were all in a sense White bohemian "slummers" (Mumford 1997) seeking rejuvenation from *The Souls of Black Folk* (1903, Anderson 2001). Plantation cafes (or Cotton Clubs), bricolage art pieces and cultural relativisms all derived a direct sense of inspi-ration and profit as early "samplers" of what many White people perceived as the unique primitivisms of African and Southern folk cultures.

At the same time, Black bohemians, cultural workers and artists took advan-tage of this precarious position as White objects, to create a multitude of New Negro subjectivities rife with both primitive stereotypes and modern inno-vations. As confining as race films, race records, race newspapers, Negro baseball leagues, Negro art, Negro history and race relations studies sound, they were also ironic positions of strength in the creation of a race market and consciousness (Baldwin 2001). Within the marketplace personas of critic Alain Locke, activist A. Philip Randolph, historian Carter G. Woodson, scholar/activist W.E.B. DuBois, blues singer Bessie Smith, writer Nella Larsen, jazz musician Louis Armstrong, anthropologist/writer Zora Neale Hurston, filmmaker Oscar Micheaux, etc., competing Black and White interests met to struggle over a multi-racial, if inequitable modern identity (Oliver 1984; Floyd 1990; Douglas 1995; Powell 1997; Spencer 1997; Davis 1998; Edkins and Marks 1999; Bowser and Spense 2000; Cottrell 2001).

The eyes of White revelers were so fixed on their new "knowledge" of a static pre-modern Negro life, that under the radar Black people created com-plex, conflicting and sometimes complicit postmodern representations of the world through nationalist, socialist, literary, feminist, scientific and commercial lenses, among so many others. Yet, all New Negro positions shared a quest

---

[10] See also *Chicago Defender*, "The Old and the New," January 3, 1920; *Chicago Whip*, "The Passing of Uncle Tom," August 9, 1919; *Chicago Whip*, "Radicals and Raids," January 10, 1920; *Chicago Whip*, "The Cause of the New Negro," January 17, 1920 and *the Messenger*, "The New Negro – What is He?" August, 1920.

to forge a modern identity relatively free from the top looking down confines of White patriarchs, patrons and/or philanthropists and their love for the social control metaphors of a Black slave and/or African primitive past. It was in these contexts and New Negro ways of "being" in the world that Black people began to contest the conventional social theories of race. New Negro scholars like Charles Johnson and E. Franklin Frazier, believed that social scientific "facts" could still provide "the intellectual tools for the redefinition of race relations and, in turn, a positive element for social change" (Blackwell and Janowitz: xiv).

Charles Johnson began his study of race relations as the Chicago Urban League's Director of Research and Records when Robert Park was president of the organization. When the League formed their Chicago Commission on Race Relations to study the Chicago race riot, Johnson was the lead researcher and author of what became the publication *The Negro in Chicago: A Study of Race Relations and a Race Riot* (1922). Johnson opposed the New Negro militancy of the era but ironically, this new sense of defiance is what afforded him the position of "native informant" to go where White scholars without a guide would have now feared. In the tradition of the *Philadelphia Negro*, Johnson gave historical context to the forces that led up to the riot. He combined this with a wealth of information on the living conditions of Negroes that challenged the misconceptions, misinformation and prejudices that for Johnson produced many of the "race problems" in the city. Johnson was a master of analyzing social theory but combined this expertise with the use of Park and Thomas' "personal document" (which were actually ethnographic methods appropriated from the social survey movement). This proto-ethnographic method would be influential in motivating students of the social sciences that quantitative and qualitative data could counter racist ideas about social development. But it was Park's general interest in public opinion, or what he called "race consciousness," that significantly influenced the study. A detailed analysis of newspaper articles and people's attitudes on race suggested that better understanding and more accurate reporting were solutions equal to adequate housing, employment and policing (Bulmer 1981, 1984).

Johnson left the U of C before completing his doctorate to become a leading figure of the New Negro Renaissance as editor of the National Urban League's *Opportunity Magazine*. Scholars contend that it was in New York and later as director of Social Sciences at Fisk University that Johnson began a very pronounced politics of bi-racial accommodation. In the spirit of many of the interracial contacts between Black artists and White patrons of the Renaissance era, Johnson spent time at *Opportunity* courting White patrons of power, wealth and prestige. As director of Social Sciences at Fisk, Johnson turned these relationships into philanthropic funding and implicitly controlled the future of young Black scholars. Johnson was noted for his sharp analysis of the powerful agrarian and industrial interests shaping the "human relations" of race and racism in his works *Shadow of the Plantation* (1934) and *Growing up in the Black Belt* (1941). At the same time, he was derided as the new "Booker T. Washington" (Jones 1974: 136–37) and Fisk was deemed, according to St. Clair Drake, "the plantation" run by "Massa Charlie" (Platt 1991: 98). Johnson ended his career as president of Fisk University where he proudly oversaw the building of the Robert Park Building of Social Sciences. While Johnson did further develop Park's theory, he remained beholden to overarching ideas about industrial civilization and its promise for Black assimilation (Johnson 1923, 1935, 1936). It is therefore fitting that upon retiring from the U of C, Park went to live out the rest of his life at Fisk (Burgess 1956; Valien 1958; Smith 1972; Robbins 1974).

The slow chipping away at Park's racial presuppositions more prominently occurred in the work of little known student, Oscar Brown and the more prolific E. Franklin Frazier (Persons 1987). Oscar Brown's 1930 dissertation, "Race Prejudice: A Sociological Study," used the history of race relations to argue, unlike Park, that conflict was not simply one phase but existed at every stage of the interaction cycle. Brown saw, what Park termed accommodation between the races during slavery, as a moment of Black subjugation at the hands of White supremacist forms of violent repression. Within Brown's conflict model, democratic strategies for equal rights were the only acceptable form of assimilation. But it was E. Franklin Frazier who would most forcefully establish a Black sociological voice at Chicago combing both the legacies of Park and DuBois to create his own vision.[11]

Even before E. Franklin Frazier stepped on the Hyde Park campus, he was an accomplished scholar and activist. Frazier was a socialist and feminist

---

[11] As an important side note, four years after Brown, the dissertation work of Black colleague, Bertram Doyle would conclude, in the spirit of Park, that the rational desires of men could not change race relations and must wait for natural changes within the "moral order" (See Doyle 1934).

member of the collegiate arm of the New Negro Movement at Howard University (Wolters 1975). He later left his position as math teacher at Tuskegee, frustrated by the university's relegation of Black labor to industrial trades. Inspired by the Black socialist ideas of DuBois and A. Philip Randolph and Chandler Owens' *The Messenger*, Frazier then self-published the anti-World War I pamphlet *God and War* (Platt 1991; Holloway 2002). While studying social sciences at Clark University, his Master's thesis contested two of the leading local lights in scientific racism, G. Stanley Hall and Frank Hankins (Bederman 1995). He then went on to research and write about the possible application of cooperative economics in Black southern communities (1923, Oct. and Nov. 1924) and even essayed a piece for Alain Locke's *The New Negro* (Locke 1925). Finally, Frazier wrote two important 1927 articles before he left for Chicago. The more controversial essay argued that Whites had a Negro Complex that generated their abnormal behavior of racism, which bordered on "insanity." The other essay warned of moving too far in either extreme of glorifying a distinct African past in ways that could discourage direct inter-racial agitation or uncritically glorifying all American traits without some sense of a Black identity. These positions put him in good stead with "Chicago School" thought and especially Park's critique of African retentions and belief that racism was a simple product of false consciousness.

At the U of C, Frazier would absorb many of the concepts of his mentors while serving as one of their staunchest critics. He quickly denounced Park's theories on racial temperament as "pseudoscientific nonsense" (Frazier 1940: 273–74; 1957: 665–68; Platt 1991: 90). Frazier was generally concerned with the affects of urbanization on Black life and used the institution of the family as his measurement of organization and disorganization. His studies, *The Negro Family in Chicago* (1932) and *The Negro Family in the United States* (1939) reveal a tense dialectic between a direct application and important reformulation of the "Chicago School's" human ecology theories. Frazier continually argued that because of the Negro's clean break with their African past and marginalization from their American present, they lacked "normal" patterns of social development. From here, Frazier evaluated the Negro's departure from American family norms (matriarchal, disintegration of Black folk culture, etc.) as deviant behavior (1939). Anthropologist Melvin Herskovitz retorted that African retentions did exist and warned against the danger of using the "accepted patterns of White family organization" to evaluate Black families as abnormal (1940: 104). This comment re-ignited a broadly relativist/universalist debate that had most prominently taken place between Robert Park and anthropologist Franz Boas.

Unlike Park, Frazier argued that disorganization was not a result of racial uniform or temperament but from the history of slavery and discrimination. Moreover, in his Chicago study, Frazier did not look at the Black Belt as a homogenous mass, ala Burgess, but at the same time, he applied the concentric circle model to Black residential zones by assigning family structure to spatial location. He mapped varying degrees of disorganization within Black areas against a model of "normative" family structures. Frazier found single-parent families without men in the first zones. Accordingly, there were direct correlations between outer residential zones and the greater amount of "durable monogamous marriages, home ownership, church membership and education of the children" (Persons 1987). Like Park, Frazier was encouraged by the level of differentiation in the Black community between the disorganized migrants and the more civilized, cultured and refined elements of the "old" settlers. However, he remained concerned that social differentiation within the Black Belt was not translating into a breakdown of the bi-racial class system between the races as Park had expected (Vlasek 1982). Moreover, Frazier argued that Park's celebration of racial consciousness presupposed a unity of Black thought, which was in fact, the domination of one set of class interests over others within the Black Belt.

As early as 1929, Frazier began developing a critique of class differentiation and Park's celebration of race consciousness within a bi-racial world of parallel Black and White capitalist institutions. In the essay, "La Bourgeoisie Noire," he argued that the Black aristocracy of "property, blood, education and family" (380), determined the interests of the Black community and discouraged Black and White worker solidarity as a threat to their status. He went on to say the New Negro Movement had retreated to a cultural nationalist approach in fear of competing with Whites in economics and politics. Frazier himself had been part of the movement but this class driven essay combined with his even more controversial book of the same name, made clear his desire to break from that past.[12] His 1957 book length *Black Bourgeoisie* continued that the Black elite was delusional about their economic status,

---

[12] V.F. Calverton's larger work, the *Anthology of American Negro Literature*, was presented as an implicit response to Locke's *The New Negro* with an intentional inclusion of economic concerns (Calverton, 1920).

which led to a preoccupation with conspicuous consumption instead of attending to the structural needs of Black communities.

To some degree, Frazier simply inverted Park's causal relationship, making class and not culture the determining factor of social disorganization. Yet, his attention to class conflict was still a critique of the Black elite on the grounds of culture. Frazier argued that this class had betrayed an older standard of respectability for the false consciousness of conspicuous consumption as an indicator of their status. Their "false" cultural lens prevented the Black bourgeoisie from confronting the fact that they never owned the means of capitalist production. This particular racial consciousness led them to adopt a class identity based on irrelevant spheres of cultural consumption. Within this framework, Frazier uncritically dismissed the Harlem Renaissance for avoiding economic concerns, the (Black) Brotherhood of Sleeping Car Porters as an "aristocratic laboring group" (1929: 383) and the national Black consumer boycott program, "Don't Buy Where You Can't Work," for adopting nationalist, and not class-based sentiments. In many ways, his prescriptions for a "proper" middle class identity were determined by pre-defined cultural norms that combined Marxist thought with the Protestant work ethic (1957; Baldwin 2003). However, it is important to recognize Frazier's work pointed out class interests, both within and between social groups, that challenged the inevitability of Park's "interaction cycle" in ways that foreshadowed later scholarship (Teele 2002).

Works by other Chicago trained Black scholars, like Horace Mann Bond's *Negro Education in Alabama: A Study of Cotton and Steel* (1939) continued to work through the tensions between class and caste analysis within the field. But the range and volume of Frazier's work reveals a much larger conceptual shift in the nation that included but surpassed the social sciences. In fact, the reception and reproduction of his scholarship almost splits at the caste/class fault line within his work. Frazier's family studies became the academic source for the infamous Moynihan Report (Rainwater and Yancey 1967; Morrison 1992) while *Black Bourgeoisie* served the interests of Black nationalist organizations in their critique of an apolitical Black elite. Unfortunately, Black behavior as the social indicator of disorganization remained the constant. Yet, Frazier's small turn from family culture to economic class, as the causal factor, spoke to something much larger than intellectual inclination. The post war era had instigated a New Negro that developed both assimilationist and nationalist strategies toward incorporation into the capitalist order. The post-

Depression era, however, inspired a burgeoning faith in an interracial working class incorporation into possibly a new social order altogether. Frazier himself, wrote *Black Bourgeoisie* as part of whom DuBois called the "Young Turks," at Howard University where a collective cadre of Black scholars pushed to offer a forthright economic analysis of race relations (Lewis 2000). At the same time, DuBois himself had just constructed his epic and radical retelling of the Reconstruction era that should have forever altered both Marxist social thought and academic historiography (1935). It is important to lay out the major themes within this shift from caste to class and how it affected social thought on race and the continued influences of race on sociology.

Cultural critic Michael Denning most eloquently and succinctly termed this seismic shift and its attendant movement as the "cultural front" (1997). Framed by the stock market crash of 1929 and the Cold War politics of the late 1940's, the promises of Park's industrial modernism, in all its forms, were pushed into a state of crisis. The capitalist vision of social relations, with its faith in technological progress and "natural" divisions between mental and manual labor and the subjects and objects of scientific study, were challenged. The children of the very ethnic immigrants that had been racially fixed as porters, laundrymen, policemen etc. by Park and Burgess, were finding their own place in the social order as members of a striking if only tenuous "Popular Front" political bloc. The literal bankruptcy of capitalist advance found this second generation in labor unions, actors on the world stage fighting fascism and imperialism abroad (Lewis 1987; Von Eschen 1997) and challenging lynch law and labor repression at home. They were also channeling new fantasies into the both public and privately funded culture industries, while fanning old flames in the 1943 nationwide race riots, or "Zoot Suit Riots," depending on the regional inflections. The particular Negro accents on what Denning calls a "laboring of American culture" (xvi), found both the "Chicago School" and its representations of the Black Belt again central in the discussion. While the loud boom of "scientific expertise" had always incorporated (many say co-opted) a diversity of utterances (fiction, journalism, social work), the social sciences now openly utilized many forms of expression. In this period the Black Belt now "occupied" the Communist leaning John Reed writing club, the New Deal sponsored Illinois Writer's Project, Sears and Roebuck's Julius Rosenwald Fund and a whole host of local fledgling periodicals that incorporated fact and fiction vertically (Bone 1986). Out of this new socio-cultural matrix emerged new "social" studies.

Among too many to mention, the Chicago "fiction" work of Gwendolyn Brooks, Richard Wright, Langston Hughes and Willard Motley was nurtured in this brave new worldview of literary realism and working-class stories. At the same time and with much overlap, the "fact" work of Black social scientists like Katherine Dunham (1959; Veve and Wilerson 1978), Allison Davis (Hillis 1995), St. Clair Drake and Horace Cayton would continue to trouble the caste/class divide. These conceptual and physical tensions set the pace for one of the most imaginatively magisterial pieces of social science scholarship ever produced: *Black Metropolis* (1945). This study emerged out of a modest WPA (Works Projects Administration) project to investigate the general social conditions surrounding the problem of juvenile delinquency in Chicago's Black Belt and became a detailed survey of the entire community.

Black Metropolis was an interdisciplinary product of the cultural front from the outset. The primary writers were anthropologist St. Clair Drake and sociologist Horace Cayton, while Richard Wright composed the introduction. The basic materials for this study were the interview documents and newspaper excerpts from the (Horace) Cayton – (Lloyd) Warner project that used quantitative and qualitative approaches. The researchers came together through the resilient and restrictive bi-racial system of research and education between the U of C and the Black College network of social science programs (Jones 1974; Stanfield 1985). In 1932, Charles Johnson offered Horace Cayton the position of Special Assistant to Secretary of the Interior, which took him all through the South analyzing the affects of New Deal legislation on Black workers (Bone 1986). From this came the study *Black Workers and the New Unions* (Cayton and Mitchell 1935).

St. Clair Drake was the product of a Garveyite father, New Negro collegiate protests at historically Black Hampton Institute (Wolters 1975) and the merging of Black radical and proletarian traditions in the significant Scottsboro case (Carter 1984; Kelley 1990). Drake began his social scientific career working under Black "Chicago School" alum Allison Davis on the project that would become *Deep South* (Davis; Gardner and Gardner 1941) and was an anthropology instructor at Dillard University under another Black Chicago alumnus, Horace Mann Bond. During the writing of *Black Metropolis*, Drake was shuttling back and forth between the ivory towers taking classes and the Black Belt conducting interviews and organizing storefront preachers (Bond and Drake 1988). Cayton was also taking courses while offering theoretical insights about "Black Belt" urbanization that would find their way into Richard Wright's 1941 photo-documentary study, *Twelve Million Black Voices*. Finally, Richard Wright studied "Chicago School" sociology, wrote at the John Reed Club and South Side Writer's Workshop while publishing in *Anvil, Partisan Review, Negro Quarterly* and *Abbott's Monthly* (Bone 1986). They were all making connections between workers of the world and the international Americanness of the Black experience while being held afloat by Rosenwald and New Deal money and community visions of freedom.

In the spirit of the cultural arm of the Popular Front, *Black Metropolis* was a bold and haunting tale about the looming seductiveness of fascism. In his introduction, Wright asks the reader to "disentangle in our minds Hilter's deeds, from what Hitler exploited. His deeds were crimes; but the hunger he exploited in the hearts of Europe's millions was a valid hunger and it is still there" (xxv). Wright made clear that the "hunger there" was not particular to Europe but also existed in America: "Do not hold a light attitude toward the slums of Chicago's South Side. Remember that Hitler came out of such a slum. Remember that Chicago could be the Vienna of American Fascism" (xx)![13] He rhetorically asked about the universal costs of the American Dream built on White life and Black death. Wright saw that none of the White political factions (communists, socialists, liberals, democrats, New Dealers etc.) had turned a real eye and offered an honest hand to the Black Belt and because of that "what happened in Europe during the past twenty years will happen here" (xxi). Even though Black observers had long made prophetic connections between fascism abroad and the U.S. brand of racial democracy at home, he justifiably remained convinced that no one would heed such warnings without more than enough proof. The social scientific work in *Black Metropolis* served as a kind of response to the call sent out in Wright's introduction. In almost 800 pages, using 20 research students, Drake and Cayton examined Black progress in employment, housing and social integration, using census survey and archival data.

They directly confronted the human ecology paradigm to expose the "Chicago Tradition" (18), as a social struggle and not some organic growth of the city. For them, urban change or fixity resulted from human behavior and force, institutional practices and political decisions. Drake and Cayton's

---

[13] Wright's comments about fascism parallel more recent warnings by sociologist Paul Gilroy about the dangerous relationship between fascism and nationalism. Moreover, Gilroy interests are directly influenced by the work of Richard Wright. (See Gilroy 1993, 2000.)

actual reproduction of the concentric circle diagram within their text (re)membered the Black Belt as "one hundred and fifty years of intense competition among native-Whites, Negroes and foreign-born for living space, economic goods and prestige" (17–18). Drake and Cayton also re-examined the post riot Chicago Commission on Race Relations report. They implicitly questioned the report's solid faith in "mutual understanding (69)" and concern over a "growing race consciousness" (71), as the core issues while ignoring the historic violent struggle over economic, political and spatial resources directed at Black people. However, their interdisciplinary methods seemed also to warn that a one-dimensional analysis of the Negro and their Black Belt dehumanized Black people as a problem to be solved and ignored the lessons their experiences brought to the larger world.

It is far from ironic that *Black Metropolis* was dedicated to Robert Park. The text deployed the diagram and mapping techniques of *The City*. But in the hands of Drake and Cayton, the once impressionistic vision of the Black ghetto was transformed into detailed cultural geographies of the many faces of Chicago's Black community. The titling of chapters eight and fourteen as "The Black Ghetto" and "Bronzeville" respectively recalled the journalistic/scientific description of the "moral regions" in *The City*. However, in the *prescriptive* juxtaposition of these particular chapters, another kind of morality tale was conveyed. The chapter "The Black Ghetto," offered detailed sociological study and statistical data to document the effects of racism on health, income, housing and a whole host of other conditions. The chapter "Bronzeville," pulled from the work of E. Franklin Frazier to argue that despite the economic homogeneity imposed on the "ghetto" there were "non-economic" factors in the creation of differentiated zones of living within the *Black Metropolis*. Yet, they did not simply argue that ghetto formation caused a dysfunctional class structure and moral order. Drake and Cayton responded directly to their chapter eight with the observation:

> 'Ghetto' is a harsh term, carrying overtones of poverty and suffering, of exclusion and subordination. In Midwest Metropolis it is used by civic leaders when they want to shock complacency into action. Most of the ordinary people in the Black Belt refer to their community as "the South Side," but everybody is also familiar with another name for the area – Bronzeville (1945: 383).

Through a use of anthropologically oriented ethnographies, *Black Metropolis* surveyed relations of labor, leisure, religion, sex and family within each of what they deemed as the most pronounced class formations in what the people called Bronzeville. Their discussion of "policy gambling" (today called lottery) remains the best analysis of this institution; challenging the boundaries between informal and formal economies and law and criminality within a racist economic system. However, this very same analytic framework exposes both the promises and pitfalls of the *Black Metropolis*.

Their ethnographic detail of daily life (including religious institutions, political organizations, dancehalls, etc.) as humane negotiations of inhuman conditions foreshadowed the best contemporary work in cultural studies. But at the same time, Drake and Cayton still implicitly measured Black institutions and class formations within a paradigm of "objective criteria." *Black Metropolis* argued that institutions like policy and figures like "race men" would no longer need to exist if racial boundaries collapsed. Many elements within the community, even though humane and not dysfunctional, were still read as responses to a larger dysfunctional America.[14]

As soon as the ink dried, perhaps even before, "Chicago School" peer Oliver Cromwell Cox argued that *Black Metropolis* was not objective enough. He criticized Drake, Cayton and Frazier for widening the definition of class to include "lifestyles," instead of limiting it to "life choices" (Bond and Drake 776–77). Cox would make his name as the "second wave's" most pronounced Marxist and accomplished theorist. In *Caste, Class and Race*, Cox offered a direct challenge to the prevailing perspective on race relations. In this study, he attacked what he called Robert Park's "Caste School" orthodoxy in race relations for describing the phenomena of racial discrimination as a cultural or moral instead of an economic condition (1942, 1944, 1945). For Cox, one cannot assume the trajectory of the nation without interrogating how racism has been a key component in the capitalist world system. In the end, he argued that unlike the cultural system of caste, "the problem of racial exploitation . . . will most probably be settled as part of the world proletarian struggle for democracy; every advance of the masses will be an actual or potential advance for the colored people" (1948: 583). Cox felt that the capitalist system was the problem and not the solution. He never wanted Black people to feel comfortable within racial identity nor America to forget that industrial progress

---

[14] Most of these insights come from a fabulous graduate class I had under the direction of political scientist Cathy Cohen in 1999. See her important social scientific work (Cohen 1999).

was predicated on a racist division of labor (Hunter 1981, 2001, Abraham and Hunter 1987; Klarland 1994; Denning 1997: 445–54).

Beneath the "Scientific" Gaze: Reading Between the Lines of Black Belt Ethnography

As we look back to move forward it becomes clear that anxieties about racial difference have been central to the fundamental organizing principles of sociological theory and method. Moreover, the conversion of Black experiences into intellectual property was predicated on the very exclusion of Black voices as both source material for sociological scholarship and as actual sociologists. However, Black resistance throughout the first half of the twentieth century continued to puncture through the thin layer of cultural cohesion proposed by the White "Chicago School" hegemony in ways that ironically opened the door to Black social scientists in the precarious position of "native informants." Black social scientists at Chicago offered trenchant caste and class critiques of the inevitability of the "interaction cycle," while still maintaining a sincere belief that once civilized, Blacks people would enter a modern, rational society allowing them to transcend their race-based limitations. The common bond is that whether biological, religious, capitalist or socialist, the "Chicago School" continued to measure "Black" behavior as delusional or, at best, a provisional state of mind en route to a prefigured stage of normality and organization.

In response to Gunnar Myrdal's most famous social study, *An American Dilemma* (1944), which explicitly argued racial identification was simply a wrong turn on the road to American democratic principles (that used many Chicago trained Black scholars), writer Ralph Ellison rhetorically asked, "Are American Negroes simply the creation of White men, or have they at least helped to create themselves out of what they found around them?" Ellison went on to reveal that much of his frustration with the social sciences in general and their reading of race and Black culture as a derivative problem or dilemma, came out of reading Park and Burgess' *Introduction to the Science of Sociology* for an undergraduate course and confronting the infamous "lady among the races" phrase. In resistance, he posited that it might take a "deeper science" to see what appear to be the Negro's distorted, temperamental reflections as actually *rejection*[s]" of a higher order and moreover, their so-called deviance as an articulation of "counter values" (1964: 315–16).

The residual traces of "The Chicago School" in its many permutations are resilient and not fading anytime soon. Books like *The Bell Curve* (1994) and *End of Racism* (1995) have resurrected Park's double inheritance of racial biology and culture. William Julius Wilson's, *The Truly Disadvantaged* (1987) focuses on family deterioration as the central problem of the Black underclass. It is clear that a wide chasm exists between the intellectual and political agendas of, for example, the *End of Racism* and *The Truly Disadvantaged*. They do however, find common ground in their attention to Black behavior as a clear indicator of a dysfunctional or pathological cultural system that led to both the social and economic marginalization of Black communities. Moreover, both Black scholars with a direct class analysis in the "Chicago School," like Frazier (1929) and Cox (1948) and some contemporary leftist scholars (Fields 1982; Gitlin 1995) variably maintain a causal base/superstructure distinction between class and race; implicitly arguing that the identity politics of race is a false consciousness that continues to erode the possibilities for a normative class solidarity. Again Black behavior or behaving Black is the root of the problem. Not many of the even most "radical" social scientists have paid adequate attention to DuBois' historical materialist insights in *Black Reconstruction* (1935). He found that contrary to Marxist orthodoxy, Northern industrial workers never became the proletarian vanguard of class-consciousness to lead revolutionary action, but were seduced by White skin privilege during the Civil War. It was Black and White southern laborers' who won the war when they headed north instigating a "Great Strike." Moreover, DuBois revealed that Black people had organized and freed themselves and the nation, without a vanguard or revolutionary class-consciousness, but within the dictates of their own religious mythologies and larger slave culture. This short departure to DuBois is significant because unlike other social scientists, he saw in slave culture not pathology or White acculturation but the unintended source for a Black radical tradition (Robinson 1983).

To this day, Black behaviors and culture are rarely examined by social scientists for the revolutionary possibilities they offer or the way in which they have continually challenged conventional theories of social development and change. Regardless of political orientation, static social scientific inquiries continue to colonize Black people and their own theorizations of the world by deploying methods that refuse to engage them as more than objects, but as peers in sociological projects. With Ellison's question in mind, perhaps its time to listen to the voices of Black people as we attempt to formulate social theories for those very people. Historian Robin Kelley (1997) pulls on the example of blind anthropologist John Langston Gwantley (1980) to show how truly "visionary" it was for him to rely on the literal insights, language and interpretive skills of his participants to theorize their own experience. Other social scientific work continues in this vein by showing the so-called normative social behaviors of "two parent homes," or conventional signs of a work ethic as "illogical" or even unrecognizable in local contexts (Scott 1982; Leadbeater and Way 1996).

Kelley observes that social scientists continue to conflate behavior and culture when "studying" Black people. Moreover, when they do examine culture it is reduced "to expressions of pathology, compensatory behavior or creative 'coping mechanism' to deal with racism and poverty" (17). Whereas, Kelley's concept of "productive play" (45), for example, engages how Black youth turn activities that have traditionally been derided as non-productive leisure into a form of labor and profit. These kinds of leisure/labor activities are left unseen or marked as abnormally derivative by traditional social scientific visions of work ethic and productive behavior. Pulling from the observations of Ellison, Gwantley and Kelley we can reformulate the "scientific gaze," and specifically trouble the line between labor and leisure. With this new vision I want to return to the "Chicago School's" Black Belt to reread the sources through a different lens and in doing so offer an alternative way of "looking" at social experience. Much of the data used by "Chicago School" studies was so prefigured by a spectral model of capitalist, functionalist or proletarian productivity that simply *reading* the sources challenges entire theoretical paradigms. However, I don't want to replace one false objective framework with another claim to the self-evident meaning of social experience.

I want to suggest that by re-situating the data within the realm of Black migrant and urban contexts that generalizable, systemic analyses and social scientific frameworks become a more collaborative process that include and don't simply contain the dissenting and even contradictory meanings that arise from a more comprehensive socio-historical worldview. In a sense I am asking for an extremely self-conscious sociology of knowledge that even situates and interrogates its own production. For example, Park and Burgess never utilized the actual voices of Black people in their imaginative explorations of race relations, so offer little to our understanding of Black experience. But their work speaks volumes about the rise of a White professional managerial class identity in early 20th century America. Whereas the data from

Charles Johnson's work, among other Black "Chicago School" social scientists, is open to more direct re-examination. Johnson was instrumental in selling a tale of rural Black peasants, as leaves being blown north to northern industry, unprepared for city living. This logic was consistently used to justify limited Black job mobility as an issue of skill and not discrimination, while also generating a need for Black reformers to train "newcomers." However, scholar Carol Marks (1989: 37) used the same Chicago Commission data to show that only twenty-five percent of Black migrants were agricultural laborers (1922: 95). A significant number in the larger seventy-five percent had between five and ten years of experience in southern cities within an array of trades and a significant rate of literacy. Moreover, this migrant familiarity with urbanity *before* coming to Chicago gives context to the many "incomprehensible" or "irrational" decisions they made in the city.

Black migrants would continue to struggle for dignity and parity in factories, homes and service industries all along their trek north. However, the insecurity of consistent labor and the broken promises of upward mobility found many disillusioned with the reformist visions that labor efficiency and thrift were the sole routes to urban civilization. Even in the south, Black people were active participants in commercialized leisure as an alternative site of labor and living. The location of dancehalls and brothels in the inner "moral regions" of Chicago's Black Belt were seen as symbols of disorganization or deviance by social scientists. Whereas, some Black women migrants understood them as places of relative autonomy or resistance to the heavy surveillance of domestic labor (Carby 1982). In *Black Metropolis*, one Chicago buffet flat prostitute exhorted, "When I see the word *maid* – why, girl, let me tell you, it just runs through me! I think I'd sooner starve" (1945: 598, emphasis theirs). The status of maid was collectively resisted because as one woman stated there was no "place to entertain your friends but the kitchen, and going in and out of the back doors. I hated all that . . . They almost make you a slave." The memory of "slavery" or slave labor was still fresh in migrants' heads and many women developed various strategies to "never work in nobody's kitchen but my own any more" (CCRR 1922: 387).

All migrants worked hard while challenging prescriptions about where hard work could take place and how much time "work" should take up in their lives. The alternative vision of work was equally acute for sharecroppers who had just left a life strictly defined by their function within a labor system. When one migrant was asked if he had gone to work everyday he replied "Goodness no . . . I had to have some days of the week off for plea-sure" (CCRR 1922: 373). This quote came again from the Chicago Commission report as an example of urban industrial "maladjustment" and the kind of behaviors that needed to be reformed. However, if social scientists worked within this migrant's context, his insistence on "pleasure" could be seen as a desire for a different kind of working civilization. As a final example, there is a significant body of rarely analyzed, interesting and many innovative dis-sertation manuscripts about the Black Belt produced by Black scholars in the U of C's school of sociology *and* divinity (Fisher 1922; Kincheloe 1929; Atwood 1930; Sutherland 1930; Smith 1935; Lewis 1936; Daniel 1940). They all com-bined cultural, economic and sociological methods and many did not work within an "ideal" model of social structure. Were they never published because they didn't fit the existing paradigms or meet the changing moods of the aca-demic publishing world (the two are many times related)? Regardless of the reason for their present absence, are we ready to recuperate *all* of these silent voices, even if they require us to transform sociological paradigms?

The point here is not to dismiss social science, but to remain critically reflective about the way we think about data, methodology and interpreta-tion and their implications for the larger social world. An honest history of the field makes clear that ethnographies and data do not just describe real-ity but, at best, mediate and at worst, become reality. The meanings that we associate with social behaviors are not simply the conclusions generated from extensive research, but have also become ways to make visible and interpret the data. There has been a direct and dangerous racial line from "scientific" theories of "disorder" and "dysfunction," to "culture of poverty" to "under-class" and finally back full circle to racialized notions of incompetence, lazi-ness and even athletic prowess. Despite volumes of critical essays, the pernicious racialized, which means sociological, cultural vision of the "Chicago School" has pervaded our academic methodologies and everyday observations. To make this point I pull on the Black radical tradition by turning to the prophetic nature of the personal, which is unfortunately dismissed as provincial or in social scientific terms not systemic, which itself is part of the problem. But in my estimation, when racial signifiers become shorthand for arbitrary char-acteristics and behaviors, we have come full circle back to, or never let go of, Robert Park and his notion of temperaments. As the example, I have a col-league who just got back a course evaluation from a student that boldly stated, "you are a terrible teacher and Black, enough said." Well I think the equation here between racial identification and social value makes my point better than I ever could, so I agree with the student . . . enough said.

Epilogue: Chess Moves on Checkerboards

> . . . *discussion of the role of the University of Chicago in reshaping the racial geography of the city's South Side is a reminder of the role of 'meds and eds' in postwar urban change . . .*

Thomas Sugrue, urban historian

> *The superficial claims of policing the campus and Hyde Park hides the reality that we live in a distrustful, colonial social order. Our colonial status is ensured by the distrust between temporary settlers (that's us the students) as a precious set of imported individuals, and the native 'other' (often called community members), the dark peoples, savage and unknown.*

Ashley P. White-Stern, U of C student[15]

After decades of "White" flight and urban disinvestment, various communities, interest groups, and political blocs are asserting an almost militant, to paraphrase Henri Lefebvre, right to the city in the present moment. From young professionals with neighborhood watched townhouse enclaves, industrial/military graveyards converted into tourist safe pleasure complexes, the informal survival economies of the working poor, to most notably universities as unabashed real estate robber barons, competing claims for urban space abound. In fact, the University of Chicago's (U of C) current chess moves in urban gentrification, especially their attempts to buy and relocate the famous Checkerboard lounge from Bronzeville to Hyde Park, have found solace in a language of Black historic preservation that reaches back to human ecology theories of early twentieth century "Chicago School" sociology. "Chicago School" human ecology and U of C acts of Black historic preservation bring together the university's century long role in determining local space allocation and appropriation directly along racial lines. Aspects of the ecological and preservationist approaches to urban change share an orientation that prizes a narrative of choice over coercion.

---

[15] Ashley P. White-Stern, "University Benevolence does not Compensate for Lasting Inequality," *Chicago Maroon* (November 22, 2004).

As a history of the present, "Black Belts and Ivory Towers" reminds observers that the U of C's current role in conceptually and concretely racializing urban space, through economic strategies of real estate ownership and now the cultural logic of historical preservation, did not just begin after World War II, but goes back to the founding of the university (Hirsch 1983). While administrators, both current and former, did not work directly with "Chicago School" sociologists, the paradigms generated from works including *The City* (1925) have proven useful in rationalizing racially uneven urban development. The ecological approach generally argues that the city is organized through a natural selection of urban space according to racial group adaptations (or temperaments), personal preferences, and cultural tastes as opposed to violent and uneven struggles for land and power. At the moment of this theoretical development, the U of C's administration played a central role in shaping the racial geography of the South Side by cordoning off the Black community and turning parts of Hyde Park into a White colonial outpost (Sugrue 2004; White-Stern 2004).

"Chicago School" social thought most directly (if only implicitly) explained away the veiled real estate power, legal restrictive covenants (Bachin 2004), land clearance policies (what the *Chicago Defender* aptly renamed Negro clearance), and municipally funded urban renewal programs of the U of C in its own back yard (Dentler and Rossi 1981). These conscious acts could be simply described as a product of the city's natural self-organization along the racial lines of "personal tastes and convenience" (Park 1925: 5). Most notably, this social scientific expert knowledge was used to put Chicago on the public policy cutting edge through its infamous, state-sponsored high rise public housing program, simply reinforcing a logic of racial temperaments with physical tenements (Carey 1975; Philpott 1978; Diner 1980; Kucklick 198; Breslau 1990).

Chicago School social thought expertly mapped residents into moral regions according to racial temperament (as opposed to racism), which helped rationalize the physical marginalization of Black communities into public housing as a natural, instead of racially motivated, process. However, now the high, physical walls have fallen. After decades of "White flight," with the U of C as a notable exception, we are witnessing an unquestionable renewed White interest in the very urban spaces that are now occupied by racial "others." In some ways, heritage tourism alongside university-sponsored educational, policing, and real estate initiatives is helping to convert what were deemed dangerous racial zones into profitable spaces of safe White consumption and even residency. The heritage tourism arm of historic preservation helps to mediate pockets of urban renaissance by bestowing cultural capital on a space (usually of an economically vulnerable racial group). In exchange, residents and merchants help re-organize that space into a consumable and safe exhibition of racial and/or ethnic authenticity that will not be available to most of the "authentic" Black people currently in residence. As Chicago's Black community has sought alternative economic solutions, their use of heritage tourism has unwittingly helped convert the university's century long, not-so invisible hand in Black "ghetto formation," into a marketable commodity. In the end, Black historic preservation/heritage tourism is helping the U of C, as the primary political and economic force, put a Black face on selective White settler re-colonization of the South Side (Mansfield and Smolcic 1989).

The current controversy surrounding the U of C's removal of the famous Checkerboard Lounge from 43rd street in Bronzeville to the university funded Harper Court shopping district in Hyde Park is telling, where explanations for this act revive a sort of neo-human ecological language. The Checkerboard controversy helps reveal the current (but not new) role of "meds and eds" (medical centers and universities) as a capitalist advanced guard in the appropriation and gentrification of urban space, here through the cultural logic of historic preservation amidst Black heritage tourism (Pugh O'Mara 2002). After over fifty years of steering Hyde Park land clearance and urban renewal programs, the university's Community Affairs Office suggests that their only failure was the creation of a dull campus and community life.[16] Therefore, critics have suggested that the seizure and relocation of the Checkerboard lounge serves as a key acquisition as university holdings move progressively north throughout the Hyde Park-Kenwood-Bronzeville neighborhoods respectively. Many argue that the U of C is attempting to cordon off expanding commercial and residential islands for a overwhelmingly White professional managerial class, even in training,[17] at "the expense of low income African-American residents."[18]

---

[16] Bruce Sagan, "The Major Story of the Last 50 Years: Urban Renewal," *Hyde Park Herald* (July 21, 2004), 3.

[17] In 2002, the *Journal of Blacks in Higher Education* ranked the U of C last for minority recruitment among selective universities. At the time approximately 4.2% of students and 2.7% of the faculty were Black at the university. See, Meredith Meyer, "Low Minority Population Plagues Diversity Effort," *Chicago Maroon* (October 20, 2004).

[18] Gregory Robinson, "Context is Key in Checkerboard Relocation," *Hyde Park Herald* (February 25, 2004), 4.

To be fair, the heritage tourism arm of historic preservation has been part of larger Black strategies to find stability within a top-heavy service (primarily information) economy, amidst a renewed White interest in the urban. The racial authenticity required by heritage tourism becomes powerful leverage in a Black urban landscape that is predominately the economic property of White non-residents. In Chicago many of the Black South Side residents, activists, government officials, and small business owners have banded together to capitalize on the growing heritage tourism industry to make claims of cultural stewardship over the space as a route to propriety. As part of this project organizers have reclaimed, from the 1930's, the name and memory of their community as Bronzeville, to position their neighborhood as a key "living museum" of sorts along the International African American Tourism landscape (Boyd 2000). One can hear and witness heroic tales of reprise, renaissance, and a bit of romance with the re-memories of a Black community that has been most recently ravaged by urban renewal, municipal disinvestment along with severe employment and housing disparities. Boarded up buildings are slowly being replaced with "new" landmarks, including a Harold Washington Cultural Center, a 47th Street Blues District, rehabilitated limestone and Brownstone housing, and the attempted restoration of community icons including the Parkway Ballroom, Gerri's Palm Tavern (which actually closed to be re-opened as a jazz and wine shop), and the Checkerboard Lounge.[19]

Tellingly, the influential National Trust for Historic Preservation defines heritage tourism as "traveling to experience the places, artifacts and activities that *authentically* represent the stories and people of the past and present" (Boyd and Timothy 2002).[20] However, cultural critic Barbara Kirshenblatt-Gimblett reminds us that while heritage is marketed as simply the recovery or preservation of something old and historically authentic, it is actually a new mode of cultural production (1998). In order to deliver heritage, which is not divorced from racial stereotypes and assumptions that shape the boundaries of historical value, the Bronzeville neighborhood must be converted into the destination of *Bronzeville*™. This emerges by staging and suppressing a living place for the requirements of an artefactual, even artificial museum

---

[19] Kari Lyderson, "Chicago's Bronzeville is Ready for a Reprise," *Washington Post* (Saturday, November 6, 2004), A03.

[20] National Trust for Historic Preservation, http://www.nationaltrust.org (viewed on Saturday November 20, 2004).

space. The early Chicago School marking and mapping of moral regions on top of complex and continually relevant histories served to explain employment and housing inequality amongst racial groups as a result of "temperamental difference[s]" and not capitalist racial inequality (Park 1925: 45). In the present, the logic behind a heritage tourism that markets cultural authenticity to consumers over-determines the meaning of Bronzeville by the services it provides within the tourist economy and makes invisible the forces that constrain Bronzeville to that very meaning.

The idea that tourists would come and experience an authentic Bronzeville from the past or present, is extremely problematic and displays how certain aspects of "authenticity-for-sale" actually helps to obscure more than it reveals. For example the celebratory proclamation that Black residents are "coming back" to Bronzeville belies the fact that Black people never left. Most of those who occupied the now destroyed "vertical ghettos" of the South Side's infamous Robert Taylor and State Street homes have been removed, likely never to return as property values have skyrocketed by 400 percent between 1990 and 2000 with little affordable housing in sight (Sugrue 2003).[21] Such facts help make it clear what particular demographic is being courted and celebrated in the current Black "homecoming." As an example, over the past few decades the city had let The Stroll, the historic Black leisure district centered at 35th and State, deteriorate into a drug zone. However, now this area has taken on new meaning as the last main corridor to the downtown central business district to be developed. Currently older Black residents who can barely afford $40 monthly rents in the last remaining Stateway Gardens building look on with disgust and longing as they watch luxury high rise apartment buildings loom over The Stroll that once was, starting at $150,000.[22] The chosen strategies of development, renaissance, and preservation have clearly been geared towards Black middle-class re-settlement within the community and White patronage of Black culture, at least initially, from without.

Within the racial matrix of heritage tourism, travelers come to know and understand the city, not by the very real histories of social struggle and inequality, but navigate urban space as a collection of consumable locations

---

[21] Kari Lyderson, "Chicago's Bronzeville is Ready for a Reprise," *Washington Post* (Saturday, November 6, 2004), A03.
[22] Ferman Mentrell Beckless, "Bronzeville Just Won't Be the Same," *Chicago Defender* (April 10, 2004), 4 and "Bronzeville's New Look," *Chicago Defender* (April 17, 2004), 4.

organically ordered by the choice to reside or congregate in places informed by distinct moral regions of racial temperament (or culture). Historic preservationist strategies of urban development celebrate the trickle down economic benefits of consumer tourism by highlighting the entrepreneurial and cultural vitality of Bronzeville's past, while present-day Bronzeville – without a mixed economic and housing base or a local consumer base with disposable income – is left with only its past to sell. The homogeneous market relations between Black heritage tourism (pole) and White consumption (metropole) reminds one of a neo-colonial system, but instead of limiting the colony to a monocrop feeder system of cotton, coal, or diamond production, the new Bronzeville is forced to collect, exhibit, and perform its cultural history for profit (Kirshenblatt-Gimblett 1998; Judd and Fanstein 1999; MacCannell 1999; Ringer 1998; Urry 1997; Alsayyad 2000; Desmond 2003). Commensurate with the ideas outlined by Robert Park and mapped out by Ernest Burgess, when one enters the heritage zone of Bronzeville and experiences the authentic jazz and blues nightlife, this becomes the unspoken personification of the Black racial and spatial temperament of musical expression, through an innate bodily vitality, with an easygoing, entertaining demeanor. Bronzeville, a name that had signified a relative resistance against White capitalist dehumanization, has been partially transformed into a complicit name brand for an updated version of tourist slumming as the bulldozing of the actual high rise slums make way for affluent re-settlement.

The results of present day poverty and ghettoization, at their most visible, are repackaged to market the unique ambience and possibly exciting dangers of even a cleaned up "ghetto life." This desiring voyeuristic aspect of the heritage tourist gaze (Urry, 2002) upon the temperamentally distinct, racial other, becomes the physical compliment to "reality" television (COPS), music styles (gangsta rap), and video games (Grand Theft Auto: *San Andreas*). The mobile voyeur is then beckoned to travel through the urban spaces of present-day foreign locales, and experience the past lives of exotic cultures (Greektown, Chinatown, 47th Street Blues alley). With the proper freeway development, the traveler even steps *out* of time with directed routes in and out of the consumed community in clear evasion of current conditions beyond their ability to provide a safe set of amusement pleasures. In fact, if there had not been overwhelming public protest, the Illinois Department of Transportation had planned to close down approximately 12 Dan Ryan Expressway ramps that would have ultimately cordoned off the predominately Black south side to direct downtown access. Notable exceptions to the proposed closures included the 31st, 35th, and 55th street exits, which bring White consumers to the Illinois Institute of Technology, White Sox Baseball Park, and the U of C respectively.[23] The ordering of urban space is represented within the cultural logic of heritage tourism (implicitly drawing from *The City*). Accordingly, cosmopolitan urbanites move freely through the city and "naturally" select zones of what Park calls "temperamental difference" for labor, living, and leisure (1925: 45). The arrangement of these zones is seemingly structured by the coalescence between the cultural and personal tastes and interests "of the individual" and the "natural environment" of, for example, the red light district, university area, or the waterfront commercial entertainment complex (1925: 45). Urban development is represented as a benevolent process, where cities are organically structured to more efficiently route consumers towards their marketplace desires, destinations, and hence destinies. It is precisely this kind of logic that helps mask the inhumane makeover of physical places, through gentrification and highway reconstruction.

Clearly, this dystopic reading of heritage tourism and historic preservation does not pay nearly enough attention to the agency of Black residents – how they have made this leisure economy work for them despite its limitations. But I want to draw attention to the underside of Black heritage tourism and historic preservation. How could the creation of "community" based on the consumer desires of primarily Black and White professionals and students actually serve as the transitional phase in a limited White urban re-colonization of the Hyde Park-Kenwood-Bronzeville community on the south side (Deutsche and Ryan 1984)? As Bronzeville was re-presenting itself for public consumption, in November of 2003 the U of C took notice and expressed a shared interest in the profitability of Black heritage tourism.[24] When the university attempted to purchase and relocate the world famous Checkerboard lounge from Bronzeville to Hyde Park, those associated with the *Restoring*

---

[23] See Virginia Groark, "Proposal for Dan Ryan Set to Shift: Ramp Closings Upset Neighbors," *Chicago Tribune* (December 21, 2003), 4; Chinta Strausberg, "Blacks Enraged Over Ramp Closings: Asks Justice Department to Halt Ryan Reconstruction," *Chicago Defender* (December 16, 2003), 1 and Stephanie Zimmerman, "IDOT Ends Panel on Ryan Expy. Work: Task Force had Offered Criticism – 'Outreach Campaign' Replaces It," *Chicago Sun-Times* (April 12, 2004), 4.
[24] Friends of the Checkerboard Lounge, "Checkerboard Move Recalls Urban Renewal Days," *Hyde Park Herald* (February 4, 2004).

Bronzeville campaign charged a "theft of culture."[25] In some respects, heritage tourism has allowed the university to put a Black face on gentrification, where an extracted Checkerboard Lounge in Hyde Park capitalizes on the cache of the "local color" of Bronzeville, without tourists ever having to enter the actual neighborhood. The debate has brought to the surface longstanding tensions between these "neighbors" and revives a reoccurring concern with the role of "meds and eds" in structuring urban life.

Both the U of C's defense of its purchase and community criticisms of the university's long and terse history in both Hyde Park and Bronzeville, consolidates a history of competing concerns amongst Black residents, university administrators, and municipal and neighborhood government officials. In the face of community resistance, U of C officials have retorted that local residents and officials had not shown interest in the lounge with their patron dollars, and furthermore, owner L.C. Thurman's decision to sell established a neutral contractual agreement between owner and buyer. Therefore, the university suggested that purchasing the Checkerboard was actually a benevolent act of historic preservation of a dying Black institution, establishing their "good neighbor" status with Bronzeville.[26] The U of C's attempt to naturalize its purchase of the Checkerboard as an act of marketplace salvation and preservation, when Bronzeville simply showed no interest, resonates with Chicago School theories that recognize the organization of urban space by "personal tastes and convenience" instead of by design and control (Park 1925: 5). However, critics' contextualization of the Checkerboard purchase as part of a much larger university design towards urban renewal challenges such a narrative that would foreground personal tastes and interests as the driving force in urban change.

Many were enthused by U of C president Don Michael Randel's recent 2004 speech, where he openly confronted the university's horrific role in urban renewal and conversely outlined "a vigorous – but vague – 'engagement' policy in neighboring communities' redevelopment."[27] But this historic reconciliation with the university's role in inhumane renewal must be read

---

[25] Paula Robinson, "This Tale of Two Cities Could Have Happier Ending," *Hyde Park Herald* (January 7, 2004), 4. and Jamie Nesbitt, "Activists Wants to Keep the Checkerboard in Bronzeville," *Hyde Park Herald* (May 19, 2004), 1.

[26] Ibid.

[27] Mike Stevens, "Learning from the 'Terrible Mistakes' of Urban Renewal," *Hyde Park Herald* (April 14, 2004), 1.

alongside present day initiatives for "off-campus nighttime entertainment options."[28] Outlining contemporary strategies of urban renewal instigated by the university give their "historic preservation" of the Checkerboard lounge new meaning. The Checkerboard purchase, in a broader context, is simply one part of a larger university initiative to exert its economic and real estate influence in the area. If one takes a long view, the university's role as landlord and architect of restrictive covenants, land clearance, and urban renewal decades earlier, encouraged a disinvestment in Bronzeville that decimated any possible patron base for institutions like the Checkerboard lounge[29] (Hirsch 1983; Bachin 2004). Their historic role in structuring the urban social order discouraged the sustainability and patronage of Black businesses. In the present, the university claim of Black historic preservation is called into further question when we consider reports of their continued refusal to meet with the Friends of the Checkerboard to help with parking needs that would have kept the lounge viable in Bronzeville *before* the U of C considered purchase.[30] Moreover, preservation initiatives are even harder to swallow in the face of university hospital expansion that has made it difficult for anyone to patronize another neighboring site of Black historic preservation, the famous DuSable museum located in Washington Park, due to the elimination of public parking.[31]

U of C expansion in all areas of real estate, policing, education, and governance have helped the university create an almost "company town" dynamic in the Hyde Park area through an efficient privatization of public life. Hospital expansion has also moved people out of "historic" residences with the demolition of for example, the Drexel Avenue homes. At the same time, the municipal influence of the university funded development organization, the South East Chicago Commission (SECC), has long influenced commercial space through zoning ordinances and a targeted enforcement of code violations. Concurrently, more and more disputes over local leases are falling into the

---

[28] Paula Robinson, "This Tale of Two Cities Could Have Happier Ending," *Hyde Park Herald* (January 7, 2004), 4.

[29] Friends of the Checkerboard Lounge, "Checkerboard Move Recalls Urban Renewal Days," *Hyde Park Herald* (February 4, 2004), 4 and Bruce Sagan, "The Major Story of the Last 50 Years: Urban Renewal," *Hyde Park Herald* (July 21, 2004), 3.

[30] Friends of the Checkerboard Lounge, "Checkerboard Move Recalls Urban Renewal Days," *Hyde Park Herald* (February 4, 2004), 4.

[31] Paula Robinson, "This Tale of Two Cities Could Have Happier Ending," *Hyde Park Herald* (January 7, 2004), 4.

hands of the U of C Real Estate Operations division.[32] Through new faculty and staff home buying incentive programs, the university is also subsidizing an increased property tax bubble farther north directly into the Bronzeville frontier complete with their own private primary educational charter school (they already own one in Kenwood) and expanded jurisdiction for the private U of C armed police force.[33] The student government also seems to be taking cues from university officials through its proposal for a controversial student and staff only shuttle that would allow university affiliates to avoid sharing public transportation with local residents en route to the Red Line CTA stop.[34]

This is all happening at the same time that public housing high rises have been destroyed with no place for low income tenants to return.[35] The university is also pushing forward with a $700 million office, parking, and retail expansion of its "South Campus" in the equally impoverished Woodlawn neighborhood that has survived their own rocky history of gentrification and urban renewal struggles with the U of C.[36] Collectively, these actions confirm the suspicions of residents that the Checkerboard lounge purchase is just the most visible controversy highlighting a development-focused, public/private cooperative land clearing. The ultimate goal is the creation of "new communities to serve affluent residences at the expense of low and moderate income residents."[37]

That influential neighborhood organizing bodies, including the New Communities Program, Quad CDC, and the historically infamous SECC are at least partially under the control of the university, makes clear that the Checkerboard's movement to Hyde Park was not simply a result of Black

---

[32] Jeremy Adragna, "Bagel Store Closes after Lease Spat with U of C," *Hyde Park Herald* (February 11, 2004), 6 and "Drexel Ave. Homes to be Razed for Hospital Tower," *Hyde Park Herald* (April 21, 2004), 1.

[33] Jeremy Adragna, "University Police Looking Northward to Bronzeville," *Hyde Park Herald* (February 11, 2004), 1 and Grace G. Dawson, "U of C Proves it Can Meet School Demands," *Hyde Park Herald* (December 8, 2004), 4.

[34] Jeremy Adragna, "U of C Kicks Off Red Line Shuttle," *Hyde Park Herald* (May 12, 2004).

[35] Kari Lyderson, "Chicago's Bronzeville is Ready for a Reprise," *Washington Post* (Saturday, November 6, 2004), A03.

[36] Robert Becker, "Woodlawn Watches Warily as U of C Stretches South," *Chicago Tribune* (October 12, 2004), 1.

[37] Gregory Robinson, "Context is Key in Checkerboard Relocation," *Hyde Park Herald* (February 25, 2004), 4.

disinterest and university salvation.[38] The U of C has initiated a new phase in urban renewal and gentrification that is tied to their historic role in property ownership, racially restrictive covenants, land clearance, and urban renewal. In this case, the university has literally served as the avant-garde, no longer simply ordering or translating moral regions of racial difference for safe travel, consumption, and control. They have initiated the actual consumption of "authentic," foreign spaces (parts of Bronzeville) by transplanting them to the seemingly safer Hyde Park. Guilty free purchase and cultural exchange takes place, without the messiness or uneasiness of the place from which the authentic culture emerged. In a similar fashion to Disney World's much-maligned World Showcase (formerly the Millennium Village), the relocation of the Checkerboard Lounge provides consumers the instant gratification of Black authenticity without its community context. Love for the cultural "other" is replaced with theft, urban renewal with removal. Such is the case with the Checkerboard lounge, a controversy that embodies the overlapping inter-sections of culture, power, and history in the 21st century urban landscape.

It is not that early "Chicago School" social thought has always intended to provide social scientific justifications for the university's capitalist expan-sions, nor can it be said that the university consciously used this academic work. Simply, "Chicago School" analyses of urban social difference – that unequal land allocations along racial lines were the product of natural moral regions or zones according to tastes and temperament and not policy and power – is the foundation on which current U of C gentrification initiatives are built. The theoretical and physical legacies of human ecology help make legible the university's appropriation of a Black historic preservation/her-itage tourism language in the Checkerboard lounge controversy. Foreshadowing the current service economy ascendancy of the "meds and eds", the U of C may have provided the blueprint for the unholy alliance between the worlds of industry and ideas, naturalizing the brutal force of land appropriation, while nullifying the resilient moments of resistance and critique.

The swiftness of innovation in the U of C's urban expansion is matched in efficiency only by the NYU and Columbia standoff at midtown for real estate supremacy of the island, Harvard's rapid advance into the Alston Brighton

---

[38] Paula Robinson, "This Tale of Two Cities Could Have Happier Ending," *Hyde Park Herald* (January 7, 2004), 4 and Bruce Sagan, "The Major Story of the Last 50 Years: Urban Renewal," *Hyde Park Herald* (July 21, 2004), 3.

corridor, and even the University of Illinois at Chicago's established dominion over Maxwell Street on the near west side. As urban medical centers and universities become one of their city's largest employers, real estate holders, policing agents and producers of knowledge, how will we begin to redefine community responsibility and urban renewal? One thing is certain: universities can no longer (never could) be considered above and beyond the messy fray of urban struggle as ideas and industry have unabashedly converged in their ivory towers. We must continue to come from behind the leafy green moats and fortifications of dusty parchment and digital regressions to ask, what will be the role of "meds and eds," and how will the ideas of their knowledge workers be used in the new culture industry empires?

Jackie Orr

The Militarization of Inner Space*

Operation Scramble

> WARNING: The following statement may contain
> secret coded messages intended to reach any of
> my allies who may reside within your borders.[1]

"[E]very American is a soldier" now, declared George
W. Bush one month after September 11, 2001.[2]
Speaking at the inaugural meeting of the Homeland
Security Council, whose opening order of business
was to beef up U.S. border operations by tightening
immigration surveillance and control, Mr. Bush's pronouncement itself performed a consequential border
crossing. His sweeping rhetorical induction of the
entire U.S. citizenry into the ranks of military com-
batants obliterated the very boundary between 'civilian' and 'soldier' on which popular understandings
of 'terrorism' fundamentally depend: would future
attacks on U.S. civilians now be acknowledged as a
targeted assault on U.S. soldiers? Mr. Bush's border
transgression, conducted in the midst and in the

---

* An earlier version of this essay appeared in *Critical Sociology*, vol. 30, no. 2 (2004).
[1] On October 10, 2001, then-National Security Adviser Condoleezza Rice made a
request to all major television networks to carry only carefully edited versions of
future videotaped statements from Osama bin Laden or his "followers." Rice suggested
that the broadcasts could be used "to send coded messages to other terrorists." In an
unprecedented joint agreement, described by one T.V. executive as a "patriotic" decision,
the networks complied. The next day, the White House made the same request to
major U.S. newspapers. See *The New York Times*, 11 October 2001, p. A1, and 12 October
2001, p. B7.
[2] Quoted in *The New York Times*, 30 October 2001, p. B5.

name of intensified border patrols, raises a few other urgent questions for the newly anointed civilian-soldier:

When was I trained for battle?

What are my weapons and how do they work?

And where, precisely, stands this "home" which the new armies of civilians are asked to secure? Which borders are we really being asked to defend? What exactly is this war into which the U.S. civilian-soldier has been involuntarily drafted?

The 'war against terrorism' is the repetitiously proffered answer to this last query. But a little bit of history and the website of the U.S. Space Command suggest another story. The U.S. Space Command was established in 1985 as the coordinating military body unifying Army, Navy, and Air Force activities in outer space. "As stewards for military space," states General Howell M. Estes III, the Space Command's ex-Commander in Chief, "we must be prepared to exploit the advantages of the space medium." In *Joint Vision 2010*, the operational plan for securing and maintaining unchallengeable "space power," the U.S. Space Command describes how "the medium of space is the fourth medium of warfare – along with land, sea, and air." The end result of the pursuit of 'space power' is the achievement of Full Spectrum Dominance: the capacity of the U.S. military to dominate in any conflict, waged in any terrestrial or extraterrestrial medium. Or, in the Space Command's words, displayed onscreen against the black, star-studded background of empty space: "U.S. Space Command – dominating the space dimension of military operations to protect U.S. interests and investment. Integrating Space Forces into warfighting capabilities across the full spectrum of conflict."[3]

The battles for which the U.S. Space Command is prepared are not futuristic science fiction scenarios. Satellite-mediated infotech warfare has arrived. The real-time military use of space-based satellites debuted in the U.S. invasion of Panama in 1989, and expanded during the first U.S.-led attack on Iraq in 1991, and in the killing fields of Kosovo (Gray 1997, Grossman 2001). "Space support to NATO's operations in Kosovo was a perfect example of how the

---

[3] All quotes are from the website of the U.S. Space Command at www.spacecom, December 2001. The website has since been altered, and many of the documents cited here are no longer displayed online. Thanks to John Burdick for originally calling my attention to the U.S. Space Command in "Terrorism and state terror," public talk presented at the Socialist Forum, Westcott Community Center, Syracuse, New York, October 14, 2001.

United States will fight its wars in the future," the Space Command reports, "Satellite-guided munitions, communications, navigation, and weather all combined to achieve military objectives . . ."[4] In the current invasion and attempted military occupation of Iraq, "space-aided warfare" wires together U.S. military command centers from Virginia to Saudi Arabia with human soldiers on the ground and automated, unmanned planes in the air (e.g. the 'Predator' and the 'Global Hawk') to create flexible networks of vision and destruction.[5] In the fall of 2004, the Pentagon announces the building of a global "war net" that will link space-based intelligence and communications satellites to new weapons technologies and to commanders and soldiers in the battlefield. The consortium of U.S. military contractors and information technology companies (including Microsoft, Sun Microsystems, Hewlett-Packard, and I.B.M.) selected to develop the necessary technologies – with a projected $24 billion budget over the next five years – plans to "weave weapons, intelligence, and communications into a seamless web," a web conceptually anchored in an ever less ethereal void of space.[6] Home to the imperial techno-hallucinations of a planetary war net, to an increasingly sophisticated and expensive infrastructure of satellites, and to a proposed network of (possibly nuclear-powered) space stations equipped with laser weaponry, 'outer space' emerges as the U.S. military's final, fantastic frontier.

With Full Spectrum Dominance as its official doctrine, the U.S. Space Command clearly articulates its 21st century mission: to ensure that the United States will remain a global power and exert global leadership during the current "globalization of the world economy." Noting with admirable sociological acumen that this globalization will create a "widening between 'haves' and 'have-nots' . . . [and] [t]his gap will widen – creating regional unrest," the U.S. Space Command announces that the new strategic situation requires "a global perspective to conduct military operations and support regional warfighting . . ."[7] The U.S. Space Command stands ready to serve.

---

[4] From the website of the U.S Space Command at www.spacecom.mil/Fact%20Sheet-MilitarySpaceForces.htm, April 22, 2002.

[5] See William J. Broad, "Allies' Vital Supply Line Now Stretches Into Orbit," *The New York Times*, 31 March 2003, p. B10; Eric Schmitt, "In the Skies Over Iraq, Silent Observers Become Futuristic Weapons," *The New York Times*, 18 April 2003, p. B8; and Eric Schmitt, "6,300 Miles From Iraq, Experts Guide Raids," *The New York Times*, 24 June 2003, p. A13.

[6] Tim Weiner, "Pentagon Envisioning a Costly Internet for War," *The New York Times*, 13 November 2004, p. A1.

[7] All quotes are from the U.S. Space Command website, December 2001.

And we – we civilian-soldiers – where do we stand? In what space really do we wage our scrambled warfare, our civilian participation in the militarized state of the nation? Are we all soldiers now in the battle for Full Spectrum Dominance of the globe? South Asia. Eurasia. East Asia. Central Asia. What boot camp has prepared us for the rigors of a perpetually ambiguous, infinitely expanding battlefield? Mosul. Ramadi. Najaf. Fallujah. Across what geography is the 'war against terrorism' really mapped? In how many dimensions must today's civilian-soldier really move?

The Bush administration's first National Security Strategy document, published in September 2002, offers the inquiring civilian-soldier some indication of the full scope of the battle plans. Twelve months after launching its boundless war against terrorism, the administration introduced its new doctrine of preemptive strikes, unilaterally pursued, against the 'perception' of threat. National security now depends, the civilian-soldier learns, on "identifying and destroying the threat before it reaches our borders . . . [W]e will not hesitate to act alone, if necessary, to exercise our right of self-defense by acting preemptively."[8] Released just as the Bush administration stepped up preparations for the invasion of Iraq, the document leads even mainstream media commentators to note, with measured alarm, its imperial posture. An editorial published in *The Atlanta Journal-Constitution* calls the National Security Strategy statement a "plan for permanent U.S. military and economic domination of every region on the globe." The editorial warns that the war against Iraq "is intended to mark the official emergence of the United States as a full-fledged global empire, seizing sole responsibility and authority as planetary policemen."[9] By the November 2004 elections, when George Bush secures another four years of executive power, a significant stream of public political discourse embraces the 'American empire' as a given: the question is no

---

[8] A published version of the document is available as *The National Security Strategy of the United States of America* (Falls Village, Connecticut: Winterhouse Editions, 2002). National Security Strategy documents, published sporadically at the discretion of the executive branch, are intended to circulate as public – and public relations – documents.

[9] Jay Bookman, "The President's Real Goal in Iraq," *The Atlanta Journal-Constitution*, 29 September 2002. Bookman traces the agenda set out in the 2002 National Security Strategy document to a report published in September 2000 by the conservative Project for a New American Century (PNAC), whose signatories included Dick Cheney, Donald Rumsfeld, Paul Wolfowitz, I. Lewis Libby, and Elliott Abrams. The genealogy allows Bookman and others to argue persuasively that the Bush administration is pursuing a military agenda imagined before the attacks of September 11, 2001, the principal architects of which are now in key positions of civilian and military power.

longer whether the U.S. is an empire, but whether it can be a beloved – and cost effective – empire.[10]

If the militarization of outer space is an essential component of Full Spectrum Dominance, and if the so-called 'war against terrorism' must be situated within broader U.S. ambitions for global empire,[11] it is perhaps useful for today's civilian-soldier to wonder just how wide and deep is a "full spectrum" of dominance? What borders must be crossed to fully dominate such an infinity of space? Does dominion in outer space require the militarization of a somewhat more covert spatial territory – a territory more spectral, less smoothly operationalized but no less necessary to planetary empire? What happens in that elusive terrain of 'inner space' as outer space becomes an overt field for fully militarized command posts? Is the 'inner' psychic terrain of today's U.S. civilian-soldier another battlefield on the way to full spectrum dominance of the globe? What kind of militarized infrastructure is needed 'inside' the soldierly civilian called upon to support the establishment of military superiority across the spectrum of spaces 'outside'?

The psychology of the civilian-soldier, the networks of everyday emotional and perceptual relations, constitute an 'inner space' that is today, I suggest, one volatile site of attempted military occupation. But the occupying forces I'm concerned with here are not those of an invasive, enemy 'other.' Rather, a partial and urgent history of how the U.S. government, media, military, and academy has enlisted the psychological life of U.S. citizens as a military asset – this is the embodied story that occupies me here.

The militarization of inner space – a complex, discontinuous story that does not crystallize into the clear knot of conspiracy but which leaves its uneven

---

[10] For a recent critical historical and geopolitical treatment of the question of U.S. empire, see Jan Nederveen Pieterse, *Globalization or Empire?* (New York: Routledge, 2004).

[11] Connections between the ambitions of the 'war against terrorism' and the space-based military imperatives of Full Spectrum Dominance are exemplified in the figure of Donald H. Rumsfeld. Until his appointment in December 2000 as Secretary of Defense, Rumsfeld chaired the Commission to Assess U.S. National Security Space Management and Organization. The Commission, charged with constructing a blueprint for the future of U.S. "military space assets," made public its unclassified report in January 2001. Citing the threat of a catastrophic "Space Pearl Harbor," the report argues forcefully and in detail for the prioritization and reorganization of military, intelligence and commercial activities in space. See the Report of the Commission to Assess U.S. National Security Space Management and Organization (Washington, D.C. 11 January 2001), available online at www.space.gov.

traces throughout the scattered archives of the 20th century United States – is now as it has been before a major concern of those most responsible for the business of war. Militarization, defined by historian Michael Geyer as "the contradictory and tense social process in which civil society organizes itself for the production of violence," constitutes at its core a border-crossing between military and civilian institutions, activities and aims (1989: 79). The militarization of inner space can be conceived, then, as the *psychological orga-nization of civil society for the production of violence*. It is not my intention to reify 'psychology' or psychological processes as if they could be separated from social, historical, or economic contexts. Quite the contrary. By naming the constructed 'inner space' of psychological activities as increasingly mili-tarized – with the events of September 11 serving as an accelerator and inten-sifier of processes that are by no means new – my hope is to deepen a critical sociological commitment to contesting the 'space' of psychology as the rad-ically social matter of political struggle, as one radically material weapon of war. Or its refusal.

While I refer to this psychological space as 'inner,' it of course is not irre-ducibly individual, and is never confined to a neat interiority. Inner space both produces and is produced by deeply social ways of seeing, and by pro-foundly cultural technologies of perception. And though I want to reject any notion of a homogeneous collective psyche, I do want to conjure the dense sociality and historicity of psychological spaces. Psychological life occupies a difficult borderland, a 'between-space' where the question and human con-fusions of what is 'inner' and 'outer' are repetitiously experienced, and consciously and unconsciously lived. Indeed, the space of psychology is the very site where everyday sensations of what's 'inside' and what's 'outside,' what's 'them' and what's 'us,' what feels safe and what seems fatally fright-ening are culturally (re)produced or resisted; it is an intensely border-conscious space. The politics of borders – how they're made and unmade, what they come to mean – is one shifting center of the politics of nationalism, of language, of memory, of race, gender, class, of terror. What has come in the modern West to be called the 'psychological' plays a dramatic, power-charged role within each of these entangled political fields. The militarization of psycho-logical space can be imagined then as a *strategic set of psychological border oper-ations* aimed at the organization of civil society for the production of violence.

The historically-specific confusion and re-configuration of the borders between the psyche of the soldier and of the civilian, between the practice of psychology and the prosecution of war, is the topic of several studies of World War II and its Cold War aftermath. "New languages for speaking about subjectivity," writes Nikolas Rose, emerged during World War II to address the new consensus that "[w]inning the war was to require a concerted attempt to understand and govern the subjectivity of the citizen" (1989: x, 21). Research on 'attitudes' and 'personality,' public opinion polling and statistical survey research, constituted new "sciences of the psyche" aimed at managing both military and civilian beliefs and behaviors; the human psyche itself became "a possible domain for systematic government in the pursuit of socio-political ends" (ibid.: 7). According to historian Laura McEnaney, with the end of the war and the rise of the U.S. national security state, the "ambient militarism" of Cold War culture translated the very meaning of national security into a "perception, a state of mind" – a profoundly psychological state in which the civilian psyche became a difficult but pervasive variable in military planning (2000: 39, 12–15). Ellen Herman chronicles the imbrications of psychological concepts and expertise into the textures of everyday life in Cold War U.S. society, arguing that efforts at "mass emotional control" in the name of national security led, by the late 1960s, to an unprecedented blurring of boundaries between public policy and private emotions (1995: 241–242).

Today, one important contributing factor to civilian-soldiers' willingness to serve may be a sanctioned ignorance of this history of previous campaigns to effectively mobilize 'inner space' in the interests of war and the organized production of violence. Remembering the militarization of psychic space as part of the full spectrum of tactics deployed in 20th century warfare may help us better grasp the multiple dimensions of danger in the present, post-September 11 contagion of terrors. "[W]hat one remembers of the past and how one remembers it depend on the social and cultural resources to which one has access," writes Fred Turner in his recent history of collective memory-making, cultural trauma, and the Vietnam war (1996: xii). Consider this text as one attempt at a public remembrance of how the inner space of psychology has been already a calculated battlefield, a terrain of cultural combat where the measure of victory includes the possibility, or impossibility, of remembering that a fight took place. If, as Turner suggests, "memory takes place simultaneously in the individual psyche and in the social domain," then what I (want to) recall is intimately tied to what you (are able to) remember (1996: xi). The psychic space of memory is a cultural and collective landscape – nobody moves around there all alone. Is it possible today to mobilize scholarly and psychic resources to disrupt what Stephen Pfohl has called "the hegemonic rhythms of public memory in the USA Today" (1992: 42)? Can a contemporary critical sociology – remembering its own insurgent origins[12] – contribute to counterhegemonic memories that are more public and more powerful?

An orbiting U.S. doctrine of Full Spectrum Dominance calls for critical terrestrial practices of full spectrum de-militarization. Economy. Culture. Society. Psyche. Perhaps it's time for a few collective flashbacks. How hard would it be to publicly remember the civilian-soldier as a central, contested figure of 20th century hot and cold wars? What difference could it make to re-frame and refuse today's 'war against terrorism' as the most recent theater of operations for securing the psychological organization of U.S. civil society for the manufacture of mass violence? Insisting on a border-crossing between the past and present tense, asking you to live briefly in the question of the boundaries between 'then' and 'now,' this text tries to contribute to an effective history of the present – one that might arrive in time for the fight for less terrorizing future spaces.[13]

Target You

"At a time of national crisis, I think it is particularly apparent that we need to encourage the study of our past."

– Lynne Cheney (October 5, 2001)[14]

---

[12] The journal *Critical Sociology*, in which this essay was first published, was previously titled *The Insurgent Sociologist* (1971–1987).

[13] The project of a "history of the present" is indebted to the work of Michel Foucault, and his efforts to engage contemporary struggles by making histories of shifting strategies of power, knowledge, and experience. Two of his most useful statements on historical methods are Foucault 1984 and 1994.

[14] Opening quote in Jerry L. Martin and Anne D. Neal, "Defending Civilization: How Our Universities Are Failing America and What Can Be Done About It" (American Council of Trustees and Alumni, November 2001). This document received significant media coverage for its argument that the U.S. academy "is the only sector of American society that is distinctly divided in its response" to the events of September 11, and included a recitation of 117 instances of campus criticism of the U.S. government post-September 11. While the document was broadly attacked within and outside the U.S. academy for its McCarthy-esque pretensions and shoddy scholarship, it's worth noting that its sponsoring organization, the American Council of Trustees and Alumni (ACTA), is the largest private financial contributor to institutions of higher education in the U.S. ACTA members reportedly gave $3.4 billion to colleges and universities in 2001.

The U.S. civilian-soldier is at least as old as a New World conquered in part by volunteer armies of white settlers and constitutionally founded on the right to own lethal weapons. But not until the advent of 20th century military and communications technologies did certain contours of today's civilian-soldier begin to take shape. Terrorists, we are told, have training camps. The 21st century civilian-soldier does too. World War II and the early years of Cold War U.S. culture, I suggest, supplied one not-so-secret training camp where the civilian-soldier was experimentally shaped by not-so-civil lessons in 'total war.'

London. Dresden. Tokyo. Hiroshima. Nagasaki.

Launched during World War II to name the new strategic situation in which the civilian home front became as important militarily as the frontlines of battle, the notion of 'total war' officially drafts the U.S. civilian-soldier into an active psychological role in the conduct of successful war.[15] In a special 1941 issue of *The American Journal of Sociology* published on the eve of U.S. entry into World War II and devoted to the problem of civilian morale, sociologist Robert E. Park observes:

> Since war has invaded the realm of the spirit, morale has assumed a new importance in both war and peace. Total war is now an enterprise so colossal that belligerent nations find it necessary not only to mobilize all their resources, material and moral, but to make present peace little more than a preparation for future war. Under these conditions so-called psychic warfare ... has assumed an importance and achieved a technical efficiency which ... has profoundly altered the character of peace, making it much harder to bear.
>
> The object of attack in psychic warfare is morale, and less that of the men in arms than of the civil population back of the lines (1941: 360).

The wartime preoccupation with civilian morale – how to build one's own and destroy the enemy's – marks an official recognition by the U.S. government and its professional knowledge-makers that, as Ellen Herman writes, "the human personality, and its diverse and unpredictable mental states were

---

[15] A succint statement of the doctrine of total war was offered in 1945 by Vannevar Bush, director of the U.S. Office of Scientific Research and Development: War, he writes, is "increasingly total war, in which the armed services must be supplemented by active participation of every element of the civilian population," quoted in Bush 1945, p. 12.

of utmost importance in prosecuting the war." The problem of morale receives enormous, well-funded attention in the U.S. throughout the war years, and becomes a pivotal concept in the construction of the ideal 20th century U.S. civilian-soldier: the notion of morale and the "control of human subjectivity" as central to military strategy "stretched the definition of war to encompass aspects of civilian social life previously considered off-limits to military policy-makers" (Herman 1995: 29–30).

Faced with the emergent challenges of total psychic warfare, U.S. social scientists in *The American Journal of Sociology* mobilize their civilian resources to consider the most promising course of social action. In the vortex of total war, where the boundaries between psychic and military tactics, soldier and civilian, home and combat zone, war and peace are set spinning – how might the civilian-solider-social scientist most effectively contribute to the allied cause?

Noted psychiatrist Harry Stack Sullivan argues for a program of "total defense" to be waged equally by the national citizen and the military con-script. Any effective "counter-strategy" for preventing civilian demoraliza-tion requires a suspension of democratic ideals and a re-education in the "rigid discipline" and mandatory cooperation characteristic of military insti-tutions. The kind of social organization required will create "a society the structure of which must be distinctly paternalistic – authoritarian – in order to win in the fight on national socialism." If such a disciplinary, authoritar-ian society can be achieved, Sullivan encourages, "we will then, I suppose, have time and ingenuity to work out a little strategy of terror of our own" (1941: 292–295).[16]

But most voices in the 1941 *AJS* issue call for more 'democratic' methods to maintain the psychological fortitude of the civilian-soldier. In a report on government-sponsored research on citizens' attitudes and opinions, sociolo-gist Edward A. Shils identifies the kind of "'intelligence' activities" that dis-tinguish a democratic government's efforts to shape civilian behavior from more overtly authoritarian information-gathering: "For a democratic gov-ernment which regards preferences not merely as objects to be manipulated

---

[16] In his most "cold-blooded proposition" in the *AJS* essay, Sullivan suggests that people who "cannot reasonably be converted into trustworthy citizens of the nation at war" might best be dealt with by placing them "out of harm's way in a civilized version of the concentration camp," p. 294.

but as a source of guidance . . . it is especially urgent to possess means of acquiring knowledge of the state of mind of its citizens." Shils celebrates the recent techniques of public opinion polling and survey research as intelligence activities befitting a democratic state. Reliable information about citizens' "state of mind" is a prerequisite for the government's effective management of "the population whose behavior it seeks to influence" (1941: 472). The social sciences – which in close collaboration with market researchers have by the early 1940s started to develop statistical techniques for gathering precisely such information – thus carve out for themselves a key role in the political administration of civilian psychology. Indeed, with the U.S. entry into the war, hundreds of sociologists, psychologists, anthropologists and educators form a "new breed of policy-oriented psychological experts," employed by civilian and military agencies to study human attitudes, behavior, opinions and emotions and to put to militarized use the new methods of sampling and survey research for large populations (Herman 1995: 54).[17]

Two entangled technological developments in the first half of the 20th century create the historical context in which the psychology of the civilian home front becomes an obsessive variable in the political calculus of war. Both developments involve enhanced and accelerated 'delivery systems' – for weapons and for words. Both developments heighten the permeability of geographic and psychological or perceptual borders. First, the invention and deployment of airplanes as instruments of war, making aerial bombardment a key strategy of industrialized warfare, ushered in a new spatial-temporal rhythm of military attack. With virtually no warning, an enemy located many hundreds of miles away could launch an aerial attack on a targeted city. The speed of the attack combined with the potential intensity of destruction posed a potent new psychological as well as material threat to the everyday life of civilians.[18]

---

[17] See also Herman, pp. 48–81. One of the most notable, if seldom noted, applications of social science research to civilian psychological management during WWII was the Sociological Research Project, an interdisciplinary team of social scientists, including psychiatrists, who worked to ensure the smooth administration and "human management" of the Poston Relocation Center, one of the internment camps for the over 100,000 Japanese-Americans 'relocated' in 1942 by the U.S. government, see Herman, pp. 25–29. On the history of survey research methods in the U.S., including the tight link with World War II government agencies and agendas, see Hyman 1991.
[18] While World War II saw the first mass use of aerial bombardment, the use of aerial warfare by Western industrialized countries against colonial territories had been

But the delivery system that amplifies most dramatically the volatility –
and military significance – of civilian psychology is the crackling black box
with the numerical dial sitting in most U.S. households by the mid-1930s. As
the first popularized form of electronic mass media, radio radically alters the
spatial-temporal rhythm of the production and reception of news and information, erasing previous boundaries of both time and space. When the 1938
radio broadcast of Orson Welles' *War of the Worlds* reportedly creates mass
panic among millions of listeners in the U.S., news commentators quickly
focus on the military implications of radio's power to influence the psychology of a mass audience.[19] While there is general agreement that "[r]adio can
spread and radio can control ideas and information essential to national
defense," there is no consensus over how this new-found weapon should be
wielded.[20] Should the state protect the public from its tendencies toward terror and initiate government control of the radio airwaves as the first line of
national defense? Or is government control of radio actually a weapon of
totalitarianism, securing a deadly monopoly on this powerful psychological
medium? Perhaps most disturbingly, what to make of the potential for this
new 'delivery system' of words and world events to broadcast theatrics and
simulations that can have just as much psychological force as real news? As
one news columnist put it, if the electrified radio voice of Adolf Hitler was
currently scaring much of Europe to its knees with "an army and an airforce
to back up his shrieking words," then what to make of the power of Orson
Welles' radio theater to "scare thousands into demoralization with nothing
at all"?[21]

U.S. social science takes note of the shifting techno-social terrain constructed
by new mass communications technologies and their capacity to rapidly mobilize psychological movements. As Princeton psychologist Hadley Cantril
writes up *The Invasion From Mars* (1940), his famous study of the 1938 'panic

inaugurated by the U.S. in Nicaragua in 1933. Occupied between world wars by U.S.
military forces and declared a 'Protectorate of the United States of America,' Nicaragua
was the site of U.S. experiments with aerial bombing against the 'Bolshevik' threat of
Augusto Cesar Sandino and his itinerate, largely rural, indigenous army of liberation.
See Galeano 1988.

[19] For a cultural history of panic and its techno-social management in the 20th century U.S., see Orr (forthcoming 2005).

[20] *Daily News*, 31 October 1938, quoted in Koch 1967, p. 22.

[21] Dorothy Thompson, "On the Record," *New York Tribune*, 2 November 1938, quoted
in Koch 1967, p. 92.

broadcast', social scientists in the special *AJS* issue also grapple with the influence of mass media on civilian psychology, publishing invited essays written by a movie studio executive and an employee of the National Broadcasting System (NBC). In "Radio and National Morale," James Angell of NBC radio explains that reasoned confidence alone is not enough to move a nation on the brink of total war. The "masses must be moved by emotional excitement and exaltation if they are to reach any high pitch of forceful action" (Angell 1941: 353–354). Movie industry executive James Wanger asserts that the "builders of morale must weave . . . a fabric of emotion around the rational aspects of democratic life . . . Men must become emotionalized, to use a clumsy word, about their country and their country's goals." Filmmakers, Wanger promises, can contribute significantly to the national cause (1941: 380–383).

How exactly will the coordinated efforts of the mass media, social scientists, and government officials to 'emotionalize' and manage psychological investments on the civilian front of total war differ from the domestic propaganda techniques of totalitarian governments?[22] "The arts and devices of spiritual warfare are many and various and more subtle no doubt than any analysis has thus far disclosed," Robert E. Park enigmatically observes (1941: 363). As the U.S. civilian-soldier materializes as a strategically conceived combatant in the crucible of a world war mediated by new mass communications technologies, the battle to establish psychological supply lines and defense systems for this most vulnerable and volatile of troops, opens out onto an unforeseen future.

Disaster on Main Street

"America will not live in peace . . ."

– Osama bin Laden (October 7, 2001)[23]

The end of World War II, rather than marking a de-militarization of the U.S. civilian-soldier, signals a deepening anxiety over his/her psychological and

---

[22] For an excellent historical discussion of how social psychology grappled with this question, self-consciously constituting itself as a necessary "science of democracy," see Rose 1996, pp. 116–149.

[23] Quoted in *The New York Times*, 8 October 2001, p. A1. Bin Laden's words end the brief videotaped statement released on October 7, hours after U.S. and British forces began bombing Afghanistan. The full quote, in translation, reads: "I swear to God that America will not live in peace before peace reigns in Palestine, and before all the army of infidels depart the land of Muhammad, peace be upon him," p. B7.

military role in the sustained tensions and proliferating dangers of the Cold War. With the United States' invention and use of atomic bombs in 1945, the character of industrialized warfare prefigured in aerial bombardment becomes exponentially more terrifying for civilian populations. In their top-secret analysis of U.S. nuclear testing in the South Pacific in 1947, the Joint Chiefs of Staff decide that the primary value of the atomic bomb is its "psychological implication," i.e. its capacity to terrorize and demoralize an enemy population without ever actually being deployed. The panic that would accompany the threat or use of nuclear weapons, they report, is a key strategic advantage for a nation on the military offensive, and a problem of the highest order for the nation planning its own defense. Military victory is assured for the country best able to exploit this potentially nerve-shattering psychological situation (Oakes 1994: 35).

A survey of U.S. public opinion is conducted during the 1947 nuclear tests and overseen by several social scientists who directed wartime military and civilian survey research agencies.[24] The findings include troubling evidence that people tend to be confused, contradictory, poorly-informed, or undecided about the grave issues of the atomic age. Indeed, responses to the survey offer "little indication that the people recognize the revolutionary significance of the new weapon." The researchers conclude that a "focusing of attention and securing [of] psychological involvement" is necessary for the U.S. public to fully participate in the government of world affairs in the new nuclear era (Cottrell and Eberhart 1948: 14–19, 59–60).

In a series of both classified and public documents produced in the late 1940s to address the civil defense problems facing U.S. planners, the findings of the 1947 Joint Chiefs of Staff's evaluation become foundational assumptions for thinking about atomic weapons. Panic and the destruction of national morale are named repeatedly as the main obstacles to the successful conduct of nuclear war. In an early instruction manual on *Panic Control and Prevention*, readers encounter the remarkable claim that:

> Mass panic can produce more damage to life and property than any number of atomic bombs. . . . If war comes, it will be a total, absolute war. Fitness of the civilian will be of equal importance with fitness of the fighter. The

---

[24] Social scientists overseeing the survey, funded by the Rockefeller Foundation and the Carnegie Corporation, include Hadley Cantril, Rensis Likert (director of the Morale Division of the United States Strategic Bombing Survey), and Leonard S. Cottrell, Jr. (director of the Survey Section of the War Department's Research Branch).

outcome of the war will depend upon the staying power of the civilian just
as much as upon that of the soldier. The fatigued civilian will be the unfit,
panic-ripe civilian (Office of Civil Defense 1951: 71–72).

The psychology of the Cold War U.S. civilian-soldier is now burdened with
nothing less than the success or demise of national security itself. With national
defense increasingly linked to psychic defense, the militarization of civilian
psychology takes on a new urgency. In this ongoing "imaginary war" for the
civilian psyche, the resources of the U.S. government, the academy, and the
corporate mass media all mobilize in an effort to "bring the public psychology into conformity with the requirements of national security policy" (Oakes
1994: 33). The effort is neither a conspiracy nor an assured success: it is experimental, creative, committed, and sustained. It does not equally target all
civilians but rather a dominantly white, middle class or upwardly-mobile
working class population who owns property, preferably a house and presumably in the suburbs.[25]

The byline reads "Moscow, 1960," and the simulated news report narrates
the historical highlights of world war as they spin out from the ill-fated Soviet
assassination attempt on the life of Yugoslavian leader, Marshal Tito, on May
10, 1952. "This was the . . . start," the report recalls, "of 32 months of unlimited catastrophe for the human race, in the course of which millions of innocent people met violent deaths. . . Among their scorched, shattered graveyards
were the atomized ruins of Washington, Chicago, Philadelphia, Detroit, New
York, London and eventually Moscow" (Sherwood 1951: 19, 22).

On May 14, 1952, the report continues, the U.S. begins dropping atomic
bombs on selected military and industrial targets in the Soviet Union, carefully avoiding civilian population centers. The round-the-clock saturation
bombing campaign continues for three months and 16 days. A year later, the
Soviet Union retaliates with the atomic bombing of civilian target cities in
the U.S., including Washington, D.C. An eyewitness account of the attack is
accompanied by a two-page illustration of the nation's capital on fire with
the caption, "Note Pentagon blazing (at upper left)" (Boyle 1951: 20).

This dramatic staging of World War III is offered up by *Collier's* magazine

---

[25] See McEnaney 2000, chapters 4–5, for the best discussion I have seen of the gender, race and class politics of Cold War civil defense discourse, including the proactive role taken by the NAACP and women's volunteer clubs to make a place for
themselves as participants in civil defense programs.

in October 1951, in a special issue entitled "Preview of the War We Do Not Want." *Collier's*, a popular weekly magazine with a wide circulation targeted mainly at a white suburban audience, designs the issue in consultation with top military, economic and political thinkers in U.S. and international affairs. The "ultimate purpose" of this fictionalized history, the editors explain, is to provide a kind of cautionary tale of "hypothetical war" amidst the anxious signs of an increasingly hot Cold War (1951: 6, 17).

Collier's hypothetical war reportage appears in the same year that the fledgling Federal Civil Defense Administration (FCDA) launches "one of the largest mass programs the nation has ever essayed": the public education and training of U.S. civilians in the "proper public attitudes and behavior" necessary to their own defense (Associated Universities, Inc., 1952: v). Created by Presidential executive order, the agency's basic mandate, spelled out in the Federal Civil Defense Act of 1950, is to provide for the civilian defense of both life and property in the event of war, including emergency communications networks to warn of enemy attack and the nationwide organization of local volunteer civil defense corps (FCDA 1952: 38).

A major theme of the FCDA's mass education and information program underlines the dangers of civilian terror in the face of atomic threat or attack. According to a pamphlet produced by the Office of Civil Defense in 1951 for local municipal leaders:

> Since the advent of the atomic bomb, unfortunate psychological reactions have developed in the minds of civilians. This reaction is one of intense fear, directed against forces that cannot be seen, felt, or otherwise sensed. The fear reaction of the uninitiated civilian is . . . of such magnitude that it could well interfere with important military missions or civil defense in time of war (1951: 63).

With "Keep Calm!" as its easy-to-remember antidote to atomic panic, the FCDA sponsors a range of print, radio, television, and cinematic messages aimed at disseminating the relevant facts and advising the appropriate behaviors. Over 20 million copies of the FCDA pamphlet, "Survival Under Atomic Attack," are distributed in 1951. In folksy prose, the text calmly describes how to avoid "losing your head" and panicking if even that worst case scenario occurs: an atomic blast catches you unawares and you "soak up a serious dose of explosive radioactivity" (U.S. Government Printing Office 1950: 12).

In April 1951, the FCDA releases the movie version of *Survival Under Atomic Attack*. Commercial distributors sell more prints of *Survival* in the first nine months than any other film in the history of the industry. In the next several years, the FCDA's mass public education program produces an instructive litany of films, newsreels, and made-for-T.V. series including *Disaster on Main Street, Operation Scramble, Bombproof, Target You, What You Should Know About Biological Warfare, Take Cover,* and *Let's Face It.*[26]

But alongside government-sponsored encouragements to Cold War civilian-soldiers to "Keep Calm!," an apparently contradictory effort to frighten the U.S. public is simultaneously underway. From its inception, the FCDA identifies "public apathy" toward civilian defense as the major obstacle to the successful conduct of its task. In a public letter to President Truman in 1952, the first director of the FCDA explains:

> The American people will respond to civil defense when they believe in its immediate necessity. Such widespread belief does not yet exist ... Too few realize that the atomic bomb changed the character of warfare and that in future conflicts the man and woman in the street and in the factory will be the prime target – that they will be in the front line of battle ... [T]here is little real understanding of the need for a balanced defense, composed of the civil and the military serving in a co-equal partnership (Caldwell in FCDA 1952: v).

In the *Report of Project East River* (1952) – an extensive study of the problems of civil defense commissioned by the FCDA, the Department of Defense, and the National Security Resources Board – the authors cite recent public opinion surveys to argue that "a major barrier to involvement and activity in civil defense" is the public's tendency to believe that an atomic attack cannot really occur in their hometown, or that the U.S. military will successfully protect the country should such an attack take place (Associated Universities, Inc., 1952: 3). *Project East River* recommends a massive public information and

---

[26] The FCDA's motion picture program involved collaboration with private industry which provided the capital, directed the films and organized their distribution; the FCDA provided information and "technical consultation." The Cold War classic "Duck and Cover" was produced through this arrangement. For a summary of media activities see FCDA, *Annual Report for 1951*, pp. 10–15; also *Annual Report for 1952*, pp. 43–49; *Annual Report for 1953*, pp. 67–77; and *Annual Report for 1954*, pp. 90–96.

training program to address public indifference and inculcate civil defense procedures as a "future way of life." Noting a dangerous heightening of military tensions with the Soviet Union, the *Project* asserts that the entire edifice of national security rests on the psychological fortitude of the civilian population. The public needs to understand that national defense today "transcends the military's ability and responsibility," and depends equally on citizens' capacity for self-help and self-protection (1952: v).

The *Project*'s findings are quickly acknowledged as the 'Bible' of civil defense. Collectively authored by Associated Universities, Inc., a Cold War think tank organized by a consortium of elite universities under contract with the Army, the *Project*'s research team includes an interdisciplinary array of sociologists, psychologists, engineers, physicists, economists, public relations personnel and educators. *Project* researchers also consult with the Psychological Strategy Board, an agency established by secret Presidential directive in 1951 and charged with the task of designing "psychological operations" – propaganda and psychological warfare planning – against enemies.[27] Although never called psychological warfare, the public information campaign outlined in the *Project* can be read as a retooling of the psychological strategies aimed at enemies abroad, now deployed for use as "emotional management techniques for psychologically manipulating" the U.S. public at home (Oakes 1994: 51). Public opinion polls, attitude surveys, in-depth interviews and personality analyses were the techniques used simultaneously to conduct psychological warfare abroad and to promote 'morale' among civilians in the U.S. (Herman 1995: 31).

And so the management of fear – avoiding the dangers of its excess (the chaos of panic), or its absence (the unpreparedness of apathy) – becomes a primary aim in constructing the ideal civilian-soldier (Oakes 1994: 62–71). In the *Project*'s plan for an informed public inoculated against the threat of mass panic, the encouragement of individual and group fear is acknowledged as

---

[27] Legally restricted to psychological affairs beyond the U.S. borders, the Psychological Strategy Board's relations to *Project East River* remained unofficial, informal, and secret. See Oakes 1994, pp. 50–51. I'm using 'psychological warfare' in the sense defined, for example, in a civil defense guide which explains: "Psychological warfare consists of activities which communicate ideas and information intended to affect the minds, emotions, and actions of people. Its purpose is to reduce [or induce] morale and the will to fight. Psychology can be used as an effective war weapon. It is often used in an attempt to soften up the citizenry, to confuse, to frighten . . . to create doubt and worry . . .," see Office of Civil Defense 1951, p. 8.

a necessary strategy. Under conditions of atomic threat, the boundary between national security and national fear is reconfigured: national security IS national fear. A nation whose civilians don't fear their own annihilation is a nation without an effective military defense system.

But by 1953, according to the picture drawn by public opinion and survey research, little has changed in the general psychology of civilian-soldiers: the public continues to be confused and psychologically distanced from the looming dangers of atomic warfare. Researchers at the University of Michigan's Survey Research Center – who start conducting government-sponsored surveys on atomic attitudes in 1946[28] – summarize their survey findings on a public uninterested in learning about the effects of atomic bombs, unaffected by conscious worry about atomic war, with unstable attitudes lacking any "logical structure" or well-developed thinking. The authors conclude that the high profile of atomic matters in the mass media and "popular fantasy," stands in stark contrast to its apparent absence in "people's conscious day-to-day thoughts." They suggest that perhaps a disavowal of anxiety is operating as a defense against intolerable feelings of fear and powerlessness in the face of the new weapons. Further research and systematic investigation are recommended (Douvan and Withy 1953: 109–111, 114–117).

Now it's 1955. The byline reads "Survival City, Nev.," and the news report narrates the highlights of the first atomic bomb dropped on a "typical" U.S. town. Part laboratory experiment, part reality, part mass-mediated spectacle, the incendiary fate of Survival City is broadcast live on CBS and NBC-TV to an estimated audience of 100 million viewers who tune in to watch the blast. The climactic televising of the explosion is preceded by two weeks of live telecasts three times daily from the test site. The town, composed of ten brick and cement houses and several prefabricated industrial buildings, is built and bombed to test the effectiveness of civil defense procedures during a simulated atomic attack. Of the 500 witnesses to the explosion in the Nevada desert, 200 are civil defense personnel. The televised test is designed to demonstrate the ferocity of atomic power, and, according to the FCDA, to bring

---

[28] Rensis Likert, director of Michigan's Survey Research Center, also directed the Morale Division of the United States Strategic Bombing Survey during World War II. The U.S.S.B.S. was a large-scale research program conducted in Germany and Japan during the final months of the war. Using a variety of techniques including survey research, the U.S.S.B.S. investigated the military, economic, social, and psychological effects of U.S. and allied bombing.

"vast numbers of Americans face to face with the enormity of the problem of survival in the nuclear age" (FCDA 1956: 6). Over 450 members of the press, including radio, television, and newsreel reporters, are stationed on "Media Hill" eight miles from ground zero. Televised interviews with the city's 'survivors' – an array of human-size mannequins placed throughout the test site – are carried out before and after the explosion (Ahlgren and Martin 1989: 26).

The alarming facts of nuclear threat and civilian survival continue in 1956 to be circulated in an array of dramatized forms, with over 22 FCDA-sponsored films available for showing on television or in schools, civic organizations, and churches. One of the films, *Operation Ivy*, documents the secret military operation carried out in the Marshall Islands on November 1, 1952, when the U.S. detonates its first hydrogen bomb, producing the largest nuclear fireball in history. The film shows the sensational atomic fireball rising up out of the sea, the shock waves rushing across the ocean surface, and the enormous mushroom cloud darkening the sky. Superimposed against the horizon of flame is a replica of Manhattan's skyline: "The fireball alone," the film narrates, "would engulf about one-quarter of the Island of Manhattan."

The public release of *Operation Ivy* is debated during a National Security Council meeting in early 1954. Discussion veers from FCDA director Val Peterson's plea for something that could "scare the American people out of their indifference," to President Eisenhower's denouncement of fear tactics and his insistence that the film be aired only if it offers "real and substantial knowledge to the people." For one reason or the other, or perhaps both, *Operation Ivy* makes its public debut on April 2, 1954, and is broadcast repeatedly over television stations throughout the day. In the media package accompanying the film's release, Peterson and the FCDA emphasize the spectacular power of the new weapon while reasserting the capacity of current civil defense strategies to absorb the new threat (Oakes 1994: 149–150).

Take Cover

"A bright line has been drawn between the civil and the savage."
– Attorney General John Ashcroft (September 21, 2001)[29]

---

[29] Quoted in *The New York Times*, 22 September 2001, p. B6.

But behind the scenes, the FCDA's assessment of the home front situation is not so sanguine. At a National Security Council meeting in January 1954, the FCDA director suggests a new strategy for testing civilians' psychological readiness for World War III. He argues for a nationwide civil defense drill that might serve as a risky but useful measure of the extent to which the U.S. public is indeed "subject to hysteria." The results of the exercise would reveal operational as well as emotional vulnerabilities in the existing civil defense infrastructure and could aid more comprehensive civil defense planning. Other Council members fear the "psychological impact" such an exercise might have, both in the U.S. and internationally, and worry over the possibility of producing a public panic (Oakes 1994: 148–149).

Ground zero is incinerated in 60 U.S. cities when 61 atomic bombs explode on their civilian targets in the early afternoon of Friday, June 15, 1955. The bombs range in explosive force from the equivalent of 20 kilotons to 5 megatons of TNT, and are delivered by air or by guided missiles launched from submarines at sea. The nationwide civil defense alert system is activated at 11:04 a.m. E.S.T., offering only a marginal advance warning of the horrific attack. By the end of the day, the massive nuclear attack on the United States kills an estimated 8 million people, injures 12 million more, destroys 6.7 million homes, and creates potentially deadly radioactive fallout conditions over approximately 63,000 square miles (FCDA 1956).

The event is called Operation Alert, a national civil defense simulation exercise designed by the FCDA in cooperation with Federal and state agencies, the White House and Cabinet members, the broadcast media, the military, organized labor, municipal governments, businesses large and small and the U.S. public. The stated goal of Operation Alert is to enhance civil defense training while testing local operational plans for attack preparedness, survival and recovery.[30] First organized in 1954, Operation Alert exercises take place each summer for the next four years. These "series of annual rehearsals for World War III," writes Cold War historian Guy Oakes, "enacted simulations

---

[30] The FCDA's concept of an 'operational plan' for local civil defense involved a "thorough analysis of items such as the most probable target area, probable damage and casualties, population distribution, industrial installations, communications, transportation systems, evacuation routes, power and water facilities, medical resources, hospitals, schools, jails, zoos, fire-fighting plans, potential assembly areas, feeding and welfare facilities, topography, prevailing winds, possible shelters, and many other items." The FCDA encouraged the development of such plans in all of the over 180 critical target areas in the U.S. See FCDA, *Annual Report for Fiscal Year 1956*, pp. 27–28.

of a nuclear attack in an elaborate national sociodrama that combined elements of mobilization for war, disaster relief, the church social, summer camp and the county fair" (1994: 84).

The FCDA's carefully planned protocols for Operation Alert direct each participating city to play out its assigned civil defense scenario as realistically as possible. During the three-day exercise in 1955, over 80 U.S. cities carry out some form of public evacuation: sixty-two cities simulate the action on paper, while another 18 conduct actual evacuations, involving at least 117,000 people. In Memphis, Tennessee, an estimated 25,000 people are evacuated from downtown office buildings. In Atlanta, Georgia, 3,500 government officials are evacuated, with 2,000 of them transported outside the city, registered and fed lunch. In Youngstown, Ohio, the entire city, led by the Mayor, evacuates. At the center of the deserted city, "adding realism to the exercise," the 554th Explosive Ordnance Detachment detonates a mock bomb (FCDA 1956).

But the climactic moment of the 1955 Operation Alert exercise is the three-day evacuation of President Eisenhower, his Cabinet, and 15,000 Federal employees to 31 undisclosed locations outside Washington, D.C. Situated somewhere in the mountains of Virginia, the secret emergency headquarters of the President become the preserve of operational continuity for the State after the nuclear obliteration of the nation's capital. Seated inside a makeshift tent before a microphone, President Eisenhower addresses the nation in a live television broadcast announcing the (simulated) nuclear emergency and the continuing survival of the nation.

The televised Presidential address is the culmination of a sophisticated, well-planned public relations and press campaign launched some six weeks before the Operation Alert exercise. The White House and FCDA coordinators of the press coverage, desiring extensive media attention for the event but also strict control of its contents, meet with executives from the broadcast industries well in advance of the simulated attack. A round-the-clock media center with the sole purpose of generating and controlling public information about Operation Alert is established in Richmond, Virginia, and equipped with state-of-the-art communications technologies for the crowds of reporters who arrive to cover the event (Oakes 1994: 86–89).

"Although the [Operation Alert] exercise showed the Nation unprepared to cope with a thermonuclear attack," the FCDA reports, "it concentrated the attention of the Nation on civil defense . . ." (1955: 35–37). Encouraged by the

concentrated attention they excite, Operation Alert exercises in each succes-
sive year grow more complex and ambitious. Each year, FCDA planners try
to design a more systematic, fully rationalized plan of action in response to
increasingly savage and extensive imaginary attacks. Searching for an ever
closer fit between simulated event and actual atomic invasion, the psychological theater of civil defense presses the borders of (im)possible terrors in
the interests of improved safety and efficient survival.

After a Cabinet-level evaluation of Operation Alert in 1956, concern is
expressed over how the exercises are affecting public attitudes. President
Eisenhower calls for a blue ribbon panel of social scientists to convene and
conduct a "thoroughgoing study of the effect on human attitudes of nuclear
weapons." The top-secret report is delivered to the President in November
1956. The panel of experts speaks in a chorus of collective bafflement. They
suppose that people are frightened by the dangers of atomic weapons and
desire to avoid war. But they are unable to report with any certainty what
the new weapons really mean to the U.S. public (Weart 1988: 135–136).

In a cabinet discussion held during the course of the extended Operation
Alert exercises in 1957, Secretary of Defense Charles Wilson reports that, due
to the realistic simulation of emergency government activities over a period
of several weeks, "people were panic stricken in large cities and were paying no attention to Government orders." Any solution to the problem of panic
risks exacerbating the potentially explosive mix of the real and the unreal
composing the elaborate sociodrama of Operation Alert: presuming the panic
is due to people's confusion over the reality of the simulated emergency operations, a statement by President Eisenhower clarifying the simulated nature
of the operations might calm the public, but be mistakenly interpreted by the
Soviets as a sign of real preparations for war, thereby touching off a defensive Soviet nuclear offensive. The fake civil defense drill, creating an actual
panic, could then explode into a real war caused by the simulated preparations to defend against it (Oakes 1994: 151).

With the real and the imaginary, the savage attack and the civil defense,
survival and extermination, terror and television, and war and its bureaucratic simulation imploding around the heads of U.S. civilian-soldiers throughout the 1950s, what historical sense to make of this psychological battleground?
Vertiginous efforts to regulate civilian psychology in the name of national
security become institutionalized, everyday concerns among workers in both
military and civilian government agencies, the university and the mass media.

The partial history I offer here of a domestic war for civilian psyches, compelled by World War II and Cold War technological and political imperatives, suggests that a militarization of psychology has been a self-conscious goal and official aim of U.S. policy for quite some time. And the shape of that militarization, the perceptions and affects promoted by such policies, has not been only about seeding blind aggression or violent arrogance in dominant U.S. culture. Militarizing civilian psyches involves the strategic deployment of fear, a considered risk of panic and terror and a productive construction of intense vulnerability and insecurity. Perhaps most maddeningly, a militarized civilian psyche is faced with a government which, while avowing its commitment to a secure national defense, at the same time wants you to know that it may not be able to protect you at all.[31]

Let's Face It

"We're going to start asking a lot of questions that heretofore have not been asked."

– George W. Bush (October 30, 2001)[32]

"What role will we assume in the historical relay of violence, who will we become in the response, and will we be furthering or impeding violence by virtue of the response that we make?"

– Judith Butler (January 2002)[33]

"Every American is a soldier" – a declaration of psychic and social fortitude announced in the absent shadow of two pillars of world trade, near the cold ashes of the nerve center of U.S. military planning and power. The militarization of inner space that such a proclamation incites and enforces is part of a history of imaginary and real constructions of the ideal U.S. civilian-soldier. Full Spectrum Dominance and its ambition to link a hegemonic multi-

---

[31] See McEnaney 2000, pp. 37–39, 53–62, for a discussion of the discourse of 'self-help' promoted by Cold War civil defense planners as they downloaded responsibility for atomic survival from the bureaucratic state to the individual and family, transforming Cold War militarization into a personal responsibility.

[32] Quoted in *The New York Times*, 30 October 2001, p. B5, in caption to photo of first meeting of the Homeland Security Council.

[33] Judith Butler, "Explanation and Exoneration, or What We Can Hear." *Theory & Event* 5, no. 4 (January 2002), e-journal at http://muse.jhu.edu/demo/theory_event/5.4butler.html, paragraph #19.

dimensional U.S. military superiority with a global economic reach, can only be built within the psychological space of a population that produces the violence demanded by such a blind, visionary conjuring of the future. The so-called 'war against terrorism' takes its place within a historical theater of cultural wars over de/militarized psychic zones.

But in the current cultural war, what role can really be played by Cold War histories of state-sponsored fear and disoriented publics? What difference does it make to know that once upon a time the U.S. government built and bombed suburban-style houses and their plastic inhabitants, ensuring the fall-out included live T.V. broadcasts from ground zero and social science surveys of public opinion before and after the blast? Does a history of the present cross paths with a theory of politics that would tell us where to go from here, after having once been there?

"A military Babel has risen out of nuclear proliferation and generalized terrorism," writes contemporary theorist and historian of war, Paul Virilio, "we're disoriented and can no longer find our way, not even in our theoretical work" (1999: 97). That was in 1999. The 'we' Virilio invokes may not include all of you. But some of us, well before September 11, 2001, lost our way in the proliferation of real and perceived terrors – and in the difficulty of confidently deciding the border between them. For me, making histories out of not-so-private memories is one way to be lost without losing my mind. For me, making histories of panic and terror is one way to participate, however crazily, in contemporary cultural wars over whether and how psychic spaces will be militarized. Today, for me, it is not surprising to hear Patricia Williams, a "mad" law professor,[34] describe the U.S. war on terrorism as a *"war of the mind*, so broadly defined that the enemy becomes anybody who makes us afraid" (2001). I know that war. I've been there before. Its casualties are never precisely calculated and the archive of its psychic and political effects is always poorly kept.

To historicize, as I try to do here, the call to psychic arms implied in George Bush's appeal to civilian "soldiers" and to track how the psychology of U.S. civilian populations became an explicit target of the national security state and its civilian institutions, is to incite public memories in the place of privatized terrors. There is no exact historical origin or parallel to the present *war of the mind*, and no easy causal accumulation of effects between the Cold

---

[34] Williams writes a column for *The Nation* called "Diary of a Mad Law Professor."

War manipulations of nuclear terror that I recall here, and the 'war against terrorism' today. The widespread anti-war feelings and politics in the U.S. in the final years of the Vietnam war, and the uneven attempts to re-militarize civilian psyches after the mostly unspeakable reality of that military defeat, are relevant to any full accounting of how psychological militarization works, or fails, or tries again.[35] But my task here is both more modest and more urgent: to find compelling psychic weapons – in the form of collective memories – with which to fight a militarization of inner spaces today.

In the aftermath of the 1991 U.S.-led war against Iraq, Thyrza Goodeve wrote that "[m]aking connections, . . . thickening the present with future visions and past complexities, forcing edges to rub up against and through their rough boundaries" was one kind of "critical survival strategy" for progressive politics under siege (1992: 53). So what does the present look like when connected to past state and media-sponsored spectacles of terror?

On Friday, April 12, 2002, an airplane buzzes McAlester, Oklahoma, covering the city with a fine spray containing pneumonic plague. The simulated bioterrorist attack infects 95 percent of the city's population. By Saturday afternoon, 120 people are dead. On the ground in McAlester, real doctors begin handing out 10,000 packets of imaginary medicine, while 700 volunteers administer fake antibiotics around the city. Local Boy Scouts, playing the role of plague-infected civilians, are rushed to the hospital or driven to the morgue. The April 2002 exercise is a follow-up to a simulation conducted at Andrews Air Force base in the (pre-September 11) summer of 2001 when officials "pretended that Iraqi-financed Afghan terrorists were spraying the smallpox virus into shopping centers in Oklahoma City, Philadelphia and Atlanta."[36]

"Seattle, May 12" the byline reads, and the news article reports at least 150 casualties when a 'dirty bomb' packed with radioactive agents explodes in an industrial area of south Seattle in the spring of 2003. "Plumes of toxic smoke fill the air for miles as firefighters in protective chemical suits milled

---

[35] See Turner 1996, pp. 83–95 for an account of the psychological politics of re-militarizing, and re-masculinizing, civilians as soldier 'heroes' in the wake of the U.S. defeat in Vietnam. See also Ronnell 1992 for a critical psychoanalytically-inflected deconstruction of the 1991 war against Iraq as a "healing" war to repair the wounds of what became called the "Vietnam war syndrome."

[36] See "Three-Day Bioterrorism Drill Begins in an Oklahoma Town" in *The New York Times*, 13 April 2002, p. A11.

through the scene . . . where overturned buses, police cars and fire engines could be seen, fake victims wandered in a daze, car fires smoldered and a few news helicopters flew overhead in the most extensive terrorism response training in the nation's history," reads the giddy report from ground zero.[37] Organized by the Department of Homeland Security at a cost of $16 million and prepared for over an 18-month period, the simulated terrorist attack involves 8,500 medical, police, fire, rescue and other personnel nationwide. It is to be followed the next day by a covert biological attack on Chicago, where volunteer victims will start to arrive in city hospitals with flulike symptoms consistent with pneumonic plague.

Manipulating the borders of the real and the imaginary, the present and the future – these are not new tactics in the battle to militarize civilian minds. If the militarization of inner space involves a *strategic set of psychological border operations*, then collectively remembering Cold War events like Operation Alert may help us recognize how these borders are once again battlefields inhabited by well-planned theaters of terror and its control, theaters extended by the mass media into the everyday lives of millions of people. Imploding a possibly horrific future into the tremulous present, radically confusing the real with a tightly choreographed imaginary of catastrophe – these forms of state-sponsored spectacle networked through channels of mass communication can be read as domestic psychological warfare. A public memory that such spectacles have been used historically to promote a politically productive fear may offer U.S. civilians one kind of psychological border defense against these mass mediated attacks.

For all the disturbing resonances, increasingly noted by contemporary critics, there is of course no simple correspondence between 1950s Cold War culture and today. Both moments involve a transition in the image of the 'enemy': from fascism to Communism in the early years of the Cold War, and from Communism to terrorism today. Both moments see the intensification of authoritarian and repressive domestic politics in the name of routing an enemy who has infiltrated national borders and resides 'inside' as well as 'outside' the United States.[38] But today's so-called 'war on terrorism' was launched in

---

[37] Sarah Kershaw, "Terror Scenes Follow Script of No More 9/11's" in *The New York Times*, 13 May 2003, p. A21.
[38] For one example of an analysis of the "eerie resonance" between dominant Cold War culture and today, see Robin 2002.

the wake of an unprecedented attack on U.S. civilian and military targets on September 11, 2001. The context in which a militarization of inner space is taking place today includes – in a dramatic difference from the Cold War – the psychological relations to violent injury and mass death experienced 'inside' the U.S. borders.

One remarkable feature of the militarization of inner space in the post-September 11 United States is how the language of psychology itself, of emotional and 'inner' experience, was quickly deployed in public discourse about the attack and its aftermath. A reductive, repetitive discourse of trauma, healing, and recovery displaced the complicated realities of violence and war, of historical and political conflict.[39] A kind of "therapeutic patriotism," mixing political authority and the authority of T.V. news networks, emerged almost immediately in the days and weeks after September 11, as the mass media addressed issues like how to talk to your children, how to manage stress, and how to express grief and mourning and begin the emotional work of healing (Aufderheide 2002). A university-wide memo circulated on September 12 at the institution where I teach noted that we were "in the midst of dealing with an incredibly traumatic event" and that all of us would be "part of the healing experience for each other." Practical antidotes to symptoms of stress were offered: strenuous physical exercise, soothing music, or keeping as busy as possible. Representative Jim McDermott, a psychiatrist, used a meeting of House Democrats in late September 2001 to explain the symptoms of post-traumatic stress disorder and suggest that he, many of his colleagues, and much of the country were probably suffering from it.[40] While the attacks on September 11 were undoubtedly traumatic, the consequences of public and personal discourse that limits that trauma to 'psychology' alone are deeply disturbing.

The contradiction here is clear: when a highly, historically militarized U.S. civilian population encounters violence against it produced by others, it has nothing but a psychologized language of inner experience to understand that violence. Many civilian-soldiers today experience the trauma of

---

[39] This aspect of the post-September 11 political landscape was immediately and incisively critique in a public statement co-authored by Paoloa Bacchetta, Tina Campt, Inderpal Grewal, Caren Kaplan, Minoo Moallem, and Jennifer Terry, "Transnational Feminist Practices Against War," later published in *Meridians: Feminism, Race, Transnationalism* 2, no. 2 (Spring 2002: 302–8).

[40] "The Psychiatrist in the House Feels the Nation's Trauma," *The New York Times*, 1 October 2001, p. A16.

September 11 without any recourse to historical or political understandings of the very violence 'we' are now asked to produce in response. As feminist theorist Laura Kipnis writes (of the political scene prior to September 11), "[W]ith trauma narratives in one sphere occluding historical consciousness in the other, it seems all the more likely that repetition and amnesia are to triumph and prevail as the identificatory modes of citizenship, rolling out the red carpet for creepy political forms . . ." (1999: 72). With objects of terror and fear defined in primarily non-political terms, a kind of antipolitics of fear emerges that threatens to erase the politics of globalization, the politics of oil, the politics of Palestine and Israel, or the politics of a Cold War that played out in many non-Western countries, including Afghanistan, Iran and Iraq. The "creepy political forms" that Kipnis warns against appear to have arrived. They include a militarization of psychic space that rests in part on an experience of violence as a strictly psychological event. The psychological organization of civilian society for the production of violence – the aim of a successful militarization of civilian psyches – proceeds today, it seems, by effectively amputating the psychological experience of traumatizing injury from issues of power or history. This may be one militarized consequence of 'therapeutic culture' or the 'therapeutic state,' theorized since the 1960s as a new formation of power in which cultural and political authority is wielded by appeal to the 'psychology' of the individual. But, even more ominously, therapeutic culture itself may be one effect of the rise of the national security state and a Cold War obsession with U.S. civilian psychology as a military playing field.[41]

Finally, perhaps most importantly, efforts to militarize post-September 11 civilian psyches lean heavily on a coded politics of meaning. If militarization always depends on the successful construction of confident borders between an evil 'them' and a good 'us,' then 'we' must notice the particular kind of border work being done today by the word 'terrorism' itself. 'Terrorism' does not only name and condemn specific acts, it also promotes a specific kind of psychological relationship. The word encodes a set of psychological meanings; it not only names but performs a form of self-other relationship. "As a

---

[41] Ellen Herman's history of the post-WWII rise of psychology as an expert and popular discourse provides the best evidence of the possible military origins of 'therapeutic culture' (though this is not a term she uses). For a recent discussion of the therapeutic state and the U.S. military see Nolan 1998, pp. 280–282.

boundary marker, the terrorist at once unsettles and stabilizes, filling a position recently vacated by the Communist in a post-Cold War era," writes Lon Troyer (2002). The unsettling threat of the 'terrorist' as radically outside cultural intelligibility and beyond moral understanding, secures for the presumably 'non-terrorist' self its own moral grounding and cultural membership. The 'terrorist' is grotesquely, yet gratifyingly, 'other.'

The historical fact that the 20th century usage of the word 'terrorism' emerged in the violent ambiguities of colonial occupation – in the violation of national, racial, ethnic, cultural, sexual, religious, linguistic, economic, and psychological borders – is not coincidental. Used, for example, by French colonial forces in the 1950s to name strategies of violent struggle by Algerian guerillas against French domination, 'terrorism' became a way to police forms of violence conducted without recourse to nationalized armies or centralized military command.[42] 'Terrorism' became a name for the violence deployed by people operating at an enormous military disadvantage, outside the boundaries of a mutually agreed upon battlefield. 'Terrorism' stages the theater of war, by force and of necessity, inside the realms of everyday life and everyday imagination and everyday fear.

But the purportedly distinguishing features of 'terrorism' – that civilians are the direct target of attack, and that the attacks are designed to create extreme fear and terror in the broader population – are, as I have tried to show here, a routinely practiced and planned-for feature of 20th century warfare. No, the difference between 'terrorism' and other forms of violence lies elsewhere. 'Terrorists' are a species of civilian-soldier who could not exist without the psychological and historical disavowal by other civilian-soldiers who refuse to remember that the boundary between civilian and military and between lethal violence and everyday life has been breached and is bleeding into almost every psyche, every 21st century civilian-soldier's nightmare of domination or sweet dream of social justice. The boundary that the word 'terrorist' really draws is between some civilian-soldiers and certain other civilian-soldiers. Historically, it is often a racialized boundary, sedimented with

---

[42] My thanks to Troy Duster who circulated his unpublished essay, "From Theater of War to Terrorism," after the attacks on September 11. Written in 1986, his overview of "the historical evolution of the very concept of contemporary terrorism," and the links between 20th century colonial battles and 'terrorism', set much of my thinking here in motion. The essay is now available online at http://www.hereinstead.com/systmpl/htmlpage13/.

histories of colonization, and economic and symbolic exploitation. Currently in the U.S., it is a racialized name used against some civilian-soldiers by other civilian-soldiers who refuse recognition of our own historical and contemporary role in the military manufacture of everyday violence. It is a name used today to mobilize and militarize U.S. civilian psychology for the production of continued, intensified violence – often against other civilians. It is a name used to describe an Iraqi citizen armed with a Kalishnakov rifle whose bullets bounce off the armored skin of a 65-ton U.S. Abrams battle tank rolling through the bombed-out streets of Fallujah. It is a word that promotes violence across unacknowledged borders, in the name of borders that don't exist. It is a secret coded message sending covert psychological instructions through political and historical, ambiguous and bloody networks of terror and fear.

Are we all soldiers now?

Were we all soldiers before?

Are we all terrorists now?

Have we all been terrorists before?

Today, 'we' must be attentive and resistant to the variety of border patrols being deployed to sustain the imaginary, as well as the material, violence of 'our' not-so-united-(psychic)-states. Historically speaking, the U.S. civilian-soldier was primarily a white man or woman who lived in a house with a relatively steady income. The complexities of the militarization of psychic space are now being lived out daily – it remains to be seen what difference racial, gender, and class differences can make in the refusal of 'our' role as loyal psychic soldiers. The cultural battle today to construct forms of 'we' that will not submit 'our' inner space to the demands of an ongoing production of violence, to a militarization of everyday life and feeling, is just that, a battle. How to practice other everyday forms of emotional and political collectivity, how to make and to feel other meanings of 'we,' is today a psychological struggle with enormous military consequences.

Charlotte Ryan

It Takes a Movement to Raise an Issue: Media Lessons from the 1997 U.P.S. Strike*

In 1997, 185,000 members of the International Brotherhood of Teamsters (IBT) led by reform president Ron Carey struck for fifteen days against United Parcel Service (U.P.S.). Making treatment of part-time workers a central issue, the Teamsters won 10,000 additional full-time jobs with benefits. They also won substantial raises and maintained the union's control of pension funds.[1] What's more, the strike galvanized national interest in the quality of life of working America. Analysts labeled the strike "'the first . . . in many years where the public has been overwhelmingly supportive of the striker.'"[2] As such, the strike represented a historical victory for social movement unionism, a reform trend promoted by many American labor activists.

"There is nothing natural about the ability to organize successfully," cautions social movement scholar, William A. Gamson upon surveying American social protest strategies across two centuries (Gamson 1975: 57). Nor is there anything natural about the ability to draw lessons from successful organizing. With

* An earlier version of this essay appeared in *Critical Sociology*, vol. 30, no. 2 (2004).

[1] International Brotherhood of Teamsters, "Half a Job is Not Enough," *IBT Research Department*, June 1997 and "Sorting It Out: What They Wanted, What They Got," *The New York Times*, August 20, 1997, p. A22.

[2] Tarpinian quoted in Adam Nagoursky, "In strike battle, teamsters use political tack," *The New York Times,* August 19, 1997, p. A1.

the intention of distilling such lessons, this paper recaps and reflects on the mass media component of the communications strategies[3] employed by the International Brotherhood of Teamsters (IBT) in the 1997 U.P.S. strike. I first review the theoretical concepts used in this paper. I next sketch the historical context attending to two interacting developments – the decline of organized labor in the late 20th century and the growing power of corporate mass media. In that context, I present the prehistory of the 1997 U.P.S. strike, the rise of social movement unionism focusing on the rise of Teamsters for a Democratic Union (TDU), and the election of TDU-supported Ron Carey as Teamster president. After a brief methodological section, I chronicle the Teamsters' communication strategies including pre-strike preparations and output during the strike. From the Teamsters' effective application of movement-building strategies to the media arena, I suggest more general lessons regarding social movements and media opportunities.

Theoretical Concepts

In sociologists' proverbial seesaw between structure and agency, strategy is the fulcrum. Rooted in the Greek word for generalship (strategia), the concept of strategy makes most sense when applied to a unit of analysis greater than the individual. While individuals can position themselves to maximize their power *within* existing structures, individuals can rarely mobilize sufficient resources to launch structural challenges. Efforts to challenge power relations in political, economic or media institutions, therefore, generally presuppose one or more collective actors composed of individuals working in concert – sharing grievances, world view, analysis, identity and resources. Collaborative efforts are even more critical when the collective actors represent marginalized social locations. Typically, marginalized challengers must address multiple structural inequalities – race/ethnicity, class, colonialisms past and present, gender, sexuality, age, language, etc.

Strategizing in the service of a marginalized constituency, collective actors evaluate existing historical conditions then position their forces (their base, allies, networks) and resources (financial, political, social, and cultural) to

---

[3] In communication strategies, I include all efforts to communicate with relevant audiences from the most direct (1–1 conversations, meetings) to flyers and in-house publication to mass media. This paper focuses primarily on the union's effort to intervene in the arenas offered by mass media, specifically, print media.

best advantage. Their goal is to weaken their opposition while expanding their forces' influence. Working under conditions not of their own making, they fully know that their challenges to existing power arrangements may stall in the face of "the material reality of oppression."[4] Strategic choice (Jasper 2004) involves identifying opportunities that play to strategists' strengths while minimizing disadvantages.

Speaking from the Chilean experience, sociologist Marta Harnacker (1974) conceptualizes strategic positioning as the conjuncture of social forces, 'la coyuntura de fuerzas.'[5] Harnacker's focus on conjuncture embeds actors in historical relationships located in specific spaces and times, while her emphasis on forces promotes attention to *collective* actors – intentional subjects, hegemonic and counter-hegemonic, who mobilize for or against other social forces, arrangements and practices. This approach avoids the recurring determinism that results from analyses that primarily question how existing structures or cultural formations reproduce inequality.

Strategic challenges entail careful long-term planning. Victory for the marginalized challenger – labor in this case – rests on overcoming structural barriers to change with available resources. When strategists misestimate the match, the social-movement challenge results, at best, in glorious failures. More commonly, collective actors plan limited challenges reaping modest results – reforms in political science parlance. Should the strategist mount repeated skirmishes that accrue and undermine existing structural inequalities, social movements expand.

Strategists may vary their approaches dramatically to match the conditions within specific institutional arenas (Rucht 1988). A winning strategy in one political, economic, social or cultural arena may not work in another. Thus, strategists concretely analyze the conditions in each arena at a given historical conjuncture before deciding how to move their players.[6] To better incorporate agency in metaphors that have stressed structural conditions, Jasper (2004) conceptualizes this process as one of "strategic choices" a phrase that echoes Raymond Williams' phase "options under pressure" (Williams in Wood

---

[4] Sharon Kurtz, personal correspondence.
[5] Harnacker's concept, "coyuntura de fuerzas," (1974) was popularized in social theory primers (cuadernitos) that influenced Latin American social movements where activists routinely discuss 'la coyuntura politica.'
[6] For an exceptional historical treatment of labor strategies, see Kimmeldorf 1999.

1996: 106). Anthropologist Sherry Ortner treads similar ground when she describes agency as skilful play within a rule-bound game:

> Social life is precisely social, consisting of webs of relationship and inter-action between multiple, shiftingly interrelated subject positions, none of which can be extracted as autonomous 'agents': and yet at the same time there is 'agency', that is, actors can play with skill, intention, wit, knowl-edge, intelligence (Ortner 1996: 12).

Extending the game metaphor, Ortner (1996) adds, "There is never only one game;" her notion of game parallels Rucht's concept of institutional arena. This study watches two interacting games – mass media as a critical public arena for the game of public discourse, and labor negotiations as a critical economic arena pitting the favored player, the trucking/delivery industry against a feisty challenger, the Teamster union representing U.P.S. workers.

At the turn of the 20th century, U.S. corporate mass media form a "mas-ter forum" – "*the* major site of contest politically, in part because all of the would-be or actual sponsors of meaning – be they authorities, members or challengers – *assume* pervasive influence" (Gamson 1998: 59 emphasis in orig-inal). As with other arenas, the mass media simultaneously interact with exist-ing socio-economic systems while maintaining their own rules, cultures, logics and market imperatives (McChesney, Croteau and Hoynes 1994, 2001, Herman and McChesney 1997). Media strategists position themselves for best advan-tage within media games embedded in a broader political and economic con-text. In planning media strategy, collective actors (within their capacity) first assess the media arena as a whole – the key institutions, their role in specific media markets,[7] and the conjunctures and tensions between governmental communications policies and business initiatives. Strategists also consider journalistic norms that shape reporters' newsgathering practices.

To negotiate access to mass media, social movement actors must maneu-ver within the news norms and routines. For instance, they must accommo-date reportorial deadlines and make a case for their story ideas within the conventions of mainstream news criteria; mainstream news stories typically are about power, understood as the actions of political leaders and other elites, about proximate events such as the weather, traffic, or flu season, and/or about the unexpected in daily life, be it humorous or tragic.[8] In initiating

---

[7] Market researchers divide the U.S. into more than 200 media markets.
[8] I describe the particular news norms governing labor coverage in detail below.

strategic challenges to existing media arrangements, collective actors use existing small opportunities provided by these news norms to build toward larger ones. Whether, when and how to tackle existing media institutions depends on the collective actor, its mission and its existing media capacity and media standing.

Media capacity – the ability to function within the news conventions of mainstream mass media[9] – varies over time and by constituency. Marginalized groups may increase their media capacity as they acquire more resources, organizational strength, popular support, etc. Media standing – the recognition by reporters of an institution or collective actor's value as a source – also can rise or fall. Thus, collective actors must evaluate their current situation to decide whether they might benefit from strategic interventions in mass media. Opportunities useful to one challenger may be inaccessible to another. Generally, national challenges require more resources than local challenges, and challenges launched without media capacity and without media standing take longer than challenges launched by actors with media capacity and standing.

In selecting a strategy, challengers must steer between under-determination and over-determination. Under-determined approaches underemphasize the formidable barriers to mass media access; knowing how to write a press release does not suffice. Communications campaigns are labor–intensive. In addition to technical skill, they require time, money, experience and relations with journalists. Over-determined approaches lean heavily on analyses of media power structures noting consolidation of ownership, overlapping boards of directorates, etc. These can obscure possibilities for social movements to communicate with broader audiences via mass media.

Despite the constraints of a market-driven mass media system, collective actors can develop and execute media strategies that expand opportunities to communicate with the large audiences dependent on mass media for information. Whether the collective actors take advantage of these narrow openings and inconsistencies in the media system depends on the conjuncture of forces – the fit between the existing power relations and the collective

---

[9] Many movements have exceptionally developed capacity to communicate via direct media – their own newsletters, websites, publications, and via alternative and opposition media. Here I concentrate on media capacity vis-à-vis corporate controlled media operating within the 200 media markets that cover the U.S.

actor – its goals, positioning, strategic and tactical skills and other strengths. The case that follows describes a collective actor, the International Brotherhood of Teamsters, executing a successful media strategy in a specific historical conjuncture – the 1997 United Parcel Service (U.P.S.) strike.

Historical Context – Organized Labor in the United States

The United States has one of the lowest union densities of any developed capitalist economy but this was not always the case. Following World War II, organized labor in the United States was on the offensive; it won 89% of nearly five thousand National Labor Relations Board (NLRB) elections bringing over a million workers into unions (Goldfield 1987: xiii). The 1947 passage of the anti-labor Taft-Hartley Act in 1947 and the purging of radicals from the Congress of Industrial Organizations (CIO) chilled union militancy, and by 1954, union density began a steady decline from 34% to less than 14% of the workforce.[10]

Many factors contributed to organized labor's dramatic decline.[11] On a political level, McCarthy-era witch-hunts coupled with the 1950s "social contract" between U.S. labor and capital creating an alliance from which American workers initially profited. Globalization theorists, however, note that the social contract left American labor ill-prepared when US corporations intensified their internationalization in the 1970s through strategic use of "plant closings, concession bargaining, union busting, export of jobs abroad, and mass layoffs" (Nissen 1999: 241). A complacent AFL-CIO leadership did not keep pace with the shifting demographics of a work force of women, immigrants, and workers of color largely concentrated in the service sector (Craver 1993: 38–39). Corporations increased aggressive anti-union activity (Freeman 1989: 118), and the decentralized trade union leaders countered nationally coordinated corporate union busting with difficulty (Freeman 1989). Weakened, organized labor lost political ground; it could not kill right-to-work laws and lost more influence as the NLRB made union elections harder to win (Tilly 1996).

---

[10] AFL-CIO, "The Union Difference; Fast Facts on Union Membership and Pay," *AFL-CIO Department of Public Policy*, 1998, Publication No. R1–292–398–10, p. 16. In states with right-to-work laws – most of the South and Southwest – the percentage falls to 7.6%.

[11] In this analysis, I draw on three literatures – labor history, communications studies and social movement theory.

The resulting membership decline sparked a vicious cycle; with fewer members, a weakened organized labor sector wielded less political clout and therefore, could not pass legislation to support union organizing, to address runaway industries, loss of net income, lengthening of the work week, the increase in contingent work (Craver 1999), and the related loss of leisure (Schor 1992).

Taking advantage of the mood set by the Civil Rights and anti-war movements, activists began to challenge labor's decline in the 1960s. Symbolic of this change was the American Federation of State, County and Municipal Employees (AFSCME) 1968 strike of municipal garbage workers in Memphis, Tennessee supported wholeheartedly by the Southern Christian Leadership Conference (SCLC). The Mineworkers' Safety Act passed in the aftermath of the 1969 Mineworkers' Black Lung strike and the 1970 Occupational Safety and Health Act were both rank-and-file supported campaigns.

Although rank-and-file activism grew in the 1970s, labor lost economic power as industries globalized, incorporated labor-reducing new technologies, and stepped up anti-union campaigns. With the 1980 election of Ronald Reagan, labor's political power dropped. The Reagan government provided corporations both tacit and explicit support for corporate anti-labor activity, the gutting of the NLRB's mediation functions being a prime example.

These defeats notwithstanding, labor activists continued to develop a new organizing model. A 1988 AFL-CIO national teleconference contrasted an *organizing model* of unionism in which union leadership routinely attends to mobilization to a narrowly conceived *servicing model* in which mobilization is left for elections, contracts or crises (Muehlenkamp 1991). The 1990s continued the revitalization of labor organizing as unions worked to refine their organizing models. (Labor Research Review 1991, Bronfenbrenner and Juravich 1998, Eisenscher 1996, Fletcher and Hurd 1998, Tillman and Cummings 1999.) Also called "social movement unionism," the approach reflected the changing composition of the American workforce and drew vital lessons from the Civil Rights and women's movements (Gooding and Casavant 1997, Kurtz 2002). Social movement unionism stressed strategic organizing, internal union democracy, cross-constituency coalition building and worldviews that extend beyond direct self-interest:

> In social movement unionism neither the unions nor their members are passive in any sense. Unions take an active lead in the streets, as well as in politics. They ally with other social movements, but provide a class vision

and content . . . That content is not simply the demands of the movements, but the activation of the mass of union members as leaders. . . . Social movement unionism implies an active strategic orientation (Moody 1997: 276).

Part of this transformation was Teamsters for a Democratic Union, the rank-and-file reform movement within the International Brotherhood of Teamsters (IBT). The IBT grew after World War II with the new interstate highway system on which the U.S. trucking industry depended. In 1957, taking advantage of the union's decentralized structure, newly elected Teamster President Jimmy Hoffa centralized control of Teamster elections, contract negotiations and pension funds (La Botz 1990). Expelled from the AFL-CIO in 1957, the Teamsters union became a household synonym for corruption and coercion; the Hoffa administration consorted with organized crime; rigged elections; and crushed dissent (Moody 1988).

By 1976, reform-oriented Teamsters after many local skirmishes united to form Teamsters for a Democratic Union (TDU); fighting for internal democracy and better contracts, TDU garnered a reputation for sober, forward-looking analyses of the trucking industry. TDU's efforts to reform the union's undemocratic by-laws also prepared rank-and-file leaders to challenge the existing national leadership. In the face of violent opposition, TDU worked for almost two decades to establish by-law reform and organizing networks needed to challenge national leadership (La Botz 1990). In 1989, a TDU-influenced court order mandated changes in the Teamster constitutions to ensure fair and democratic elections. In 1994, TDU efforts bore fruit with the election of reform candidate, Ron Carey, a former United Parcel Service (U.P.S.) worker and president of a 7000-strong New York City local.

The Teamsters union had long represented United Parcel Service workers and U.P.S. workers' own reform movement, UPSurge, played a powerful role in the establishment of TDU. The victory of Carey and the social union agenda he and TDU represented created a springboard for U.P.S. workers to organize the national strike of 1997. The second favorable shift in political opportunity came with the appointment of a sympathetic Secretary of Labor by the Clinton Administration in 1996. Clinton's first Secretary of Labor, Robert Reich, criticized the use of contingent labor, and his replacement, Alexis Herman, played a role in the U.P.S. strike.

Historical Context – The Mass Media and Social Contests

No media campaign succeeds without sponsorship (Gamson 1993), but not all message sponsors are equal in the eyes of a corporate media intent on expanding profitability and market share. Half to two-thirds of all U.S. news stories come from government sources. Public relations firms, primarily working for corporate clients shuttle another 40–50% of stories to newsrooms (Nimmo and Combs 1983: 24). Such insider sponsors have crucial advantages: plentiful resources and contacts; messages that reinforce rather than question accepted values; and organizational cultures well suited to the news-making practices of mainstream media outlets (Ryan 1991). Media outlets, explains economist and long-time media critic Edward Herman, marginalize labor not by conspiracy but by the combined power of

> industry structure, common sources, ideology, patriotism, and the power of the government and top media sources to define newsworthiness and frameworks of discourse. Self-censorship, market forces, and the norms of news practices may produce and maintain a particular viewpoint as effectively as formal state censorship (Herman 1985: 89).

Organized labor, despite its considerable resources, generally approaches the institutional arena of mainstream media as an outsider. The constraints are many but can be lumped in three categories – market imperatives, news norms and routines and cultural/ideological assumptions *about* workers and unions and *by* workers and unions.

Market Imperatives

As businesses in a free-market economy, mainstream media operations make money by expanding market share, targeting the most desirable market segments – those mostly likely to consume advertisers' products – while trimming other production costs, especially labor. Editors assign reporters to beats serving lucrative market segments and cut beats serving smaller and less lucrative market niches.

Labor reporting has particularly suffered in an advertising-driven media system. With only 13% of 100 million US workers unionized, editors have cut the once common labor beat replacing it with workplace beats geared to upscale professionals (Mort 1992: 81).

James Warren, former labor reporter for the *Chicago Tribune*, concludes that Business Page coverage of labor is inadequate: "Business editors have a skewed view on these stories and the business section tends to be a bulletin board for corporate America" (Tasini 1990: 7).

News Norms and Routines

News norms are reporters' routine ways to produce stories fast daily, standardized routines for gathering facts, identifying reliable sources, etc. In their schooling and on the job, reporters learn that it is more cost-effective and professionally advantageous to go along with existing norms. The effects on labor are multiple.

Mainstream news norms adopt the point of view of investors, management and consumers, investors, or management but rarely that of labor (Croteau and Hoynes 1994). With the labor beat a professional dead end, reporters rarely explore working-class American life critically. That public broadcasting is similarly limited may come as more of a surprise (Croteau, Hoynes and Carragee 1994). Other studies describe labor reporting as sporadic and focused on conflict (Hartman 1979). Media's tendency to cover labor only during strikes and work conflicts reinforces labor's image as combative. Finally, media fails to cover labor in the context of a shifting global economy. More commonly, journalists treat stories about unemployment rates, public education, welfare, crime and unemployment as morality plays not as the social costs of global economic transformations.[12]

Studies of source patterns – who's quoted, at what length, in what location in the story – demonstrate that journalists' news-gathering practices favor easily accessed institutionalized sources (Ryan 1991). What's more, reporters treat government and corporations, all massive and comparatively well endowed, as representing a general national interest. In contrast, ironically, when workers join forces to gather the necessary resources to sponsor media messages, they become suspect in journalists' eyes as "special interests." Consequently, journalists apply different standards of evidence to labor activists than to politicians or public leaders. They do not grant activists an automatic right to reply to charges. What's more, while journalists grant public officials and academics the respected role of neutral, "objective" observer of events, they disallow this role for labor. A study of coverage of industrial relations in England, for instance, found that mainstream media obscured indepen-

---

[12] There are rare exceptions, such as Bill Moyers' special, *Minimum Wages*, 1992.

dent working-class perspectives, ignored management's activities, and presented government solely as a positive force. Workers' actions were discussed primarily as they affected consumers (Hartman 1979). Even when labor funds academic studies, credibility does not necessarily ensue. Herman finds that reporters often identify labor-funded studies as such while not so labeling corporate-sponsored studies (Herman 1996).

Cultural Myths and Stereotypes of Working Class Life

Since World War II, journalism recruits primarily from the upper and upper middle-class college-educated. Most journalists are unfamiliar with working-class life in general and the perspective of organized labor in particular. They tend to reflect popular stereotypes of workers and organized labor. U.S. mainstream journalists usually interview industrial workers in bars, and farmers in sight of silos (Hill 1982). Images of corrupt labor leaders, union violence, greed and ineffectiveness abound, while complex coverage of industrial relations is rare. Common are portrayals of organized labor as powerful but corrupt, self-serving bureaucracies, eager to strike for their narrow self-interest (Puente 1986). Counter-poised are positive images of the consumer as king, the workplace as a private, not a public concern and the corporate executives as caretakers of an American economy that rewards the meritorious (Martin 2004). Thus labor is cast as "the bad guy"[13] and corporate interests as "the good guy" who wants the "little guy" citizen-consumer to be treated as a king. Casting is essential for subsequent agenda setting; the "good guys" want to shape social policy and "little guys" should support them.

Lacking independent experience, editors tend to assign and reporters tend to write stories, which reinforce the themes listed above. Coverage of the 1997 U.P.S. strike for instance, raised many of these themes. To create counter-images, the Teamsters union launched a major initiative.

The Issue of Resources

The labor movement devotes more resources to media than many other social movements. Nonetheless, policy analysts would be naive to ignore the relative resource disparity between corporations and unions. Compared to

---

[13] Media images of workers and business leaders are predominantly male (Croteau and Hoynes 1994).

well-researched and packaged corporate media campaigns, labor's efforts to cover workers routinely are under-resourced (Douglas 1986, Puette 1992, Ryan 1991). What's more, organized labor remains suspicious of mainstream media and often avoids reporters whom corporations court (Mort 1998). The net effect is that reporters can cover a corporate campaign with far more ease than a labor campaign.

New technologies[14] held promise as egalitarian resources but have more often exacerbated the polarization of news media into elite and mass-commercial forms. In an epoch in which "power and influence depend on the control and strategic use of information" (Bennett 1988: x), the information explosion is not available to all, the drive for profits having stunted its promise.

Strategic Choices – Options under Pressures

Discerning one's strategic options amidst the constraints and contradictions of existing media systems, can easily lead social movement organizations from apathy to despair. Many social movement organizations react by boycotting mainstream media and building their own independent media, an approach much in evidence in both the American Left and Christian Right.[15] Boycotting mainstream media, however, ignores cracks in media institutions which can serve as potential media opportunities born of contradictions in the massive market-driven system.

Building on accepted convention, organized labor can angle for media coverage during strikes and work actions, then work to make that coverage "explode outward." Labor has its own independent media and communications networks where it can test its approaches. What's more, cable and Internet have weakened the stranglehold of the large networks. Finally, reporters, downsized and sped-up, may be more open to well-organized communications campaigns that meet news criteria.

Labor can also leverage its strengths to counter the weaknesses of a media-saturated society; cynical general publics may ignore corporate communications campaigns and respond to face-to-face encounters with "average citizens."

---

[14] Internet use by media outlets and labor is rapidly changing. This paper cannot address this in depth. Analysts warn that reporter dependence on internet sources may further marginalize under-resourced organizations.

[15] The Christian Right uses this strategy effectively, moving back into mainstream visibility after consolidating an Evangelical base, and sustaining independent media to create the base for new campaigns.

While corporations can create impressions of mobilization by hiring consultants to flood Congress with orchestrated grassroots responses, corporations cannot easily create relationships that stand solid in a fight. Corporations cannot, for instance, follow organized labor as it talks to neighbors, co-workers and fellow church congregants.

Mass media also becomes newly interested in labor as labor's base of support grows and 'makes news' through organizing. Both anti-sweatshop and justice-for-janitors campaigns have won mainstream media coverage by integrating intentional communications and organizing campaigns. In both cases, organizers embedded communications strategies in broader political organizing strategies. As the U.P.S. strike suggests, if it takes a village to raise a child, it takes a social movement to raise an issue.

The 1997 U.P.S. – Teamster Strike

In 1997, 185,000 United Parcel Service (U.P.S.) employees represented by the International Brotherhood of Teamsters (IBT), won a five-year contract with major "quality-of-work-life" concessions, a victory that labor journalist Kim Moody called, "A microcosm of what US labor is and what it might become" (Moody 1999: 97). The six-month contract campaign culminating in a fifteen-day strike, blended formal negotiations with picket lines, rallies, and other support activities. Announcing, "Good jobs for working families are going to be won on the picket lines and in the community – not at the negotiating table,"[16] the union organized broad national and international coalitions of community, religious and labor supporters. Teamster contract demands centered on several issues:

- **Part-time work at U.P.S.:** Over 60% of U.P.S.'s 1997 workforce was part-time, an 18% increase in ten years. In some cities, the workforce was almost all part-time (76% in San Francisco; 90% in Louisville; 72% in Newark/Northern New Jersey). Many workers had accepted part-time employment at U.P.S. with a promise of full-time work in the future but 83% of jobs created at U.P.S. since 1993 were part-time. Many workers were part-time in name only: at least 10,000 working up to 35 hours/week without the

---

[16] Carey quoted in International Brotherhood of Teamsters, "Carey, AFL-CIO Pres. Sweeney Walk Picket Line in Chicago," *IBT Media Advisory*, August 6, 1997.

benefits or pay scale of full-time U.P.S. workers. Since 1982, part-time pay
had stagnated at $8.00 while full-time pay scales rose from $13.46 to $19.95.

- **Workplace safety:** In 1994, U.P.S. raised the weight limit on packages from
  70 to 150 pounds without adequate safety measures, a change that had
  resulted in an injury rate of 33.8 injuries for every 100 workers, 2.5 times
  higher than the national average. Meanwhile, U.P.S. lobbied Congress to
  cut OSHA's budget and limit its power to monitor and respond to workplace safety violations.

- **Pensions and Sub-contracting:** The union opposed U.P.S. proposals to take
  control of the union pension fund. It wanted to restrict subcontracting to
  low-wage, non-union subsidiaries that would impact workers' pay, health,
  benefits and pension coverage.

The IBT won all its critical demands. Most notably, it won a commitment to
convert 2,000 part-time jobs per year into 10,000 more full-time jobs over the
course of five years. It won pay-raises of $3.10/hr. for full and $4.10/hr. part-
time workers and bans on job sub-contracting (save for peak holiday periods).
The union maintained control of the pension fund and also negotiated increases
in company pension contributions. In turn, the union conceded to a five-year
contract.[17]

Teamsters for a Democratic Union called the U.P.S. strike, "North America's
biggest labor victory of the 1990's."[18] To Teamster communication coordinator, Rand Wilson, the strike represented, "the labor movement operating on
all cylinders – a total team effort by an awful lot of people" (Wilson 1998).
Explaining the strike's success, TDU similarly credited "the year-long contract campaign launched by the International Union."[19]

Methodology

Like several chapters in this anthology (Brooks, Lindsey, Orr), I use textual
analysis as a methodology of choice. Anthropologist Sherry Ortner (1996),
however, urges scholars to pair textual analyses with "studies of the ways in
which people resist, negotiate, or appropriate some feature of their world"

---

[17] "Sorting It Out: What They Wanted, What They Got," *The New York Times*, August
20, 1997, p. A22.
[18] Teamsters for a Democratic Union, "Ken Hall on the 1997 U.P.S. Victory," Accessed
July 19, 2002 at www.tdu.org/U.P.S.
[19] Teamsters for a Democratic Union, "Lessons of the 1997 U.P.S. Contract Campaign,"
Accessed July 19, 2002 at www.tdu.org/U.P.S.

(Ortner 1996: 2). By linking textual analysis to studies of historically embedded agency, Ortner argues, scholars can correct for problems with over-determinism that ignore possibilities for agency, and under-determinism that ignores historically shaped constraints.

Studies at the interface of media and social movements provide fertile ground for theorists wanting to link texts and the agents who make and react to them. In this case I look at two types of text: the Teamsters' press releases – messages the collective actor proactively and reactively created and sponsored – and the resulting media coverage. The historical conjuncture is the United Parcel Service strike of 1997.

As is common in case study research (Yin 1989, Stake 1994), I use both primary and secondary sources to reconstruct the Teamsters' communication strategy during the 1997 U.P.S. strike. For information on Teamster strategy (rank-and-file and communications organizing), I draw on published accounts by AFL-CIO communications staff (Mort 1999, Baldwin 1999), a published account by the IBT communications coordinator and the director (Witt and Wilson 1999), speeches (Wilson 1998, Hall 1997), and Teamster publications.[20] Additionally, to document Teamster union "sponsor activity," I analyze press releases issued by the IBT national communication staff in a nine-month period beginning six months before the strike and continuing afterward. Using the strike as a critical discourse moment (Chilton 1987), I then analyze newspaper coverage. The strike lasted fifteen days (August 4–August 20, 1997) and received ample coverage in most "newspapers of record," e.g., newspapers recognized as authoritative voices whose coverage represents a historical record and generally set the agenda for broadcast media.[21] To measure the Teamsters' presence in mainstream news coverage, I sample print coverage of the strike in two newspapers of record – the nationally oriented *New York Times* and the regional newspaper of record, *The Boston Globe*. For the period studied,[22] the sample includes 50 *New York Times* and 42 *Boston Globe*

---

[20] I am particularly grateful to Rand Wilson who provided Teamster press releases for the six months preceding the campaign and the actual campaign. He also read and commented on the case. Wilson served as a communications coordinator for the IBT during the U.P.S. strike.

[21] It is common for a TV or radio newscaster to begin his/her story, "A Washington Post story today. . . ."

[22] July 29–August 26, 1997. The news sample included the week preceding the strike, the strike itself and one post-strike week.

articles. I first construct a coverage journal to capture the flow of the news coverage. Noting Teamster communications staff activity before and during the strike, I subject the articles to frame analysis, a method described in Gamson and Lasch (1983) and Ryan (1991).

Juxtaposing union-generated and media-generated sources against the concrete conjuncture of U.P.S. workers and owners competing in governmental, public and media arenas/games allows me to track how an intentional subject was able to challenge hegemonic forces. Organizers for the Teamsters' union, building on relationships and understandings developed over twenty years by TDU and other IBT organizing campaigns, made strategic choices which increased their power. I focus primarily on one choice – messages/frame sponsorship amidst the pressure/constraints of mainstream news.

A coverage journal – *The Boston Globe* and *New York Times*

While the U.P.S. strike was "breaking news," its coverage followed an engrained formula – an epic struggle with a beginning, middle, and end. In the aftermath, a chorus of experts joined the actors in debating the meaning of the struggle.

The Beginning

Initial *Boston Globe* and *New York Times* coverage offered ritualized summarizes of opposing sides. The article, "High Stakes for Two Titans,"[23] for instance, discusses part-time work from two perspectives – the union calling for fair pay for essentially full-time work, the company arguing that competition from non-union delivery services makes lower wages necessary. Both papers covered two classic themes: the strike's impact on consumers and its potential damage to the economy (Puette 1992). Typical consumer-oriented articles included "Phish-Fest Tix held up by U.P.S. Strike"[24] and "For Brides and Businesses, Thinly Veiled Frustration."[25] Among articles focusing on economic damage were these: "U.P.S. Strike Disrupts Thousands of Firms"[26] and "Small Businesses Suffer the Most from U.P.S. Strike."[27] Puette (1992) argues that

---

[23] Steven Greenhouse, *The New York Times*, August 5, 1997, p. A1. Note that the headlines here suggest the framing pursued within the story.
[24] Jim Sullivan, *The Boston Globe*, August 5, 1997, p. E6.
[25] Lynda Richardson, *The New York Times*, August 6, 1997, A17.
[26] Diane E. Lewis, *The Boston Globe*, August 5, 1997, p. D1.
[27] Dirk Johnson, *The New York Times*, August 9, 1997, p. A1.

both themes – "Pity the Consumer" and "Unions are conflictual and resulting strikes hurt the economy" – implicitly blame strikers for inconveniencing average citizens.

As the national newspaper of record, *The New York Times* focused more on the negotiation process and the federal government's role while national strike activities provided human interest.[28]

The Middle

Wrapping up the strike's first week, *The Boston Globe* presented four articles assessing the strike, its impact and the importance of work as a "hot button issue."[29] While these articles fully present corporate U.P.S.' perspective and rehash the Teamster "organized crime" image, even at this mid-point of the strike, Teamster mobilization and the union's contract demands had already impacted coverage. The company-prioritized pension issue was downplayed while two *New York Times* articles in this first week explored the union's concern over part-time jobs. "Strike Points to Inequality in 2-tier Job Market"[30] reads one headline.

The End

If the union's framing was receiving increasing play by the first week's end, by the end of the strike (week two), the union's framing had become prominent. Coverage of the union's frame grew as the strike campaign achieved organizing landmarks, which reporters recognized as signifying strength: international unions were honoring the strike, the federal government had refused to force a vote or intervene via the Taft-Hartley Act, picket lines were being maintained nationally, and strong strike support events were happening broadly across the country. *Globe* and *New York Times* reporters took particular note of two developments which to them represented a growing momentum on the part of the union: other unions were pledging support including money,[31] and polls were showing massive public

---

[28] See for instance, the same day articles Steven Greenhouse, "No Talks and Very Few Deliveries in U.P.S. Strike," *The New York Times*, August 6, 1997, A17 and Dirk Johnson, "Angry Voices of Pickets Reflect Sense of Concern," *The New York Times*, August 6, 1997, p. A16.

[29] Diane E. Lewis, "Hot Button Issue," *The Boston Globe*, August 10, 1997, p. E2.

[30] Louis Uchitelle, *The New York Times*, August 8, 1997, p. A22.

[31] Tina Cassidy, "Officials Join Teamsters at Rally," *The Boston Globe*, August 9, 1997,

support.[32] On August 20, 1997, as *Boston Globe* and *New York Times* articles announced a tentative agreement to end the 15-day strike, U.P.S. and the union engaged in a contest to frame what the settlement meant. A *Boston Globe* article entitled "Teamsters Victory Seen as 'Watershed'"[33] begins, "Don't expect a raise tomorrow. But labor's victory in the strike against U.P.S. suggests American workers are now in a better position – whether they belong to a union or not." The lead then cites a private industry economic forecaster explaining; "The pendulum is shifting to labor, which is probably good, because workers haven't participated in the country's prosperity." *New York Times* coverage was far more qualified. A front-page article entitled, "A victory for labor: but how far will it go?"[34] reported U.P.S. threats of 15,000 layoffs and quoted a U.P.S. spokesperson, "'We're taking the attitude that no one wins in a strike.'" Two articles covered union gains while two others cited potential "bigger losses," "probable drop" in business, and clients' now "strained loyalties." A follow-up op-ed by a U.P.S. consultant criticized union public relations tactics and warned of dire long-term consequences caused by union demands. Attention was focused on Carey, whom the article described as a charismatic, but unscrupulous leader.[35]

A media victory: The chorus expounds

Toward the end of the strike (August 16–August 20), experts cited in both *Boston Globe* and *New York Times* articles agreed that the union was winning the strike and that a well-run public relations campaign had played a pivotal role in mobilizing the Teamsters' members, supporters, and a broader general public.[36] What's more, experts argued, the public support shown the Teamsters and documented in the media, would improve the general negotiating climate for other unions: *Business Week* quoted rueful U.P.S. vice-

F1 and Steven Greenhouse, "Labor Unions Plan a Teamsters Loan to Sustain Strike," *The New York Times*, August 13, 1997, A1.

[32] Diane E. Lewis, "UPS Strike: Public Opinion Union Arsenal," *The Boston Globe*, August 19, 1997, D1.

[33] Charles Stein, August 20, 1997, E1.

[34] Steven Greenhouse, *The New York Times*, August 20, 1997, A1.

[35] Jeffrey Sonnenfeld, "In the dignity department, U.P.S. wins [Op-ed]," *New York Times*, August 24, 1997, p. F14.

[36] Diane E. Lewis, "UPS Strike: Public Opinion Union Arsenal," *The Boston Globe*, August 19, 1997, D1 and Adam Nagourney, "In Strike Battle, Teamsters Borrow Page from Politics," *The New York Times*, August 16, 1997, A1.

chairman John Alden, "If I had known that it was going to go from negotiating for U.P.S. to negotiating for part-time America, we would've approached it differently."[37]

Communications staff Rand Wilson stressed that broader labor organizing profited from the public awareness raised by the strike:

> In all, the Teamsters Union had more organizing successes in 1997 than in any year in recent memory, and after the strike I heard lots of anecdotes from other union organizers about how the U.P.S. victory inspired unorganized workers to contact them as well (Wilson 1998).

Agency: Teamster Staff Strategically Sponsor Stories

The Teamsters "played the (communications) game better so far (than U.P.S.) – a point begrudgingly made by U.P.S. officials and outside observers."[38] Union staff forged "sophisticated campaigns aimed at turning opinion in Washington," wielding communications skills that "will become a permanent part of labor relations."[39]

This media success was not pre-ordained – a rare instance of truth speaking for itself. Rather, Teamster media success resulted from careful planning, preparation and follow-up; in the year preceding the strike, Teamster communications staff had mounted an extensive communications strategy to complement a yearlong organizing strategy. Moreover, media coverage of the union's message increased only when the union's multi-faceted strike support activities won over large and visible publics. Advance preparation facilitated mass mobilization.

The Preparation Phase

Staff for the Teamsters' national communications department released over thirty media advisories and press statements in the six-month contract campaign. In the five months preceding the strike, six press releases – roughly one per month – highlighted contract issues. During the strike, press releases

---

[37] Paul Magnuson and Nicole Harris, "A Wake-up Call for Business," September 1, 1997, p. 28.
[38] Adam Nagourney, "In Strike Battle, Teamsters Borrow Page from Politics," *The New York Times*, August 16, 1997, A1.
[39] Ibid.

increased to one per day, 24 press releases in a three-week period. Behind this barrage was a well-organized communications staff, which began planning coverage of contract negotiations and the subsequent strike over nine months in advance. In short, over the course of the campaign, staff spent hours preparing press statements, fact sheets, calling reporters, staffing press tables, etc. While union members and existing staff can accomplish the above for an occasional event, a sustained organizing drive or strike needs staff with dedicated labor time to conduct all the above operations.

Involving Rank-and-File in Framing Issues

There is no media strategy without an organizing strategy; in such campaigns, organizing staff and communications staff work hand-in-hand. Teamsters' communications staff "surveyed members' priorities, and gave local leaders, stewards, and activists leaflets and an 8-minute video to help them use the survey as an organizing tool" (Wilson 1998). The communications staff discussed survey results with organizing staff and engaged in extensive research and writing. This culminated in the framing of a clear message. Simultaneously the Education Department set up member-to-member communication networks, which helped mobilize members to participate in actions preceding the strike. These actions and networks built cooperation between part-timers and full-timers. Without networks and communications mechanisms, organizing staff would not have been able to mobilize members and supporters for key actions.

Making Issues Newsworthy

To signal the newsworthiness of the contract negotiations, union press releases routinely highlighted several points most notably that in covering 185,000 workers the U.P.S. contract represented the largest contract being negotiated in 1997. The depth of union support for a strike (at 95% a nearly unanimous strike vote) as well as the breadth of external support – nationally and internationally – served further claims of newsworthiness. To illustrate this depth and breadth of support, the union held mobilizations that made the issues tangible and visual for reporters. Teamster communication staff, Rand Wilson recalls:

> We held "Don't Break Our Backs" rallies where injured U.P.S. workers spoke and members presented more than 5,000 grievances on special "EZ" grievance forms. The next month we handed out tens of thousands of Teamster

whistles and invited people to use them on the job and outside their centers to) "Blow the Whistle" on U.P.S. for undermining good jobs.

Solidarity demonstrations were held that same day by U.P.S. workers in a number of European countries – where the company had invested billions of dollars to expand its services.

About six weeks before contract expiration, more than a hundred thousand Teamsters signed petitions telling U.P.S. that "We'll Fight for More Full-Time Jobs" (1998).

Once the strike began, Teamsters launched a series of coordinated events. Perhaps most eye-catching for mainstream media was the Teamster wedding: Teamster member, Deborah Burdette of Anderson, South Carolina and her fiancée held their wedding outside her U.P.S. center, while her coworkers, instead of throwing rice, waved picket signs reading, "Part-Time America Won't Work" (Wilson 1998).

Documenting Issues

Three background studies authorized by the union gave the communications department a wealth of evidence to document the legitimacy of their main contract demands especially the demand for "good full-time jobs" which paid wages that would support a family. Studies and reviews of U.P.S.'s own statistics were crystallized into fact sheets to accompany press releases. Facts recurrently bulleted in flyers and press releases included these:

- Over 1/2 U.P.S. workers were part-time, an increase of 18% in ten years. In some cities, 90% of U.P.S. workers were part-time.
- Only 40,000 of 182,000 part-timers hired in 1996 worked at U.P.S. at year's end – a 400% turnover.
- Three-quarters of departing part-timers cited lack of full time work as a reason.
- While the company routinely promised part-timers the possibility of full-time work in the future, U.P.S. pre-strike contract proposals only promised 1,000 full-time slots.
- At least 10,000 part-timers actually worked full time, but were paid on a part-time pay scale ($8.00 rather than $19.95) for the same work as full-timers.
- U.P.S. had the worst safety record in industry, 2.5 times worse than the post office. Without adequate safety precautions, U.P.S. had raised weight restrictions from 70 to 150 lb. in 1994.

Mobilizing

As described above, prior to contract negotiations, the union identified priority issues and researched its concerns. It also began to mobilize members and educate the public through a series of pre-negotiation events. Negotiations opened with a contract rally in March. A die-in for Worker's Memorial Day highlighted health and safety issues in April. Teamsters in other countries rallied to support U.P.S. workers in May. In June, just before the strike authorization vote in July, President Ron Carey toured five states and a study was released documenting problems caused by part-time work.

The events created news hooks, reasons for reporters to cover the issues the union wanted to highlight (part-time work; health and safety, etc.). What's more, the union took seriously the need not only to hold events, but also to approach the media for coverage. In the five months preceding the strike, the Teamster communication department issued seven press releases publicizing the previously mentioned events. At a U.P.S. distribution center in Jonesboro, Arkansas, for instance, a supervisor told workers wearing contract campaign stickers to remove them or leave, and fired their union steward. Workers walked out and over to a local television station which covered the incident. In light of the coverage, management backed down.

Sponsoring the Message

Long before the strike began, the union had worked to frame a coherent message about what their issues signified, a process which will be explained in more detail in the next section. For the union, the issue underlying quality of work life was the right to "good jobs for America's working families." Contract issues, campaign events, press releases, selection of spokespersons, etc. carried this message intentionally. The coherence with which the union frame was transmitted resulted from careful, thoughtful planning, and many discussions at local and national meetings. Communications staff Rand Wilson recalls,

> Working with the field staff, our communications strategy was geared toward getting members involved and helping them speak for themselves. . . . For months, we talked with our members about how we were fighting – not just for more cents per hour – but for the future of good jobs that all communities need.
>
> And that preparation paid off when reporters went out to ask members what was going on. A few hours after picket lines went up, the national

Reuters news wire was quoting a rank-and-file U.P.S. driver, Randy Walls from Atlanta, saying, "We're striking for every worker in America. We can't have only low service-industry wages in this country." The *Minneapolis Star-Tribune* quoted Mark Dray, a U.P.S. *full*-timer for 25 years: "The whole world's going to part-time. Used to be the American dream was to get a good job and own your own home with a white picket fence. Now it's hoping you win the lottery." And part-timer Mike McBride told the *Cleveland Plain Dealer*: "This strike is not for today. It's . . . about 10 years down the line. If we don't stand up, we might as well pack our bags" (Wilson 1998).

The union combined direct and mass communication; some U.P.S. drivers covered their routes explaining strike issues to their regular customers. Through such events, the union sponsored its story just as government and corporations routinely sponsor theirs (Witt and Wilson 1999).

Framing the Union's Message

When Teamsters' communication staff strategically sponsored news stories, they interwove five critical ingredients: 1) skilled staff with 2) adequate labor power to 3) sponsor activities that 4) strategically position the 5) union's message. To this message element, the framing of the story itself, I now turn. In framing facts into a coherent story line, sources name the issue, define who is a player with the right to speak, say who's responsible and target possible solutions. Of these, most pivotal is naming the issue; issue definition commonly becomes a battleground. "We've basically been at a war of words,'" acknowledged a U.P.S. spokesperson toward the end of the strike.[40]

In U.P.S. contract battles, the union and U.P.S. management saw different facts and stories as important, the differences stemming from basic disagreements about how to run the economy and society. The union argued that it is in society's interest to provide a living wage for workers: "What this country needs is good, decent, full-time jobs."[41] In contrast, U.P.S. argued that workers' interests lies in protecting the company's health, a variant on the slogan, *What's good for GM is good for the nation*: "U.P.S. executives have

---

[40] Adam Nagourney, "In Strike Battle, Teamsters Borrow Page from Politics," *The New York Times*, August 16, 1997, A1.
[41] Carey in Charles Stein, "In UPS Strike, Courting Public Opinion." *The Boston Globe*, August 10, 1997, p. A8.

repeatedly argued that they already have the highest labor costs in the shipping industry and that if they give in to the union's demands, then nonunion competitors like Federal Express and Roadway Package Systems, known as RPS, will capture more market share. Kerr Sternad, a U.P.S. spokesman, said, 'I can tell you that the teamsters and any other experts are blind if they don't see the fact that a significant portion of our business is going to nonunion competitors and all of our business is at risk to those nonunion competitors.'"[42]

	Union's standpoint: Fair pay for hard work	Company standpoint: Business necessity
What is the issue?	The issue is whether an American worker, in exchange for his or her labor, can expect to receive sufficient compensation to cover a family's food, clothing, shelter, health care, education and retirement costs.	The issue is whether United Parcel Service can continue to maintain its market share if union demands for compensation make U.P.S. lose its competitive edge (as contrasted to competing firms paying non-union wages).

Labor and management's diverging perceptions represent a framing contest – a struggle to define the issue, the key players with standing and the range of viable solutions. Framing a story, in short, has less to do with an absolute truth than with an issue's significance from where one sits. For example, Teamster stories emphasized working conditions while U.P.S. management stories stressed the need to control costs in order to maintain a competitive edge.

Operating from different frames, opponents routinely perceive each other as distorting the truth. Jeffrey Sonnenfeld, U.P.S. management consultant, for instance, charged that Ron Carey

> brilliantly confused journalists, customers, academicians, and most important, U.P.S. workers by seizing legitimate concerns about the 'new social

---

[42] Steven Greenhouse, "A glass half full or half empty?" *The New York Times,* August 18, 1997, p. A15.

contract' in the workplace and using them against a company that staunchly lived by the principles of loyalty and justice in the old social contract.[43]

Rather than pose this as deceit or bias, it helps to recognize that Teamsters and the U.P.S. both focused on "truths" relevant for their arguments. For U.P.S., this meant asking how the company could maintain a competitive edge in a globalized international transport industry. For the Teamsters, it met addressing a deteriorating American standard of living. Documenting the American dream's demise was therefore directly relevant for the union. In contrast, for U.P.S. management, documenting the lost American dream was not relevant.

Underlying Assumptions about Labor

As mentioned previously, beyond specific labor-management battles, reporters hold generic understandings of labor, management and the economy which prime them to be more receptive to some stories and less so to others. Most commonly, reporters think of unions as a special interest. Implicitly, they are operating within a pluralist understanding – society as composed of competing interest groups moderated by the balancing hand of government which has as its mandate to even up the playing field and to keep the rules of competition clean. Everyone has an interest; no one is altruistic.

In sharp contrast is organized labor's perception of itself as a warrior in a crusade for equity and social justice; labor assumes an uneven playing field; the powerless must unite or be crushed.

Reporters, attempting to be objective in a battle between what they understand as two special interests – labor and management – tend to side with the free-market stand-in for the citizen – the consumer. Thus a preponderance of coverage focuses on how the strike hurts consumers – both individuals and businesses – dependent on U.P.S. Journalists portray government sometimes as a mediator, sometimes as a power bloc being wooed by the contending parties. In addition, since most journalists have limited experience with working people and unions, they tend to uncritically incorporate stereotypes of unions.

---

[43] "In the dignity department, U.P.S. wins [Op-ed]," *New York Times*, August 24, 1997, p. F14.

Union frame: Fair wage for hard work

What is the issue? The issue is whether American workers, in exchange for their labor, can expect their salaries to cover food, clothing, shelter, health care, education and retirement costs.

From the union's standpoint, who are the vested players?

"US" (labor)	• 185,000 hard working U.P.S. workers, promised full-time jobs but stuck in part-time jobs which pay half of what a full time job pays for the same work.
"Them"	• "Big Brown," United Parcel Service which is making a billion dollars in profits each year, while forcing an increasing percentage of its work-force into part-time insecure jobs which are low-paying, unsafe, and dead-ended.
Other players	• Gov't. which could play a positive role in forcing U.P.S. to the table.
	• Working America especially other organized workers who could be allies. "Issues behind this strike reach directly into the living rooms and pocketbooks of every working family in America" (Sweeney, IBT 8–6–97).
	• Members of the general public – church groups, women, etc. who maybe directly affected by the rise of low-wage jobs.
Who or what's responsible?	U.P.S., which is putting profits before its employees. Long-term this hurts a previously strong company, lowering productivity, increasing injuries and worker turnover: "U.P.S. is a billion-dollar company that can afford to provide good full-time jobs with pensions and health care." Carey 3–10–97
What is range of possible solutions?	Union contract demands for more full-time jobs, increases in hourly rates for part-time and full-time workers, new regulations to protect workers from packages heavier than 70 lb., limitations on sub-contracting, secured pension provisions, etc.

At times, U.P.S. spokespersons promoted these themes. They targeted Carey as a corrupt union boss promoting a conflictual strike to distract the union's members and the broader public from his own legal problems.[44] To the extent that these themes do, in fact, resonate with the perceptions of broad publics with little direct union experience, they can be found coming not exclusively from the company, but from the mouth of the "man-in-the-street." The interpretive power of the reporter and editor rests in their ability to decide which "man-in-the-street" represents the American citizens' common wisdom. For instance, *Times* reporter, Steven Greenhouse, quotes James Kelly, chairman of U.P.S., "The part-time job at U.P.S. is a great job," then followed the quote with this man-on-the-street reaction: "(Kelly's) type of argument resonated with Richard Arzola, a commercial printing salesman, in East Austin, Texas. 'I don't support the strike at all,' he said. 'We don't need unions. At one time, maybe back in the '40's or '30's, but now you don't need a union. Those guys are getting a pretty deal to work.'"[45]

Discussion

The Democratic Clinton Administration opened potential political opportunities for organized labor. Teamsters, for instance, could reckon that the Clinton Labor Department would sympathize with contingent labor. To take advantage of new opportunities, however, labor had to mobilize its internal resources and allied networks. To accomplish this, Teamster leaders on local, regional and national levels, built on networks forged by TDU and other union reformers.

Similarly, in the media arena, the Teamsters needed to build on their indigenous resources to exercise their option to promote their perspectives on the U.P.S. strike in national mass media. They also incorporated resources from allies using research by labor scholars and support from politicians, and other unions in the U.S. and internationally. The successful communication campaign built on a well-researched organizing campaign and relied on the Teamsters' internal communications infrastructure – a skilled national staff, communications networks, and the recruitment and careful preparation of

---

[44] "Behind the Teamsters Strike," *The New York Times*, August 7, 1997, p. A30.
[45] Steven Greenhouse, "A Victory For Labor, But How Far Will it Go?" *The New York Times*, August 20, 1997, A1.

leaders/spokespersons. This was a communications campaign that exploded outward.

In each case, the union's communications strategy framed the problematic working conditions of part-time workers as a violation of the American dream, a frame that resonated with the many other American workers lacking job security, benefits and a living wage. In framing their campaign as representing a social crisis affecting many Americans, not just Teamster members, the union avoided the common labeling of unions and strikers in particular as narrow special interests and expanded their ability to mobilize.

> The campaign proved that working people will be attracted to a labor movement that is
>
> One,   a movement *of workers*, not just officials;
>
> Two,   a movement of *all* workers, not just its members; and
>
> Three, a *fighting force* for working people, not just a bureaucratic service institution.
>
> (Wilson and Witt 1998)

Lessons for Social Movements

The 1997 Teamster (IBT) strike against United Parcel Service (U.P.S.) suggests several generalizable lessons about communications strategies for collective actors that validate Howard Kimmeldorf's general conclusion that in skirmishes with capital, labor gains ground when it successfully establishes the organizational infrastructure that allows it to sustain collective challenges (156). For the modern historical era, this infrastructure includes mass media. The Teamsters' communication strategy focused on collective action and the strengthening of a collective actor in different geographical regions and levels – local, regional and national. It built on two decades of organizing infrastructure created by Teamsters for a Democratic Union (TDU) and other Teamsters. The Teamster internal communication infrastructure – staff, outlets, rank-and-file trainings – made the external media campaigns viable. Second, the strategy was grounded in an analysis of power relations – the "lay of the land" in the media arena. This was not simply parallel lists of constraints and opportunities, but a holistic assessment of Harnacker's "coyuntura de fuerzas," (historical conjuncture) taking note of the indigenous resources and networks built through two decades of reform battles in the Teamsters' union, the election of a Democratic Administration, the rising American dissatisfaction with decline in working conditions, and massive structural shifts in the mass media. The strategy exploited small openings that could be expanded building on indigenous resources, synergistic alliances and trans-formative practices.

The Clinton election and appointment of labor-receptive Cabinet members opened opportunities for organized labor, but the ability to exercise their options in economic, political and communication arenas rested squarely on the hard-won resources of reformers within the trade union movement. In this case, the International Brotherhood of Teamsters was able to build on two decades of internal democratization to launch a major national strike grounded in the mobilizing strategies of social movement unionism.

To interpret this victory exclusively in terms of the national shift in polit-ical winds distorts social movement dynamics by downplaying internal growth dynamics – how small changes can accrue to "explode outward" in scholar-activist Richard Healey's graphic phrase.[46] In the two decades preceding the 1997 strike, Teamsters for a Democratic Union and other reform-oriented pockets of teamsters fought internally to challenge a criminally-connected union leadership and to democratize their union (La Botz, 1990). From these battles grew the indigenous resources critical in the 1997 strike; these included broadened networks that created coalitions regionally, nationally and inter-nationally as well as democratic culture and transformative practices that prepared local Teamsters, their spouses and supporters to develop and con-vey reform frames, first through independent channels and later, through mass media. Entrée into mass media was gained by meeting routine prac-tices regarding news criteria and spokespersons, then transforming and expanding them via Teamster mobilizations. A national communications staff consolidated the practices creating vertical lines of communication that com-plemented the local and regional horizontal networks (Morris 1986). In other words, within their own union, disenfranchised workers had to form a col-lective actor and strengthen their power prior to challenging management. From this internal vibrancy grew the communications strength that allowed the union to succeed in the master forum – the mass media – during the U.P.S. strike.

---

[46] See www.grassrootspolicy.org

Afterward

Shortly after its 1997 U.P.S. victory, the Teamsters' union cascaded into tur-
moil when Teamster president Ron Carey was charged with accepting illegal campaign contributions. By 2000, Republicans won the White House, the
economy stagnated, and de-unionization accelerated. Buffeted by these losses
and the 911 shift to war, labor organizers did not turn the 1997 U.P.S. victory
into the upsurge they desired. Though they continued to exercise strategic
options, they were constrained by increasing pressures from opposing forces
in industry, government, and ongoing pressures within mass media.

Much remains to be learned about how intentional subjects form, consider
and execute challenges to hegemonic forces, how they consolidate gains, learn
from losses, address internal differences and inequalities, and cope with the
unintended consequences of their intentional efforts. Many theorists operating from indigenous, postcolonial and subaltern perspectives see answering
these questions as important. Ortner (1996: 8) argues, "the denial of the intentional subject and of 'agency,' both misreads and works against the intellectual and political interests of women, minorities, postcolonial, and other
subaltern subjects." Jan Mohamed and Lloyd (1987: 16) further urge theorists
to realize that for the already marginalized "the non-identity of minorities
remains the sign of material damage to which the only coherent response is
struggle, not ironic distanciation."

In exploring how best to struggle, marginalized collective actors could collaborate with social theorists who tend to locate themselves within the academic arena. For academic social theorists, however, choosing to collaborate
with marginalized subjects may heighten the risks and pressures of academic life. As they watch the daily clock and the tenure clock, social theorists
playing the academic game make ongoing classed, raced, gendered choices –
where to position themselves, on whom to gaze, with whom to relate what
stories and how to disseminate resulting insights. Deciding whose accounts
count, social theorists make strategic choices under very real pressures. To
pursue Jan Mohamed and Lloyd's suggestion, one potential strategic choice
for the theorist might be to position oneself with intentional subjects to document and reflect on collective attempts at resistance. Even if partial, provisional or imperfect, such collective challenges merit our attention.

William R. Wood

(Virtual) Myths*

Give me a map then, let me see how much /
Is left for me to conquer all the world

– Tamburlaine

I

In the fall of 2000, Norway's coastline expanded by
some 16,000 miles. Mapmakers conceded a roughly
45 percent error in the old calculations. An engineer
with the Norwegian Mapping Authority explained
that a new computer program was able to measure
and calculate thousands of tiny inlets and islands
that had been missed or miscalculated in earlier
estimates. "The land is the same," noted Trygve
Hegheim, head of the map service in Sognog Fjordane
County, who also noted that work had already started
on revising official figures.

What does it mean to say the land is "the same"?
Hegheim is not speaking of social changes brought
about by this discovery. Rather, his argument is a
technical one. The mass of the land has not been
altered. The coastline did not grow. Nothing has
changed except the degree and sophistication of measurement techniques, where cruder mapping technologies have been replaced with more exacting
digital mapping technologies.

* An earlier version of this essay appeared in *Critical Sociology*, vol. 30, no. 2 (2004).

Indeed, the compelling point of this rather odd acquisition of coastline lies in an assumption of mundane continuity, a transition from old to new. Once charted by cartographers and explorers, the Norwegian coastline begins to break free from the error of human calculation and the limitations of the human eye itself. Representation becomes more precise, more able to depict the world as it actually is. The vision of the land, in the eye of the satellite, becomes complete.

II

This assumption of continuity (i.e. Hegheim's assertion that nothing has changed) can be understood not only technically, but also epistemologically. Modern technologies of representation demand a high degree of separation between subject and object, between the act of viewing and the act of being viewed. This demarcation runs the gamut of the Western philosophical and scientific cannon, where the works of Plato and Augustine remain profoundly analogous to those of modern science in their resolve to distinguish subject and object, body and soul, light and dark. Francis Bacon's famous dictum that nature must be "bound in service," where it is the job of science to "torture nature's secrets from her," brings to light this abyss between the natural world and the human one. The corporeal passivity of nature, of the body, stand in marked contrast to the productive activities of the mind, the soul, and the will.

Bacon's infamous dictum represents more than a division of subject/object in Western epistemology. It represents an historical epistemology highly correlated to the dominance of visual experience and knowledge. Marshall McLuhan's well-known phrase "an ear for an eye" suggests that such an emphasis of the visual, at the expense of other senses, was based in the rise of print and mass literacy. Martin Jay (1993: 187), however, has argued that the privileging of vision has much earlier roots. "From the shadows playing on the wall of Plato's cave and Augustine's praise of divine light to Descartes' ideas available to a 'steadfast mental gaze' and the Enlightenment's faith in the data of our senses, the ocularcentric underpinnings of our philosophical tradition have been undeniably persuasive." For Jay, Western philosophy and epistemology have always evidenced a high degree of ocularcentrisim. Even so, he argues, the work of those such as Bacon represents a shift away from the Neo-Platonic emphasis on light, or even Descartes' Cartesian perception, towards what Ian Hacking (1975: 33) calls "positivist seeing," a type of vision less related to the Cartesian "active rendering of the object transparent to the mind" and more akin to a type of "passive blunting of light rays on opaque, impenetrable 'physical objects' which are themselves passive and indifferent to the observer." Such a "passivity" or "indifference" of the physical object, still inchoate in the work of Bacon and other late Renaissance empiricists, nevertheless anticipates the more defined positivism of Comte, Bentham and Mill, where the scientific investigation and description of sensory experience, and in particular vision, become the only forms of legitimate knowledge about the physical world.

That positivism has as its core the requisite centrality of vision, of objects "themselves passive and indifferent" is evident in the cartographic projects of sixteenth and seventeenth century Europe. In this regard, cartography provides its own history of Western epistemology and the subsequent rise of "positivistic seeing" as legitimate knowledge. Though Ptolemy's *Geography* had been rediscovered and translated in the thirteenth century, it was not until the sixteenth century that European mapmakers such as Münster began to incorporate Leon Battista Alberti's discovery of linear perspective into chorographic (i.e. regional) maps, looking directly down upon land from a position of relative omniscience. Cosgrove (1984: 48) notes of Battista, "[H]e create[d] a technique which became fundamental to the realist representation of space and the external world. The artist, through perspective, establishes the arrangement or composition and thus the specific time, of the events described, determines – in both senses – the 'point of view' to be taken by the observer, and controls through framing the scope of reality revealed." The point of view in linear perspective becomes externalized from events or locations depicted in paintings and maps. In the case of mapmaking, the incorporation of Battista's linear perspective was most notable not for what was present, but rather for what was now absent. "Realist representation of three-dimensional space on a two-dimensional surface through linear perspective directs the external world towards the individual located outside that space. It gives the eye absolute mastery over space" (Cosgrove 1984: 48). What was now absent, in these earliest of modern maps, was the self itself, the subjective perspective that had throughout the Middle Ages tied the mapreader to the land through a particular point of view – usually a hilltop overlooking a city or region. The view from these earliest of modern maps became the view from nowhere, and the view from everywhere.

More than rendering space as the domain of the individual eye, mapping techniques developed and employed by European cartographers began to rearticulate their vision of space as one more amenable to the eye/I of both commerce and conquest. In the "realist representation" of three-dimensional spaces on two-dimensional surfaces, mapping became increasingly directed towards the survey and private appropriation of land (Cosgrove 1984: 46, 49). This was a substantial break from medieval *mappamundi* and T-O maps, with their assumptions of the Parousia and the time/space of Christian eschatology. In a very real sense, time and space parted ways on the earliest of these modern maps. The cosmological space of God's dominion was usurped by the space of increasing privatization and commercialization of land. Eschatological time was replaced with an increasing sense of market time, technological time, productive time.

III

The French sociologist Henri Lefebvre (1991: 21) surmised that it was Marx who was responsible for such emphasis of time over space in the social sciences. "In the wake of [the] fetishization of space in the service of the state [Hegel], philosophy and practical activity were bound to seek a restoration of time. Hence Marx's vigorous reinstatement of historical time as revolutionary time." In his recasting of Hegel's philosophy, Marx's history of the world became a temporal and secular history, explained not by the movement of spirit or even the will of God, but rather by a material dialectic. "The history of all hitherto existing society is the history of class struggle," wrote Marx and Engels in *The Communist Manifesto*. Lefebvre's observation illuminates how the space of the state, understood by Hegel as the highest synthesis of spirit and consciousness, becomes with Marx the culmination of specific historical-material antecedents (Marx 1998 [1848]: 50).

This assumption of dialectical time and undialectical space is analogous in many regards to the division of subject/object in Western epistemology. In this matter, it is perhaps more the influence of Charles Darwin than (as often argued) Hegel that speaks to Marx's emphasis on temporal dialectical processes. It is no coincidence that Marx sought to dedicate a portion of *Das Kapital* to Charles Darwin, who refused the offer. For if Marx's formulation of the material temporal dialectic of class struggle was itself a driving force in the study and understanding of society, it was greatly influenced by Darwin's discovery of biological evolutionary principles. The epistemological demarcation of subject and object, already visually distinguishable in Renaissance painting and cartography, become transparent in the works of Darwin and Marx. To understand the world, for Darwin, was to understand the histories of evolution, the particularities of species adaptation and the survival of organisms, a world fundamentally detached from human subjectivity itself. Likewise, to understand the history of the world for Marx was to understand the histories of production, capital accumulation and the division of labor. "Men make their own history," argued Marx in *The Eighteenth Brumaire of Louis Napoleon,* "but they do not make it as they please; they do not make it under self-selected circumstances, but under circumstances existing already, given and transmitted from the past" (Marx 2000: 329). The past, present and future were, for both thinkers, the harbinger of change and action, in species adaptation as much as in class conflict. Space, on the other hand, was largely relegated to the status of a backdrop for the activity of men and of nature.

IV

Hegheim's comment about the land being "the same" underscores the division between time and space, where the Norwegian coastline seems to appear *ex nihilo,* out of the nothingness of human productivity. If it is true, as Michel Foucault (1980: 70) has argued, that within social theory "a devaluation of space has prevailed for generations," a critical redress of this devaluation has become increasingly apparent in theories seeking to historicize a dialectics of space. Such theories ask not only how space is related to time (in particular Marx's dialectical materialism) but also how space itself is fabricated and transformed within larger relations of power, and in particular the capitalism of the late twentieth century. A central premise of these inquiries is the construction and articulation of space as a primary and not a secondary factor in critical studies of social relations. Space is not merely transformed through temporal processes, but rather stands as a central point of contestation and struggle. *How* space is defined greatly influences both temporal processes and the relations of power that occur within them.

This redress seeks not only to counter Marx's apparent valuation of time over space, but also inquires into how Marx and others *did* address the relationship of space and time, and why their analyses have been hitherto neglected. In the case of Marx, while Lefebvre correctly links Marx's work to the "vigorous reinstatement of historical time," it is also the case that Marx (1973: 539) did address the question of space in relation to time, specifically in relation to the circulation of capital:

> [Capital] . . . strives to annihilate this space [of circulation] with time, i.e., to reduce to a minimum the time spent in motion from one place to another. The more developed the capital, therefore, the more extensive the market over which it circulates, which forms the spatial orbit of its circulation, the more does it strive simultaneously for an ever greater extension of the market and for the greater annihilation of space by time.

Capital seeks to destroy the limitations of space(s) that impede rates of acquisition, or more specifically surplus accumulation and subsequent reinvestment of capital. In this regard, space remains both adversarial and fallow in relation to capital, reminiscent of Bacon's famous dictum that nature must be "bound in service" and it is the job of science to "torture nature's secrets from her." In this case, it is not the space of "nature" as natural resources or scientific law, but rather the space of geographical limitations, the space of tradition, the space of inactivity. Any space that impedes the orbit of capital accumulation must be overcome. Space becomes dynamic, in Marx's analysis, only in relation to labor and time. Like all things before the torrent of capitalism, it too must melt into thin air.

Max Weber as well wrote of the ordering of space in particular arrangements conducive to disciplinary tactics, essential to rational task-making and decreased specialization (1946: 259):

> No special proof is necessary to show that military discipline is the ideal model for the modern capitalist factory, as it was for the ancient plantation. In contrast to the plantation, organizational discipline in the factory is founded upon a completely rational basis. With the help of appropriate methods of measurement, the optimum profitability of the individual worker is calculated like that of any material means of production.

Central to Weber's organizational discipline is an emphasis not only on the arrangement of spaces (i.e. the factory floor), but also the manner in which bodies themselves are arranged. "The masses are uniformly conditioned and trained for discipline in order that their optimum of physical and psychic power in attack may be rationally calculated" (Weber 1946: 254); where rational calculation include not only the specialization of labor and utilization of advancing technologies of production, but also the disciplining of the body itself as a mechanism through which labor and technology can freely operate. It is this last premise by which Frederick Taylor and Henry Ford, with their respective emphases on divisional labor and assembly line production, fundamentally transformed the relationship between the body and labor in the twentieth century.

Yet neither Marx nor Weber addressed the organizational and disciplinary practices of capitalism as *productive* of space. Rather, they spoke to ways in which *existing* space is overcome, rerouted, arranged, utilized and managed. In this vein, the works of world systems theorists such as Fernand Braudel, Immanuel Wallerstein and Giovanni Arrighi stand as an important addition to the spatial sensibilities present in the work of Marx and Weber. In pushing their respective analyses beyond the boundaries of the factory, the military, or the nation-state itself, Braudel, Wallerstein, Arrighi and others have conceptualized the spatial arrangements of capitalism as an emerging world system, cutting into the territories it subsumes and subsequently rearranging them according to a core/periphery relationship.

The idea of a cope/periphery relationship in relation to modern capitalism is both useful and problematic in terms of space, for while it articulates an understanding of capitalism as dependant upon regionally specific spatial and geographic arrangements, the discussion of space is limited by an inattention to how these spaces themselves became articulated, configured, produced. It was Braudel who first analyzed the role of geographical and topographical determinants in the formulation of core/peripheral global regions of capital movement and production. His work evidences sensitivity to the importance of accounting for space and territory as not merely or only contingent upon a temporal dialectic. Rather, specific geographical attributes of countries or territories, for example Britain's historical insulation from land armies, stand as significant causal factors in the situation of core, semi peripheral, and peripheral regions; hence his axiom that "geography proposes, history disposes" (Braudel 1992: 523).

Nevertheless, it remains problematic that, as with Marx and Weber, the world systems theorists do not question how territory itself becomes articulated and produced in this ever-emerging world system. In relation to the hegemon, territory merely seems to appear, and it is an emphasis upon the articulation and arrangements of territory, rather than an analysis of the production and representation of space itself as an aspect of capitalism, which pervades the bulk of world systems literature.

Regardless of this inattention, it remains an important empirical finding of world systems theory that capitalism both inscribes new territory, as well as re-inscribes existing territory, often in a discursive and even contradictory fashion. Arrighi's *The Long Twentieth Century* exemplifies the idea that cycles of capital accumulation have definitive affinities to spatial arrangements. Arrighi attributes to Marx the recognition that capitalism has boundaries it cannot breach without the destruction and rearticulation of production processes. Working within Marx's theory of the movement of capital (MCM'), Arrighi (1994: 14) argues that Marx, "failed to notice the sequence of leading capitalist states . . . [Venice, Holland, Britain, and the United States] . . . consists of units of increasing size, resources, and world power."[1] Although intrinsically linked to the nation-state, capital eventually outgrows its core and moves elsewhere. Indeed, the geographical mobility of capital has proved one of its most adaptive elements.

Arrighi moreover maintains that this movement is hardly continuous. "Long periods of crises, restructuring and reorganization, in short, of discontinuous change, have been far more typical of the history of the capitalist world economy than those brief moments of generalized expansion along a definitive developmental path like the one that occurred in the 1950s and 1960s" (Arrighi 1994: 1). Within these periods of discontinuity, the acquisition of new territory – and with it both material resources and new markets – has provided a large impetus for the movement of capital. In this sense, the idea that each new cycle of accumulation demands the acquisition of new territory, as well as the re-articulation of existing territory, stands as an important assertion of world systems theory.

V

The work of Arrighi begins to broach an important distinction between the discovery (or even conquest) of space and the production of space. It also begins to allow for the introduction of an analysis of capitalism and its relationship to dominant Western European epistemological assumptions of space.[2]

---

[1] By MCM', Marx (1990: 247–257) means the historical movement of money to commodities and back to money again.

[2] Feminist scholarship, post-colonial studies and post-structuralism have also devoted significant attention to the relationship between capitalism and its ability to produce and define space. This is especially important in thinking not only about large-scale

In the historical movement of capital from Northern Italy to Holland to Britain and then the United States, Arrighi connects the power of capital and empire to its apparent need both to produce more space as well as to constantly redefine its existing spaces. What is not discussed in Arrighi's work, and what is vital to these histories, is the (re)discovery of spatial technologies such as Ptolemaic cartography and geography that played a central role in the success of European colonialism and imperialism. "Together with other tools of the geographic trade – globes, atlases, prints, paintings, travel narratives – maps provided the means to construct, no less than project, an image of power and possession abroad. No mere semblance of empire, maps furnished monarchs and merchants the very materials out of which distant empires could be fashioned" (Schmidt 1997: 551).

Here Schmidt interjects the map itself into the history of colonialism and capitalism. No mere "semblance of empire," the map becomes central to both the ideology and production of empire itself. It is thus no mistake that large portions of the so-called "third world," as well as indigenous populations in the industrialized world have sought to rearticulate narratives of the "New World", Asia and Africa not as histories of "discovery," but rather as histories of usurpation and annihilation. Where Arrighi's work has focused on the movement of markets and capital, for example, the work of those like Walter Mignolo has focused more on the techniques involved in the conquest of what he calls "Amerindian" cultures and societies, including the almost total elimination of indigenous geographical representations of space and time in lieu of those afforded through European cartographic methodologies.

In showing that European representations of space were neither the only nor the best representations of the New World, Mignolo's work complicates narratives of discovery so central to Renaissance and early modern European empire building. That maps were central to these narratives is not surprising, considering their ability to represent the space as fundamentally distinct from time. Conversely, according to Mignolo, Amerindian maps tended to converge spatial representations with time and social or cultural life. Thus, even as Mignolo (1995: 248) notes, "it would be erroneous to retain a homogenous picture of pre-Columbian cosmologies . . . the configuration of space in Mesoamerican and Andean civilization was largely abstract, in contrast to

---

spatial analysis, as in the case of states, but in analyses of small and micro spaces such as the home, the workplace, and public and common spaces.

the European T/O maps, which were based on knowledge of land configuration . . . and unconnected with time." Early modern European maps eviscerated both time and culture from their cartographic representations of the New World, something that many pre-Columbian maps did not do.[3] The European maps, so dependent on technologies of spatial uniformity, became in this manner technologies unto themselves, both in the production of empire and in the epistemology and ideology that accompanied and informed it.

Ideologically, the demarcation of time, space, and culture is evident even in the earliest European maps of the Americas, where in 1503 Amerigo Vespucci referred to discovered lands as "novus" or new, revealing an "unconscious arrogance and deep [European] belief that what was . . . not known had to be, of necessity, new; that what was not known . . . did not exist" (Mignolo 1995: 264). The time and cultures of so-called New World civilizations were, in effect, erased within the spaces of European cartography. In their place arose images and symbols of savagery and cannibalism, mixed with the promise of unspoiled and untamed lands – a type of barbaric Eden full of both peril and promise.

European cartography did something more than ideologically vilify and barbarize pre-Columbian cultures, however. It interpolated a uniform system of coordinates into previously disparate territories, encapsulating wildly diverging topographies, cultures and histories under a comprehensive rubric of latitude and longitude. David Nally (2002) notes, "Put differently, 'turning land into paper' requires a whole host of spatial practices including encoding global space in a unified representational pattern based on geometric projection (measurements); transforming spatial complexities into different pictorial codes (cartographies); and the mediation of space by embodied sub-

---

[3] Walter Mignolo's (1992: 820) work on cartography and colonization is central to any discussion concerning the mapping of the "New World." Mignolo notes that Amerindian cartographers encompassed painting, mapping, and writing into their work, and that the "*tlaculio* was a man of many functions, contrary to the increasing European specialization and distinction between the geographer, the historian and the painter." This disjuncture allowed for a mobilization on the part of the European colonizers, an "overpowering force of European cartography in the colonization of space and the process of putting the Americas on the map, which was at the same time a process of concealing the Amerindian's representation of space." His work suggests a critique not of technique, nor of sophistication, but rather of a particular type of representation which allowed the Europeans to successfully represent land in a manner conducive to both the domination of persons and facilitation of commerce and conquest.

jects moving through the landscape (narratives)." Lands and people, once disparate, could now be unified under a technical language of grids and spatial conformity.

Such a uniform co-ordination of spatial representation stands as a central achievement in Europe's race towards colonization and the auspices of early capitalism.[4] In this sense the history of modern mapmaking cannot be (although often is) separated from the history of European colonization, war and the development of markets. The immense profitability of conquest and new possible markets for raw materials and finished goods created a high demand for maps. McLuhan notes (1994: 157–158) that maps commanded both a high price as well as a significant effort on the part of rulers to keep maps of the New World secret. David Harvey (1990: 228) argues moreover that "the [European] mapping of the world opened up a way to look upon space as open to appropriation for private uses," and in the rush toward establishing trade routes and colonial settlements, "[t]he cost of cartographic ignorance – militarily as well as in trade and commerce – was so enormous that the incentive to procure good maps overwhelmed any other reservations." With this in mind, perhaps the real discovery of those earliest explorers and monarchs was not the land itself, but rather the particular representation of space that, in a very real and brutal manner, engendered the production and extraction of wealth from Asia, Africa and the Americas.

If European cartography effectively erased Amerindian representations of the world, it was similarly effective in redefining Europe's view of its own space and territory. This echoes Arrighi's insistence that discontinuous change, and not merely generalized expansion, lay at the heart of capital movement. For where European cartography abetted its colonial aspirations in the New World, it also accompanied significant social and economic changes in Europe. Such changes tended to favor merchants and finance capitalists at the expense of monarchy. The well-known painting of Elizabeth I by Ditchley illuminates the fact that emerging technologies of cartography and representation had the effect of conceptually separating the monarchy from the land.

In his book *The Condition of Postmodernity*, David Harvey (1990: 247) references Ditchley's painting as an example "which helps [to] explain the support that the Renaissance maps of England supplied to individualism, nationalism

---

[4] What Marx refers to as "primitive accumulation."

Figure 1. The Ditchley Portrait of Elizabeth I (1592).

and parliamentary democracy at the expense of dynastic privilege." Harvey does not elaborate further on why this particular image helps explain how this new system of mapmaking contributed to the growth of individualism and parliamentary democracy. Indeed, he cites Helgerson, who argues that maps could just as easily serve to support a strongly centralized monarchy (Harvey 1990: 227). In the painting, Elizabeth stands as an imposing figure *over* the map of Europe, and it is possible to read this work as a *representation* of the English monarchy's quest for hegemony and domination in Europe, where the light of the heavens shines upon the West, and darkness shrouds the East. It is the West that has become the center of commerce and conquest, and by this time the English monarchy had begun to actualize the benefits, and taste the fruits, of enlightenment cartography.

The portrait of Elizabeth does something else as well, something that provides an important clue to Harvey's enigmatic proposition above. As Shelburne and Holt (1997) note, in the space of the medieval world, "conventionally the monarch *is* the land. The strange and iconic Ditchley portrait of Queen Elizabeth seeks to reiterate this point by imposing Elizabeth on a map of England. But the portrait makes this equation at the price of admitting a disjunction: she's on the land, not of it or in it." This distinction opened "a conceptual gap between the land and its ruler," a gap that Helgerson argues "would eventually span battlefields" (Helgerson 1994: 114). The battlefields Helgerson has in mind, according to Shelburne and Holt (1997) are:

a strange episode in the history of English mapmaking. The first atlas of Britain (i.e., England and Wales) was published in 1579 by Christopher Saxton under royal sponsorship. The maps in Saxton's atlas became standard, and they were repeatedly copied, for instance in the Atlas of John Speed. One copy, printed in 1644 claims that "this map was reduced from the county maps of Mr. Saxton by order of Oliver Cromwell for the use of his armies (Helgerson 1994: 108)." The Queen's (by then the King's) maps are also those of his revolting subjects: the land is up for grabs.[5]

In the Ditchley painting, the land is up for grabs because the map can stand alone, without Elizabeth or any other monarch. Moreover, one can imagine, as did Cromwell, a different figurehead standing in dominion over the map. For while the feudal world operated largely under the divine right of a contract of *fee*, "a conditional right to occupy and exploit the land" (Coquillette 1999: 96) the demarcation of Elizabeth and the map impart a new spatial sensibility devoid of absolute dominion. It is this disjuncture Harvey and Helgerson find interesting. No longer synonymous with the land, the monarch becomes one among many who struggle to achieve and maintain control over it.

In the context of the Cromwellian revolution and English Civil Wars (1642–1651), the portrait of Elizabeth takes on added significance. For if the land was conceptually "up for grabs" in the painting itself, the first British enclosure movement beginning in 1534 ushered in a radically different understanding of land rights and use.[6] While the first enclosure movement was small in scale when compared to later enclosures, it nevertheless enabled a conceptual distinction between land and ownership. This conceptual possibility, impossible a century prior, was almost certainly tied to emerging capital markets, including both an increase in demand for textile commodities as well as significant developments in trade routes. Barrington Moore (1966: 14–16), for example, has argued that the English landed aristocracy in the

---

[5] As Harvey notes, "Helgerson . . . argues that Christopher Saxon's collections of country maps of Britain, published in 1579, not only allowed the English, for the first time, to take 'effective visual and conceptual possession of the physical kingdom in which they lived,' but also strengthened the sense of individual and local powers within a framework of national loyalties" (Harvey 1990: 228).

[6] The first enclosure movement, dating approximately from 1534 to 1603, was the beginning in a series of British laws designed to forcibly remove serfs from the estates of landed aristocracy and other "common" lands. During this time, land which had previously been used primarily for the production of foodstuffs became valuable as the market for textiles and other commodity crops increased.

fifteenth and sixteenth centuries found themselves caught between an absolutist monarchy and an increasingly wealthy urban class. In the framework of increasing commercialization, the aristocracy was forced to either adopt more commercial outlooks concerning land, or perish. The landed aristocracy, who for so long had generally abided the peasant class to the degree that they were able to eek out a living on "their land," moved towards a much different use of the land, one governed less by noble obligation or even the state of incipit local economies, and more by the growth of urban markets in which commodities could be traded and sold for profit. Moreover, according to Wallerstein (1974: 77–78) at this point in time:

> There was not only a price rise, but a wage lag ... Hamilton argued [1929: 355–56] that as prices rose, wages and rents failed to keep abreast of prices because of institutional rigidities – in England and France, but not in Spain. This created a gap, a sort of windfall profit, which was the major source of capital accumulation in the sixteenth century. "In England and France the vast discrepancy between prices and wages, born of the price revolution, deprived laborers of a large part of the incomes they had hitherto enjoyed, and diverted this wealth to the recipients of other distributive shares ... Rents, as well as wages, lagged behind prices; so landlords gained nothing from labour's loss ... The windfalls thus received, along with gains from the East India trade ... and the stupendous profits obtainable supplied an incentive for the feverish pursuit of capitalistic enterprise."

Stated otherwise, this rise in prices could not sustain an aristocracy whose major source of income was rents from peasants or tenant farmers. Commodity crops and textiles, and in particular wool, served to supplant the falling rents. In turn, the peasants and tenant farmers, who for so long had survived largely from the land and small cottage industries, were removed, often quite brutally.

Even where the removal of peasants from their land was a mere foreshadowing of later and larger enclosures, it was nevertheless significant enough for Cromwell to draw his insurgency. Thus, it is not only in Ditchley's painting where the land becomes up for grabs, but in the first enclosure movement and ensuing challenge to noble control where land itself begins to take on the now familiar tones of private property, what Harvey (1990: 254) has called "freely alienable parcels of private property, to be bought and traded at will upon the market." In this important regard, these new technologies of spatial representation served not only the nobility, as well as merchants and explorers engaged in foreign conquest and trade, but also landowners and the emerging bourgeoisie in their push toward the private appropriation of land.

VI

In the case of European cartography and its relation to both the "New World" as well as to Western Europe's movement toward a private appropriation of land, we see an echo of Harvey's quarrel with the history of social theory. If such theory has, within the last one hundred or so years, tended to "broadly assume either the existence of some pre-existing spatial order within which temporal processes operate," (Harvey 1990: 205) the predominant histories of Europe and its colonial conquests have reduced space to a mere contingency. Marx's "annihilation of space" becomes nothing more than the history of increasing technologies which serve to make markets smaller and more accessible, as for example in the transition from carriage to automobile to airplane.

There remains, however, another important aspect of this equation, one that recognizes not only the increased mastery over territory, but rather the production of space itself as a vital element in the growth of Western capitalism. It is not enough to say, as the textbooks do, that land was "discovered." It is also not enough to say that territory was conquered or made more readily malleable through increased technology and larger markets. Rather, the specific processes through which space itself enters into the means and relations of production must remain central to any history that seeks to uncover the specific crossroads between capitalism and representation.

An inquiry of this sort is useful in the consideration of colonial "discovery" as well as the establishment of private property in the first and ensuing enclosure movements. It is also crucial in understanding the full force of Marx's statement. Capital does not merely seek to overcome the physical limitations of the land. It also transforms land into space in a manner that renders it uniformly pliable for both the facilitation and turnover of capital. Thus, while the "land" itself may retain unique characteristics, the manner in which it is represented in the emerging maps of fifteenth and sixteenth centuries converges uniformly under a grid of latitude and longitude amenable to conquest as well as commerce. To conceptualize capitalism as a world system is to understand then not only the acquisition and expropriation of ever-increasing areas in the search for materials, markets and profit. Instead, if, "with each crisis, [capitalism] mutates into a larger sphere of activity and a wider field of penetration, of control, investment and transformation (Jameson 1998: 139)," it is because it has produced the very territory itself, as well as the mechanisms of control, investment and transformation through which it operates.

VII

Returning to the Norwegian map, these histories of conquest must give pause to even the most innocuous geographical representations. What exactly is at stake in the representation of territory? For colonial Europe, wracked by war, famine and an economic system increasingly dependent on liquidity, the representation of space provided both a means as well as an ideological justification for increased dominion. Indeed, the map was, and remains, a particularly useful tool in this case for the reason that it removes space from considerations of power, conveniently erasing any traces of its maker.

For now, we are confronted with a 16,000-mile long epistemological suture. Very quickly this wound will heal and be sublimated into new textbooks, new computer models, new representations which are *more correct*. Yet conceptually, this suture remains present and allows us to speak more concisely about what Gilles Deleuze and Felix Guattari call processes of "reterritorialization." For while the world systems theorists have shown us that, historically, capitalism is always both extending its geographical boundaries as well as reconfiguring existing ones, the work of Deleuze and Guattari (1983: 259) moves beyond the notion of mere geographic re-articulation:

> [O]n the one hand, capitalism can proceed only by continually developing the subjective essence of abstract wealth or production for the sake of production, that is, "production as an end in itself, the absolute development of the social productivity of labor," but on the other hand and at the same time, it can do so only in the framework of its own limited purpose, as a determinate mode of production, "production of capital," 'the self-expansion of existing capital." Under the first aspect capitalism is continually surpassing its own limits, always deterritorializing further, "displaying a cosmopolitan, universal energy which overthrows every restriction and bond," but under the second, strictly complementary, aspect, capitalism is continually confronting limits and barriers that are interior and immanent to itself, and that, precisely because they are immanent, let themselves be

overcome only provided they are reproduced on a wider scale (always more territorialization – local, world-wide, planetary).

It is not merely geographic space that is reconfigured in the movement of capitalism. Rather, capitalism seeks to define, articulate and produce a multiplicity of spaces, both in hitherto undefined realms as well as in existing and familiar territories. Perhaps this is what Hannah Arendt (1958: 253) had in mind when she observed that, "Under modern conditions, not destruction but conservation spells ruin because the very durability of conserved objects is the greatest impediment to the turn over process, whose constant gain in speed is the only constant left wherever it has taken hold." Or as Deleuze and Guattari (1983: 257) profess, capitalism must always deterritorialize with one hand what is reterritorialized with the other.

Historically, for Marx and Arrighi, such territorialization is not haphazard in that the manic logic of Marx's cycles of accumulation (MCM′) are connected to both the increasing geographical scope of new markets as well as the saturation of existing markets. As Jameson (1998: 153) notes, "in any specific region of production . . . there comes a moment in which the logic of capitalism – faced with the saturation of local and even foreign markets – determines an abandonment of that specific kind of production . . ." In this manner, the movement of capital and the abandonment of specific types of production are arguably as old as capitalism itself.

The work of Michel Foucault, among others, offers the proposition that one locus of (re)territorialization is the human body itself. In his work, Foucault diagrams a new mechanism of power, "more dependent upon bodies and what they do than upon the earth and its products. It is a mechanism of power," writes Foucault (1980: 104), "which permits time and labour, rather than wealth and commodities, to be extracted from bodies." Here, Foucault is speaking about the disciplining of bodies, the historical shift from a discontinuous power of the sovereign to a type of power which functions through "a tightly knit grid of material coercions . . . which introduces a genuinely new economy of power [which] must be able to simultaneously . . . increase the subjected forces and to improve the efficacy and force of that which subjects them" (Foucault 1980: 104).

There is sufficient precedent in the "arrangement" of bodies so integral to increased productive efficiency. Frederick Taylor, in his *Principles of Scientific Management* (1911) proposed this idea almost a century ago. Weber spoke similarly of the arrangement of disciplined bodies on the factory floor and in the ranks of armies. Foucault is not speaking, however, merely of increased economic efficiency in production. Rather, he is speaking also of the notion of a transition to an economy of bodies themselves. If for Marx, the physical corpus of the laborer is required in order to extract exchange value from raw materials (even if the surplus value arises from the exploitation of the laborer), Foucault suggests the possibility that particular regimes of discipline serve to supplant (or at least accentuate) commodity production as a prerequisite for the extraction of time and labour from bodies.

Foucault's work on the early modern prison details a history of the movement to such an economy:

> The failure of the project was immediate, and it was realized virtually from the start. In 1820 it was already understood that the prisons, far from transforming criminals into honest citizens, serve only to manufacture new criminals . . . Prisons manufactured delinquents, but delinquents turned out to be useful, in the economic domain as much as the political . . . For example, because of the profits that can be made in the exploitation of sexual pleasure, we find the establishment in the nineteenth century of the great prostitution business, which was possible only thanks to the delinquents who served as the medium for the capitalization of everyday, paid-for sexual pleasure . . . [Moreover] As it was initially conceived, penal labour was an apprenticeship not so much in this or that trade as in the virtues of labor itself. Pointless work, for pointless work's sake . . . from the 1830s, it became clear that in fact the aim was not to retrain delinquents . . . but to regroup them within a clearly demarcated, card-indexed milieu which could serve as a tool for economic or political ends (Foucault 1980: 40–42).

Here Foucault is speaking of something quite different than increased individuated economic efficiency, in the Weberian or even Marxist sense. Instead of bodies being trained in particular tasks oriented toward increased production, it is bodies themselves that serve as both producer and product. In Foucault's example of penal labor, the body of the criminal has been largely abandoned as a site of productive economy. In it place arises a body which serves as a mechanism of inscription through which criminality is written, coaxed, confessed. The truth of the body lies no longer in its productive capacity *per se*, but rather in its particular arrangements in a larger economy.

Much of the force of Foucault's work lies not in the mapping of criminality, nor even in the history of penalization. It lies rather in what he saw as the formulation of discursive disciplinary regimes that constituted the body as an object, and not merely a subject, within capitalism.[7] His work followed numerous "genealogies" – the prison, the clinic, the asylum, the couch. Within these apparently disparate milieus exists a body required to confess the truth of its nature – the criminal, the patient, the homosexual. If Foucault's economy of the body represents within these genealogies a process of "reterritorialization," then what is the truth that the body confesses today? Almost certainly there are many. Let us propose, however, that a primary one at the beginning of the twenty-first century is the truth of biology.

VIII

In the case of the Norwegian coastline, these 16,000 miles begin to look less like a discovery, and more an abandonment of one type of production in lieu of another. The productive process of "turning land into paper" fades against the new productive impetus of turning land into digital information. The coastline itself is reterritorialized in the language of the new cartography, in the language of digital informatics, where the eye of the satellite "completely blurs the line between cartography and satellite imagery" (Wood 1993: 92).

Digital cartography has replaced the maps of yesteryear. The new images of land and space emerge as so many "millions of pixels that [have] been transmitted from . . . satellites" (Wood 1993: 92). Lest one imagine for a moment, however, that this new map represents the real Norwegian coastline, Denis Wood (1993) has the following to say about the Geosphere mapping project, the "original" satellite maps of the Earth:[8]

---

[7] One criticism of Foucault's work on the body has been his lack of nuance in relation to gender and race. In regard to Foucault's work on the prison, Angela Davis (1998: 96–7) notes, "As interesting as it may be to examine the influences of the earlier European models on the emergent US prison system, what may help us to understand the way in which this system would eventually incorporate, sustain and transform structures of racism is an examination of the impact of slavery on US systems of punishment." Davis is rightly concerned that Foucault's "body" is in fact the ubiquitous white male body, and that the history of antebellum incarceration in the South follows a decidedly different lineage. In light of Davis' critique, we should consider Deleuze and Guattari's notion of reterritorialization in the widest possible terms, where bodies can be both subjected to the cruelest forms of exploitation as well as functioning as territory for the production of wants, needs, and desires. The Black Woman in American cultural and economic history is a prime example of the exploitation of labor and the facilitation of "criminal" desire.

[8] According to the Geosphere project (http://www.geosphere.com/imagery.html), the Geosphere image of the earth "is the original satellite map of Earth, showing the

The GeoSphere map embodies its own ideological commitments every bit as much as do the mappaemundi, the Ptolemaic maps and the maps of the nineteenth century. Like many of his predecessors, Van Sant opted to run the equator across the heart of his map, to put the Atlantic in its middle and to orient it north up. Van Sant openly acknowledges that he filtered and modified the . . . data in a number of deliberate subjective ways. The exclusion of clouds itself omits a distinctive dominant feature of the earth as seen from space. In places where cloud free images were unavailable, the researchers artificially subtracted the clouds, pixel by pixel . . . River systems have been thickened to make them more visible, and false color was applied – ironically, to make the vegetative cover appear more real . . . The lighting and coloration of the Van Sant map emphasize the natural aspects of the earth while omitting the landmarks of human society. W.T. Sullivan . . . created a nearly antithetical map that focuses instead on the impact of humans (Wood 1993).

Two important points come to light from Wood's cartographic confession. First, the production of representation commences irrespective of any "real" object. Wood's work offers an alternative to the proposition that differing maps are merely a product of differing tools, biases or mediums of representation. Maps do not merely fail in their ability to truly depict objective representations. Rather, they actively produce the notion of objective space itself.

The other important point in relation to Wood's comment is the realization the production of representation is, and always must be, connected to relations of power. The creation of an objective other allows for space (as opposed to time) to be "treated as a fact of nature, 'naturalized' through the assignment of common-sense everyday meanings" (de Certeau 1984: 121). Van Sant's predilections regarding the filtering and presentation of data are more than the subjective position of an author. As de Certeau (1984: 121) notes, the map itself functions as a "totalizing stage," on which is played out

world as it appears from space. The image was first published as the title page of the 1990 National Geographic World Atlas . . . Since its creation, it has been the best-selling image in the world . . . The cloud free image was created from multiple whole Earth mosaics of satellite scenes, utilizing two visual bands and three thermal bands from the NOAA TIROS satellite. Each of the satellite mosaics was itself a full 43,200 × 21,600 pixels resolution image. These were combined with high resolution hydrology and elevation databases."

the "eliminat[ion] little by little . . . the practices which produce it." In the case of European expansionism, the rediscovered Ptolemaic map became a practice of the, "rhetorical visualization of the unknown, an invitation to *fill the blank space*, and to explore that previous inauspicious West beyond the ocean sea" (Harvey and Woodward 1991: 6–8).[9] Lefebvre (1991: 8–9) proposes that, to take seriously a "science of space" (i.e. a systematic analysis of the relation of space and time to the historical contingencies of capitalism), one must take into account the manner in which space "represents the political use of knowledge . . . [remembering] that knowledge under this system is integrated in a more or less 'immediate' way into the forces of production . . . [and] implies an ideology designed to conceal that use, along with the conflicts intrinsic to the highly interested employment of a supposedly disinterested knowledge."

In this manner, "discovery" is substituted in lieu of "production," where spaces and objects become naturalized within a process of never-ceding reterritorialization. "Discovered" objects wait patiently outside the realm of human affairs in the world of nature. As such, they are not susceptible to contingencies of power that might seek to resist their truths. They serve the important role of eviscerating the human element from their existence. For Martin Heidegger, this was the compelling relationship between capitalism and technology. In situating "discovered" objects within the boundaries of the productive economy (and specifically capitalism – a recognition made with Marx) in which the very notion of the concept of the object itself is produced, either with or without the production of the actual object, Heidegger (1977: 16–17) was encouraging his reader to forego the myth of discovery:

> The revealing that holds sway throughout modern technology does not unfold into a bringing-forth in the sense of a *poiēsis*. The revealing which rules in modern technology is a challenging [*Herausfordern* – a calling forth or summoning to action, provocation], which puts to nature the unreasonable demand that it supply energy that can be extracted and stored as such . . . The earth now reveals itself as a coal mining district, the soil as a mineral deposit . . . even the cultivation of the field has come under the grip of another kind of setting-in-order, which *sets* upon nature . . . Agriculture is now the mechanized food industry. Air is now set upon to yield nitrogen, the earth to yield ore, ore to yield uranium . . .

---

[9] My emphasis.

A distinction remains. Heidegger was speaking of already transformed objects... tilled soil, processed nitrogen, mined uranium, dammed rivers. Yet whether or not these objects have actually undergone a transformation was of secondary consideration for Heidegger. Instead, he confronted modern technology as an ordering revealing – an unmasking of the standing of the object only in relation to the ordering of other objects. His portrayal of the forester typifies this proposition of the ordering revealing. The woodsman who, "in the wood, measures the felled timber and to all appearances walks the same forest path in the same way as did his grandfather, is today commanded by profit-making in the lumber industry, whether he knows it or not. He is made subordinate to the orderability of cellulose, which for its part is challenged forth by the need for paper, which is then delivered to newspapers and illustrated magazines" (Heidegger 1977: 17–18). Trees, as all objects, even without ever having been touched, stand ready as objects *on call for inspection.* They are already usurped into what he calls the "standing reserve." The transformation of objects into a standing reserve is peculiar to an economic and social system that demands that all things (made visible) be brought into a productive network of relations.[10] If the map serves as an invitation to fill in blank space, it is because the space itself has been produced as standing reserve. All objects which become visible the under such a gaze find their truth, in part, in their ability to be mapped, to be opened up and transformed (produced) as not merely a subject, but rather as Foucault understood, as objects of knowledge.

For Heidegger, humans are not exempted in an ordering of standing reserve, centered on the continual expansion of production. In manner similar to trees, rivers, land, water, they become themselves resources even as they participate in the production of such an ordering.[11] "The current talk about human

---

[10] I use the term 'made visible' here in recognition of the fact that, just as the traces of production are erased from the naturalized map, surplus economies and populations (particularly those of the third world) are erased from the virtual map – whether it be a map of discourse which cannot allow the word 'genocide' to remain visible, or maps of information flows which illuminate the flow of capital and information while rendering the rest of the world as nothingness. For examples of these maps see < http://mappa.mundi.net/maps/maps_021/> for a map of international aggregate news flow, and < http://mappa.mundi.net/maps/maps_020/> for a map of international Internet topography.

[11] Heidegger notes, however, "Yet precisely because man is challenged more originally than are the energies of nature, i.e., into the process of ordering, he is never transformed into mere standing-reserve. Since man drives technology forward, he takes part in ordering as a way of revealing." *Question*, 18.

resources, about the supply of patients for a clinic, gives evidence of this" (Heidegger 1977: 18).[12] Much like Foucault's supply of criminals to the prison, the supply of patients to the clinic denotes a fundamental shift from a Marxist analysis that understands human labor-power as the commodity central to capitalism. Free labor, for Marx, cannot exist without a market for commodities, i.e. a transformation on a societal scale from an economy of use-value to an economy of exchange-value. Yet for Marx, commodities require labor to extract value, and while value may come from the expropriation of surplus labor (and not from the commodity itself), a tree is no good either to the worker or the owner in a capitalist economy until it has been transformed. Heidegger's concern, however, was not of the transformative power of capitalism *per se*, but rather the creation of the actual objects themselves. Thus, one might say that "nature" grows trees, and capitalism turns those trees into pulp or timber. Heidegger's work suggests an opposite position. It is, in modern capitalism, impossible to conceive of trees outside the ordering process of the standing reserve. "Nature," does not create trees, nor is excess coastline discovered. They are themselves produced. In as much as Marx's recognition still applies to elements of productive economies, namely the production of goods, the work of Foucault and Heidegger suggest that it is the body itself which is fast becoming the predominate object of production, and not merely a subject from which labor power can be exploited.

IX

The myth of discovery, however, is a vital one in the case of the production of bodies as objects, as much as it was to (and remains central in) narratives of colonial conquest. The maintenance of a subject/object epistemology has its own history in the body, a history analogous to European histories of colonial conquest. In the early sixteenth century, some thirty years after the expedition of Columbus, Vesalius opened up the body to the medical gaze. If it is true that, at this time, capitalism was producing new cartographic representations in its "feverish pursuit of profit," cannot the same be said about

---

[12] Today, the supply of patients to the clinic has extended to the supply of prisoners in the United States. Often corporations contract with prisons, or even run the prisons for profit, and are guaranteed a minimum number of prisoners for newly built facilities and the requisite labor.

Figure 2. Title Page of *De Humani Corporis Fabrica*, Andreas Vesalius (1543).

the body where, within a short time of the arrival of the surgeon's gaze, medicine was seeking to (re)territorialize what it had only previously opened up? As Foucault's work illustrates, medicine sought to naturalize its newly opened spaces in a manner not dissimilar from that of other explorers. By the beginning of the eighteenth century, the foundation of the clinic as an institution of knowledge was able to "present [the practical knowledges of medicine] as the restitution of an eternal truth in a continuous historical development in which events alone have been of a negative order: oblivion, illusion, concealment" (Foucault 1994: 57). Much like the geographical maps of the empire, "this way of rewriting history itself evaded a much truer but much more complex history. It masked that other history by assimilating to clinical method all the study of cases, in the old sense of the word; and, therefore, it authorized all subsequent simplifications whereby clinical medicine became simply the examination of the individual" (Foucault 1994: 57). Here we find echoes of Mignolo's work, where European cartography has erased pre-Columbian representations of land/space/time/culture, becoming instead merely "the examination of land."

Vesalius occupies an interesting historical position, and his *De Fabrica* presents an odd spectacle. Here the corpse is laid open—not only to the gaze of the practitioner—but also to the public. Lind (1949: p. ax) tells us that public dissections were common in the Renaissance. Previous to the Renaissance, the practice of cutting open bodies for medical purposes was largely forbidden under Church law. But here, in the public dissection of the body, the corpse is itself produced, in a manner concomitant with the production of space occurring at the same time in European history. Both representations, land and body, are virtually doubled, and brought under the auspices of an objectifying gaze. In his discussion of Vesalius, Robert Romanyshyn makes the distinction between "dead body" and "corpse" in describing the fundamental effect of opening up the body for medical purposes. For where the dead body was both visible (in that death was not hidden away from the living) and dynamic (in that the body of the dead held significant emotive and spiritual power) in medieval Europe, the corpse becomes something quite different under the rubric of medical science. "It offers a life which is both divorced from birth and death, a sanitized life, as purified and cleansed of the smell of death as it is detached from the mess of life. It offers, in short, a life which destined to become a mechanism, a life in which the Vesalian corpse will soon become a machine" (Romanyshyn 1989: 127–8).

The body as machine illuminates the convergence of a subject/object epistemology firmly rooted in the entrails of productive (re)territorialization. It also illuminates the successful integration of Christian views of women into a proto-technical view of the body. For where men were borne into the image of God (and women borne into the image of man), these earliest technical representations took for granted the primacy of the male image as machine. As much as Christian views of gender linked men to the higher objectivity of God, they also linked women to the base subjectivity of bodily experience – desire, temptation and impurity. That the earliest anatomical maps of the body were almost exclusively male bring to light the full force of Deleuze and Guattari's insistence that existing spaces are not merely abandoned, but rather re-territorialized. In this case, such a (re)territorialization accommodated both existing structures of gendered power as well as the burgeoning scientific-medical demarcation of subject and object, in this case the subject of the dead body and the object of anatomical representation.

Where the image of women was erased or disavowed in the body as machine, the public as spectator disappeared not long after. By the end of the eighteenth century, the public spectacle of the opening of the body, evident in Vesalius' *De Fabrica*, disappeared almost entirely from the viewing of the corpse. The last public dissection in Britain occurred in 1830. By the time of the lithograph below (1883), the process of discovery occurred entirely behind closed doors. The space of the body, or more accurately, the production of the maps of the body, becomes the exclusive domain of professionals. No

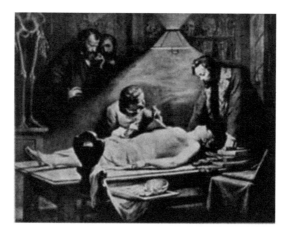

Figure 3. Lithograph of Public Dissection (1883).

longer conducted for the edification of the public, the technical acuity required of the anatomist now excluded the prying eyes of spectators, even while such work was conducted ostensibly for their benefit. It is the beginning of an era in medicine which Arney and Bergan (1984: 8–28) call the "disappearance of the experiencing person."

This disappearance constitutes the rise of pathology as the legitimating medical methodology. "Reiser tells us that the physician at the beginning of the seventeenth century . . . relied chiefly on three techniques to diagnose illness: 'the patient's statement in words which described his symptoms; the physicians observations of the signs of the illness, his patient's physical appearance and behavior'" (Arney and Bergan 1984: 12). By the end of the nineteenth century, however, any reliance on the patient's experience had given way to a look into the body itself. "The rule physicians had to follow was look into the body and see the disease . . . The patient's speech about his experience of his body and the physician's experience of the patient disappeared from the medical encounter" (Arney and Bergan 1984: 12).

The map of the interior of the body became the locus of medical truth. "You may take notes for twenty years, from morning to night at the bedside of the sick," wrote Reiser (1978: 1), "and all will be to you only a confusion of symptoms, which, not being united at one point, will necessarily present only a train of incoherent phenomena. *Open up a few bodies*; this obscurity will soon disappear, which observation alone would have never been able to dissipate." The truth of the body under the medical gaze becomes a technical truth. The confession of the illness must come from deep within the body itself – indeed only those who can open the body up can decipher this confession. It is a confession in which the person plays a secondary role. It is no longer experience that reveals illness, but rather technique.

Under this regime, the maps of the anatomists became increasingly detailed, giving way to a structured ordering in which the language of biological systems – respiratory, vascular, immune – came to resemble that of a complex machine. Such and ordering was no doubt appropriate in relation to the rise of an increasingly mechanistic and industrial society. However far removed these systems remain today from the experiences of the patient (i.e. how does one experience an immune system?), the image and representation of the body as a complex machine, knowable through the increased mapping of the simplest components and functions, persists. Indeed, the imagery of the body as machine, as a composition of systems, exists still as a primary map and metaphor. It is, in another sense however, what Arney and Bergen call a *pentimento* – the term used to describe old paintings where one image has been painted over another, but the old image remains ghostly visible.

X

The image of the body as a machine is indeed becoming a ghostly one. Arney and Bergen's *pentimento* is highly akin to the epistemological suture present in the discord of the two Norwegian coasts, where the image of the old coastline fades against the strength of the new one. And much like the new coastline, the new image of the body is a digital one. In this image, the materiality of the body and the land cede to a new episteme, dependent no longer on the cartographic tools of the of the geographer or the anatomical charts of the physician, but rather on a type of representation discernable only to the digital eye. Where the maps of the cartographers required exploration (and conquest), and the maps of the anatomists required dissection, the embodiment of land and flesh is eviscerated through a mapping process far less brusque.

In understanding the centrality of the discovery myth, both to the Western epistemological demarcation of subject/object and specifically to maps, it is not surprising that this new technical form of representation has engendered its own peculiar narrative. "This time around, nature is cast in the image of the computer and the language of physics, chemistry, mathematics and information sciences" (Rifkin 1998: 211). This story, like those before it, begins with a map, an opening of "empty spaces" which lend themselves, in this case, to a ceaseless and perhaps real-time reterritorialization. "There's been a general increase in information processing over the last 550 million years, and particularly in the last 150 million years," writes E.O. Wilson (in Levin 1992: 138). "Information processing," according to Francisco Kayla, is the degree to which organisms adapt to their environment through "the ability to retain and process information about the environment, and to react accordingly, [allowing] the organism to seek out suitable environments . . . and avoid unstable ones." (in Levin 1992: 211). Organisms, in this manner, *do not* mean people, animals, or even living things. Organisms, from the standpoint of cybernetics, merely denote particular arrangements of information that interact with larger informational flows. Thus, Norbert Weiner (1954: 38) could state without much hesitation that, "the physical functioning of the living individual and the operations of some of the newer communicating machines are precisely parallel in their analogous attempts to control entropy through feedback." It is not that machines are becoming more like people, nor even people more like machines. Rather, the materiality of both becomes subordinate to a compatibility of digital language and communication that links them together.

Information theory allows E.O. Wilson to rewrite the history of the world as the evolution of an autopoietic (i.e. self-producing and sustaining) system. It matters little that "information processing" – the idea that information has a distinct existence outside of the "markers which embody it" – emerged only "in the wake of WWII" (Hayles 1999: 14, 25).[13] Within the last fifty years, a fundamental shift occurred which has allowed those like Wilson to speak not merely of information as conceptually distinct from material objects, but rather as having its own history, its own beginning and end, its own telos. In this history, the existing maps of the body become obsolete; as antiquated as the maps of the explorers who utilize the stars in order to locate their fixed position on a map, and as outdated as the physician who charts the biological systemic centers of the body.

Indeed, there are no fixed positions, no longitude or latitude, no heart or

---

[13] According to Hayles (1999: 14), "By 1948, the distinction [between informational patterns and material objects] had coalesced sufficiently for [Norbert] Weiner to articulate it as a criterion that any adequate theory of materiality would be forced to meet."

brain. As Pfohl (1997) notes, "Inside and out, cybernetics offers a model of 'circular causation' . . . Which comes first: the cybernetic chicken or a golden egg? The answer, of course, is neither. Both are circularly caused: interactively, dynamically, reciprocally. Not mechanically, but in information-governed energetic exchange . . . By making informational objects out of each other, ceaseless and circular cybernetic communicators alter the environments within which they and others energetically interact." Thus, while genetics and the ideal of the gene existed before the "discovery" of the double helix, it is only with the formulation of cybernetic principals that Watson and Crick begin the process of liberating the truth of the body from the body itself. "In a long molecule," wrote Watson and Crick (1953: 967), "many different permutations are possible, and it therefore seems likely that the precise sequence of the bases is the code which carries the genetical information."[14] If the heart lies at the center of the circulatory system, and the brain at the center of the nervous system, the gene has no corresponding biological system. The only "system" in which it functions is in the systems of information exchange, in the language of code. In this sense, where Vesalius was compelled to tear open to the body and force its anatomical confessions, the truth of the gene requires no such intrusion.

The anatomical maps of those like Vesalius were an extrapolation of the general from the specific. By opening up one body, it was possible to ascertain the general functions of the species insofar as these maps were intended to *represent* all bodies or functions thereof. How odd then that the new map of biology, the genetic map, is a map of the specific which derivates its truth from the most general. That is to say, the map of the human gene is a map of *no person at all*. It is a totally virtual map. Indeed, there exists no individual in the world whose genetic code resembles this map. Where the white male body was the archetype for the maps of the anatomists (and much of medicine), the map of the gene is a map of nobody, and (we are told) of everybody.[15] Borges' tale of the map becomes Baudrillard's tale of the simulacrum. For in Borges' myth, the map has a corresponding object from which

---

[14] As Keller (1995: 19) notes, while for Watson and Crick this 'code' was more metaphorical than actual, it was nevertheless seminal because "it authorized the expectation . . . that biological information does not increase in the course of development, it is already fully contained in the gene."

[15] According to the geneticists, all humans share some 99.9% of all genes.

its representation is conceived. Baudrillard's simulacrum is not merely the triumph of the subjective map over it objective counterpart. Rather it is the map with no original.

In his work *The Order of Things*, Foucault (1973: 231–232) argued that by 1795 a transformation had occurred (largely in the work of Cuvier) which allowed the natural sciences to introduce a precise and technical definition of life. In what Foucault termed the "era of biology," the natural sciences moved away from Aristotelian systems of classification, towards the principle of the "organic," the deduction of the living and the non-living through the classification of biological function. In the opening up of corpses, physicians and anatomists began a new process of classification through the mapping of organic structure and function. In the tracing of such functions, these maps charted the biological division between organic and inorganic, between life and death. In the case of the gene, however, the "map" of Watson and Crick's double helix in turn virtualizes the space of the body itself, so that the division of organic and inorganic ceases to have any functional meaning. Weiner's (1954: 38) insistence that "the physical functioning of the living individual and the operations of some of the newer communicating machines are precisely parallel" makes sense only in the conceptualization of the body, or more specifically the gene, as information which can easily transverse the boundaries so dear to the mapmakers of the body.

Lefebvre's (1991: 8–9) earlier claim, that space "represents the political use of knowledge," becomes here particularly germane. For "[remembering] that knowledge under this system is integrated in a more or less 'immediate' way into the forces of production . . . [and] implies an ideology designed to conceal that use," the map of the human genome (as in E.O. Wilson's history) eliminates all competing maps. As early as 1924, T.H. Morgan observed, "It is clear that whatever the cytoplasm contributes to [embryonic] development is almost entirely under the influence of genes carried from the chromosome, and therefore may in a sense be said to be indifferent" (1924: 728). Cytoplasmic indifference? Or rather impotence. In the face of the gene, the fleshy cells and their requisite maps are relegated to the realms of yesteryear. They, more than anything, become the *pentimentos* of bioinformatics.

XI

Bioinformatics is not only a story about the history of the body represented. It is also a story about the peculiar relationship of space to the incessant demands of capitalism, where space as the political use of knowledge *is* "integrated in a more or less 'immediate' way into the forces of production." For if the gene is the new map of the body, it employs tactics similar to those maps of the physicians and cartographers, tactics designed to bring forth the "invisible" and the "discovered" into the forces of production.

That this map is virtual should not incur surprise. Virtuality lies at the heart of the modern cartographic project. If there is anything new, it is rather the speed and totality in which the virtual project of bioinformatics has transformed the body itself into a space amenable for (re)territorialization. As Marx testified, capitalism must always seek to overthrow its limitations and boundaries. Indeed, it continues to colonize and seek profits wherever it can, including the production of goods and services. But it is in the logic of Heidegger's "standing reserve," which finds its fruition in the gene itself, where the manic crossroads of cybernetic information and the incessant mapping of capitalism meet. In this space the logic of the new economy adaptability, flexibility, rapid deployment, flux – meets with the nothingness of information. The labor required of the body in Marx's surplus accumulation gives way to the harvesting of the body itself. In this logic, flesh becomes a commodity to be used, grown, cloned, sexualized, and annihilated. But the code of the body is laid bare to continual and incessant reterritorialization. The anatomical maps of biological systems drew upon the metaphor of body as machine, with no small influence from the rise of the industrial revolution where the body became machine-like in many regards. The informational coding of the body is hardly metaphor. Code can be rewritten as soon as it is functionally complete. Machines, on the other hand, require more vested amounts of time.

XII

The emergence of the modern cartographic project and Heidegger's standing reserve *is* the coded body, continually open to reterritorialization, continually processed through increasing schemes of complex spatial representation (increasing mapping of the gene, all of our genes). And if genetics and molecular biology have left the molecule in favor of the message, they have not left the regime of what Ivan Illich calls "health as one's responsibility" – the historical emergence in the late twentieth century of a new subjectivity closely tied to both the knowledge of the body under modern medicine, and the increasing breadth of confessionality as self-knowledge. It is a subjectivity not of the body-machine, but rather the informational systems view of the body, where the body itself becomes an organism constantly in communication with itself and its environment. "Health as function, process, mode of communication, health as an orienting behavior that requires management" is how Illich (1990) describes this new understanding of health. It is a subjectivity that demands constant monitoring of the self-as-organism for states of disequilibria. The physician and the patient "no longer regard a sick man as a broken machine, but . . . look upon him as an energy system in which the balances of force has been distributed. An up-to-date definition of illness would, therefore, be to the effect that that it is an upsetting of the equilibrium of an energy system" (Walker 1942: 29).[16] The language here is of course striking in its similarity to Weiner's insistence on the parallel attempts of "living individuals" and "communicating machines" to control entropy through feedback.

The gene is the new standard of life for the virtual self. The language of life and death, once the prerogative of theologians and then physicians, becomes sublimated in a discourse which refuses to recognize either. This new standard is not merely the result of an increase in technical knowledge, nor a simple shift from theology to anatomy to genetics. It is both epistemological and ontological; it tells us both how we should proceed with our investigations of life, and how we are to understand ourselves. The language of the gene – the code – has been subsumed into the larger discourse of who we are – our secrets, our desires, our truths. It allows us to, in the language of Foucault, experience ourselves as subjects. But these are not subjects of desire in the Christian or even psychoanalytic sense. For where the Christian confession sought salvation, it brought with it a knowledge of the body as a dark and dangerous place, to be avoided yes, but which also allowed a certain economy of pleasure through the constant guarding against its desirous stirrings. Likewise, psychoanalysis allowed for the scientific legitimization of

---

[16] This quote is taken from Arney and Bergen (1984: 72), as indeed much of the discussion here concerning the "disappearance of the experiencing person" and the rise of pathology as a state of disequilibria.

a sexual discourse that, in turn, constituted an economy of pleasure in which one could both "discover" what had remained hidden, and speak about it at length. While notably different, both are rooted deep within the body, deep beneath the fleshy boundary of the skin that demarcates one sinner from another, this neurotic from that one. Both of these confessional techniques contain a type of liberation, along with an economy of power. The sinner is liberated from his sins, the neurotic from her past.

No, rather these are control-communication-information subjects in a discourse Albert Borgmann (1992) has called one of prediction and control. It is a discourse eminently suited for the information age, a discourse that mitigates the liberation of the sinner or the neurotic, a discourse of "health," a logic which situates individuals on trajectories with no definitive end. Health and pleasure become optimal management. Machines, on the one hand, can be "fixed." Informational systems can only be managed and contained. When "disease" becomes a state of disequilibrium for an immune system – far removed from the dis-comfort of earlier experiencing subjects, all organisms as subjects to the second law of thermodynamics (entropy) are to some degree, diseas-ing from birth. It is no coincidence that Weiner's work sought explicitly to counter entropy. An informational systems (i.e. cybernetic) management approach demands constant guard against disequilibrium. The more the body strives to give in to "entropy," the more it becomes then enemy of health. Indeed, it is life (and not death) that becomes the enemy of the organism.

Bodies have always been more difficult to manage than organisms. And while genetics and the ideal of the gene existed before the "discovery" of the double helix, with the advent of cybernetics, which as Hayles (1999: 2) argues "presumes a conception of information as a (disembodied) entity that can flow between carbon-based organic components and silicon-based electronic components to make protein and silicon operate as a single system," genetics can finally liberate the truth of the body entirely from the body itself.

Epilogue

The newly discovered Norwegian coastline is not far removed from the bioinformatic body. The mere fact that both entities – human and geographical "bodies" – can be subsumed under the larger logic of digital informatics suggests that Morgan's "cytoplasmic indifference" extends far beyond the human body itself. Rita Charon (2000: 556), a clinician and medical sociologist, notes,

"The practice of medicine requires powerful instruments for visualizing patients' bodies. We now know that we must see clearly the lives of patients as well as their bodies." The separation of patients' lives from their bodies here denotes a more traditional medical perspective, one not dissimilar from the desire to look beneath the skin and locate pathologies. The movement into patients' lives, however innocuous it may be on the part of the practitioner, is the movement towards a virtualized subjectivity, where all aspects of one's life become relevant as information, as potential variables in the maintenance of optimum health. It is the movement towards a totalizing cartography in which real-time representation becomes virtually real. The real coastline of Norway now lies in the eye of the machine, as the real self lies in the sequence of proteins which, we are told, make us uniquely human.

Where the Geosphere map is a map of nothing and the world, the map of the human genome is a map of no one and every person. At the heart of this virtual project exists an economy of bodies and objects, required to make themselves known for the sake of their health, their security, their integrity. It is no mistake that the history of mapping, at least in the West, is inexorably tied to the history of domination, colonialism and capitalism. It is also no mistake that the tactic of "discovery" runs central to the history and sustenance of an epistemology predicated on the division of subject/object, and insistent on the primacy of time over space.

In its completion of the common laboratory mouse genome, Celera Genomics refused to publish the findings in a scientific journal. Instead, they will sell this information only to their paying customers. Celera is also the company that completed the map of the human genome, in no small part from information gleaned from the Human Genome Project (Connor 2002).[17] It is no different for human DNA. We do not need social theory to tell us this, the newspapers do a fine job.[18]

Under a biological systems approach to the body, medical and pharmaceutical companies hawked their wares for the majority of the last century, marketing products and procedures (vaccines, antibiotics, drugs, surgeries,

---

[17] The race between Celera Genomics and the HGP to decode the human genome reveals many parallels to the earlier European race to map the new world. The myth of discovery remains central, even as the ability to represent determines how such space is understood scientifically, and utilized commercially.

[18] Bailey, Britt, "Think you own your own genes, think again," *San Francisco Chronicle*, March 29, 2001, p. A-25.

etc.) that sought efficacy on all bodies. It was the age of economies of scale and, in a nefarious sense, it paid to keep the body alive within a regime of health. Under a bioinformatics approach, however, it is the code itself which emerges as currency. This transition is evident in the shift away from the production of generalized medicines toward tailored drug therapies, genetic manipulation, and biotechnology generally:

> [T]he era of "one size fits all" medication is ending, as physicians learn to read a patient's unique genetic code and to tailor treatments accordingly . . . A massive effort now underway to catalog the variations in DNA is ushering all fields of medicine into what researchers call the "post-genomic era," when DNA tests will be as routine as blood pressure and temperature checks . . . But the era of personalized medicine cannot materialize until more people are willing to have their DNA scanned for links between genetic variation and disease.[19]

Here is the (re)territorialization of Deleuze and Guattari (1983: 259), where "capitalism is continually confronting limits and barriers that are interior and immanent to itself and that, precisely because they are immanent, let themselves be overcome only provided they are reproduced on a wider scale . . ." Yet not only a wider scale, but on virtual scale where the body itself is no longer limited by its fleshy cytoplasm. Individuated "therapies" have the advantage not only of being immensely profitable, they also confront the barrier of the body, reinscribing its organs and skin even while colonizing its genes. "One size fits all" medication (i.e. antibiotics) is fine for the Third World, which has become its biggest client. Yet the human genome is ultimately more flexible in its applicability to a just-in-time medical model, and the map from which it can draw efficacy is almost infinitely larger.

Heidegger's standing reserve becomes the virtual body. The (re)territorialization of space moves from body-as-machine to the coded body, as the maps of the land move from the decorated and ornate to the digital. The epistemological suture of the Norwegian coastline becomes apparent only in consideration of its ironic insistence on difference. As it acquires increased territory through increased technical (and virtual) sophistication, it does so only through a language that renders its borders inconsequential.

---

[19] Fischer, Joannie, "Snipping away at human disease: Into the era of individually tailored therapies," *U.S. News & World Report*, Vol. 129, No. 16, 2000, p. 58.

Figure 4. Advertisement *Hitachi* (2004).

Biotechnology already understands this. Advanced Cell Technology, arguing from the standpoint of the "new ecology," suggests that cloning can help to reverse the eminent extinction of wildlife species. According to the *New York Times*, biotech firms have, "urged zoos and wildlife officials to begin collecting and freezing tissue samples of endangered species."[20] If the Pandas in the wild die, and the ones in the zoo become ill, not to worry. According to Robert Lanza, vice president Advanced Cell Technology "For a few dollars of electricity you can preserve the genes of all the pandas in China."

Although such a statement appears absurd, it is decidedly not. Recently, the consumer electronics company Hitachi ran an ad that succinctly sums up the virtualization of the body. Although the ad is directed towards consumers of digital electronics, the mere fact that this image and the accompanying text *make any sense at all* is perhaps the clearest indication that the body itself has become a virtual entity. The irony of this ad lies in the proposition that data has any "weight." Indeed, the savvy consumer presumably understands this, and we are meant to understand the difference between digital repre-

---

[20] Pollack, Andrew, "Cloning Used in an Effort to Preserve Rare Species," *New York Times*, October 9, 2000, Online edition, available at http://www.nytimes.com/2000/10/09/science/09CLON.html.

sentations and "real life," with one being decidedly more important than the other.

Bioinformatics tells another tale, however. The truth of this 7 pounds and 3 ounces lies far beneath the skin and bones and flesh. In the world of digital information and the mapping of the virtual body, we "and all other animals, are machines created by our genes" (Dawkins 1990: 2). The body-as-machine, for so long the preeminent medical and metaphorical approach to the body, becomes itself a baroque ornamentation of "cytoplasmic indifference" against the currency of bioinformatics.

Ramón Grosfoguel

Geopolitics of Knowledge and Coloniality of Power: Thinking Puerto Rico and Puerto Ricans from the Colonial Difference*

This essay provides an alternative reading of Puerto Rico and Puerto Ricans within the "modern world-system" (Wallerstein 1979), or, as Walter Mignolo has recently proposed, the "modern/colonial world-system" (Mignolo 2000). It uses a modified version of the world-system approach (Wallerstein 1979) to Puerto Rico's history, political-economy, urbanization processes as well as to Puerto Rican political strategies, migration processes and modes of incorporation as colonial/racial subjects within the United States' empire. The unit of analysis used here is not a "society", but a "historical system." I conceptualize Puerto Rico and Puerto Ricans as part of broader time and spatial processes in the modern/colonial world-system. Yet, by "situating" or "geopolitically locating" the knowledge produced in this chapter from a "Puerto Rican location," it reinterprets important aspects of the world-system approach. I use "Puerto Rican perspective" in quotation marks because I do not want either to essentialize, or to pretend to represent the voices of Puerto Ricans. Instead, I take as a point of departure some voices and expressions of Puerto Rican subaltern thinking.

* The original version of this essay appeared as the introduction to Grosfoguel (2003).

It might seem anachronistic to talk about colonies and colonialism today. However, a world-system approach from a "Puerto Rican perspective" offers a unique opportunity to reinterpret the modern/colonial world and to question the "common sense" assumption that the world has been "decolonized". This is not due to the obvious fact that Puerto Rico is still a colony of the United States, nor is it an attempt to make of Puerto Rico a "model" for understanding the rest of the periphery in the capitalist world-economy. Instead, I intend to rethink the modern world-system from multiple Puerto Rican locations and experiences, which reveal the limitations of the so-called "decolonization" of the modern world, both in terms of the global political-economy and the dominant geoculture and imaginary. Considering Puerto Rico as a Caribbean "modern colony," in that it has access to metropolitan citizenship and welfare transfers, calls for a rethinking of the purported decolonization of the so-called "independent" Caribbean. "Independent" republics in the Caribbean experience the crude exploitation of the capitalist world-system without the metropolitan transfers that Puerto Rico receives as a "modern colony." Puerto Rican subaltern groups articulate their opposition to the formation of a nation-state in the island as a rejection of neo-colonialism's crude realities in neighboring Caribbean countries. Moreover, Puerto Rican migrants in the United States experience the effects of racism as a hegemonic imaginary of the modern/colonial world-system. The Puerto Rican experience illustrates how racial/colonial ideologies have not been eradicated from metropolitan centers which remain in grave need of a socio-cultural decolonization. A "Puerto Rican perspective/location" can highlight global processes that the world-system approach does not emphasize; these include "global symbolic strategies" (Grosfoguel 1994) and "global coloniality" (Quijano 1993).

Puerto Rico's postwar political-economy and mass migration to the metropolis are incomprehensible if one does not account for the global geopolitical symbolic/ideological strategies employed by the United States during the Cold War and U.S. colonial/racist social imaginary. Puerto Rico was transformed into a Cold War "symbolic showcase" of the U.S. developmentalist policies toward the periphery of the world-economy as opposed to the Soviet model. The world-system's use of the notion of "geoculture" to address "global ideologies" is insufficient to understand "showcase" strategies in the world-system. Bourdieu's concept of "symbolic capital" and Quijano's notion of "coloniality of power" can redress these limitations. Although Bourdieu developed the concept of "symbolic capital" for micro-social analysis, it is a powerful tool when applied to conceptualize symbolic strategies at a global scale related to the "manufacturing of showcases."

The United States developed global symbolic/ideological strategies during the Cold War to showcase a peripheral region or an ethnic group as opposed to a challenging peripheral country or ethnic group in order to gain symbolic capital toward its developmentalist model. These strategies are not superstructural or epiphenomenonal, they are material and constitutive of global political-economic processes. Strategies of "symbolic capital" are economically expensive because they entail the investment of capital in non-profitable forms such as credits, aid and assistance programs. Nevertheless, symbolic profits could translate into economic profits in the long run. How to explain the so-called "Southeast Asian miracle" without an understanding of global ideological/cultural strategies? Since the 1950s, the United States has showcased several peripheral countries in different regions of the world where communist regimes represented a challenge such as Greece vis-à-vis Eastern Europe; Taiwan vis-à-vis China; South Korea vis-à-vis North Korea in the 1960s; Puerto Rico vis-à-vis Cuba in the 1980s; Jamaica vis-à-vis Grenada; Costa Rica vis-à-vis Nicaragua. Other showcases include Brazil in the 1960s (the so-called Brazilian miracle) and, more recently, Mexico and Chile in the 1990s as post-Cold War neo-liberal showcases. Compared to other countries, all of these showcases received disproportionately large sums of U.S. foreign aid, favorable conditions for economic growth such as flexible terms to pay their debts, special tariff agreements that made commodities produced in these areas accessible to the metropolitan markets, and/or technological transfers. Most of these showcases success lasted for several years, subsequently failing. However, they were crucial to produce an ideological hegemony over Third World peoples in favor of developmentalist programs. Developmentalist ideology is a crucial constitutive element in the hegemony of the "West;" the capitalist world-system gains credibility by developing a few successful peripheral cases. These are civilizational and cultural strategies to gain consent and to demonstrate the "superiority" of the "West".

In seeking to understand these strategies, one must also employ the concept of "coloniality," developed by Peruvian sociologist Aníbal Quijano. This notion accounts for the entangled, heterogeneous and mutually constitutive relations between the international division of labor, global racial/ethnic hierarchy and hegemonic Eurocentric epistemologies in the modern/colonial world-system. Coloniality on a world-scale, with the United States as the undisputed hegemon over non-European people, characterizes the global-ization of the capitalist world-economy today. The old colonial hierarchies of West/non-West remain in place and are entangled with the so-called "new international division of labor." Herein lies the relevance of the distinction between colonialism and coloniality. Coloniality refers to the continuity of colonial forms of domination produced by colonial cultures and structures in the modern/colonial world-system. "Coloniality of power" refers to a cru-cial structuring process in the modern/colonial world-system that articulates peripheral locations in the international division of labor, subaltern group political strategies, and Third World migrants' inscription in the racial/eth-nic hierarchy of metropolitan global cities.

Although Puerto Rico still has a colonial administration, its location as a "modern colony" in the Caribbean poses a particular kind of "coloniality" that contrasts with the "coloniality" of so-called "independent" republics in the region. Puerto Rico benefits from massive annual metropolitan transfers that never reach the shores of Caribbean nation-states. Moreover, the International Monetary Fund (IMF) and the World Bank (WB), as discipli-nary agencies of peripheral countries in the capitalist world-economy, never intervene in Puerto Rico's affairs due to its status as a "modern colony" of the United States. The prosperity of the Puerto Rican "modern colony" rela-tive to Caribbean nation-states that struggled for freedom and independence constitutes a tragic historical irony. This phenomenon cannot be understood from a nationalist nor a colonialist perspective that assumes automatic decol-onization after the formation of a nation-state or from an approach that takes the nation-state as the unit of analysis.

Beyond Colonialist and Nationalist Discourses

Arguments over Puerto Rico's status are frequently divided between nation-alist and colonialist interpretations of Puerto Rico and Puerto Ricans. Colonialist positions do not question the unequal power relationships between Puerto Rico and the United States despite the fact that Puerto Rico is still under the territorial clause of the United States. While the United States selectively con-fronts the lack of democratic and human rights around the world, it main-tains a colonial administration in its "backyard" and refuses to organize a democratic referendum on Puerto Rico's status. The real concern keeping U.S. political leaders from authorizing a referendum is that Puerto Ricans will vote for statehood. Why is statehood a matter of such concern? The explanation must be sought in the global geopolitical changes of the last decade of the twentieth century.

The end of the Cold War shifted United States priorities towards Puerto Rico. The island had long been a "symbolic showcase" of the United States developmentalist model for the Third World and an important U.S. military stronghold during the Cold War. During the Cold War era, billions of dollars were transferred to the island to serve the global United States' interests. With Cold War priorities a thing of the past, the U.S. today, through neo-colonial ("independent" or "autonomous") arrangements, maintains the military use of Puerto Rico and the exploitation of its labor force and can justify significant cuts to United States federal transfers to the island. Neo-colonialism is "the colony without the benefits of the modern colony." Moreover, the dominant neo-liberal ideology together with the disciplinary institutions of global capitalism – IMF, WB, World Trade Organization (WTO), General Agreement on Tariffs and Trade (GATT) – and the increased autonomization of transnational corporations from nation-states, have made colonial administrations obsolete. Although Quijano uses the concept of "global coloniality" to refer to the condition of "independence without decolonization" in Latin America since the nineteenth century, one can use this term to designate the regime of power that predominates today in the modern/colonial world-system. Global coloniality, as opposed to global colonialism, is today the dominant form of core-periphery relationships in the capitalist world-economy. Core powers and transnational corporations exploit and dominate the periphery without the expense of colonial administrations. Thus, "independence" is no longer a subversive solution from the point of view of the imperial elites because there is no real "independence" or "sovereignty" in the periphery of the modern/colonial world-system.

The concept of "coloniality of power" is useful here to transcend the common held assumption of both colonialist and nationalist discourses which states that with the end of colonial administrations and the formation of nation-states in the periphery we are living in a post-colonial, decolonized world. The entanglement between a global division of labor of core-periphery relationships and a global racial/ethnic hierarchy of Western and non-Western people, formed during several centuries of European colonial expansion, was not significantly transformed with the end of colonialism and the formation of nation-states in the periphery. The transition from global colonialism to global coloniality transformed the global forms of domination, but not the structure of core-periphery relationships at a world-scale. New disciplinary institutions formed after the Second World War such as the IMF and the WB as well as military organizations such as NATO, intelligence agencies and the Pentagon, keep the periphery in a subordinate position. The end of the Cold War era intensified the processes of global coloniality. Thus, one implication of thinking in terms of a modern/colonial world-system, as opposed to simply a modern world-system, is that it questions in a more overt form the myth of decolonization and the assumption that modernity is somehow a more advanced stage of "progress" and "development" after, before or simply disconnected from colonialism and coloniality. From a modern/colonial world-system approach, modern peripheral nation-states, mostly composed of non-Western peoples, are still colonial in relation to the hegemonic European/Euro-American core states. Moreover, the impact of the European colonial expansion still informs the racial/ethnic hierarchies and the "imagined community" at the nation-state level. Thus, continuities from colonial times are as important as discontinuities.

Although this global context explains why the U.S. elites are no longer fearful of "independence" or "autonomy" in Puerto Rico, it does not provide a key to understanding why "statehood" has become the new "subversive" option in their eyes. The admission of Puerto Rico as the fifty-first state of the union would mean an increase of approximately 3 billion dollars in federal transfers to the island. Even more important, it would signal the full incorporation – with equal rights – of the first Afro-Latino Caribbean state. This cultural dimension has important political implications for the twenty-first century. Although Euro-American Anglo elites have been the colonizing force in the United States, their colonial control over the economic, political, and cultural structures of the U.S. empire will be increasingly threatened with the growth of non-white Spanish-speaking populations within U.S. borders. Latinos are a subordinated group in the hegemonic, and still colonial, imaginary of the United States. The recent congressional debates over the status question of Puerto Rico are deeply affected by the cultural and demographic Latin-Americanization of the United States in the twenty-first century.

Unlike territory subsumed by the U.S. colonial expansion to the west of the North American continent, Puerto Rico is not a settler or population colony. It has been an "exploitation colony," which has had important implications for the island's cultural politics. Civil society in Puerto Rico is dominated by Spanish language. There is no significant Anglo population on the island that has questioned the dominant culture and language as there were in the settler colonialisms of places such as California or Texas. Anglos are a minority on the island and the elected representatives of a future Puerto Rican state in Congress would all be Spanish-speaking "Latinos" who would promote an "estadidad jíbara," a statehood platform that affirms local Puerto Rican identity and Spanish language. The incorporation of the island as the fifty-first state would have dramatic implications for the future demise of "English Only" struggles, opening doors for the future consolidation of bilingual cultural and political struggles in California, New Mexico, Florida, New York and other states with large Latino populations. A Puerto Rican state could create an important precedent that Anglo elites would be unable to suppress easily given the future demographic transformations of the empire in the first century of the new millennium. Many U.S. elites made clear the cultural politics of language when they attempted to impose "English" as a pre-condition for the statehood option in a referendum on Puerto Rico's status. This is all the more striking given that none of the other fifty states has ever had such a requirement and the U.S. has no official language. Further, U.S. elites never required fluency in English when Puerto Ricans were drafted to fight in all U.S. twentieth century wars, nor when citizenship was imposed on Puerto Ricans in 1917, nor when the island was incorporated as a colonial territory in 1898. The threat of the "Latinization" of the United States in the twenty-first century to the racial/ethnic hierarchy of the empire and to white supremacy was deployed politically by many Euro-American Anglo Congressional representatives who were opposed to offer "statehood" as an option during the House of Representative's (March 4, 1998) debate over the Young Bill which was designed to promote a referendum on the future status of the island.

Puerto Rican people are fully aware of the political and economic implications of becoming a neo-colonial "independent" or "autonomous" territory. Fewer than 10 percent of the voters support either of these options. The neo-colonial domination and exploitation of the so-called "independent" Caribbean islands by the United States symbolizes for many Puerto Ricans what the future may hold if the island becomes a pseudo-independent republic. After a hundred years of colonialism, neo-colonialism represents for Puerto Ricans an expropriation of social and civil rights conquered through painful and difficult struggles under United States citizenship. "Independence" and "sovereignty" in the Caribbean periphery are a fictional narrative of the hegemonic developmentalist geoculture of the modern/colonial world-system. This explains the low percentages of pro-independence votes in local status referendums (not recognized by the federal government) and elections during the last forty years in Puerto Rico.

Although Puerto Ricans have a strong sense of identity and cultural nationalism, subalternity is not expressed through political nationalism. Subalternity in Puerto Rico has historically deployed "jaibería" – "subversive complicity" or "ambiguous" identification strategies (see Grosfoguel, Negron-Muntaner, and Georas 1997) – to struggle against the "coloniality of power" of both American elites and local "blanquito" elites. "Puerto Rican-ness" is mobilized as a distinct "national identity" against inconvenient U.S. policies in the island or as an "ethnic identity" in the United States to claim rights and resources. When unwanted decisions are ruled by local courts in Puerto Rico, subaltern groups go to the Federal court to overrule the decision; vice-versa, Federal decisions are challenged in local courts. I have used the term "ethnonation" to refer to this double identification strategy (Grosfoguel, Negron-Muntaner, and Georas 1997). This Duboisean "double consciousness" of a simultaneous interior/exterior cultural and political location has also been mobilized against local "blanquito" elites. When local elites complain about federal increases in minimum wages that compromise their profits, subaltern groups mobilize their United States citizenship to stake their claim to certain rights. Puerto Rican subaltern struggles mobilize discourses and strategies of "national" and/or "ethnic" identity (depending on the particular context) while simultaneously demanding an improvement of civil and social rights within the United States empire.

Nationalist discourses in Puerto Rico fall into the trap of a colonialist underestimation of Puerto Rican agency and subalternity. Puerto Rican nationalist discourses portray the "Puerto Rican masses" as "colonized," "docile" and "ignorant" due to their consistent rejection of "independence" for the island and the "ambiguity" of their political and identification strategies. Similar to colonialist/Eurocentric positions, nationalist ideologues do not recognize the cultural and political strategies deployed by Puerto Rican subaltern subjects as valid forms of knowledge and politics. Similarly to the United States' "new right," Puerto Rican nationalists favor "workfare" as opposed to "welfare" and portray Puerto Rican popular demands for parity in federal funding as claims to foster "laziness" in the island.

The concept of "colonial difference" (Mignolo 2000) is crucial here to overcome the paternalistic and elitist limits of both nationalist and colonialist discourses. If the modern world is constituted by a colonial difference, if there is no modernity without coloniality and, therefore, we live in a modern/colonial world, then, knowledge is not produced from a universal location and we need to epistemologically account for the geopolitics of our knowledge production. The notion of "colonial difference" is crucial to geopolitically locate the forms of thinking and cosmologies produced by subaltern subjects as opposed to hegemonic global designs. From which location in the colonial divide is knowledge produced? Nationalist and colonialist discourses are thinking from a power position in the colonial divide of the modern/colonial world, while subaltern subjects are thinking from the subordinate side of the colonial difference. Colonialist discourses reproduce the North-South global colonial divide, while nationalist discourses reproduce an "internal" colonial divide within national formations. The knowledge, critical insights and political strategies produced from the subordinate side of the colonial difference serve as point of departure to go beyond colonialist and nationalist discourses. Rather than underestimating the subaltern, we should take seriously their cosmologies, thinking, and political strategies as a point of departure to our knowledge production.

After one hundred years of fighting U.S. wars and serving as cheap labor for U.S. corporations, Puerto Ricans deserve equal civil and social rights within the United States. The designation of "laziness" is a typical racist slogan used by "white" imperial elites in the United States and "white" Creole elites in Puerto Rico to dismiss subaltern struggles for equal rights. The complex and paradoxical situation is that nationalist discourses in Puerto Rico make similar arguments regarding the "laziness" of subaltern groups. Nationalist discourses contend that "people do not know better," they are ideologically "colonized," and as such are in need of a nationalist vanguard to enlighten the "masses." The subaltern rejection of nationalist solutions to the colonial question in Puerto Rico is represented by nationalist discourses as a "colonial mentality." Rather than reproduce the local elite's condescending colonialist perception of the Puerto Rican subaltern groups' strategies in their everyday life and political interventions, I opt to understand them as valid forms of knowledge and political intervention given the "coloniality of power" under which they live. Rather than dismiss the knowledges produced by these subaltern subjects as "colonial" and I take them as points of departure to rethink not only Puerto Rico and Puerto Ricans but the modern/colonial world-system itself.

The political implication here is not to propose that the periphery of the modern/colonial world-system should imitate Puerto Rico, Curazao or Martinique and become "modern colonies" of empires. This is not only impossible due to the core powers opposition to incorporate the periphery into metropolitan citizenship rights, it is also not desirable by non-Western peoples. The situation in Martinique and Puerto Rico dramatizes the need for a global redistribution of wealth from core to periphery. How else can one explain that a banana worker in Martinique, as opposed to one in Dominica or St. Lucia, or a maquiladora worker in Puerto Rico, as opposed to one in the Dominican Republic or Haiti, has access to signifiers of First World living standards such as mass consumption, telephones, refrigerator, VCR, decent housing conditions and a car? Workers in Puerto Rico and Martinique experience exploitation similar to the workers in the neighbor Caribbean nation-states. However, the main difference between Caribbean modern colonies and Caribbean nation-states, is the existence in the former of core-periphery redistributive wealth mechanisms such as access to metropolitan welfare programs and resources that offset the inequalities produced by core-periphery exploitation. These mechanisms do not exist in the Caribbean nation-states where there is only core exploitation without core redistribution of wealth. This is what subaltern groups in locations like Puerto Rico and Martinique are articulating in their critique and rejection of neo-colonial independence. Thus, if we take this subaltern critique seriously, what this experience dramatizes is the need to create global mechanisms to redistribute wealth from North to South. Global problems of exploitation and domination cannot have a colonial or a nation-state level solution. A global problem requires post-colonial global solutions beyond nationalism and colonialism.

Post-Coloniality and World-Systems: A Call for a Dialogue

A "Puerto Rican perspective" can modify some assumptions of world-system analysis. Most world-system analyses focus on how the international division of labor and the geopolitical military struggles are constitutive of capitalist accumulation processes at a world-scale. This approach is a useful point of departure; however the peculiar incorporation of Puerto Rico and Puerto Ricans into the United States forces me to take more seriously ideological/symbolic strategies as well as the colonial/racist culture of the modern/colonial world-system in my analysis. World-system analysis has recently developed the concept of geoculture to refer to global ideologies. However, the geoculture concept uses an infrastructure-superstructure paradigm. For reasons that will be developed below, I take ideological/symbolic strategies and colonial/racist culture as constitutive, together with capitalist accumulation processes and the inter-state system, of the core-periphery relationships at a world-scale. These different structures and processes form a heterarchy (Kontopoulos 1993) of heterogeneous, complex and entangled hierarchies that cannot be accounted for in the infrastructure/superstructure paradigm.

Post-coloniality shares with the world-system approach a critique of developmentalism, Eurocentric forms of knowledge, gender inequalities, racial hierarchies and the cultural/ideological processes that foster the subordination of the periphery in the capitalist world-system. Both approaches also share a critique of what I call "feudalmania." Several centuries ago, European elites established a discursive opposition between peripheral "backwardness, obscurantism and feudalism" while Europe was represented as "advanced, civilized and modern." Leopoldo Zea called this process, paraphrasing Rodó, the new "northernmania" (*nordomanía*), that is, the attempt by dominant elites to construct new "models" in the North which would stimulate development while in turn developing new forms of colonialism (Zea 1986: 16–17). The subsequent nineteenth century characterization of the periphery as "feudal" or in a backward "stage" by Western elites and Latin American Creole elites of European descent served to justify the periphery's subordination to the masters from the North, and is part of what I call "feudalmania" which continued throughout the twentieth century and into the present.

"Feudalmania" is a device of what Johaness Fabian calls "temporal distancing" (1983) to produce a knowledge that denied coevalness between the periphery and the so-called "advanced European countries." The "denial of coevalness" creates a double ideological mechanism. First, it conceals European/Euro-American responsibility in the exploitation of the periphery. By not sharing the same historical time or geographical space, each region's destiny is conceived as unrelated to the other's. Second, by living in different temporalities, wherein Europe is purportedly at a more advanced stage of development than the rest of the world, a notion of European superiority emerges. Thus, Europe was the "model" to imitate and the developmentalist goal was to "catch up." This is expressed in the dichotomies civilization/

savagery, developed/underdeveloped, West/the Rest and so forth. The world-system approach provides a radical critique of these Eurocentric developmentalist ideologies while post-colonial criticism provides a radical critique to the "Orientalist" and "Occidentalist" construction of non-European people as inferior others, implied in developmentalist and culturalist discourses.

However, the critical insights of both approaches emphasize different determinants. While post-colonial critiques emphasize colonial culture, the world-system approach emphasizes the endless accumulation of capital on a world-scale. Post-colonial critiques emphasize agency; the world-system approach emphasizes structure. Some scholars of the post-colonial theory such as Gayatri Spivak (1988) acknowledge the importance of the international division of labor as constitutive of the capitalist system while some scholars of the world-system approach such as Immanuel Wallerstein acknowledge the importance of cultural processes such as racism and sexism as inherent to historical capitalism. However, the two camps in general are still divided over the culture vs. economy and the agency vs. structure debates. This is partly inherited from the "two cultures" that divide the sciences from the humanities, premised upon the Cartesian dualism of mind over matter.

With very few exceptions, most post-colonial theorists come from fields of the humanities such as literature, rhetoric, and cultural studies. Only a small number of scholars in the field of post-coloniality come from the social sciences, in particular from anthropology. On the other hand, world-system scholars are mainly from disciplines in the social sciences such as sociology, anthropology, political science, and economics. Very few of them come from the humanities, with the exception of historians, who tend to have more affinities with the world-system approach. I have emphasized the disciplines that predominate in both approaches because I think that these disciplinary boundaries are constitutive of some of the theoretical differences between both approaches.

Post-colonial criticism characterizes the capitalist system as a cultural system. They believe that culture is the constitutive element that determines economic and political relations in the capitalist system (Said 1979). By contrast, most world-system scholars emphasize the economic relations at a world-scale as constitutive of the capitalist world-system. Cultural and political relations are instrumental to, or epiphenomenon of, the capitalist accumulation processes. The fact is that world-system theorists have difficulties theorizing culture while post-colonial theorists have difficulties conceptualizing political-economic processes. The paradox is that many world-system scholars acknowledge the importance of culture, but do not know what to do with this recognition and do not articulate the importance of culture in a non-reductive way. And in a parallel fashion, many post-colonial scholars acknowledge the importance of political-economy but do not know how to integrate it into cultural analysis without reproducing a "culturalist" type of reductionism. Thus, both literatures fluctuate between the danger of economic reductionism and the danger of culturalism.

I propose that the culture vs. economy dichotomy is a "chicken-egg" dilemma – that is, a false dilemma, coming from what Immanuel Wallerstein has called the legacy of nineteenth century liberalism (1991: 4). This legacy implies the division of the economic, political, cultural and social as autonomous arenas. According to Wallerstein, the construction of these "autonomous" arenas and their materialization in separate disciplinary knowledge domains in the social sciences, on the one hand, and the humanities, on the other, are a pernicious result of liberalism as a geoculture of the modern world-system. In a critical appraisal of world-system analysis, Wallerstein (1991) states that:

> World-system analysis intends to be a critique of nineteenth century social science. But it is an incomplete, unfinished critique. It still has not been able to find a way to surmount the most enduring (and misleading) legacy of nineteenth century social science – the division of social analysis into three arenas, three logics, three levels – the economic, the political and the socio-cultural. This trinity stands in the middle of the road, in granite, blocking our intellectual advance. Many find it unsatisfying, but in my view no one has yet found the way to dispense with the language and its implications, some of which are correct but most of which are probably not (4). [A]ll of us fall back on using the language of the three arenas in almost everything we write. It is time we seriously tackled the question . . . we are pursuing false models and undermining our argumentation by continuing to use such language. It is urgent that we begin to elaborate alternative models (271).

We have yet to develop a new language that accounts for the complex processes of the modern/colonial world-system without relying on the old liberal language of the three arenas. For example, the fact that we characterize the modern world-system as a world-economy misleads many people into thinking that world-system analysis is about analyzing the so-called "economic logic" of the system. This is precisely the kind of interpretation Wallerstein attempts to avoid in his critique to the three autonomous domains. However, as Wallerstein himself acknowledges, the language we use in world-system analysis is still caught in the old language of nineteenth century social science. To dispense of this language is a huge challenge. What if capitalism is a world-economy, not in the limited sense of an economic system, but in that of a historical system defined as ". . . an integrated network of economic, political and cultural processes the sum of which hold the system together" (Wallerstein 1991: 230)? We need to find new concepts and a new language to account for the complex entanglement of gender, racial, sexual and class hierarchies within global geopolitical, geocultural and geo-economic processes of the modern world-system where the ceaseless accumulation of capital is affected by, integrated into, constitutive of and constituted by those hierarchies. In order to find a new language for this complexity, we need to go "outside" our paradigms, approaches, disciplines and fields. I propose that we examine the metatheoretical notion of "heterarchies" developed by Greek social theorist, sociologist and philosopher Kyriakos Kontopoulos (1993) as well as the notion of "coloniality of power" developed by the Peruvian sociologist Aníbal Quijano (1991, 1993, 1998) in this effort.

Heterarchical thinking (Kontopoulos 1993) is an attempt to conceptualize social structures with a new language that breaks with the liberal paradigm of nineteenth century social science. The old language of social structures is a language of closed systems, that is, of a single, overarching logic determining a single hierarchy. To define a historical system as a "nested hierarchy" as the Gulbenkian commission proposed, undermines our argument by continuing to use a metatheoretical model that corresponds to closed systems – precisely the opposite of what World-System approach attempts to do. In contrast, heterarchies move us beyond closed hierarchies into a language of complexity, open systems, entanglement of multiple and heterogeneous hierarchies, structural levels, and structuring logics. The notion of "logics" here is redefined to refer to the heterogeneous entanglement of multiple agents' strategies. The idea is that there is neither autonomous logics nor a single logic, but multiple, heterogeneous, entangled complex processes within a single historical reality. The notion of entanglement is crucial here and is close to Wallerstein's notion of historical systems understood as "integrated networks of economic, political and cultural processes." The moment multiple hierarchical relationships are considered to be entangled, according to Kontopoulos', or integrated, according to Wallerstein, no autonomous logics or domains remain. The notion of a single logic runs the risk of reductionism which is the contrary to complex systems while the notion of multiple logics runs the risk of dualism. The solution to these ontological questions (the reductionist/autonomist dilemma) in heterarchical thinking is to go beyond the monism/dualism binary opposition and to talk about an emergentist materialism that implies multiple processes at different structural levels within a single historical material reality. Heterarchies keep in use of the notion of "logics" only for analytical purposes to make certain distinctions, or to abstract certain processes, so that processes once conceived as integrated or entangled in a concrete historical process acquire a different structural effect and meaning. Heterarchical thinking provides a language for what Immanuel Wallerstein calls a new way of thinking that can break with the liberal nineteenth century social sciences and focus on complex, historical systems.

The notion of "coloniality of power" is also helpful in terms of the culture vs. economy dilemma. Quijano's work provides a new way of thinking about this dilemma that both post-colonial and world-system analysis attempts to address. In Latin America, most dependentistas privileged the economic and political relations in social processes at the expense of cultural and ideological determinations. Culture was perceived by the dependentista school as instrumental to capitalist accumulation processes. In many respects, dependentistas reproduced some of the economic reductionism of orthodox Marxist approaches. This led to two problems: first, an underestimation of the colonial/racial hierarchies; and, second, an analytical impoverishment that could not account for the complexities of heterarchical political-economic processes.

Dependency ideas must be understood as part of the *longue durée* of modernity ideas in Latin America. Autonomous national development is a central ideological theme of the modern world-system since the late eighteenth century. Dependentistas reproduced the illusion that rational organization and development can be achieved from the control of the nation-state. This contradicted the position that development and underdevelopment are the result of structural relations within the capitalist world-system. Although dependentistas defined capitalism as a global system beyond the nation-state, they still believed it was possible to delink or break with the world system at the nation-state level (Frank 1970, Frank 1969). This implied that a socialist revolutionary process at the national level could insulate the country from the global system. However, as we know today, it is impossible to transform a system that operates on a world-scale by privileging the control/administration of the nation-state (Wallerstein 1992b). No "rational" control of the nation-state would alter the location of a country in the international division of labor. "Rational" planning and control of the nation-state contributes to the developmentalist illusion of eliminating the inequalities of the capitalist world-system from a nation-state level.

In the capitalist world-system, a peripheral nation-state may experience transformations in the form of its incorporation to the capitalist world-economy, a minority of which might even move to a semi-peripheral position. However, to break with, or transform, the whole system from a nation-state level is completely beyond their range of possibilities (Wallerstein 1992a; 1992b). Therefore, a global problem cannot have a national solution. This is not to deny the importance of political interventions at the nation-state level. The point here is not to reify the nation-state and to understand the limits of political interventions at this level for the long-term transformation of a system that operates at a world-scale. The nation-state, although still an important institution of historical capitalism, is a limited space for radical political and social transformations. Collective agencies in the periphery need a global scope in order to make an effective political intervention in the capitalist world-system. Social struggles below and above the nation-state are strategic spaces of political intervention that are frequently ignored when the focus of the movements privileges the nation-state. Social movements' local and global connections are crucial for effective political interventions. In part, the dependentistas overlooked this because of their tendency to privilege the nation-state as the unit of analysis and because of the economistic emphasis of their approaches. This oversight had terrible political consequences for the Latin American left and the credibility of the dependentista political project.

For most dependentistas, the "economy" was the privileged sphere of social analysis. Categories such as "gender" and "race" were frequently ignored, and when used they were reduced to either class or economic interests. Aníbal Quijano (1993) is one of the few exceptions to this approach. "Coloniality of power" is a concept that attempts to integrate as part of a heterogeneous structural process the multiple relations in which cultural, political and economic processes are entangled in capitalism as a historical system. At the center of "coloniality of power" is social power and the entanglement of capitalist accumulation processes with a racial/ethnic hierarchy and its derivative classification of superior/inferior, developed/underdeveloped and civilized/barbarian people. Similar to world-systems analysis, the notion of "coloniality" conceptualizes the process of colonization of the Americas and the constitution of a capitalist world-economy as part of the same entangled process. The construction of a global racial/ethnic hierarchy was simultaneous, coeval in time and space, to the constitution of an international division of labor with core-periphery relationships at a world-scale. As mentioned before, for Quijano there is no "pre" or "post" racial/ethnic hierarchy at a world-scale in relation to the capitalist accumulation process. Since the initial formation of the capitalist world-system, the ceaseless accumulation of capital was entangled with a racist, homophobic and sexist culture. The international division of labor was heterarchically entangled with racial/ethnic, gender and sexual hierarchies. The European colonial expansion was lead by European heterosexual males. Everywhere they went, they exported their cultural prejudices and formed heterarchical structures of sexual, gender, class and racial hierarchies. Thus, in "historical capitalism" the process of peripheral incorporation into the ceaseless accumulation of capital was entangled with homophobic, sexist and racist practices and cultures.

As opposed to world-system analysis, what Quijano emphasizes with his notion of "coloniality" is that there is no overarching capitalist accumulation logic that can instrumentalize ethnic/racial divisions and precede the formation of a global colonial, Eurocentric culture. The "instrumentalist" approach is reductive and is caught in the old language of nineteenth century social science. Since its initial formation, capitalist accumulation was always entangled in a non-reductive way to a Eurocentric culture. The relationship between Western and non-Western peoples through colonial culture was always entangled with social power, the international division of labor and the capitalist accumulation processes. Moreover, Quijano uses the notion of "coloniality" as opposed to "colonialism" in order to call our attention to the historical continuities between colonial and so-called "post-colonial" times. The fact that colonialism as a political-juridical administration has almost disappeared from the inter-state system, does not mean colonial relations have also disappeared.

One implication of the notion of "coloniality of power" is that the world has not fully decolonized. The first decolonization was incomplete. It was limited to the juridical-political "independence" from the European imperial states. The "second decolonization" will have to address heterarchies of entangled racial, ethnic, sexual, gender and economic relations that the "first decolonization" left untouched. As a result, the world needs a "second decolonization," different from and more radical than the first. As opposed to the "first decolonization," the "second decolonization" is a long-term process that cannot be reduced to an event.

The pernicious influence of coloniality in all of its expressions at different levels (global, national, local) as well as its Eurocentric knowledge structures have been reflected in the anti-systemic movements around the world. For example, many leftist projects in Latin America, following the dependentista underestimation of racial/ethnic hierarchies, have reproduced White Creole domination over non-European people within their organizations and when controlling state power. The Latin American "left" never radically problematized the racial/ethnic hierarchies that were built during the European colonial expansion and that are still present today in Latin America's "coloniality of power." The conflicts between the Sandinistas and the Mizquitos in Nicaragua emerged as part of the reproduction of the old racial/colonial hierarchies (Vila 1992). This was not, as Sandinistas would have us believe, a conflict created by the CIA. The Sandinistas reproduced the historical "coloniality of power" between the Pacific coast and the Atlantic coast in Nicaragua. The White Creole elites in the Pacific coast hegemonized the political, cultural and economic relations that subordinated Blacks and Indians in the Atlantic coast. As such, the differences between the Somocista dictatorship and the Sandinista regime in this regard were not that great. Similarly, Cuban White elites hegemonized the power positions in the post-revolutionary period (Moore 1988). The number of Blacks and Mulattos in power positions is minimal and does not correspond to their demographic status as the numerical majority. Again, we see that the historical continuities of the "coloniality of power" are greater than the discontinuities. Thus, "coloniality" refers to the long-term continuities of the racial hierarchies from the time of European colonialism to the formation of nation-states in the Americas. Today there is a "coloniality of power" despite the disappearance of direct colonial administrations. No radical project in Latin America can be successful without dismantling these colonial/racial hierarchies. This affects not only the scope of "revolutionary processes" but also the democratization of the social hierarchies. The underestimation of the problem of coloniality has greatly contributed to the popular disillusionment with "leftist" projects in Latin America.

The second problem with the dependentista underestimation of cultural and ideological dynamics is that it impoverished their own political-economy approach. Ideological/symbolic strategies as well as Eurocentric forms of knowledge are constitutive of the political-economy of the capitalist world-system. Global symbolic/ideological strategies are an important structuring logic of the core-periphery relationships in the capitalist world-system. For instance, core states develop ideological/symbolic strategies by fostering "Occidentalist" (Mignolo 1995) forms of knowledge that privileged the "West over the Rest." This is clearly seen in developmentalist discourses which became a "scientific" form of knowledge in the last fifty years. This knowledge privileged the "West" as the model of development. Developmentalist discourse offers a colonial recipe on how to become like the "West."

Although the dependentistas struggled against these universalist/Occidentalist forms of knowledge, they perceived this knowledge as a "super-struture" or an epiphenomenon of some "economic infrastructure." Dependentistas never perceived this knowledge as constitutive of Latin America's political-economy. Constructing peripheral zones such as Africa and Latin America as regions with a "problem" related to "stages of development" concealed Western responsibility in the exploitation of these continents. The construction of "pathological" regions in the periphery as opposed to the normal development patterns of the "West" justified an even more intense political and economic intervention from imperial powers. By treating the "Other" as "underdeveloped" and "backward," metropolitan exploitation and domination were justified in the name of the "civilizing mission."

A component of Quijano's "coloniality of power" is his critique of Eurocentric forms of knowledge. According to Quijano, the privileging of Eurocentric forms of knowledge is simultaneous with the entangled process of core-periphery relations and racial/ethnic hierarchies. The ascribed superiority of European knowledge in many areas of life was an important aspect of the coloniality of power in the world-system. Subaltern knowledges were excluded, omitted, silenced and/or ignored. This is not a call for a fundamentalist or an essentialist rescue mission for authenticity. The point here is to put the colonial difference (Mignolo 2000) at the center of the process of knowledge production. Subaltern knowledges are those knowledges at the intersection of the traditional and the modern. They are hybrid, transcultural forms of knowledge, not in the traditional sense of syncretism or "mestizaje," but in Aimé Cesaire's sense of the "miraculous arms" or what I have called "subversive complicity" with the system. These are forms of resistance that resignify dominant forms of knowledge from the point of view of the non-Eurocentric rationality of subaltern subjectivities thinking from border epistemologies.

They constitute what Walter Mignolo (2000) calls a critique of modernity from the geo-political experiences and memories of coloniality. According to Mignolo (2000), this is a new space that deserves further explorations as a new critical dimension to modernity/coloniality and, at the same time, as a space from where new utopias can be devised. This has important implications for knowledge production. Are we going to produce a new knowledge that repeats or reproduces the universalistic, Eurocentric God's eye view? To say that the unit of analysis is the world-system, not the nation-state, is not equivalent to a neutral God's-eye view of the world. I believe that world-system analysis takes the side of the periphery, workers, women, racialized/colonial subjects and anti-systemic movements in the process of knowledge production. This means that although world-systems take the world as a unit of analysis, they are taking a non-universal, particular perspective of the world. Still, world-system analysis has not found a way to fully incorporate subaltern knowledges in our process of knowledge production. Without this there can be no decolonization of knowledge and no utopistics beyond Eurocentrism. The complicity of the social sciences with the coloniality of power in knowledge production and imperial global designs calls for new institutional and non-institutional locations from which the subaltern can speak and be heard.

Geopolitics of Knowledge and the Imaginary of the Modern/Colonial World

It is important as scholars to recognize that we always speak from a specific location in the gender, class, racial and sexual hierarchies of a particular region in the modern/colonial world-system. Our knowledges, as the feminist thinker Donna Haraway (1991) contends, are always already "situated," but I will add, following Quijano (1993) and Mignolo (2000), that they are "situated" within the axis of the colonial difference produced by the "coloniality of power" in the modern/colonial world-system. The Western/masculinist idea that we can produce knowledges that are unpositioned, unlocated, neutral and universalistic is one of the most pervasive mythologies in the modern/colonial world-system. Universal/global designs are always already situated in local histories (Mignolo 2000). Those in power positions in the European/Euro-American vs. non-European hierarchy of the modern/colonial world often think in terms of global designs or universalistic knowledges to control and dominate colonized/racialized/subordinated peoples in the capitalist world-system. The colonial difference formed by centuries of European colonial expansion in the modern/colonial world-system is always constitutive of processes of knowledge production. To speak from the subaltern side of the colonial difference forces us to look at the world from angles and points of view critical of hegemonic perspectives. This requires an effort on our part. "Border thinking" or "border epistemology" are precisely the terms used by Walter Mignolo (2000), inspired by the work of Chicana and Chicano scholars such as Gloria Anzaldúa (1987), Norma Alarcón (1981) and José David Saldívar (1997) to refer to this in-between location of subaltern knowledges, critical of both imperial designs (global coloniality) and anti-colonial nationalist strategies (internal coloniality).

We still live in a world where the dominant imaginary is still colonial. The global hegemonic colonial culture involves a very intricate and uneven set of narratives with long histories that are re-enacted in the present through complex mediations. Post-colonial literatures have contributed greatly to the discussion of these narratives as they are produced and reproduced in the constitution of one group's superiority over an-Other. The process of "Othering" people has operated through a set of narrative oppositions between the West and the Rest, civilized and savage, intelligent and stupid, hard-working and lazy, superior and inferior, masculine and feminine (sexual and racist narratives have been entangled), pure and impure, clean and dirty and so forth. World-systemic historical/structural processes constituted these narratives and I can only simplify and schematically designate them here: the dynamics of European Modernity (e.g. citizenship, nation-building, democracy, civil/social rights), European colonial expansion, colonial modernities and white/masculinist supremacy.

The capitalist world-system was formed by the Spanish/Portuguese expansion to the Americas (Wallerstein 1979; Quijano and Wallerstein 1992; Mignolo 1995; 2000). This first modernity (1492–1650) built the foundations of the racist/colonial culture we are living today. Simultaneous to its expansion to the Americas in 1492, the Spanish Empire expelled Arabs and Jews from their land in the name of the "purity blood" (*pureza de la sangre*). This "internal border" against Arabs and Jews was built simultaneously with the "external border" against people from other geographical zones (Mignolo 2000). The Spanish and Portuguese expansion to the Americas constructed the racial categories that would be later generalized to the rest of the world (Quijano and Wallerstein 1992). No one defined themselves as Blacks in Africa, Whites in

Europe, or Indians in the Americas before the European expansion to the Americas. All of these categories where invented as part of the European colonization of the Americas (Quijano and Wallerstein 1992). The formation of the international division of labor or a capitalist world-system occurred simultaneously with the formation of a global racial/ethnic hierarchy – There is no "pre" nor "post" to their joint constitution. The superiority of the Westerners over non-Westeners in terms of a racial narrative of superior/inferior peoples was constructed in this period. This is why Mignolo (2000) states that "Occidentalism" (dominant discourse of the first modernity) is the socio-historical condition of possibility for the emergence of Orientalism (dominant discourse of the second modernity). Christianity was also central to the constitution of the colonial imaginary of the system.

During the second modernity (1650–1945) the core of the world-system shifted from Spain and Portugal to Germany, The Netherlands, England and France. The emergence of Northwestern Europe as the core of the capitalist world-system continued, expanded and deepened the "internal imaginary border" (against Jews, Arabs, Gypsies, etc.) and the "external imaginary border" built during the first modernity (against the Americas and later expanded to include other geographical zones). The second modernity added a new border between Northwestern Europeans and Iberian peoples to the old racial/colonial hierarchies. Hispanic/Latin Southern European cultures were constructed as inferior to the Northwestern Europeans. This hierarchical division within Europe would spread to North America and be reenacted in the context of the US imperial expansions of 1848 (Mexican-American War) and 1898 (Spanish-American War). The U.S. colonization of Northern Mexico, Cuba and Puerto Rico formed part of the white Anglo hegemony in the nineteenth century colonial expansions of the second modernity. Hispanic cultures were subalternized and the notion of "whiteness" acquired different and new meanings. In the context of the U.S. colonial expansion, white Spaniards were expelled from the notion of "whiteness." "Hispanics" were constructed as part of the inferior others excluded from the superior "white European" races. To make matters even more complicated, in the United States, the notion of whiteness expanded to include groups that were internal colonial subjects of Europe under Northwestern European hegemony (particularly, Irish, Eastern Europeans, Italians and Jews). At the time, European Orientalist discourses were also being articulated in relation to the colonized populations of Asia, Africa and the Middle East. The history of the second modernity is crucial to understanding the present racialization of Puerto Ricans or Mexicans of all colors in the United States and Anglo-White-American hegemony. The hegemonic White/Black divide does not exhaust the multiple racisms deployed and developed in the Unites States' colonial expansion. Given the social construction of race, "whiteness" is not merely about skin color. There are other markers that racialize people located on the "wrong side" of the colonial difference (such as accent, language or demeanor).

The capitalist world-system expanded to cover the whole planet during the second modernity (Wallerstein 1979). European (understood not merely in geographic terms, but in the broader sense of White European supremacy) and Euro-American nation building, struggles for citizenship rights and development of parliamentary regimes were inscribed in a global colonial/racist imaginary that established "internal" and "external" borders (Quijano 1993; Mignolo 2000). The invisibility of global coloniality in the process of building modern nation-states in nineteenth century Europe and the Americas shows how powerful and ingrained its colonial/racist culture was and still is. While categories of modernity such as citizenship, democracy and nation-building were acknowledged for the dominant Northwestern Europeans, the colonial "others" were submitted to coerced forms of labor and authoritarian political regimes in the periphery and semi-periphery. The Latin American periphery is no exception. White elites continued to dominate the power relations of the newly independent republics of South and Central America in the nineteenth century. Latin American independence, achieved in struggle against Spain and Portugal, was hegemonized by Euro-American elites. It was not a process of social, political, cultural or economic decolonization. Blacks, mulattos, Native-Americans and people of color remained in subordinated and disenfranchised positions in the "coloniality of power" constitutive of the emerging nation-states. Colonialism gave way to coloniality, that is, "independence without decolonization."

The post-1945 processes of nation-building in the great majority of the periphery of the world-economy are still informed by these colonial legacies and by the colonial/racial culture built during centuries of European colonial expansion. The Eurocentric colonial culture is an ideology that is not geographically limited to Europe, but rather is constitutive of the geoculture and imaginary of the modern world-system. Thus, modernity is always already constituted by coloniality. As Walter Mignolo (2000) states, we are living in a "modern/colonial capitalist world-system." The myth that we live in a decolonized world needs to be challenged. Contesting this myth requires that we take a "situated" view of these legacies within an axis of colonial difference. This has crucial epistemological implications for how we produce knowledge, how we shape new concepts and new language for dialogue. Challenging this myth also has crucial political implications in terms of how we conceive social change, struggles against inequality, scientific disciplines, utopian thinking, democracy, and decolonization.

Discussion: Neo-Culture of Poverty Approach and New Racisms

Political and epistemological challenges to the myths of decolonization give rise to new understandings of new racisms. Racism is a pervasive phenomenon that is constitutive not only of social relations in the United States, but of the imaginary of the capitalist world-system as a whole since the 1500s. Racism dominates the "common sense" of the modern/colonial world-system despite the changing meanings of "racist discourses" in the last 500 years. "Biological racist discourses" have now been replaced by what is called the "new racism" or "cultural racist" discourses. Historically, "scientific knowledges" and "racism" have been complicit discourses and practices. Sociobiology or eugenics was a type of knowledge produced in the name of science to justify or articulate "biological racist discourses." The most recent manifestation of the complicity between racism and science is the relationship between "culture of poverty approaches" and the new "cultural racisms." The "new racism" contends that the failure of "colonial/racialized" groups is not due to "inferior genes" or "inferior IQ" (although this is still a pervasive and popular perception, including some academic attempts to revive it), but rather to "improper" cultural habits and/or an "inferior" culture. This emphasis on culture over genes is what characterized the new "cultural racisms" dividing the world between groups with a superior culture and groups with an inferior or inadequate culture. This "new racism" has been legitimized by academic approaches that portray the high poverty rates among people of color both in the core and the periphery in terms of their traditional, inadequate, underdeveloped and inferior cultural values and/or practices.

The "new economic sociology" which includes a variety of approaches, has emerged as a field of research on migrant incorporation. As elaborated by some scholars (Portes and Zhou 1992; Portes and Sessenbrener 1993), the new economic sociology represents a return to "culture of poverty" assumptions, but with a more sophisticated terminology.[1] This provides a good example of the complicity between knowledges produced in the social sciences and new racial formations in metropolitan centers. According to this approach, the social capital of an ethnic community is central in understanding why certain ethnic groups are successful and others fail in the labor market (Portes and Zhou 1992). In contrast to the structural and individualist approaches, the "new economic sociology" calls for micro-network explanations of poverty and inequality in America (Portes and Zhou 1992). Social capital, the central concept in this approach, is defined as "those expectations for action within a collectivity that affect the economic goals and goal-seeking behavior of its members, even if these expectations are not oriented toward the economic sphere" (Portes and Sessenbrenner 1993: 1323). These expectations are the result of the community's micro-networks. This approach attempts to center the analysis on the "internal" dynamics of an ethnic community or the inner workings of micro-networks in order to understand how social capital affects economic behavior in an ethnic community. One of these mechanisms is "enforceable trust," which is said to be an integral part of the economic trans-actions that emerge from the internal sanctioning capacity of an ethnic com-munity. Cubans in Miami are put forward as an example of the positive aspects of this form of social capital and as a group that has purportedly "made it" in the American mainstream without massive government assis-tance (Portes and Sessenbrenner 1993; Portes and Zhou 1992). The emergence of the Cuban enclave in Miami is explained as the result of "character" loans given with no collateral by Cuban bank officials for business start-ups to fel-low exiles based on their business reputation back in Cuba (Portes and Zhou 1992; Portes and Sessenbrenner 1993; Portes and Stepick 1995). This narra-tive about the emergence of the Cuban ethnic economy in Miami omits the role of global political-economic forces in the capital formation of Cuban entrepreneurs and the coloniality of power related to it. Because of the cen-trality of the Cuban example in this approach, an unpacking of the broader structural processes that account for capital formation within this community and that exemplify the role of global processes in the formation, structuring,

---

[1] Important exceptions to this approach within the "new economic sociology" lit-erature are excellent works by Roger Waldinger (1986; 1996) and Mark Granovetter (1985.) Both Waldinger and Granovetter have a more complex and structural con-ceptualization, as opposed to a culturalist understanding of the economic sociology notions of "embeddedness" and "networks."

and reproduction of micro-community networks is central to a critique of the approach.

Cuban businesses were formed mainly by the institutional policies the United States' government deployed as part of the Cold War. Cuban exiles became a symbolic showcase of the superiority of capitalism over socialism (Pedraza-Bailey 1985). The success of Cubans in the United States was crucial for the United States to gain symbolic capital vis-à-vis the Soviet model. In order to advance its geopolitical goals and global designs during the Cold War, the United States channeled massive state resources to the Cuban refugees. Through the Cuban Refugee Program under the Health, Education and Welfare Department (HEW) of the United States, Cubans received welfare payments, job training, bilingual language programs, educational support, subsidized college loans, health care services, help in job search efforts and money for resettling out of Miami. Moreover, the initial capital for many Cuban entrepreneurs was raised through the privileged support offered by the Small Business Administration (SBA).

Cubans unwittingly became an example of how successful an ethnic group could be if they received the proper welfare programs like education, health, job training and English as a second language courses (DeFreitas 1991). This contrasts strongly with the portrait of Cubans as an ethnic group that has "made it" through their own micro-networks at a community level, without massive government assistance (Portes and Sessenbrenner 1993; Portes and Zhou 1992). My argument is not that social networks at a community level are unimportant, but rather that micro-networks are embedded in broader power relations and social structures that constrain or enable the access to capital, information and resources by community level micro-networks. It is a reductionist approach to simply focus on the relation between micro-networks and capital formation or marginalization in the labor market without studying how mediating structures and social relations at a macro and meso level shape the labor market incorporation of ethnic communities.

Research done in the vein of this "neo-culture of poverty" approach contrasts the "success" of Cubans in Miami with the "failure" of colonial/racial subjects within the United States empire such as Puerto Ricans in the South Bronx or African-Americans in the inner city (Portes and Sessenbrenner 1993). According to this approach, African-American youth and second "generation" Puerto Ricans are a negative example of a particular type of social capital called "bounded solidarity" that is born out of common adversity. The "neo-culture of poverty" approach states that to call someone a "wannabe" exercises group pressure that discourages him/her from seeking or pursuing "outside" opportunities. Moreover, they portray the Haitian-American teenagers dilemma in Miami as ". . . torn between parental expectations for success through education and an inner city youth culture [African-Americans] that denies such a thing is possible" (Portes and Sessenbrenner 1993: 1342).

I am not denying that such group pressures exist. The argument is that such pressures are the result of a particular location in broader social/colonial structures. As Pierre Bourdieu (1977) reminds us, the *habitus* of an individual is always related to the "internal" dispositions of a relational position in a broader field of power relations. Thus, the African-American and Puerto Rican youth skepticism towards education is not necessarily a false perception due to a negative social capital but probably a more realistic understanding of their possibilities within an educational system that penalizes individuals who are born in low-income, segregated and racialized communities. The United States is the only Western metropole with no national public educational system. The resources and quality of public schools depend on the income and property taxes of local communities. People born in impoverished, discriminated communities are penalized for the rest of their life for not having access to the proper education. By centering the explanation of poverty or marginality in the negative cultural practices of an ethnic community, the "neo-culture of poverty" approach erases: (1) the structural conditions of discrimination faced by young Puerto Ricans, Chicanos, Haitian-Americans or African-Americans such as lack of access to high quality education and labor market opportunities; (2) the "coloniality of power" and the colonial history of subordination structuring the racial oppression, residential segregation and exploitation that Puerto Ricans, African-Americans, Chicanos and other colonial/racialized minorities have experienced in the United States; and (3) the class differences among the groups involved in the ethnic micro-networks which conditions their access to resources and capital.

The underlying implication of the "neo-culture of poverty" approach is that Cubans are an example of a positive version of social capital due to their "superior" cultural practices while Puerto Ricans and African-Americans are an example of negative social capital due to their 'inferior" cultural practices. This is strikingly similar to what the culture of poverty approach argued thirty years ago. The main difference is that the "neo-culture of poverty" approach replaced the term "cultural values" of the old culture of poverty approach for the more contemporary term "social capital," treated as equivalent to "cultural practices" and analytically central to explain an ethnic community's failure or success in the labor market. This serves as an example of the complicit relationship between scholarly knowledge production and "cultural racist/colonial" discourses. This "neo-culture of poverty approach" provides the so-called "scientific knowledge" that legitimate the claims made by new "cultural racist" discourses about the "social failure" of certain racial/ethnic groups in terms of their "cultural inadequacy" or "cultural inferiority." By embedding these "cultural racist/colonial" discourses into understandings of coloniality of power and "modern/colonial capitalist world system" we embark upon new projects of social change.

References

Abbott, Andrew. 1999. *Department and Discipline: Chicago Sociology at One Hundred.* Chicago: Univeristy of Chicago Press.

Abraham, Sameer and Herbert Hunter. 1987. *Race, Class and the World System: The Sociology of Oliver C. Cox.* New York: Monthly Review Press.

Acker, Joan. 1990. "Hierarchies, Jobs, Bodies: A Theory of Gendered Organizations." Gender and Society 4(2): 139–158.

Ahlgren, Carol and Frank Edgerton Martin. 1989. "From Dante to Doomsday: How a City Without People Survived a Nuclear Blast." Design Book Review 17 (Winter): 26–28.

Alarcon, Norma. 1981. Chicana's Feminist Literature: A Re-vision through Malintzin/or Malintzin: Putting Flesh Back on the Object. In Cherrie Moraga and Gloria Anzaldua, eds., *This Bridge Called My Back: Writing by Radical Women of Color.* Watertown, MA: Persephone Press.

Albelda, Randy, Nancy Folbre and the Center for Popular Economics. 1996. *The War on the Poor: A Defense Manual.* New York: The New Press.

Aldridge, A. Owen. 1971. "American Burlesque at Home and Aboard: Together with the Etymology of Go-Go Girls." Journal of Popular Culture 5(3): 555–575.

Alfred, Gerald R. 1995. *Heeding the Voices of Our Ancestors: Kanhawake Mohawk Politics and the Rise of Native Nationalism.* Toronto: Oxford.

Alfred, Gerald R. 1999. *Peace, Power, Righteousness : An Indigenous Manifesto.* New York: Oxford.

Alsayyad, Nezar. 2000. *Consuming Tradition, Manufacturing Heritage: Global Norms and Urban Forms in the Age of Tourism.* London: Routledge.

Andersen, Margaret. 2001. *Thinking About Women: Sociological Perspectives on Sex and Gender, Fifth Edition.* Boston: Allyn & Bacon.

Anderson, Benedict. 1991. *Imagined Communities.* New York: Verso.

Anderson, Elijah. 1990. *Streetwise.* Chicago: University of Chicago Press.

Anderson, Elijah. 2000. *Code of the Street: Decency, Violence & Moral Life of the Inner City.* New York: W.W. Norton & Co.

Anderson, Paul Allen. 2001. *Deep River: Music and Memory in Harlem Renaissance Thought.* Durham: Duke University Press.

Angell, James R. 1941. "Radio and National Morale." The American Journal of Sociology 47(3): 352–359.

Anzaldua, Gloria. 1987. *Borderlands/La Frontera: The New Mestiza.* San Francisco: Aunt Lute Books.

Appadurai, Arjun. 1990. "Disjuncture and Difference in the Global Cultural Economy." Public Culture 2(2): 1–24.

Appadurai, Arjun. 1996. *Modernity at Large: Cultural Dimensions of Globalization.* Minneapolis: University of Minnesota Press.

Appiah, Kwame Anthony. 1993. *In My Father's House: Africa in the Philosophy of Culture.* New York: Oxford.

Arendt, Hannah. 1958. *The Human Condition*. Chicago: University of Chicago Press.

Arney, William Ray and Bernard Bergen. 1984. *Medicine and the Management of Living: Taming the Last Great Beast*. Chicago: University of Chicago Press.

Arrighi, Giovanni. 1994. *The Long Twentieth Century*. New York: Verso.

Asociación de Maquiladoras A.C. (AMAC). 1989. *Analysis Turnover*. Unpublished Internal document.

Associated Universities, Inc. 1952. *Report of the Project East River*. New York: Associated Universities, Inc.

Atwood, J.H. 1930. *The Attitudes of Negro Ministers of the Major Denominations in Chicago toward the Fact of Division Between Negro and White Churches*. Unpublished Ph.D. dissertation, Divinity School, University of Chicago.

Aufderheide, Pat. 2002. Therapeutic Patriotism and Beyond. Television Archive website at http://tvnews3.televisionarchive.org/tvarchive/html/article_pal.html (June).

Bacchetta, Paola, Tina Campt, Inderpal Grewal, Caren Kaplan, Minoo Moallem, and Jennifer Terry. 2002. "Transnational Feminist Practices Against War." Meridians: Feminism, Race, Transnationalism 2(2).

Bachin, Robin. 2004. *Building the South Side: Urban Space and Civic Culture in Chicago, 1890–1919*. Chicago: University of Chicago Press.

Baerresen, Donald. 1971. *The Border Industrialization Program of Mexico*. Lexington, MA: Heath Lexington Books.

Bagdikian, Ben. 1978. "The Best News Money Can Buy." Human Behavior (October): 63–67.

Bagdikian, Ben. 2000. *The Media Monopoly, Sixth Edition*. Boston: Beacon Press.

Baird, Peter and Ed McCaughan. 1979. *Beyond the Border*. New York: North American Congress on Latin America.

Baker, Houston Jr. 1991. *Workings of the Spirit: The Poetics of Afro-American Women's Writing*. Chicago: University of Chicago Press.

Baker, Houston. 1987. *Modernism and the Harlem Renaissance*. Chicago: University of Chicago Press.

Baker, Lee. 1998. *From Savage to Negro: Anthropology and the Construction of Race, 1896–1954*. Berkeley: University of California Press.

Baldwin, Davarian L. 2001. *Chicago's New Negroes: Race, Class and Respectability in the Midwestern Black Metropolis, 1915–1935*. Unpublished Ph.D. dissertation, American Studies, New York University.

Baldwin, Davarian L. 2003. "Out From the Shadow of E. Franklin Frazier?: Middle-Class Identity and Consumer Citizenship in the Black Metropolis." Journal of Urban History 9(6): 778–793.

Baldwin, Marc. 1999. Public Policy and the Two-Thirds Majority. In Jo-Ann Mort, ed., *Not Your Father's Labor Movement*. New York: Verso.

Balshaw, Maria. 2000. *Looking for Harlem: Urban Aesthetics in African American Literature*. Sterling Virginia: Pluto Press.

Bannister, Robert. 1979. *Science and Myth in Anglo-American Social Thought*. Philadelphia: Temple University Press.

Baron, Ava. 1991. Gender and Labor History: Learning from the Past, Looking to the

Future. In Ava Baron, ed., *Work Engendered: Toward a New History of American Labor*. Ithaca: Cornell University Press.

Barton, Bernadette. 2002. "Dancing on the Mobius Strip: Challenging the Sex War Paradigm." Gender & Society 16(5): 585–602.

Bates, Beth Thompkins. 2001. *Pullman Porters and the Rise of Protest Politics in Black America, 1925–1945*. Chapel Hill, UNC Press.

Baudrillard, Jean. 1993. *Simulations*. New York: Semiotext[e].

Beckett, Katherine and Theodore Sasson. 2000. *The Politics of Injustice: Crime and Punishment in America*. Thousand Oaks, CA: Pine Forge Press, Inc.

Bederman, Gail. 1995. *Manliness and Civilization: A Cultural History of Gender and Race in the United States, 1880–1917*. Chicago: University of Chicago Press.

Beekman, Scott Michael. 1998. *This Judas Iscariot: Cyril Briggs and the African Blood Brotherhood's Relationship with Marcus Garvey and the Universal Negro Improvement Association, 1918–1922*. Unpublished Ph.D. dissertation, Ohio State University.

Benally, Herbert John. 1994. "Navajo Philosophy of Learning and Pedagogy." Journal of Navajo Education 12(1): 23–31.

Benally, Herbert John. 1998. Navajo Ways of Knowing. In Max O. Hallman, ed., *Traversing Philosophical Boundaries*. Belmont, CA: Wadsworth.

Bendix, Reinhard. 1977. *Max Weber: An Intellectual Portrait*. Berkeley: University of California Press.

Benedict, Jeff. 2000. *Without Reservation: The Making of America's Most Powerful Indian Tribe and Foxwoods, the World's Largest Casino*. New York: HarperCollins.

Benería, Lourdes and Martha Roldán. 1987. *The Crossroads of Class and Gender*. Chicago: University of Chicago Press.

Benjamin, Walter. 1968 (1940). *Illuminations*, edited by Hanah Arendt. New York: Schocken Books.

Bennett, W. Lance. 1988. *News: The Politics of Illusion*. New York: Longman.

Berger, John. 1972. *Ways of Seeing*. London: Penguin Books.

Bergeron, Suzanne. 2001. "Political Economy Discourses of Globalization and Feminist Politics." Signs 26(4): 983–1006.

Bhavnani, Kum-Kum, John Foran and Priya Kurian. 2003. An Introduction to Women, Culture and Development. In Kum-Kum Bhavnani, John Foran and Priya A. Kurian, eds., *Feminist Futures: Re-imagining Women, Culture and Development*. London: Zed Books.

Binder, Carroll. 1927. *Chicago and the New Negro*. Chicago: Chicago Daily News.

Blackmar, Frank W. 1909. "(Review of) Studies in the American Race Problem, by Alfred H. Stone." American Journal of Sociology 16(6): 837–839.

Blackwell, James and Morris Janowitz, eds. 1974. *Black Sociologists: Historical and Contemporary Perspectives*. Chicago: University of Chicago Press.

Bledstein, Burton. 1976. *The Culture of Professionalism: The Middle Class and the Development of Higher Education*. New York: Norton.

Bogart, William. 1996. *Simulation of Surveillance: Hypercontrol in Telematic Societies*. Minneapolis: University of Minnesota Press.

Boles, Jacqueline and Albeno P. Garbin. 1974. "Stripping for a Living: An Occupational Study of the Night Club Stripper." Sociology and Social Research 58:136–144.

Bond, George Clement and John Gibbs St. Clair Drake. 1988. "A Social Portrait of John Gibbs St. Clair Drake: An American Anthropologist." American Ethnologist 15(4): 762–781.

Bond, Horace Mann. 1939. Negro Education in Alabama: A Study in Cotton and Steel. New York: Octagon Books.

Bone, Robert. 1986. "Richard Wright and the Chicago Renaissance," Callaloo 28(Summer): 446–468.

Bonilla-Silva, Eduardo. 2001. White Supremacy and Racism in the Post-Civil Rights Era. New York: Lynne Rienner Publishers.

Bontemps, Arna. 1972. The Harlem Renaissance Remembered. New York: Dodd and Mead.

Bordo, Susan. 1993. Unbearable Weight: Feminism, Western Culture, and the Body. Berkley, Los Angeles, and London: University of California Press.

Borgmann, Albert. 1992. Crossing the Postmodern Divide. Chicago: University of Chicago Press.

Boudieu, Pierre. 1977. Outline of a Theory of Practice. Cambridge: Cambridge University Press.

Bowser, Benjamin. 1981. "The Contributions of Blacks to Sociological Knowledge: A Problem of Theory and Role to 1950." Phylon 42(2): 180–193.

Bowser, Pearl and Louise Spense. 2000. Writing Himself into History: Oscar Micheaux, His Silent Films and His Audiences. New Brunswick: Rutgers University Press.

Boyd, Michelle. 2000. "Reconstructing Bronzeville: Racial Nostalgia and Neighborhood Redevelopment." Journal of Urban Affairs 22(2):107–122.

Boyd, Stephen and Dallen Timothy. 2002. Heritage Tourism. Reading, MA: Longman Publishing Group. Michigan.

Boyer, Paul S. 1984. Urban Masses and Moral Order in America, 1820–1920. Cambridge: Harvard University Press.

Boyle, Hal. 1951. "Washington Under the Bomb." Collier's 27(October).

Bracey, John, August Meier and Eliot Rudwick. 1973. The Black Sociologists: The First Half Century. In Joyce Ladner, ed., The Death of White Sociology. New York: Vintage Books.

Braudel, Fernand. 1984. The Perspective of the World: Civilization and Capitalism, 15th–18th Century, Volume 3. New York: Harper & Row.

Brennan, Teresa. 1993. History After Lacan. New York: Routledge.

Brennan, Teresa. 2000. Exhausting Modernity: Grounds for a New Economy. New York: Routledge.

Breslau, Daniel. 1990. "The Scientific Appropriation of Social Research: Robert Park's Human Ecology and American Sociology." Theory and Society 19(4): 417–446.

Brewster, Zachary. W. 2003. "Behavioral and Interactional Patterns of Strip Club Patrons: Tipping Techniques and Club Attendance." Deviant Behavior 24: 221–243.

Brodkin Sachs, Karen. 1993. How Did Jews Become White Folks? In Gregory, Steven and Roger Sanjek, eds., Race. New Brunswick, NJ: Rutgers University Press.

Bronfenbrenner, Kate and Tom Juravich. 1998. It Takes More than House Calls: Organizing to Win. In Kate Bronfenbrenner, Sheldon Friedman, Richard Hurd, Rudolph Oswald and Ronald Seeber, eds., *Organizing to Win*. Ithaca: Cornell University Press.

Brooks, Abigail. 2004. "'Under the Knife and Proud of It:' An Analysis of the Normalization of Cosmetic Surgery." Critical Sociology 30(2): 207–239.

Broschart, Kay. 1991. Ida B. Wells-Barnett. In Maro Jo Deegan, ed., *Women in Sociology*. Westport, CT: Greenwood Press.

Brown, Oscar. 1930. *Race Prejudice: A Sociological Study*. Unpublished Ph.D. dissertation, Department of Sociology, University of Chicago.

Bruckert, Chris. 2002. *Taking It Off, Putting It On: Women in the Strip Trade*. Toronto: Women's Press.

Brush, Pippa. 1998. "Metaphors of Inscription: Discipline, Plasticity and the Rhetoric of Choice." Feminist Review 58: 22–43.

Bulmer, Martin. 1981. "Charles S. Johnson, Robert E. Park and the Research Methods of the Chicago Commission on Race Relations, 1919–22: An Early Experiment in Applied Social Research." Ethnic and Racial Studies 4(3): 265–288.

Bulmer, Martin. 1984. *The Chicago School of Sociology: Institutionalization, Diversity and the Rise of Sociological Research*. Chicago: University of Chicago Press.

Bunyan, John. 1981. *The Pilgrim's Progress*. New York: New American Library-Signet Classic.

Burg, David. 1976. *Chicago's White City of 1893*. Lexington: University Press of Kentucky Press.

Burgess, Ernest. 1925. The Growth of the City: An Introduction to a Research Project. In Robert Park, Ernest Burgess, and Roderick McKenzie, eds., *The City*. Chicago: University of Chicago Press.

Burgess, Ernest. 1956. "Charles S. Johnson: Social Scientist and Race Relations." Phylon (4th Qtr.).

Bush, Vannevar. 1945. *Science: The Endless Frontier*. Washington, D.C.: U.S. Government Printing Office.

Butler, Judith. 1990. *Gender Trouble: Feminism and the Subversion of Identity*. New York: Routledge.

Butler, Judith. 1993. *Bodies That Matter: On the Discursive Limits of Sex*. New York: Routledge.

Cajete, Gregory A. 1994. *Look to the Mountain: An Ecology of Indigenous Education*. Durango, CO: Kivaki.

Calloway, Colin G. 1983. "An Uncertain Destiny: Indian Captivities on the Upper Connecticut River." Journal of American Studies 17: 189–210.

Canby, William C., Jr. 2004. *American Indian Law in a Nutshell, 4th ed*. St. Paul, MN: West Publishing.

Cantril, Hadley. 1940. *The Invasion from Mars: A Study in the Psychology of Panic*. Princeton: Princeton University Press.

Cappetti, Carla. 1985. "Sociology of Existence: Richard Wright and the Chicago School." MELUS 12(2): 25–43.

Cappetti, Carla. 1993. *Writing Chicago: Modernism, Ethnography and the Novel*. New York: Columbia University Press.

Carby, Hazel. 1987. *Reconstructing Womanhood: The Emergence of the Afro-American Woman Novelist*. New York: Oxford University Press.

Carby, Hazel. 1992. "Policing the Black Woman's Body in an Urban Context." Critical Inquiry 18(Summer): 738–57.

Carey, J.T. 1975. *Sociology and Public Affairs: The Chicago Sociology School*. Beverly Hills, CA: Sage Publications.

Carrillo, Jorge and Alberto Hernández. 1985. *Mujeres Fronterizas en la Industria Maquiladora*. Mexico City: Secretaría de Educación Pública and Centro de Estudios Fronterizos del Norte de México.

Carrillo, Jorge and Miguel Angel Ramírez . 1990. "Maquiladoras en la frontera norte: Opinión sobre los sindicatos." Frontera Norte 2(4): 121–152.

Carrillo, Jorge. 1985. *Conflictos Laborales en la Industria Maquiladora*. Tijuana: Centro de Estudios Fronterizos del Norte de México.

Carter, Dan T. 1984. *Scottsboro: A Tragedy of the American South*. Baton Rouge, LA: LSU Press.

Catanzarite, Lisa and Myra Strober. 1993. "The Gender Recomposition of the Maquiladora Labor Force." Industrial Relations 32(1): 133–147.

Cayton, Horace and George S. Mitchell. 1935. *Black Workers and the New Unions*. College Park, MD: McGrath Publishing.

Cayton, Horace and St. Clair Drake. 1945. *Black Metropolis: A Study of Negro Life in a Northern City*. Chicago: University of Chicago Press.

Charon, Rita. 2000. To Listen, To Recognize. In Phil Brown, ed., *Perspectives in Medical Sociology*. Prospect Heights, IL: Waveland Press.

Chicago Commission on Race Relations (CCRR). 1922. *The Negro in Chicago: A Study of Race Relations and a Race Riot*. Chicago: University of Chicago Press.

Childs, Peter and R.J. Patrick Williams. 1999. *An Introduction to Post-colonial Theory*. New York: Prentice-Hall.

Chilton, Paul. 1987. "Metaphor, Euphemism and the Militarization of Language." Current Research on Peace and Violence 10: 7–19.

Chin, Elizabeth. 2000. *Purchasing Power: Black Kids and American Consumer Culture*. Minneapolis: University of Minnesota Press.

Cicourel, Aaron. 1964. *Method and Measurement in Sociology*. New York: Free Press.

Clark, Veve and Margaret Wilkerson, eds. 1978. *Kaiso: Katherine Dunham, An Anthology of Writings*. Berkeley: Institute for the Study of Social Change, CCEW Women's Center, University of California.

Clifford, James and George Marcus, eds. 1986. *Writing Culture: The Poetics and Politics of Ethnography*. Berkeley: University of California Press.

Clifford, James. 1988. *The Predicament of Culture: Twentieth Century Ethnography, Literature and Art*. Cambridge, MA: Harvard University Press.

Clough, Patricia. 1998. *The End(s) of Ethnography: From Realism to Social Criticism, Second Edition*. New York: Peter Lang Publishing.

Cohen, Cathy. 1999. *The Boundaries of Blackness: AIDS and the Breakdown of Black Politics*. Chicago: University of Chicago Press.

Cohen, Jay S. 2001. *Over Dose: The Case Against the Drug Companies: Prescription Drugs, Side Effects, and Your Health*. New York: Jeremy P. Tarcher/Putnam.

Collins, Patricia Hill. 1990. *Black Feminist Thought: Knowledge, Consciousness, and the Politics of Empowerment*. New York: Routledge.

Collins, Patricia Hill. 2000. *Black Feminist Thought, Second Edition*. New York: Routledge.

Conklin, John. 1998. *Criminology, Sixth Edition*. Boston: Allyn & Bacon.

Connell, R.W. 1987. *Gender & Power*. Stanford, CA: Stanford University Press.

Conyers Jr., John. 2000. Carter Goodwin Woodson's Biographical Sketch. In James L. Conyers, ed., *Carter G. Woodson*. New York: Garland.

Cook, Daniel. 2004. *The Commodification of Childhood: Personhood, the Children's Wear Industry and the Rise of the Child-Consumer, 1917–1962*. Durham: Duke University Press.

Cook-Lynn, Elizabeth. 1996. *Why I Can't Read Wallace Stegner and Other Essays: A Tribal Voice*. Madison: University of Wisconsin.

Cooper, Frank. 2002. "The Un-balanced Fourth Amendment: A Cultural Study of the Drug War, Racial Profiling and ARVIZU." Villanova Law Review 47(4): 851–895.

Cooper, H.E. 1929. "Variety, Vaudeville, Virtue, Naughty Nineties to Respectability." Dance Magazine (December): 23–37.

Coquillette, Daniel R. 1999. *The Anglo-American Legal Heritage*. Durham, NC: Carolina Academic Press.

Cosgrove, Denis. 1985. "Prospect, perspective and the evolution of the landscape idea." Transactions of the Institute of British Geographers, New Series 10(1): 45–62.

Cottrell, Leonard S., Jr., and Sylvia Eberhart. 1948. *American Opinion on World Affairs in the Atomic Age*. Princeton: Princeton University Press.

Cottrell, Robert. 2001. *The Best Pitcher in Baseball: The Life of Rube Foster, Negro League Giant*. New York: NYU Press.

Cox, Oliver Cromwell. 1942. "The Modern Caste School of Race Relations." Social Forces 21(2): 218–226.

Cox, Oliver Cromwell. 1944. "Racial Theories of Robert E. Park, et al. Journal of Negro Education." 13(4): 452–463.

Cox, Oliver Cromwell. 1945. "Race, and Caste: A Definition and a Distinction." American Journal of Sociology. 50(5): 360–368.

Cox, Oliver Cromwell. 1948. *Caste, Class and Race*. New York: Modern Reader Paperbacks.

Craver, Charles. 1993. *Can Unions Survive?* New York: New York University Press.

Cravey, Altha. 1998. *Women and Work in Mexico's Maquiladoras*. Lanham: Rowman and Littlefield Publishes, Inc.

Cronon, William. 1991. *Nature's Metropolis: Chicago and the Great West*. New York: W.W. Norton and Company.

Croteau, David and William Hoynes. 1994. *By Invitation Only: How Media Limit Political Debate*. Monroe, ME: Common Courage Press.

Croteau, David and William Hoynes. 2001. *The Business of Media: Corporate Media and the Public Interest*. Monroe ME: Common Courage Press.

Croteau, David, William Hoynes and Kevin Carragee. 1996. "The Political Diversity of Public Television: Polysemy, the Public Sphere, and the Conservative Critique of PBS." Journalism and Mass Communication Monographs 157: 1–55.

D'Sousa, Dinesh. 1995. *The End of Racism: Principles for a Multiracial Society*. New York: Free Press.

Dahlgren, Peter, and Colin Sparks, eds. 1991. *Communication and Citizenship: Journalism and the Public Sphere*. London: Routledge.

Daley, Elizabeth. 1994. *Labor and the Mass Media: A Case Study and Survey of the Literature*. Center for Labor Research, Ohio State University. Working Paper Series: WP-011.

Daniel, Vattel Elbert. 1940. *Ritual in Chicago's South Side Churches for Negroes*. Unpublished Ph.D. dissertation, Department of Sociology, University of Chicago.

Davis, Allison, Burleigh Gardner and Mary Gardner. 1941. *Deep South: A Social Anthropological Study of Caste and Class*. Chicago: University of Chicago Press.

Davis, Angela. 1988. *Blues Legacies and Black Feminisms*. New York: Pantheon Books.

Davis, Angela. 1998. *The Angela Y Davis Reader*. Malden, MA: Blackwell.

Davis, Kathy. 1991: "Remaking the She-Devil: A Critical Look at Feminist Approaches to Beauty." Hypatia 6: 20–43.

Davis, Kathy. 1995. Reshaping the Female Body: The Dilemma of Cosmetic Surgery. New York: Routledge.

Davis, Kathy. 1997. *Embodied Practices: Feminist Perspectives on the Body*. London: Sage.

Davis, Kathy. 1999. "Cosmetic Surgery in A Different Voice: The Case Of Madame Noel." Women's Studies International Forum 22: 473–488.

Dawkins, Richard. 1990. *The Selfish Gene*. Oxford: Oxford University Press.

De Certeau, Michel. 1984. *The Practice of Everyday Life*. Berkeley: University of California Press.

De la O. Martínez, María Eugenia. 1991. *Reconversión industrial en la industria maquiladora electronica: Cuatro estudios de caso participación femenina en Ciudad Juárez*, Chihuahua. Unpublished Manuscript, Tijuana.

De la Rosa Hickerson, Gustavo. 1979. *La contratación colectiva en las maquiladoras: Analisis de un caso de sobreexplotación*. Unpublished Professional Thesis, Ciudad Juárez, Escuela de Derecho, Universidad Autónoma.

Deegan, Mary Jo, ed. 2002. *The New Woman of Color: The Collected Works of Fannie Barrier Williams*. Dekalb, IL: Northern Illinois University Press.

Deegan, Mary Jo. 1981. "Early Women Sociologists and the American Sociological Society: Patterns of Inclusion and Exclusion." American Sociologist 16 (February): 14–24.

Deegan, Mary Jo. 1988b. "W.E.B. DuBois and the Women of Hull House, 1896–1899." American Sociologist 19(4): 301–311.

Deegan, Mary Jo. 1988. *Jane Adams and the Men of the Chicago School, 1892–1918*. New Brunswick, NJ: Transaction Books.

Deegan, Mary Jo. 2002. *Race, Hull-House, and the University of Chicago: A New Conscience Against Ancient Evils*. Westport, CT: Praeger.

DeFreitas, Gregory. 1991. *Inequality at Work: Hispanics in the U.S. Labor Force*. New York: Oxford University Press.

Deleuze, Gilles and Felix Guattari. 1983. *Anti-Oedipus: Capitalism and Schizophrenia*. Minneapolis: University of Minnesota Press.

Deloria, Ella. 1994. *Speaking of Indians*. New York: Friendship.

Denning, Michael. 1997. *The Cultural Front: The Laboring of American Culture in the Twentieth Century*. London: Verso.

Dentler, Robert and Peter Rossi. 1981. *The Politics of Urban Renewal*: The Chicago Findings. Westport, CT: Greenwood Press.

Derrida, Jacques. 1981 [1972]. *Positions*, translated by Alan Bass. Chicago: University of Chicago Press.

Desarollo Economico de Ciudad Juárez. 1991. *Ciudad Juárez en Cifras*. Ciudad Juárez: Desarollo Económico.

Desmond, Jane. 2001. *Staging Tourism: Bodies on Display from Waikiki to Sea World*. Chicago: University of Chicago Press.

Deutsche, Roslaind and Cara Gendel Ryan. 1984. "The Fine Art of Gentrification." October 31 (Winter): 91–111.

Dibble, Vernon. 1975. *The Legacy of Albion Small*. Chicago: University of Chicago Press.

Diner, Stephen. 1980. *A City and its Universities: Public Policy in Chicago, 1892–1919*. Chapel Hill: UNC Press.

Dodson, Lisa. 1999. *Don't Call Us Out of Name: The Untold Lives of Women and Girls in Poor America*. Boston: Beacon Press.

Donaldson, Sam. 1987. *Hold On, Mr. President*. New York: Random House.

Douglas, Ann. 1995. *Terrible Honesty: Mongrel Manhattan in the 1920s*. New York: Farrar, Straus and Giroux.

Douglas, Sara. 1986. *Labor's News: Unions and the Mass Media*. Norwood, NJ: Ablex.

Douvan, Elizabeth and Stephen B. Withy. 1953. "Some Attitudinal Consequences of Atomic Energy." The Annals of the American Academy of Political and Social Science 290 (November): 108–117.

Doyle, Bertram. 1934. *The Etiquette of Race Relations in the South*. Unpublished Ph.D. dissertation, Department of Sociology, University of Chicago.

DuBois, W.E.B. 1935. *Black Reconstruction*. New York: Harcourt Brace.

DuBois, W.E.B. 1940. *Dusk of Dawn*. New York: Harcourt and Brace.

DuBois, W.E.B. 1989 [1903]. *Souls of Black Folk*. New York: Penguin Books.

DuBois, W.E.B. 1996 [1899]. *Philadelphia Negro*. Philadelphia: University of Pennsylvania Press.

Dunham, Katherine. 1959. *A Touch of Innocence: Memoirs of Childhood*. New York: Harcourt Brace.

Edin, Kathryn and Laura Lein. 1997. *Making Ends Meet*. New York: Russell Sage Foundation.

Edkins, Diana and Carole Marks, eds. 1999. *Stylemakers and Rulebreakers of the Harlem Renaissance*. New York: Crown Publishers.

Egan, R. Danielle. 2000. *The Phallus Palace: Sexy Spaces, Desiring Subjects and Fantasy of Objects*. Unpublished Ph.D. Dissertation, Boston College.

Egan, R. Danielle. 2003. "I'll be Your Fantasy Girl, If You'll be My Money Man: Mapping Desire, Fantasy and Power in Two Exotic Dance Clubs." Journal of Psychoanalysis, Culture and Society 8(1): 109–120.

Eisenchier, Michael. 1996. *Critical Juncture: Labor at the Crossroads*. Boston: Center for Labor Research.

Eisenschier, Michael. 1999. Labor: Turning the Corner Will Take More than Mobilization. In Tillman, R. and Cummings, M., eds., *The Transformation of U.S. Unions; Voices, Visions, and Strategies from the Grassroots*. Boulder, CO: Lynne Rienner Publishers.

Eller, Jack David and Reed M. Coughlan. 1993. "The Poverty of Primordialism: The Demystification of Ethnic Attachment," Ethnic and Racial Studies 16(2): 183–202.

Ellison, Ralph. 1964. *Shadow and Act*. New York: Random House.

Enloe, Cynthia. 1989. *Bananas, Beaches and Bases: Making Feminist Sense of International Politics*. Berkeley: University of California Press.

Entman, Robert. 1989. *Democracy Without Citizens*. New York: Oxford University Press.

Epstein, Edward J. 1973. *News from Nowhere: Television and the New*. New York: Vintage.

Erdoes, Richard and Alfonso Ortiz, eds. 1984. *American Indian Myths and Legends*. New York: Pantheon Books.

Erikson, David and Tewksbury, Richard. 2000. "The Gentlemen in the Club: A Typology of Strip Club Patrons." Deviant Behavior: An Interdisciplinary Journal 21: 271–293.

Ewick, Patricia and Susan S. Silbey. 1992. "Conformity, Contestation, and Resistance: An Account of Legal Consciousness." New England Law Review 26(3): 731–749.

Fabian, Johannes. 1983. *Time and the Other*. New York: Columbia University Press.

Fanon, Frantz. 1967 [1952]. *Black Skin, White Masks*. New York: Grove Press.

Farough, Steven. 2001. *Contemporary White Masculinities*. Unpublished Ph.D. Dissertation, Department of Sociology, Boston College.

Farough, Steven. 2004. "The Social Geographies of White Masculinities." Critical Sociology 30(2): 241–264.

Farris, Robert E.L. 1967. *Chicago Sociology, 1920–1937*. San Francisco: Chandler.

Feagin, Joe. 2001. *Racist America: Roots, Current Realities, and Future Reparations*. New York: Routledge.

Featherstone, Mike and Turner, Bryan, S. 1991. *The Body: Social Process and Cultural Theory*. London: Sage.

Federal Civil Defense Association. 1952. *Annual Report for 1951*. Washington, D.C.: U.S. Government Printing Office.

Federal Civil Defense Association. 1953. *Annual Report for 1952*. Washington, D.C.: U.S. Government Printing Office.

Federal Civil Defense Association. 1954. *Annual Report for 1953*. Washington, D.C.: U.S. Government Printing Office.

Federal Civil Defense Association. 1955. *Annual Report for 1954*. Washington, D.C.: U.S. Government Printing Office.

Federal Civil Defense Association. 1956. *Annual Report for Fiscal Year 1955*. Washington, D.C.: U.S. Government Printing Office.

Ferguson, Ronald F. 2001. Community Revitalization, Jobs, and the Well-being of the Inner-City Poor. In Sheldon H. Danziger and Robert H. Haveman, eds., *Understanding Poverty*. New York: Russell Sage.

Fernandez-Kelly, Maria Patricia. 1983. *For We Are Sold, I and My People: Women and Industry in Mexico's Frontier*. Albany: State University of New York Press.

Ferree, Myra Marx, William A. Gamson, Jürgen Gerhards, and Dieter Rucht. 2002. *Shaping Abortion Discourse: Democracy and the Public Sphere in Germany and the United States*. New York: Cambridge University Press.

Field, Les W. 1999. "Complicities and Collaborations: Anthropologists and the 'Unacknowledged Tribes' of California." Current Anthropology 40(3): 193–201.

Fields, Barbara J. 1982. Ideology and Race. In J. Morgan Kousser and James McPherson, eds., *Region, Race and Reconstruction*. New York: Oxford University Press.

Fine, Michelle, Lois Weis, Linda C. Powell, and L. Mun Wong, eds. 1997. *Off White: Readings on Race, Power, and Society*. New York: Routledge.

Fish, V.K. 1985. "Hull House: Pioneer in Urban Research During its Creative Years." History of Sociology (6) (1).

Fisher, Miles Mark. 1922. *The Olivet Baptist Church*. Unpublished Masters Thesis, Divinity School, University of Chicago.

Flacks, Dick. 2005. The Question of Relevance in Social Movement Studies. In David Croteau, ed., *Rhyming Hope and History: Activists, Academics and Social Movement Scholarship*. Minneapolis: University of Minnesota Press.

Fletcher, Bill and Richard Hurd. 1998. Beyond the Organizing Model: The Transformation Process in Local Unions. In Kate Bronfenbrenner, Sheldon Friedman, Richard Hurd, Rudolph Oswald and Ronald Seeber, eds., *Organizing to Win*. Ithaca: Cornell University Press.

Floyd, Samuel. 1990. *Black Music of the Harlem Renaissance: A Collection of Essays*. New York: Greenwood Press.

Forbes, Jack D. 1990. "The Manipulation of Race, Caste, and Identity: Classifying AfroAmericans, Native Americans and Red-Black People." Journal of Ethnic Studies 17(4): 1–51.

Foucault, Michel. 1979 (1975). *Discipline and Punish: The Birth of the Prison*. New York: Vintage Books.

Foucault, Michel. 1980. *History of Sexuality Volume 1: An Introduction*. New York: Vintage Press.

Foucault, Michel. 1980. *Power/Knowledge: Selected Interviews and Other Writings 1972–1977*, edited by Colin Gordon. New York: Pantheon Books.

Foucault, Michel. 1984. Nietzsche, Genealogy, History. In Paul Rabinow, ed., *The Foucault Reader*. New York: Pantheon.

Foucault, Michel. 1994. *The Birth of the Clinic*. New York: Vintage Books.

Foucault, Michel. 1994. Two Lectures. In Nicholas B. Dirks, Geoff Eley, and Sherry B. Ortner, eds., *Culture/Power/History: A Reader in Contemporary Theory*. Princeton: Princeton University Press.

Frank, André Gunder. 1969. *Latin America: Underdevelopment or Revolution*. New York: Monthly Review Press.

Frank, André Gunder. 1970. *Capitalismo y Subdesarrollo en América Latina*. México: Siglo XXI.

Frank, Katherine. 1998. "The Production of Identity and the Negotiation of Intimacy in a Gentleman's Club." Sexualities 2: 175–201.

Frank, Katherine. 2002. *G-Strings and Sympathy: Strip Club Regulars and Male Desire.* Durham: Duke University Press.

Frank, Thomas. 1997. *The Conquest of Cool.* Chicago: The University of Chicago Press.

Frankenberg, Ruth. 1993. *White Women, Race Matters: The Social Construction of Whiteness.* Minneapolis, MN: University of Minnesota Press.

Fraser, Nancy and Linda Gordon. 1994. "A Genealogy of Dependency: Tracing a Keyword of the U.S. Welfare State." Signs 19: 309–336.

Fraser, Nancy. 1995. What's Critical about Critical Theory. In J. Meehan, ed., *Feminists Read Habermas.* London: Routledge.

Frazier, E. Franklin. 1924b. "Cooperatives: The Next Step in the Negro's Business Development." Southern Workman 53(November): 505–509.

Frazier, E. Franklin. 1924a. "Some Aspects of Negro Business." Opportunity 2(October): 293–297.

Frazier, E. Franklin. 1925. Durham: Capital of the Black Middle Class. In Alain Locked, ed., *The New Negro: Voices of the Harlem Renaissance.* New York: Albert and Charles Boni Inc.

Frazier, E. Franklin. 1927a. "The Pathology of Race Prejudice." Forum 77(6): 856–862.

Frazier, E. Franklin. 1927. Racial Self-Expression. In Charles S. Johnson, ed., *Ebony and Topaz.* New York: National Urban League.

Frazier, E. Franklin. 1929. La Bourgeoisie Noire. In V.F. Calverton, ed., *Anthology of American Negro Literature.* New York: Modern Library.

Frazier, E. Franklin. 1932. *The Negro Family in Chicago.* Chicago: University of Chicago Press.

Frazier, E. Franklin. 1939. *The Negro Family in the United States.* Chicago: University of Chicago Press.

Frazier, E. Franklin. 1940. *Negro Youth at the Crossways: Their Personality Development in the Middle States.* Washington, D.C.: The American Council of Education.

Frazier, E. Franklin. 1947. "Sociological Theory and Race Relations." American Sociological Review 12(3): 265–271.

Frazier, E. Franklin. 1957. *The Black Bourgeoisie: The Rise of a New Middle Class.* New York: Free Press.

Frazier, E. Franklin. 1957. *The Negro in the United States.* New York: Macmillan.

Frazier, E. Franklin. 1968. *E. Franklin Frazier on Race Relations,* edited by G. Franklin Edwards. Chicago: University of Chicago Press.

Freeman, Carla. 2001. "Is Local: Global as Feminine: Masculine? Rethinking the Gender of Globalization." Signs 26(4): 1007–1038.

Freeman, Richard. 1989. The Changing State of Unionism around the World. In Wei-Chiao Huang, ed., *Organized Labor at the Crossroads.* Kalamazoo, MI: W.E. Upjohn Institute.

Frobel, Folker, Jurgen Heinrichs and Otto Kreye. 1980. *The New International Division of Labor: Structural Unemployment in Industrialized Countries and Industrialization in Developing Countries.* Cambridge: Cambridge University Press.

Fuentes, Annette and Barbara Ehrenreich. 1983. *Women in the Global Factory*. Boston: South End Press.

Furner, Mary O. 1975. *Advocacy and Objectivity: A Crisis in the Professionalization of American Social Science, 1865–1905*. Lexington: University of Kentucky Press.

Galeano, Eduardo. 1988. *Century of the Wind*. New York: Pantheon Books.

Gallagher, Charles. 2003. "Color-blind Pleasures: The Social and Political Functions of Erasing the Color Line In Post Race America." Race, Gender & Class 10(4).

Gamson, Josh. 1989. "Silence, Death, and the Invisible Enemy." Social Problems 36: 351–367.

Gamson, William A. 1975. *The Strategy of Social Protest*. Homewood, IL: Dorsey Press.

Gamson, William A. 1988. Political Discourse and Collective Action. In *From Structure to Action: Social Movement Participation Across Cultures*, edited by B. Klandermans, H. Kriesi and S. Tarrow. Greenwich, CT: JAI Press.

Gamson, William A. 1990 [1975]. *The Strategy of Social Protest, Second Edition*. Belmont, CA: Wadsworth Publishing Company.

Gamson, William A. 1992. *Talking Politics*. Cambridge: Cambridge University Press.

Gamson, William A. 1998. Social Movements and Cultural Change. In Marco Giugni, Doug McAdam and Charles Tilly, eds., *From Contention to Democracy*. New York: Rowman and Littlefield Publishers.

Gamson, William A. and Andre Modigliani. 1989. "Media Discourse and Public Opinion on Nuclear Power: A Constructionist Approach." American Journal of Sociology 95: 1–37.

Gamson, William A. and Gadi Wolfsfeld. 1993. "Movements and Media as Interacting Systems." The Annals of the American Academy of Political and Social Science 528: 114–125.

Gamson, William A. and Kathryn Lasch. 1983. The Political Culture of Social Welfare Policy. In S. E. Spiro and E. Yuchtman-Yaar, eds., *Evaluating the Welfare State: Social and Political Perspectives*. New York: Academic Press.

Gamson, William A., Bruce Fireman and Steven Rytina. 1982. *Encounters with Unjust Authority*. Homewood, IL: The Dorsey Press.

Gamson, William A., David Croteau, William Hoynes and Theodore Sasson. 1992. "Media Images and the Social Construction of Reality." Annual Review of Sociology 18: 373–93.

Gamson, William and Kathryn Lasch. 1983. *The Political Culture of Social Welfare Policy*. In Shimon E. Spiro ed., Evaluating the Welfare State: Social and Political Perspectives. New York: Academic Press.

Gans, Herbert. 1979. "Symbolic Ethnicity: The Future of Ethnic Groups and Cultures in America." Ethnic and Racial Studies 2(1): 1–20.

Gans, Herbert. 1980. *Deciding What's News*. New York: Vintage Books.

Garland, Davis. 2001. *The Culture of Control: Crime and Social Order in Contemporary Society*. Chicago: University of Chicago Press.

Garnham, Nicholas. 1986. The Media and the Public Sphere. In Peter Golding, Graham Murdock and Paul Schlesinger, eds., *Communicating Politics*. New York: Holmes and Meier.

Garroutte, Eva Marie. 2003. *Real Indians: Identity and the Survival of Native America.* Berkeley: University of California.

Gates Jr., Henry Louis. 1988. "The Trope of a New Negro and the Reconstruction of the Image of the Black." Representations 24(Fall): 129–155.

Gerhards, Jürgen. 1996. *Discursive and Liberal Publics.* Working Paper, WZB.

Gerstle, Gary and John Mollenkopf, eds. 2001. *E pluribus unum?: Contemporary and Historical Perspectives on Immigrant Political Incorporation.* New York: Russell Sage.

Geyer, Michael. 1989. The Militarization of Europe, 1914–1945. In John R. Gillis, ed., *The Militarization of the Western World.* New Brunswick: Rutgers University Press.

Gibson-Graham, J.K. 1996. *The End of Capitalism (as we knew it).* Cambridge, MA: Blackwell.

Giddens, Anthony. 1979. *Central Problems in Social Theory.* Berkeley: University of California Press.

Giddens, Anthony. 1991. *Modernity and Self Identity: Self and Society in the Late Modern Age.* Cambridge: Polity Press.

Gilbert, Dennis and Kahl, Joseph. 1993. *The American Class Structure: A New Synthesis, Fourth Edition.* Belmont, CA: Wadsworth Publishing Co.

Gilbert, James. 1991. *Perfect Cities: Chicago's Utopias of 1893.* Chicago: University of Chicago Press.

Gillespie, Rosmary. 1996. "Women, the Body and Brand Extension in Medicine: Cosmetic Surgery and the Paradox of Choice." Women and Health 24: 69–83.

Gilroy, Paul. 1993. *The Black Atlantic: Modernity and Double Consciousness.* Cambridge: Harvard University Press.

Gilroy, Paul. 2000. *Against Race: Imagining Political Culture Beyond the Color Line.* Cambridge: Belknap of Harvard Univ. Press.

Giltin, Todd. 1995. *The Twilight of Common Dreams: Why America is Wracked by Culture Wars.* New York: Metropolitan Books.

Ginsburg, Faye D. 1989. *Contested Lives: The Abortion Debate in an American Community.* Berkley: University of California Press.

Giroux, Henry A. 1997. *Channel Surfing: Racism, the Media, and the Destruction of Today's Youth.* New York: St. Martin's Griffin.

Gitlin, Todd. 1980. *The Whole World Is Watching.* Berkeley: University of California Press.

Glasgow University Media Group. 1976. *Bad News.* London: Routledge and Kegan Paul.

Glasgow University Media Group. 1980. *More Bad News.* London: Routledge and Kegan Paul.

Glasgow University Media Group. 1982. *Really Bad News.* London: Writers and Readers.

Goddard, Terrell Dale. 1999. "The Black Social Gospel in Chicago, 1896–1906." Journal of Negro History 84(3): 227–246.

Goffman, Erving. 1974. *Sigma: Notes on the Management of Spoiled Identity.* New York: Jason Aronson.

Goffman, Erving. 1995 [1962]. *Stigma.* Upper Saddle River, NJ: Prentice Hall.

Goggins, Jacqueline. 1993. *Carter G. Woodson: A Life in Black History*. Baton Rouge: Louisiana State Press.

Goldfield, Michael. 1987. *The Decline of Organized Labor in the United States*. Chicago: University of Chicago Press.

Goodeve, Thyrza. 1992. Watching For What Happens Next. In Nancy J. Peters, ed., *War After War*. San Francisco: City Lights Books.

Gooding, Cheryl and Kathleen Casavant. 1997. *Women and the Labor Movement in Massachusetts*. Boston: Center for Labor Research.

Goodman, Nelson. 1978. *Ways of Worldmaking*. Indianapolis: Hackett.

Gordon, Avery. 1997. *Ghostly Matters: Haunting and the Sociological Imagination*. Minneapolis: University of Minnesota Press.

Gordon, David, Richard Edwards and Michael Reich. 1982. *Segmented Work, Divided Workers: The Historical Transformation of Labor in the United States*. Cambridge: Cambridge University Press.

Gouldner, Alvin W. 1979. *The Future of Intellectuals and the Rise of the New Class*. New York: Seabury.

Granovetter, Mark. 1985. "Economic Action and Social Structure: The Problem of Embeddedness." American Journal of Sociology 91: 481–510.

Gray, Chris Hables. 1997. Postmodern War: The New Politics of Conflict. New York: The Guilford Press.

Grewal, Inderpal and Caren Kaplan. 1994. *Scattered Hegemonies: Postmodernity and Transnational Feminist Practices*. Minneapolis: University of Minnesota Press.

Griffen, Susan. 1978. *Women and Nature: The Roaring Inside of Her*. San Francisco: Sierra Club Books.

Griffin, Farah Jasmine. 1995. *"Who Set You Flowin'?": The African-American Migration Narrative*. New York: Oxford University Press.

Grillo, Trina and Stephanie Wildman. 1995. Obscuring the Importance of Race: The Implication of Making Comparisons between Racism and Sexism (or Other-isms). In Richard, Delgado, ed., *Critical Race Theory: The Cutting Edge*. Philadelphia: Temple University Press.

Grosfoguel, Ramón, Negrón-Muntaner, Frances and Georas, Chloe. 1997. Beyond Nationalist and Colonialist Discourses: The Jaiba Politics of the Puerto Rican Ethno-Nation. In Frances Negrón-Muntaner and Ramón Grosfoguel, eds., *Puerto Rican Jam!: Rethinking Colonialist and Nationalist Discourses*. Minnesota: University of Minnesota Press.

Grosfoguel, Ramón. 1994. "World Cities in the Caribbean: The Rise of Miami and San Juan." REVIEW XVII 3:351–81.

Grosfoguel, Ramón. 2003. *Colonial Subjects: Puerto Ricans in a Global Perspective*. Berkeley: University of California Press.

Grossman, James. 1989. *Land of Hope: Chicago, Black Southerners and the Great Migration*. Chicago: University of Chicago Press.

Grossman, Karl. 2001. *Weapons In Space*. New York: Seven Stories Press.

Grosz, Elizabeth. 1994. *Volatile Bodies: Towards A Corporeal Feminism*. Bloomington: Indiana University Press.

Guigni, Marco G., Doug McAdam, and Charles Tilly, eds. 1998. *From Contention to Democracy.* New York: Rowman and Littlefield.

Guy Standing. 1989. "Global Feminization through Flexible Labor." World Development 17(7): 1077–1095.

Gwantley, John Langston. 1980. *Drylongso: A Self-Portrait of Black America.* New York: Random House.

Habermas, Jürgen. 1987 [1981]. *The Theory of Communicative Action.* Boston: Beacon Press.

Habermas, Jürgen. 1989 [1962]. *The Structural Transformation of the Public Sphere.* Cambridge, MA: MIT Press.

Hacking, Ian. 1973. *Why Does Language Matter To Philosophy.* Cambridge: Cambridge University Press.

Haiken, Elizabeth. 1997. *Venus Envy: A History of Cosmetic Surgery.* Baltimore: The John's Hopkins University Press.

Hales, Katherine. 1999. *How We Have Become Posthuman: Virtual Bodies in Cybernetics, Literature and Informatics.* Chicago: University of Chicago Press.

Hall, Jacqueline Dowd. 1979. *Revolt Against Chivalry: Jesse Daniel Ames and the Women's Campaign against Lynching.* New York: Columbia University Press.

Hall, Stuart, et al. 1978. *Policing the Crisis: Mugging, the State, and Law and Order.* New York: Holmes and Meier Publishers Inc.

Hallin, Daniel, and Paolo Mancini. 1984. "Speaking of the President: Political Structure and Representational Form in U.S. and Italian Television News." Theory and Society 13: 829–850.

Hamilton, Earl J. 1929. "American Treasure and the Rise of Capitalism." Economica IX, 27 (Nov.).

Haraway, Donna. 1989. *Primate Visions.* New York: Routledge.

Haraway, Donna. 1991. *Simians, Cyborgs, and Women: The Invention of Nature.* New York: Routledge.

Haraway, Donna. 1997. *Modest_Witness@Second_Millennium FemaleMan_Meets_Oncomouse: Feminism and Technoscience.* New York: Routledge.

Harding, Sandra. 1987. Introduction: Is There a Feminist Method? In Sandra Harding, ed., *Feminism and Methodology.* Bloomington: Indiana University Press.

Hardt, Michael and Negri, Antonio. 2004. *Multitudes: War and Democracy in the Age of Empire.* New York: Penguin Press.

Harlan, Louis. 1972. *Booker T. Washington: The Making of a Black Leader, 1856–1901.* New York: Oxford University Press.

Harnacker, Marta. 1974. *Los Conceptos Elementales de Materialismo Historico.* Buenos Aires: Siglo XXI.

Harris, Neil. 1978. Museums, Merchandising, and Popular Taste: The Struggle for Influence. In Ian Quimby, ed., *Material Culture and the Study of American Life.* New York: W.W. Norton.

Harrod, Howard. 2000. *The Animals Came Dancing: Native American Sacred Ecology and Animal Kinship.* Tucson: University of Arizona.

Hartigan Jr., John. 1999. *Racial Situations: Class Predicaments of Whiteness in Detroit.* Princeton, NJ: Princeton University Press.

Hartland, Edwin Sidney. 1909–1910. *Primitive Paternity: The Myth of Supernatural Birth in Relation to the History of the Family*. London: D. Nutt.

Hartman, Edward G. 1948. *The Movement to Americanize the Immigrant*. New York: Columbia University Press.

Hartman, Paul. 1979. "News and Public Perceptions of Industrial Relations." Media, Culture and Society 1: 256.

Harvey, David. 1990. *The Condition of Postmodernity*. Cambridge, MA: Blackwell.

Harvey, J. Brian and David Woodward. 1991. "An Alternative to Mapping History." Americas 43(5–6): 6–8.

Harvey, Lee. 1987. *Myths of the Chicago School of Sociology*. Aldershot, England: Gower.

Haskell, Thomas. 1977. *The Emergence of Professional Social Science: The American Social Science Association and the Nineteenth Century Crisis of Authority*. Urbana: University of Illinois Press.

Haskell, Thomas. 1984. *The Authority of Experts*. Urbana: University of Illinois Press.

Hausbeck, Katherine and Barbara Brent. 2000. Inside Neveda's Brothel Industry. In Weitzer, ed., *Sex for Sale: Prostitution, Pornography and the Sex Industry*. New York: Routledge.

Hayles, N. Katherine. 1999. *How We Became Post-Human*. Chicago: University of Chicago Press.

Hays, Sharon. 2003. *Flat Broke With Children: Women in the Age of Welfare Reform*. Oxford: Oxford University Press.

Heidegger, Martin. 1977. *The Question Concerning Technology and Other Essays*. New York: Harper.

Helbling, Mark. 1999. *The Harlem Renaissance: The One and the Many*. Westport, Connecticut: Greenwood Press.

Helgerson, Richard. 1992. *Forms of Nationhood: The Elizabethan Writing of England*. Chicago: University of Chicago Press.

Herman, Andrew. 1999. *The 'Better Angels' of Capitalism*. Boulder, CO: Westview Press.

Herman, Edward and Noam Chomsky. 1988. *Manufacturing Consent: The Political Economy of the Mass Media*. New York: Pantheon.

Herman, Edward and Robert McChesney. 1997. *The Global Media: The New Missionaries of Corporate Capitalism*. London: Cassell.

Herman, Edward. 1985. "Diversity of News: Marginalizing the Opposition." Journal of Communications (Summer): 89–101.

Herman, Edward. 1992. *Beyond Hypocrisy*. Boston: South End Press.

Herman, Edward. 1996. "News That's Fit for Power." Nation (January 22): 3.

Herman, Ellen. 1995. *The Romance of American Psychology: Political Culture in the Age of Experts*. Berkeley: University of California Press.

Hernstein, Richard J. and Charles Murray. 1994. *The Bell Curve: Intelligence and Class Structure in American Life*. New York: Free Press.

Herskovitz, Melville. 1940. "The American Negro Family." Nation 150 (January 27).

Hill, Joe. 1982. "The Brown Bag Beat." Working Papers (January-February): 68–72.

Hill, Mike. 2004. *After Whiteness: Unmaking an American Majority*. New York: New York University Press.

Hill, Robert A., ed. 1983. *The Marcus Garvey and Universal Negro Improvement Association Papers, Vol. I, 1826–August 1919*. Berkeley: University of California Press.

Hillis, Michael R. 1995. "Allison Davis and the Study of Race, Social Class and Schooling." Journal of Negro Education 64(1): 33–41.

Hine, Darlene Clark. 1996. *Speak Truth to Power: Black Professional Class in the United States*. Brooklyn: Carson Publishing.

Hinkle, Roscoe C and Gisela Hinkle. 1954. *The Development of Modern Sociology: It's Nature and Growth in the United States*. New York: Random House.

Hirsch, Arnold. 1983. *Making the Second Ghetto: Race and Housing in Chicago, 1940–1960*. Cambridge: Cambridge University Press.

Hodge, Frederick Webb, ed. 1968 [1912]. *Handbook of American Indians North of Mexico. Part I*. Smithsonian Institution Bureau of American Ethnology Bulletin 30. St. Clair Shores, MI: Scholarly.

Hofferth, Sandra and John F. Sandberg. 2001. Changes in American Children's Time, 1981–1997. In Timothy J. Owens and Sandra L. Hofferth, eds., *Children at the Millennium: Where Have We Come From? Where Are We Going?* New York: JAI.

Hofstadter, Richard. 1944. *Social Darwinism in American Thought*. Boston: Beacon Press.

Hollander, Jocelyn. 2002. "Resisting Vulnerability: The Social reconstruction of Gender in Interaction." Social Problems 49(9): 474–496.

Holloway, Jonathan Scott. 2002. *Confronting the Veil: Abram Harris Jr., E. Franklin Frazier and Ralph Bunche*. Chapel Hill: University of North Carolina Press.

Holt, Douglas B. 2002. "Why Do Brands Cause Trouble? A Dialectic Theory of Consumer Culture and Branding." Journal of Consumer Research 29(1): 70–90.

Hooks, Bell. 1992. *Black Looks: Race and Representation*. Boston: South End Press.

Horsman, Reginald. 1981. *Race and Manifest Destiny: The Origins of American Racial Anglo-Saxonism*. Cambridge: Harvard University Press.

Hoyt, Michael. 1984. "Downtime for Labor." Columbia Journalism Review (March–April): 36–40.

Huggins, Nathan. 1971. *The Harlem Renaissance*. New York: Oxford University Press.

Hughes, C. Alvin. 1984. "The Negro Sanhedrin Movement." The Journal of Negro History 69(1): 1–13.

Hunter, Herbert. 2001. *The Sociology of Oliver C. Cox: New Perspectives*. Stamford, CT: JAI Press.

Hunter, Herbert. 1981. *The Life and Work of Oliver C. Cox*. Unpublished Ph.D. dissertation, Boston University.

Hurst, Charles. 2001. *Social Inequality: Forms, Causes, and Consequences, Fourth Edition*. Boston: Allyn and Bacon.

Hurston, Zora Neale. 1963. *Mules and Men*. Bloomington: Indiana University Press.

Hurston, Zora Neale. 1981. *The Sanctified Church*. Berkeley: Turtle Island.

Hutchinson, George. 1995. *The Harlem Renaissance in Black and White*. Cambridge, MA: Harvard University Press.

Hyman, Herbert. 1991. *Taking Society's Measure: A Personal History of Survey Research*. New York: Russell Sage Foundation.

Iglesias Prieto, Norma. 1985. *La Flor Más Bella de la Maquiladora*. Mexico City: Secretaría de Educación Pública and Centro de Estudios Fronterizos del Norte de México.

Illich, Ivan. 1990. *Health as One's Own Responsibility – No Thank You!* Trans. Jutta Mason, Internet resource, http://homepage.mac.com/tinapple/illich/1990_health_responsibility.PDF.

Instituto Nacional de Estadistíca, Geografía e Informática (INEGI). 1990. *Estadistíca de la Industria Maquiladora de Exportación, 1975–1988*. Mexico City: INEGI.

Instituto Nacional de Estadistíca, Geografía e Informática (INEGI). 1991a. *Avance de Información Económica*. Mexico City: INEGI.

Instituto Nacional de Estadistíca, Geografía e Informática (INEGI). 1991b. *Estadistíca de la Industria Maquiladora de Exportación, 1979–1989*. Mexico City: INEGI.

Instituto Nacional de Estadistíca, Geografía e Informática (INEGI). 1996. *Estadistíca de la Industria Maquiladora de Exportación, 1990–1995*. Mexico City: INEGI.

Iyengar, Shanto and Donald Kinder. 1987. *News that Matters: Television and American Opinion*. Chicago: University of Chicago Press.

Iyengar, Shanto. 1991. *Is Anyone Responsible?* Chicago: University of Chicago Press.

Jameson, Fredric. 1998. *The Cultural Turn*. New York: Verso.

Jan Mohamed, Abdul and David Lloyd. 1987. "Introduction: Minority Discourse: What is to be Done?" Cultural Critique 7(Fall): 5–18.

Janowitz, Morris. 1965. "Review of Shadow and Act, by Ralph Ellison." American Journal of Sociology 70(6): 732–734.

Jasper, James. 2004. "A Strategic Approach to Collective Action: Looking for Agency is Social Movement Choices." Mobilization: An International Journal 9(1): 1–16.

Jay, Martin. 1993. *Downcast Eyes: The Denegration of Vision in Twentieth-Century French Thought*. Los Angeles: University of California Press.

Jenkins, Henry. 1998. *The Children's Culture Reader*. New York: New York University Press.

Jiménez Betancourt, Rubí. 1989. Participación Femenina en La Industria Maquiladora. Cambios recientes. In Jennifer Cooper et al., eds., *Fuerza de Trabajo Femenina Urbana en México, Volumen Segundo*. Mexico City: UNAM.

Jocks, Christopher. 1997. "Response: American Indian Religious Traditions and the Academic Study of Religion: A Response to Sam Gill." Journal of the American Academy of Religion 65(1): 169–76.

Johnson, Charles S. 1923. "How Much of the Migration was a Flight From Persecution." Opportunity 1(October): 272–274.

Johnson, Charles S. 1934. *Shadow of the Plantation*. Chicago: University of Chicago Press.

Johnson, Charles S. 1935. "Incidence Upon the Negro." American Journal of Sociology 40(6): 737–745.

Johnson, Charles S. 1936. "The Conflict of Caste and Class in an American Industry." American Journal of Sociology 42(2): 55–65.

Johnson, Charles S. 1941. *Growing up in the Black Belt*. Washington D.C.: American Council on Education.

Johnson, Eloise. 1997. *Rediscovering the Harlem Renaissance: The Politics of Exclusion*. New York: Garland Publishing.

Jones, Butler. 1974. The Tradition of Sociology Teaching in Black Colleges: The Unheralded Professionals. In James Blackwell and Morris Janowitz, eds., *Black Sociologists: Historical and Contemporary Perspectives*. Chicago: University of Chicago Press.

Judd, Dennis and Susan Fanstein. 1999. *The Tourist City*. New Haven: Yale University Press.

Kasson, John. 1978. *Amusing the Millions: Coney Island at the Turn of the Century*. New York: Hill and Wang.

Katz, Michael B. and Thomas J. Sugrue. 1998. *W.E.B. DuBois, Race, and the City; The Philadelphia Negro and its Legacy*. Philadelphia: University of Pennsylvania.

Kaw, Eugenia. 1993. "Medicalization of Racial Features. Asian American Women and Cosmetic Surgery." Medical Anthropology Quarterly 7(1): 74–89.

Keane, John. 1991. *The Media and Democracy*. London: Polity Press.

Keller, Evelyn Fox. 1995. *Refiguring Life*. New York: Columbia University Press.

Kelley, Robin D.G. 1990. *Hammer and Hoe: Alabama Communists During the Great Depression*. Chapel Hill: University of North Carolina Press.

Kelley, Robin D.G. 1997. *Yo' Mama's Dysfunktional: Fighting the Culture Wars in Urban America*. Boston: Beacon Press.

Kelling, George L. 1996. *Fixing Broken Windows: Restoring Order and Reducing Crime in Our Communities*. New York: Martin Kessler Books.

Kelly, Delos. 2003. Bureaucratic Slots and Client Processing. In Delos Kelly and Edward J. Clarke, eds., *Deviant Behavior*. New York: Worth Books.

Kempadoo, Kamala. and Doezema, Jo, eds. 1998. *Global Sex Wokers: Rights, Resistance, and Redefinition*. New York: Routledge.

Kenney, William. 1993. *Chicago Jazz: A Cultural History, 1904–1930*. New York: Oxford University Press.

Key, R. Charles. 1978. Society and Sociology: The Dynamics of Black Sociological Negation. Phylon 39(1): 35–48.

Kimmeldorf, Howard. 1999. *Battling for American Labor: Wobblies, Craft Workers, and the Making of the Union Movement*. Berkeley CA: University of California Press.

Kincheloe, Samuel C. 1929. *The Prophet*. Unpublished Ph.D. dissertation, Department of Sociology, University of Chicago.

Kingfischer, Catherine Pelissier. 1996. *Women in the American Welfare Trap*. Philadelphia: University of Pennsylvania Press.

Kipnis, Laura. 1999. "The Stepdaughter's Story: Scandals National and Transnational." Social Text 58(17): 59–73.

Kirby, Katherin. 1996. *Indifferent Boundaries: Spatial Concepts of Human Subjectivity*. New York: Guilford Press.

Kirshenblatt-Gimblett, Barbara. 1998. *Destination Culture: Tourism, Museums, and Heritage*. Berkeley: University of California Press.

Klandermans, Bert. 1992. The Social Construction of Protest and Multiorganizational Fields. In Aldon Morris and Carol Mueller, eds., *Frontiers in Social Movement Theory*. New Haven: Yale University Press.

Klarlan, Susan. 1994. "The Origins of Racism: The Critical Theory of Oliver C. Cox." Mid-American Review of Sociology 18(1 and 2).

Kline, Stephen. 1993. *Out of the Garden: Toys and Children's Culture in the Age of TV Marketing*. London: Verso.

Koch, Howard. 1967. *The Panic Broadcast*. New York: Avon Books.

Kontopoulos, Kyriakos. 1993. *The Logics of Social Structures*. Cambridge: Cambridge University Press.

Kopinak, Kathryn. 1989. "Living the Gospel through Service to the Poor: The Convergence of Political and Religious Motivations in Organizing Maquiladora Workers in Juárez, Mexico." Socialist Studies: A Canadian Annual 5: 217–245.

Krupat, Arnold. 1989. *The Voice in the Margin: Native American Literature and the Canon*. Berkeley: University of California.

Kucklick, H. 1980. "Chicago Sociology and Urban Planning Policy: Sociological Theory as Occupational Ideology." Theory and Society 9(6): 821–845.

Kurtz, Lester P. 1984. *Evaluating Chicago Sociology: A Guide to Literature, with an Annotated Bibliography*. Chicago: University of Chicago Press.

Kurtz, Sharon. 2002. *Workplace Justice: Organizing Multi-Identity Movements*. Minneapolis: University of Minnesota Press.

La Botz, Dan. 1990. *Teamsters for a Democratic Union: Rank and File Rebellion*. New York: Verso Press.

Lal, Barbara Ballis. 1987. "Black and Blue in Chicago: Robert E. Park's Perspective on Race Relations in Urban America, 1914–44." The British Journal of Sociology 38.

Lal, Barbara Ballis. 1990. *The Romance of Culture in an Urban Civilization: Robert E. Park on Race and Ethnic Relations in Cities*. New York: Routledge.

Law, Lisa. 2000. *Sex Work in Southeast Asia: The Place of Desire in a Time of AIDS*. New York: Routledge.

Leadbeater, Bonnie J. Ross and Niobe Way, eds. 1996. *Urban Girls: Resisting Stereotypes, Creating Identities*. New York: New York University Press.

Lears, T. Jackson. 1981. *No Place of Grace: Antimodernism and the Transformation of American Culture, 1890–1920*. New York: Pantheon.

Lee, Martin and Norman Solomon. 1990. *Unreliable Sources: A Guide to Detecting Bias in News Media*. New York: Carol Publishing Group

Lefebvre, Henri. 1991. *The Production of Space*. Oxford: Blackwell.

Lengermann, Patricia. 1979. "The Founding of the American Sociological Review." American Sociological Review 44(2): 185–198.

Levin, Roger. 1992. *Complexity: Life at the Edge of Chaos*. New York: Macmillan.

Levine, Lawrence. 1988. *Highbrow/Lowbrow: The Emergence of Cultural Hierarchy in America*. Cambridge, MA: Harvard University Press.

Lewis, David J. and Richard Smith. 1980. *American Sociology and Pragmatism: Mead, Chicago Sociology and Symbolic Interactionism*. Chicago: University of Chicago Press.

Lewis, David Levering. 1981. *When Harlem was in Vogue*. New York: Oxford University Press.

Lewis, David Levering. 1987. *The Race to Fashoda: European Colonialism and African Resistance in the Scramble for Africa*. New York: Weidenfield & Nicolson.

Lewis, David Levering. 1993. *W.E.B. DuBois – Biography of a Race, 1868–1919*. New York: Henry Holt.

Lewis, David Levering. 2000. *W.E.B. DuBois: The Fight for Equality and the American Century, 1919–1963*. New York: H. Holt.

Lewis, Hylan. 1936. *Social Differentiation in the Negro Community*. Unpublished Masters thesis, Department of Sociology, University of Chicago.

Lewis, Russell. 1983. "Everything Under One Roof: World's Fairs and Department Stores in Paris and Chicago." Chicago Historical Review 12(Fall).

Liepe-Levinson, Katherine. 2002. *Strip Show: Performances of Gender and Desire*. New York: Routledge.

Lim, Linda. 1983. Capitalism, Imperialism, and Patriarchy: The Dilemma of Third-World Women Workers in Multinational Factories. In June Nash and Patricia Fernandez-Kelly, eds., *Women, Men and the International Division of Labor*. Albany: State University of New York Press.

Lind, L.R. 1949. *The Epitome of Andreas Vesalius*. New York: Macmillan.

Lindner, Rolf. 1996. *The Reportage of Urban Culture: Robert Park and the Chicago School*. New York: Cambridge University Press.

Locke, Alain, ed. 1925. *The New Negro: Voices of the Harlem Renaissance*. New York: Albert and Charles Boni Inc.

Lown, Judy. 1990. *Women and Industrialization: Gender at Work in Nineteenth-Century England*. Minneapolis: University of Minnesota Press.

Lutz, Nancy Melissa. 1988. Images of Docility: Asian Women and the World Economy. In Joan Smith et al., eds., *Racism, Sexism and the World System*. New York: Greenwood Press.

Lyman, Stanford. 1992. *Militarism, Imperialism, and Race Accommodation*. Fayetteville: University of Arkansas Press.

Macannell, Dean. 1999. *Tourist: A New Theory of the Leisure Class*. Berkeley: University of California Press.

MacLeod, Jay. 1997. *Ain't No Makin' It: Aspirations and Attainment in a Low-Income Neighborhood*. Boulder, CO: Westview Press.

Madge, John. 1962. *The Origins of Scientific Sociology*. Glencoe, IL: Free Press.

Malinowski, Bronislaw. 1979. The Role of Magic and Religion. In William A. Lessa and Evon Z. Vogt, eds. *Reader in Comparative Religion: An Anthropological Approach, Fourth Edition*. New York: Harper and Row.

Mansfield, Carol and Elizabeth Smolcic. 1989. *Black Heritage Tourism: Exploitation or Education?* Washington D.C.: Partners for Livable Places.

Marks, Carol. 1989. *Farewell – We're Good and Gone: The Great Black Migration*. Bloomington: Indiana University Press.

Martin, Christopher. 2004. *Framed! Labor and the Corporate Media*. Ithaca, NY: Cornell University Press.

Martindale, Don. 1976. "American Sociology Before World War II." Annual Review of Sociology 2: 121–143.

Marx, Karl. 1973. *Grundisse*. London: New Left Review.

Marx, Karl. 1990. *Capital, Volume 1*. Penguin: New York.

Marx, Karl. 2000. *Karl Marx: Selected Writings*, edited by David McLellan. Oxford: Oxford University Press.

Mass Praxis. 1994. *Obstacles to Participatory Action Research*. Unpublished Paper, College of Public and Community Service, UMASS-Boston.

Massey, Doreen. 1994. *Space, Place, and Gender*. Minneapolis: University of Minnesota Press.

Massey, Douglas and Nancy Denton. 1993. *American Apartheid: Segregation and the Making of the Underclass*. Cambridge, MA: Harvard University Press.

Mathews, Fred H. 1977. *Quest for an American Sociology: Robert E. Park and the Chicago School*. Montreal: McGill University Press.

McAdam, Doug, John D. McCarthy, and Mayer N. Zald, eds. 1996. *Comparative Perspectives on Social Movements*. Cambridge: Cambridge University Press.

McArdle, Andrea. 2001. *Zero Tolerance: Quality of Life and The New Police Brutality in New York City*. New York: New York University Press.

McChesney, Robert. 1999. *Rich Media; Poor Democracy*. Urbana: University of Illinois.

McClintock, Anne. 1993. The Angel of Progress: Pitfalls of the Term 'Post-Colonialism.' In Patrick Williams and Laura Chrisman, eds., *Colonial Discourse and Post-Colonial Theory: A Reader*. London: Harvester Wheatsheaf.

McCormack, Karen. 2002. *Welfare (M)Others: Discourse, Discipline and Resistance*. Unpublished Ph.D. Dissertation, Boston College.

McEnaney, Laura. 2000. *Civil Defense Begins at Home: Militarization Meets Everyday Life in the Fifties*. Princeton: Princeton University Press.

McLuhan, Marshall. 1994. *Understanding Media*. Cambridge, MA: The MIT Press.

McMurray, Linda. 1991. *Recorder of the Black Experience: A Biography of Monroe Nathan Work*. Baton Rouge: Louisiana State University Press.

McNeal, James U. 1999. *The Kids Market: Myths and Realities*. Ithaca: Paramount Market.

Melucci, Alberto. 1989. *Nomads of the Present*. Philadelphia: Temple University Press.

Messner, Steven and Richard Rosenfeld. 1997. *Crime and the American Dream, Second Edition*. Belmont, CA: Wadsworth Publishing Company.

Mignolo, Walter D. 1992. "On the Colonization of Amerindian Languages and Memories: Renaissance Theories of Writing and Discontinuity of the Classical Tradition," Comparative Studies in Society and History 34(2): 301–330.

Mignolo, Walter D. 1992. "The Darker Side of the Renaissance: Colonization and the Discontinuity of the Classical Tradition." Renaissance Quarterly 45(4): 808–828.

Mignolo, Walter D. 1994. Afterword: Writing and Recorded Knowledge in Postcolonial Situations. In Elizabeth Hill Boone and Walter D. Mignolo. *Writing Without Words: Alternative Literacies in Mesoamerica and the Andes*. Durham: Duke.

Mignolo, Walter D. 1995. *The Darker Side of the Renaissance: Literacy, Territoriality, and Colonization*. Ann Arbor: The University of Michigan Press.

Mignolo, Walter. 2000. *Local Histories/Global Designs: Essays on the Coloniality of Power, Subaltern Knowledges and Border Thinking*. Princeton: Princeton University Press.

Milkman, Ruth. 1987. *Gender at Work: The Dynamics of Job Segregation by Sex during World War II*. Urbana: University of Illinois Press.

Miller, David Reed. 1994. Definitional Violence and Plains Indian Reservation Life: Ongoing Challenges to Survival. In William B. Taylor and Franklin Pease, eds., *Violence, Resistance, and Survival in the Americas*. Washington: Smithsonian

Miller, Tyler G. 2004. *Living in the Environment, 13th Edition*. Pacific Grove, CA: Brooks/Cole (Thomson).

Mills, C. Wright. 1959. *The Sociological Imagination*. New York: Oxford University Press.

Mohanty, Chandra Talpade. 1991. Introduction: Cartographies of Struggle. In Chandra Talpade Mohanty, Ann Russo and Lourdes Torres, eds., *Third World Women and the Politics of Feminism*. Bloomington: Indiana University Press.

Molotch, Harvey. 1979. Media and Movements. In Zald and McCarthy, eds., *The Dynamics of Social Movements*. Boston: Little, Brown.

Momaday, N. Scott. 1989. The Center Holds. In N. Scott Momaday and Charles L. Woodard, *Ancestral Voice: Conversations with N. Scott Momaday*. Lincoln: University of Nebraska Press.

Momaday, N. Scott. 1997. 1974 interview with Lawrence J. Evers. In Matthias Schubnell, ed., *Conversations with N. Scott Momaday*. Jackson: University Press of Mississippi.

Moody, Kim. 1997. *Labor in a Lean World*. New York: Verso Press.

Moody, Kim. 1999. The Dynamics of Change. In Ray Tillman and Michael Cummings, eds., *The Transformation of U.S. Unions*. Boulder, CO: Lynne Rienner Publishers.

Mooney, James. 1992. *James Mooney's History, Myths, and Sacred Formulas of the Cherokees*. Asheville, NC: Historical Images.

Moore Jr., Barrington. 1966. *The Social Origins of Dictatorship and Democracy*. Boston: Beacon Press.

Moore, Carlos. 1988. *Castro, the Blacks and Africa*. Los Angeles: Center for Afro-American Studies at University of California, Los Angeles.

Morgan, Kathryn Pauly. 1991. "Women and the Knife: Cosmetic Surgery and the Colonialization of Women's Bodies." Hypatia 6: 26–53.

Morgan, T.H. 1924. Mendelian Heredity in Relation to Cytology. In E.V. Cowdry, ed., *General Cytology*. Chicago: University of Chicago Press.

Morris, Aldon. 1986. *The Origins of the Civil Rights Movement*. New York: Free Press.

Morrison, Toni. 1992. *Race-ing Justice, En-gendering Power: Essays on Anita Hill, Clarence Thomas, and the Construction of Social Reality*. New York: Pantheon.

Morrow, Phyllis and William Schneider, eds. 1995. *When Our Words Return: Writing, Hearing and Remembering Oral Traditions of Alaska and the Yukon*. Logan: Utah State.

Mort, Jo-Ann. 1992. "How the Media Cover Labor: The Story That's Not Being Told." Dissent 39: 81–85.

Mort, Jo-Ann. 1999. *Not Your Father's Labor Movement*. New York: Verso.

Moses, Wilson. 1978. *The Golden Age of Black Nationalism, 1850–1925*. Oxford University Press.

Mudimbe, V.Y., ed. 1992. *The Surreptitious Speech: Presence Africaine and the Politics of Otherness 1947–1987*. Chicago: University of Chicago.

Muehlenkamp, Robert. 1991. "Organizing Never Stops." Labor Research Review 17 (Spring): 1–5.

Mumford, Kevin. 1997. *Interzones: Black/White Sex Districts in Chicago and New York in the Early Twentieth Century.* New York: Columbia University Press.

Murphy, Alexandra. 2003. "The Dialectical Gaze: Exploring the Subject-Object Tension in the Performances of Women Who Strip." Journal of Contemporary Ethnography, 32(3): 305–335.

Myrdal, Gunnar. 1944. *An American Dilemma: The Negro Problem and Modern Democracy.* New York: Harper and Row.

Nagel, Joane. 1996. *American Indian Ethnic Renewal: Red Power and the Resurgence of Identity and Culture.* New York: Oxford.

Nally, David. 2002. "The Production of Space." Canadian Literature 174. Internet resource, http://www.canlit.ca/reviews/unassigned/5574_nally.html.

Nance, Susan. 2002. "Respectability and Representation: The Moorish Science Temple, Morocco, and Black Public Culture in 1920s Chicago." American Quarterly 54(4): 623–659.

Navarro, Jose Manuel. 2002. *Creating Tropical Yankees: Social Science Textbooks and U.S. Ideological Control in Puerto Rico, 1898–1908.* New York: Routledge.

Nimmo, Dan and J. Combs. 1983. *Mediated Political Realities.* New York: Longmans.

Nissen, Bruce. 1999. Cross-Border Alliances in the Era of Globalization. In Ray Tillman and Michael Cummings, eds., *The Transformation of U.S. Unions.* Boulder, CO: Lynne Rienner Publishers.

Nolan, James. 1998. *The Therapeutic State: Justifying Government at Century's End.* New York: New York University Press.

Oakes, Guy. 1994. *The Imaginary War: Civil Defense and American Cold War Culture.* New York: Oxford University Press.

Office of Civil Defense, Sacramento, CA. 1951. *Instructor's Manual and Teaching Outline: Panic Control and Prevention.* Sacramento: California State Printing Office.

Oliver, Paul. 1984. *Songsters and Saints: Vocal Traditions on Race Records.* Cambridge: Cambridge University Press.

Olsen, Alexandra and John Voss. 1979. *The Organization of Knowledge in Modern America.* Baltimore: Johns Hopkins University Press.

Omi, Michael and Howard Winant. 1986. *Racial Formation in the United States from the 1960's to the 1980's.* New York: Routledge.

Omi, Michael and Howard Winant. 1994. *Racial Formation in the United States, Second Edition.* New York: Routledge.

Orr, Jackie. Forthcoming. *Panic Diaries: A Genealogy of Panic Disorder.* Durham: Duke University Press.

Ortner, Sherry. 1996. *Making Gender: The Politics and Erotics of Culture.* Boston: Beacon Press.

Park, Robert and Ernest W. Burgess. 1921. *Introduction to the Science of Sociology.* Chicago: University of Chicago Press.

Park, Robert and Herbert Miller. 1921. *Old War Traits Transplanted.* New York: Harper.

Park, Robert E. 1905. "A City of Racial Peace." The World To-Day IX (August).

Park, Robert E. 1908. "Agricultural Extension Among the Negroes." The World To-Day XV (August).

Park, Robert E. 1913. "Negro Home Life and Standards of Living." Annals of the American Academy of Political and Social Science (Sept.).

Park, Robert E. 1913. "Racial Assimilation in Secondary Groups, with Particular Reference to the Negro." American Sociological Society VIII. Reprinted in Race and Culture (1950).

Park, Robert E. 1918. "Education in its Relation to the Conflict and Fusion of Cultures: With Special Reference to the Problems of the Immigrant, the Negro and Missions," Publication of the American Sociological Society XIII.

Park, Robert E. 1921. Temperaments, Tradition and Nationality. In Robert Park and Ernest W. Burgess, eds., Introduction to the Science of Sociology. Chicago: University of Chicago Press.

Park, Robert E. 1921. The City as a Social Laboratory. In T.V. Smith and L. White, eds., Chicago. Chicago: University of Chicago Press.

Park, Robert E. 1923. "Negro Race Consciousness as Reflected in Race Literature." American Review I (Sept.-Oct.) Reprinted in Race and Culture (1950).

Park, Robert E. 1925. Magic, Mentality and City Life. In Robert Park, Ernest Burgess, and Roderick McKenzie, eds., The City. Chicago: University of Chicago Press.

Park, Robert E. 1925. The City: Suggestions for the Investigation of Human Behavior in the Urban Environment. In Robert Park, Ernest Burgess, and Roderick McKenzie, eds., The City. Chicago: University of Chicago Press.

Park, Robert E. 1926. "Review of six books on black American songs, spirituals, poetry." American Journal of Sociology 31(6): 821–824.

Park, Robert E. 1926. "Review of The New Negro." American Journal of Sociology 31: 6 (May).

Park, Robert E. 1926. Untitled review essay of six literary, musical and cultural books. American Journal of Sociology 31(5): 675–677.

Park, Robert E. 1928. "Review of ten books on black American songs, folklore, drama and poetry." American Journal of Sociology 36(6): 988–995.

Park, Robert E. 1931. "Mentality of Racial Hybrids." American Journal of Sociology 36(1): 534–551.

Park, Robert E. 1941. "Morale and the News." The American Journal of Sociology 47(3): 360–377.

Park, Robert E. 1950. Race and Culture. New York: Free Press.

Park, Robert, Ernest W. Burgess and Roderick McKenzine. 1925. The City. Chicago: University of Chicago Press.

Patterson, Orlando. 2002. Emerging Patterns of Race and Ethnicity in the Twenty-first Century America. Lecture at Assumption College (February 4).

Pearson, Ruth. 1986. Female Workers in the First and Third Worlds: The Greening of Women's Labor. In K. Purcell et al., eds., The Changing Experience of Employment. London: Macmillan and the British Sociological Association.

Pearson, Ruth. 1991. Male Bias and Women's Work in Mexico's Border Industries. In Diane Elson, ed., Male Bias in the Development Process. Manchester: Manchester University Press.

Pedraza, Silvia and Ruben G. Rumbaut, eds. 1996. *Origins and Destinies: Immigration, Race, and Ethnicity in America*. Belmont, CA: Wadsworth.

Pedraza-Bailey, Silvia. 1985. *Political and Economic Migrants in America: Cubans and Mexicans*. Austin: University of Texas Press.

Peña, Devon. 1997. *The Terror of the Machine: Technology, Work, Gender, and Ecology on the US-Mexican Border*. Austin: University of Texas Press.

Perry, Pamela. 2002. *Shades of White: White Kids & Racial Identities in High School*. Durham, NC: Duke University Press.

Persons, Stowe. 1987. *Ethnic Studies at Chicago, 1905–45*. Urbana: University of Illinois Press.

Peterson, R.A. and L.P. Sharpe. 1974. "A Study of Recruitment and Socialization into Two Deviant Female Occupations." Sociology Symposium 11: 1–14.

Pfohl, Stephen. 1992. *Death at the Parasite Cafe: Social Science (Fictions) and the Postmodern*. New York: St. Martin's Press.

Pfohl, Stephen. 1994. *Images of Deviance and Social Control: A Sociological History*. New York: McGraw-Hill.

Pfohl, Stephen. 1997. "The Cybernetic Delirium of Norbert Wiener." CTHEORY 20(1–2). Internet resource, http://collection.nlcbnc.ca/100/201/300/ctheory/articles/1997/art44a.txt.

Phelps, Howard. 1919. "Negro Life in Chicago." Half Century Magazine (May).

Philpott, Thomas. 1978. *The Slum and the Ghetto: Neighborhood Deterioration and Middle Class Reform, Chicago, 1880–1930*. New York: Oxford University Press.

Pieterse, Jan Nederveen. 2004. *Globalization or Empire?* New York: Routledge.

Pile, Stephen. 1996. *Body and the City: Psychoanalysis, Space and Subjectivity*. London: Routledge.

Pile, Stephen. 1997. Introduction. In Stephen Pile and Michael Keith, ed., *Geographies of Resistance*. London: Routledge.

Pinderhughes, Howard. 1993. "The Anatomy of Racially Motivated Violence in New York City." Social Problems 4(4): 478–492.

Platt, Anthony M. 1991. *E. Franklin Frazier Reconsidered*. New Brunswick: Rutgers University Press.

Polletta, Francesca. 1996. "Book Review." Contemporary Sociology 25: 483–485.

Pope, Harrison, Katherine A. Phillips and Robert Olivardia. 2000. *The Adonis Complex: The Secret Crisis of Male Body Obsession*. New York: Free Press.

Portes, Alejandro and Julia Sensenbrenner. 1993. "Embeddedness and Immigration: Notes on the Social Determinants of Economic Action." American Journal of Sociology 98(6): 1320–50.

Portes, Alejandro and Min Zhou. 1992. "Gaining the upper hand: economic mobility among immigrant and domestic minorities." Ethnic and Racial Studies 15(4): 491–522.

Portes, Alejandro and Stepick III, Alex. 1993. *City on the Edge: The Transformation of Miami*. Berkeley: University of California Press.

Powell, Richard J. 1997. Re/Birth of a Nation. In Richard J. Powell and David A. Bailey, eds., *Rhapsodies in Black: Art of the Harlem Renaissance*. The Institute of International Visual Arts, Berkeley: University of California Press.

Prakash, Gyan. 1992. "Postcolonial Criticism and Indian Historiography," Social Text 31/32: 8–19.

Puette, William. 1992. *Through Jaundiced Eyes: How the Media View Organized Labor.* Ithaca: ILR Press.

Pugh-O'Mara, Margaret. 2002. *Cities of Knowledge; Cold War Politics, Universities, and the Roots of the Information Age Metropolis.* Unpublished Ph.D. dissertation, University of Pennsylvania.

Quadagno, Jill. 1996. *The Color of Welfare: How Racism Undermined the War on Poverty.* Oxford: Oxford University Press.

Quattro, Leah De. 2003. *Popular Music as a Site of Agency, Labor and Discourse: Black Cultural Production in Liverpool.* Unpublished BA Thesis, Boston College.

Quijano, Aníbal and Wallerstein, Immanuel. 1992. "Americanity as a Concept, or the Americas in the Modern World-System." International Journal of Social Sciences 134: 583–591.

Quijano, Aníbal. 1991. "Colonialidad y Modernidad/Racionalidad." Perú Indígena 29: 11–21. "Race Psychology: Standpoint and Questionnaire with Particular Reference to the Immigrant and the Ne

Quijano, Aníbal. 1993. 'Raza', 'Etnia' y 'Nación' en Mariátegui: Cuestiones Abiertas. In Roland Forgues, ed., *José Carlos Mariátgui y Europa: El Otro Aspecto del Descubrimiento.* Lima, Perú: Empresa Editora Amauta S.A.

Quijano, Aníbal. 1998. La Colonialidad del Poder y la Experiencia Cultural Latinoamericana. In Roberto Briceño-León and Heinz R. Sonntag, eds., *Pueblo, Epoca yDesarrollo: La Sociología de América Latina.* Caracas: Nueva Sociedad.

Quijano, Aníbal. 2000. "Coloniality of Power, Ethnocentrism, and Latin America." NEPANTLA 1(3): 533–580.

Rainwater, Lee and William L. Yancey. 1967. *The Moynihan Report and the Politics of Controversy.* Cambridge: MIT Press.

Rambo-Ronai, Carol. 1992. The Reflexive Self through Narrative: A Night in the Life of an Erotic Dancer/Researcher. In Carolyn Ellis and Michael G. Flaherty, ed., *Investigating Subjectivity: Research on Lived Experience.* Thousand Oaks, CA: Sage.

Rambo-Ronai, Carol. 1993. *Deviance and Resistance in the Biographical Work of Exotic Dancers.* Unpublished Ph.D. Dissertation, University of Florida.

Raushenbush, Winfred. 1979. *Robert E. Park: Biography of a Sociologist.* Durham: Duke University Press.

Raymond, Chris Anne. 1985. Risk in the Press: Conflicting Journalistic Ideologies. In Dorothy Nelkin, ed., *The Language of Risk.* Beverly Hills, CA: Sage Publications.

Reed, Christopher Robert. 1988. "Organized Racial Reform in Chicago During the Progressive Era: The Chicago NAACP, 1910–1920." Michigan Historical Review 14(1): 75–99.

Reed, Christopher Robert. 1997. *The Chicago NAACP and the Rise of Black Professional Leadership, 1910–1966.* Bloomington: Indiana University Press.

Reilly, John. 1982. "Richard Wright Preaches the Nation: 12 Million Black Voices." Black American Literature Forum 16(6): 116–119.

Reiser, Stanley Joel. 1978. *Medicine and the Reign of Technology.* Cambridge: Cambridge University Press.

Rhode, Deborah. 1997. *Speaking of Sex: The Denial of Gender Inequality*. Cambridge, MA: Harvard University Press.

Richardson Greene, Lorraine. 1919. *The Rise of Race Consciousness in the American Negro*. Unpublished Master's thesis, Department of Sociology, University of Chicago.

Richardson, Laurel. 1991. "Postmodern Social Theory: Representational Practices." Sociological Theory 9(2): 173–179.

Richardson, Laurel. 1997. *Fields of Play: Constructing an Academic Life*. New Brunswick, NJ: Rutgers University Press.

Richter, Daniel K. 1992. *The Ordeal of the Longhouse: The Peoples of the Iroquois League in the Era of European Colonization*. Chapel Hill: University of North Carolina.

Rifkin, Jeremy. 1998. *The Biotech Century*. New York: Penguin.

Rifkin, Jeremy. 1998. *Harnessing the Gene and Remaking the World: The Biotech Century*. New York: Tarcher Putnum.

Rigney, Lester-Irabinna. 1997. "Internalisation of an Indigenous Anti-colonial Cultural Critique of Research Methodologies: A Guide to Indigenous Research Methodology and Its Principles." Wicazo sa Review 14(2): 109–21.

Rigney, Lester-Irabinna. 2001. "A First Perspective of Indigenous Australian Participation in Science: Framing Indigenous Research towards Indigenous Australian Intellectual Sovereignty." Kaurna Higher Education Journal 7: 1–13.

Ringer, Gregory. 1998. *Destinations: Cultural Landscapes of Tourism*. London: Routledge.

Robb, Frederick, ed. 1927. *The Negro in Chicago: 1779–1927, Volume 1–2*. Chicago: Washington Intercollegiate Club of Chicago.

Robbins, Richard. 1974. Charles S. Johnson. In James Blackwell and Morris Janowitz, eds., *Black Sociologists*. Chicago: University of Chicago Press.

Roberts, Lee et al. 2004. "Mortality before and after the 2003 invasion of Iraq: cluster sample survey." The Lancet (October 29). Available at http://image.thelancet.com/extras/04art10342web.pdf.

Robin, Corey. 2002. "Primal Fear." Theory and Event 5(4). E-journal at http://muse/jhu.edu/demo/theory_events/5.4.

Robinson, Cedric. 1983. *Black Marxism: The Making of the Black Radical Tradition*. London: Zed Books.

Rochberg-Halton, Eugene. 1989. Life, Literature and Sociology in Turn-of-the-Century Chicago. In Simon Bronner, ed., *Consuming Vision*. New York: Norton.

Rodgers, Daniel T. 1998. *Atlantic Crossings: Social Politics in a Progressive Age*. Cambridge: Harvard University Press.

Romanyshyn, Robert D. 1989. *Technology as Symptom and Dream*. London : Routledge.

Ronnell, Avital. 1992. Support Our Tropes. In Nancy J. Peters, ed., *War After War*. San Francisco: City Lights Books.

Roosens, Eugene E. 1989. *Creating Ethnicity: The Process of Ethnogenesis*. Newbury Park, CA: Sage.

Rose, Nikolas. 1989. *Governing the Soul: The Shaping of the Private Self*. New York: Routledge.

Rose, Nikolas. 1996. *Inventing Our Selves: Psychology, Power, and Personhood*. Cambridge: Cambridge University Press.

Rosenbaum, Ruth. 1994. *Market Basket Survey: A Comparison of the Buying Power of Maquiladora Workers in Mexico and UAW Assembly Workers in GM Plants in the US.* San Antonio: Coalition for Justice in the Maquiladoras.

Ross, Andrew. 1984. *The Chicago Gangster Theory of Life: Nature's Debt to Society.* London: Verso.

Ross, Dorothy. 1991. *The Origins of American Social Science.* New York: Cambridge University Press.

Rotella, Carlo. 2004. *Good With Their Hands: Boxers, Bluesmen, and Other Characters from the Rust Belt.* Berkeley: University of California Press.

Rucht, Dieter. 1988. Themes, Logics, and Arenas of Social Movements: A Structural Approach. In Klandermans. Kriesi and Tarrow, eds., *International Social Movement Research, Volume I.* Greenwich, CT: JAI Press.

Rucht, Dieter. 1995. Parties, Associations, and Movements as Systems of Political Interest Mediation. In J. Thesing and W. Hofmeister, eds. *Political Parties in Democracy.* Sankt Augustin: Konrad-Adenauer-Stiftung.

Rushdie, Salman. 1991. Commonwealth Literature Does Not Exist. In Salman Rushdie, *Imaginary Homelands: Essays and Criticism 1981–1991.* New York: Viking.

Russell, Katheryn. 1998. *The Color of Crime.* New York: New York University Press.

Ryan, Charlotte. 1991. *Prime Time Activism: Media Strategies for Grassroots Organizing.* Boston: South End Press.

Rydell, Robert. 1985. *All The World's A Fair: Visions of Empire At American International Expositions, 1876–1916.* Chicago: University of Chicago Press.

Safa, Helen. 1986. Runaway Shops and Female Employment: The Search for Cheap Labor. In Eleanor Leacock and Helen Safa, eds., *Women's Work: Development and the Division of Labor by Gender.* Massachusetts: Bergin and Garvey Publishers.

Said, Edward. 1979. *Orientalism.* New York: Vintage Books.

Saldivar, Jose David. 1997. *Border Matters.* Berkeley and Los Angeles: University of California Press.

Salzinger, Leslie. 2003. *Genders in Production: Making Workers in Mexico's Global Factories.* Berkeley: University of California Press.

Sandoval, Chela. 1997. Theorizing White Consciousness. In Ruth Frankenberg, ed., *Displacing Whiteness: Essays in Social and Cultural Criticism.* Durham, NC: Duke University Press.

Santiago, Guadalupe and Hugo Almada Mireles. 1991. *Condiciones actuales de trabajo en la industria maquiladora de Ciudad Juárez.* Ciudad Juárez: Centro de Estudios Regionales y Comunicación Alternativa (CERCA).

Sassen, Saskia. 1998. *Globalization and Its Discontents.* New York: New Press.

Sasson, Theodore. 1995. *Crime Talk: How Citizens Construct a Social Problem.* New York: Aldine de Gruyter.

Schmidt, Benjamin. 1997. "Mapping an Empire: Cartographic and Colonial Rivalry in Seventeenth-Century Dutch and English North America." William and Mary Quarterly, Third Series 54(3): 549–578.

Schmitter, Philippe C. 1977. "Modes of Interest Mediation and Models of Societal Change in Western Europe." Comparative Political Studies 10: 7–26.

Schneider, David. 1984. *A Critique of the Study of Kinship*. Ann Arbor: University of Michigan Press

Schon, Donald A. and Martin Rein. 1994. *Frame Reflection: Toward the Resolution of Intractable Policy Controversies*. New York: Basic Books.

Schor, Juliet B. 2004. *Born to Buy: The Commercialized Child and the New Consumer Culture*. New York: Scribner.

Schor, Juliet. 1992. *The Overworked American*. New York: Basic Books.

Scott, Daryl. 1997. *Contempt and Pity: Social Policy and the Image of the Damaged Black Psyche, 1880–1996*. Chapel Hill: UNC Press.

Scott, David. 1996. *Behind the G-String: An Exploration of the Stripper's Image, Her Person and Her Meaning*. London: McFarland Press.

Scott, James C. 1985. *Weapons of the Weak: Everyday Forms of Peasant Resistance*. New Haven, CT: Yale University Press.

Scott, James C. 1990. *Domination and the Arts of Resistance: Hidden Transcripts*. New Haven, CT: Yale University Press.

Scott, Joan. 1988. *Gender and the Politics of History*. New York: Columbia University Press.

Scott, Patricia Bell. 1982. Debunking Sapphire: Toward a Non-Racist and Non-Sexist Social Science. In Gloria T. Hull, Patricia Bell Scott and Barbara Smith, eds., *All the Women are White, All the Blacks are Men, But Some of Us are Brave: Black Women's Studies*. New York: The Feminist Press.

Seiter, Ellen, 1993. *Sold Separately: Parents & Children in Consumer Culture*. New Brunswick: Rutgers University Press.

Serrin, William. 1991. "The Wages of Work." The Nation 252(3): 80–2.

Shaiken, Harley and Stephen Herzenberg. 1987. *Automation and Global Production: Automobile Engine Production in Mexico, the United States, and Canada*. San Diego: Center for US-Mexican Studies, UCSD.

Shaiken, Harley. 1990. *Mexico in the Global Economy: High Technology and Work Organization in Export Industries*. San Diego: Center for US-Mexican Studies, UCSD.

Shaiken, Harley. 1994. "Advanced Manufacturing and Mexico: A New International Division of Labor." Latin American Research Review 29(3): 39–71.

Shelburne, Steve and Lynn Holt. 1997. *The Early Modern Construction of Space*. Internet Resource, http://www2.centenary.edu/forbidden/shelbur1.htm.

Sherwood, Robert. 1951. "The Third World War." Collier's 27(October).

Shils, Edward A. 1941. "A Note on Governmental Research on Attitudes and Morale." The American Journal of Sociology 47(3): 472–480.

Sidel, Ruth. 1996. *Keeping Women and Children Last: America's War on the Poor*. New York: Penguin Books.

Siu, Paul Chang Pang. 1987. In John Kwo Wei Tchen ed., *The Chinese Laundryman: A Study of Social Isolation*. New York: New York University Press.

Sklair, Leslie. 1993. *Assembling for Development: The Maquila Industry in Mexico and the United States*. San Diego: Center for US-Mexican Studies, UCSD.

Sklar, Kathryn Kish. 1991. Hull-House Maps and Papers. In Martin Bulmer, Kevin Bales and Kathryn Kish, eds., *The Social Survey in Historical Perspective, 1880–1940*. Cambridge: Cambridge University Press.

Small, Albion and George Vincent. 1894. *An Introduction to the Study of Society*. New York: American Books.

Small, Albion. 1907. "Points of Agreement among Sociologists." Publications of the American Sociological Society, Volume 1.

Smith, Charles U. 1972. "Contributions of Charles S, Johnson to the Field of Sociology." Journal of the Social and Behavioral Sciences (Spring).

Smith, Dennis. 1988. *The Chicago School: A Liberal Critique of Capitalism*. New York: St. Martin's Press.

Smith, Dorothy. 1999. "[Book Review:] Ghostly Matters: Haunting and the Sociological Imagination." Contemporary Sociology 28(1): 120–121.

Smith, Herbert. 1935. *Three Negro Preachers in Chicago*. Unpublished Masters thesis, Divinity School, University of Chicago.

Smith, Linda Tuhiwai. 1999. *Decolonizing Methodologies: Research and Indigenous Peoples*. New York: Zed Books.

Snipp, Matthew C. 1986. "Who Are American Indians? Some Observations about the Perils and Pitfalls of Data for Race and Ethnicity," Population Research and Policy Review 5: 247–52.

Snow, David, and Robert D. Benford. 1988. Ideology, Frame Resonance, and Participant Mobilization. In Bert Klandermans, Hanspeter Kriesi and Sidney Tarrow, eds., *From Structure to Action: Comparing Social Movement Research across Cultures*. Greenwich, CT: JAI Press.

Snow, David, and Robert D. Benford. 1992. Master Frames and Cycles of Protest. In Aldon Morris and Carol Mueller, eds., *Frontiers in Social Movement Theory*. New Haven: Yale University Press.

Spear, Alan. 1967. *Black Chicago*. Chicago: University of Chicago Press.

Spencer, Jon Michael. 1997. *The New Negroes and Their Music: The Success of the Harlem Renaissance*. Knoxville: University of Tennessee Press.

Spinney, Robert. 2000. *The City of Big Shoulders: A History of Chicago*. Dekalb, Il: NIU Press.

Spitzer, Eliot. 1999. *The New York City Police Department's "Stop & Frisk" Practices: A Report to the People of the State of New York From The Office Of The Attorney General*. New York: Office of the New York State Attorney General.

Spivak, Gayatri. 1988. "Can the Subaltern Speak?" In Cary Nelson and Lawrence Grossberg, eds., *Marxism and the Interpretation of Culture*. Urbana: University of Illinois Press.

Spivak, Gayatri. 1988. *In Other Words: Essays in Cultural Politics*. New York: Routledge, Kegan and Paul.

Stake, Robert. 1994. Case Studies. In Norman Denzin and Yvonna Lincoln, eds., *Handbook of Qualitative Research*. Thousand Oaks, CA: Sage Publications.

Stanfield, John. 1982. "The Negro Problem within and beyond the Institutional Nexus of Pre-World War I Sociology." Phylon 43(3): 187–201.

Stanfield, John. 1985. *Philanthropy and Jim Crow in American Social Science*. Westport CT: Greenwood Press.

Steinberg, Shirley R. and Joe L. Kincheloe, 1997. *Kinderculture: The Corporate Construction of Childhood*. Boulder: Westview.

Stone, Alfred. 1908. "Is Race Friction Between Blacks and Whites in the United States Growing and Inevitable?" American Journal of Sociology 13(5): 676–697.

Stone, Alfred. 1908. *Studies in the American Race Problem*. New York.

Stone, Alfred. 1921. Conflict and Accommodation. In Robert Park and Ernest Burgess, eds., *Introduction to the Science of Sociology*. Chicago: University of Chicago Press.

Stover, Dale. 2001. "Postcolonial Sun Dancing at Wakpamni Lake," Journal of the American Academy of Religion 69(4): 817–36.

Strickland, Arvarh. 1966. *History of the Chicago Urban League*. Urbana: University of Illinois Press.

Sugrue, Thomas. 2003. "Revisiting the Second Ghetto." Journal of Urban History 29(3): 281–290.

Sullivan, Deborah. 2001. *Cosmetic Surgery: The Cutting Edge of Commercial Medicine in America*. New Brunswick, NJ: Rutgers University Press.

Sullivan, Harry Stack. 1941. "Psychiatric Aspects of Morale." The American Journal of Sociology 47(3): 277–301.

Sutherland, Robert Lee. 1930. *An Analysis of Negro Churches in Chicago*. Unpublished Ph.D. Dissertation, Divinity School, University of Chicago.

Swidler, Ann. 1986. "Culture in Action: Symbols and Strategies." American Sociological Review 51: 273–86.

Tarrow, Sidney. 1998. *Power in Movement: Social Movements and Contentious Politics*. New York: Cambridge University Press.

Tasini, Jonathan. 1990. "Lost in the Margins: Labor and the Media." Extra! (Summer): 2–11.

Taylor, Frederick Winslow. 1967 [1912]. *The Principles of Scientific Management*. New York: Norton.

Taylor, Therman Ray. 1981. *Cyril Briggs and the African Blood Brotherhood: Another Radical View of Race and Class During the 1920's*. Unpublished Ph.D. Dissertation, University of California, Santa Barbara.

Teele, James, ed. 2002. *E. Franklin Frazier and Black Bourgeoisie*. Columbia: University of Missouri Press.

Thiong'o, Ngugi wa. 1986. *Decolonising the Mind: the Politics of Language in African Literature*. Portsmouth, NH: Heinemann.

Thomas, W.I. 1904. "The Psychology of Race Prejudice." American Journal of Sociology 9: 593–611.

Thomas, W.I. 1912. "Race Psychology: Standpoint and Questionnaire with Particular Reference to the Immigrant and the Negro." American Journal of Sociology 17(6): 725–775.

Thomas, W.I. and Florian Znaniecki. 1918–1920. *The Polish Peasants in Europe and America, Volumes 1–4*. Chicago: University of Chicago Press.

Thompson, Stith. 1929. *Tales of the North American Indians*. Cambridge, MA: Harvard University Press.

Thornton, Russell. 1997. "Tribal Membership Requirements and the Demography of 'Old' and 'New' Native Americans," Population Research and Policy Review 16: 33–42.

Tiano, Susan. 1994. *Patriarchy on the Line: Labor, Gender and Ideology in the Mexican Maquila Industry*. Philadelphia: Temple University Press.

Tillman, Ray and Michael Cummings, eds. 1999. *The Transformation of U.S. Unions*. Boulder, CO: Lynne Rienner Publishers.

Tilly, Chris. 1996. *Half a Job; Bad and Good Part-time Jobs in a Changing Labor Market*. Philadelphia: Temple University Press.

Trachtenberg, Alan. 1982. *The Incorporation of America: Culture and Society in the Gilded Age*. New York: Hill and Wang.

Troyer, Lon. 2002. "The Calling of Counterterrorism." Theory & Event 5(4). E-journal at http://muse/jhu.edu/demo/theory_events/5.4.

Tuchman, Gaye. 1978. *Making the News*. New York: The Free Press.

Turner, Fred. 1996. *Echoes of Combat: Trauma, Memory, and the Vietnam War*. Minneapolis: University of Minnesota Press, 1996.

Tuttle, William. 1970. *Race Riot: Chicago in the Red Hot Summer of 1919*. New York: Antheneum.

Urry, John. 1997. *Touring Cultures: Transformations of Travel & Theory*. London: Routledge.

Urry, John. 2002. *The Tourist Gaze*. Thousand Oaks, CA: Sage Publications.

Valien, Preston. 1958. "Sociological Contributions of Charles S. Johnson." Sociology and Social Research (March-April).

Valladolid, Julio and Frédérique Apffel-Marglin. 2001. Andean Cosmovision and the Nurturing of Biodiversity. In John A. Grim, ed., *Indigenous Traditions and Ecology: The Interbeing of Cosmology and Community*. Cambridge, MA: Harvard University Press.

Van Waas, Michael. 1981. *The Multinational's Strategy for Labor: Foreign Assembly Plants in Mexico's Border Industrialization Program*. Unpublished Ph.D. Dissertation, Stanford University.

Van Waas, Michael. 1982. "Multinational Corporations and the Politics of Labor Supply." The Insurgent Sociologist 11(3): 49–57.

Vera, Beatriz. Undated. *Informe Preliminar*. Unpublished Manuscript, Ciudad Juárez.

Veysey, Laurence. 1965. *The Emergence of the American University*. Chicago: University of Chicago Press.

Vila, Carlos M. 1992. *La Costa Atlantica de Nicaragua*. Mexico D.F.: Fondo de Cultura Economica.

Virilio, Paul. 1999. *The Politics of the Very Worst*. New York: Semiotext(e).

Vizenor, Gerald. 1994. *Manifest Manners: Postindian Warriors of Survivance*. Hanover, NH: Wesleyan/New England University Press.

Vlasek, Dale. 1982. E. Franklin Frazier and the Problem of Assimilation. In Hamilton Cravens, ed., *Ideas in America's Cultures: From Republic to Mass Society*. Ames: Iowa State University Press.

Von Eschen, Penny. 1997. *Race Against Empire: Black Americans and Anticolonialism, 1937–1957*. Ithaca: Cornell University Press.

Wacker, Fred. 1976. "American Dilemma: The Racial Theories of Robert E. Park and Gunnar Myrdal." Phylon 37(2): 117–125.

Wacker, Fred. 1983. *Ethnicity, Pluralism, and Race: Race Relations Theory in America before Myrdal*. Westport, CT: Greenwood Press.

Wacker, Fred. 1995. The Sociology of Race and Ethnicity in the Second Chicago School. In Gary Fine, ed., *A Second Chicago School? The Development of Postwar American Sociology*. Chicago: University of Chicago Press.

Waldinger, Roger. 1986. *Through the Eye of the Needle: Immigrants and Enterprise in New York's Garment Trades*. New York: New York University Press.

Waldinger, Roger. 1996. *Still the Promised City?: African-Americans and New Immigrants in Postindustrial New York*. Cambridge, MA: Harvard University Press.

Walker, Kenneth. 1942. *Circle of Life: A Search for an Attitude to Pain, Disease, Old Age and Death*. London: Jonathan Cape.

Wall, Cheryl. 1997. *Women of the Harlem Renaissance*. Bloomington: Indiana University Press.

Wallerstein, Immanuel. 1974. *The Modern World-System*. New York: Academic Press.

Wallerstein, Immanuel. 1979. *The Capitalist World-Economy*. Cambridge and Paris: Cambridge University Press and Editions de la Maison des Sciences de l'Homme.

Wallerstein, Immanuel. 1991. *Unthinking Social Science*. Cambridge: Polity Press.

Wallerstein, Immanuel. 1992a. *The Concept of National Development, 1917–1989: Elegy and Requiem*. American Behavioral Scientist 35(4–5): 517–29.

Wallerstein, Immanuel. 1992b. The Collapse of Liberalism. In Ralph Miliband and Leo Panitich, eds., *The Socialist Register 1991*. London: Merlin Press.

Wanger, Walter. 1941. "The Role of Movies in Morale." The American Journal of Sociology 47(3): 378–383.

Warrior, Robert Allen. 1995. *Tribal Secrets: Recovering American Indian Intellectual Traditions*. Minneapolis: University of Minnesota.

Warrior, Robert. 1999. "The Native American Scholar: Toward a New Intellectual Agenda." Wicazo sa Review 14(2): 46–55.

Washington, Booker T. 1969 [1909]. *The Story of the Negro: The Rise of a Race from Slavery*. Gloucester, MA: Peter Smith II.

Washington, Booker T. 1986 [1901]. *Up from Slavery*. New York Penguin Books.

Washington, Booker T., Fannie Barrier Williams and N.B. Wood. 1969 [1901]. *A New Negro for a New Century*. New York: Arno Press.

Waters, Mary. 1990. *Ethnic Options: Choosing Identities in America*. Berkeley, CA: University of California Press.

Watson J.D. and Crick F.H.C. 1953. "Genetic Implications of the structure of Deoxyribonucleic Acid." Nature 171: 964–967.

Watson, Steve. 1995. *The Harlem Renaissance*. New York: Pantheon Books.

Watts, Jerry. 1983. "On Reconsidering Park, Johnson, DuBois, Frazier and Reid: Reply to Benjamin Bowser's The Contribution of Blacks to Sociological Knowledge." Phylon 44(4): 273–291.

Weart, Spencer R. 1988. *Nuclear Fear: A History of Images*. Cambridge: Harvard University Press.

Weaver, Jace. 1997. *That the People Might Live: Native American Literatures and Native American Community*. New York: Oxford.

Weaver, Jace. 1998. From I-Hermeneutics to We-Hermeneutics: Native Americans and the Post-Colonial. In Jace Weaver, ed., *Native American Religious Identity: Unforgotten Gods*. Maryknoll, NY: Orbis.

Weber, Max. 1946. The Meaning of Discipline. In Gerth and Mills, eds., *From Max Weber: Essays in Sociology*. New York: Oxford University Press.

Weber, Max. 1949. *The Methodology of the Social Sciences*, translated and edited by Edward Shils and Henry Finch. New York: The Free Press.

Weber, Max. 1958a. *From Max Weber*, H.H. Gerth and C.W. Mills, eds. New York: Oxford University Press.

Weber, Max. 1958b. *The Protestant Ethic and the Spirit of Capitalism*. New York: Charles Scribner's Sons.

Weber, Max. 1930. *The Protestant Ethic and the Spirit of Capitalism*. London: Routledge.

Weedon, Chris. 1997. *Feminist Practice & Poststructuralist Theory, Second Edition*. Cambridge, MA: Blackwell.

Weiner, Norbert. 1954. *The Human Use of Human Beings*. New York: Avon Books.

Wellman, David. 1993. *Portraits of White Racism, Second Edition*. New York: Cambridge University Press.

Wells-Barnett, Ida B. 1970. *Crusade for Justice: The Autobiography of Ida B. Wells*, edited by Alfreda M. Duster. Chicago: University of Chicago Press.

Wells-Barnett, Ida B. 2002 [1892]. *On Lynchings*, with an introduction by Patricia Hill Collins. Amherst, N.Y: Humanity Books.

Wetstein, Matthew E. 1996. *Abortion Rates in the United States*. Albany, NY: State University of New York Press.

White-Sax, Barbara. 1999. "Wealthy, Savvy Kids Have Their Say." Drug Store News (7 June 7): 63.

Williams, Fannie Barrier. 1905. "Social Bonds in the 'Black Belt' of Chicago." Charities 15 (7 Oct.).

Williams, Linda. 1999. *Hard Core: Power, Pleasure and the Frenzy of the Visible*. Berkley: University of California Press.

Williams, Patricia. 1991. *The Alchemy of Race and Rights: A Diary of a Law Professor*. Cambridge: Harvard University Press.

Williams, Patricia. 2001. "This Dangerous Patriot's Game." The Observer (December 2).

Wilson, Mabel O. 1996. *Making a Civilization Paradigm: Robert Park, Race, Urban Ecology*. Unpublished paper, American Studies Seminar, New York University.

Wilson, Rand. 1998. Unpublished Speech at Cornell University.

Wilson, William Julius. 1987. *The Truly Disadvantaged: The Inner City, The Underclass and Public Policy*. Chicago: University of Chicago Press.

Wilson, William Julius. 1996. *When Work Disappears: The World of the New Urban Poor*. New York: Random House.

Winant, Howard. 1994. *Racial Conditions: Politics, Theory, Comparisons*. Minneapolis, MN: University of Minnesota Press.

Wintz, Cary, ed. 1996. *The Harlem Renaissance, 1920–1940*. New York: Garland Publishing.

Wintz, Cary. 1997. *Black Culture and the Harlem Renaissance*. Houston Texas: Rice University Press.

Wirth, Louis. 1928. *The Ghetto*. Chicago: University of Chicago Press.

Witt, Matt and Rand Wilson. 1998. Part-Time America Won't Work. In Jo-Ann Mort, ed., *Not Your Father's Labor Movement*. New York: Verso.

Wolf, Diane. 1990. "Daughters, Decisions and Domination: An Empirical and Conceptual Critique of Household Strategies." Development and Change 21: 43–74.

Wolters, Raymond. 1975. *The New Negro on Campus: Black College Rebellions of the 1920's*. Princeton: Princeton University Press.

Wood, Denis. 1993. "The Power of Maps (maps are subjective)." Scientific American 268(5): 88–94.

Wood, Ellen Meiksins. 1996. *Democracy Against Capitalism: Renewing Historical Materialism*. Cambridge: Cambridge University Press.

Work, Monroe. 1900. "Crime Among Negroes of Chicago: A Social Study." American Journal of Sociology 6(2): 204–223.

Work, Monroe. 1903. *Negro Real Estate Holders of Chicago*. Unpublished Masters Thesis, Department of Sociology, University of Chicago.

Wright Jr., Richard R. 1901. *The Industrial Conditions of Negroes in Chicago*. Unpublished BD Thesis, Divinity School, University of Chicago.

Wright Jr., Richard R. 1965. *87 Years Behind the Black Curtain: An Autobiography*. Philadelphia: Rare Book Co.

Wright Jr., Richard R. 1969 [1911]. *The Negro in Pennsylvania: A Study in Economic History*. New York: Arno Press.

Yin, Robert. 1989. *Case Study Research: Design and Methods, Second Edition*. Newbury Park, CA: Sage Publications.

Young, Gay and Beatriz Vera. 1984. *Extensive Evaluation of Centro de Orientación de la Mujer Obrera, A.C. in Ciudad Juárez*. Unpublished Manuscript, Inter-American Foundation, Ciudad Juárez.

Yu, Henry. 2001. *Thinking Orientals: Migration, Contact and Exoticism in Modern America*. Oxford University Press.

Yudelman, Sally. 1987. *Hopeful Openings: A Study of Five Women's Development Organizations in Latin America and the Caribbean*. West Hartford: Kumarian Press.

Zea, Leopoldo. 1986. Introducción. In Leopoldo Zea, ed., *América Latina en Sus Ideas*. México: Unesco and Siglo XXI.

Zorbaugh, Harvey. 1929. *The Gold Coast and the Slum*. Chicago: University of Chicago Press.

Zukin, Sharon. 1995. *The Cultures of Cities*. Cambridge, MA: Blackwell.

About the Authors and Editors

PATRICIA AREND is a Ph.D. Candidate in Sociology at Boston College. Her areas of interest are gender, race, class, sexuality, consumption and social theory. Her dissertation examines "white weddings" in consumer society.

DAVARIAN L. BALDWIN is an Assistant Professor of History at Boston College where his teaching and research focuses on Black cultural studies, the social production of knowledge, critical urban studies, and social and political theory. He has published previously in Black Renaissance/Renaissance Noire, Journal of Urban History, American Studies, and various collected anthologies. His book *Chicago's New Negroes: Race, Class, and Respectability in the Black Metropolis, 1910–1935* (University of North Carolina Press, forthcoming 2006), examines the mass consumer marketplace as a crucial site of intellectual life in the early twentieth century.

ABIGAIL BROOKS is a Ph.D. Candidate in Sociology at Boston College. Her areas of interest include feminist theory, sociology of gender, critical gerontology and feminist age studies, sociology of the body, science and technology studies, and social theory. Her dissertation investigates women's lived experiences and interpretations of growing older against the contextual backdrop of growing prevalence, acceptance, and approval of cosmetic surgery.

R. DANIELLE EGAN is an Assistant Professor in the Department of Sociology at St. Lawrence University. She is currently finishing her manuscript entitled *The Phallus Palace: Sexy Spaces, Desiring Subjects and the Fantasy of Objects* and is co-editing an anthology *Flesh For Fantasy: The Production and Consumption of Exotic Dance* with Katherine Frank. Her current research is on desire, power and the pedagogical process.

STEVEN D. FAROUGH is Assistant Professor of Sociology at Assumption College, where he teaches social theory, research methodology and courses on race and gender. His current research is on white masculinities. Steven sees his research on white masculinities connecting to his theoretical and methodological orientation as a sociologist in general – to use contemporary social theory and qualitative methods to study how the relationship between language, identity, social organization, and power works within the daily lives of relatively privileged people.

WILLIAM A. GAMSON is a Professor of Sociology and co-directs, with Charlotte Ryan, the Media Research and Action Project (MRAP) at Boston College. He has most recently co-authored, *Shaping Abortion Discourse: Democracy and the Public Sphere in Germany and the United States* (2002) and is the author of *Talking Politics* (1992) and *The Strategy of Social Protest* (2nd edition, 1990) among other books and articles on political discourse, the mass media and social movements. He is a past president of the American Sociological Association and a Fellow of the American Academy of Arts and Sciences.

EVA MARIE GARROUTTE is an Associate Professor of Sociology at Boston College and an enrolled citizen of the Cherokee Nation. Her book, *Real Indians: Identity and the Survival of Native America* (2003, University of California) develops the perspective of Radical Indigenism. Ongoing research, funded by the National Institute on Aging, examines doctor patient communication with American Indian elders.

RAMÓN GROSFOGUEL is Professor in the Department of Ethnic Studies at UC-Berkeley and Research Associate of the Maison des Science de l'Homme in Paris. He has published many articles on Caribbean migration to Western Europe and the United States. His latest book is *Colonial Subjects: Puerto Ricans in a Global Perspective* (University of California Press, 2003).

ARTHUR AND MARILOUISE KROKER are the editors of *CTHEORY*, an online international journal of theory, technology, and culture. They have also authored and edited numerous articles and books, including *Digital Delirium, Hacking the Future, The Possessed Individual,* and *Technology and the Canadian Mind.*

DENISE LECKENBY is a Ph.D. Candidate in Sociology at Boston College. Her areas of interest include qualitative methodology, feminist methodology, feminist theory, and sexuality. She is coeditor of *Women in Catholic Higher Education: Border Work, Living Experiences, and Social Justice* (2003).

DELARIO LINDSEY is a Ph.D. Candidate in Sociology at Boston College. His areas of interest include world cities, social control, race, and frame critical analysis.

KAREN MCCORMACK is a visiting Assistant Professor of Sociology at Wellesley College. The article in this anthology is an excerpt from her dissertation entitled Welfare (M)Others: Discourse, Discipline and Resistance. Her current research focuses on the changing meaning of marriage and the family.

JACKIE ORR is an Associate Professor of Sociology at Syracuse University. She teaches and writes in the fields of cultural politics, contemporary theory, and feminist studies of technoscience and psychiatry. Her book, *Panic Diaries: A Genealogy of Panic Disorder* (Duke University Press, forthcoming 2005), chronicles the entanglements of bodies, pills, computers, capital, war, and (social) scientific discourses that have shaped and re-shaped 'panic' in the 20th century United States.

STEPHEN PFOHL is a Professor of Sociology and Chairperson of the Sociology Department at Boston College. He is the author of a wide variety of books and articles on topics ranging from the politics of deviance and social control to studies in social theory and contemporary culture. Pfohl's books include *Death at the Parasite Cafe* (1992) and *Images of Deviance and Social Control* (1994). Stephen is also a Past-President of the Society for the Study of Social Problems.

CHARLOTTE RYAN, a former labor and community organizer, co-directs the Boston College Media Research and Action Project. Her work focuses on the interplay between social movements and communications systems. She co-wrote *Rhyming Hope and History* (2005) and *Communicating Change* (2005).

LESLIE SALZINGER is an Associate Professor of Sociology at Boston College. She is an ethnographer whose research explores the cultural constitution of economic processes and the creation of subjects within political economies. Her book, *Genders in Production: Making Workers in Mexico's Global Factories* (University of California Press, 2003) focuses on the formation and consequences of gendered subjectivities in transnational production on Mexico's northern border. Her current research investigates the social constitution of markets and value among peso/dollar traders in banks located in New York and Mexico City.

CHARLES SARNO is Assistant Professor of Sociology at Holy Names University in Oakland, CA. His essay in this volume is excerpted from his dissertation entitled *Power and the Spirit: Methodological Studies in a Black Apostolic Church*.

JULIET SCHOR is Professor of Sociology at Boston College. She is the author or editor of numerous books, including *Born to Buy: The Commercialized Child and the New Consumer Culture* (2004), *The Overworked American: The Unexpected Decline of Leisure* (1992); and *The Overspent American: Upscaling, Downshifting and the New Consumer* (1998). She is also a founding board member of the Center for a New American Dream.

AIMEE VAN WAGENEN is a Ph.D. Candidate in Sociology at Boston College. Her dissertation investigates identity, public health and power in the science and practice of HIV prevention and education.

WILLIAM WOOD is a Ph.D. Candidate in Sociology at Boston College. He is currently finishing his dissertation on juvenile restorative justice. William has also earned a Master of Divnity degree from Union Theological Seminary in New York City, where he studied religious history and social theory.

Index

STUDIES IN CRITICAL SOCIAL SCIENCES

ISSN 1537-4234

1. LEVINE, Rhonda F. (ed.) *Enriching the Social Imagination.* How Radical Sociology Changed the Discipline. 2004. ISBN 90 04 13992 3
2. COATES, Rodney D. (ed.) *Race and Ethnicity.* Across Time, Space and Discipline. 2004. ISBN 90 04 13991 5
3. PODOBNIK, B. & T. REIFER (eds.) *Transforming Globalization.* Challenges and Opportunities in the Post 9/11 Era. 2005. ISBN 90 04 14583 4
4. PFOHL, S., A. VAN WAGENEN, P. AREND, A. BROOKS & D. LECKENBY (eds.) *Culture, Power, and History.* Studies in Critical Sociology. 2005. ISBN 90 04 14659 8